Rick Steves'®

PROVENCE &
THE FRENCH RIVIERA

2010

Pont du Gard · Côtes du Rhône · Grand Canyon du Verdon · Nîmes · Monaco · Antibes · Nice · Camargue · Aix-en-Provence · Cassis · Marseille

AVALON
TRAVEL

CONTENTS

Top Destinations in Provence & the French Riviera

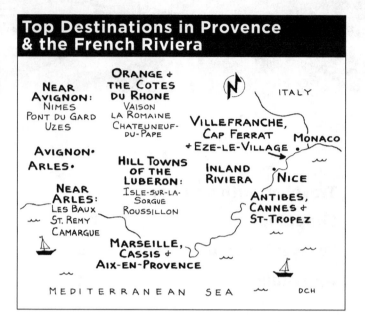

NEAR AVIGNON:
NIMES
PONT DU GARD
UZES

ORANGE & THE COTES DU RHONE
VAISON LA ROMAINE
CHATEUNEUF-DU-PAPE

ITALY

VILLEFRANCHE, CAP FERRAT + EZE-LE-VILLAGE

MONACO

AVIGNON•
ARLES•

HILL TOWNS OF THE LUBERON:
ISLE-SUR-LA-SORGUE
ROUSSILLON

INLAND RIVIERA

NICE

NEAR ARLES:
LES BAUX
ST. REMY
CAMARGUE

ANTIBES, CANNES + ST-TROPEZ

MARSEILLE, CASSIS + AIX-EN-PROVENCE

MEDITERRANEAN SEA

DCH

INTRODUCTION

Provence and the French Riviera are an intoxicating bouillabaisse of enjoyable cities, warm stone villages, Roman ruins, contemporary art, and breathtaking coastlines steaming with sunshine and stirred by the wind. There's something about the play of light in this region, where natural and man-made beauty mingle to dazzle the senses and nourish the soul. It all adds up to *une magnifique* vacation.

Provence and the Riviera stretch along France's southeast Mediterranean coast from the Camargue (south of Arles) to Monaco, and ramble north along the Rhône Valley into the Alps. The regions combined are about the same size as Massachusetts—you can take a train or drive from one end to the other in just three hours—yet they contain more sightseeing opportunities and let's-live-here villages than anywhere else in France. Marseille and Nice, the country's second- and fifth-largest cities, provide good transportation and an urban perspective to this otherwise relaxed region, where every day feels like a lazy Sunday.

In Provence, gnarled sycamores line the roads that twist their way through stone towns and between oceans of vineyards. France's Riviera is about the sea and money—it's populated by a yacht-happy crowd wondering where the next "scene" will be. While Provence feels older and more *español* (with paella on menus and bullfights on Sundays), the Riviera feels downright Italian—with fresh-Parmesan-topped pasta and red-orange, pastel-colored buildings. For every Roman ruin in Provence, there's a modern-art museum in the Riviera. Provence is famous for its wines and wind, while the bikini and ravioli were invented on the Riviera.

This book covers the predictable biggies, from jet-setting beach resorts to remote canyons, but it also mixes in a healthy

INTRODUCTION

Provence and the French Riviera

dose of Back Door intimacy. Along with Pont du Gard, Nice, and Avignon, we'll introduce you to our favorite villages. You'll sample delicious wineries and explore untouristy Roman ruins. You'll marvel at ancient monuments, take a canoe trip down the meandering Sorgue River, and settle into a shaded café on a made-for-movies square. Claim the ideal beach to call home, and at day's end, dive headfirst into a sunset from a hill-town perch. You'll try tasty-yet-affordable wines while feasting on a healthy cuisine heavy on olives, tomatoes, and spices. Just as important, you'll get on a first-name basis with many of our Provençal friends—hoteliers, restaurateurs, vintners, and lots more.

This book is selective, including only the most exciting sights and romantic villages. There are *beaucoup de* Provençal hill towns... but we cover only the most intriguing. And while there are scads of beach towns on the Riviera, we recommend the top three.

The best is, of course, only our opinion. But after spending more than half of our adult lives writing and lecturing about travel, guiding tours, and gaining an appreciation for all things French, we've developed a sixth sense for what touches the traveler's imagination.

About This Book

Rick Steves' Provence & the French Riviera 2010 is a personal tour guide in your pocket. Better yet, it's actually two tour guides in your pocket: The co-author of this book is Steve Smith. Steve lived in France as a child and has been traveling to France—as a guide, researcher, homeowner, and devout Francophile—every year since 1985. He has restored an old farmhouse in Burgundy and today keeps one foot on each side of the Atlantic. Together, Steve and I keep this book up-to-date and accurate (though for simplicity, from this point "we" will shed our respective egos and become "I").

I update this book every year in person. The telephone numbers and hours of sights listed in this book are accurate as of mid-2009—but even with annual updates, things change. For the very latest, visit www.ricksteves.com/update. Also at my website, you'll find a valuable list of reports and experiences—good and bad—from fellow travelers (www.ricksteves.com/feedback).

This book consists of two obvious parts: Provence and the Riviera (although almost everything covered in this book is officially considered part of the "Provence–Alpes–Côte d'Azur region" by the French government). The Provence half highlights Arles and Avignon, and their day-trip destinations; the photogenic hill towns of the Côtes du Rhône and Luberon; and the coastal towns of Marseille and Cassis, and nearby Aix-en-Provence. On the high-rolling French Riviera, I cover the waterfront destinations of Nice, Villefranche-sur-Mer, Cap Ferrat, Monaco, Antibes, Cannes, and St-Tropez—plus the best of the inland hill towns and the truly grand Grand Canyon du Verdon.

The introductions to **Provence** and **The French Riviera** acquaint you with the history, cuisine, and wine of the places you'll be visiting, and give practical advice on what to see, how to get around, and lots more. Don't overlook the valuable tips in these chapters.

In the destination chapters, you'll find these sections:

Planning Your Time suggests a schedule, with thoughts on how best to use your limited time in each place.

Orientation includes specifics on city transportation, helpful hints, easy-to-read maps, and tourist information (note that tourist information is abbreviated **TI** in this book).

Sights, described in detail, are rated:

▲▲▲—Don't miss.

▲▲—Try hard to see.

▲—Worthwhile if you can make it.

No rating—Worth knowing about.

Self-guided walks help you explore these fascinating towns and places on foot: Avignon, Nîmes, Arles, Aix-en-Provence, Les Baux, Isle-sur-la-Sorgue, Roussillon, Monaco, Antibes, Villefranche-sur-Mer, and Cannes. (A few of the in-depth walks and tours get their own chapters: a stroll along Nice's promenade des Anglais, a walk through Old Nice, and a guided visit to the Chagall Museum.) I also include a few self-guided **driving tours,** allowing you to explore the Côtes du Rhône wine road, the Grand Canyon du Verdon, and inland hill towns of the Riviera with the knowledge of a local.

Sleeping describes my favorite hotels, from good-value deals to cushy splurges.

Eating serves up a range of options, from inexpensive take-out joints to fancier restaurants.

Connections outlines your options for traveling to destinations by train and bus, plus route tips for drivers.

The book also includes detailed chapters on these key topics:

Traveling with Children offers general tips and destination-specific advice, like kid-friendly hotels and restaurants. Both co-authors have kids (from 8 to 22 years old), and we've used our substantial experience traveling with children to improve this book. Our kids have greatly enriched our travels, and we hope the same will be true for you.

Shopping has suggestions for this region's best souvenirs and bargains. Steve's wife, who had a business importing French products to the US, contributes her shopping-savvy advice every year.

France: Past and Present gives you a quick overview of the country.

The **appendix** is a traveler's tool kit, with telephone tips, useful phone numbers, recommended books and films, a festival list, climate chart, handy packing checklist, hotel reservation form, French survival phrases, and lots more. I also provide detailed information on transportation for getting around the region by train, bus, or car.

Browse through this book and select your favorite sights. Then have a *fantastique* trip! Traveling like a temporary local, you'll get the absolute most out of every mile, minute, and euro. I'm happy that you'll be visiting the places I know and love, and meeting my favorite French people.

Planning

This section will help you get started on planning your trip—with advice on trip costs, when to go, and what you should know before you take off.

Travel Smart

Your trip to France is like a complex play—easier to follow and really appreciate on a second viewing. While no one does the same trip twice to gain that advantage, reading this book in its entirety before your trip accomplishes much the same thing.

Design an itinerary that enables you to visit museums and festivals (see page 463) on the right days. Note holidays, specifics on sights, and days when sights are closed. If you're using public transportation, read up on the tips for trains and buses (see pages 448 and 450 of the appendix). If you're renting a car, peruse my driving tips and study the examples of road signs (see page 453).

Be sure to mix intense and relaxed periods in your itinerary. To maximize rootedness, minimize one-night stands (and, where possible, opt for three-night stands). Every trip—and every traveler—needs at least a few slack days (for picnics, laundry, people-watching, and so on). Pace yourself. Assume you will return.

Reread this book as you travel, and visit local tourist information offices. Upon arrival in a new town, lay the groundwork for a smooth departure; write down the schedule for the train or bus that you'll take when you leave. Use taxis in the big cities, bring along a water bottle, and linger in the shade.

As you travel, take advantage of the Internet and phones to make your trip run smoothly. By going online (at Internet cafés or your hotel) and using the phone (buy a phone card or carry a mobile phone), you can get tourist information, learn the latest on sights (special events, English tour schedules, etc.), book tickets and tours, make reservations, reconfirm hotels, research transportation

Best Two-Week Trip of Provence & the French Riviera by Car

Day Plan

1 Fly into Nice. Settle in at your hotel, then take a walk along the promenade des Anglais up to Castle Hill (see the Welcome to the Riviera Walk chapter). Sleep in or near Nice.

2 Start the morning with my self-guided tour of Old Nice (see the Old Nice Walk chapter), allowing time to smell the *fougasse* and sample a *café.* Spend your afternoon at one or more of Nice's fine museums (see the Chagall Museum Tour chapter). Have dinner on the beach. Sleep in or near Nice.

3 Take the bus to nearby Villefranche-sur-Mer, explore, and have lunch. Consider my recommended seaside walks in Cap Ferrat, or the one-hour boat cruise from Nice's port. Everyone should spend the afternoon or evening in almost-neighboring Monaco. Sleep in or near Nice.

4 First thing in the morning, pick up your rental car in Nice. Drive north to Vence or Grasse (you choose), then continue on to the Gorges du Verdon and sleep in tiny Aiguines or Moustiers-Ste-Marie.

5 Continue west into the Luberon and explore the villages of *La Provence Profonde.* Stay in or near Roussillon.

6 Spend your day sampling hill towns in the Luberon. Taste a village market, then drive over the hills to the valley of the Côtes du Rhône. Sleep in or near Vaison la Romaine (Monday arrival is ideal since market day is Tuesday). If you're here from late June to late July, when the lavender blooms, the drive to Vaison la Romaine via Sault is a must.

7 Explore Vaison la Romaine's upper medieval village and lower Roman city. Set sail along the Côtes du Rhône wine road (following my self-guided driving tour) and visit a winery or wine cooperative. Tour little Le Crestet and take a walk above Gigondas. Sleep in or near Vaison la Romaine.

8 Start your day touring the Roman Theater in Orange and consider a quick stop in Châteauneuf-du-Pape. Continue south and set up in Avignon. In the afternoon, take my

connections, and keep in touch with your loved ones.

Connect with the culture. Set up your own quest for the best café, bell tower, crêpe, or whatever. Enjoy the friendliness of your French hosts. Slow down and be open to unexpected experiences. Ask questions—most locals are eager to point you in their idea of the right direction. Keep a notepad in your pocket for organizing your thoughts. Wear your money belt, and learn the local currency and how to estimate prices in dollars. Those who expect to travel smart, do.

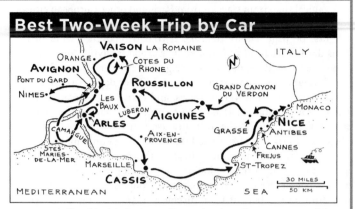

Best Two-Week Trip by Car

self-guided Avignon walks and enjoy dinner on one of the town's many atmospheric squares. Sleep in Avignon.

9 Relax in Avignon this morning, then divide the rest of your day between Nîmes and Pont du Gard. If the weather's good, bring your swimsuit and float on your back below the 2,000-year-old Pont du Gard. Sleep in Avignon.

10 Take a joyride through the Camargue (if it's summer, when flamingos are scarce, visit Les Baux this morning rather than tomorrow evening) and wind up in Arles (big market day on Saturday). Sleep in Arles.

11 Spend your day in Arles. Drive to Les Baux for dinner. Sleep in Arles.

12 Drive to Cassis and stop for lunch and a midday visit to Aix-en-Provence or Marseille (Marseille is dicier by car). Set up in Cassis and watch the sun set from the old port while you savor a bouillabaisse dinner. Sleep in Cassis.

13 Spend all day in Cassis enjoying *la vie douce.* Take a boat trip to the *calanques,* watch the *pétanque* balls roll, and end your day with a drive up Cap Canaille. Sleep in Cassis.

14 Drive to St-Tropez and spend your morning carousing along its old port (searching for Brigitte Bardot). In the afternoon, drive to Nice via the scenic detour from Fréjus to Cannes. Sleep in Nice.

15 Trip over.

Trip Costs

Five components make up your total trip cost: airfare, surface transportation, room and board, sightseeing and entertainment, and shopping and miscellany.

Airfare: Nice is the handiest airport for Provence and the Riviera (though Marseille is attracting more airlines every year). A basic round-trip flight from the US to Nice or Paris costs $800–1,600, depending on where you fly from and when (cheaper in winter). Smaller budget airlines provide bargain service—often more economical than train travel—from Paris and other European cities to places such as Marseille, Avignon, and Montpellier (see "Cheap Flights" on page 458 for details). If your trip covers a wide area, consider saving time and money in Europe by flying "open jaw" (into one city and out of another—e.g., into Nice and out of Paris).

Surface Transportation: Allow $30 per day per person for public transportation (trains, buses, and taxis), or $50 per day per person for a rental car (based on two people sharing) for rental fees, tolls, parking, gas, and insurance. Car rental and leases are cheapest if arranged from the US. Train passes only make sense if you are traveling to regions beyond Provence and the Riviera, as distances within this region are short, and point-to-point fares are reasonable. Remember that married couples, seniors, students, and families can benefit from discounts (*réduction*, ray-dook-see-own). Railpasses are normally available only outside of Europe (see "Transportation," page 444, for more details on car rental, rail trips, and bus travel).

Room and Board: You can thrive in Provence and the Riviera on $135 a day per person for room and board. A $135-a-day budget allows an average of $12 for breakfast, $18 for lunch, $40 for dinner with drinks, and $65 for lodging (based on two people splitting the cost of a $130 double room). That's definitely doable. Students and tightwads do it on $50 a day ($25 per bed, $25 for meals and snacks).

Sightseeing and Entertainment: Allow about $10 per major sight (Arles' Roman Arena-$8, Nice's Chagall Museum-$9, Pont du Gard combo-ticket-$17), $6 for minor ones (e.g., climbing church towers), $25 for guided walks, and $35 for splurge experiences (e.g., bullfights or concerts). Arles and Avignon each offer a money-saving museum pass (details listed in this book)—and most of Nice's museums are free. An overall average of $20–25 a day for sightseeing and entertainment works for most. Don't skimp here. After all, this is the driving force behind your trip—you came to sightsee, enjoy, and experience Provence and the French Riviera.

Shopping and Miscellany: Figure $5 per ice-cream cone, coffee, or soft drink. Shopping can vary in cost from nearly nothing to a small fortune (for tips on stretching your euros, see the Shopping chapter). Good budget travelers find that this category has little to do with assembling a trip full of lifelong and wonderful memories.

Sightseeing Priorities

Depending on the length of your trip, here are my recommended priorities:

6 days: Arles and day trips to Pont du Gard and Les Baux, a night in a Côtes du Rhône village, and Nice with a day trip to Monaco

 9 days, add: Avignon and Cassis
12 days, add: Luberon, Grand Canyon du Verdon, and Antibes
14 days, add: Nîmes, Marseille, Aix-en-Provence, and the
                Camargue

For a day-by-day itinerary of a two-week trip, see this chapter's two recommended routes (by car, and by train and bus).

When to Go

With more than 300 days of sunshine per year, Provence and the Riviera enjoy France's sunniest weather. Spring and fall are best, with generally comfortable weather—though crowds can be a problem if you're not careful, particularly during holiday weekends and major events (May is worst—see "Major Holidays and Weekends" sidebar, page 25). April can be damp, and any month can be windy.

Summer means festivals, lavender, steamy weather, long hours at sights, and longer lines of cars along the Riviera. Europeans vacation in July and August, jamming the Riviera, the Gorges du Verdon, and Ardèche (worst from mid-July through mid-Aug), but leaving the rest of this region relatively calm. While many French businesses close in August, the traveler hardly notices.

September brings the grape harvest, when small wineries are off-limits to taste-seeking travelers (for information on wine-tasting, see page 48). Late fall delivers beautiful foliage and a return to tranquility in normally crowded places.

While you can find mild, sunny weather in any season, Provence is famous for its bone-chilling temperatures when the wind blows (see page 52). Winter travel is OK in Nice and Avignon, but you'll find smaller cities and villages buttoned up tight. Sights and tourist-information offices keep shorter hours, and some tourist activities (such as English-language castle tours) vanish altogether. To get the latest weather forecast in English, dial 08 99 70 11 11, then press 1. Also see the climate chart in the appendix.

Thanks to Provence's temperate climate, fields of flowers greet the traveler much of the year:

May: Wild red poppies *(coquelicots)* sprout.

June: Lavender begins to bloom in the lower hills of Provence, generally during the last week of the month.

July: Lavender is in full swing in Provence, and sunflowers are awakening. Cities, towns, and villages everywhere overflow with carefully tended flowers.

August–September: Sunflowers flourish.

October: In the latter half of the month, the countryside glistens with fall colors (since most trees are deciduous). Vineyards go for the gold.

Best Two-Week Trip of Provence & the French Riviera by Train and Bus

Note that on Sundays, fewer trains run, and bus service often disappears.

Day   Plan

1   Fly into Nice. Settle in at your hotel, then take a walk along the promenade des Anglais and up to Castle Hill (see the Welcome to the Riviera Walk chapter). Sleep in or near Nice.

2   Start the morning with my self-guided tour of Old Nice (see the Old Nice Walk chapter), allowing time to smell the fougasse and sample un café. Spend your afternoon at one or more of Nice's fine museums (see the Chagall Museum Tour chapter). Have dinner on the beach. Sleep in or near Nice.

3   Rent a bike, or take a train or the bus to nearby Villefranche-sur-Mer, explore, and have lunch. Consider my recommended seaside walks in Cap Ferrat, or take the one-hour boat cruise from Nice's port. Everyone should spend the afternoon or evening in almost-neighboring Monaco. Sleep in or near Nice.

4   Take a bus north to Vence and St-Paul-de-Vence. Stop for a stroll and visit the Fondation Maeght and/or Matisse's Chapel of the Rosary. Sleep in Vence or back in Nice.

5   Take a train from Nice to Isle-sur-la-Sorgue via Marseille (best to arrive on Sat or Wed and awaken the next morning for market day). Wander and explore the town. Consider a canoe ride down the crystal-clear Sorgue River. Sleep in Isle-sur-la-Sorgue.

6   Enjoy market day this morning, then take a train to Avignon. Take my self-guided Avignon walks this afternoon and enjoy dinner on one of Avignon's many atmospheric squares. Sleep in Avignon.

7   Day-trip to Nîmes and the Pont du Gard aqueduct in the

Know Before You Go

Your trip is more likely to go smoothly if you plan ahead. Check this list of things to arrange while you're still at home.

You need a **passport**—but no visa or shots—to travel in France. You may be denied entry into certain European countries if your passport is due to expire within three to six months of your ticketed date of return. Get it renewed if you'll be cutting it close. It can take up to six weeks to get or renew a passport (for more on passports, see www.travel.state.gov). Pack a photocopy of your passport in your luggage in case the original is lost or stolen.

morning. If the weather's good, bring your swimsuit and float on your back below the 2,000-year-old Pont du Gard. Explore Avignon in the afternoon and spend the night there.

8 Take a morning bus to Vaison la Romaine (market day is Tue, so a Mon arrival is ideal). Set up in Vaison la Romaine for two nights. Few buses run to Vaison la Romaine, though there is always a morning bus from Avignon. Explore Vaison la Romaine's upper medieval village and lower Roman city this afternoon.

9 Tour the wine villages near Vaison la Romaine. Take a mini-van tour of the wine road (see "Tours of Provence," page 40), bike to Séguret and Gigondas, or hike to Le Crestet for lunch (taxi back). Check out Vaison la Romaine's wine cooperative. Sleep in Vaison la Romaine.

10 Take a morning bus to Orange, visit the theater, then hop a train to Arles (big market day on Sat). Check into Arles for the next two nights.

11 Take a taxi (or, in summer, a bus) to Les Baux and have breakfast with a view. Return to Arles by taxi and spend your afternoon there; or take a taxi from Les Baux to St. Rémy-de-Provence, explore there, then catch a bus back to Arles.

12 Hop the train to Cassis. Take a boat trip to the calanques, watch the pétanque balls roll, and end your day with a taxi ride up Cap Canaille. Sleep in Cassis.

13 Take a train to Aix-en-Provence. Have lunch and take my self-guided walking tour of the city, then return home to Cassis and watch the sunset from the old port while you savor a bouillabaisse dinner. Sleep in Cassis.

14 Take the short train ride into Marseille (check your bag at the station), explore the city, then take a train back to Nice. Sleep in Nice.

15 Trip over.

Check to see if you'll be visiting France during any **holidays or festivals,** when rooms can cost more and get booked up quickly. (See "Major Holidays and Weekends" sidebar on page 25).

Call your **debit- and credit-card companies** to let them know the countries you'll be visiting so they'll accept (and not deny) your international charges. Confirm what your daily withdrawal limit is; consider asking to have it raised so you can take out more cash at each ATM stop. Ask about international transaction fees.

If you're interested in **travel insurance,** do your homework before you buy. Compare the cost of the insurance to the likelihood of your using it and your potential loss if something goes wrong. For details on the many kinds of travel insurance, see www.rick steves.com/plan/tips/insurance.htm.

If you'll be **traveling with children,** read over the list of pre-trip suggestions on page 415.

If you're planning on **renting a car** in France, you'll need your driver's license.

All **high-speed trains** in France require a seat reservation—book as early as possible, as these trains fill fast. If you're taking an overnight train (especially to international destinations), and you need a *couchette* (overnight bunk) or sleeper—and you *must* leave on a certain day—consider booking it in advance through a US agent (such as www.raileurope.com), even though it may cost more. (For more on train travel, see page 444 and www.rick steves.com/rail.)

Since **airline carry-on restrictions** are always changing, visit the Transportation Security Administration's website (www.tsa .gov/travelers) for an up-to-date list of what you can bring on the plane with you...and what you have to check.

Practicalities

Emergency Telephone Numbers: In France, dial 17 for police help or 15 for a medical emergency.

Time: In France—and in this book—you'll use the 24-hour clock. It's the same through 12:00 noon, then keep going: 13:00, 14:00, and so on. For anything past 12, subtract 12 and add p.m. (14:00 is 2:00 p.m.)

France, like most of continental Europe, is generally six/nine hours ahead of the East/West Coasts of the US. The exceptions are the beginning and end of Daylight Saving Time: Europe "springs forward" the last Sunday in March (two weeks after most of North America), and "falls back" the last Sunday in October (one week before North America). For a handy online time converter, try www.timeanddate.com/worldclock.

Business Hours: You'll find much of rural France closed weekdays from noon to 14:00 (lunch is sacred). On Sunday, most businesses are closed (family is sacred), though some small stores such as *boulangeries* (bakeries) are open until noon, special events and weekly markets pop up, and museums are open all day (but public transportation options are fewer). On Monday, some businesses are closed until 14:00 and sometimes all day. Smaller towns are often quiet and downright boring on Sundays and Mondays, unless it's market day. Saturdays are virtually weekdays (without the rush hour).

Where Do I Find Information On...?

Credit Card Theft	See page 15.
Packing Light	See the packing list on page 469.
Phoning	See "How to Dial" on page 435.
Language	See page 471.
Making Hotel Reservations	See page 468.
Tipping	See page 16.
Tourist Information Offices	See page 433.
Updates to This Book	See www.ricksteves.com/update

Shopping: The Shopping chapter, near the end of this book, offers tips on how to enjoy Provence's market days. For the nuts-and-bolts details on clothing-size conversions, see page 466 of the appendix. For customs regulations and VAT refunds (the tax refunded on large purchases made by non-EU residents), see page 17.

Watt's Up? Europe's electrical system is different from North America's in two ways: the shape of the plug (two round prongs) and the voltage of the current (220 volts instead of 110 volts). For your North American plug to work in Europe, you'll need an adapter, sold inexpensively at travel stores in the US. As for the voltage, most newer electronics or travel appliances (such as hair dryers, laptops, and battery chargers) automatically convert the voltage—if you see a range of voltages printed on the item or its plug (such as "110–220"), it'll work in Europe. Otherwise, you can buy a converter separately in the US (about $20).

Discounts: Although discounts aren't listed in this book, seniors (age 60 and over), students with International Student Identification Cards, teachers with proper identification, and youths under 18 or even 26 often get discounts. Always ask. Some discounts are available only for EU citizens. To inquire about a senior discount, ask, *"Réduction troisième âge?"* (ray-dook-see-ohn twah-zee-ehm ahzh). To get a teacher or student ID card, visit www.statravel.com or www.isic.org.

News: Americans keep in touch via the *International Herald Tribune* (published almost daily throughout Europe and online at www.iht.com). Other newsy sites are http://news.bbc.co.uk and www.europeantimes.com. Every Tuesday, the European editions of *Time* and *Newsweek* hit the stands with articles of particular interest to European travelers. Sports addicts can get their daily fix online or from *USA Today*. Many hotels have CNN and BBC television channels.

Money

This section offers advice on getting cash, using credit and debit cards, dealing with lost or stolen cards, and tipping.

Cash from ATMs

Throughout Europe, cash machines (ATMs) are the standard way for travelers to get local currency. Travelers checks are a waste of time in banks and a waste of money in fees.

As an emergency backup, bring several hundred dollars (in easy-to-exchange $20 bills). Avoid currency exchange booths—they're known for enticing come-ons, but lousy rates and/or outrageous fees. If you have foreign currency to exchange, take it to a bank.

Bring plastic—debit and credit cards. It's smart to bring two cards, in case one gets demagnetized or eaten by a temperamental machine. To withdraw money from an ATM—known as a *retrait* or *distributeur (de billets)*—you'll need a debit card (ideally with a Visa or MasterCard logo for maximum usability), plus a PIN code. Know your PIN code in numbers; there are only numbers—no letters—on European keypads.

Before you go, confirm with your bank that your card will work overseas, and alert them that you'll be making withdrawals in Europe. Otherwise, the bank may not approve transactions if it perceives unusual spending patterns. (Your credit-card company may do the same thing—let them know about your travel plans, too.) Also ask about international fees; see "Credit and Debit Cards," below.

When using an ATM, try to take out large sums of money to reduce your per-transaction bank fees. If the machine refuses your request, try again and select a smaller amount (some cash machines limit the amount you can withdraw—don't take it personally). If that doesn't work, try a different machine.

To keep your cash safe, use a money belt—a pouch with a strap that you buckle around your waist like a belt and wear under your clothes. Thieves target tourists. A money belt provides peace of mind, allowing you to carry lots of cash safely. Don't waste time every few days tracking down a cash machine—withdraw a week's worth of money, stuff it in your money belt, and travel!

Credit and Debit Cards

For purchases, Visa and MasterCard are more commonly accepted than American Express. Just like at home, credit or debit cards work easily at larger hotels, restaurants, and shops, but smaller businesses prefer payment in local currency (in small bills—break large bills at a bank or larger store). If receipts show your credit-card number, don't toss these thoughtlessly.

Exchange Rate

1 euro (€) = about $1.40

To convert prices in euros to dollars, add about 40 percent: €20 = about $28, €50 = about $70. (You can check www .oanda.com for the most up-to-date exchange rates and to print out a cheat sheet.) Just like the dollar, the euro is broken down into 100 cents. You'll find coins ranging from 1 cent to 2 euros, and bills from 5 euros to 500 euros.

Fees: Credit and debit cards—whether used for purchases or ATM withdrawals—often charge additional, tacked-on "international transaction" fees of up to 3 percent plus $5 per transaction. Note that if you use a credit card for ATM transactions, it's technically a "cash advance" rather than a "withdrawal"—and subject to an additional cash-advance fee.

To avoid unpleasant surprises, call your bank or credit-card company before your trip to ask about these fees. If the fees are too high, consider getting a card just for your trip: Capital One (www .capitalone.com) and most credit unions have low-to-no international transaction fees.

If merchants offer to convert your purchase price into dollars (called dynamic currency conversion, or DCC), refuse this "service." You'll pay even more in fees for the expensive convenience of seeing your charge in dollars.

Dealing with "Chip and PIN": Some parts of Europe (especially France, Great Britain, Ireland, the Netherlands, and Scandinavia) are adopting a "chip and PIN" system for their credit and debit cards. These "smartcards" come with an embedded microchip, and cardholders enter a PIN instead of signing a receipt. In most cases, you can still use your credit or debit card at the cashier and sign the receipt the old-fashioned way. A few merchants might insist on the PIN—making it helpful for you to know the PIN for your credit card (ask your credit-card company); in a pinch, use cash or your debit card and PIN instead.

Your US credit and debit cards will not work in train- or Métro-ticket machines, at self-service gas pumps, or at freeway tollbooths. But sometimes there's a cashier nearby who can take your credit or debit card and make it work.

Damage Control for Lost Cards

If you lose your credit, debit, or ATM card, you can stop people from using it by reporting the loss immediately to the respective global customer-assistance centers. Call these 24-hour US numbers collect: Visa (410/581-9994), MasterCard (636/722-7111), and American Express (623/492-8427). For another option (with the same results), you can call these toll-free numbers in France: Visa (08 00 90 11 79) and MasterCard (08 00 90 13 87). American Express has a Paris office, but the call isn't free (01 47 77 70 00, English spoken). Diners Club has offices in the US (702/797-5532, call collect) and Britain (from France, dial 00-44-1695-53760).

At a minimum, you'll need to know the name of the financial institution that issued you the card, along with the type of card (classic, platinum, or whatever). Providing the following information will allow for a quicker cancellation of your missing card: full card number, whether you are the primary or secondary cardholder, the cardholder's name exactly as printed on the card, billing address, home phone number, circumstances of the loss or theft, and identification verification (your birth date, your mother's maiden name, or your Social Security number—memorize this, don't carry a copy). If you are the secondary cardholder, you'll also need to provide the primary cardholder's identification-verification details. You can generally receive a temporary card within two or three business days in Europe.

If you promptly report your card lost or stolen, you typically won't be responsible for any unauthorized transactions on your account, although many banks charge a liability fee of $50.

Tipping

Tipping *(donner un pourboire)* in France isn't as automatic and generous as it is in the US, but for special service, tips are appreciated, if not expected. As in the US, the proper amount depends on your resources, tipping philosophy, and the circumstances, but some general guidelines apply.

Restaurants: At cafés and restaurants, a 10–15 percent service charge is always included in the bill *(service compris)*, though it's appropriate to tip up to 5 percent extra for superior service. When you hand your payment plus a tip to your waiter, you can say, "*C'est bon*" (say bohn), meaning, "It's good" (and you don't want any change back). If you order a meal at a counter, don't tip.

Taxis: To tip the cabbie, round up. For a typical ride, round up to the next euro on the fare (for a €13 fare, give €14); for a long ride, round to the nearest €10 (for a €75 fare, give €80). If the cabbie hauls your bags and zips you to the airport to help you catch your flight, you might want to toss in a little more. But if you feel like you're being driven in circles or otherwise ripped off, skip the tip.

Special Services: It's thoughtful to tip a couple of euros to someone who shows you a special sight and who is paid in no other way. Tour guides at sights sometimes hold out their hands for tips

(€1–2) after they give their spiel; if I've already paid for the tour, I don't tip extra, unless they really impressed me. At hotels, porters expect a euro for each bag they carry (another reason to pack light). Leaving the maid a euro per overnight at the end of your stay is a nice touch. In general, if someone in the service industry does a super job for you, a tip of a couple of euros is appropriate, but not required.

When in doubt, ask. If you're not sure whether (or how much) to tip for a service, ask your hotelier or the tourist information office; they'll fill you in on how it's done on their turf.

Getting a VAT Refund

Wrapped into the purchase price of your French souvenirs is a Value-Added Tax (VAT) of about 19.6 percent. If you purchase more than €175 (about $245) worth of goods at a store that participates in the VAT-refund scheme, you're entitled to get most of that tax back. Getting your refund is usually straightforward and, if you buy a substantial amount of souvenirs, well worth the hassle. If you're lucky, the merchant will subtract the tax when you make your purchase. (This is more likely to occur if the store ships the goods to your home.) Otherwise, you'll need to:

Get the paperwork. Have the merchant completely fill out the necessary refund document, *Bordereau de Vente a l'Exportation*, also called a "cheque." You'll have to present your passport at the store.

Get your stamp at the border or airport. Process your cheque(s) at your last stop in the EU (e.g., at the airport) with the customs agent who deals with VAT refunds. It's best to keep your purchases in your carry-on for viewing, but if they're too large or dangerous (such as knives) to carry on, track down the proper customs agent to inspect them before you check your bag. You're not supposed to use your purchased goods before you leave. If you show up at customs wearing your chic new French ensemble, officials might look the other way—or deny you a refund.

Collect your refund. You'll need to return your stamped document to the retailer or its representative. Many merchants work with a service, such as Global Refund (www.globalrefund.com) or Premier Tax Free (www.premiertaxfree.com), which have offices at major airports, ports, or border crossings. These services, which extract a 4 percent fee, can refund your money immediately in your currency of choice or credit your card (within two billing cycles). If the retailer handles VAT refunds directly, it's up to you to contact the merchant for your refund. You can mail the documents from home, or quicker, from your point of departure (using a stamped, addressed envelope you've prepared or one that's been provided by the merchant). You'll then have to wait—it could take months.

Customs for American Shoppers

You are allowed to take home $800 worth of items per person duty-free, once every 30 days. The next $1,000 is taxed at a flat 3 percent. After that, you pay the individual item's duty rate. You can also bring in duty-free a liter of alcohol (slightly more than a standard-size bottle of wine; you must be at least 21), 200 cigarettes, and up to 100 non-Cuban cigars. You may take home vacuum-packed cheeses; dried herbs, spices, or mushrooms; and canned fruits or vegetables, including jams and vegetable spreads. Baked goods, candy, chocolate, oil, vinegar, mustard, and honey are OK. Fresh fruits or vegetables are not. Meats are generally not allowed, though canned pâtés are permitted if made from geese, duck, or pork. Note that you'll need to carefully pack any bottles of wine and other liquid-containing items in your checked luggage, due to limits on liquids in carry-ons. To check customs rules and duty rates before you go, visit www.cbp.gov, and click on "Travel," then "Know Before You Go."

Sightseeing

Sightseeing can be hard work. Use these tips to make your visits to Provence's and the Riviera's finest sights meaningful, fun, efficient, and painless.

Plan Ahead

Set up an itinerary that allows you to fit in all your must-see sights. For a one-stop look at opening hours in the bigger cities, see the "At a Glance" sidebars for Arles, Avignon, Marseille, Nice, and Monaco. Most sights keep stable hours, but you can easily confirm the latest by calling the local TI.

If you'll be visiting during a holiday, find out if a particular sight will be open by phoning ahead or checking its website. And don't put off visiting a must-see sight—you never know when a place will close unexpectedly for a holiday, strike, or restoration.

When possible, visit major sights in the morning (when your energy is best) and save other activities for the afternoon. Hit the highlights first, then go back to other things if you have the stamina and time.

Going at the right time can also help you avoid crowds and traffic jams. This book offers tips on specific sights. Ideally, visit the following sights on weekdays, and arrive early or late: Les Baux, Pont du Gard, Séguret, Roussillon, Fontaine de Vaucluse, Nice's Chagall and Antibes' Picasso museums, St-Paul-de-Vence, Eze-le-Village, and St-Tropez. The *calanques* near Cassis are best early, but not late.

Read ahead. To get the most out of the self-guided tours

and sight descriptions in this book, read them before you visit. Several cities offer sightseeing passes that are worthwhile values for serious sightseers; plan ahead.

At Sights

All sights have rules, and if you know about these in advance, they're no big deal.

At churches—most of which offer interesting art (usually free) and a cool, welcome seat—a modest dress code is encouraged (no bare shoulders or shorts).

Some important sights have metal detectors or conduct bag searches that will slow your entry, and major museums and sights require you to check daypacks and coats. They'll be kept safely. If you have something you can't bear to part with, stash it in a pocket or purse. To avoid checking a small backpack, carry it under your arm like a purse as you enter. From a guard's point of view, a backpack is generally a problem while a purse is not. If you check a bag, the attendant may ask you (in French) if it contains anything of value—camera, phone, money, passport—since these cannot be checked.

Photography is sometimes banned at major sights. Look for signs or ask. If cameras are allowed, flashes or tripods are usually not. Flashes damage oil paintings and distract others in the room. Even without a flash, a handheld camera will take a decent picture (or you can buy postcards or posters at the museum bookstore). Video cameras are generally allowed.

Museums may have special exhibits in addition to their permanent collection. Some exhibits are included in the entry price; others come at an extra cost (which you may have to pay even if you don't want to see the exhibit).

Many sights rent audioguides, which offer useful recorded descriptions in English (about €6). If you bring along your own pair of headphones and a Y-jack, you can sometimes share one audioguide with your travel partner and save money. Guided tours in English are most likely to be offered during peak season (around €8) and range widely in quality.

Expect changes—artwork can be on tour, on loan, out sick, or shifted at the whim of the curator. To adapt, pick up any available free floor plans as you enter. Ask the museum staff if you can't find a particular painting. Say the title or artist's name, or point to the photograph in this book, and ask for its location by saying, *"Où est?"* (oo ay).

Important sights often have an on-site café or cafeteria (usually a good place to rest and have a snack or light meal). The WCs at many sights are free and clean.

Many places sell postcards and guidebooks that highlight

their attractions. Before you leave, scan the postcards and thumb through the biggest guidebook (or skim its index) to be sure you haven't overlooked something that you'd like to see.

Most sights stop admitting people 30–60 minutes before closing time, and some rooms close early (generally about 45 minutes before the actual closing time). Guards usher people out, so don't save the best for last.

Every sight or museum offers more than what is covered in this book. Use this information as an introduction—not the final word.

Sleeping

Accommodations in Provence and the Riviera are a good value and generally easy to find. Choose from one- to four-star hotels (two stars is my mainstay), bed-and-breakfasts *(chambres d'hôte,* usually cheaper than hotels), hostels, campgrounds, and even homes *(gîtes,* rented by the week). I like hotels and B&Bs that are clean, small, central, traditional, friendly, and a good value. Most places I list have at least four of these six virtues. For tips on making reservations, see page 27.

Types of Accommodations
Hotels
In this book, the price for a double room will range from €40 (very simple, toilet and shower down the hall) to €300-plus (maximum plumbing and more), with most clustering at around €80–110.

The French have a simple hotel rating system based on amenities (zero through four stars, indicated in this book by * through ****). One star is modest, two has most of the comforts, and three is generally a two-star with a fancier lobby and more elaborately designed rooms. Four stars offer more luxury than you usually have time to appreciate. Two- and three-star hotels are required to have an English-speaking staff, though virtually all hotels I recommend have someone who speaks English (unless I note otherwise in the listing). The number of stars does not usually reflect room size or guarantee quality. Some two-star hotels are better than many three-star hotels. One- and two-star hotels are inexpensive, but some three-star (and even a few four-star hotels) offer good value, justifying the extra cost. Unclassified hotels (no stars) can be bargains or depressing dumps.

Most hotels have lots of doubles and a few singles, triples, and quads. Traveling alone can be expensive, as singles (except for the rare closet-type rooms that fit only one twin bed) are simply doubles used by one person—so they cost about the same as

Types of Rooms

Study the price list on the hotel's website or posted at the desk, so you know your options. Receptionists often don't mention the cheaper rooms—they assume you want a private bathroom or a bigger room. Here are the types of rooms and beds:

une chambre sans douche et WC	room without a private shower or toilet (uncommon these days)
une chambre avec cabinet de toilette	room with a toilet but no shower (some hotels charge for down-the-hall showers)
une chambre avec bain et WC	room with private bathtub and toilet
une chambre avec douche et WC	room with private shower and toilet
chambres communiquantes	connecting rooms (ideal for families)
un grand lit	double bed (55 inches wide)
deux petits lits	twin beds (30–36 inches wide)
un lit single	a true single room
un lit de cent-soixante	queen-size bed (literally 160 centimeters, or 63 inches wide)
le king size	a king-size bed (usually two twins pushed together)
un lit pliant	folding bed
un bérceau	baby crib
un lit d'enfant	child's bed

a double. Room prices vary within each hotel depending on size, and whether the room has a bath or shower, and twin beds or a double bed (tubs and twins cost more than showers and double beds). A triple is often the same as a double room, with a double or queen-size bed plus a sliver-size single. Quad rooms usually have two double beds. Hotels cannot legally allow more in the room than what's shown on their price list. Modern hotels generally have a few family-friendly rooms that open to each other *(chambres communiquantes)*.

Given the economic downturn, some hoteliers might be willing to make a deal. I'd suggest emailing several hotels to ask for their best price. Comparison-shop and make your choice. As you look over the listings, you'll notice that many hotels promise special prices to my readers who book direct (without using a room-finding service or hotel-booking website, which take a commission). To get these rates, mention this book when you reserve,

INTRODUCTION

Keep Cool

If you're planning to visit southern France in the summer, the extra expense of an air-conditioned room can be money well spent. Most hotel rooms with air-conditioners come with a control stick (like a TV remote) that generally has the same symbols and features: fan icon (click to toggle through wind power, from light to gale); louver icon (choose steady airflow or waves); snowflake and sunshine icons (cold air or heat, depending on season); clock ("O" setting: run *X* hours before turning off; "I" setting: wait *X* hours to start); and the temperature control (20 or 21 degrees Celsius is comfortable; also see the thermometer diagram on page 467).

then show the book upon arrival. During slow times, or for long stays, rooms might be offered for even less than listed. To get the best deal, ask for their best price possible, and identify yourself as a Rick Steves reader.

Hotels in France must charge a daily tax *(taxe du séjour)* of about €1 per person per day. While some hotels include it in the price list, most add it to your bill.

You can save as much as €25 by finding the rare room without a private shower or toilet. A room with a bathtub usually costs more than a room with a shower (and is generally larger). Hotels often have more rooms with tubs than showers and are inclined to give you a room with a tub (which the French prefer).

A double bed is usually cheaper than twins, though rooms with twin beds tend to be larger, and French double beds are smaller than American double beds. Many hotels have queen-size beds (a bed that's 63 inches wide—most doubles are 55 inches). To learn if a hotel has queen-size beds, ask, *"Avez-vous des lits de cent-soixante?"* (ah-vay-voo day lee duh sahn-swah-sahnt). Some hotels push two twins together under king-size sheets and blankets to make *le king size*.

If you prefer a double bed (instead of twins) and a shower (instead of a tub), you need to ask for it—and you can save up to €20. If you'll take either twins or a double, ask generically for *une chambre pour deux* (room for two) to avoid being needlessly turned away.

Hotel lobbies, halls, and breakfast rooms are off-limits to smokers, though they can light up in their rooms. Still, I rarely smell any smoke in the hundreds of rooms I check each year. Some hotels have non-smoking rooms or floors—ask about them if this is important to you. If your room smells of smoke, ask for another one.

Most hotels offer some kind of breakfast, but it's rarely included in the room rates. The price of breakfast usually correlates with the price of the room: The more expensive the room, the

Sleep Code

(€1 = about $1.40, country code: 33)
To help you sort easily through these listings, I've divided the rooms into three categories based on the price for a standard double room with bath:

$$\$\$\$ \quad \textbf{Higher Priced}$$
$$\$\$ \quad \textbf{Moderately Priced}$$
$$\$ \quad \textbf{Lower Priced}$$

To give maximum information in a minimum of space, I use the following code to describe the accommodations. Prices listed are per room, not per person. When a price range is given for a type of room (such as double rooms listing for €100–130), it means the price fluctuates with the season, size of room, or length of stay.

S = Single room (or price for one person in a double).
D = Double or twin.
T = Triple (generally a double bed with a single).
Q = Quad (usually two double beds).
b = Private bathroom with toilet and shower or tub.
s = Private shower or tub only (the toilet is down the hall).
* = French hotel rating system, ranging from zero to four stars.

According to this code, a couple staying at a "Db-€90" hotel would pay a total of €90 (about $126) for a double room with a private bathroom. You can assume a hotel takes credit cards unless you see "cash only" in the listing. Unless otherwise noted, hotel staff speak basic English, and breakfast is not included (but is usually optional).

If I list "Internet access," there's a public terminal in the lobby for guests to use. If I list "Wi-Fi", you can generally access it in your room (usually for free), but only if you have your own laptop.

---

more expensive the breakfast. This per-person charge can add up, particularly for families, so beware. While hotels hope that you'll buy their breakfast, it's optional unless otherwise noted (for more on breakfast, see "Eating," later in this chapter).

Some hotels, especially in coastal resort towns, strongly encourage their peak-season guests to take *demi-pension* (half-pension)—that is, breakfast and either lunch or dinner. By law, they can't require you to take half-pension unless you are staying three or more nights, but, in practice, many do during summer. While the food is usually good, it limits your ability to shop around. I've indicated where I think *demi-pension* is a good value.

Rooms are safe. Still, keep cameras and money out of sight. Towels aren't routinely replaced every day; drip-dry and conserve. Extra pillows and blankets are often in the closet or available on request. To get a pillow, ask for *"Un oreiller, s'il vous plaît"* (un oh-ray-yay, see voo play).

Your hotelier, a good source of advice, can direct you to the nearest launderette or Internet café. Some hoteliers will ask you to sign their *Livre d'Or* (literally "Golden Book," for client comments). They take this seriously and enjoy reading your remarks. To avoid the time-wasting line at the reception desk in the morning (or a last-minute dispute over the bill), ask if you can settle your bill the evening before you leave.

Modern Hotel Chains: France is littered with sterile, ultramodern hotels, usually located on cheap land just outside of town, providing drivers with low-stress accommodations. The antiseptically clean and cheap Formule 1 and ETAP chains (about €40–50/room for up to three people), the more attractive Ibis hotels (€80–100 for a double), and the cushier Mercure and Novotel hotels (€110–170 for a double) are all run by the same company, Accor (www.accorhotels.com). While far from quaint, these can be a good value (particularly if you find deals on their website), and some are centrally located. A smaller chain, Kyriad, offers good prices and quality (France tel. 08 25 00 30 03, overseas tel. 33 1 64 62 46 46—push 1 to make a reservation, www.kyriad.com; these telephone numbers also work for eight affiliated chains, including Clarine, Climat de France, and Campanile). For a long listing of various hotels throughout France, see www.france.com.

Bed-and-Breakfasts

B&Bs (*Chambres d'hôte*, abbreviated CH in this book) are generally found in smaller towns and rural areas. They're a great deal, offering double the cultural intimacy for much less than most hotel rooms—and helping to compensate for the low value of the dollar. While you may lose some hotel conveniences—such as lounges, in-room phones, daily bed-sheet changes, and credit-card payments—I happily make the trade-off for the personal touch and lower rates. You'll find B&Bs in this book and through local tourist offices, often listed by the owner's family name. It's always OK to ask to see the room before you commit. While some CHs post small *Chambres* or *Chambres d'hôte* signs in their front windows, many are found only through the local tourist office.

I recommend reliable CHs that offer a good value and/or unique experience (such as CHs in renovated mills, châteaux, and wine *domaines*). While *chambres d'hôte* have their own star-rating system, it doesn't quite correspond to the hotels' rating system. So, to avoid confusion, I haven't listed these stars for CHs. But

Major Holidays and Weekends

Popular places are even busier on weekends...and inundated on three-day weekends. Holiday weekends can make towns, trains, roads, and hotels more crowded than in summer. Book your accommodations and train trips well in advance if you'll be traveling during busy times.

In 2010, expect unusually big crowds on: Easter weekend and the two weeks following it (April 2-18, busiest April 2-11); Labor Day weekend (April 30-May 2); Ascension weekend (May 13-16); Pentecost weekend (May 21-23); Bastille Day (July 14) and the week during which it falls; Assumption weekend (Aug 13-15); and the winter holidays (Dec 19-Jan 2—note that Christmas week is quieter than the week of New Year's). All Saints' Day (Nov 1) and Armistice Day (Nov 11) are usually quiet, but holidays nonetheless. For information on festivals, see page 463 of the appendix.

most of my recommended CHs have private in-room bathrooms, and some have common rooms with refrigerators. Doubles with breakfast generally cost €55-75 (breakfast may or may not be included—ask). *Tables d'hôte* are CHs that offer an optional, reasonably priced, home-cooked dinner (usually a fine value, must be requested in advance). While your hosts may not speak English, they will almost always be enthusiastic and pleasant.

Hostels

You'll pay about €20 per bed to stay at a hostel *(auberge de jeunesse)*. People of any age are welcome if they don't mind dorm-style accommodations or meeting other travelers. Cheap meals are sometimes offered, and kitchen facilities may be available. Expect youth groups in spring, crowds in the summer, snoring, and great variability in quality from one hostel to the next. Family and private rooms are sometimes available on request, but it's basically boys' dorms and girls' dorms. You usually can't check in before 17:00 and must be out by 10:00. There is often a 23:00 curfew. Official Hostelling International (HI) hostels are marked with a triangular sign that shows a house and a tree. Some hostels accept reservations only by email. If you'll be staying for several days in an HI hostel, consider buying a membership card before you go (www.hihostels.com).

Camping

In Europe, camping is more of a social than an environmental experience. It's a great way for American travelers to make European friends. Camping costs about €15-20 per campsite per night, and almost every destination recommended in this book has a campground within a reasonable walk or bus ride from the town center and train station. A tent and sleeping bag are all you need. Many campgrounds have small grocery stores and washing machines, and some even come with discos and miniature golf. Hot showers are better at campgrounds than at many hotels. Local TIs have camping information. You'll find more detailed information in the annually updated *Michelin Camping France*, available in the United States and at most French bookstores.

Gîtes and Apartments

Throughout France, you can find reasonably priced rental homes, and nowhere are there more options than in Provence and the Riviera. Because this region is so small, you could rent one home in Provence and one in the Riviera, and day-trip to most of the sights described in this book.

Gîtes (pronounced "zheet") are country homes (usually urban-ites' second homes) that the government rents out to visitors who want a week in the countryside (the homes are rented for at least a week at a time, from Saturday to Saturday). The objective of the *gîte* program was to save characteristic rural homes from aban-donment and to make it easy and affordable for families to enjoy the French countryside. The government offers subsidies to reno-vate such homes, then coordinates rentals to make it financially feasible for the owner. Today, France has more than 8,000 *gîtes*. One of your co-authors restored a farmhouse a few hours north of Provence, and even though he and his wife are American, they received the same assistance that French owners get.

Gîtes are best for drivers (they're usually rural, with little public-transport access) and ideal for families and small groups (since they can sleep many for the same price). Homes range in comfort from simple cottages and farmhouses to restored châteaux. Most have at least two bedrooms, a kitchen, a living room, and a bathroom or two—but no sheets or linens (though you can usu-ally rent them for extra). Like hotels, all *gîtes* are rated for comfort from one to four (using ears of corn—*épis*—rather than stars). Two or three *épis* are generally sufficient quality, but I'd lean toward three for more comfort. Prices generally range from €350–1,200 per week, depending on house size and amenities such as pools. For more information on *gîtes* in Provence, visit www.provence -guide.com, www.gites-de-france.com/gites, or www.gite.com.

Apartments, less common than *gîtes*, are available in cities and in towns along the Riviera (one-week minimum rentals). Avignon, Aix-en-Provence, Nice, and other Riviera towns have the biggest selection. It's usually more expensive to stay in an apartment than in a *gîte*.

You'll find long lists of homes and apartments for rent through TIs and on the Internet. Here are two good independent sources to consider: **France Homestyle** is run by Claudette, a service–oriented French woman from Seattle who handpicks every home and apartment she lists (US tel. 206/325-0132, www.francehome style.com, info@francehomestyle.com). Or try **Ville et Village,** which has a bigger selection of higher-end places (US tel. 510/559-8080, www.villeetvillage.com, rentals@villeetvillage.com).

Phoning

To make an international call to France to line up hotel reservations, you'll need to know its country code: 33. To call from the US or Canada, dial 011-33-local number (drop the initial 0 from the local number). If calling France from another European country, dial 00-33-local number (without the initial 0). For more information on telephoning, see page 435.

Making Reservations

Given the quality of the accommodations I've found for this book, I recommend that you reserve your rooms in advance, particularly if you'll be traveling during peak season. Book several months ahead, or as soon as you've pinned down your travel dates. Note that some national holidays merit your making reservations far in advance (see "Major Holidays and Weekends" sidebar). Just like at home, holidays that fall on a Monday, Thursday, or Friday can turn the weekend into a long holiday, so book the entire weekend well in advance.

Requesting a Reservation: To reserve, contact hotels directly by email, phone, or fax. Email is the clearest and most economical way to make a reservation. Or you can go straight to the hotel website; many have secure online reservation forms and can instantly inform you of availability and any special deals. But be sure you use the hotel's official site and not a booking agency's site—otherwise you may pay higher rates than you should. If you're phoning from the US, be mindful of time zones (see page 12). Most hotels listed are accustomed to guests who speak only English.

The hotelier wants to know these key pieces of information (also included in the sample request form on page 468 and at www.ricksteves.com/reservation):

- number and type of rooms
- number of nights
- date of arrival
- date of departure
- any special needs (e.g., bathroom in the room or down the hall, twin beds vs. double bed, air-conditioning, quiet, view, ground floor, etc.)

When you request a room, use the European style for writing dates: day/month/year. For example, for a two-night stay in July, I would request: "1 double room for 2 nights, arrive 16/07/10, depart 18/07/10." (Consider carefully how long you'll stay; don't just assume you can tack on extra days once you arrive.)

If you don't get a reply to your email or fax, it usually means the hotel is already fully booked (but you can try sending the message again, or call to follow up).

Confirming a Reservation: If the hotel's response includes its room availability and rates, it's not a confirmation. You must tell them that you want that room at the given rate. The hotelier will usually request your credit-card number for a one-night deposit to hold the room. While you can email your credit-card information (I do), it's safer to share that personal info via phone call, fax, two successive emails, or secure online reservation form (if the hotel has one on its website).

Canceling a Reservation: If you must cancel your reservation, it's courteous to do so with as much advance notice as possible—at least three days. Simply make a quick phone call or send an email. Family-run hotels and *chambres d'hôte* lose money if they turn away customers while holding a room for someone who doesn't show up. Understandably, many hotels bill no-shows for one night.

Some hotels require seven days' notice, while most want three days; otherwise, you might lose a deposit. Or you might be billed for the entire visit if you leave early. Ask about cancellation policies before you book.

If canceling via email, request confirmation that your cancellation was received to avoid being accidentally billed.

Reconfirm Your Reservation: Always call to reconfirm your room reservation a day or two in advance from the road. Smaller hotels and *chambres d'hôte* appreciate knowing your time of arrival. If you'll be arriving after 17:00, be sure to let your hotelier know. On the small chance that a hotel loses track of your reservation, bring along a hard copy of their emailed or faxed confirmation.

Reserving Rooms as You Travel: If you enjoy having a flexible itinerary, you can make reservations as you travel, calling hotels or *chambres d'hôte* a few days to a week before your visit. If you prefer the freedom of traveling without any reservations at all, you'll have greater success snaring rooms if you arrive at your destination early in the day. When you anticipate crowds (weekends are worst), call hotels at about 9:00 on the day you plan to arrive, when the hotel clerk knows who'll be checking out and just which rooms will be available. If you encounter a language barrier, ask the fluent receptionist at your current hotel to call for you.

Eating

The French eat long and well—nowhere more so than in the south. Relaxed and tree-shaded lunches with a chilled rosé, three-hour dinners, and endless afternoons at outdoor cafés are the norm. Local cafés, cuisine, and wines should become a highlight of any French adventure. It's sightseeing for your palate. Even if the rest of you is sleeping in cheap hotels, let your taste buds travel first class in France. (They can go coach in England.) You can eat well without going broke—but choose carefully: You're just as likely to blow a small fortune on a mediocre meal as you are to dine wonderfully for €20. For specific suggestions on what to order where, see my cuisine suggestions in the introductions to Provence (page 44) and the Riviera (page 264).

Dining indoors improved dramatically for non-smokers after a recent law mandated that all café and restaurant interiors be smoke-free. Today the only smokers you'll find are at outside tables, which—unfortunately—may be exactly where you want to be.

Waiters probably won't overwhelm you with friendliness (their tip is included in the bill, so there's less schmoozing than we're used to at home). Notice how hard they work. They almost never stop. Cozying up to clients (French or foreign) is probably the last thing on their minds. To get a waiter's attention, say, "*S'il vous plaît*" (see voo play)—"please."

Breakfast

You'll almost always have the option of breakfast at your hotel, which is pleasant and convenient. *Petit déjeuner* (puh-tee day-zhuh-nay) starts with café au lait, hot chocolate, or tea, and a roll with butter and marmalade. Some hotels offer only this classic continental breakfast for about €8, while others put out a buffet breakfast for about €10–15 (cereal, yogurt, fruit, cheese, croissants, juice, and the occasional hard-boiled egg)—which I usually spring for.

If all you want is coffee or tea and a croissant, the corner café is cheaper (though you get more coffee at your hotel). Go local at the café and ask for *une tartine* (oon tart-een; baguette slathered with butter or jam) with your café au lait. To keep it really cheap, pick up some fruit at a grocery store and pastries at your favorite *boulangerie* (bakery), and have a picnic breakfast, then savor your coffee at the bar *(comptoir)* while standing, like the locals do. For a less atmospheric alternative, some fast-food places offer very cheap breakfasts.

Picnics

For most lunches—*déjeuner* (day-zhuh-nay)—I picnic, munch a take-away sandwich from a *boulangerie,* or get a crêpe from a *crêperie.*

Picnics can be first-class affairs and adventures in high cuisine. Be daring. Try the smelly cheeses, ugly pâtés, sissy quiches, and miniscule yogurts. Local shopkeepers are accustomed to selling small quantities of produce. Try the tasty salads-to-go and ask for a plastic fork *(une fourchette en plastique)*. A small container is *une barquette*.

Gather supplies early for a picnic lunch; you'll probably visit several small stores to assemble a complete meal, and many close at noon for their lunch break. Look for a *boulangerie*, a *crémerie* or *fromagerie* (cheeses), a *charcuterie* or *traiteur* (deli items, prepared salads, meats, and pâtés), an *épicerie* or *magasin d'alimentation* (small grocery with fruit, veggies, drinks, and so on), and a *pâtisserie* (delicious pastries). While wine is taboo in public places in the US, it's *pas de problème* in France.

Open-air markets *(marchés)* are fun and photogenic, and they close at about 13:00 (many are listed in this book; local TIs have complete lists). There's much more information about these wonderful Provençal experiences in the Shopping chapter (see "Market Day" on page 420). Local *supermarchés* are less colorful but cheaper, more efficient, and offer adequate quality. Department stores often have supermarkets in the basement. On the outskirts of cities, you'll find the monster *hypermarchés*. Drop in for a glimpse of hyper-France in action.

In stores, unrefrigerated soft drinks, bottled water, and beer are one-third the price of cold drinks. Milk, bottled water, and boxed fruit juice are the cheapest drinks. Avoid buying drinks to go at streetside stands; you'll find them for far less in a shop. Try to keep a water bottle with you. Water quenches your thirst better and cheaper than anything you'll find in a store or café. I drink tap water throughout France, filling my bottle in hotel rooms as I go.

Sandwiches and Other Quick Bites

Everywhere in Provence and the Riviera, you'll find bakeries and small stands selling baguette sandwiches, quiche, and pizza-like items to go for about €4. Usually filling and tasty, they also streamline the picnic process. (If you don't want your sandwich drenched in mayonnaise, ask for it *sans mayonnaise;* sahn my-oh-nehz.) Here are some sandwiches you'll see:

Anything *à la provençal* (ah lah proh-vehn-sahl): A sandwich with marinated peppers, tomatoes, and eggplant.

Fromage (froh-mahzh): Cheese (white on beige).

Jambon beurre (zhahn-bohn bur): Ham and butter (boring for most).

Jambon crudités (zhahn-bohn krew-dee-tay): Ham with tomatoes, lettuce, cucumbers, and mayonnaise.

Poulet crudités (poo-lay krew-dee-tay): Chicken with tomatoes, lettuce, maybe cucumbers, and always mayonnaise.

Saucisson beurre (saw-see-sohn burr): Thinly sliced sausage and butter.

Thon crudités (tohn krew-dee-tay): Tuna with tomatoes, lettuce, and sometimes cucumbers, but definitely mayonnaise.

Look also for grilled *panini* sandwiches *à la italienne.*

Café Culture

French cafés and brasseries provide budget-friendly meals and a refuge from museum and church overload. At either, feel free to order only a bowl of soup or a salad or *plat* (main course) for lunch, dinner, or any time of day.

Cafés and brasseries usually open by 7:00, but closing hours vary. Unlike restaurants, which open only for lunch and dinner and close in between, some cafés and all brasseries serve food throughout the day (though with a more limited menu than at restaurants), making them the best option for a late lunch or an early dinner. (Note that many cafés in smaller towns close their kitchens from about 14:00 until 18:00.)

If you're a novice, it's easier to sit and feel comfortable when you know the system. Check the price list first, which by law must be posted prominently. There are two sets of prices: You'll pay more for the same drink if you're seated at a table *(salle)* than if you're seated at the bar or counter *(comptoir)*. For tips on beverages, see next page.

Standard Menu Items: *Croque monsieur* (grilled ham-and-cheese sandwich) and *croque madame* (*croque monsieur* with a fried egg on top) are generally served day and night. Sandwiches are least expensive, but plain—and much better at the *boulangerie*. To get more than a piece of ham *(jambon)* on a baguette, order a sandwich *crudité*, which means garnished with veggies. Omelets come lonely on a plate with a basket of bread. The daily special—*plat du jour* (plah dew zhoor), or just *plat*—is your fast, hearty, and garnished hot plate for €10–15. At most cafés, feel free to order only *entrées* (which in French means the starter course); many find these lighter and more interesting than a main course. A vegetarian can enjoy a tasty, filling meal by ordering two *entrées*. Regardless of what you order, bread is free; to get more, just hold up your bread basket and ask, *"Encore, s'il vous plaît?"*

Salads: They're typically large—one is perfect for lunch or a light dinner. To get salad dressing on the side, order *"la sauce à côté"* (lah sohs ah co-tay). Among the classics are:

Salade niçoise (nee-swahz), a specialty from Nice, usually includes green salad topped with green beans, boiled potatoes, tomatoes, anchovies, olives, hard-boiled eggs, and lots of tuna.

Salade au chèvre chaud is a mixed green salad topped with warm goat cheese on toasted bread croutons.

Salade composée is "composed" of any number of ingredients, such as *lardons* (bacon), *comté* (a Swiss-style cheese), Roquefort (bleu cheese), *œuf* (egg), *noix* (walnuts), and *jambon* (ham, generally thinly sliced).

Salade paysanne usually comes with potatoes *(pommes de terre)*, walnuts *(noix)*, tomatoes, ham, and egg.

Salade aux gesiers has chicken gizzards (and often slices of duck).

Restaurants

Choose restaurants filled with locals. Consider my suggestions and your hotelier's opinion, but trust your instincts. If a restaurant doesn't post its prices outside, move along. Refer to my restaurant recommendations to get a sense of what a reasonable meal should cost.

Restaurants in the south open for dinner at 19:00 and are typically most crowded about 20:30 (the early bird gets the table). Last seating is usually about 21:00 (22:00 in cities and on the French Riviera, possibly earlier in small villages during the off-season).

If a restaurant serves lunch, it generally begins at 11:30 and goes until 14:00, with last orders taken about 13:30. In contrast, most cafés and brasseries offer a minimal menu (or more) all day (described earlier under "Cafe Culture").

If you ask for the *menu* (muh-noo) at a restaurant, you won't get a list of dishes; you'll get a fixed-price meal. *Menus*, which usually include three courses, are generally a good value if you're hungry: You'll get your choice of soup, appetizer, or salad; your choice of three or four main courses with vegetables; plus a cheese course and/or a choice of desserts. Service is included *(service compris* or *prix net)*, but wine and other drinks are generally extra.

Many restaurants offer cheaper versions of their *menu*, allowing you to select two courses, rather than three. These pared-down *menus* are sometimes called *formules* and feature an *entrée et plat* (first course and main dish), or *plat et dessert* (main dish and dessert). Most restaurants offer a reasonable *menu-enfant* (kids' menu).

Ask for *la carte* (lah kart) if you want to see a menu and order à la carte, like the locals do. Request the waiter's help in deciphering the French. Consider his or her recommendations and anything *de la maison* (of the house), as long as it's not an organ meat *(tripes, rognons,* and *andouillette)*. Galloping gourmets should bring a menu translator; the *Rick Steves' French Phrase Book*, with a menu decoder, works well for most travelers. Wines are often listed in a separate *carte des vins*.

Coffee and Tea Lingo

By law, the waiter must give you a glass of tap water with your coffee or tea if you request it; ask for *"Un verre d'eau, s'il vous plaît"* (uhn vayr doh, see voo play).

Provence is known for its herbal and fruit teas. Look for *tilleul* (linden), *verveine* (verbena), or interesting blends such as *poire–vanille* (pear–vanilla).

Coffee

French	Pronounced	English
un café allongé (also called *café longue*)	uhn kah-fay ah-lohn-zhay (kah-fay lohn)	closest to an American cup of coffee
un express	uhn ex-press	shot of espresso
une noisette	oon nwah-zeht	espresso with a shot of milk
café au lait	kah-fay oh lay	coffee with lots of steamed milk (closest to an American latte)
un grand crème	uhn grahn krehm	big café au lait
un petit crème	uhn puh-tee krehm	small café au lait
un décaffiné	uhn day-kah-fee-nay	decaf—available for any of the above drinks

Tea

French	Pronounced	English
un thé nature	uhn tay nah-tour	plain tea
un thé au lait	uhn tay oh lay	tea with milk
un thé citron	uhn tay see-trohn	tea with lemon
une infusion	oon an-few-see-yohn	herbal tea

Remember that in France, an *entrée* is the first course, and *le plat* or *le plat du jour* (plate of the day) is the main course with vegetables. In the south, I usually order *une entrée* and *un plat* from *la carte* (often as a fixed-price, two-course *menu* or *formule*), then find an ice cream or crêpe stand and take a dessert stroll. If that sounds like too much, just order *un plat*. Because small dinner salads are usually not offered à la carte, two travelers can split a big salad (usually several salad options), then each get a *plat* (this also works well for other starter courses).

Beverages

Water: The French are willing to pay for bottled water with their meal (*eau minérale;* oh mee-nay-rahl) because they prefer the taste

How Was Your Trip?

Were your travels fun, smooth, and meaningful? If you'd like to share your tips, concerns, and discoveries, please fill out the survey at www.ricksteves.com/feedback. I value your feedback. Thanks in advance—it helps a lot.

over tap water. Badoit is my favorite carbonated water (*l'eau gazeuse;* loh gah-zuhz). If you prefer a free pitcher of tap water, ask for *une carafe d'eau* (oon kah-rahf doh). Otherwise, you may unwittingly buy bottled water.

Wine and Beer: House wine at the bar is cheap and good in this region (about €3/glass at modestly priced places). At a restaurant, a bottle or carafe of house wine costs €8–18. To get inexpensive wine, order regional table wine (*un vin du pays;* uhn van duh pay) in a pitcher (*un pichet;* uhn pee-shay), rather than a bottle. Note, though, that finer restaurants usually offer only bottles of wine.

If all you want is a glass of wine, ask for *un verre de vin rouge* for red wine or *vin blanc* for white wine (uhn vehr duh van roozh/blahn). A half-carafe of wine is *un demi-pichet* (uhn duh-mee pee-shay); a quarter-carafe (ideal for one) is *un quart* (uh kar).

The local beer, which costs about €4 at a restaurant, is cheaper on tap (*une pression;* oon pres-yohn) than in the bottle (*bouteille;* boo-teh-ee). France's best beer is Alsatian; try Kronenbourg or the heavier Pelfort. *Une panaché* (oon pah-nah-shay) is a refreshing French shandy (beer and lemon soda).

Regional Specialty Drinks: For a refreshing before-dinner drink, order a *kir* (pronounced "keer")—a thumb's level of *crème de cassis* (black currant liqueur) topped with white wine. In Provence, try sweet wines such as Muscat de Beaumes de Venise or Rasteau (Vin Doux Naturel). Both should be served chilled (from the fridge, never with ice cubes) and can be enjoyed before dinner or with some desserts; they're terrific with foie gras, melons, peaches, or Roquefort cheese. Look also for sparkling wines, usually inexpensive versions of the pricey Champagne.

If you like brandy, try a *marc* (regional brandy) or an Armagnac, cognac's cheaper twin brother. *Pastis,* the standard southern France aperitif, is a sweet anise (licorice) drink that comes on the rocks with a glass of water. Cut it to taste with lots of water.

Soft Drinks: For a fun, bright, nonalcoholic drink of 7-Up with mint syrup, order *un diabolo menthe* (uhn dee-ah-boh-loh mahnt); for 7-Up with fruit syrup, order *un diabolo grenadine* (think Shirley Temple). Kids love the local orange drink (*orange pressé;* oh-rhan-juh preh-say, you'll need to add sugar) and the flavored syrups mixed with bottled water (*sirops à l'eau;* see-roh ah loh). In France, *limonade* (lee-moan-ahd) is Sprite or 7-Up. The ice cubes melted after the last Yankee tour group left.

Traveling as a Temporary Local

We travel all the way to Europe to enjoy differences—to become temporary locals. You'll experience frustrations. Certain truths that we find "God-given" or "self-evident," such as cold beer, ice in drinks, bottomless cups of coffee, hot showers, and bigger being better, are suddenly not so true. One of the benefits of travel is the eye-opening realization that there are logical, civil, and even better alternatives.

With a history rich in human achievement, France is an understandably proud country. To enjoy its people, you need to celebrate the differences. A willingness to go local ensures that you'll enjoy a full dose of French hospitality.

Americans are enjoying a surge in popularity in Europe these days. But if there is a negative aspect to the French image of Americans, it's that we are big, loud, aggressive, impolite, rich, and a bit naive.

The French place a high value on speaking quietly in restaurants and on trains. Listen while on the bus or in a restaurant—the place can be packed, but the decibel level is low. Try to adjust your volume accordingly to show respect for their culture.

While the French look bemusedly at some of our Yankee excesses—and worriedly at others—they nearly always afford us individual travelers all the warmth we deserve. Judging from all the happy feedback I receive from travelers who have used this book, it's safe to assume you'll enjoy a great, affordable vacation—with the finesse of an independent, experienced traveler.

Thanks, and *bon voyage!*

Back Door Travel Philosophy
From Rick Steves' Europe Through the Back Door

Travel is intensified living—maximum thrills per minute and one of the last great sources of legal adventure. Travel is freedom. It's recess, and we need it.

Experiencing the real Europe requires catching it by surprise, going casual..."Through the Back Door."

Affording travel is a matter of priorities. (Make do with the old car.) You can eat and sleep—simply, safely, and enjoyably—anywhere in Europe for $120 a day plus transportation costs. In many ways, spending more money only builds a thicker wall between you and what you traveled so far to see. Europe is a cultural carnival, and time after time, you'll find that its best acts are free and the best seats are the cheap ones.

A tight budget forces you to travel close to the ground, meeting and communicating with the people. Never sacrifice sleep, nutrition, safety, or cleanliness to save money. Simply enjoy the local-style alternatives to expensive hotels and restaurants.

Connecting with people carbonates your experience. Extroverts have more fun. If your trip is low on magic moments, kick yourself and make things happen. If you don't enjoy a place, maybe you don't know enough about it. Seek the truth. Recognize tourist traps. Give a culture the benefit of your open mind. See things as different, but not better or worse. Any culture has plenty to share.

Of course, travel, like the world, is a series of hills and valleys. Be fanatically positive and militantly optimistic. If something's not to your liking, change your liking.

Travel can make you a happier American, as well as a citizen of the world. Our Earth is home to six and a half billion equally precious people. It's humbling to travel and find that other people don't have the "American Dream"—they have their own dreams. Europeans like us, but with all due respect, they wouldn't trade passports.

Thoughtful travel engages us with the world. In tough economic times, it reminds us what is truly important. By broadening perspectives, travel teaches new ways to measure quality of life.

Globetrotting destroys ethnocentricity, helping us understand and appreciate other cultures. Rather than fear the diversity on this planet, celebrate it. Among your most prized souvenirs will be the strands of different cultures you choose to knit into your own character. The world is a cultural yarn shop, and Back Door travelers are weaving the ultimate tapestry. Join in!

PROVENCE

"There are treasures to carry away in this land, which has not found a spokesman worthy of the riches it offers."

—Paul Cézanne

This magnificent region is shaped like a giant wedge of quiche. From its sunburned crust, fanning out along the Mediterranean coast from the Camargue to Marseille, it stretches north along the Rhône Valley to Orange. The Romans were here in force and left many ruins—some of the best anywhere. Seven popes, artists such as Vincent van Gogh and Paul Cézanne, and author Peter Mayle all enjoyed their years in Provence. This destination features a splendid recipe of arid climate, oceans of vineyards, dramatic scenery, captivating cities, and adorable hill-capping villages.

Explore the ghost town that is ancient Les Baux, and see France's greatest Roman ruins, the Pont du Gard aqueduct and the theater in Orange. Admire the skill of ball-tossing *boules* players in small squares in every Provençal village and city. Spend a few starry, starry nights where Van Gogh did, in Arles. Youthful but classy Avignon bustles in the shadow of its brooding Palace of the Popes. Stylish and self-confident Aix-en-Provence lies 30 minutes from the sea and feels more Mediterranean. It's a short hop from Arles or Avignon into the splendid scenery and villages of the Côtes du Rhône and Luberon regions. Should you need an urban fix—and feel the need to really understand southern France—Marseille is a must. If you prefer a Provençal beach fix, find Cassis, just east of Marseille.

Choose a Home Base

With limited time, make Arles or Avignon your sightseeing base—particularly if you have no car. Italophiles prefer smaller

PROVENCE

Provence

Arles, while poodles pick urban Avignon. Many enjoy nights in both cities. (With a car, head for St. Rémy or the hill towns.)

Arles has a blue-collar quality; the entire city feels like Van Gogh's bedroom. It also has this region's best-value hotels and is handy to Les Baux, St. Rémy, and the Camargue.

Avignon—three times larger than Arles—feels sophisticated, with more nightlife and shopping. Avignon makes a good base for non-drivers thanks to its convenient public-transit options (within 45 minutes, you can reach Pont du Gard, Uzès, and St. Rémy by bus; and Arles, Nîmes, Isle-sur-la-Sorgue, and Aix-en-Provence by train—and Marseille is just one hour away).

Or, for drivers who prefer a smaller-town base, **St. Rémy** is manageable and centrally located. It offers a nice range of hotels with free and easy parking, good restaurants, and a few sights of its own. Or you can sleep in one of Provence's many hill towns, or out in the countryside; the towns of **Vaison la Romaine** (in the Côtes du Rhône region) and **Roussillon** (in the Luberon) are two good but remote options.

Planning Your Time

The bare minimum you should spend in Provence is three days: one day for sightseeing in Arles and Les Baux (Arles is best on Wed or Sat, when it's market day); a day for Pont du Gard and Nîmes; and a full day for Orange and the Côtes du Rhône villages. Add two more days to explore Avignon; Uzès or St. Rémy; and more Provençal villages. Allow an additional two days in Cassis, using one of them for a day trip to Marseille or Aix-en-Provence (or both). Ideally, see the cities—Arles, Nîmes, Avignon, Aix-en-Provence, and Marseille—by train, then rent a car for the countryside.

To measure the pulse of rural Provence, spend at least a few nights in the smaller towns. (They come to life on market days, but can be quiet on Mondays, when shops are shuttered tight.) I've described many towns in the Côtes du Rhône and Luberon. The Côtes du Rhône is ideal for wine connoisseurs and an easy stop for those heading to or from the north. The Luberon is for hill-town lovers and works well for travelers heading east, toward Aix-en-Provence or the Riviera. Don't day-trip to these very different areas; nights spent in Provençal villages are what books are written about. One or two nights in each area make for a terrific start.

The small port town of Cassis is a wonderful Mediterranean meander between Provence and the Riviera (and more appealing than most Riviera resorts). It has easy day-trip connections to Marseille and Aix-en-Provence.

Depending on the length of your trip, here are my recommended priorities for Provence:

3 days:	Arles and Les Baux; Pont du Gard and Nîmes; and Orange and Côtes du Rhône villages
5 days, add:	Avignon and either St. Rémy or Uzès
7 days, add:	Cassis, Marseille, Aix-en-Provence
9 days, add:	Luberon hill towns, Camargue

Getting Around Provence

By Bus or Train: Public transit is good between cities and decent to some towns, but marginal at best to the villages. Frequent trains link Avignon, Arles, and Nîmes (about 30 min between each).

Avignon has good train connections with Orange, and decent service to Isle–sur-la-Sorgue. Marseille is well-connected to all cities in Provence, with frequent service to Cassis and Aix-en-Provence (about 30 min to each).

Buses connect many smaller towns, though service can be sporadic. From Arles, you can catch a bus to Stes-Maries-de-la-Mer (in the Camargue) or St. Rémy. From Avignon, you can bus to Pont du Gard, St. Rémy, Uzès, Isle-sur-la-Sorgue (also by train), and less easily to Vaison la Romaine and some Côtes du Rhône villages. St. Rémy, Isle-sur-la-Sorgue, and Uzès are the most accessible small towns.

While a tour of the villages of the Côtes du Rhône or Luberon is best on your own by car, excellent minivan tours and basic bus excursions are available. (TIs in Arles and Avignon have information on bus excursions to regional sights that are hard to reach *sans* car; see "Tours of Provence," below.)

By Car: The region is made-to-order for a car. The yellow Michelin Local maps #332, #340, or #528 are a godsend. I've described key sights and a variety of full-day drives deep into the countryside. Be wary of thieves: Park only in well-monitored spaces and leave nothing valuable in your car.

Avignon (pop. 100,000) is a headache for drivers. Arles (pop. 52,000) is easier, but still urban. Les Baux and St. Rémy work well from Arles or Avignon (or vice versa). Nîmes and Pont du Gard are a short hop west of Avignon and on the way to or from Languedoc. The town of Orange ties in tidily with a trip to the Côtes du Rhône villages and with destinations farther north. If you're heading north from Provence, consider a three-hour detour through the spectacular Ardèche Gorges (see page 179 in the Orange and the Côtes du Rhône chapter). The Luberon villages are about halfway between Arles or Avignon and Aix-en-Provence (consider basing yourself in little Lourmarin for day trips to Aix-en-Provence). And if you're continuing on to the Riviera, be lured into the Grand Canyon du Verdon detour (see the Inland Riviera chapter). Most drivers will prefer exploring congested Marseille by taking a train from Cassis or Aix-en-Provence (both towns have easy parking at their train stations and frequent trains and buses to the center of Marseille).

Tours of Provence

It's possible to take half-day or full-day excursions to most of the sights described in this book (best from Avignon). Most TIs have brochures on excursions and can help you make a reservation. Here are several good options to consider:

Wine Safari—Dutchman Mike Rijken runs a one-man show, taking travelers through the region he adopted more than 20 years

Top 10 Roman Sights in Provence

1. Pont du Gard aqueduct and its museum
2. Roman Theater in Orange
3. Ancient History Museum in Arles
4. Maison Carrée in Nîmes
5. Arena in Nîmes
6. Arena in Arles
7. Roman city of Glanum (in St. Rémy)
8. Ruined aqueduct near Fontvieille
9. Roman city of Vaison la Romaine
10. St. Julien Bridge (near Roussillon)

Top 10 Provençal Towns and Villages

1. Roussillon (beautiful hill town sitting atop a huge ochre deposit, giving it a red-rock appeal, popular with American tourists)
2. Uzès (chic town with manicured pedestrian streets, popular with European tourists)
3. Joucas (adorable little village where flowers and stones are lovingly maintained, popular with artists)
4. Brantes (spectacularly situated cliff village with little tourism)
5. Lourmarin (lovely upscale village, busy in the day but quiet at night)
6. Le Crestet (an overlooked village with a sensational hilltop location and one commercial enterprise)
7. Séguret (a linear hillside village with memorable views and many day-trippers, but few overnighters)
8. Gigondas (world-famous wine village with a nice balance of commercial activity and quiet)
9. Vaison la Romaine (a popular midsize town with Roman ruins and lots of activity, spanning both sides of a river)
10. Nyons (an overlooked midsize town with a few pedestrian streets; famous for its olive oil and ideal climate)

ago. Mike came to France to train as a chef, later became a wine steward, and has now found his calling as a driver/guide. His English is fluent, and while his focus is wine and wine villages, Mike knows the region thoroughly and is a good teacher of its history (€55/half-day, €100/day, priced per person, group size varies from 2 to 6; pickups possible in Arles, Avignon, Lyon, Marseille, or Aix-en-Provence; tel. 04 90 35 59 21, mobile 06 19 29 50 81, www.winesafari.net, mikeswinesafari@wanadoo.fr).

Imagine Tours—Unlike most tour operators, this is a nonprofit organization with a focus on cultural excursions. It offers personalized tours allowing visitors to discover the "true heart of

How About Them Romans?

Provence is peppered with intriguing Roman ruins and museums. In fact, many scholars claim the best-preserved ancient Roman buildings are not in Italy, but in France—for example, the Arena and Maison Carrée in Nîmes. Since these attractions make up a big part of your sightseeing agenda in this region, it's worth learning about how they came to be.

Classical Rome endured from about 500 B.C. through A.D. 500—spending about 500 years growing, 200 years peaking, and 300 years declining. In 49 B.C., Julius Caesar defied the Republic by crossing the Rubicon River in northern Italy, conquering Provence (and ultimately all of France)—and killing about a third of its population in the process. He erected a temple to Jupiter on the future site of Paris' Notre-Dame Cathedral.

The concept of one-man rule lived on with his grandnephew, Octavian (whom he had also adopted as his son). Octavian killed Brutus, eliminated his rivals (Mark Antony and Cleopatra), and united Rome's warring factions. He took the title "Augustus" and became the first in a line of emperors who would control Rome for the next 500 years—ruling like a king, with the backing of the army and the rubber-stamp approval of the Senate. Rome morphed from a Republic into an Empire: a collection of many diverse territories ruled by a single man.

Augustus' reign marked the start of 200 years of peace, prosperity, and expansion known as the *Pax Romana.* At its peak (c. A.D. 117), the Roman empire had 54 million people and stretched from Scotland in the north to Egypt in the south, as far west as Spain and as far east as modern-day Iraq. To the northeast, Rome was bounded by the Rhine and Danube Rivers. On Roman maps, the Mediterranean was labeled *Mare Nostrum* ("Our Sea"). At its peak, "Rome" didn't just refer to the city, but to the entire civilized Western world.

The Romans were successful not only because they were good soldiers, but also because they were smart administrators and businessmen. People in conquered territories knew they had joined the winning team and that political stability would replace barbarian invasions. Trade thrived. Conquered peoples were welcomed into the fold of prosperity, linked by roads, education, common laws and gods, and the Latin language.

Provence, with its strategic location, benefited greatly from Rome's global economy and grew to become an important part of its worldwide empire. After Julius Caesar conquered Gaul, Emperor Augustus set out to Romanize it, building and renovating cities in the image of Rome. Most cities had a theater (some had several), baths, and aqueducts; the most important ones had sports arenas. The Romans also erected an infrastructure of roads, post offices, schools (teaching in Latin), police stations, and water-supply systems.

With a standard language and currency, Roman merchants

were able to trade wine, salt, and olive oil for foreign goods. The empire invested heavily in cities that were strategic for trade. For example, the Roman-built city of Arles was a crucial link in the trade route from Italy to Spain, so they built a bridge across the Rhône River and fortified the town.

A typical Roman city (such as Nîmes, Arles, Orange, or Vaison la Romaine) was a garrison town, laid out on a grid plan with two main roads: one running north—south (the *cardus*), the other east—west (the *decumanus*). Approaching the city on your chariot, you'd pass through the cemetery, which was located outside of town for hygienic reasons. You'd enter the main gate and speed past warehouses and apartment houses to the town square (forum). Facing the square were the most important temples, dedicated to the patron gods of the city. Nearby, you'd find bathhouses; like today's fitness clubs, these served the almost sacred dedication to personal vigor. Also close by were businesses that catered to the citizens' needs: the marketplace, bakeries, banks, and brothels.

Aqueducts brought fresh water for drinking, filling the baths, and delighting the citizens with bubbling fountains. Men flocked to the stadiums in Arles and Nîmes to bet on gladiator games, and eager couples attended elaborate plays at theaters in Orange, Arles, and Vaison la Romaine. Marketplaces brimmed with exotic fruits, vegetables, and animals from the far reaches of the empire. Some cities in Provence were more urban 2,000 years ago than they are today. For instance, Roman Arles had a population of 100,000—double today's size.

In these cities, you'll see many rounded arches. These were constructed by piling two stacks of heavy stone blocks, connecting them via an arch (supported with wooden scaffolding), then inserting an inverted keystone where the stacks met. *Voilà!* The heavy stones were able to support not only themselves, but also a great deal of weight above the arch. The Romans didn't actually invent the rounded arch, but they exploited it far better than their predecessors, stacking arches to build arenas and theaters, stringing them side by side for aqueducts, stretching out their legs to create barrel-vaulted ceilings, and building freestanding "triumphal" arches to celebrate conquering generals.

When it came to construction, the Romans' magic building ingredient was concrete. A mixture of volcanic ash, lime, water, and small rocks, concrete—easier to work than stone, longer-lasting than wood—served as flooring, roofing, filler, glue, and support. Builders would start with a foundation of brick, then fill it in with poured concrete. They would then cover important structures, such as basilicas, in sheets of expensive marble (held on with nails), or decorate floors and walls with mosaics—proving just how talented the Romans were at turning the functional into art.

Provence." The itineraries adapt to your interests, and the volunteer guides will meet you at your hotel or the departure point of your choice (€150/half-day, €275/day, prices are for up to 4 people, tel. 06 89 22 19 87, fax 04 90 24 84 26, mobile 06 89 22 19 87, www.imagine-tours.net, imagine.tours@gmail.com).

Wine Uncovered—Passionate Englishman (is that an oxymoron?) Olivier Hickman takes small groups on focused tours of selected wineries in Châteauneuf-du-Pape and in the villages near Vaison la Romaine. Olivier is serious about French wine, knows his subject matter inside and out, and wants to help you learn. He offers in-depth tastings at two wineries for €40 per person (his minimum fee is €110) and full-day tours for €70 per person. If you need transportation, he can help arrange it (tel. 06 75 10 10 01, www.wine-uncovered.com, olivier.hickman@wine-uncovered.com).

François Marcou—For a fun and distinctly French perspective on wines of the Côtes du Rhône region, François offers different itineraries each day. He is based in Avignon and will pick up travelers at their hotel, the TI, or the train station (€75/person for all-day wine tours that include 4–5 tastings, tel. 06 28 05 33 84, www.avignon-wine-tour.com, avignon.wine.tour@modulonet.fr).

Visit Provence—Based in Avignon, this company provides a variety of guided tours to most destinations covered in this book. They have eight-seat minivans and English commentary (about €60/half-day, €100/day; they'll pick you up at your hotel in Avignon). Ask about their cheaper big-bus excursions, or consider hiring a van and driver for your own private use (plan on €210/half-day, €400/day, tel. 04 90 14 70 00, check website for current destinations, www.provence-reservation.com).

Madeleine's Culinary and Active Adventures—This effervescent American expat plans small group tours from Avignon and Arles to visit food artisans and wineries. Madeleine also leads kid-friendly hikes in the countryside (€250/day, flat rate for 2–6 people, tel. 06 82 15 51 74, www.cuisineprovencale.com).

Provence's Cuisine Scene

Provence has been called France's "garden market," stressing farm-fresh food (vegetables, fruit, and meats) prepared in a simple way, and meant to be savored with family and friends. Grilled foods are typical, as are dishes derived from lengthy simmering—in part a reflection of long days spent in the fields. Colorful and lively, Provençal cuisine hammers the senses with an extravagant use (by French standards) of garlic, olive oil, and herbs. Order anything *à la provençal,* and you'll be rewarded with aromatic food heightened by rich and pungent sauces. Thanks to the proximity of the Riviera, many seafood dishes show up on Provençal menus (see

"The Riviera's Cuisine Scene," page 264).

Unlike other French regional cuisines, the food of Provence is inviting for nibblers. Appetizers (hors d'oeuvres) often consist of bowls of olives (try the plump and full-flavored black *tanche* or the green, buttery *picholine*), as well as plates of fresh vegetables served with lusty sauces ready for dipping. These same sauces adorn dishes of hard-boiled eggs, fish, or meat. Look for tapenade, a paste of pureed olives, capers, anchovies, herbs, and sometimes tuna. True anchovy-lovers seek out *anchoïade* (a spread of garlic, anchovy, and parsley) or *bagna cauda* (warm sauce of anchovies and melted butter or olive oil).

Aioli—a rich, garlicky mayonnaise spread over vegetables, potatoes, fish, or whatever—is another Provençal favorite. In the summertime, entire village festivals celebrate this sauce. Watch for signs announcing *aioli monstre* ("monster aioli"), and for a few euros, dive into a very local eating experience (pass the breath mints, please).

Despite the heat, soup is a favorite in Provence. *Soupe au pistou* is a thin yet flavorful vegetable soup with a sauce (called *pistou*) of basil, garlic, and cheese—pesto minus the pine nuts. Or try *soupe à l'ail* (garlic soup, called *aigo bouido* in the local dialect). For seafood soups, see "The Riviera's Cuisine Scene."

Provençal main courses venerate fresh vegetables and meats. (Eat seafood on the Riviera and meat in Provence.) Ratatouille is a mixture of Provençal vegetables (eggplant, zucchini, onions, and peppers are the usual suspects) in a thick, herb-flavored tomato sauce. It's readily found in charcuteries and often served at room temperature, making it the perfect picnic food. Ratatouille veggies also show up on their own, stuffed and served in spicy sauces. Look for *aubergines* (eggplants), *tomates* (tomatoes), *poivrons* (sweet peppers), and *courgettes* (zucchini—especially *fleurs de courgettes*, stuffed and batter-fried zucchini flowers). *Tians* are gratin-like vegetable dishes named for the deep terra-cotta dish in which they are cooked and served. *Artichauts à la barigoule* are stuffed artichokes flavored with garlic, ham, and herbs (*barigoule* is from the Provençal word for thyme, *farigoule*). Also look for *riz de Camargue*—the reddish, chewy, nutty-tasting rice that has taken over the Camargue area, which is otherwise useless for agriculture.

The famous herbs of Provence influence food long before it's cooked. The locally renowned lambs of the *garrigue* (shrub-covered hills), as well as rabbits and other small edible beasts in Provence, dine on wild herbs and spicy shrubs—essentially pre-seasoning their delicate meat. Regional specialties include lamb (*agneau,* most often leg of lamb, *gigot d'agneau*), grilled and served no-frills, or the delicious *lapin à la provençale*—rabbit served with garlic, mustard, tomatoes, and herbs in white wine. Locals have a curious passion for quail *(caille).* These tiny, bony birds are often grilled and served with any variety of sauces, including those sweetened with Provençal cherries or honey and lavender. *Daube,* named for the traditional cooking vessel *daubière,* is generally beef simmered in wine with spices and herbs—and perhaps a touch of orange zest—until it is spoon-tender; it's then served with noodles or the local rice. *Taureau* (bull's meat), usually raised in the marshy Camargue, melts in your mouth.

By American standards, the French undercook meats: *bleu* (bluh) is virtually raw (just flame-kissed); rare or *saignant* (seh-nyahn) is close to raw; medium or *à point* (ah pwahn) is rare; and well-done or *bien cuit* (bee-yehn kwee) is medium. (Since French cows are raised on grass rather than corn, the beef is leaner than in the US, so limiting the cooking time keeps the meat tender.)

There are a few dishes to avoid: *Pieds et paquets* is a scary dish of sheep's feet and tripe (no amount of Provençal sauce can hide the flavor here). *Tourte de blettes* is a confused "pie" made with Swiss chard; both savory and sweet, it can't decide whether it should be a first course or dessert (it shows up as both).

Eat goat cheese *(fromage de chèvre)* in Provence. Look for *banon de banon* or *banon à la feuille* (dipped in *eau-de-vie* to kill bad mold, then wrapped in a chestnut leaf), spicy *picodon* (the name means "spicy" in the old language), or the fresh, creamy *brousse du Rove* (often served mixed with cream and sugar for dessert). On Provençal cheese platters, you'll often find small rounds of bite-size chèvres, each flavored with a different herb or spice—and some even rolled in chopped garlic (more breath mints, please).

Desserts tend to be fairly light and fruit-filled, or traditionally French. There are fresh tarts made with seasonal fruit, Cavaillon melons (served cut in half with a trickle of the sweet Rhône wine Beaumes de Venise), and ice cream or sorbet sweetened with honey and flavored with various herbs such as lavender, thyme, or rosemary.

Wines of Provence

Provence was the first area in France to be planted with grapes, in about 600 B.C., by the Greeks. Romans built on what the Greeks started, realizing even back then that Provence had an ideal climate for producing wine: mild winters and long, warm summers (but not too hot—thanks to the cooling winds). This sun-baked, wine-happy region offers Americans a chance to sample wines blended

French Wine Lingo

Here are the steps you should follow when entering any wine-tasting:

    1. Greetings, Sir/Madam: *Bonjour, Monsieur/Madame.*

    2. We would like to taste a few wines: *Nous voudrions déguster quelques vins* (noo voo-dree-ohn day-goo-stay kehl-kuh van).

    3. We want a wine that is _____ and _____: *Nous voudrions un vin _____ et _____* (noo voo-dree-ohn uhn van _____ ay_____).

    Fill in the blanks with your favorites from this list:

English	French	Pronounced
wine	*vin*	van
red	*rouge*	roozh
white	*blanc*	blahn
rosé	*rosé*	roh-zay
light	*léger*	lay-zhay
full-bodied, heavy	*robuste*	roh-boost
fruity	*fruité*	frwee-tay
sweet*	*doux*	doo
tannic	*tannique*	tah-neek
jammy	*confituré*	koh-fee-tuh-ray
fine	*fin, avec finesse*	fan, ah-vehk fee-nehs
ready to drink (mature)	*prêt à boire*	preh tah bwar
not ready to drink	*fermé*	fair-may
oaky	*goût de la chêne*	goo duh lah sheh-nuh
from old vines	*de vieille vignes*	duh vee-yay-ee veen-yah
sparkling	*pétillant*	pay-tee-yahn

*With the exception of the fortified white Beaumes de Venise, few Provençal wines would be considered "sweet."

from several grapes—resulting in flavors unlike anything we get at home (yes, we have good Cabernet Sauvignons, Merlots, and Pinot Noirs, but Rhône wines are new to most of us). Provence's shorts-and-T-shirt climate and abundance of hearty, reasonably priced wines make for an enjoyable experience, particularly if you're willing to learn. See "Provençal Wine-Tasting 101," later in this chapter, for the basics.

In France, wine production is strictly controlled by the government to preserve the overall quality. This ensures that vintners use specified grapes that grow best in that region and follow certain grape-growing procedures. The *Appellation d'Origine Contrôlée* (AOC) label found on many bottles is the government's seal of approval indicating that a wine has met a series of requirements. The type and percentages of grapes used, vinification methods, and taste are all controlled and verified.

Provençal vintners can blend wines using a maximum of 13 different grapes (5 white and 8 red)—unique in France. (In Burgundy and Alsace, only one grape variety is used for each wine—so Pinot Noir, Chardonnay, Riesling, Tokay, and Pinot Gris are each 100 percent from that grape.) This blending allows Provençal winemakers great range in personalizing their wine. For reds, most vintners blend half a dozen or so different grapes. The most prevalent grapes are Grenache, Mourvèdre, Syrah, Carignan, and Cinsault. The white grapes include Grenache-Blanc, Roussanne, Marsanne, Bourboulenc, and Clairette.

There are three primary growing areas in Provence: Côtes du Rhône, Côtes de Provence, and Côteaux d'Aix-en-Provence. A few wines are also made along the Provençal Mediterranean coast. All regions produce rich, fruity reds and dry, fresh rosés. Only about 5 percent of wine produced here is white. Most Provençal whites are light and tart, with plenty of citrus, and work best as a pre-dinner drink or in a *kir*.

In Provence, I generally drink rosé instead of white. Don't confuse these rosés with the insipid blush stuff found in the US; French rosé is often crisp and fruity, a perfect match to the hot days and Mediterranean cuisine. Rosé wines are made from red grapes whose juice is white, until crushed with their skins. The white juice is left in contact with the dark-red skins just long enough to produce the pinkish color (no more than 24 hours). Rosés from Tavel (20 minutes north and west of Avignon) are the most respected, but you'll find many good producers at affordable prices in other areas as well. Americans unaccustomed to drinking rosés should give them a try here.

Provençal Wine-Tasting 101

The American wine-tasting experience (I'm thinking Napa Valley) is generally informal, chatty, and entrepreneurial (logo-adorned baseball caps and golf shirts). Although Provençal vintners are welcoming, and more easygoing than in other parts of France, it's still a serious, wine-focused experience. Your hosts are not there to make small talk, and they're likely to be "all business." For some people, it can be overwhelming to try to make sense of the vast range of options among Provençal wines, particularly when faced with a no-

nonsense winemaker or sommelier. Take a deep breath, do your best to follow my instructions below, and don't linger anywhere you don't feel welcome (I've tried to identify which places are most accepting of wine novices). Visit several private wineries or stop by a *cave coopérative*—an excellent opportunity to taste wines from a number of local vintners in a single, less intimidating setting.

Provençal winemakers are happy to work with you...*if* they can figure out what you want (which they expect you to know). When you enter a winery, it helps to know what you like (drier or sweeter, lighter or full-bodied, fruity or more tannic, and so on). The people serving you may know those words in English, but you'd be wise to learn and use these key words in French (see "French Wine Lingo" sidebar). Avoid visiting places between noon and 14:00—many are closed, and those that aren't would rather be at lunch.

For reds, you'll be asked if you want to taste younger wines that still need maturing or older wines, ready to drink now. (Whites and rosés are always ready to drink.) The French like to sample younger wines and determine how they will taste in a few years, allowing them to buy bottles at cheaper prices and stash them in their cellars. Americans want it now—for today's picnic. While many Americans like a big, full-bodied wine, most French tend to prefer more subtle flavors. They judge a wine by virtue of what food it would go well with—and a big, oaky wine would overwhelm most French cuisine.

Remember that the vintner is hoping you'll buy at least a bottle or two. If you don't, you may be asked to pay a minimal fee for the tasting. They know that Americans can't take much wine with them, and they don't expect to make a big sale, but they do hope you'll look for their wines in the US. Some of the places I list will ship your purchase home—ask.

Côtes du Rhône Wines

The Côtes du Rhône, which follows the Rhône River from just south of Lyon to near Avignon, is the king of Provence wines. Our

focus is on the southern, Provençal section, roughly from Vaison la Romaine to Avignon (though wine-lovers should take note of the big, complex reds found in the northern Rhône wines of St. Joseph, Hermitage, and Cornas, as well as the seductive white of Condrieu). The wines of the southern Rhône are consistently good—and sometimes exceptional. The reds are full-bodied, rosés are dry and fruity, and whites are dry and fragrant, often with hints of flowers. Côtes du Rhône whites aren't nearly as good as the reds, though the rosés are refreshing and ideal for lunch on the terrace. For more on this wine region, including a self-guided driving tour of local villages and vintners, see the Côtes du Rhône chapter.

Many sub-areas of the southern Côtes du Rhône are recognized for producing distinctly good wines, and have been awarded their own *appellations* (like Châteauneuf-du-Pape, Gigondas, Beaumes de Venise, Côtes de Ventoux, Tavel, and Côtes du Luberon). Wines are often named for the villages that produce them. The "Côtes du Rhône Villages" is a smaller appellation on the eastern side of the Côtes du Rhône. There are just over 20 villages in this appellation, including Séguret, Sablet, Rasteau, and Cairanne. As it is the top wine for vintners in these villages, there are strict guidelines for production.

Here's a summary of what you might find on a Côtes du Rhône *carte des vins* (wine list):

Châteauneuf-du-Pape: Wines from this famous village are almost all reds (often blends; the most dominant grapes are typically Grenache, Mourvèdre, and Syrah). These wines have a velvety quality and can be spicy, with flavors of licorice and prunes. Châteauneuf-du-Pape wines merit lengthy aging. Considered among the best producers are Château de Beaucastel, Le Vieux Télégraphe, and Château la Nerthe. You can easily find their wines in North America. It's also worth seeking out lesser-known names and smaller wineries (many of which are listed in this book).

Gigondas: These wines have many of the same qualities as Châteauneuf-du-Pape, but are lesser known and therefore cheaper. Gigondas red wines are spicy, meaty, and can be pretty tannic. Again, aging is necessary to bring out the full qualities of the wine. Look for Domaine du Terme, Château de Montmirail, or Domaine de Coyeux for good quality.

Beaumes de Venise: While reds from this village are rich and flavorful, Beaumes de Venise is most famous for its Muscat—a sweet, fragrant wine usually served as an apéritif or with dessert. It often has flavors of apricots and peaches, and it should be consumed within two years of bottling. Try Domaine de Coyeux, Domaine de Durban, and Château Redortier.

Rasteau: This village sits across the valley from Gigondas and shares many of its qualities at lower prices. Rasteau makes fine rosés, robust (at times "rough") and fruity reds, and a naturally sweet wine (Vin Doux Naturel). Their Côtes du Rhône Villages can be excellent. The cooperative in Rasteau is good, though you should not miss a visit to Domaine des Girasols.

Sablet: This village lies down in the valley below Gigondas and makes decent, fruity, and inexpensive reds and rosés.

On the Wine Label

appellation	area in which a wine's grapes are grown
bouchonné	"corked" (spoiled from a bad cork)
bouquet	bouquet (the fragrance when first opened)
cave	cellar
cépage	grape variety (Syrah, Chardonnay, etc.)
côte, côteau	hillside or slope
domaine	wine estate
étiquette	label
fût, tonneau	wine barrel
grand vin	excellent wine
millésimé	wine from a given year
mis en bouteille au château/à la domaine	estate-bottled (bottled where it was made)
vin de table	table wine (can be a blend of several wines)
vin du pays	wine from a given area (a step up from *vin de table*)

Tavel: The queen of French rosés is 20 minutes north and west of Avignon, close to Pont du Gard. Tavel produces a rosé that is dry, crisp, higher in alcohol, and more full-bodied than other rosés from the region. Look for any rosé from Tavel.

Côtes de Provence Wines

The lesser-known vineyards of the Côtes de Provence run east from Aix-en-Provence almost to St-Tropez. Many wines from this area are sold in an unusual curvy bottle (which makes me feel tipsy before I've had a sip). Typical grapes are Cinsault, Mourvèdre, Grenache, Carignan, and a little Cabernet Sauvignon and Syrah. The wines are commonly full-bodied and fruity, and are meant to be drunk when they're young. It's common to chill reds from this area—and they can be delicious. They cost less than Côtes du Rhônes and have similar characteristics. But the region is most famous for its "big" rosés that can be served with meat and garlic dishes (rosé accounts for 60 percent of production).

For one-stop shopping, make a point to find the superb **La Maison des Vins Côtes de Provence** on RN-7 in Les Arcs-sur-Argens (a few minutes north of the A-8 autoroute,

Le Mistral

Provence lives with its vicious mistral winds, which blow 30-60 miles per hour, about 100 days out of the year. Locals say it blows in multiples of threes: three, six, or nine days in a row. The mistral clears people off the streets and turns lively cities into ghost towns. You'll likely spend a few hours or days taking refuge—or searching for cover. The winds are strongest between noon and 15:00.

When the mistral blows, it's everywhere, and you can't escape. Author Peter Mayle said it could blow the ears off a donkey (I'd include the tail). Locals say it ruins crops, shutters, and roofs (look for stones holding tiles in place on many homes). They'll also tell you that this pernicious wind has driven many people crazy (including young Vincent van Gogh). A weak version of the wind is called a *mistralet*.

The mistral starts above the Alps and Massif Central mountains and gathers steam as it heads south, gaining momentum as it screams over the Rhône Valley (which acts like a funnel between the Alps and Pyrénées) before exhausting itself when it hits the Mediterranean. While this wind rattles shutters throughout the Riviera and Provence, it's strongest over the Rhône Valley...so Avignon, Arles, and the Côtes du Rhône villages bear its brunt. While wiping the dust from your eyes, remember the good news: The mistral brings clear skies.

about halfway between Aix-en-Provence and Nice). This English-speaking wine shop and tasting center represents hundreds of producers, selling bottles at vineyard prices and offering free tastings of up to 16 wines (June–Oct daily 10:00–19:00; Nov–May Mon–Sat 10:00–18:00, closed Sun; tel. 04 94 99 50 20, www .caveaucp.fr).

Côteaux d'Aix-en-Provence Wines

This large wine region, between Les Baux and Aix-en-Provence, produces some interesting reds, whites, and rosés. Commonly used grapes are the same as in Côtes de Provence, though several producers (mainly around Les Baux) use a higher concentration of Cabernet Sauvignon, which helps distinguish their wines. The vintners around Les Baux produce some exceptionally good wines, and many of their vineyards are organic. Try Domaine d'Eole or Domaine Gourgonnier.

Provençal Mediterranean Wines

Barely east of Marseille, Cassis and Bandol sit side by side, overlooking the Mediterranean. Though very close together, they are designated as separate wine-growing areas because of the distinctive nature of their wines. Cassis is one of France's smallest wine regions and is known for its strong, fresh, and very dry whites (made with the Marsanne grape)—arguably the best white wine in Provence. Bandol is known for its luscious, velvety reds. This wine, aged in old oak and made primarily from the Mourvèdre grape, is my favorite.

ARLES

By helping Julius Caesar defeat Marseille, Arles (pronounced "arl") earned the imperial nod and was made an important port city. With the first bridge over the Rhône River, Arles was a key stop on the Roman road from Italy to Spain, the Via Domitia. After reigning as the seat of an important archbishop and a trading center for centuries, the city became a sleepy backwater of little importance in the 1700s. Vincent van Gogh settled here a hundred years ago, but left only a chunk of his ear (long gone). American bombers destroyed much of Arles in World War II as the townsfolk hid out in its underground Roman galleries. But today Arles thrives again, with its evocative Roman ruins, an eclectic assortment of museums, made-for-ice-cream pedestrian zones, and squares that play hide-and-seek with visitors.

Orientation to Arles

Arles faces the Mediterranean, turning its back on Paris. While the town is built along the Rhône, it largely ignores the river—which is all for the best, since it's the part of Arles most damaged by Allied bombers in World War II (and therefore the least appealing today).

Landmarks hide in Arles' medieval tangle of narrow, winding streets. Virtually everything is close—but first-timers can walk forever to get there. Hotels have good, free city maps, and Arles provides helpful street-corner signs that point you toward sights and hotels. Racing cars enjoy Arles' medieval lanes, turning sidewalks into tightropes and pedestrians into leaping targets.

Tourist Information

The **main TI** is on the ring road boulevard des Lices, at esplanade Charles de Gaulle (April–Sept daily 9:00–18:45; Oct–March Mon–Sat 9:00–16:45, Sun 10:00–13:00; tel. 04 90 18 41 20, www .arlestourisme.com). There's also a **train station TI** (Mon–Fri 9:00–13:30 & 14:30–16:45, closed Sat–Sun).

At either TI, pick up the city map, note the bus schedules (displayed in binders), and get English information on nearby destinations such as the Camargue wildlife area (described in the next chapter). Ask about "bullgames" (Provence's more humane version of bullfights—see "Events in Arles," page 70) and walking tours of Arles. Skip the useless €1 brochure describing several walks in Arles, including one that locates Van Gogh's "easels" (better explained on page 66). Both TIs charge €1 to reserve hotel rooms.

Arrival in Arles

By Train: The train station is on the river, a 10-minute walk from the town center. Before heading into town, get what you need at the train station TI (see above). There's no baggage storage at the station, but you can walk 10 minutes to stow it at Hôtel Régence (see "Helpful Hints," later).

To reach the town center, turn left out of the train station and walk 10 minutes; or wait for the free Starlette bus (3/hr, Mon–Sat only) at the shelter across the street. Taxis generally wait in front of the station, but if you don't see any, call the posted telephone numbers, or dial 04 89 73 36 00 (rates are fixed, allow about €10 to any of my recommended hotels).

By Bus: The Centre-Ville bus station is a few blocks below the main TI, located on the ring road at 16–24 boulevard Georges Clemenceau.

By Car: Arles' only parking garage is Parking des Lices, near the TI on boulevard des Lices (€8/24 hrs). Most hotels have parking nearby—ask for detailed directions (€1.50/hr at most meters, free 12:00–14:00 & 19:00–9:00). For most hotels, first follow signs to *Centre-Ville*, then *Gare SNCF* (train station). You'll come to a big roundabout (place Lamartine) with a Monoprix department store to the right. You can park along the city wall and find your hotel on foot; the hotels I list are no more than a 10-minute walk away (best not to park here overnight due to theft concerns and markets on Wed and Sat). Fearless drivers can plunge into the narrow streets between the two stumpy towers via rue de la Calade, and follow signs to their hotel. Again, theft is a problem; leave nothing in your car, and trust your hotelier's advice on where to park.

Helpful Hints

Market Days: The big markets are on Wednesdays and Saturdays. For all the details, see page 70.

Meetings and Festivals: An international photo event jams hotels in early July. The let-'er-rip, twice-a-year Féria draws crowds over Easter and in mid-September (see www.arlestourisme .com for dates).

Internet Access: Cyber Café Taxiphone will make you feel like you're surfing in Morocco (daily 10:00–22:00, 31 rue Augustin Tardieu).

Baggage Storage and Bike Rental: The recommended Hôtel Régence (see page 72) will store your bags for €3–5 each (daily 7:30–22:00 mid-March–mid-Nov, closed in winter). They also rent bikes (€6/hr, €14/day, one-way rentals within Provence possible, same hours as baggage storage). Ask about their electric bikes—handy on windy days, but with limited power. From Arles, you can ride to Les Baux (20 miles round-trip, very steep climb) or into the Camargue (40 miles round-trip, forget it in the wind)—provided you're in great shape.

Laundry: There's a launderette at 12 rue Portagnel (daily 7:00–21:30, you can stay later to finish if you're already inside, English instructions).

Car Rental: Avis is at the train station (tel. 04 90 96 82 42), and **Europcar** and **Hertz** are downtown (Europcar is at 2 bis avenue Victor Hugo, tel. 04 90 93 23 24; Hertz is closer to place Lamartine at 10 boulevard Emile Combes, tel. 04 90 96 75 23).

Local Guide: Charming **Jacqueline Neujean,** an excellent guide, knows Arles and nearby sights intimately and loves her work (€90/2 hrs, tel. & fax 04 90 98 47 51).

English Book Exchange: A small exchange is available at the recommended **Soleileis** ice-cream shop (see page 78).

Language and Cooking Courses: Food-lovers enjoy cooking classes and market tours offered by local B&B owner/amateur historian Erick Vedel (see page 72). Madeleine Vedel offers a wide range of excursions, including countryside hikes, organic-winery tours, and artisan visits where you can pick wild asparagus, harvest grapes, or make chocolate (www.cuisine provencale.com).

Public Pools: Arles has three public pools (indoor and outdoor). Ask at the TI or your hotel.

Boules: The local "*boul*ing alley" is by the river on place Lamartine. After their afternoon naps, the old boys congregate here for a game of *pétanque* (see page 196 for details on this popular local pastime).

Getting Around Arles

In this flat city, everything's within walking distance. Only the Ancient History Museum requires a long walk (take a taxi for €10, or a public bus for €0.80—details on page 60). The elevated riverside promenade provides Rhône views and a direct route to the Ancient History Museum (to the southwest) and the train station (to the northeast). Keep your head up for *Starry Night* memories, but eyes down for decorations by dogs with poorly trained owners.

Arles' **taxis** charge a set fee of about €10, but nothing except the Ancient History Museum is worth a taxi ride. To call a cab, dial 04 89 73 36 00 or 04 90 96 90 03.

The free **Starlette bus** circles the town (3/hr, Mon–Sat only), but is only useful for access to the train station.

Sights in Arles

Most sights cost €3–6, and while any sight is worth a few minutes, many aren't worth their individual admission price. The TI sells three different monument passes (called Passeports). **Le Passeport Avantage** covers almost all of Arles' sights (€13.50, under 18 for €12; Fondation Van Gogh discounted); the €9 **Le Passeport Arelate** covers Arles' four Roman sights, including the Ancient History Museum; and the €9 **Le Passeport Liberté** lets you choose any five monuments (one must be a museum). Depending on your interests, one of the €9 Passeports is probably best.

Start at the Ancient History Museum for a helpful overview (drivers should try to do this museum on their way into Arles), then dive into the city-center sights. Remember, many sights stop selling tickets 30–60 minutes before closing (both before lunch and at the end of the day). To make the most of Arles' Roman history, refer to the sidebar on page 42.

▲▲Ancient History Museum
(Musée de l'Arles et de la Provence Antiques)

Begin your town visit here—it's Roman Arles 101. Located on the site of the Roman chariot racecourse (the arc of which is built into

the parking lot), this air-conditioned, all-on-one-floor museum is just west of central Arles along the river. Models and original sculptures (with almost no posted English translations, but a fair handout) re-create the Roman city, making workaday life and culture easier to imagine.

ARLES

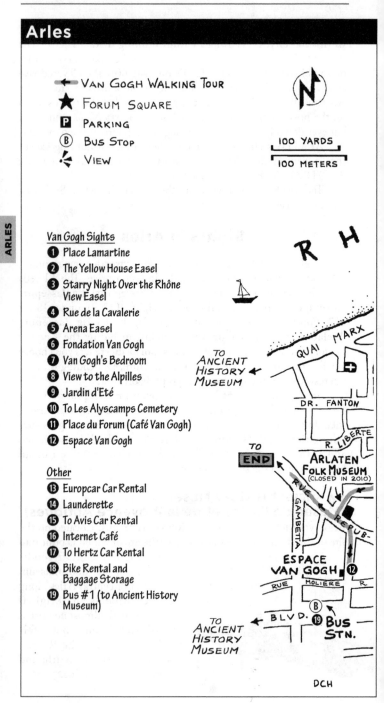

Arles

Van Gogh Walking Tour
★ Forum Square
P Parking
Ⓑ Bus Stop
View

Van Gogh Sights
❶ Place Lamartine
❷ The Yellow House Easel
❸ Starry Night Over the Rhône View Easel
❹ Rue de la Cavalerie
❺ Arena Easel
❻ Fondation Van Gogh
❼ Van Gogh's Bedroom
❽ View to the Alpilles
❾ Jardin d'Eté
❿ To Les Alyscamps Cemetery
⓫ Place du Forum (Café Van Gogh)
⓬ Espace Van Gogh

Other
⓭ Europcar Car Rental
⓮ Launderette
⓯ To Avis Car Rental
⓰ Internet Café
⓱ To Hertz Car Rental
⓲ Bike Rental and Baggage Storage
⓳ Bus #1 (to Ancient History Museum)

100 YARDS
100 METERS

RH

TO ANCIENT HISTORY MUSEUM

QUAI MARX

DR. FANTON

R. LIBERTE

TO END

ARLATEN FOLK MUSEUM (CLOSED IN 2010)

RUE GAMBETTA

REPUB-

ESPACE VAN GOGH ⓬

RUE   MOLIERE   R.

TO ANCIENT HISTORY MUSEUM

BLVD.   Ⓑ ⓳ BUS STN.

DCH

ARLES

TO
TRAIN
STATION
& ⑮

TO LES BAUX,
FONTVIEILLE
& AVIGNON

AVE. STALIN

③

START

②

MONOPRIX

PLACE
LAMAR-
TINE

①

PETANQUE

GATE

BLVD.

RUE   JULES FERRY

CAVALERIE

EMILE COMBES

REATTU
MUSEUM

QUAI LAMARTINE

RUE JOUVEAU

R. L. BLUM

④

⑱

PLACE
VOLTAIRE

R. CONDORCET

DORMOY

GRAND PRIEURE

RUE DU QUATRE SEPT.

R. AMPH.

VOLTAIRE

⑯

RUE PORTAGNEL

⑰

⑭

RUE DU

RUE DE HOTEL DE VILLE

SAUVAGE

RUE

SUISSES

R. TARDIEU

R.   REFUGE

RUE DES ARENES

⑤

ENTER

ROMAN
ARENA

⑦

⑧

★

⑪

R. DIDEROT

⑥

FOND.
V.G.

NOTRE
DAME

R. BALZE   RUE CALADE

WC

ST.
TROPHIME

PLACE
REPUB-
LIQUE

PORTE
DE CLOITRE

PORTE DE LAURE

ANCIENT
CITY
WALLS

LIQUE

RUE

JARDIN
D'ETE

CLASSICAL
THEATER

ROTONDE

JAURES

CLOISTERS

⑨

MONTEE VAUBAN

BLVD. EMILE COMBES

DES   LICES

⑬

V. HUGO

POST
& TAXIS

P

PLAYGROUND

R. E. FASSIN

TO ⑩

TO LES AYLSCAMPS
CEMETERY

TO ⑩

ONE

Cost, Hours, Location: €6, daily April–Oct 9:00–19:00, Nov–March 10:00–18:00, presqu'île du Cirque Romain.

Information: Ask for the English booklet, which provides a helpful if not in-depth background on the collection, and inquire whether there are any free English tours (usually daily July–Sept at 17:00, 90 min). Tel. 04 90 18 88 88, www.arles-antique.cg13.fr.

Getting There: To reach the museum by foot from the city center (a 25-min walk), turn left at the river and take the riverside path to the big, blue, modern building. The **taxi** ride costs €10 (museum can call a taxi for your return). **Bus #1** gets you within a few minutes' walk (€0.80, 3/hr Mon–Sat, none Sun). Catch the bus in Arles (clockwise direction on boulevard des Lices), then get off at the Musée de l'Arles Antique stop (before the stop, you'll see the bright-blue museum ahead on the right). Turn left as you step off the bus, and follow the sidewalk. (To return to the center, the bus stop is across the street from where you got off.)

◑ Self-Guided Tour: A huge map of the Roman Arles region greets visitors and shows the key Roman routes accessible to Arles. Find the impressive row of pagan and early-Christian sarcophagi (from the second to fifth centuries). These would have lined the Via Aurelia outside the town wall. In the early days of the Church, Jesus was often portrayed beardless and as the good shepherd, with a lamb over his shoulder.

Next, you'll see models of every Roman structure in (and near) Arles. These are the highlight for me, as they breathe life into the buildings as they looked 2,000 years ago. Start with the model of Roman Arles, and imagine the city's splendor. Find the Forum—still the center of town today, though only two columns survive. The model of the Roman city—with the Arena and huge racecourse—shows that an emphasis on sports is not unique to modern America. It also illustrates how little Arles seems to have changed over two millennia, with its houses still clustered around the city center, and warehouses still located on the opposite side of the river.

Look for individual models of the major buildings shown in the city model: the elaborately elegant forum; the floating bridge that gave Arles a strategic advantage (over the widest, and therefore slowest, part of the river); the theater (with its glorious stage wall); the Arena (with its movable stadium cover to shelter spectators from sun or rain); and the circus, or chariot racecourse. Part of the original racecourse was just outside the windows, and while long gone, it must have resembled Rome's Circus Maximus in its day—its

Arles at a Glance

▲▲▲**Roman Arena** This big amphitheater, once used by gladiators, today hosts summer "bullgames" and occasional bullfights. **Hours:** Daily May–Sept 9:00–18:00, March–April and Oct 9:00–12:00 & 14:00–18:00, Nov–Feb 10:00–12:00 & 14:00–16:30. See page 65.

▲▲**Ancient History Museum** Filled with models and sculptures, this is Roman Arles 101. **Hours:** Daily April–Oct 9:00–19:00, Nov–March 10:00–18:00. See page 57.

▲▲**Forum Square** Lively, café-crammed square that was once the Roman forum. **Hours:** Always open. See page 62.

▲▲**St. Trophime Church and Cloisters** Church with exquisite Romanesque entrance. **Hours:** Church open daily April–Sept 9:00–12:00 & 14:00–18:30, Oct–March 9:00–12:00 & 14:00–17:00; cloisters open daily March–Oct 9:00–18:00, Nov–Feb 10:00–17:00). See page 63.

▲▲**Fondation Van Gogh** Small gallery with works by major contemporary artists paying homage to Van Gogh (but no Vincent originals). **Hours:** April–June daily 10:00–18:00, July–Sept daily 10:00–19:00, Oct–March Tue–Sun 11:00–17:00, closed Mon. See page 65.

▲**Arlaten Folk Museum** Shares the treasures and pleasures of Provençal life from the 18th and 19th centuries—but closed for renovation in 2010.

Classical Theater Ruined Roman theater, recently restored and still used for events. **Hours:** Daily May–Sept 9:00–19:00, March–April and Oct 9:00–12:00 & 14:00–18:00, Nov–Feb 10:00–12:00 & 14:00–17:00. See page 64.

Réattu Museum Decent, mostly modern art collection in a fine 15th-century mansion. **Hours:** Daily July–mid-Sept 10:00–19:00, March–June and mid-Sept–Oct 10:00–12:30 & 14:00–17:30, Nov–Feb 13:00–17:00. See page 66.

ARLES

obelisk is now the centerpiece of Arles' place de la République.

Finally, check out the 3-D model of the hydraulic mill of Barbegal, with its 16 waterwheels and eight grain mills cascading down a nearby hillside (well worth a side-trip if you have a car—see page 88).

Other rooms in the museum display pottery, jewelry, fine metal and glass artifacts, and well-crafted mosaic floors that make it clear that Roman Arles was a city of art and culture. The many statues that you see are all original, except for the greatest—the *Venus of Arles*, which Louis XIV took a liking to and had moved to Versailles. It's now in the Louvre—and, as locals say, "When it's in Paris…bye-bye."

In Central Arles

Ideally, visit these sights in the order listed below. I've included some walking directions to connect the dots.

▲▲**Forum Square (Place du Forum)**—Named for the Roman forum that once stood here, this square was the political and religious center of Roman Arles. Still lively, this café-crammed square is a local watering hole and popular for a *pastis* (see "Eating in Arles," page 76). The bistros on the square, while no place for a fine dinner, can put together a good-enough salad or *plat du jour*—and when you sprinkle on the ambience, that's €10 well spent.

At the corner of Grand Hôtel Nord-Pinus, a plaque shows how the Romans built a foundation of galleries to make the main square level (to compensate for Arles' slope down to the river). The two columns are all that survive from the upper story of the entry to the Forum. Steps leading to the entrance are buried (the Roman street level was about 20 feet below you); you can get a glimpse by peeking through the low windows next to Hôtel d'Arlatan, a block below place du Forum on rue Sauvage.

The statue on the square is of **Frédéric Mistral** (1830–1914). This popular poet, who wrote in the local dialect rather than in French, was a champion of Provençal culture. After receiving the Nobel Prize in Literature in 1904, Mistral used his prize money to preserve and display the folk identity of Provence. He founded the regional folk museum (the Arlaten Folk Museum, which is closed in 2010) at a time when France was rapidly centralizing. (The local mistral wind—literally "master"—has nothing to do with his name.)

The **bright-yellow café**—called Café Van Gogh/Café la Nuit—was the subject of one of Vincent van Gogh's most famous works in Arles. While his painting showed the café in a brilliant yellow from the glow of gas lamps, the facade was bare limestone, just like the other cafés on this square. The café's current owners have painted it to match Van Gogh's version…and to cash in on the Vincent-crazed hordes who pay too much to eat or drink here.

• *Walk a block uphill (past Grand Hôtel Nord Pinus) and turn left. Walk through the Hôtel de Ville's vaulted entry (or take the next right if it's closed), and pop out onto the big…*

Republic Square (Place de la République)—This square used to be called "place Royale"…until the French Revolution. The obelisk was the former centerpiece of Arles' Roman Circus. The lions at its base are the symbol of the city, whose slogan is (roughly) "the gentle lion." Find a seat and watch the peasants—pilgrims, locals, and street musicians. There's nothing new about this scene.

• *Near the corner of the square where you entered, look for...*

▲▲**St. Trophime Church**—Named after a third-century bishop of Arles, this church sports the finest Romanesque main entrance (west portal) I've seen anywhere.

Like a Roman triumphal arch, the church facade trumpets the promise of Judgment Day. The tympanum (the semicircular area above the door) is filled with

Christian symbolism. Christ sits in majesty, surrounded by symbols of the four evangelists: Matthew (the winged man), Mark (the winged lion), Luke (the ox), and John (the eagle). The 12 apostles are lined up below Jesus. It's Judgment Day... some are saved and others aren't. Notice the condemned (on the right)—a chain gang doing a sad bunny-hop over the fires of hell. For them, the tune trumpeted by the three angels above Christ is not a happy one. Below the chain gang, St. Stephen is being stoned to death, with his soul leaving through his mouth and instantly being welcomed by angels. Ride the exquisite detail back to a simpler age. In an illiterate medieval world, long before the vivid images of our Technicolor time, this was a neon billboard over the town square.

Enter the church (free, daily April–Sept 9:00–12:00 & 14:00–18:30, Oct–March 9:00–12:00 & 14:00–17:00). Just inside the door on the right, a chart locates the interior highlights and helps explain the carvings you just saw on the tympanum.

Tour the church counterclockwise. The tall 12th-century Romanesque nave is decorated by a set of tapestries showing scenes from the life of Mary (17th century, from the French town of Aubusson). Amble around the Gothic apse. Just to the left of the high altar, check out the relic chapel—with its fine golden boxes that hold long-venerated bones of obscure saints. Farther down is a chapel built on an early-Christian sarcophagus from Roman Arles (dated about A.D. 300). The heads were lopped off during the French Revolution.

This church is a stop on the ancient pilgrimage route to Santiago de Compostela in northwest Spain. For 800 years, pilgrims on their way to Santiago have paused here...and they still do today. As you leave, notice the modern-day pilgrimages advertised on the far right near the church's entry.

• *Leaving the church, turn left, then left again through a courtyard to enter the cloisters.*

The adjacent **cloisters** are worth a look, with many small columns that were scavenged from the ancient Roman theater (enter at the far end of the courtyard). Enjoy the sculpted capitals, the rounded 12th-century Romanesque arches, and the pointed 14th-century Gothic ones. On the second floor, you'll walk along an angled rooftop designed to catch rainwater—notice the slanted gutter that channeled the water into a cistern (€3.50, daily March–Oct 9:00–18:00, Nov–Feb 10:00–17:00).

• Turn left out of the cloisters, then take the first right on rue de la Calade to reach the...

Classical Theater (Théâtre Antique)—This first-century B.C. Roman theater once seated 10,000...just like the theater in Orange. But unlike Orange, here in Arles there was no hillside to provide support. This theater was an elegant, three-level structure with 27 arches radiating out to the street level. From the outside, it looked much like a halved version of Arles' Roman Arena. For more on Roman theaters, see page 149.

Walk to a center aisle and pull up a stone seat. To appreciate the theater's original size, look to the upper-left side of the tower and find the protrusion that supported the highest of three seating levels. The structure required 33 rows of seats to accommodate demand. During the Middle Ages, the old theater became a convenient town quarry—St. Trophime Church was built from theater rubble. Precious little of the original theater survives today, although considerable effort is under way to rebuild sections of the seating area and turn it once again into a top venue, with seating for 3,000 spectators.

Two lonely Corinthian columns are all that remain of a three-story stage wall that once featured over 100 columns and statues painted in vibrant colors. The orchestra section is defined by a semicircular pattern in the stone in front of you. Stepping up onto the left side of the stage, look down to the slender channel that allowed the brilliant-red curtain to disappear below, like magic. The stage, which was built of wood, was about 160 feet across and 20 feet deep. Go backstage and browse through broken bits of Rome, and loop back to the entry behind the grass (€3; daily May–Sept 9:00–19:00, March–April and Oct 9:00–12:00 & 14:00–18:00, Nov–Feb 10:00–12:00 & 14:00–17:00). Budget travelers can peek over the fence from rue du Cloître, and see just about everything for free.

• A block uphill is the...

▲▲▲**Roman Arena (Amphithéâtre)**—Nearly 2,000 years ago, gladiators fought wild animals here to the delight of 20,000 scream-

ing fans. Today, local daredevils still fight wild animals
here—"bullgame" posters
around the Arena advertise
upcoming spectacles (see page
70). A lengthy restoration process is well under way, giving
the amphitheater an almost
bleached-teeth whiteness.

In Roman times, games were free (sponsored by city bigwigs), and fans were seated by social class. The many exits allowed for rapid dispersal after the games—fights would break out among frenzied fans if they couldn't leave quickly. Through medieval times and until the early 1800s, the arches were bricked up and the stadium became a fortified town—with 200 humble homes crammed within its circular defenses. Three of the medieval tow-ers survive (the one above the ticket booth is open and rewards those who climb it with terrific views). To see two still-sealed arches—complete with cute medieval window frames—turn right as you leave, walk to the Andaluz restaurant, and look back to the second floor (€6, daily May–Sept 9:00–19:00, March–April and Oct 9:00–18:00, Nov–Feb 10:00–17:00). For more on Roman amphitheaters, see page 129.

• *Turn left out of the Arena and walk uphill to find the...*

▲▲**Fondation Van Gogh**—A refreshing stop for any art-lover, and especially interesting to Van Gogh fans, this small gallery features works by contemporary artists who pay hom-age to Vincent through thought-provoking interpretations of his works. Many pieces are explained in English by the artists. The black-and-white photographs (both art and shots of places that Vincent painted) complement the paintings. Unfortunately, this collection is often on the road July through September, when non–Van Gogh material is on display here (€6, €4 with Le Passeport Avantage; great collection of Van Gogh souve-nirs, prints, and postcards for sale in gift shop; April–June daily 10:00–18:00; July–Sept daily 10:00–19:00; Oct–March Tue–Sun 11:00–17:00, closed Mon; facing Arena at 24 bis rond-point des Arènes, tel. 04 90 49 94 04, www.fondationvangogh-arles.org). For more on Vincent, see the next section, "Van Gogh Sights in and near Arles."

• *The next two attractions are back across town. The Arlaten Folk Museum (closed in 2010) is close to place du Forum, and the Réattu Museum is near the river.*

▲Arlaten Folk Museum (Musée Arlaten/Museon Arlaten)—
This museum, which normally explains the ins and outs of daily Provençal life, is closed for renovation in 2010 (www.museon arlaten.fr).

Réattu Museum (Musée Réattu)—Housed in the former Grand Priory of the Knights of Malta, this mildly interesting, mostly modern art collection includes 57 Picasso drawings (some two-sided and all done in a flurry of creativity—I liked the bullfights best), a room of Henri Rousseau's Camargue watercolors, and an unfinished painting by the Neoclassical artist Jacques Réattu... but none with English explanations. Occasional special exhibits show off the museum's impressive permanent collection, which is mostly in storage (€4, €2 extra for special exhibits, daily July–mid-Sept 10:00–19:00, March–June and mid-Sept–Oct 10:00–12:30 & 14:00–17:30, Nov–Feb 13:00–17:00, last entry 30 min before closing for lunch or at end of day, 10 rue du Grand Prieuré, tel. 04 90 96 37 68, www.museereattu.arles.fr).

Van Gogh Sights in and near Arles

In the dead of winter in 1888, the 35-year-old Dutch artist Vincent van Gogh left big-city Paris for Provence, hoping to jump-start his floundering career. He was inspired. Coming from the gray skies and flat lands of the north, Vincent was bowled over by everything Provençal—the sun, bright colors, rugged landscape, and unspoiled people. For the next two years he painted furiously, cranking out a masterpiece every few days.

None of the 200-plus paintings that Van Gogh did in the south can be found today in the city that so moved him. But you can walk the same streets he knew and see places he painted, marked by about a dozen steel-and-concrete "**easels**," with photos of the final paintings for then-and-now comparisons. The TI has a €1 brochure that locates all the easels (those described in this book are easily found without the brochure—see the map on page 58). Small stone markers with yellow accents embedded in the pavement lead to the easels.

• *Take a walk in Vincent's footsteps (roughly north to south through Arles' center) and watch his paintings come to life. Start at* **place Lamartine** *and find the stone easel across the grass from the Civette Arlesienne bistro.*

Vincent arrived in Arles on February 20, 1888, to a foot of snow. He rented a small house on the north side of place Lamartine. The house was destroyed in 1944 by an errant bridge-seeking bomb, but the four-story building behind it—where you see the Civette Arlesienne—still stands (find it in the painting). The house had four rooms, including a small studio and the cramped trapezoid-shaped bedroom made famous in paintings. It was painted yellow inside and out, and Vincent named it..."The Yellow House." You can see a re-creation of his bedroom from this house by the Arena (described later).

In late March, spring finally arrived. In those days, a short walk away from place Lamartine led to open fields. Donning his straw hat, Vincent set up his easel outdoors and painted quickly, capturing what he saw and felt—the blossoming fruit trees, gnarled olive trees, peasants sowing and reaping, jagged peaks, and windblown fields, all lit by a brilliant sun that drove him to use ever-brighter paints.

ARLES

• *Walk to the river (passing a monument in honor of two American pilots killed in action during the liberation of Arles) and find the easel in the wall where ramps lead down to the river.*

One night, Vincent set up along this river west of place Lamartine and painted the stars boiling above the city skyline— *Starry Night over the Rhône*. To his sister Wilhelmina, Van Gogh wrote, "At present I absolutely want to paint a starry sky. It often seems to me that night is still more richly colored than the day; having hues of the most intense violets, blues, and greens. If only you pay attention to it, you will see that certain stars are lemon-yellow, others pink or a green, blue, and forget-me-not brilliance." Come back at night to match his painting with today's scene. (Note: This painting is not the *Starry Night* you're thinking of— keep reading.)

• *Turn around and walk through the small park, then go into town between the stone towers along* **rue de la Cavalerie.**

Van Gogh walked into town the same way, underneath the arch and along this street. Arles' 19th-century red light district was just east of rue de la Cavalerie, and the far-from-home Dutchman spent many lonely nights in its bars and brothels.

• *Pass through place Voltaire, continue walking up rue Voltaire to the* **Arena,** *and then find the easel at the top of the Arena steps, to the right.*

All summer long, fueled by sun and alcohol, Vincent painted the town. He loved the bullfights in the Arena, and sketched the colorful surge of the crowds, spending more time studying the people than watching the bullfights. (Near the Arena, the Fondation Van Gogh—described on page 65—exhibits paintings by artists inspired by Van Gogh.) On the opposite side of the Arena, near Andaluz restaurant, you can visit a re-creation of Vincent's humble bedroom during his time in Arles (€3, daily 10:00–18:00).

• *Walk up the cobbled lane next to Andaluz restaurant, then keep left in the parking lot to find a viewpoint.*

This view to the **Alpilles Mountains** more or less matches what Vincent would have seen. Imagine him hauling his easel into those fields under intense sun, leaning against a ferocious wind. Vincent carried his easel as far as the medieval abbey of **Montmajour,** that bulky structure three miles straight ahead. The St. Paul Hospital where he was eventually treated in St. Rémy is on the other side of the Alpilles, several miles beyond Montmajour.

• *Continue past the upper end of the Arena, turn left, and walk out rue de Porte de Laure. Step down into the park and find the easel on the last path before the street to the right.*

Vincent spent many a sunny day painting the leafy **Jardin d'Eté.** In another letter to his sister, Vincent wrote, "I don't know whether you can understand that one may make a poem by arranging colors.... In a similar manner, the bizarre lines, purposely selected and multiplied, meandering all through the picture may not present a literal image of the garden, but they may present it to our minds as if in a dream." Vincent never made real friends, though he palled around with (and painted) his mailman and a Foreign Legionnaire. (The fact that locals pronounced his name "vahn-saw van gog" had nothing to do with his psychological struggles here.) Packing his paints and a picnic in a rucksack, he day-tripped to the old Roman cemetery of **Les Alyscamps** (a 10-min detour from this route, across the busy street and to the left).

• *Continue down the path and exit the gardens at the far-right corner. Walk past the Classical Theater on rue du Cloître, and take the first left on rue de la Calade. Continue to **place du Forum,** and locate an easel one café down from the yellow Café Van Gogh.*

In October, lonely Vincent—who dreamed of making Arles a magnet for fellow artists—persuaded his friend Paul Gauguin to come. He decorated Gauguin's room with several humble canvases of sunflowers (now some of the world's priciest paintings), knowing that Gauguin had admired a similar painting he'd done in Paris. At first, the two got along well. They spent days side by side, rendering the same subject in their two distinct styles. At night, they hit the bars and brothels. Van Gogh's well-known *Café at Night* captures the glow of an absinthe buzz at Café Van Gogh on place du Forum.

After two months together, the two artists clashed over art and personality differences. The night of December 23, they were drinking absinthe at the café when Vincent suddenly went ballistic. He threw his glass at Gauguin. Gauguin left. Walking through place Victor Hugo, Gauguin heard footsteps behind him and turned to see Vincent coming at him, brandishing a razor. Gauguin quickly fled town. The local paper reported what happened next: "At 11:30 p.m., Vincent Vaugogh [*sic*], painter from Holland, appeared at the brothel at no. 1, asked for Rachel, and gave her his cut-off earlobe, saying, 'Treasure this precious object.' Then he vanished." He woke up the next morning at home with his head wrapped in a bloody towel and his earlobe missing.

• *From here, retrace your steps a bit, then walk through the place de la République, turn right in the far corner, and find the Arlaten Folk Museum. Turn left on rue Président Wilson, and find Espace Van Gogh (on the right). There's an easel in the center of the courtyard.*

Vincent was checked into the local hospital—today's **Espace Van Gogh** cultural center. It surrounds a courtyard garden that the

ARLES

artist loved and painted during his month here, as he was being treated for blood loss as well as for hallucinations and severe depression that left him bed-ridden. The citizens of Arles circulated a petition demanding that the mad Dutchman be kept under medical supervision. (The Espace is free, but only the courtyard is open to the public.)

In the spring of 1889, the bipolar genius (a modern diagnosis) transferred to the **St. Paul Monastery and Hospital in St. Rémy-**

de-Provence (see page 92), where he spent a year, thriving in the care of doctors and nuns. Painting was part of his therapy, so they gave him a studio to work in, and he produced more than 100 paintings. Alcohol-free and institutionalized, he did some of his wildest work. With thick, swirling brushstrokes and surreal colors, he made his placid surroundings throb with restless energy. Today at the hospital in St. Rémy, you can see a replica of his room and his studio, plus many scenes he painted *in situ* like these in Arles—the courtyard, the plane trees, the view out the upstairs window of nearby fields, and the rugged Alpilles Mountains.

In the spring of 1890, Vincent left Provence to be cared for by a doctor in Auvers-sur-Oise, north of Paris. On July 27, he wandered into a field and shot himself. He died two days later.

The next easels are less central, but easily located and worth the effort for Van Gogh fans: the **Trinquetaille Bridge,** on the river walkway toward the Ancient History Museum (the current bridge is a 1951 replacement); and the most famous, the **Langlois Drawbridge** (1.5 miles south of town along a Rhône canal—today's bridge is a 1926 duplicate of the original).

Events in Arles

ARLES

▲▲**Wednesday and Saturday Markets**—Twice a week in the morning, Arles' ring road erupts into an open-air market of fish, flowers, produce, and you-name-it. The Wednesday market runs along boulevard Emile Combes, between place Lamartine and bis avenue Victor Hugo; the segment nearest place Lamartine is all about food, and the upper half features clothing, tablecloths, purses, and so on. On the first Wednesday of the month, it's a flea market, with less produce. The Saturday market is along boulevard des Lices near the TI. Join in, buy flowers, try the olives, sample some wine, and swat a pickpocket. Both markets are open until 12:00.

Part of the market has a North African feel, thanks to the Algerians and Moroccans who live in Arles. They came to do the lowly city jobs that locals didn't want, and now they mostly do the region's labor-intensive agricultural jobs (picking olives, harvesting fruit, and working in local greenhouses; see sidebar on page 223).

▲▲**Bullgames (Courses Camarguaises)**—Occupy the same seats that fans have used for nearly 2,000 years, and take in Arles' most memorable experience—the *courses camarguaises* in the ancient Arena. These nonviolent "bullgames" are more sporting than bloody Spanish bullfights. The bulls of Arles (who, locals stress, "die of old age") are promoted in posters even more boldly than their human foes. In the bullgame, a ribbon *(cocarde)* is laced between the bull's horns. The *razeteur*, with a special hook, has 15 minutes to snare the ribbon. Local businessmen

encourage a *razeteur* (dressed in white with a red cummerbund) by shouting out how much money they'll pay for the *cocarde*. If the bull pulls a good stunt, the band plays the famous "Toreador" song from *Carmen*. The following day, newspapers report on the games, including how many *Carmens* the bull earned.

Three classes of bullgames—determined by the experience of the *razeteurs*—are advertised in posters: The *course de protection* is for rookies. The *trophée de l'Avenir* comes with more experience. And the *trophée des As* features top professionals. During Easter and the fall rice-harvest festival *(Féria du Riz),* the Arena hosts actual Spanish bullfights (look for *corrida*) with outfits, swords, spikes, and the whole gory shebang. Bullgame tickets run €5–15, while bloody bullfights are pricier (€14–80). Schedules change every year—ask at the TI or check online at www.arenes-arles.com.

Don't pass on a chance to see *Toro Piscine,* a silly spectacle for warm summer evenings where the bull ends up in a swimming pool (uh-huh...get more details at TI). Nearby villages stage *courses camarguaises* in small wooden bullrings nearly every weekend; TIs have the latest schedule.

Sleeping in Arles

Hotels are a great value here; many are air-conditioned, though few have elevators. The Calendal, Musée, and Régence hotels offer exceptional value.

$$$ Hôtel le Calendal*** is a seductive place located between the Arena and Classical Theater. Enter an expertly run hotel with airy lounges and a lovely palm-shaded courtyard. Enjoy the elaborate €12 buffet breakfast, have lunch in the courtyard or at the inexpensive sandwich bar (daily 12:00–15:00), and take advantage of their four free laptops for guests. You'll also find a Jacuzzi and a "spa" with a Turkish bath, hot pool, and massages at good rates. The quite-comfortable rooms sport Provençal decor and come in all shapes and sizes (standard Db-€80–95, Db with balcony-€129, Tb-€120–140, Qb-€160, price depends on room size, air-con, Wi-Fi, reserve ahead for parking-€10, just above Arena at 5 rue Porte de Laure, tel. 04 90 96 11 89, fax 04 90 96 05 84, www.lecalendal.com, contact@lecalendal.com).

$$$ Hôtel d'Arlatan***, built on the site of a Roman basilica, is classy in every sense of the word. It has sumptuous public spaces, a tranquil terrace, a designer pool, a turtle pond, and antique-filled rooms, most with high, wood-beamed ceilings and stone walls. In the lobby of this 15th-century building, a glass floor looks down into Roman ruins (standard Db-€137, bigger Db-€157, Db/Qb suites-€180, apartments-€200–250, excellent buffet breakfast-€14, air-con, bathrobes, ice machines, elevator, Wi-Fi, parking-€16, 1 block below place du Forum at 26 rue Sauvage, tel. 04 90 93 56 66, fax 04 90 49 68 45, www.hotel-arlatan.fr, hotel-arlatan@wanadoo.fr).

$$ Hôtel du Musée** is a quiet and affordable manor-home hideaway tucked deep in Arles (tricky to find by car). This delightful refuge comes with 28 air-conditioned and wood-floored rooms, a flowery two-tiered courtyard, and snazzy art-gallery lounges.

ARLES

Sleep Code

(€1 = about $1.40, country code: 33)
S = Single, **D** = Double/Twin, **T** = Triple, **Q** = Quad, **b** = bathroom,
s = shower only, * = French hotel rating system (0-4 stars).
Unless otherwise noted, credit cards are accepted and English
is spoken.

To help you sort easily through these listings, I've divided
the rooms into three categories based on the price for a
standard double room with bath:

$$$ Higher Priced—Most rooms €80 or more.
 $$ Moderately Priced— Most rooms between €55–80.
  $ Lower Priced—Most rooms €55 or less.

Lighthearted Claude and English-speaking Laurence, the gracious
owners, are eager to help (Sb-€50, Db-€60–70, Tb-€70–85,
Qb-€90, Wi-Fi, laptop available for guests, garage-€10, follow signs to *Réattu Museum* to 11 rue du Grand Prieuré, tel. 04
90 93 88 88, fax 04 90 49 98 15, www.hoteldumusee.com, contact
@hoteldumusee.com).

$$ Hôtel de la Muette**, with reserved owners Brigitte and
Alain, is another good choice. Located in a quiet corner of Arles,
this low-key hotel is well-kept, with stone walls, wood beams, and
air-conditioning. The just-renovated rooms are very sharp (Db-€66–
76, Tb-€77, Qb-€92, buffet breakfast with eggs-€8, Internet access
and Wi-Fi, garage-€7, 15 rue des Suisses, tel. 04 90 96 15 39, fax 04
90 49 73 16, www.hotel-muette.com, hotel.muette@wanadoo.fr).

$$ A Bed and Breakfast in Arles, run by gentle chef Erick
Vedel, combines a laid-back B&B experience with five spacious
and funky-but-comfy rooms with optional cooking workshops.
Breakfast includes home-made crêpes, jams, and fresh-squeezed
orange juice (Db-€70–80, extra bed-€15, good family room, across
from launderette at 11 rue Portagnel, tel. & fax 04 90 49 69 20,
www.cuisineprovencale.com, actvedel@wanadoo.fr). Foodies
should check out their website for the affordable range of gourmet
cooking classes.

$$ Hôtel Acacias**, just off place Lamartine and inside
the old city walls, is a modern pastel paradise. Its smallish well-
maintained and well-priced rooms have all the comforts (standard
Sb or Db-€53, larger Db-€64–78, extra bed-€15, breakfast-€6, air-
con, elevator, Wi-Fi, 1 rue Marius Jouveau, tel. 04 90 96 37 88, fax 04
90 96 32 51, www.hotel-acacias.com, contact@hotel-acacias.com).

$ Hôtel Régence**, the best budget deal in Arles, has a river-
front location, immaculate and comfortable Provençal rooms, good

beds, safe parking, and easy access to the train station (Db-€48–55, Tb-€60–65, Qb-€70–75, buffet breakfast-€6, choose river view or quieter courtyard rooms, most rooms have showers, air-con, no elevator but only two floors, Internet access and Wi-Fi; from place Lamartine, turn right immediately after passing between towers to reach 5 rue Marius Jouveau; tel. 04 90 96 39 85, fax 04 90 96 67 64, www.hotel-regence.com, contact@hotel-regence.com). The gentle Nouvions speak some English.

$ Hôtel Voltaire* rents 12 small and spartan rooms with ceiling fans and nifty balconies overlooking a caffeine-stained square. Located a block below the Arena, it's perfect for starving artists. Smiling owner "Mr." Ferran (fur-ran) loves the States (his dream is to travel there), and hopes you'll add to his postcard collection (D-€30, Ds-€34, Db-€40, 1 place Voltaire, tel. 04 90 96 49 18, fax 04 90 96 45 49, levoltaire13@aol.com). They also serve a good-value lunch and dinner (described under "Eating in Arles," later).

Near Arles

Many drivers, particularly those with families, prefer staying outside Arles in the peaceful countryside, with easy access to the area's sights. See also "Sleeping in Les Baux" on page 86.

$$$ Le Peiriero***, 15 minutes from Arles in the town of Fontvieille, is a pooped parent's dream come true, with a grassy garden, massive pool, table tennis, badminton, massage parlor, indoor children's play area, and even a few miniature golf holes. The spacious family-loft rooms, capable of sleeping up to five, have full bathrooms on both levels. This complete retreat also comes with a terrace café and a well-respected restaurant, and helpful owners, the Levys (streetside Sb or Db-€96–116, gardenside Db-€130, Db with terrace-€140, loft-€210, dinner *menu*-€29, €35 for breakfast and dinner, air-con, Wi-Fi, free parking, just east of Fontvieille on road to Les Baux, 34 avenue des Baux, tel. 04 90 54 76 10, fax 04 90 54 62 60, www.hotel-peiriero.com, info@hotel-peiriero.com). Just a short drive from Arles and Les Baux (and 20 minutes from Avignon), little Fontvieille slumbers in the shadows of its big-city cousins—though it has its share of restaurants and boutiques.

$$$ Mas du Petit Grava is a vintage Provençal farmhouse 15 tree-lined minutes east of Arles. Here California refugee Jim and Ike offer four large and well-cared-for rooms with tubs, tiles, and memories of Vincent (Jim is a huge Van Gogh fan). A lovely garden surrounds a generously sized pool, but what draws most here are Jim and Ike (Db-€110–130, includes a fine breakfast, free Wi-Fi, tel. 04 90 98 35 66, www.masdupetitgrava.net). From Arles, drive east on D-453 toward St. Martin de Crau; 2.5 kilometers (about 1.5 miles) after passing through Raphèle, turn left on Route Saint Hippolite.

Arles Hotels and Restaurants

← VAN GOGH WALKING TOUR
★ FORUM SQUARE
P PARKING
Ⓑ BUS STOP
⚡ VIEW

ARLES

1 Hôtel le Calendal
2 Hôtel d'Arlatan
3 Hôtel du Musée
4 Hôtel de la Muette
5 "A Bed and Breakfast in Arles"
6 Hôtel Acacias
7 Hôtel Régence
8 Hôtel Voltaire
9 To Le Peiriero & Domaine de Laforest
10 To Mas du Petit Grava
11 Le 16 & Au Bryn du Thym Restaurants
12 Bistrot à Vins Restaurant
13 La Guele de Loup Restaurant
14 La Cuisine de Comptoir Rest.
15 Café de la Major (Coffee/Tea)
16 Le Grillon Restaurant
17 Le Criquet Restaurant
18 L'Atelier & A Côté Rests.
19 Soleileis Ice Cream

TO ANCIENT HISTORY MUSEUM ←

QUAI MARX
DR. FANTON
R. LIBERTE
ARLATEN FOLK MUSEUM (CLOSED IN 2010)
RUE GAMBETTA
REPUB-
ESPACE VAN GOGH
RUE MOLIERE R.
TO ANCIENT HISTORY MUSEUM ←
BLVD.
Ⓑ BUS STN.

100 YARDS
100 METERS

DCH

ARLES

$$ Domaine de Laforest is ideally located a few minutes below Fontvieille, near the aqueduct of Barbegal. It's a big 320-acre spread engulfed by vineyards, rice fields, and swaying trees. The sweet owners (Sylvie and mama Mariette) have eight two-bedroom apartments with great weekly rates that may be rented for fewer days when available (€310, €400, or €600 per week, air-con, Internet and Wi-Fi in main building, pool, big lawn, swings, mosquitoes can be a problem, 1000 route de l'Aqueduc Romain, tel. 04 90 54 70 25, fax 04 90 54 60 50, www.domaine-laforest.com, contact@domaine-laforest.com).

Eating in Arles

ARLES

You can dine well in Arles on a modest budget—in fact, it's hard to blow a lot on dinner here (most of my listings have *menus* for €22 or less). The bad news is that restaurants here change regularly, so double-check my suggestions. Before dinner, go local on place du Forum and enjoy a *pastis*. This anise-based apéritif is served straight in a glass with ice, plus a carafe of water—dilute to taste.

For **picnics,** a big, handy Monoprix supermarket/department store is on place Lamartine (Mon–Sat 8:30–19:25, closed Sun).

On or near Place du Forum

Great atmosphere and mediocre food at fair prices await on place du Forum. By all accounts, the garish yellow Café Van Gogh is worth avoiding. A half-block below the Forum, on rue du Dr. Fanton, lies a lineup of more tempting restaurants (including the first three listed below).

Le 16, with warm ambience inside and out, is an affordable place to enjoy a fresh salad (€9, bright and creative), good €12 *plats*, or a €21 three-course *menu* (closed Sat–Sun, 16 rue du Dr. Fanton, tel. 04 90 93 77 36).

Au Bryn du Thym, almost next door, has long been reliable and specializes in traditional Provençal cuisine—the bull steak is delicious. Arrive early for an outdoor table or call ahead, and let hardworking and sincere Monsieur and Madame Colombaud take care of you. Monsieur does *le cooking* while Madame does *le serving* (€19 three-course *menu*, closed Tue, 22 rue du Dr. Fanton, tel. 04 90 49 95 96).

Bistrot à Vins appeals to wine-lovers who enjoy pairing food and drink. You'll dine to light jazz at this warm, cozy bistro, which is well-run by affable Ariane. She speaks enough English and offers simple, tasty dishes (€10–16) designed to highlight her reasonably priced wines—many available by the glass (indoor dining only, closed Mon–Tue, 2 rue du Dr. Fanton, tel. 04 90 52 00 65).

La Guele de Loup is a small, traditional place with a loyal following (reserve ahead) and fine blend of Provençal and classic French cuisine served in an intimate setting (€30 three-course *menu*, closed Wed, 39 rue des Arènes, tel. 04 90 96 96 69).

At **La Cuisine de Comptoir,** locals of all ages abandon Provençal decor at this cool little bistro. Welcoming owners Alexandre and Vincent serve light *tartine* dinners—a light and delicious cross between pizza and bruschetta, served with soup or salad for just €10 (a swinging deal). Sit at the counter and watch *le chef* at work (closed Sun, indoor dining only, just off place du Forum's lower end at 10 rue de la Liberté, tel. 04 90 96 86 28).

Café de la Major is the place to go to recharge with some serious coffee or tea (closed Sun, 7 bis rue Réattu, tel. 04 90 96 14 15).

Near the Roman Arena

For about the same price as on place du Forum, you can enjoy regional cuisine with a point-blank view of the Arena. Because they change regularly, the handful of (mostly) outdoor eateries that overlook the Arena are pretty indistinguishable.

Le Grillon is reliable and serves good salads, crêpes, and *plats du jour* for €9–12 with great views of the Arena (closed Wed, at the top of the Arena on rond-point des Arènes, tel. 04 90 96 70 97).

Le Criquet is a sweet little place serving Provençal classics at good prices two blocks above the Arena (€18 three-course *menu*, closed Mon, indoor dining only, 21 rue Porte de Laure, tel. 04 90 96 80 51).

Hôtel le Calendal (recommended in "Sleeping in Arles," earlier) serves lunch in its lovely courtyard (€15, daily 12:00–15:00) or delicious little sandwiches for €2 each (three make a good meal) at its small café.

Hôtel Voltaire (recommended in "Sleeping in Arles," earlier) is an unspoiled place serving simple three-course lunches and dinners to loyal clientele for €12 and hearty *plats* and salads for €8–10—try the *salade fermière* or the filling *assiette Provençale* (closed Sun evening, a few blocks below the Arena at 1 place Voltaire, tel. 04 90 96 49 18).

A Gastronomic Dining Experience

One of France's most recognized chefs, Jean-Luc Rabanel, has created a sensation with two different-as-night-and-day dining options 50 yards from place de la République (at 7 rue des Carmes). They sit side by side, both offering indoor and terrace seating.

L'Atelier is so intriguing that people travel great distances just for the experience. Diners fork over €90 (at lunch, you'll spoon out €55) and trust the chef to create a memorable meal...which he does. There is no menu, just an onslaught of delicious taste sensations served on artsy dishes. Don't plan on a quick dinner and don't come for the setting—it's a contemporary, shoebox-shaped dining room, but several outdoor tables are also available. The get-to-know-your-neighbor atmosphere means you can't help but join the party (closed Mon–Tue, best to book ahead, friendly servers will hold your hand through this palate-widening experience, tel. 04 90 91 07 69, www.rabanel.com).

A Côté saddles up next door offering a warm wine bar/bistro ambience and top-quality cuisine for far less. Here you can sample the famous chef's talents for as little as €6 (tapas plate) or as much as €30 (three-course *menu*, smallish servings). You'll also find reasonable prices for wine (from €3 a glass) and a helpful staff (daily, tel. 04 90 47 61 13).

And for Dessert...

Soleileis has Arles' best ice cream, with all-natural ingredients and unusual flavors such as *fadoli*—olive oil. There's also a shelf of English books for exchange (open daily 14:00–18:30, across from recommended Le 16 restaurant at 9 rue du Dr. Fanton).

Arles Connections

From Arles by Train to: Paris (11/day, 2 direct TGVs—4 hrs, 9 with transfer in Avignon—5 hrs), **Avignon Centre-Ville** (11/day, 20 min, less frequent in the afternoon), **Nîmes** (9/day, 30 min), **Orange** (4/day direct, 35 min, more frequently with transfer in Avignon), **Aix-en-Provence Centre-Ville** (10/day, 2 hrs, requires at least 1 transfer in Marseille), **Marseille** (20/day, 1–2 hrs), **Cassis** (7/day, 2 hrs), **Carcassonne** (8/day, 2.5–4 hrs, 5 with transfer in Nîmes or Narbonne), **Beaune** (10/day, 4.5 hrs, 9 with transfer in Nîmes or Avignon and Lyon), **Nice** (11/day, 3.75–4.5 hrs, most require transfer in Marseille), **Barcelona** (2/day, 6 hrs, transfer in Montpellier), **Italy** (3/day, transfer in Marseille and Nice; from Arles, it's 4.5 hrs to Ventimiglia on the border, 8 hrs to Milan, 9.5 hrs to Cinque Terre, 11 hrs to Florence, and 13 hrs to Venice or Rome).

From Arles Train Station to Avignon TGV Station: If you're connecting from Arles to the TGV in Avignon, it's easiest to take the SNCF bus directly from Arles' train station to Avignon's TGV station (10/day, 1 hour). Another option—which takes the same amount of time, but adds more walking—is to take the regular train from Arles to Avignon's Centre-Ville Station, then catch the *navette* (shuttle bus) to the TGV station from there.

From Arles Bus Station to: **Nîmes** (6/day, 1 hr), **St. Rémy-de-Provence** (3/day Mon–Sat April–Oct, none Sun or Nov–March, 50 min), **Fontvieille** (6/day, 10 min), **Camargue/Stes-Maries-de-la-Mer** (5/day Mon–Sat, 3/day Sun, 1 hr). The bus station is at 16–24 boulevard Georges Clemenceau (2 blocks below main TI, next to Café le Wilson). Bus info: tel. 04 90 49 38 01 (unlikely to speak English).

To Les Baux: From Arles, a bus runs to **Les Baux** only July through August (6/day, 35 min). For other ways to reach Les Baux, see page 81.

NEAR ARLES

Les Baux • St. Rémy
• The Camargue

The diverse terrain around Arles harbors many worthwhile and easy day trips. The medieval ghost town of Les Baux haunts the eerie Alpilles Mountains, while chic and compact St. Rémy-de-Provence awaits just over the hills, offering Roman ruins and memories of Vincent van Gogh. For an entirely different experience, the flat Camargue knocks on Arles' southern door with sandy beaches, saltwater lakes, rice paddies, flamingos, wild horses, and wild black bulls.

Planning Your Time

Because public transportation in this area is sparse, these sights are easiest to reach by car, taxi, or minivan tour. For a memorable one-day road trip from Arles or Avignon, spend the morning in Les Baux (before the crowds), have lunch in St. Rémy and explore its sights, then finish at the Roman aqueduct of Barbegal. Non-drivers can do the same day trip (without the aqueduct) by bus and taxi. If you have more time or are a nature or bird-watching buff, head for the Camargue.

Les Baux

The hilltop town of Les Baux crowns the rugged Alpilles (ahl-pee) Mountains, evoking a tumultuous medieval history. Here, you can imagine the struggles of a strong community that lived a rough-and-tumble life—thankful more for their top-notch fortifications than for their dramatic views. It's mobbed with tourists most of the day, but Les Baux rewards those who arrive by 9:00 or after 17:30. (While the hilltop citadel's entry closes at the end of

Near Arles

the day, once you're inside, you're welcome to live out your fondest medieval fantasies all night long.) Sunsets are dramatic, the castle is brilliantly illuminated after dark, and nights in Les Baux are pin-drop peaceful. If you like what you see here, but want a more off-the-beaten-path experience, head for the Luberon and find the Fort de Buoux (see page 215).

Getting to Les Baux

By Car: Les Baux is a 20-minute drive from Arles: Follow signs for *Avignon*, then *Les Baux*. Drivers can combine Les Baux with St.

Rémy (15 min away) and the ruined Roman aqueduct of Barbegal (both described later in this chapter).

By Bus: From Arles, direct bus service to Les Baux runs only July through August (6/day, 35 min, via Abbey of Montmajour, Fontvieille, and Paradou).

You can also combine Les Baux and St. Rémy into a worthwhile day trip from Arles or Avignon: From either city, take the bus to St. Rémy (50 min, from Arles: 3/day Mon–Sat April–Oct, none Sun or Nov–March; from Avignon: 6/day Mon–Sat, 3/day Sun); then take a taxi to Les Baux, and another taxi back to your home base (see below).

By Taxi: Count on €37 for a taxi one-way from Arles to Les Baux (€45 after 19:00), and allow €15 one-way from St. Rémy (tel. 06 80 27 60 92).

By Minivan Tour: The best option for many is a minivan tour, which can be both efficient and economical (easiest from Avignon; see page 40).

Orientation to Les Baux

Les Baux is actually two visits in one: castle ruins perched on an almost lunar landscape, and a medieval town below. Savor the castle, then tour—or blitz—the lower streets on your way out. While the town, which lives entirely off tourism, is packed with shops, cafés, and tourist knickknacks, the castle above stays manageable since crowds are dispersed over a big area. The lower town's polished-stone gauntlet of boutiques is a Provençal dream-come-true for shoppers.

Tourist Information

The TI is immediately on the left as you enter the village (daily 9:00–17:30, later in summer, tel. 04 90 54 34 39, www .lesbauxdeprovence.com). Ask about combo-ticket deals, such as the castle ruins and Cathédrale d'Images for €13 (saves €3), and the €15.50 **Les Baux Jours pass,** which covers the castle ruins, the Cathédrale d'Images, and the Yves Brayer Museum (saves €4.50). You'll also see deals combining Les Baux with other sights in the region (such as the theater in Orange). The TI can also call a cab for you.

Arrival in Les Baux

Drivers must pay €4 to park anywhere. Don't be tempted by the first parking spots you see; drive right to the top and park as close as possible to the entry. Pay at the machine just below the town entry (next to telephone, WC, and bakery).

Walk up the cobbled street into town, where you're greeted

first by the TI. From here, the main drag leads directly to the castle—just keep going uphill (a 10-min walk).

Sights in Les Baux

▲▲▲The Castle Ruins (The "Dead City")

The sun-bleached ruins of the "dead city" of Les Baux are carved into, out of, and on top of a rock 650 feet above the valley floor. Many of the ancient walls of this striking castle still stand as a

testament to the proud past of this once-feisty village.

Cost and Hours: €8 (ask about family rates), includes excellent audioguide, daily July–Aug 9:00–20:00, Easter–June and Sept–Oct 9:00–19:00, Nov–Easter 9:30–17:00. If you are inside the castle when the entry closes, you can stay as long as you like. From April to October, medieval pageantry, tournaments, or fun-for-kids demonstrations enliven the mountaintop. If you bring your lunch, enjoy the picnic tables.

History: Imagine the importance of this citadel in the Middle Ages, when the Lords of Baux were notorious warriors. (How many feudal lords could trace their lineage back to one of the "three kings" of Christmas-carol fame, Balthazar?) In the 11th century, Les Baux was a powerhouse in southern France, controlling about 80 towns. The Lords of Baux fought the counts of Barcelona for control of Provence...and eventually lost. But while in power, these guys were mean. One ruler enjoyed forcing unransomed prisoners to jump off his castle walls.

In 1426, Les Baux was incorporated into Provence and France. Not accustomed to subservience, Les Baux struggled with the French king, who responded by destroying the fortress in 1483. Later, Les Baux regained some importance and emerged as a center of Protestantism. Arguing with Rome was a high-stakes game in the 17th century, and Les Baux's association with the Huguenots brought destruction again in 1632 when Cardinal Richelieu (under King Louis XIII) demolished the castle. Louis rubbed salt in the wound by billing Les Baux's residents for his demolition expenses. The once-powerful town of 4,000 was forever crushed.

➲ Self-Guided Tour: Buy your ticket in the old olive mill, inspect the models of Les Baux before its 17th-century destruction, and then pick up your audioguide after entering the sight. The audioguide follows posted numbers counterclockwise around the rocky spur. Take full advantage of this tool—as you wander

Les Baux

1 Le Mas d'Aigret
2 Le Mas de l'Esparou B&B
3 Hostellerie de la Reine Jeanne
4 To Le Mazet des Alpilles B&B
5 Joel Durand Chocolates

NOT TO SCALE

TO ST REMY VIA MOST SCENIC ROUTE

CAVES DE SARRAGAN

CATHEDRALE D'IMAGES

D-17

TO ARLES & FONTVIEILLE

CHAPEL OF PENITENTS

EYGUIERES GATE

MUSEUM OF SANTONS

PLACE LOUIS JOU

R. PORTE MAGE

CEM.

WC

ST. VINCENT

YVES BRAYER MUSEUM

RUE DE LA CALADE

UPHILL!

GRAND RUE F. MISTRAL

TOWN

CASTLE RUINS

CHAPEL

RUE TRENCAT

TICKETS & ENTRY TO "DEAD CITY"

R. DU CHATEAU

R. NEUVE

CITY HALL

RENAISSANCE WINDOW

R. DE LORME

C L I F F S

TO ST REMY

P PARKING

VIEW

LOWER TOWN WALK

TO MAUSSANE, PARADOU, ABBEY DE MONTMAJOUR, ARLES, 4 & BARBEGAL

DCH

around, key in the number for any of the 30 narrated stops that interest you.

As you walk on the windblown spur (*baux* in French), you'll pass kid-thrilling medieval siege weaponry (go ahead, try the battering ram). Good displays in English and images help reconstruct the place. Try to imagine 4,000 people living up here. Notice the water-catchment system (a slanted field that caught rainwater and drained it into cisterns—necessary during a siege) and find the reservoir cut into the rock below the castle's highest point. Look for post holes throughout the stone walls that reveal where beams once supported floors.

For the most sensational views, climb to the blustery top of the citadel. Hang on. The mistral wind just might blow you away.

The St. Blaise chapel across from the entry/exit runs videos with Provençal themes (plays continuously; just images and music, no words).

▲Lower Town

After your castle visit, you can shop and eat your way back through the new town. Or you can escape some of the crowds by following my short tour, below, which covers these minor but worthwhile sights as you descend (all stay open at lunch except the Yves Brayer Museum).

• *On the main drag (grand rue Frédéric Mistral), a few blocks below the castle exit, is the...*

Manville Mansion City Hall—The 15th-century city hall flies the red-and-white flag of Monaco, a reminder that the Grimaldi family (which has long ruled the tiny principality of Monaco) owned Les Baux until the French Revolution (1789). In fact, in 1982, Princess Grace Kelly and her royal husband, Prince Rainier Grimaldi, came to Les Baux to receive the key to the city.

Twenty yards up rue Nueve, the fine 1571 **Renaissance** window frame, marking the site of a future Calvinist museum, stands as a reminder of this town's Protestant history. This was probably a place of Huguenot worship—the words carved into the lintel, *Post tenebras lux,* were a popular Calvinist slogan: "After the shadow comes the light."

• *At the end of rue Nueve, head right on rue des Fours to get to the...*

Yves Brayer Museum (Musée Yves Brayer)—This enjoyable museum lets you peruse three floors of paintings (Van Gogh–like Expressionism, without the tumult) by Yves Brayer (1907–1990), who spent his final years here in Les Baux. Like Van Gogh, Brayer was inspired by all that surrounded him. Brayer picked up inspiration from his travels through Morocco, Spain, and the rest of the Mediterranean world (€4, daily 10:00–12:30 & 14:00–18:30, tel. 04 90 54 36 99). Pick up the descriptive English sheet at the entry.

• *Next door is...*

St. Vincent Church—This 12th-century Romanesque church was built short and wide to fit the terrain. The center chapel on the right (partially carved out of the rock) houses the town's traditional Provençal processional chariot. Each Christmas Eve, a ram pulled this cart—holding a lamb, symbolizing Jesus, and surrounded by candles—through town to the church.

• *Around the corner (to the left as you leave the church) are public WCs. Directly in front of the church is a vast view, making clear the strategic value of this rocky bluff's natural fortifications. A few steps away is the...*

Chapel of Penitents—Notice the nativity scene painted by Yves Brayer, illustrating the local legend that says Jesus was born in Les Baux. On the opposite wall, find his version of a starry night. Leaving the church, turn left. Wash your shirt in the old-town "laundry"—with a pig-snout faucet and 14th-century stone washing surface designed for short women.

• *Heading downhill at the junction on rue de la Calade, you'll pass cafés with wonderful views, the town's fortified wall, and one of its two gates. After passing a free (and curiously evangelical) "museum of aromas and perfumes," you hit the awe-inspiring...*

Museum of Santons—This free museum displays a collection of *santons* ("little saints"), popular folk figurines that decorate local Christmas mangers. Notice how the nativity scene "proves" once again that Jesus was born in Les Baux. These painted clay dolls show off local dress and traditions (with good English descriptions). Find the old couple leaning heroically into the mistral.

Joel Durand Chocolates—Farther along, you'll find this shop, with tasty samples. Figure out their letter-code system and find your favorite.

Near Les Baux

A half-mile beyond Les Baux, D-27 (toward Maillane) leads to dramatic views of the hill town. There are pullouts and walking trails at the pass, and two sites that fill cool, cavernous caves in former limestone quarries dating back to the Middle Ages. (The limestone is easy to cut, but gets hard and nicely polished when exposed to the weather.) Speaking of quarries, in 1821, the rocks and soil of this area were found to contain an important mineral for making aluminum. It was named after the town: bauxite.

Caves de Sarragan—The best views of Les Baux are from this parking lot, occupied by the Sarragan Winery (which invites you in for a taste). While this place looks like it's designed for groups, the friendly, English-speaking staff welcomes individuals (free, daily April–Sept 10:00–12:00 & 14:00–19:00, Oct–March until 18:00, tel. 04 90 54 33 58, www.caves-sarragan.com).

▲▲**Cathédrale d'Images**—This similar cave nearby offers a mesmerizing sound-and-slide show with a different program every year. The show thrills visitors no matter what the program, as 48 projectors flash countless images set to music on the quarry walls as you wander around. The 2009 program featured the life of Pablo Picasso; check their website for the 2010 theme (€8, March–Dec daily 10:00–18:00, closed Jan–Feb, tel. 04 90 54 42 65, www.cathedrale-images.com). Dress warmly, since the cave is cool.

D-27 continues to St. Rémy, allowing for a handy loop trip (to complete the loop, return from St. Rémy to Les Baux via D-5).

Sleeping in Les Baux

Many of these accommodations are actually scattered around the countryside surrounding Les Baux.

$$$ Le Mas d'Aigret*, barely east of Les Baux on the road to St. Rémy, is a well-run, lovely refuge that crouches under

Sleep Code

(€1 = about $1.40, country code: 33)
S = Single, **D** = Double/Twin, **T** = Triple, **Q** = Quad, **b** = bathroom,
s = shower only, * = French hotel rating system (0–4 stars).
Unless otherwise noted, credit cards are accepted and English
is spoken.

To help you easily sort through these listings, I've divided
the rooms into three categories, based on the price for a
standard double room with bath:

$$$ **Higher Priced**—Most rooms €80 or more.
$$ **Moderately Priced**—Most rooms between €55–80.
$ **Lower Priced**—Most rooms €55 or less.

For more accommodations in this area, see page 93.

Les Baux. Lie on your back and stare up at the castle walls rising beyond the swimming pool, or enjoy valley views from the groomed terraces (Db with no view-€95, larger Db with balcony and view-€150, Tb/Qb-€200, two cool troglodyte rooms-€170–200, half-pension option with big breakfast and good dinner for about €40 per person, air-con, rooms have some daytime road noise, tel. 04 90 54 20 00, fax 04 90 54 44 00, www.masdaigret .com, contact@masdaigret.com, Dutch Marieke and French Eric).

$$ Le Mas de l'Esparou *chambre d'hôte*, a few minutes below Les Baux toward Paradou, is welcoming and kid-friendly, with three spacious rooms, a big swimming pool, table tennis, and distant views of Les Baux. Sweet Jacqueline loves her job, and her lack of English only makes her more animated (Db-€68, extra bed-about €16, includes breakfast, cash only, between Les Baux and Maussane les Alpilles on D-5, look for white sign with green lettering, tel. & fax 04 90 54 41 32).

$$ Hostellerie de la Reine Jeanne**, an exceptional value, is a good place to watch the sun rise and set from Les Baux. Warmly run by Gaelle and Marc, this place offers a handful of sufficiently comfy rooms above a busy (and good-value) restaurant (standard Ds-€52, standard Db-€58, Db with view deck-€62–72, Tb-€70–80, cavernous family suite-€105, air-con in half the rooms, ask for *chambre avec terrasse*, good *menus* from €16, 150 feet to your right after entry to the village of Les Baux, tel. 04 90 54 32 06, fax 04 90 54 32 33, www.la-reinejeanne.com, reine.jeanne@wanadoo.fr).

$ Le Mazet des Alpilles is a small home with three tidy, air-conditioned rooms just outside the unspoiled village of Paradou, five minutes below Les Baux. It may have rooms when others don't (Db-€55, ask for largest room, includes breakfast, cash only, air-con, child's bed available, pleasant garden, follow brown signs from D-17, in Paradou look for route de Brunelly, tel. 04 90 54 45 89, www.alpilles.com/mazet.htm, lemazet@wanadoo.fr). Sweet Annick speaks just enough English.

Eating in Les Baux

You'll find quieter cafés with views along my self-guided tour route (described above). The recommended **Hostellerie de la Reine Jeanne** offers friendly service and good-value meals indoors or out (€12 salads, €16 *menus*, try the *salade Estivale*, open daily).

Sights Between Les Baux and Arles

The following stops are easiest for drivers.

Abbey of Montmajour—This brooding hulk of a ruin, just a few minutes' drive from Arles toward Les Baux, was once a thriving abbey and a convenient papal retreat (c. A.D. 950). Today, the vacant abbey church is a massive example of Romanesque architecture and an overpriced sight (€7.50; May–Aug daily 10:00–18:30; Sept–April Tue–Sun 10:00–17:00, closed Mon; tel. 04 90 54 64 17). Film buffs will appreciate this sight as the setting for *The Lion in Winter,* where Eleanor of Aquitaine (played by Katherine Hepburn) battled with her husband, Henry II (Peter O'Toole). For more on abbeys, see "Medieval Monasteries" on page 208.

The surrounding fields were a favorite of Van Gogh's, who walked here from Arles to paint his famous wheat fields. Now they're rice fields, which wouldn't have looked nearly as good on canvas.

▲**Roman Aqueduct of Barbegal**—To be all alone with evocative Roman ruins, drivers can take a quick detour to the crumbled arches of ancient Arles' principal aqueduct.

From the parking area, follow the dirt path through the olive grove and along the aqueduct ruins for 200 yards. Approaching the bluff with the grand view, you'll see that the water canal is split into two troughs: One takes a 90-degree right turn and heads for Arles; the other goes straight to the bluff and over, where it once sent water cascading down to power eight grinding mills. Romans grew wheat on the vast fields you see from here, then brought it down to the mega-watermill of Barbegal. Historians figure that this mill produced enough flour each day to feed 12,000 hungry Romans. If you saw the model of this eight-tiered mill in Arles' Ancient History Museum (see page 57), the milling is easy to visualize—making a visit here quite an exciting experience.

Returning to your car, find the broken bit of aqueduct—it's positioned like a children's playground slide—and take a look at the waterproofing mortar that lined all Roman aqueducts.

Getting There: Coming from Arles, take D-17 toward Fontvieille; then, three kilometers (less than 2 miles) before Fontvieille, look for signs for *L'Aqueduc Romain* on D-82 (it's signed coming from Fontvieille to Arles as well, on the left). In less than three kilometers, park at the dirt pullout (no sign—it's just after the *Los Pozos Blancos* sign, where the ruins of the aqueduct cross the road). Leave no valuables visible in your car; the gravel twinkles with the remains of broken car windows.

St. Rémy-de-Provence

Sophisticated and sassy, St. Rémy (sahn ray-mee) gave birth to Nostradamus and cared for a distraught artist. Today, it caters to

shoppers and Van Gogh fans. A few minutes from the town center, you can visit the once-thriving Roman city called Glanum, the mental ward where Vincent van Gogh was sent after lopping off his lobe, and an art center dedicated to his memory. Best of all is the chance to elbow your way through its raucous Wednesday market (until 12:30). A ring road—which local drivers mistake for a racecourse—hems in a pedestrian-friendly center that's well-stocked with fine foods, pottery boutiques, art galleries, and the latest Provençal fashions.

Getting to St. Rémy

By Car: From Les Baux, St. Rémy is a spectacular 15-minute drive over the hills and through the woods. Roads D-5 and D-27 each provide scenic routes between these towns, making a loop drive between them worthwhile. The most scenic approach is on D-27; from Les Baux, take the road toward Maillane that passes the Cathédrale d'Images. Take advantage of the many good pullouts and get out of your car for that view. From St. Rémy to Les Baux, follow signs for *Tarascon*, and you'll see the D-27 turnoff to Les Baux in a few miles. Parking in St. Rémy is tricky; it's easiest at the TI lot (€1/3 hours, free Mon–Sat 12:00–14:00 and all day Sun). Parking on place Charles de Gaulle is always free, but farther from the center (leave the ring road on avenue Frédéric Mistral).

By Bus: Buses run from Arles (3/day Mon–Sat April–Oct, none Sun or Nov–March) and Avignon (6/day Mon–Sat, 3/day

Sun) to St. Rémy. If arriving at St. Rémy by bus, get off on the ring road at the stop called République. The TI is a block up avenue Durand Maillane (to the right).

By Taxi: From Les Baux, allow €15 one-way; from Avignon, count on €35 (tel. 06 80 27 60 92 or 06 09 52 71 54). St. Rémy's four taxis park on place de la République, next to the bus stop.

Orientation to St. Rémy

From St. Rémy's circular center, it's a 15-minute walk along a busy road with no sidewalk to Glanum and the St. Paul Monastery (Van Gogh's mental hospital).

Tourist Information

The TI is two blocks toward Les Baux from the ring road (Mon–Sat 9:00–12:30 & 14:00–18:00, Sun 10:00–12:00—except closed Sun Oct–April; tel. 04 90 92 05 22, www.saintremy-de-provence .com). At the TI, pick up a town map, bus schedules, hiking guides, and a map tracing Van Gogh's favorite painting locations with *in situ* copies of the painted scenes (the *Starry Night* panel is just outside the TI). They can also call a taxi for you. Get information about the English "In the Footsteps of Van Gogh" walking tours (€8, 1.5 hours, departs TI at 10:00 usually on Tue, Thu, and Fri; also occasional afternoon tours of the town; requires reservation). Skip the overpriced Citypod audioguide, a quick 30-minute tour of the town (€5, at TI).

Sights in St. Rémy

St. Rémy's best attractions are outside the town center: the ruins at Glanum and the Vincent van Gogh sights nearby. This cluster of sights is an unappealing 15-minute walk south of the TI. If you're driving, you can park for free at the St. Paul Monastery (coming from Les Baux, it's the first right after passing Glanum) and walk five minutes to Glanum from there (or pay €2.50 to park at the Glanum site).

▲Glanum Ruins

These crumbling stones are the foundations of a Roman market town, located at the crossroads of two ancient trade routes between Italy and Spain. A heavy Roman arch and tower stand across the road as proud reminders of the town's glory days, and indicate how much larger the town was back then (the Roman city was about seven times larger than the visible ruins). The arch marked the entry into Glanum, and the tower is a memorial to the grandsons of Emperor Augustus Caesar.

St. Rémy Area

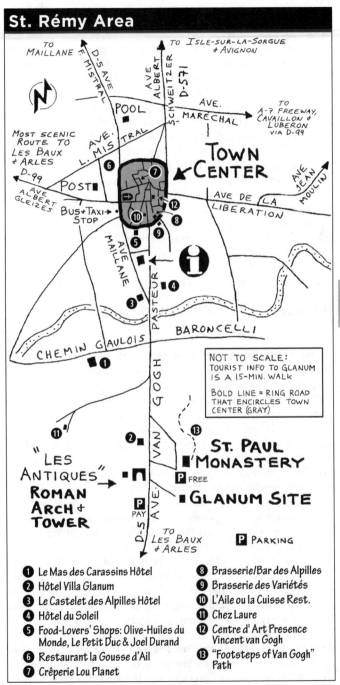

NOT TO SCALE:
TOURIST INFO TO GLANUM
IS A 15-MIN. WALK

BOLD LINE = RING ROAD
THAT ENCIRCLES TOWN
CENTER (GRAY)

① Le Mas des Carassins Hôtel
② Hôtel Villa Glanum
③ Le Castelet des Alpilles Hôtel
④ Hôtel du Soleil
⑤ Food-Lovers' Shops: Olive-Huiles du Monde, Le Petit Duc & Joel Durand
⑥ Restaurant la Gousse d'Ail
⑦ Crêperie Lou Planet
⑧ Brasserie/Bar des Alpilles
⑨ Brasserie des Variétés
⑩ L'Aile ou la Cuisse Rest.
⑪ Chez Laure
⑫ Centre d'Art Presence Vincent van Gogh
⑬ "Footsteps of Van Gogh" Path

NEAR ARLES

While the ruins are, well...ruined, their setting at the base of the rocky Alpilles is lovely. It's also shadeless, so if it's hot, come early or late. These ruins highlight the range and prosperity of the Roman Empire, and along with other Roman monuments in Provence, they paint a more complete picture of Roman life. About 2,500 people lived in Glanum at its zenith. While this was an important town, with grand villas, temples, a basilica, a forum, a wooden dam, and aqueducts, it was not important enough to justify an arena or a theater (such as those in Arles, Nîmes, and Orange). For more on Roman history, see page 42.

The free English handout, the exhibits in the entry, and the helpful information panels scattered about the site all help put this picture together. Still, eager Romanophiles will want to spring for the well-done "Itineraries" book (€7). Stroll up Glanum's main street and see remains of a market hall, a forum, thermal baths, reservoirs, and more. The view from the belvedere justifies the effort (€7, under 18 free, daily April–Sept 9:00–18:30, Oct–March 10:30–17:00, parking-€2.50, tel. 04 90 92 23 79). There's a pleasant on-site café with Roman specialties and classic snack fare.

Retracing Van Gogh's Steps

For more on Vincent van Gogh's time in this region, see page 66 in the Arles chapter.

St. Paul Monastery and Hospital (Le Monastère St. Paul de Mausole)—Just below Glanum is the still-functioning mental hospital (Clinique St. Paul) that treated Vincent van Gogh from 1889 to 1890. Pay €4 and enter Vincent's temporarily peaceful world: a small chapel, intimate cloisters, a re-creation of his room, and a small lavender field with six (of my favorite) paintings copied on large displays. Read the thoughtful English explanations about Vincent's tortured life. Amazingly, he completed 143 paintings and over 100 drawings in his 53 weeks here—none of which remain anywhere nearby today. The contrast between the utter simplicity of his room (and his life) and the multimillion-dollar value of his paintings today is jarring. The site is managed by Valetudo, a center specializing in art therapy (daily April–Sept 9:30–18:45, Oct–March 10:30–17:30, tel. 04 90 92 77 00).

Around the complex, you'll see panels of Vincent's works—some located right where he painted them. Several are located along the short road into the site (the TI has a map with a list of the reproductions). Stand among flamelike cypress trees, gaze over the distant skyline of St. Rémy, and realize you're in the midst of Van Gogh's most famous work, *The Starry Night*.

Centre d'Art Présence Vincent van Gogh—This center in old St. Rémy is an ongoing tribute to the painter, and features a small room of reproductions and worthwhile video presentations (usually with English subtitles). The theme changes each year, though the subject always remains Vincent van Gogh. Upstairs is a rotating exhibit that reflects the enormous influence of Vincent's work on contemporary artists. You'll also find a worthwhile collection of works by Cubist precursor Albert Gleizes (€3.30, Tue–Sun 10:00–12:30 & 14:00–19:00, closed Mon, inside the ring road on rue Estrine, tel. 04 90 92 34 72).

Sleeping in St. Rémy

(€1 = about $1.40, country code: 33)
$$$ Le Mas des Carassins*, a 15-minute walk from the center, is impeccably run by friendly Michel and Pierre. Luxury is affordable here. Your hosts pay careful attention to every detail, from the generously sized pool and gardens to the muted room decor and optional €30 home-cooked dinner (available only on weekdays). Reservations are smart—its 14 rooms fill fast (standard Db-€126, deluxe Db-€159, Db with terrace-€179, suite-€202, extra bed-€20, includes breakfast, air-con, Wi-Fi, table tennis, look for signs 200 yards toward Les Baux from TI, 1 Chemin Gaulois, tel. 04 90 92 15 48, fax 04 90 92 63 47, www.hoteldescarassins.com, info@hotel descarassins.com).

$$$ Hôtel Villa Glanum* is a modern hotel on the main road (some traffic noise) across from the St. Paul Monastery and the Glanum ruins. It's a 15-minute walk from the town center with tight but well-maintained rooms. The best rooms, which come with higher rates, are in bungalows around the pretty pool and lush gardens (Db-€90–120, Tb-€140, Qb-€150, cheaper off-season, 46 avenue Van Gogh, tel. 04 90 92 03 59, fax 04 90 92 00 08, www .villaglanum.com, contact@villaglanum.com).

$$ Le Castelet des Alpilles* is way Old World, but the location is good (halfway between St. Rémy's old town and the Roman ruins), the terrace is big, the price is fair, and the rooms are plenty comfortable. Most are big and airy, and the balcony rooms have views of the Alpilles (Db-€72–82, Db with air-con and view balcony-€100, Tb-€118, Wi-Fi, 6 place Mireille, tel. 04 90 92 07 21, fax 04 90 92 52 03, www.castelet-alpilles.com, hotel.castel .alpilles@wanadoo.fr).

$$ Hôtel du Soleil, an easy walk from St. Rémy's center, is a budget traveler's refuge, with simple, air-conditioned, and spotless rooms clustered around a pleasant courtyard and pool. Happy Monsieur Monset is behind the desk (standard Sb/Db-€66, bigger Sb/Db-€82, Tb-€95, 3 rooms have small terraces, 2-room apartment-€110–130, Internet access and Wi-Fi, easy parking, a block above the TI at 35 avenue Pasteur, tel. 04 90 92 00 63, fax 04 90 92 61 07, www.hotelsoleil.com, info@hotelsoleil.com).

Food-Lovers' Guide to St. Rémy

Wednesday is market day in St. Rémy, but you don't have to fast until then. Foodies will appreciate the three shops gathered on the ring road in St. Rémy, near the turnoff to Les Baux.

Start at **Olive-Huiles du Monde,** where you can belly up to a wine bar–like setting and sample the best olive oil and vinegar in the area. The friendly staff speaks English and is happy to spoon up samples of three olive oils and two surprisingly tasty vinegars. Check out the fine display of other products made from olive oil and the good truffle display (daily 10:00–12:30 & 15:00–19:00, 16 boulevard Victor Hugo, tel. 04 90 15 02 33).

Le Petit Duc, across the road, offers a remarkable introduction to antique cookies. Let friendly owner/chef Hermann, who speaks some English, and sweet Marie, who tries, take you on a mornings-only kitchen tour (daily 10:00–13:00 & 15:00–19:00, 7 boulevard Victor Hugo, tel. 04 90 92 08 31).

Just one whiff from **Joel Durand Chocolates** will lure chocoholics inside. Ask for a sample and learn the letter-coded system. The lavender is surprisingly good (daily 9:30–12:30 & 14:30–19:30, a few doors down from Le Petit Duc at 3 boulevard Victor Hugo, tel. 04 90 92 38 25).

Eating in St. Rémy

The town is packed with fine restaurants, each trying to outdo the other. Join the evening strollers and compare.

La Gousse d'Ail is no secret, but even so, it's a reliable and warm place for a mini-splurge (*menus* from €32, closed Thu, on the ring road just after the turnoff to Maillane at 6 boulevard Marceau, tel. 04 90 92 16 87).

Crêperie Lou Planet, on pleasant place Favier, is cheap and peaceful, with outdoor seating in summer, delicious crêpes, and good salads. Owner Jean has been here for 25 years and still hasn't changed the menu (daily April–Sept 12:00–22:00, behind Hôtel de Ville).

Brasserie/Bar des Alpilles sits on the ring road offering a great salad selection and good standard café fare, including pasta dishes for €9 (daily lunch and dinner, 21 boulevard Victor Hugo, tel. 04 90 92 0 17).

Brasserie des Variétés has good kids' menus, along with computers and Wi-Fi (daily, #32 on the ring road, tel. 04 90 92 42 61).

L'Aile ou la Cuisse offers a chic and fresh salad bar for €12, and elegant dinner meals (€16–28 *plats*, €40 *menus*). It's a friendly and funky place with delicious cuisine and gorgeous desserts (in front of the Hôtel de Ville at 5 rue de la Commune, tel. 04 32 62 00 25).

Chez Laure is a simple, local, and relaxed outdoor restaurant. It's located a mile from St. Rémy in a park-like setting with toys available for kids (open daily, €10 lunch *menu*, €18 dinner *menu*, on route du Lac, tel. 04 90 92 51 99). To find the restaurant, look for signs between the Glanum ruins and the TI (see map on page 91).

The Camargue

The Camargue region occupies the vast delta of the Rhône River, and it is one of Europe's most important wetlands. This marshy area exists where the Rhône splits into two branches (big and little), just before it flows into the Mediterranean. Over the millennia, a steady flow of sediment has been deposited at the mouth of the rivers—thoroughly land-locking villages that once faced the sea.

Since World War II, farmers have converted large northern tracts of the Camargue to rice fields, making the delta a major producer of France's rice. Salt is the other key industry in the Camargue—you can see vast salt marshes and evaporation beds around the town of Salin de Giraud. Because the salt marshes were long considered useless, the land has remained relatively untouched, leaving it a popular nature destination today.

Today the Camargue Regional Nature Park is a protected and "wild" area, where pink flamingos, wild bulls, nasty boars, nastier mosquitoes (in every season but winter—come prepared), and the famous white horses wander freely through lagoons and tall grass. For more on these animals, see "The Wildlife of the Camargue" sidebar.

The Camargue's subtle wetlands beauty makes it a worthwhile joyride for some, but a take-it-or-leave-it sight for many (unless it's spring and you've never seen a flamingo in flight). The Everglades-like scenery is a birder's paradise, and occasional bulls and wild horses add to the enjoyment. But for avid city sightseers, this can feel like a big swamp—interesting to drive through, but where's the excitement? Read ahead and decide for yourself (tel. 04 90 97 86 32, www.parc-camargue.fr, info@parc-camargue.fr). Since the birds are fewest and the mosquitoes are greatest in summer, I'd pass on the Camargue at that time.

However, if you have children who can't take the city anymore, a picnic on the long sandy beach at plage d'Arles may be just what the doctor ordered. Also called plage de Piemanço, this public beach is 10 kilometers (6 miles) after Salin de Giraud (see map on page 82). Bring everything you might need, as there are no vendors, but the sand is soft and the sea is warm.

Getting to the Camargue

There are several ways beyond a car to experience the Camargue: horseback, mountain bikes, and jeep safaris. All three options are available in Stes-Maries-de-la-Mer, and jeep safaris are also offered from Arles (ask at TI). Hiking is not good in the Camargue, as there are few decent trails (check www.kustgids.nl/camargue-en). The best biking is across the Digue (dike) to Phare de la Gacholle (see below).

By Scenic Drive: There are two primary driving routes from Arles through the Camargue: to Stes-Maries-de-la-Mer (town described under "Sights in the Camargue"), and toward Salin de Giraud.

My favorite route is toward **Salin de Giraud:** Leave Arles on D-570 toward Stes-Maries-de-la-Mer, passing the D-36 turnoff to Salin de Giraud (you'll return along this route). After a stop at the Camarguais Museum, continue along D-570, then turn left on D-37 toward Salin de Giraud and follow it as it skirts the Etang de Vaccarès lagoon. The lagoon itself is off-limits, but this area has views and good opportunities to get out of the car and smell the marshes. Turn right off D-37 onto the tiny road at Villeneuve, following La Capelière and La Fiélouse.

Make time for a stop at **La Capelière** (headquarters for Camargue sightseers), where you can pick up an excellent map, ask the eager staff questions, and enjoy a small exhibit and one-mile walking trail with some English information on the Camargue (modest trail fee). Birders can look at the register to see what birds have been spotted recently (observations in English are in red).

The best part of the Camargue (particularly in spring) awaits at **La Digue de la Mer,** about 10 scenic kilometers (six miles) past La Capelière. A rough dirt road rising above water on both sides greets travelers; it's time to get out of your car and stroll (though you can drive on for a few miles to Phare de la Gacholle). This is a critical reproduction area for flamingos (about 5,000 offspring annually), so it's your best chance to see groups of mamas and papas up close and personal. If you rented a mountain bike, now would be the right time to use it: It's about eight bumpy but engaging miles between water and sand dunes to Stes-Maries-de-la-Mer.

The Wildlife of the Camargue

In this nature reserve, amusing flamingos and countless other bird species flourish—attracting bird-watchers from all over the world. Once an endangered species, the flamingos flock here because of all that salt—which is why they come to the Camargue rather than to, say, the sandy beaches of the Riviera. Ten thousand flamingos leave here each fall, heading to warmer climates, and then return in March to pink up the Camargue (a visit here in the spring reaps big, pink rewards). To see a formation of these long and clumsy-looking birds in flight is an experience you won't soon forget.

The black bulls are raised for bullfights (by local cowboys called *gardians*) and eventually end up on plates in Arles' restaurants (you may have met one already). The *gardians*, who have patrolled the Camargue on local horses for centuries, add a Wild West aura to the region. The region's unique small horses—born brown or black, later turning light gray or white—are one of the oldest breeds in the world, and may have existed in the area since prehistoric times.

With the continual loss of wetlands throughout the world, it's critical that places like this remain preserved, and that we understand their significance.

For the fastest way back to Arles, backtrack to D-37 at Villeneuve, then follow D-36. If driving to Stes-Maries-de-la-Mer, there are several parking lots and plenty of on-street parking for drivers.

By Bus: Buses serve the Camargue (stopping at Camarguais Museum and Stes-Maries-de-la-Mer) from Arles' bus station (5/day Mon–Sat, 3/day Sun, 1 hour, tel. 04 90 96 36 25).

Sights in the Camargue

Camarguais Museum (Musée Camarguais)—Located in a traditional Camargue barn on the road to Stes-Maries-de-la-Mer, this well-designed folk museum does a good job of describing the natural features and cultural traditions of the Camargue. The costumes, tools, and helpful exhibits come with some English explanations (look for handouts and small screens), and there's a two-mile nature trail (€5; May–Sept daily 9:00–18:00; Oct–April Wed–Mon 10:00–17:00, closed Tue; 8 miles from Arles on D-570 toward Stes-Maries-de-la-Mer at Mas du Pont de Rousty farmhouse, tel. 04 90 97 10 82).

Stes-Maries-de-la-Mer—At the western end of the Camargue lies this whitewashed, Spanish-feeling seafront town with acres of flamingos, bulls, and horses at its doorstep. From the bus stop, walk to the church (10 min) to get oriented. The place is so popular that it's best avoided on weekends and during holidays. It's a French Coney Island—a trinket-selling, perennially windy place.

The town is also famous as a mecca for the Roma (also known as Gypsies). Every May, Roma from all over Europe pile in their caravans and migrate to Stes-Maries-de-la-Mer to venerate the statue of Saint Sarah. Legend has it that Mary Magdalene made landfall here in a boat with no oars after an epic journey across the Mediterranean from Egypt. Fleeing persecution for practicing the new and unpopular Christian faith, she was accompanied by two other "Stes-Maries": Mary Jacobe, the mother of the apostle James, and Mary Salome, the mother of the apostles James and John. Also in the boat was "Black Sarah," an Egyptian servant. Sarah collected alms for the poor; over time, her request for handouts became associated with the Roma people, who embrace her as their patron saint. Today's impressive spectacle to honor Sarah is like a sprawling flea market spilling out from the town.

At other times, the town of Stes-Maries-de-la-Mer has little to offer except its beachfront promenade, bullring, and towering five-belled fortified church. The church interior is worth a look for its unusual decorations and artifacts, including the statue of St. Sarah (church entry free, €2 to climb to roof for Camargue and sea views). Avoid the women with flowers and the assertive palm readers, who often cluster near the church—they want your money, not your friendship.

Most tourists come to take a horse, jeep, or bike into the Camargue—and there's no lack of outfits ready to take you for a ride. The TIs in Arles (see page 55) and Stes-Maries-de-la-Mer have long lists (Stes-Maries-de-la-Mer TI open daily April–Sept 9:00–19:00, until 20:00 in summer, Oct–March 9:00–17:00, tel. 04 90 97 82 55, www.saintesmaries.com). You can rent bikes (for the ride out to La Digue de la Mer) and get advice on the best route at Le Vélo (19 rue de la République, tel. 04 90 97 74 56). Jeep excursions run about €30 for 2.5 hours; Camargue-Decouverte is one of many outfits based in Arles (1 rue Emile Fassin, tel. 04 90 96 69 20, www.camargue-decouverte.com). Les Cabanes de Cacharel gives top-notch horseback tours (€13/1 hour—too short to see much, €25/2 hours, €37/3 hours, route de Cacharel in Stes-Maries-de-la-Mer, tel. 04 90 97 84 10, www.camargueacheval .com, info@camargueacheval.com).

Aigues-Mortes—This strange walled city, on the western edge of the Camargue (20 miles from Nîmes), was built by Louis IX as a jumping-off point for his Crusades to the Holy Land. Although Aigues-Mortes was a strategically situated royal port city, it was actually never near the sea—ships reached it via canals that were dug through an immense lagoon. Today its tall towers and thick fortifications seem oddly out of place, surrounded by nothing but salt marshes and flamingos. The name "Aigues-Mortes" means "Dead Waters," which says it all. Skip it unless you need more souvenirs and crowded streets, although drivers can detour to Aigues-Mortes, between Nîmes and Arles, for a quick-and-easy taste of the Camargue. Aigues-Mortes and Nîmes are linked by buses (6/day, 50 min) and trains (6/day, 45 min).

AVIGNON

Famous for its nursery rhyme, medieval bridge, and brooding Palace of the Popes, contemporary Avignon (ah-veen-yohn) bustles and prospers behind its mighty walls. During the 68 years (1309–1377) that Avignon starred as the *Franco Vaticano*, it grew from a quiet village into a thriving city. With its large student population and fashionable shops, today's Avignon is an intriguing blend of medieval history, youthful energy, and urban sophistication. Street performers entertain the international throngs who fill Avignon's ubiquitous cafés and trendy boutiques. If you're here in July, be prepared for big crowds and higher prices, thanks to the rollicking theater festival. (Reserve your hotel far in advance.) Clean, sharp, and popular with tourists, Avignon is more impressive for its outdoor ambience than for its museums and monuments. See the Palace of the Popes, and then explore the city's thriving streets and beautiful vistas from the parc des Rochers des Doms.

Orientation to Avignon

The cours Jean Jaurès, which turns into rue de la République, runs straight from the Centre-Ville train station to place de l'Horloge and the Palace of the Popes, splitting Avignon in two. The larger eastern half is where the action is. Climb to the parc des Rochers des Doms for the town's best view, tour the pope's immense palace, lose yourself in Avignon's back streets (see my "Discovering Avignon's Back Streets" self-guided walk), and find a shady square to call home. Avignon's shopping district fills the traffic-free streets near where rue de la République meets place de l'Horloge.

Tourist Information

The main TI is between the Centre-Ville train station and the old town, at 41 cours Jean Jaurès (April–Oct Mon–Sat 9:00–18:00—until 19:00 in July, Sun 9:45–17:00; Nov–March Mon–Fri 9:00–18:00, Sat 9:00–17:00, Sun 10:00–12:00; tel. 04 32 74 32 74, www.avignon-tourisme.com). From April through mid-October, a branch TI office, called Espace Ferruce, is open at St. Bénezet Bridge (daily 10:00–13:00 & 14:00–18:00, but it can be slow with just one person working). At either TI, get the good tear-off map. If you're staying a while, pick up the free and handy *Guide Pratique* (info on car and bike rentals, hotels, apartment rentals, events, and museums).

Everyone should pick up the free **Avignon Passion Pass** (valid 15 days, for up to five family members). Get the pass stamped when you pay full price at your first sight, and then receive reductions at the others (for example, €2 less at the Palace of the Popes and €3 less at the Petit Palais). The discounts add up—always show your Passion Pass when buying a ticket. The pass comes with the Avignon "Passion" map and guide, which includes several good (but tricky-to-follow) walking tours.

Arrival in Avignon

By Train

Avignon has two train stations: TGV (linked to downtown by frequent shuttle buses) and Centre-Ville. While most TGV trains serve only the TGV train station, some serve Centre-Ville—verify your station in advance.

TGV Station (Gare TGV): This shiny new station, on the outskirts of town, has no baggage storage (bags can be stored only at Centre-Ville Station).

To get to the city center, take the *navette*/**shuttle bus** (marked *Navette/Avignon Centre;* €1.20, buy ticket from driver, 3/hr, 15 min). To find the bus stop, leave the station by the north exit *(sortie nord)*, walk down the stairs, and find the long bus shelter to the left. In downtown Avignon, you'll arrive at a stop located three blocks from the city's main TI and two blocks from Centre-Ville Station (just inside the city walls, in front of the post office on cours Président Kennedy—see map on page 106). A **taxi** ride between the TGV station and downtown Avignon costs about €15 (to find taxis, exit the TGV station via *sortie nord*).

To pick up a **rental car** at the TGV train station, walk out the south exit *(sortie sud)* to find the *location de voitures* in the parking lot. If you're driving directly to Arles, St. Rémy-de-Provence, Les Baux, or the Luberon, leave the station following signs to *Avignon Sud,* then *La Rocade.* You'll soon see exits to Arles (best for St. Rémy and Les Baux) and Cavaillon (for Luberon villages).

If you're heading from the Avignon TGV train station to the **Arles train station,** you can catch a direct SNCF bus from the TGV station's bus stop (10/day, 1 hour, schedule available at any information booth inside the TGV station).

Centre-Ville Station **(Gare Avignon Centre-Ville):** All non-TGV trains (and a few TGV trains) serve the central station. You can stash your bags here—exit the station to the left and look for the *consignes* sign (daily May–Sept 6:00–22:00, Oct–April 10:00–18:00, confirm closing time when you leave your bag). To reach the town center, cross the busy street in front of the station and walk through the city walls onto cours Jean Jaurès. The TI is three blocks down, at #41.

By Bus

The dingy bus station *(gare routière)* is 100 yards to the right as you leave the Centre-Ville train station (beyond and below Ibis Hôtel).

By Car

Drivers entering Avignon follow *Centre-Ville* and *Gare SNCF* (train station) signs. You'll find central pay lots (about €10/half-day, €14/day) in the garage next to Centre-Ville Station, at the Parking Jean Jaurès under the ramparts across from the train station; or at the Parking Palais des Papes (follow signs on the riverside road, boulevard St. Lazare, just past St. Bénezet Bridge). Some free parking is available near the city walls (on boulevard Saint-Roch near Porte de la République), and there are two free lots nearby with free shuttle buses to the center (follow *P Gratuit* signs): One is just across Daladier Bridge (pont Daladier), and the other is along the river past the Palace of the Popes, just northeast of the walls. Leave nothing in your car. Hotels have advice for smart overnight parking and get big discounts at pay lots.

Helpful Hints

Book Ahead for July: During the July theater festival, rooms are rare—reserve very early or stay in Arles (see page 71) or St. Rémy (page 93).

Internet Access: The TI has a current list, or ask your hotelier.

English Bookstore: Try **Shakespeare Bookshop** (Tue–Sat 9:30–12:00 & 14:00–18:30, closed Sun–Mon, 155 rue Carreterie, in Avignon's northeast corner, tel. 04 90 27 38 50).

Festival d'Avignon

The last thing Avignon needs is an excuse to party. Still, every July since 1947, a theater festival envelops the city, creating a Mardi Gras–like atmosphere. Contemporary theater groups come from throughout Europe, and each year the festival showcases a different theater director or artist. The program is announced in May, and most tickets are booked immediately—hotels are 80 percent full by March. The festival is indoors, but venues overflow into the streets. The organizers need 20 different locations for the performances, from actual theater spaces to small chapels to the inner courtyard of the Palace of the Popes, which seats 2,000. There's also a "fringe festival," called Avignon-Off, which adds another 100 venues and countless amateur performances; and a children's theater festival, with storytellers, dance, musicals, and marionettes. In July, the entire city is a stage, with mimes, fire-breathers, singers, and musicians filling the streets. Most of the performances are in French, some are occasionally in English, and many dance performances don't require language at all (www.festival-avignon.com and www.avignonleoff.com).

Baggage Storage: You can leave your bags at Centre-Ville Station (see "Arrival in Avignon," earlier).

Laundry: The launderette at 66 place des Corps-Saints, where rue Agricol Perdiguier ends, has English instructions and is handy to most hotels (daily 7:00–20:00).

Grocery Store: Carrefour City is central and has long hours (Mon–Sat 7:00–21:00, Sun 9:00–12:00, 2 blocks from the TI, toward place de l'Horloge on rue de la République).

Bike Rental: The TI has the latest on bike rentals. You'll enjoy riding on the Ile de la Barthélasse, but biking is better in Isle-sur-la-Sorgue (described in the Hill Towns of the Luberon chapter) and Vaison la Romaine (described in the Orange and the Côtes du Rhône chapter).

Car Rental: The TGV train station has the car-rental agencies (open long hours daily).

Shuttle Boat: A free shuttle boat, the *Navette Fluviale*, plies back and forth across the river (as it did in the days when the town had no functioning bridge) from near St. Bénezet Bridge (daily July–Aug 11:00–21:00, Sept–June roughly 10:00–12:30 & 14:00–18:00, 3/hr). It drops you on the peaceful Ile de la Barthélasse, with its riverside restaurant (see page 122), grassy walks, and bike rides with terrific city views. If you stay on the island for dinner, check the schedule for the last return boat—or be prepared for a pleasant 25-minute walk back to town.

Avignon at a Glance

▲▲**Parc des Rochers des Doms** Park and ramparts at the hilltop where Avignon was first settled, with great views of the Rhône River Valley and the famous broken bridge. **Hours:** Daily April–Sept 7:30–20:00, Oct–March 7:30–18:00. See page 108.

▲▲**St. Bénezet Bridge** The "pont d'Avignon" of nursery-rhyme fame, once connecting Vatican territory to France. **Hours:** Daily mid-March–Oct 9:00–19:00, until 20:00 July and Sept, until 21:00 in Aug, Nov–mid-March 9:30–17:45. See page 109.

▲▲**Scenic Squares** Numerous hide-and-seek squares ideal for postcard-writing and people-watching—pick your favorite: place des Corps-Saints, place St. Pierre, place des Châtaignes (adjacent to place St. Pierre), place Crillon, place St. Didier (near recommended Caveau du Théâtre Restaurant), and the big place Pie (see map on page 106). **Hours:** Always open.

▲**Palace of the Popes** Fourteenth-century Gothic palace built by the popes who made Avignon their home. **Hours:** Daily mid-March–Oct 9:00–19:00, until 20:00 July and Sept, until 21:00 in Aug, Nov–mid-March 9:30–17:45. See page 110.

▲**Tower of Philip the Fair** Massive tower across St. Bénezet Bridge, featuring the best view over Avignon and the Rhône basin. **Hours:** April–Sept daily 10:00–12:30 & 14:00–18:30; Oct–Nov Tue–Sat 10:00–12:30 & 14:00–17:00, closed Sun–Mon; closed Dec–March. See page 114.

Petit Palace Museum "Little palace" displaying the Church's collection of medieval Italian painting and sculpture. **Hours:** June–Sept Wed–Mon 10:00–13:00 & 14:00–18:00, Oct–May Wed–Mon 9:30–13:00 & 14:00–17:30, closed Tue year-round. See page 108.

Synagogue Thirteenth-century synagogue rebuilt in a Neoclassical Greek-temple style. **Hours:** Mon–Fri 10:00–12:00 & 15:00–17:00, closed Sat–Sun. See page 112.

Fondation Angladon-Dubrujeaud Museum with a small but enjoyable Postimpressionist collection, including art by Cézanne, Van Gogh, Daumier, Degas, and Picasso. **Hours:** Wed–Sun 13:00–18:00, closed Mon–Tue. See page 114.

Calvet Museum Fine-arts museum with a good collection and English audioguide. **Hours:** Wed–Mon 10:00–12:00 & 13:00–18:00, closed Tue. See page 114.

AVIGNON

Commanding City Views: Walk or drive across Daladier Bridge for a great view of Avignon and the Rhône River (there's a good walking path across the bridge, along the river). You can enjoy other impressive vistas from the top of parc des Rochers des Doms, from the tower in the Palace of the Popes, and from the end of the famous, broken St. Bénezet Bridge.

Tours in Avignon

Walking Tours—The TI offers informative two-hour English walking tours of Avignon (€11, discounted with Avignon Passion Pass, €17 includes a tour of the Popes' Palace; April–Oct daily at 10:00, Nov–March on Sat only; depart from main TI, Sun departures from ticket room at Palace of the Popes; themes vary daily).

Tourist Trains—Two little trains, designed for tired tourists, leave regularly from the Palace of the Popes (mid-March–mid-Oct daily 10:00–19:00). One does a town tour (€7, 3/hr, 45 min, English commentary), and the other choo-choos you sweat-free to the top of the park, high above the river (€1 one-way, schedule depends on demand, no commentary).

Guided Excursions—Several minivan tour companies based in Avignon offer tours to destinations described in this book, including Pont du Gard, the Luberon, and the Camargue (about €60–75/ person for all-day tours). See "Tours of Provence" on page 40 (note that guides Madeleine Vedel and François Marcou both live in Avignon), or ask the TI to book you a tour.

Self-Guided Walks

Combine these two walks—one ("Welcome to Avignon") covering the major sights, and the other ("Discovering Avignon's Back Streets") along the lanes less taken—to get below the surface of this historic city.

▲▲Welcome to Avignon

Before starting this walk—which connects the city's top sights—be sure to pick up the Avignon Passion Pass at the TI, then show it when entering each attraction to receive discounted admission (explained earlier, under "Tourist Information").

• *Start your tour where the Romans did, on place de l'Horloge, in front of City Hall (Hôtel de Ville).*

Place de l'Horloge

This café square was the town forum during Roman times and the market square through the Middle Ages. (Restaurants here

Avignon

200 YARDS
200 METERS

ILE DE LA BARTHELASSE

RIVER

TO P & LYON VIA D-225 & A-7

ST. BENEZET BRIDGE

Petit Palais Museum

BLVD. ST-LAZARE

RHONE

PARK (ROCHERS DES DOMS)

POND

PALACE OF THE POPES

TERRACE

BLVD. DU RHONE

DALADIER BRIDGE

TO VILLENEUVE & P

PLACE CRILLON

ST. ETIENNE

R. GROTTES

R. BALANCE

PLACE SQUARE

PLACE DE L'HORLOGE

TO 7

PEYRO

V. LEGAT

CROIX

ST. PIERRE

RUE CARNOT

ALLE DE L'OUILLE

BLVD DE L'OUILLE

REMPART L'OUILLE

RUE JOSEPH

PASSAGE L'ORAT.

ST. AGRICOL

MARCHANDS

ROUG.

R. CARR.

P. CAR

VIEUX PIE

PL. PIE

SYNAGOGUE

PL. PIG.

R. THIERS

MARKET

R. BONNETERIE

RUE V. HUGO

CALVET MUSEUM

RUE VERNET

R. DE LA REPUBLIQUE

R. ROI RENE

PLACE ST. DIDIER

Fondation ANGLADON

RUE DES LICES

PEINT

WATERWHEEL

BLVD. RASPAIL

R. ST. CHARLES

JAURES

FABRE

RUE

PERD.

PLACE DES CORPS-SAINTS

OLD CITY WALLS

TO NIMES VIA A-9

POST B

COURS JFK

COURS

ST. MICHEL

DCH

BLVD.

ST. ROCH

BUS STN.

TRAIN STN. "CENTRE-VILLE"

TO ARLES & TGV TRAIN STN.

View

--- **Ped. Path**

P **Parking**

B **Main Bus Stop**

← **Self-Guided Walk**

1 Start of Welcome to Avignon Walk
2 Views & Orientation Table
3 Best View of Bridge & Stairs to Ramparts
4 Hôtel la Mirande (Start of Discovering Back Streets Walk)
5 TGV Shuttle & Bus #11 Stop

6 Launderette
7 To Shakespeare Bookshop
8 Carrefour City Grocery
9 City Hall
10 Tourist Train Stop
11 Shuttle Boat Stops (2)

AVIGNON

offer good people-watching, but they also have less ambience and low-quality meals—you'll find better squares elsewhere to hang your beret in.) Named for a medieval clock tower that the City Hall now hides (find plaque in English), this square's present popularity arrived with the trains in 1854. Walk a few steps to the center of the square, and look down the main drag, rue de la République. When the trains came to Avignon, proud city fathers wanted a direct, impressive way to link the new station to the heart of the city (just like in Paris)—so they plowed over homes to create rue de la République and widened place de l'Horloge. This main drag's Parisian feel is intentional—it was built not in the Provençal manner, but in the Haussmann style that is so dominant in Paris. For example, notice that buildings have slate roofs rather than tile.

• *Walk uphill past the carousel (public WCs behind). You'll see a golden statue of Mary, floating high above the buildings. Veer right at the street's end, and continue into...*

Palace Square (Place du Palais)

This grand square is lined with the Palace of the Popes, the Petit Palais, and the cathedral. In the 1300s, the Vatican moved the entire headquarters of the Catholic Church to Avignon. The Church bought Avignon and gave it a complete makeover. Along with clearing out vast spaces like this square and building this three-acre palace, the Church erected more than three miles of protective wall, with 39 towers, "appropriate" housing for cardinals (read: mansions), and residences for the entire Vatican bureaucracy. The city was Europe's largest construction zone. Avignon's population grew from 6,000 to 25,000 in short order. (Today, 13,000 people live within the walls.) The limits of pre-papal Avignon are outlined on city maps: Rues Joseph Vernet, Henri Fabre, des Lices, and Philonarde all follow the route of the city's earlier defensive wall.

The Petit Palais (Little Palace) seals the uphill end of the square and was built for a cardinal; today, it houses medieval paintings (museum described later). The church just to the left of the Palace of the Popes is Avignon's cathedral. It predates the Church's purchase of Avignon by 200 years. Its small size reflects Avignon's modest, pre-papal population. The gilded Mary was added in 1854, when the Vatican established the doctrine of her Immaculate Conception. Mary is purposefully taller than the Palace of the Popes. The Vatican never accepted what it called the "Babylonian Captivity" and had a bad attitude about Avignon long after the pope was definitively back in Rome. There hasn't been a French pope since the Vatican returned to Rome—over 600 years. That's what I call a grudge.

Directly across the square from the palace's main entry stands a cardinal's residence built in 1619 (now the Conservatoire National de Musique). Its fancy Baroque facade was a visual counterpoint to the stripped-down Huguenot aesthetic of the age. During this time, Provence was a hotbed of Protestantism—but, buried within this region, Avignon was a Catholic stronghold. Notice the stumps in front and nearby. Nicknamed *bites*, slang for the male anatomy, they effectively keep cars from double-parking in areas designed for people. Many of the metal ones slide up and down by remote control to let privileged cars come and go.

• *You can visit the massive Palace of the Popes (described on page 110) now, but it works better to visit that palace at the end of this walk, then continue directly to the "Back Streets" walk, described later.*

Now is a good time to take in the...

Petit Palace Museum (Musée du Petit Palais)

This former cardinal's palace now displays the Church's collection of mostly medieval Italian painting (including one delightful Botticelli) and sculpture. All 350 paintings deal with Christian themes. A visit here before going to the Palace of the Popes helps furnish and populate that otherwise barren building, and a quick peek into its courtyard shows the importance of cardinal housing (€6, €2 English brochure, June–Sept Wed–Mon 10:00–13:00 & 14:00–18:00, Oct–May Wed–Mon 9:30–13:00 & 14:00–17:30, closed Tue year-round, at north end of Palace Square, tel. 04 90 86 44 58).

• *From Palace Square, we'll head up to the rocky hilltop where Avignon was first settled, then drop down to the river. With this short loop, you can enjoy a park, hike to a grand river view, walk a bit of the wall, and visit Avignon's beloved broken bridge—an experience worth ▲▲. Begin by walking up to the...*

▲▲Parc des Rochers des Doms

While the park itself is a delight—with a sweet little café and public WCs—don't miss the climax: a panoramic view of the Rhône River Valley and the broken bridge. You'll pass fresh water as you climb (fill your bottle). There's a huge terrace in the north side of the park, with an orientation table and information plaques, but its views are inferior to the smaller viewpoint described below (park gates open daily April–Sept 7:30–20:00, Oct–March 7:30–18:00).

For the best views (and the favorite make-out spot for local teenagers later in the evening), find the small terrace behind the odd zodiac display (across the grass from the pond-side park café—good prices for food and drinks). On a clear day, the tallest peak you see, with its white limestone cap, is Mont Ventoux ("Windy Mountain"). Below and to the right, you'll spot free passenger ferries shuttling across the river (great views from path on other side of the river), and tucked amidst the trees on the far side of the river, a highly recommended restaurant, Le Bercail. The island in the river is the Ile de la Barthélasse, a nature preserve where Avignon can breathe.

St. André Fortress (across the river on the hill; see info plaque) was built by the French in 1360, shortly after the pope moved to Avignon, to counter the papal incursion into this part of Europe. The castle was barely across the border in the kingdom of France. Avignon's famous bridge was a key border crossing, with towers on either end—one French and one Vatican. The one across the river is the Tower of Phillip the Fair (described below).

• *From this viewpoint, take the stairs to the left (closed at night) down to the tower. As the stairs spiral down, just before St. Bénezet Bridge, catch a glimpse of the...*

Ramparts

The only bit of the rampart you can walk on is accessed from St. Bénezet Bridge (fee to enter). When the pope came in the 1360s, small Avignon had no town wall...so he built one. What you see today was restored in the 19th century.

• *When you come out of the tower on street level, exit outside the walls and walk left, going under the new bridge to find the old bridge's entrance.*

▲▲St. Bénezet Bridge (Pont St. Bénezet)

This bridge, whose construction and location were inspired by a shepherd's religious vision, is the "pont d'Avignon" of nursery-rhyme fame. The ditty (which you've probably been humming all day) dates back to the 15th century: *Sur le pont d'Avignon, on y danse, on y danse, sur le pont d'Avignon, on y danse tous en rond* ("On the bridge of Avignon, we will dance, we will dance, on the bridge of Avignon, we will dance all in a circle").

But the bridge was a big deal even outside of its kiddie-tune fame. Built between 1171 and 1185, it was the only bridge crossing the mighty Rhône in the Middle Ages. It was damaged several times by floods and subsequently rebuilt, until 1668, when most of it was knocked down by a disastrous icy flood. Lacking a government stimulus package, the townsfolk decided not to rebuild this time, and for more than a century, Avignon had no bridge across the Rhône. While only four arches survive today, the original bridge was huge: Imagine a 22-arch, 3,000-foot-long bridge extending from Vatican territory to the lonely Tower of Philip the Fair, which marked the beginning of France (see displays of the bridge's original length). A Romanesque chapel on the bridge is dedicated to St. Bénezet. While there's not much to see on the bridge, the audioguide included with your ticket tells a good enough story. It's also fun to be in the breezy middle of the river with a fine city view.

Cost and Hours: €4.50, €13 combo-ticket includes Palace of the Popes, same hours as the Palace of the Popes (see below), last entry one hour before closing, tel. 04 90 27 51 16. The ticket booth is housed in what was a medieval hospital for the poor (funded by bridge tolls). Admission includes a small room dedicated to the song of Avignon's bridge and your only chance to walk a bit of the ramparts (enter both from the tower).

• *To get to the Palace of the Popes from here, exit left, then turn left again back into the walls. Walk to the end of the short street, then turn right following signs to Palais des Papes. After a block, look for the brown signs leading you left under the passageway, and up the stairs to Palace Square and the...*

▲Palace of the Popes (Palais des Papes)

In 1309, a French pope was elected (Pope Clément V). At the urging of the French king, His Holiness decided he'd had enough of unholy (and dangerous) Italy. So he loaded up his carts and moved to Avignon for a secure rule under a supportive king. The Catholic Church literally bought Avignon (then a two-bit town), and popes resided here until 1403. Meanwhile, Italians demanded a Roman pope, so from 1378 on, there were twin popes—one in Rome and one in Avignon—causing a schism in the Catholic Church that wasn't fully resolved until 1417.

A visit to the mighty yet barren papal palace comes with an audioguide that leads you along a one-way route and does a credible job of overcoming the complete lack of furnishings. It teaches the basic history while allowing you to tour at your own pace.

As you wander, ponder that this palace—the largest surviving Gothic palace in Europe—was built to accommodate 500 people as the administrative center of the Vatican and home of the pope. This was the most fortified palace of the age (remember, the pope left

Rome to be more secure). Nine popes ruled from here, making this the center of Christianity for 100 years. You'll walk through the pope's personal quarters (frescoed with happy hunting scenes), see many models of how the various popes added to the building, and learn about its state-of-the-art plumbing. The rooms are huge. The "pope's chapel" is twice the size of the adjacent Avignon cathedral.

While the last pope checked out in 1417, the Vatican owned Avignon until the French Revolution in 1789. During this interim period, the pope's "legate" (official representative...normally a nephew) ruled Avignon from this palace. Avignon residents, many of whom had come from Rome, spoke Italian for a century after the pope left, making it a linguistic ghetto within France. In the Napoleonic age, the palace was a barracks, housing 1,800 soldiers. You can see cuts in the wall where high ceilings gave way to floor beams. Climb the tower (Tour de la Gâche) for grand views and a rooftop café with surprisingly good food at very fair prices.

A room at the end of the tour (called *la boutellerie*) is dedicated to the region's wines, of which they claim the pope was a fan. Sniff "Le Nez du Vin"—a black box with 54 tiny bottles designed to develop your "nose." (Blind-test your travel partner.) The nearby village of Châteauneuf-du-Pape is where the pope summered in the 1320s. Its famous wine is a direct descendant of his wine. You're welcome to taste here (€6 for three to five fine wines and souvenir tasting cup).

Cost and Hours: €10.50, €13 combo-ticket includes St. Bénezet Bridge, daily mid-March–Oct 9:00–19:00, until 20:00 July and Sept, until 21:00 in Aug, Nov–mid-March 9:30–17:45, last entry one hour before closing, tel. 04 90 27 50 74, www.palais-des -papes.com.

• *You'll exit at the rear of the palace, where my "Back Streets" walking tour begins (see below). Or, to return to Palace Square, make two rights after exiting the palace.*

▲▲Discovering Avignon's Back Streets

Use the map in this chapter or the TI map to navigate this easy, level 30-minute walk. This self-guided tour begins in the small square (place de la Mirande) behind the Palace of the Popes. If you've toured the palace, this is where you exit. Otherwise, from the front of the palace, follow the narrow, cobbled rue Peyrollerie, carved out of the rock, around the palace on the right side as you face it.

• *Our walk begins at the...*

Hôtel la Mirande: Located on the square, Avignon's finest hotel welcomes visitors. Find the atrium lounge and consider a coffee break amid the understated luxury (€12 afternoon tea served daily 15:00–18:00, includes a generous selection of pastries). Inspect the royal lounge and dining room (recommended on page

122); cooking demos are offered in the basement below. Rooms start at €450 in high season.

• *Turn left out of the hotel and left again on rue Peyrollerie ("Coppersmiths Street"), then take your first right on rue des Ciseaux d'Or. On the small square ahead you'll find the...*

Church of St. Pierre: The original chestnut doors were carved in 1551, when tales of New World discoveries raced across Europe. (Notice the Indian headdress, top center.) The fine Annunciation (lower right) shows Gabriel giving Mary the exciting news in impressive Renaissance 3-D. Now take 10 steps back from the door and look way up. The tiny statue breaking the skyline of the church is the pagan god Bacchus, with oodles of grapes. What's he doing sitting atop a Christian church? No one knows.

• *Follow the alley to the left, which was covered and turned into a tunnel during the town's population boom. It leads into what was the cloister of St. Pierre—named for chestnut trees (place des Châtaignes), but now replaced by plane trees. The practical atheists of the French Revolution destroyed the cloister, leaving only faint traces of the arches along the church side of the square. For recommended restaurants near the Church of St. Pierre, see "Eating in Avignon," later in this chapter. Continue around the church and cross busy place Carnot to the Banque Chaix. Find the classy...*

15th-Century Building: Across the lane to the right, with its beams showing, is a rare vestige from the Middle Ages. Notice how this building widens the higher it gets. A medieval loophole based taxes on ground-floor square footage—everything above was tax-free. Walking down the pedestrian street, rue des Fourbisseurs ("Street of the Animal Furriers"), notice how the top floors almost meet. Fire was a constant danger in the Middle Ages, as flames leapt easily from one home to the next. In fact, the lookout guard's primary responsibility was watching for fires, not the enemy. Virtually all of Avignon's medieval homes have been replaced by safer structures.

• *Turn left from rue des Fourbisseurs onto the traffic-free rue du Vieux Sextier ("Street of the Balance," for weighing items); another left under the first arch leads 10 yards along rue B. Lyon to Avignon's...*

Synagogue: Jews first arrived in Avignon with the Diaspora (exile) of the first century. Avignon's Jews were nicknamed "the Pope's Jews" because of the protection that the Vatican offered to Jews expelled from France. While this synagogue dates from the 1220s, in the mid-19th century it was completely rebuilt in a Neoclassical Greek-temple style by a non-Jewish architect. This is the only synagogue under a rotunda that you'll see anywhere. It's an intimate, classy place dressed with white colonnades and walnut furnishings. To visit the synagogue, press the buzzer and friendly Rabbi Moshe Amar will be your guide (free, Mon–Fri

10:00–12:00 & 15:00–17:00, closed Sat–Sun, 2 place Jerusalem, tel. 04 90 55 21 24).

• *Retrace your steps to rue du Vieux Sextier and turn left, then continue to the big square and find the big, boxy...*

Market (Les Halles): In 1970, the town's open-air market was replaced by this modern one. The market's jungle-like green wall reflects the changes of seasons and helps mitigate its otherwise stark exterior (open Tue–Sun until 13:00, closed Mon). Step inside for a sensual experience of organic breads, olives, and festival-of-mold cheeses. The rue des Temptations cuts down the center. Cafés and cheese shops are on the right—as far as possible from the stinky fish stalls on the left. Follow your nose away from the fish and have a coffee with the locals.

• *Exit out the back door of Les Halles, turn left on rue de la Bonneterie ("Street of Hosiery"), and track the street for five minutes to the plane trees, where it becomes...*

Rue des Teinturiers: This "Street of the Dyers" is a tie-dyed, tree- and stream-lined lane, home to earthy cafés and galleries. This was the cloth industry's dyeing and textile center in the 1800s (a *teinturier* is a dyer). The stream is a branch of the Sorgue River. Those stylish Provençal fabrics and patterns you see for sale everywhere were first made here, after a pattern imported from India.

About three small bridges down, you'll pass the Grey Penitents chapel. The upper facade shows the GPs, who dressed up in robes and pointy hoods to do their anonymous good deeds back in the 13th century (long before the KKK dressed this way). As you stroll on, you'll see the work of amateur sculptors, who have carved whimsical car barriers out of limestone.

Trendy restaurants on this atmospheric street are recommended under "Eating in Avignon."

• *Farther down rue des Teinturiers, you'll come to the...*

Waterwheel: Standing here, imagine the Sorgue River—which hits the mighty Rhône in Avignon—being broken into several canals in order to turn 23 such wheels. In about 1800, waterwheels powered the town's industries. The little cogwheel above the big one could be shoved into place, kicking another machine into gear behind the wall. (For more on the Sorgue River and its waterwheels, see my self-guided walk of Isle-sur-la-Sorgue, page 185.) Across from the wheel at #41 is **La Cave Breysse**, offering regional wines by the glass and good lunch fare (described under "Eating in Avignon").

• *To return to the real world, double back on rue des Teinturiers and turn left on rue des Lices, which traces the first medieval wall. (Lice is the no-man's-land along a wall.) You'll pass a four-story arcaded building that was a home for the poor in the 1600s, an army barracks in the 1800s, a fine-arts school in the 1900s, and a deluxe condominium today (much of this neighborhood is going high-class residential). Eventually you'll return to rue de la République, Avignon's main drag.*

More Sights in Avignon

Most of Avignon's top sights are covered by the walking tours, described earlier. With more time, consider these options.

Fondation Angladon-Dubrujeaud—Visiting this museum is like being invited into the elegant home of a rich and passionate art collector. It mixes a small but enjoyable collection of art from Postimpressionists (including Paul Cézanne, Vincent van Gogh, Honoré Daumier, Edgar Degas, and Pablo Picasso) with re-created art studios and furnishings from many periods. It's a quiet place with a few superb paintings (€6, Wed–Sun 13:00–18:00, closed Mon–Tue, 5 rue Laboureur, tel. 04 90 82 29 03, www.angladon .com).

Calvet Museum (Musée Calvet)—This fine-arts museum impressively displays its collection, highlighting French Baroque works. While the museum goes ignored by most, you'll find a few diamonds in the rough upstairs: Géricault, Soutine, and one painting each from Manet, Sisley, Bonnard, Dufy, and Vlamnick (€6, includes audioguide, Wed–Mon 10:00–12:00 & 13:00–18:00, closed Tue, in the quieter western half of town at 65 rue Joseph Vernet, antiquities collection a few blocks away at 27 rue de la République—same hours and ticket, tel. 04 90 86 33 84, www .musee-calvet.org).

Near Avignon, in Villeneuve-lès-Avignon
▲Tower of Philip the Fair (Tour Philippe-le-Bel)—Built to protect access to St. Bénezet Bridge in 1307, this massive tower offers a terrific view over Avignon and the Rhône basin. It's best late in the day (€2.20; April–Sept daily 10:00–12:30 & 14:00–18:30; Oct–Nov Tue–Sat until 17:00, closed Sun–Mon; closed Dec–March; tel. 04 32 70 08 57). To reach the tower from Avignon, drive (5 min, cross Daladier Bridge, follow signs to *Villeneuve-lès-Avignon*), or take bus #11 (2/hr, catch bus in front of post office on cours Président Kennedy, second shelter down—see map on page 106).

Sleeping in Avignon

Hotel values are better in Arles. Avignon is particularly popular during its July festival (see sidebar on page 103), when you must book ahead (expect inflated prices). Drivers should ask about parking deals.

Near Avignon's Centre-Ville Station

The first five listings are a five- to ten-minute walk from the Centre-Ville train station. (For hotels Colbert, Parc, and Splendid, turn right off cours Jean Jaurès on rue Agricol Perdiguier.)

$$$ Hôtel Bristol*** is a big, professionally run place on the main drag, offering predictable "American" comfort including spacious public spaces, large rooms, a big elevator, air-conditioning, and a generous buffet breakfast (Db–€84–98, bigger Db-€120, Tb-€142, Qb-€145–180, 44 cours Jean Jaurès, tel. 04 90 16 48 48, fax 04 90 66 22 72, www.bristol-hotel-avignon.com, contact @bristol-avignon.com).

$$ Hôtel Colbert** is a solid two-star hotel and a good midrange bet, with well-maintained and nicely decorated rooms in many sizes. Your efficient hosts—Patrice, Annie, and *le chien* Brittany—care for this restored manor house, with its warm public spaces and sweet little patio (Sb-€45–65, small Db-€78, bigger Db-€80–90, no triples available, air-con, Wi-Fi, 7 rue Agricol Perdiguier, tel. 04 90 86 20 20, fax 04 90 85 97 00, www.lecolbert -hotel.com, contact@avignon-hotel-colbert.com).

$ Hôtel du Parc* is a spotless value with white walls, tiny bathrooms, and stone accents. It's scrupulously managed by entertaining Avignon native Madame Rous, who bakes her own bread and pastries for breakfast—and even made the bedspreads by hand (S-€30, Ss-€40, Ds-€50–62, Ts-€72, no TVs or phones, tel. 04 90 82 71 55, fax 04 90 85 64 86, http://perso.modulonet.fr/hoduparc, hotel.parc@modulonet.fr). This place is cheaper and homier than Hôtel le Splendid, across the street.

$ Hôtel le Splendid* rents 17 simple but cheery rooms with wood floors and small but sharp bathrooms (Sb-€48, Db-€60, bigger Db with air-con-€70, Tb with air-con-€80, three Db apartments-€90, extra person-€10, discounts for stays longer than one week, 17 rue Agricol Perdiguier, tel. 04 90 86 14 46, fax 04 90 85 38 55, www.avignon-splendid-hotel.com, contacthotel@infonie.fr).

$ At Hôtel Boquier**, engaging Madame Sendra offers 12 quiet, good-value, and well-maintained rooms under wood beams in a central location (small Db-€55, bigger Db-€68, Tb-€78, Qb-€90, extra bed-€10, air-con, no elevator, Internet access and Wi-Fi, parking-€7, near the TI at 6 rue du portail Boquier, tel. 04 90 82 34 43, fax 04 90 86 14 07, www.hotel-boquier.com, contact@hotel-boquier.com).

AVIGNON

Sleep Code

(€1 = about $1.40, country code: 33)
S = Single, **D** = Double/Twin, **T** = Triple, **Q** = Quad, **b** = bathroom, **s** = shower only, * = French hotel rating system (0-4 stars). Unless otherwise noted, credit cards are accepted and English is spoken.

To help you easily sort through these listings, I've divided the rooms into three categories, based on the price for a standard double room with bath:

$$$ Higher Priced—Most rooms €85 or more.
$$ Moderately Priced—Most rooms between €65-85.
$ Lower Priced—Most rooms €65 or less.

In the Center, near Place de l'Horloge

$$$ Hôtel d'Europe****, with Avignon's most prestigious address, lets peasants sleep royally without losing their shirts—but only if you land one of the 10 surprisingly reasonable "standard" rooms. Enter a fountain-filled courtyard, linger in the lounges, and savor every comfort. The hotel is located on the handsome place Crillon, near the river (standard Db-€180, superior Db-€350, prestige Db-€495, breakfast-€17, elevator, Internet access, garage-€17, near Daladier Bridge at 12 place Crillon, tel. 04 90 14 76 76, fax 04 90 14 76 71, www.heurope.com, reservations@heurope.com). The hotel's restaurant is Michelin-rated (one star) and serves an upscale €55 *menu* in its formal dining room or front courtyard.

$$$ Hôtel Mercure Cité des Papes*** is a modern chain hotel within spitting distance of the Palace of the Popes. It has 89 smartly designed small rooms (Sb-€115, Db-€130–170, many rooms have views over place de l'Horloge, air-con, elevator, 1 rue Jean Vilar, tel. 04 90 80 93 00, fax 04 90 80 93 01, www.mercure.com, h1952@accor.com).

$$$ Hôtel Pont d'Avignon***, just inside the walls near St. Bénezet Bridge, is part of the same chain as the Hôtel Mercure Cité des Papes, with the same prices for its 87 rooms (direct access to a garage makes parking easier than at the other Mercure hotel, elevator, on rue Ferruce, tel. 04 90 80 93 93, fax 04 90 80 93 94, www.mercure.com, h0549@accor.com).

$$ At Hôtel de Blauvac**, friendly owner Veronica manages 16 mostly spacious, plush-carpeted, high-ceilinged rooms (many with an additional upstairs loft). It's a faded old manor home with a sky-high atrium and elevated rates. Its location near the pedestrian zone means reliable noise at night, and the lack of air-conditioning means you'll want the windows open (Sb-€72–82, Db-€77–87,

AVIGNON

Avignon Hotels

1. Hôtel Bristol
2. Hôtel Colbert
3. Hôtel du Parc
4. Hôtel le Splendid
5. Hôtel Boquier
6. Hôtel d'Europe
7. Hôtel Mercure Cité des Papes
8. Hôtel Pont d'Avignon
9. Hôtel de Blauvac
10. Hôtel Médiéval
11. Villa Agapè B&B
12. To Le Clos du Rempart Rooms & Lumani B&B
13. To Auberge Bagatelle Hostel & Jardin de Bacchus Rooms

Tb-€92–102, Qb-€107, €10 less off-season, Internet access and Wi-Fi, 1 block off rue de la République at 11 rue de la Bancasse, tel. 04 90 86 34 11, fax 04 90 86 27 41, www.hotel-blauvac.com, blauvac@aol.com).

$$ Hôtel Médiéval** is burrowed deep a few blocks from the Church of St. Pierre. Built as a cardinal's home, this massive stone mansion has a small garden and friendly-as-they-get Mike at the helm. It has 35 wood-paneled, air-conditioned, unimaginative rooms (Sb-€49, Db-€59–74, bigger Db or Tb-€83–90, kitchenettes available but require 3-night minimum stay, Wi-Fi, 5 blocks east of place de l'Horloge, behind Church of St. Pierre at 15 rue Petite Saunerie, tel. 04 90 86 11 06, fax 04 90 82 08 64, www .hotelmedieval.com, hotel.medieval@wanadoo.fr).

Chambres d'Hôte

$$$ Villa Agapè, just off busy place de l'Horloge (right in the center of town), is an oasis of calm and good taste. Run by friendly Madame de La Pommeraye, the villa has three handsomely decorated rooms, a quiet courtyard, lots of stairs, lovely public spaces, and a soaking pool to boot (Db-€100–160, extra person-€30, includes breakfast, 2-night minimum, cash only, closed in July, Internet access and Wi-Fi, from place de l'Horloge it's one block down on left above the pharmacy at 13 rue St. Agricol—ring buzzer, tel. & fax 04 90 85 21 92, mobile 06 07 98 71 30, www .villa-agape.com, michele@villa-agape.com). For a weeklong stay, ask about renting her entire house, where you get Madame's room, study, and kitchen (€2,500–3,300).

$$$ At **Le Clos du Rempart,** a 10-minute walk from the center, Madame Assad rents two comfortable rooms and one apartment on a peaceful courtyard with Middle Eastern decor (Db-€120–150 depending on season and room size, 2-bedroom apartment for 4 with kitchen-€800–1,100/week, includes breakfast, cash only, air-con, Wi-Fi, 1 parking spot in garage, inside the walls east of the Popes' Palace at 35–37 rue Crémade—call or check website for directions, tel. & fax 04 90 86 39 14, www .closdurempart.com, aida@closdurempart.com).

$$$ Lumani provides the ultimate urban refuge just inside the city walls, a 15-minute walk from the Popes' Palace. In this graceful old manor house, gentle Elisabeth and Jean welcome guests to their art-gallery-cum-bed-and-breakfast that surrounds a fountain-filled courtyard with elbow room. She paints, he designs buildings, and both care about your experience in Avignon. The five rooms are decorated with flair; no two are alike and all overlook the shady garden (small Db-€100, big Db-€140, Db suites-€170, extra person-€30, includes breakfast, credit cards OK except American

AVIGNON

Express, Internet access and Wi-Fi, music studio, parking-€10 or easy on street, 37 rue de Rempart St Lazare, tel. 04 90 82 94 11, www.avignon-lumani.com, lux@avignon-lumani.com).

On the Outskirts of Town

$ Auberge Bagatelle's hostel offers dirt-cheap beds, a lively atmosphere, café, grocery store, launderette, great views of Avignon, and campers for neighbors (D-€42, Ds-€45, T-€62, Ts-€64, Tb-€72, Q-€76, Qb-€97, dorm bed-€18, across Daladier Bridge on Ile de la Barthélasse, bus #10 from main post office, tel. 04 90 86 71 31, fax 04 90 27 16 23, www.aubergebagatelle.fr, auberge .bagatelle@wanadoo.fr).

Near Avignon

$$ At Jardin de Bacchus, just 15 minutes northwest of Avignon and convenient to Pont du Gard, enthusiastic and English-speaking Christine and Erik offer three rooms in their rural farmhouse overlooking little Tavel's famous vineyards (Db-€80–90, 2-night minimum or add €30, fine dinner possible, Wi-Fi, tel. 04 66 90 28 62, www.jardindebacchus.fr, jardindebacchus@free.fr). For details on their cooking classes, see page 443 in the appendix.

Eating in Avignon

Skip the overpriced places on place de l'Horloge and find a more intimate location for your dinner. Avignon has many delightful squares filled with tables ready to seat you.

Near the Church of St. Pierre

The church divides two enchanting squares. One is quiet and intimate, the other is lively.

L'Epicerie, sitting alone on an intimate square, serves the highest-quality and highest-priced cuisine around the Church of St. Pierre, with a focus on products from the south of France. Expect lots of color and a dash of spice (€18–24 *plats*, closed Sun off-season, cozy interior good in bad weather, 10 place St. Pierre, tel. 04 90 82 74 22).

On Place des Châtaignes: Pass under the arch by L'Epicerie restaurant and enter enchanting place des Châtaignes, with a tasty commotion of tables. Peruse your options. The **Crêperie du Cloître** makes acceptable €6 salads and €6 dinner crêpes (daily, cash only). **Restaurant Nem,** tucked in the corner, is Vietnamese and family-run (*menus* from €12, cash only). **Pause Gourmande** is a small lunch-only eatery with €9 *plats du jour* and always a veggie option (closed Sun).

Place Crillon

This large and trendy square just off the river attracts a stylish crowd and houses a variety of dining choices. **Restaurant les Artistes** is popular (€16 three-course *menu*, daily, tel. 04 90 82 23 54); **La Comédie** serves €9 crêpes and salads with mod seating (daily); **La Piazza** is *solo Italiano* (€16 three-course *menu*, daily); and **Café Le Crillon** is most refined and more pricey (closed Sun).

Place des Corps-Saints

You'll find several youthful and reasonable eateries with tables sprawling under big plane trees on this locally popular square. **Cuisine et Comptoire** attracts the café crowd (closed Sun), though I enjoy the €10 pizzas and friendly service at **Le Pili** (daily, tel. 04 90 27 39 53). **Zeste** is a friendly deli offering fresh soups, pasta salads, wraps, smoothies, and more. Get it to go, or eat inside or on the scenic square—all at unbeatable prices (€10 three-course *menu*, daily, tel. 09 51 49 05 62).

By the Market (Les Halles)

Here you'll find a good selection of eateries with good prices. **Restaurant Françoise** is a pleasant café and tea salon, where fresh-baked tarts—savory and sweet—and a variety of salads and soups make a healthful meal, and vegetarian options are plentiful (€6–12 dishes, Mon–Sat 8:00–19:00, closed Sun, free Wi-Fi, 6 rue Général Leclerc, tel. 04 32 76 24 77).

Rue des Teinturiers

This "tie-dye" street has a wonderful concentration of eateries popular with the natives, and justifies the long walk. It's a youthful and trendy area, recently spiffed up with a canalside ambience and little hint of tourism. Survey the eateries listed here before choosing (all line up near the waterwheel).

La Cave Breysse is a fun and colorful pause before dinner. Midday or evening, the owners would love to serve you a fragrant €2.50 glass of regional wine. Choose from the blackboard by the bar that lists all the bottles open today, then join the gang outside by the canal. In the evening, this place is a hit with the young local crowd for its wine (flexible hours, usually Tue–Sat 12:00–14:30 & 18:00–22:30, closed Sun–Mon, no food in evening; across from waterwheel at 41 rue des Teinturiers).

L'Empreinte is good for North African cuisine. Choose a table in its tent-like interior, or sit canalside on the cobbles (copious

Avignon Restaurants

1. Church of St. Pierre Eateries
2. Place Crillon Eateries
3. Place des Corps-Saints Eateries
4. Restaurant Françoise
5. La Cave Breysse Wine Bar & L'Empreinte Restaurant
6. To Restaurant Numéro 75
7. L'Isle Sonnante
8. La Compagnie des Comptoirs
9. Le Caveau du Théâtre
10. Hôtel la Mirande Restaurant
11. Le Bercail Rest.

couscous or *tajine* for €13–16, take-out and veggie options available, daily, 33 rue des Teinturiers, tel. 04 32 76 31 84).

Restaurant Numéro 75 is worth the walk (just past where the cobbles end on rue de Teinturiers), filling the Pernod mansion (of *pastis* liquor fame) and a large, romantic courtyard with outdoor tables. The menu is limited to Mediterranean cuisine, but everything's *très* tasty. It's best to go with the options offered by your young black-shirted server (€20 two-course lunch *menu* with wine and coffee, dinner *menus:* €27/appetizer and main course or main course and dessert, €33/3 courses; Mon–Sat 12:00–14:00 & 20:00–22:00, closed Sun, 75 rue Guillaume Puy, tel. 04 90 27 16 00).

Elsewhere in Avignon

At **L'Isle Sonnante,** join chef Boris and his wife Anne to dine intimately in their formal and charming one-room *bistrot*. You'll choose from a small menu offering only fresh products and be served by owners who care (*menus* from €28, closed Sun–Mon, 100 yards from the carousel on place de l'Horloge at 7 rue Racine, tel. 04 90 82 56 01, best to book ahead).

La Compagnie des Comptoirs is the brainchild of famous twin-brother chefs who established a following in southern France with their inventive cuisine. Enter a white world of cool bars, sleek interiors, and a grand courtyard (the restaurant's highlight). This is where young Avignon professionals meet to enjoy foods from the Mediterranean basin. Come for a great-value lunch (€15 two-course *menu*) or splurge for a fine dinner (€45 with wine, closed Sun evening, 83 rue Joseph Vernet, tel. 04 90 85 99 04).

Le Caveau du Théâtre is a welcoming place where Richard invites diners to have a glass of wine or dinner at a sidewalk table, or inside in one of two carefree rooms (€13 *plats*, €18 *menus*, fun ambience for free, closed for lunch Sat and all day Sun, 16 rue des Trois Faucons, tel. 04 90 82 60 91).

Hôtel la Mirande is the ultimate Avignon splurge. Reserve ahead here for understated elegance and Avignon's top cuisine (€35 lunch *menu*, €105 dinner tasting *menu*; closed Tue–Wed—but for a price break, dine in the kitchen with the chef on these "closed" days for €85 including wine; behind Palace of the Popes, 4 place de la Mirande, tel. 04 90 86 93 93, fax 04 90 86 26 85).

Across the River

Le Bercail offers a fun opportunity to get out of town (barely) and take in *le fresh air* with a terrific riverfront view of Avignon, all while enjoying inexpensive Provençal cooking served in big portions. Book ahead, as this restaurant is popular (*menus* from €17, serves late, daily April–Oct, tel. 04 90 82 20 22). To get there, take the free shuttle boat (located near St. Bénezet Bridge) to the Ile de la Barthélasse, turn right, and walk five minutes. As the boat usually stops running at about 18:00 (except in July–Aug, when it runs until 21:00), you can either taxi home or walk 25 minutes along the pleasant riverside path and over Daladier Bridge.

Avignon Connections

Trains

Remember, there are two train stations in Avignon: the suburban TGV Station and the Centre-Ville Station in the city center (€1.20 shuttle buses connect to both stations, buy ticket from driver, 3/hr, 15 min). TGV trains usually serve the TGV train station only, though a few depart from Centre-Ville train station (check your station). Only Centre-Ville Station has baggage storage (see "Arrival in Avignon," page 101). Car rental is available only at the TGV Station. Some cities are served by slower local trains from Centre-Ville Station as well as by faster TGV trains from the TGV Station; I've listed the most convenient stations for each trip.

From Avignon's Centre-Ville Station **by Train to: Arles** (11/day, 20 min, less frequent in the afternoon), **Orange** (10/day, 15 min), **Nîmes** (14/day, 30 min), **Isle-sur-la-Sorgue** (10/day on weekdays, 5/day on weekends, 30 min), **Lyon** (10/day, 2 hrs, also from TGV Station—see below), **Carcassonne** (8/day, 7 with transfer in Narbonne, 3 hrs), **Barcelona** (2/day, 6 hrs, transfer in Montpellier).

From Avignon's TGV Station to: Arles (by SNCF bus, 10/day, 50 min), **Nice** (20/day, most via TGV, 4 hrs, most require transfer in Marseille), **Marseille** (10/day, 1 hr), **Cassis** (7/day, 2 hrs), **Aix-en-Provence TGV** (10/day, 25 min), **Lyon** (12/day, 1.5 hrs, also from Centre-Ville Station—see above), **Paris'** Gare de Lyon (9/day in 2.5 hrs, more connections with change—3–4 hrs), **Paris'** Charles de Gaulle airport (7/day, 3 hrs).

Buses

The bus station *(gare routière)* is just past and below the Ibis Hôtel, to the right as you exit the train station (info desk open Mon–Sat 8:00–19:30, closed Sun, tel. 04 90 82 07 35). Nearly all buses leave from this station (buy tickets on bus, small bills only). The biggest exception is the SNCF bus service from the Avignon TGV train station to Arles (explained on page 78). The Avignon TI has schedules. Service is reduced or nonexistent on Sundays and holidays. Check your departure time beforehand and make sure to verify your destination with the driver.

From Avignon to Pont du Gard: Buses go to this famous old aqueduct (3/day, 50 min, departs from bus station, usually from stall #11), but the schedule doesn't work well for day-trippers from

Avignon; instead, consider a taxi one-way and bus back, or for more worthwhile day trip, see my suggested train/bus excursion that combines Nîmes and Pont du Gard (page 125).

By Bus to Other Regional Destinations: Uzès (3/day Mon–Sat, none Sun, 1 hr, stops at Pont du Gard); **St. Rémy-de-Provence** (6/day Mon–Sat, 3/day Sun, 40 min, handy way to visit its Wed market); **Orange** (3–5/day, 45 min; train is much faster); **Isle-sur-la-Sorgue** (6/day Mon–Sat, 3–4/day Sun, 45 min); **Lourmarin** (3/day, 90 min); **Vaison la Romaine, Nyons, Sablet,** and **Séguret** (5/day during school year, called *période scolaire*, 3/day otherwise and 1/day from TGV station, 75–90 min; faster to change to train at Orange); **Gordes** (via Cavaillon, 1/day, none Wed or Sun, 2 hrs, spend the night or taxi back to Cavaillon).

NEAR AVIGNON

Nîmes, Pont du Gard, and Uzès

While Avignon lacks Roman monuments of its own, some of Europe's greatest Roman sights are an easy, breezy day trip away. (To get the most out of these sights, read the "How About Them Romans?" sidebar on page 42 before you visit.) The Pont du Gard aqueduct is a magnificent structure to experience, as is the city it served 2,000 years ago, Nîmes, which wraps a variety of intriguing Roman monuments together in a bustling, bigger-city package. The pedestrian-friendly town of Uzès, between Nîmes and Pont du Gard, offers a refreshing break from power monuments and busy cities. Combining these three sights makes a memorable day trip into the Languedoc region. Traveling by car, you'll drive scenic roads (particularly D-979 between Uzès and Nîmes) that show off the rugged *garrigue* landscape that this area is famous for.

Planning Your Time

Consider getting away from the tourists and spending a night in classy Nîmes or cozy Uzès. If you're on a tighter schedule, don't worry—this region's sights are easy to cover in a day trip from Avignon, even without a car.

By Taxi, Train, or Bus: With only three buses a day connecting Avignon with Pont du Gard and Uzès, you need to plan carefully. If you only care about Pont du Gard and are pressed for time, consider taking a €42 taxi from Avignon there, then take the early-afternoon bus back. But if you have the time and patience, public transit is a good option. Double-check all schedules at Avignon's TI and at bus stops at least five minutes early, pay the driver (no big bills), and always verify your stop and direction with the bus driver. Here are three plans to consider (unless noted, connections for these trips work every day but Sunday—when buses are too infrequent):

Early Riser: Take the 7:40 bus from Avignon to Pont du Gard (45 min) and be the first at the famous bridge, then continue on to Nîmes (11:25 departure, Mon–Fri only) for some sightseeing before returning from Nîmes to Avignon (trains almost hourly).

Late Riser: Sleep in, and take the 12:05 bus from Avignon, arriving at Pont du Gard at 12:50. Then take the early-afternoon bus (about 14:45) on to Nîmes (40 min). After sightseeing in Nîmes, return by train to Avignon (trains almost hourly).

All-Day Trip: For a rewarding all-day excursion, take a morning train from Avignon's Centre-Ville Station to Nîmes (leaves at about 9:00, 30 min). After sightseeing there, take the 13:00 bus from Nîmes to Pont du Gard (40 min), then catch a 16:00 bus to Uzès (20 min). Wind down with an afternoon stroll through Uzès, and take the last bus from Uzès back to Avignon at 18:30. This lands you back in Avignon at 19:25—just in time for dinner. *Bonne route!*

Nîmes

Most travelers make time in their schedules for Arles and Avignon, but ignore Nîmes. While Arles and Avignon have more touristic appeal, Nîmes—which feels richer and surer of itself—is refreshingly lacking in overnight tourists. This thriving town of classy shops and serious businesses is studded with world-class Roman monuments and laced with traffic-free lanes. (And if you've visited the magnificent Pont du Gard, you gotta be curious where all that water went.)

Since the Middle Ages, Nîmes has exported a famous fabric: The word "denim" actually comes from here (*de Nîmes* = "from Nîmes"). Denim caught on in the United States in the 1800s, when a Bavarian immigrant, Levi Strauss, exploited its use in the American West.

Today, Nîmes is officially in the Languedoc region (for administrative purposes only), yet historically the town has been a key player in the evolution of Provence. Only 30 minutes by train from Arles or Avignon (€8 one-way to either), and three hours from Paris on the TGV, Nîmes is worth a visit if you want a taste of today's urban Provence. The city keeps its clean, peaceful, and pedestrian-polished old center a secret for its well-heeled residents. (Locals admit they don't need the tourist money as much as other Provençal towns.) While most visitors understandably prefer sleeping in Arles or Avignon, a night here provides a good escape from tourist crowds and a truer taste of a Provençal city.

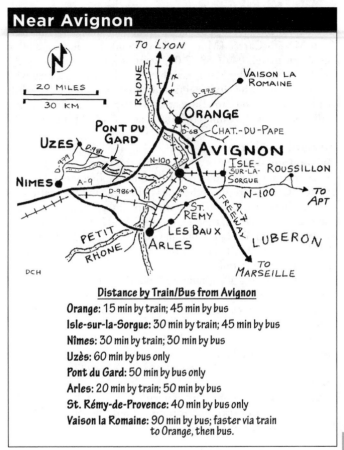

Near Avignon

Distance by Train/Bus from Avignon

Orange: 15 min by train; 45 min by bus
Isle-sur-la-Sorgue: 30 min by train; 45 min by bus
Nîmes: 30 min by train; 30 min by bus
Uzès: 60 min by bus only
Pont du Gard: 50 min by bus only
Arles: 20 min by train; 50 min by bus
St. Rémy-de-Provence: 40 min by bus only
Vaison la Romaine: 90 min by bus; faster via train
to Orange, then bus.

Orientation to Nîmes

Nîmes ("neem") has no river or natural landmark to navigate by, so it's easy to become disoriented. For a quick visit, limit yourself to the manageable triangle within the ring of roads formed by boulevard Victor Hugo, boulevard Amiral Courbet, and boulevard Gambetta.

The town's landmarks are connected by short walks: It's 10 minutes from the train station to the Arena, 10 minutes from the Arena to the Roman temple of Maison Carrée, and 10 minutes from Maison Carrée to either the Castellum or the Fountain Garden. Apart from seeing this handful of ancient monuments, appreciate the city's virtually traffic-free old center—a delight for browsing, strolling, sipping coffee, and people-watching.

Tourist Information

The helpful TI is a few steps out the front door and across the street from Maison Carrée (Mon–Sat 8:30–19:00, Sun 10:00–18:00, 6 rue Auguste, tel. 04 66 58 38 00, www.ot-nimes.fr). Pick up the excellent *Discovering Nîmes* pamphlet, which includes a map with a description of the city's sights and museums, and a worthwhile old-town walk. You can also rent an MP3-player audioguide for a walking tour of Old Nîmes (€8, €10/2 people, leave ID as deposit).

Arrival in Nîmes

By Train and Bus: Trains and buses use the same station (handy if you're combining Pont du Gard with Nîmes). There is no baggage storage. Confirm return schedules before leaving the station, as service can be sparse. The bus station and information office are at the rear of the train station (Mon–Fri 7:30–12:30 & 14:00–18:30, closed Sat–Sun). Buses to Pont du Gard generally leave from stalls 2 or 3 (look for the shelters to the right as you walk out the back door of the train station).

The Arena is a 10-minute walk out the front of the train station. Head up the left side of avenue Feuchères, veer left at the end of the street, then curve right and you'll see the Arena (to find its entrance, walk counterclockwise around the Arena). The Maison Carrée and TI are an enjoyable 10-minute stroll from the Arena through Nîmes' traffic-free old town.

By Car: Follow signs for *Centre-Ville* and *TI,* then *Arènes Parking,* and pay to park underneath the Arena. In this huge garage, make a note of where you parked. If it's full, Parking des Feuchères is nearby (behind the train station), and Parking Maison Carrée is close to the TI.

Helpful Hints

Summer Thursdays: The "Jeudi de Nîmes" (Thursdays of Nîmes) tradition turns the entire old center of town into a festival of shops, street music, and liveliness on Thursday nights in July and August from 18:00 until late.

Internet Access: Netgames is behind Maison Carrée at 25 place du Maison Carrée (daily 9:00–24:00, lots of young gamers).

Laundry: There's a clean launderette near the recommended Hôtel la Baume at 14 rue Nationale (daily 7:00–21:00).

Taxi and Tours: Call 04 66 29 40 11 for a cab. It's €42 to Pont du Gard.

Car Rental: At the station, you'll find **Avis** (tel. 04 66 29 66 36), **Europcar** (tel. 04 66 29 07 94), and **Hertz** (tel. 04 66 76 25 91).

Train Tickets: The small **SNCF Boutique** office, centrally located in the old town, is an easy place to check schedules or buy train tickets without having to go to the station (Tue–Sat 8:30–18:50, closed Sun–Mon, 11 rue de l'Aspic).

Local Guide: Sylvie Pagnard is a delightful guide whose walking tours are top quality and top price. She does regional tours and has a car (€140/3 hrs, €360/8 hrs, tel. 04 66 20 33 14, mobile 06 03 21 37 33, sylviepagnard@aol.com).

Tourist Train: It departs from the esplanade with the fountain, in front of the Arena (€5, daily April–Oct, nearly hourly at the bottom of the hour, does not run Nov–March, 35 min).

View and WCs: Ride the glass elevator to the top-floor café of the Museum of Contemporary Art for a great view over the ancient Maison Carrée and a quiet break above the world. The museum is in the glass building that faces the monument, and the elevator is inside near the front door (Tue–Sun 10:00–18:00, closed Mon). The basement has good WCs (same hours as café).

Self-Guided Walk

Welcome to Nîmes

I've described Nîmes' best sights below in a logical walking order for a good daylong visit, starting from the Arena (near the train station, with easy parking underground). Many of the sights I mention are free; the major exception is the Arena.

▲▲Arena (Amphithéâtre)

Nîmes' Arena dates from about A.D. 100 and is more than 425 feet in diameter and 65 feet tall. Considered the best-preserved arena

of the Roman world, it's a fine example of Roman engineering... and propaganda. In the spirit of "give them bread and circuses," it was free. No gates, just 60 welcoming arches, numbered to allow entertainment-seekers to come and go freely. The agenda was to create a populace that was thoroughly Roman—enjoying the same activities and entertainment, all thinking as one (not unlike Americans' nationwide obsession with the same reality-TV shows). The 24,000 seats could be filled and emptied in minutes (through passageways called *vomitoires*).

Cost and Hours: €8, includes audioguide, daily March–Oct 9:00–18:00, June–Aug until 19:00, Nov–Feb closes at 17:00, last ticket sold 45 min before closing, may close for special events—check at TI. Buy the €10 combo-ticket if you plan to visit the Maison Carrée and the Tour Magne (tower in the Fountain Garden—not worth the climb).

Nîmes

NEAR AVIGNON

● **Self-Guided Tour:** Climb to the very top—it's a rare opportunity to enjoy the view from the nosebleed seats of a Roman arena. An amphitheater is literally a double theater: two theaters facing each other, designed so that double the people could view a *Dirty Harry* spectacle (without the fine acoustics provided by the back wall of a theater stage). You may think of this as a "colosseum," but that's not a generic term. Rome's Colosseum was a one-of-a-kind arena—named for a colossal statue of Nero that stood nearby.

The floor where the action took place was the *arena* (literally, "sand"—which absorbed the blood, as in bullfights today). The Arena's floor, which covered passages and storage areas underneath, came with the famous elevator for surprise appearances of wild animals. (While Rome could afford exotic beasts from the tropics, places like Nîmes made do with snarling local beasts...bulls, wild boars, lots of bears, and so on.) The standard fight was as real as professional wrestling is today—mostly just crowd-pleasing. Thumbs down and kill the guy? Maybe in Rome, but only rarely (if ever) here.

1. New Hôtel la Baume
2. Hôtel de l'Amphithéâtre
3. Hôtel Brasserie des Arènes
4. Place aux Herbes Eateries
5. Place du Marché Eateries
6. Rest. Café Ciel de Nîmes
7. Place des Esclafidous Eateries
8. Covered Produce Market
9. Launderette
10. Internet Café
11. SNCF Boutique (Train Tickets)

→ SELF-GUIDED WALK

— RING ROAD ENCLOSING OLD TOWN

⚐ VIEW

P PARKING

NEAR AVIGNON

After Rome fell, and stability was replaced by Dark Age chaos, a huge structure like this was put to good use—bricked up and made a fortress (just like the Roman Arena in Arles). In the 13th century, after this region was incorporated into France, the Arena became a gated community housing about 700 people—with streets, plumbing, even gardens on the top level. Only in 1809 did Napoleon decide to scrape away the people and make this a historic monument, thus letting the ancient grandeur of Roman France shine.

Two fun multimedia exhibits bring bullfighting and gladiating to life on the Arena's ground floor (was that Kirk Douglas in those tight shorts?). Since 1850, Nîmes' Arena has been a venue for spectacles, even Spanish-style bullfights. An inflatable dome added in 1988 provides a roof over the lower seats (from the glass half-walls down), giving the city a winter venue of 7,000 seats to watch ice-skating, opera, and concerts. Acts from Elton John to Depeche Mode have played here.

Roman Nîmes

Born a Celtic city (about 500 B.C.), Nîmes joined the Roman Empire in the first century B.C. Because it had a privileged status within the Roman Empire, Nîmes was never really considered part of the conquered barbarian world. It rated highly enough to merit one of the longest protective walls in the Roman world and to have a 30-mile-long aqueduct (Pont du Gard) built to serve its growing population.

Today, the physical remains of Roman Nîmes testify to its former importance. The city's emblem—a crocodile tied to a palm tree—is a reminder that Nîmes was a favorite retirement home for Roman officers who conquered Egypt. (The crocodile is Egypt, and the palm tree symbolizes victory.) All over town, little bronze croc-palm medallions shine on the sidewalks. In the City Hall, 400-year-old statues of crocodiles actually swing from the top of a monumental staircase.

• *From the Arena, head to Maison Carrée via a stroll through Nîmes' "conservation zone"—the Old City. With your back to the Arena's ticket office, follow rue des Arènes into place du Marché and the heart of the...*

▲▲Old City

Those coming to Nîmes only for its famous Roman sights are enchanted by its carefully preserved old center. Here, you can study how elements in the buildings from the medieval and Renaissance times artfully survive: Shop interiors incorporate medieval brick with stone arches; windows expose Gothic finery; and Renaissance staircases grace peaceful courtyards.

Place du Marché has an inviting café ambience, including a wispy palm-tree-and-crocodile fountain (Nîmes' emblem in Roman times—see "Roman Nîmes," above). **Le Courtois Café/ Pâtisserie** is the class act of the square—check out its old-time interior (good lunch stop). It's been family-run since 1892. If you have a sweet tooth, let the sweet women serve you the house specialty, a dipped-in-chocolate *nélusko* (€3.50, somewhere between a cake and a cookie—the oldest recipe of the house); or a Nîmes specialty, *caladon* (literally "cobble" like on the street—a hard honey-and-almond cookie; open daily 8:00–19:30, tel. 04 66 67 20 09).

• *Leave the square, heading past the crocodile on rue des Broquiers, then turn left on rue de l'Aspic, the town's primary shopping spine. Rue de l'Aspic leads to place de l'Horloge, the center of the old town. From here, pedestrian-friendly streets fan out in all directions, including directly to Maison Carrée (described later). Take rue de la Madeleine, the first street to the right as you enter place de l'Horloge, to the...*

▲Place aux Herbes

This inviting square is the site of Nîmes' oldest market. Marking the center of the old town, it's a good hub for a bit of sightseeing. There are several good places to eat or to have a drink on or near the square (see "Eating in Nîmes," page 137). The next three sights are on or within a block of this square:

Nîmes Cathedral: While its Romanesque facade survives from the 12th century, the cathedral's interior—gutted over centuries of dynastic squabbles, Reformation, and Revolution—is unremarkable Neo-Romanesque, mostly from the 19th century.

Museum of Old Nîmes: Taking a left out of the cathedral leads to this humble single-floor museum, inhabiting a 17th-century bishop's palace. The museum highlights life in the city, starting with the Middle Ages, and provides the best chance to bring the intriguing architectural remnants of historic Nîmes to life. You'll also learn the story of indigo, 19th-century denim wear, and early Levis (free, no English but basics are easy to understand, Tue–Sun 10:00–18:00, closed Mon, tel. 04 66 76 73 70).

Old-Time Spice Shop: L'Huilerie Epicerie is a charming time warp displaying spices and herbs, oils, and candy (Mon–Sat 9:00–12:00 & 15:00–19:00, closed Sun; a block off place aux Herbes, down the small lane past Le Petit Moka café at 10 rue des Marchands). To revel in more of Nîmes' medieval atmosphere, find the nearby Passage du Vieux Nîmes.

• *When you're ready to move on, return to place de l'Horloge, turn right, and follow rue de Gazan past the clock tower to the...*

Covered Produce Market

Les Halles Centre Commerciale looks like a big black modern parking garage, but the ground floor is a thriving, colorful market hall, well worth exploring (daily until 13:00).

• *A right out of the covered market on rue Général Perrier leads to the...*

▲▲Maison Carrée

This temple rivals Rome's Pantheon as the most complete and beautiful building that survives from the Roman Empire. (There's

nothing inside but a tacky 3-D history movie, so we'll focus on its magnificent exterior.) The temple survived in part because it's been in constant use for the last thousand years—as a church, City Hall, private stable, archives during the Revolution, people's art gallery after the Revolution (like Paris' Louvre), and finally as the monument you visit today. It's a textbook example of a "pseudo-peripteral temple" (surrounded by columns, half of which support the roof over a porch, and half of which merely decorate the rest of the building) and a "six-column temple" (a standard proportion—if it's six columns wide, it must be 11 columns deep).

The lettering across the front is long gone, but the tiny surviving "nail holes" presented archaeologists with a fun challenge: Assuming each letter would leave a particular series of nail holes as evidence, derive the words. Archaeologists agree that this temple was built to honor Caius and Lucius, the grandsons (and adopted sons) of Emperor Augustus. And from this information, they date the temple from the year A.D. 4.

Maison Carrée ("Square House"—named before they had a word for "rectangle") was the centerpiece of a fancy plaza surrounded by a U-shaped commercial, political, and religious forum. This marked the core of Roman Nîmes. As was the case in all Roman temples, only the priest went inside. Worshippers gathered for religious rituals at the foot of the steps. Climb the steps as a priest would—starting and ending with your right foot...*dexter* (from the Latin for "right") rather than *sinister* ("left"). Put your right foot forward for good karma.

Inside, the ***Heroes of Nîmes* movie** tells the story of six heroic locals, each vying to be "the most heroic citizen of noble Nîmes." While entertaining, this 3-D film—covering 2,000 years in 20 minutes—insults the building it fills (€4.50, every 30 min, daily 10:00–19:00, soundtrack in Latin and French with English subtitles).

The modern building facing the temple is Nîmes' **Carrée d'Art** ("Square of Art"), designed by British architect Lord Norman Foster. It's home to the city's Museum of Contemporary Art (Tue–Sun 10:00–18:00, closed Mon, good view café and WCs—see page 129).

• *If you haven't visited the TI yet, do it now (across the street and a few steps up from Maison Carrée; see "Tourist Information," page 128). Then walk down rue Molière with the Museum of Contemporary Art on your left. Dogleg right until you hit the canal, then follow the canal left until you reach the...*

▲Spring of Nemo in the Fountain Garden

Centuries before the Romans arrived in Nîmes, the Spring of Nemo was here (named, like the town itself, for a Celtic god). When the Romans built a shrine to Emperor Augustus around the spring, rather than bulldoze the Nemo temple, they built alongside it and welcomed Nemo into their own pantheon (as was their more-gods-the-merrier tradition). Today, the spring remains, though the temple is gone.

Walk into the center of the Fountain Garden (Jardin de la Fontaine) and look into the canal. In the early 1700s, Nîmes needed a reliable source of water for its textile industry—to power its mills and provide water for the indigo dyes for the fabric *serge de Nîmes* (denim). About 1735, the city began a project to route a canal through the city and discovered this Roman temple. The city eventually agreed to fund a grander project that ultimately resulted in what you see today: a lavish Versailles-type park, complete with an ornate network of canals and boulevards. This was just 50 years after the construction of Versailles, and to the French, this place has a special significance. These were the first grand public gardens not meant for a king, but for the public. The industrial canals built then still wind throughout the city.

• *Hiding behind trees in the back-left corner of Fountain Garden, find the...*

▲▲Temple of Diana

This first-century "temple," which modern archaeologists now believe was more likely a Roman library, has long been considered one of the best examples of ancient stonework. Its roof—a round Roman barrel vault laced together with still-visible metal pegs—survived until a blast during the Catholic–Protestant Wars of Religion in the 1500s.

At first glance, all the graffiti is obnoxious. But it's actually part of the temple's story. For centuries, France had a highly esteemed guild of stone-, metal-, and woodworkers called the Compagnons, founded by Gothic-church builders in the Middle Ages. As part of their almost mystic training, these craftsmen would visit many buildings—including the great structures of antiquity (such as this one)—for inspiration. Walk through the side aisle for a close look at the razor-accurate stonework and the 17th-, 18th-, and 19th-century signatures of the Compagnon craftsmen inspired by this building. Notice how their signatures match their era—no-nonsense "Enlightened" chiseling of the 18th century gives way to ornate script in the Romantic 19th century.

Cost and Hours: The park and temple are free and open daily (April–mid-Sept 7:30–22:00, mid-Sept–March 7:30–18:30). Skip the hike up to Tour Magne (at top of gardens), which has two remaining levels of a Roman tower; the view is worth neither the sweat nor the €3 fee. Instead, have a well-deserved coffee break or snack at the park's café, located next to the Temple of Diana.

• *To reach the next sight (about a 15-min walk away), backtrack out of the park, turning left at the canal (quai de la Fontaine). At the busy corner, keep left and merge onto busy boulevard Gambetta. In a few blocks, turn left on rue Ménard, which leads to the....*

▲Castellum

This small excavation site, sitting next to the street, shows a modest-looking water distribution tank that was the grand finale of the 30-mile-long Pont du Gard aqueduct.

Discovered in the 1850s, this is one of only two known Roman distribution tanks (the other is in Pompeii). The water needs of Roman Nîmes grew beyond the capacity of its local springs. Imagine the jubilation on the day (in A.D. 50) that this system was finally operational. Suddenly, the town had an abundance of water—for basic needs as well as for cool extras like public fountains. Notice the plugged hole marking the end of the aqueduct, a pool, a lower water channel, and the water-distribution holes. The lower channel served top-priority needs, providing water via stone and lead pipes to the public wells that graced neighborhood squares. The higher holes—which got wet only when the supply was plentiful—routed water to the homes of the wealthy, to public baths, and to nonessential fountains.

The excavation site is free to visit and always open. (For more on this impressive example of Roman engineering, see the "Pont du Gard" section, later in this chapter.)

Sleeping in Nîmes

$$$ New Hôtel la Baume*, a few blocks from the cathedral, is a business-class hotel with 34 sizeable and well-designed rooms featuring every comfort. This beautiful Renaissance building dates

NEAR AVIGNON

Sleep Code

(€1 = about $1.40, country code: 33)
S = Single, **D** = Double/Twin, **T** = Triple, **Q** = Quad, **b** = bathroom, **s** = shower only, ***** = French hotel rating system (0-4 stars). Unless otherwise noted, credit cards are accepted and English is spoken.

To help you easily sort through these listings, I've divided the rooms into three categories, based on the price for a standard double room with bath:

$$$ Higher Priced—Most rooms €85 or more.
  $$ Moderately Priced—Most rooms between €60-85.
    $ Lower Priced—Most rooms €60 or less.

from the 1600s (Sb-€115, Db-€145–150, Tb-€175, look for deals on their website, air-con, elevator, 21 rue Nationale, tel. 04 66 76 28 42, fax 04 66 76 28 45, www.new-hotel.com/labaume, nimeslabaume @new-hotel.com).

$$ Hôtel de l'Amphithéâtre** is ideally located on a pedestrian street a spear's toss from the Arena. It's quiet—unless there's a concert at the Arena—with well-kept rooms run by helpful Hervé and Nathalie (small Db-€55–66, larger Db-€68–83, no elevator, 3 of the 15 rooms have air-con, 4 rue des Arènes, tel. 04 66 67 28 51, fax 04 66 67 07 79, hotel-amphitheatre @wanadoo.fr).

$ Hôtel Brasserie des Arènes* occupies a privileged location facing the Arena. Its 11 basic rooms above a modern café—some rooms with kitchenettes—provide one-star comfort at fair rates (Db-€45–52, Tb-€50–55, no air-con or elevator, 4 boulevard des Arènes, tel. 04 66 67 23 05, fax 04 66 67 76 93, www.brasserie -arenes.com, hotel@brasserie-arenes.com).

Eating in Nîmes

Enjoy the elegance of Nîmes by eating lunch on one of its fine squares. Sadly, most of these cafés close at dinner.

Place aux Herbes: This square, beautifully situated in the shadow of the cathedral, boasts several popular and hardworking bistros. **Restaurant ô Délices** and **Le Petit Moka** both serve fresh salads, crêpes, and *tartines.*

Place du Marché: A block from the Arena, this square is home to **Mogador Café,** serving tasty, light lunches (salads, crêpes, and lots of veggies), and **Le Courtois Café/Pâtisserie,** with its trademark desserts (described on page 132).

Overlooking the Maison Carrée: **Restaurant Café Ciel de Nîmes** fills a terrace atop the city's Norman Foster–designed contemporary art gallery, offering diners great views of the Roman temple. Facing the temple, you'll see the terrace atop the modern building on your right (€10 *plats du jour,* €12 salads, €16 three-course workday lunch special, Tue–Sun 10:00–18:00, closed Mon, place de la Maison Carrée, tel. 04 66 36 71 70).

Place des Esclafidous: Several tempting places line this cute little square two blocks behind the cathedral (find the post office on rue Crémieux and walk behind it). At **Restaurant les Magnolias,** you'll dine in a cozy interior or on a peaceful terrace; meals are reasonable, and the service is friendly (*menus* from €18, big salads for €10, daily for dinner, tel. 04 66 21 64 01). **La Table de Clair** is across the square, with eclectic ambience and *très* tasty cuisine (€20–33 *menus,* dinner only, closed Sun, tel. 04 66 67 55 61).

Nîmes Connections

Trains and buses depart from the same station in Nîmes (see "Arrival in Nîmes," page 128). If traveling by bus, plan to arrive early at the station to double-check your schedule. Ask at the bus information office in the rear of the train station for the next bus to your destination and which stall it leaves from (most likely stall 2 or 3; look for shelters to your right as you walk outside). Buy your ticket from the driver (about €7 one-way to Pont du Gard, avoid big bills). Route numbers posted on the buses themselves usually do not correspond with those on paper timetables, so verify your destination with the driver.

From Nîmes by Train to: Arles (9/day, 30 min), **Avignon** (14/day, 30 min), **Aigues-Mortes** in the Camargue (6/day, 45 min), **Carcassonne** (8/day, 2.5 hrs, transfer in Narbonne), **Paris** (10/day, 3 hrs).

By Bus to: Uzès (8/day Mon–Fri, 6/day Sat, 2/day Sun, 1 hr, €8), **Pont du Gard** (5/day Mon–Sat, 2/day Sun and off-season, 40 min; check return times before you leave, tel. 04 66 29 27 29, www .stdgard.fr), **Aigues-Mortes** in the Camargue (6/day, 50 min), **Arles** (6/day, 1 hr).

Pont du Gard

Throughout the ancient world, aqueducts were like flags of stone that heralded the greatness of Rome. A visit to this sight still works to proclaim the wonders of that age. This perfectly preserved Roman aqueduct was built in about 19 B.C. as the critical link of a 30-mile canal that, by dropping one inch for every 350 feet, supplied nine million gallons of water per day (about 100 gallons per second) to Nîmes—one of ancient Europe's largest cities. Though most of the aqueduct is on or below the ground, at Pont du Gard it spans a canyon on a massive bridge—one of the most remarkable surviving Roman ruins anywhere. Wear sturdy shoes if you plan to climb around the aqueduct (footing is tricky), and bring swimwear if you plan to backstroke below the monument.

Getting to Pont du Gard

The famous aqueduct is between Remoulins and Vers-Pont du Gard on D-981, 17 miles from Nîmes and 13 miles from Avignon.

By Car: Pont du Gard is a 25-minute drive due west of Avignon (follow N-100 from Avignon, tracking signs to *Nîmes* and *Remoulins,* then *Pont du Gard* and *Rive Gauche*), and 45 minutes northwest of Arles (via Tarascon on D-15). While parking

Pont du Gard

— ROAD   🔭 VIEW

--- PATH   🅿 PARKING

NOT TO SCALE:
MUSEUM TO PONT DU GARD
IS A 5-MINUTE WALK

PONT DU GARD

TRAIL ALONG CANAL

BEST VIEW

CANAL TUNNEL

TO CANAL RUINS

GARRIGUE NATURAL AREA

🅿 (RIVE DROITE) DON'T PARK HERE

TO REMOULINS & NIMES

GARDON RIVER

MUSEUM COMPLEX

CINEMA, LUDO (KIDS' SPACE), INFO, SHOP, WC & RESTAURANT

❸

🅿 (RIVE GAUCHE) PARK HERE

D-981

TO UZÈS

D-981

❷

❶ ROUNDABOUT

TO REMOULINS, NIMES, AVIGNON, ARLES & A-9 FREEWAY

DCH

❶ Bus Stop from Avignon & Nîmes
❷ Bus Stop to Avignon & Nîmes
❸ Bus Stop (Summer & Weekends)

is available on the Rive Droite (Right Bank), it's farther away from the museum than parking on the Rive Gauche (Left Bank). If going to Arles from Pont du Gard, follow signs to *Nîmes* (not Avignon), then follow D-986 and then D-15 to Arles.

By Bus: Buses run to Pont du Gard (on the Rive Gauche side) from Nîmes, Uzès, and Avignon. Combining Pont du Gard with Nîmes and/or Uzès makes a good day-trip excursion from Avignon (see "Planning Your Time," at the beginning of this chapter).

Buses stop at the traffic roundabout 300 yards from the aqueduct (see map above). In summer and on weekends, however, buses usually drive into the Pont du Gard site and stop at the parking lot's ticket booth. Confirm where the bus stops at the parking booth inside the Pont du Gard site.

At the roundabout, the stop for buses coming from Avignon and Nîmes (and going to Uzès) is on the side opposite Pont du Gard; the stop for buses to Nîmes and to Avignon is on the same side as Pont du Gard (a block to your left as you exit Pont du Gard onto the main road). Make sure you're waiting for the bus on the correct side of the traffic circle (stops have schedules posted), and use your hand to signal the bus to stop for you (otherwise, it'll chug on by). Buy your ticket when you get on, and verify your destination with the driver.

By Taxi: From Nîmes or Avignon, it's about €42 for a taxi ride to Pont du Gard. If you're staying in Avignon and only want to see Pont du Gard (and not Nîmes or Uzès), consider splurging on a taxi to the aqueduct in the morning, then take the early-afternoon bus back.

Orientation to Pont du Gard

There are two riversides to Pont du Gard: the Left Bank (Rive Gauche) and Right Bank (Rive Droite). Park on the Rive Gauche, where you'll find the museums, ticket booth, ATM, cafeteria, WCs, and shops—all built into a modern plaza. You'll see the aqueduct in two parts: first the fine museum complex, then the actual river gorge spanned by the ancient bridge. Tickets are sold at the information desk by the café and in the gift shop.

Cost: While it's free to see the aqueduct itself, the optional activities cost extra: parking (€5), museum (€7), corny film (€4), and a kids' space called *Ludo* (€5, scratch-and-sniff experience in English of various aspects of Roman life and the importance of water). The extensive outdoor *garrigue* natural area, featuring historic crops and landscapes of the Mediterranean, is free (though €4 buys you a helpful English booklet). All these attractions are designed to give the sight more meaning—and they do—but for most visitors, only the museum is worth paying for. Those on a budget can skip the pay sights, just pay €5 for parking, and enjoy the aqueduct for free.

The €12 **combo-ticket** (€9 for kids ages 6–17) covers all sights and parking, and includes the €4 booklet to the *garrigue* natural area. If you want to see all the sights, this is a good value. Families save with the €24 **family ticket** (covers two parents and up to four kids). If you get a combo-ticket, check the movie schedule; the romancing-the-aqueduct 25-minute film is silly, but it offers good information in a flirtatious French-Mediterranean style...and a cool, entertaining, and cushy break.

For an extra €6, you can rent an **audioguide** with detailed explanations of the aqueduct in English. Ask ahead about **guided walks** on top of the aqueduct (called "Musée Plus," combine with museum visit for a few extra euros).

Hours: The museum is open May–Sept Tue–Sun 9:30–19:00, Mon 13:00–19:00; Oct–April until 17:00; closed two weeks in Jan.

NEAR AVIGNON

The aqueduct itself is free and open until 1:00 in the morning, as is the parking lot. Tel. 08 20 90 33 30, www.pontdugard.fr.

Canoe Rental: Floating under Pont du Gard by canoe is an experience you won't soon forget. Collias Canoes will pick you up at Pont du Gard (or elsewhere, if pre-arranged) and shuttle you to the town of Collias. You'll float down the river to the nearby town of Remoulins, where they'll pick you up and take you back to Pont du Gard (€18/person, €9/child under 12, usually 2 hours, though you can take as long as you like, good idea to reserve the day before in July–Aug, tel. 04 66 22 85 54).

Plan Ahead for Swimming: Pont du Gard is perhaps best enjoyed on your back and in the water—bring along a swimsuit, and sandals for the rocks.

Sights at Pont du Gard

▲**Museum**—In this state-of-the-art museum (well-presented in English), you'll enter to the sound of water and understand the critical role fresh water played in the Roman "art of living." You'll see examples of lead pipes, faucets, and siphons; walk through a mock rock quarry; and learn how they moved those huge rocks into place and how those massive arches were made. While actual artifacts from the aqueduct are few, the exhibit shows the immensity of the undertaking as well as the payoff. Imagine the excitement as this extravagant supply of water finally tumbled into Nîmes. A relaxing highlight is the scenic video of a helicopter ride along the entire 30-mile course of the structure, from its start at Uzès all the way to the Castellum in Nîmes.

▲▲▲**Viewing the Aqueduct**—A park-like path leads to the aqueduct. Until a few years ago, this was an actual road—adjacent to the aqueduct—that had spanned the river since 1743. Before you cross the bridge, pass under it and hike about 300 feet along the riverbank for a grand viewpoint from which to study the world's second-highest standing Roman structure. (Rome's Colosseum is only 6 feet taller.)

This was the biggest bridge in the whole 30-mile-long aqueduct. It seems exceptional because it is: The arches are twice the width of standard aqueducts, and the main arch is the largest the Romans ever built—80 feet (so it wouldn't get its feet wet). The bridge is about 160 feet high and was originally about 1,100 feet long. Today, 12 arches are missing, reducing the length to 790 feet.

While the distance from the source (in Uzès) to Nîmes was only 12 miles as the eagle flew, engineers chose the most economical route, winding and zigzagging 30 miles. The water made the trip in 24 hours with a drop of only 40 feet. Ninety percent of the aqueduct is on or under the ground, but a few river canyons like this required bridges. A stone lid hides a four-foot-wide, six-foot-tall chamber lined with waterproof mortar that carried the stream for more than 400 years. For 150 years, this system provided Nîmes with good drinking water. Expert as the Romans were, they miscalculated the backup caused by a downstream corner, and had to add the thin extra layer you can see just under the lid to make the channel deeper.

The bridge and the river below provide great fun for holidaygoers. While parents suntan on rocks, kids splash into the gorge from under the aqueduct. Some daredevils actually jump from the aqueduct's lower bridge—not knowing that crazy winds scrambled by the structure cause painful belly flops (and sometimes even accidental deaths). For the most refreshing view, float flat on your back underneath the structure.

The appearance of the entire gorge changed in 2002, when a huge flood flushed lots of greenery downstream. Those floodwaters put Roman provisions to the test. Notice the triangular-shaped buttresses at the lower level—designed to split and divert the force of any flood *around* the feet of the arches rather than *into* them. The 2002 floodwaters reached the top of those buttresses. Anxious park rangers winced at the sounds of trees crashing onto the ancient stones...but the arches stood strong.

The stones that jut out—giving the aqueduct a rough, unfinished appearance—supported the original scaffolding. The protuberances were left, rather than cut off, in anticipation of future repair needs. The lips under the arches supported wooden templates that allowed the stones in the round arches to rest on something until the all-important keystone was dropped into place. Each stone weighs four to six tons. The structure stands with no mortar—taking full advantage of the innovative Roman arch, made strong by gravity.

Hike over the bridge for a closer look and the best views. Steps lead up a high trail (marked *panorama*) to a superb viewpoint (right at the top; best views are after the trail starts descending). You'll also see where the aqueduct meets a rock tunnel. Walk through the tunnel and continue for a bit, following a

NEAR AVIGNON

trail that meanders along the canal's path. Back on the museum side, steps lead up to the other end of the aqueduct and along a trail that eventually leads to surviving bits of the aqueduct system (follow red-and-yellow trail markers). Remains of this part are scant because of medieval cannibalization—frugal builders couldn't resist the precut stones as they constructed local churches. The ancient quarry (about a third of a mile downstream on this side) may be open to the public...someday.

Uzès

Like Nîmes and Pont du Gard, this intriguing, less-trampled town is officially in Languedoc, not Provence. Uzès (oo-zehs) feels like it

must have been important—and it was, as a bishopric from the fifth century until 1789. It's best seen slowly on foot, with a long coffee break in its arcaded and mellow main square, place aux Herbes (not so mellow during the colorful Wednesday morning market and even bigger all-day Saturday market).

By car, Uzès is 10 minutes from Pont du Gard and 30 minutes from Nîmes and Avignon. It offers a welcome small-town break from serious sightseeing. Go local and overnight here. Arrive on Tuesday or Friday nights to enjoy the next morning's market.

The town itself—traffic-free and tastefully restored—is the sight. In spite of all those bishops, there are no important museums. You can follow the TI's self-guided walking tour, but skip the dull and overpriced Palace of the Duché de Uzès (€12, French-only tour). The town's tasteful boutiques are numerous, as are English-speakers. (The toy shop Au Bois de mon Coeur under the arcade at 8 Place aux Herbes has special treats for kids.) The unusual circular tower called Tour Fenestrelle is all that remains of a 12th-century cathedral. Even if you're not a plant enthusiast, pop into the **Medieval Garden,** a "living herbarium" with plants thought to have curative qualities. The garden is at the foot of the King's and Bishop's towers. The €4 entrance fee includes a little shot of lemongrass tea lovingly delivered by the volunteers who care for this sight (April–Sept daily 14:00–18:00 plus 10:30–12:30 on Sat–Sun and daily in July–Aug, until 17:00 in Oct, closed Nov–March, English handout and some information posted, tel. 04 66 22 38 21).

The **Musée du Bonbon** of Haribo (think gummy bears) lies just outside Uzès and makes a worthwhile detour for the kids (July–Aug daily 10:00–19:00; Sept–June Tue–Sun 10:00–13:00 & 14:00–18:00, closed Mon; 1.5 miles from Uzès on the road to Avignon and Pont du Gard, tel. 04 66 22 74 39).

Getting to Uzès

Uzès is a short hop west of Pont du Gard. It's well-served by **bus** from Nîmes (8/day Mon–Fri, 6/day Sat, 2/day Sun, 1 hr, €8), but less so from Avignon (3/day Mon–Sat, none Sun, 1 hr, stops at Pont du Gard). **Drivers** will circle the old town on the busy ring road. The TI and both hotels that I list are on this ring road.

Tourist Information

The TI sits at the top of the ring road (on place Albert 1er). Pick up the brief self-guided tour brochure in English (June–Sept Mon–Fri 9:00–18:00, Sat–Sun 10:00–13:00 & 14:00–17:00; Oct–May Mon–Fri 9:00–12:30 & 14:00–18:00, Sat 10:00–13:00, closed Sun; tel. 04 66 22 68 88, www.uzes-tourisme.com).

Sleeping in Uzès

(€1 = about $1.40, country code: 33)
Pale-green signs direct drivers to hotels from the ring road.

$$$ Hôtel du Général d'Entraigues*** is a cool 15th-century stone-cozy hotel with 36 rooms and hard-to-find staff. It combines traditional and modern touches with a flowery terrace and pool (Db-€80–170, most about €90, skip the €12 continental breakfast, air-con in most rooms; coming from Pont du Gard or Nîmes, it's virtually the first building you see on the ring road; place de l'Evêché, tel. 04 66 22 32 68, fax 04 66 22 57 01, www.leshotelsparticuliers.com, entraigues@leshotelsparticuliers.com).

$$$ L'Hostellerie Provençale** is an intimate place with nine cushy and thoughtfully appointed rooms (all with air-con) just off the ring road a few blocks after the TI. It's well-known for its adorable and delectable restaurant (Db-€90–140, Wi-Fi, parking garage-€10, 4-course dinner *menus* from €35, 1 rue de la Grande Bourgade, tel. 04 66 22 11 06, fax 04 66 75 01 03, www.hostellerieprovencale.com, contact@hostellerieprovencale.com).

Eating in Uzès

When the weather cooperates, it's hard to resist meals on place aux Herbes, which is lined with appealing café options. **La Renaissance** is a fair bet, with salads, pizzas, and *plats du jour* from about €10 to €13, plus a €20 *menu* (open daily for lunch and dinner, 6 place aux Herbes, tel. 04 66 03 11 82). **Terroires,** on the other side of the square, serves modern, light cuisine such as *tartines*, tapas, and great salads, all made with regional products (€13 *plats*, closed Mon).

The creative **Bistro Burger** serves gourmet Charolais burgers for €10 and has good wines by the glass (many options including kids' and vegetarian *menus*, daily 12:00–22:00, 19 place aux Herbes, tel. 04 66 20 21 03). Beware: Only Americans eat their burgers with their hands—the French use a knife and fork.

Le Zanelli Italian dishes up pizzas and more and is located on the most prized terrace in the center of Uzès, place Nicolas Froment (allow €8–18, daily July–Aug, otherwise closed Tue–Wed, tel. 04 66 03 01 93).

To dine well indoors, find the restaurant **La Parenthèse** in the recommended **l'Hostellerie Provençale** (closed Sun–Mon, described earlier).

ORANGE AND THE COTES DU RHONE

*Orange • Châteauneuf-du-Pape
• Vaison la Romaine • Best of the
Côtes du Rhône Villages
• More Côtes du Rhône Drives*

The sunny Côtes du Rhône wine road—one of France's best—starts at Avignon's doorstep. It winds north through a mountainous landscape carpeted with vines, peppered with warm stone villages, and presided over by the Vesuvius-like Mont Ventoux. The wines of the Côtes du Rhône (grown on the *côtes,* or hillsides, of the Rhône River Valley) are easy on the palate and on your budget. But this hospitable place offers more than famous wine—its hill-capping villages inspire travel posters, its Roman ruins inspire awe, and the people you'll meet are welcoming...and, often, as excited about their region as you are. Yes, you'll have good opportunities for enjoyable wine-tasting, but there is also a soul to this area...if you take the time to look.

Located 20 minutes north of Avignon, the ancient town of Orange has vineyards on its outskirts. But it's because of its well-preserved Roman Theater that Orange gets (and deserves) attention.

Planning Your Time

Vaison la Romaine is the small hub of this region, offering limited bus connections with Avignon and Orange, bike rental, and a mini-Pompeii in the town center. Nearby, you can visit the impressive Roman Theater in Orange, drive to the top of Mont Ventoux, follow my self-guided driving tour of Côtes du Rhône villages and wineries, and pedal to nearby towns for a breath of fresh air. The vineyards' centerpiece, the Dentelles de Montmirail mountains, are laced with a variety of exciting trails ideal for hikers.

To explore this area, allow two nights for a good start. Drivers should head for the hills (read this chapter's self-guided driving tour before deciding where to stay). Those without wheels find that Vaison la Romaine is the only practical home base (or, maybe better, consider a minivan tour—see next page).

Getting Around the Côtes du Rhône

By Car: Pick up the Michelin Local maps #332 or #528 to navigate your way around the Côtes du Rhône. (Landmarks like the Dentelles de Montmirail and Mont Ventoux make it easy to get your bearings.) I've described my favorite driving route in a self-guided driving tour, later in this chapter.

If your plan is to connect the Côtes du Rhône with the **Luberon,** you can do it scenically via Mont Ventoux (follow signs to *Malaucène*, then to *Mont Ventoux*, allowing 2 hours to Roussillon). This route is one of the most spectacular in Provence. Or, faster, you can zip between the Luberon by taking the autoroute via Orange and Cavaillon. A third, more direct route takes you through the traffic-snarled, difficult-to-navigate city of Carpentras, which should be avoided. Get advice from your hotelier.

By Bus: Buses run to Vaison la Romaine from Orange and Avignon (3–5/day, 45 min from Orange, 1.5 hrs from Avignon) and connect several wine villages (including Gigondas, Sablet, and Beaumes de Venise) with Vaison la Romaine and Nyons to the north. Another line runs from Vaison la Romaine to Carpentras, serving Crestet (below Le Crestet), Malaucène, and Le Barroux (2/day, tel. 04 90 36 09 90). Both routes provide scenic rides through this area.

By Train: Trains get you as far as Orange (from Avignon: 10/day, 15 min); from there, buses make the 45-minute trip to Vaison la Romaine.

By Minivan Tour: Various all-day minivan excursions to this area leave from Avignon. For a wine-focused tour, I recommend three individuals who can expertly guide you through the region. For all tours to this area, see "Tours of Provence" on page 40.

Côtes du Rhône Market Days

Monday: Bedoin (intimate market, between Vaison la Romaine and Mont Ventoux)

Tuesday: Vaison la Romaine (great market with produce and antiques/flea market)

Wednesday: Malaucène (good and less-touristy market with produce and antiques/flea market, near Vaison la Romaine), Buis les Barronies (on recommended loop drive north into the Drôme Provençale), and Sault (handy if you're driving to the Luberon area)

Thursday: Nyons (great market with produce and antiques/flea market) and Vacqueyras

Friday: Châteauneuf-du-Pape (small market) and Carpentras (big market)

Saturday: Valréas (small market north of Vaison la Romaine)

Orange

Orange is notable for its Roman arch and grand Roman Theater. Orange was a thriving city in ancient times—strategically situated on the Via Agrippa, connecting the important Roman cities of Lyon and Arles. It was actually founded as a comfortable place for Roman army officers to enjoy their retirement. Even in Roman times, career military men retired after only 20 years. Does the emperor want thousands of well-trained, relatively young guys hanging around Rome? No way. What to do? "How about a nice place in the south of France...?"

Orientation to Orange

Tourist Information

The unnecessary TI is located next to the fountain and parking area at 5 cours Aristide Briand (April–Sept Mon–Sat 9:30–19:00, Sun 10:00–13:00 & 14:00–18:30; Oct–March Mon–Sat 10:00–13:00 & 14:00–17:30, closed Sun; tel. 04 90 34 70 88).

Arrival in Orange

By Train: Orange's **train station** is a level 15-minute walk from the Roman Theater (or an €8 taxi ride, tel. 06 09 51 32 25). The recommended Hôtel de Provence across from the station will keep your bags (see "Sleeping in Orange," later). To walk into town from the train station, head straight out of the station (down avenue Frédéric Mistral), merge left onto Orange's main shopping street (rue de la République), then turn left on rue Caristie; you'll run into the Roman Theater's massive stage wall.

By Bus: Buses stop at the gare SNCF and at place Pourtoules, two blocks from the Roman Theater (walk to the hill and turn right to reach the theater, bus station tel. 04 90 34 15 59, www .vaucluse.fr/86-reseau-departemental.htm).

By Car: Follow *Centre-Ville* signs, then *Théâtre Antique* signs, and park as close to the Roman Theater's huge wall as possible; the easiest option is Parking Théâtre Antique (by the fountain and the TI). Those coming from the autoroute will land here by following *Centre-Ville* signs; others should follow *Centre-Ville* signs, then *Office du Tourisme* signs, to find this parking. To reach the theater, walk to the hill and turn left.

Orange

*Map labels:*

TO GAP

ARC DE TRIOMPHE

N

AVE ARTAUD

AVE. DE L'ARC DE TRIOMPHE

200 YARDS
200 METERS

P PARKING
V VIEW

MEYNE RIVER

RUE ST. JEAN

PLACE ST. JEAN

R. LA COUR

R. VICTOR HUGO

BLVD.

RUE DU NOBLE

DALADIER

R. CARISTIE

CATHEDRAL

A. BRIAND

RUE DU TANNEURS

TO A-7 FREEWAY

RUE

ST. MARTIN

PL. CLEM.

PL. REB.

R. PONT NEUE

R. DE LA REPUBLIQUE

AVE. FABRE

AVE. FRED. MISTRAL

TO VAISON LA ROMAINE

COURS

COURS

PL. HERBES

R. PONTILLAC

PLACE FRERES MOUNET

ENTER

R. ST. FLOR.

PL. LIB.

RUE CONTRASCARPE

TO TRAIN STN. & HOTEL DE PROVENCE

AVE. DES THERMES

RUE DE TOURRE

EXCAVATIONS

MONTÉE DU CHALONS

RUE POURTOULES

Post

ROMAN THEATER

ESCALIER EST

COURS POURTOULES

BUS STN.

P

ST. EUTROPE HILL

RUE A. BLANC (D-68)

AVE. GEN. LECLERC

TO CHATEAUNEUF-DU-PAPE

TO AVIGNON VIA N-7

DCH

Sights in Orange

▲▲Roman Theater (Théâtre Antique)—Orange's ancient theater is the best-preserved in existence, and the only one in Europe with its acoustic wall still standing. (Two others in Asia Minor also survive.)

Cost, Hours, Information: €8, daily April–Sept 9:00–18:00, until 19:00 in summer, Oct–March 9:30–17:30 except closes at 16:30 Nov–Feb, tel. 04 90 51 17 60, www.theatre-antique.com.

The Côtes du Rhône Area

Your ticket includes an informative audioguide, a fun film covering 2,000 years of history (called *Phantom of the Theater*), and entrance to the small museum across the street (Musée d'Art et d'Histoire). Pop in to the museum to see a few theater details and a rare grid used as the official property-ownership registry—each square represented a 120-acre plot of land.

Cheap Trick: Vagabonds wanting to see the theater for free can hike up nearby stairs (*escalier est* off rue Pourtoules is closest) to view it from the bluff high above.

Map legend:
- **COTES DU RHONE DRIVING TOUR**
- **DROME PROVENCALE DRIVING TOUR**

Map labels: TO SERRES, D-94, D-64, STE-JALLE, D-108, D-546, FAUCON, D-5, BUIS LES BARONNIES, D-72, D-40, ENTRECHAUX, BRANTES, D-41, MALAUCENE, MONT VENTOUX, D-974, COL DE TEMPETES, D-164, D-19, D-974, BEDOIN, D-942, SAULT, TO LUBERON (SCENIC ROUTE)

5 MILES
10 KM

DCH

Cafés: A shaded café-filled square (place de la République) is two blocks from the theater up rue Ségond Weber.

⊙ Self-Guided Tour: After you enter (to the right of the actual theater), you'll see a huge dig—the site of the Temple to the Cult of the Emperor. Look for signs to the worthwhile movie (English subtitles) that gives you a good visual sense of how the theater looked to the Romans.

Enter the theater, then climb the steep stairs to find a seat high up to appreciate the acoustics (eavesdrop on people by the stage). Contemplate the idea that 2,000 years ago, Orange residents enjoyed grand spectacles with high-tech sound and lighting effects—such as simulated thunder, lightning, and rain.

A grandiose Caesar overlooks everything, reminding attendees of who's in charge. If it seems like you've seen this statue before, you probably have. Countless sculptures identical to this one were mass-produced in Rome and shipped throughout the empire to grace buildings like this theater for propaganda purposes. To save money on shipping and handling, only the heads of these statues were changed with each new ruler. The permanent body wears a breastplate emblazoned with the imperial griffon (body of a lion, head and wings of an eagle) that only the emperor could wear. When a new emperor came to power, new heads were made in Rome and shipped off throughout the empire to replace the pop-off heads on all these statues. (Imagine Barack Obama's head on George W. Bush's body.)

Archaeologists believe that a puny, vanquished Celt was included at the knee of the emperor, touching his ruler's robe respectfully—a show of humble subservience to the emperor. It's interesting to consider how an effective propaganda machine can con the masses into being impressed by their leader.

The horn has blown. It's time to find your seat: row two, number 30. Sitting down, you're comforted by the "EQ GIII" carved into the seat (*Equitas Gradus* #3...three rows for the Equestrian order). You're not comforted by the hard limestone bench (thinking it'll probably last 2,000 years). The theater is filled with 10,000 people. Thankfully, you mix only with your class, the nouveau riche—merchants, tradesmen, and city big shots. The people seated above you are the working class, and way up in the "chicken roost" section is the scum of the earth—slaves, beggars, prostitutes, and youth hostellers. Scanning the orchestra section (where the super-rich sit on real chairs), you notice the town dignitaries hosting some visiting VIPs.

OK, time to worship. They're parading a bust of the emperor from its sacred home in the adjacent temple around the stage. Next is the ritual animal sacrifice called *la pompa* (so fancy, future generations will use that word for anything full of such...pomp). Finally, you settle in for an all-day series of spectacles and dramatic entertainment. All eyes are on the big stage door in the middle—where the Julia Roberts and Brad Pitts of the day will appear. (Lesser actors come out of the side doors.)

The play is good, but many come for the halftime shows—jugglers, acrobats, and striptease dancers. In Roman times, the theater was a festival of immorality. An ancient writer commented, "The vanquished take their revenge on us by giving us their vices through the theater."

With an audience of 10,000 and no amplification, acoustics were critical. A roof originally covered the stage, somewhat like the glass-and-iron stage roof you see today (recently installed to protect the stage wall). The original was designed not to protect the stage from the weather, but to project the voices of the actors into the crowd. For further help, actors wore masks with leather caricature mouths that functioned as megaphones. The side walls originally rose as high as the stage wall and supported a retractable roof that gave the audience some protection from the sun. After leaving the theater, look up to the stage wall from the outside and notice the supports for poles that held the roof in place.

The Roman Theater was all part of the "give them bread and circuses" approach to winning the support of the masses (not unlike today's philosophy of "give them tax cuts and *American Idol*"). The spectacle grew from 65 days of games per year when the theater was first built (and when Rome was at its height) to about 180 days each year by the time Rome finally fell.

▲**Roman "Arc de Triomphe"**—Technically the only real Roman arches of triumph are in Rome's Forum, built to commemorate various emperors' victories. The great Roman arch of Orange is actually a municipal arch erected (in about A.D. 19) to commemorate a general, named Germanicus, who protected the town. The 60-foot-tall arch is on a noisy traffic circle (north of city center, on avenue Arc de Triomphe).

Sleeping in Orange

(€1 = about $1.40, country code: 33)
$$ Hôtel de Provence**, at the train station, is air-conditioned, quiet, comfortable, and affordable. Friendly Madame Verbe runs this traditional place with grace (Db-€60–70, Tb-€75–95, small rooftop pool, café, 60 avenue Frédéric Mistral, tel. 04 90 34 00 23, fax 04 90 34 91 72, www.hoteldeprovence84.com, hoteldeprovence84@orange.fr).

Orange Connections

From Orange by Train to: Avignon (10/day, 15 min), **Arles** (4/day direct, 35 min, more with transfer in Avignon), **Lyon** (16/day, 2 hrs).

By Bus to: Châteauneuf-du-Pape (1/day, none Sun, 30 min), **Vaison la Romaine** (3–5/day, 45 min), **Avignon** (3–5/day, 45 min—take the train instead). Buses to Vaison la Romaine and other wine

THE CÔTES DU RHONE

villages depart from the gare SNCF and from place Pourtoules (turn right out of the Roman Theater, and right again onto rue Pourtoules).

Near Orange: Châteauneuf-du-Pape

This most famous of the Côtes du Rhône wine villages is busy with tourists eager to sample its famous product and stroll its climbing lanes. While I prefer the less-famous wine villages farther north (described under "The Best of the Côtes du Rhône Villages," later in this chapter), this welcoming wine-drenched town makes an easy day trip from Avignon, and works well with a visit to nearby Orange.

Châteauneuf-du-Pape means "New Castle of the Pope," named for the pope's summer retreat—now a ruin capping the beautiful-to-see but little-to-do hill town (more interesting during the Friday market). Wine-loving popes planted the first vines here in the 1300s. The pope's crest is embossed on all bottles of this deservedly famous wine.

Approaching from Avignon, signs announce, "Here start the vineyards of Châteauneuf-du-Pape." Pull over and stroll into a vineyard with a view of the hill town. Notice the rocky soil—perfect for making a good wine grape. Those stones retain the sun's heat (plentiful here) and force the vines to struggle, resulting in a lean grape—lousy for eating, but ideal for producing big wines (see "Côtes du Rhône Wines," page 49). Eight different grapes are blended to make the local specialty, which has been strictly controlled for 80 years. Grenache is the most prominent grape in the blend. The most interesting white wines in Provence are also made here (a blend of up to five grapes), but the reds are what attract most visitors.

The **Wine Museum** (Musée du Vin) provides useful background for your Côtes du Rhône exploration (free, daily 9:00–12:00 & 14:00–18:00, on route d'Avignon, at start of the village if coming from Avignon, tel. 04 90 83 70 07). After a brief self-guided tour of the winemaking process (English explanations in the notebooks reward good students), enjoy a tasting. You'll need to tell them what you want; see "French Wine Lingo," page 47. For a clear contrast, taste a "ready-to-drink" wine (*prêt à boire;* preh tah bwar), then a wine from "old vines" (*vieille vignes;* vee-yay-ee veen-yuh).

A handy way to sample this prestigious product is to find the **Cave du Verger des Papes,** where Jean-Baptiste is dying to help you understand the wines of Châteauneuf-du-Pape. Speaking fluent English and offering wines from 50 different producers (including his own) in his stone-vaulted tasting cellar, he provides an ideal introduction to the area wines (careful—he's a good salesman, and pushes his wines in particular). You'll taste two whites and four reds, and if you like what you taste, he can ship directly to your home at fair rates (March–Dec daily 11:00–19:00, closed Jan–Feb, tel. 04 90 83 50 94, www.caveduverger.com). On foot, follow brown *Château* signs to the top of town. By car, drive to the very top of the village, following *Château* signs (fine views at the top), park at the ruined castle, then stroll a block into the village. And if you're visiting the village of Gigondas on this chapter's wine road tour, ask about their new *cave* there.

The town **TI** has a long list of other wineries that welcome visitors (Mon–Sat 9:00–12:30 & 14:00–18:00, closed Sun, place du Portail, tel. 04 90 83 71 08).

Eating in Châteauneuf-du-Pape: If it's time to eat, **La Mère Germaine** has been the place to go in Châteauneuf since 1922, and still offers the town's most attractive combination of ambience and cuisine. Green booths, rose walls, and a happy loyal clientele decorate the bistro (daily for lunch and dinner, €16 lunch *plats*, €20–24 *menus*, just up from the TI at 3 rue de Commandant Lemaitre, tel. 04 90 83 54 37).

Côtes du Rhône

The Côtes du Rhône region features classic Provençal scenery, characteristic villages, cozy wineries, fields of fragrant lavender, and excellent restaurants. If you're sleeping in this area, Vaison la Romaine is a handy home base. Then delve into the region's highlights by following my self-guided driving tour. With more time, dig deeper into the Côtes du Rhône with a drive up Mont Ventoux, a spin around the Drôme Provençale, or a visit to the Ardèche Gorges.

Vaison la Romaine

With quick access to vineyards, villages, and Mont Ventoux, this lively little town of 6,000 makes a great base for exploring the Côtes du Rhône region by car or by bike. You get two villages for the price of one: Vaison la Romaine's "modern" lower city has worthwhile Roman ruins

Vaison la Romaine

B Bus Stop
P Parking
-- Trail

CAVE LA ROMAINE

AVE. G. PERRY

AVE. ST. QUENIN

TO VILLEDIEU, BOLLENE & ORANGE

AVE. MITTERAND

AVE. DES CHORALIES

TO ⑫

PLAYGROUND

POOL

PUYMIN ROMAN RUINS

MUSEUM

AVE. J. MAZEN

AVE. GEN. DE GAULLE

RUE BERN. NOEL

ENTER

R. COL. PARA

LA VILLASSE ROMAN RUINS

POST

RUE BURRUS

COURS POMPEE

TAULIGNAN ⑦

⑩

CATHEDRAL

R. TROGUE

GRAND RUE

⑪

④ ⑨

AVE. VICTOR HUGO

AVE. JULES FERRY

VILLE-

PL. MONTFORT

BASSE

QUAI PASTEUR

QUAI P. GONTARD

⑤

OUVEZE

⑥

PED. ZONE

RUE LOUIS

TO ⑮

QUAI DE VERDUN

ROMAN BRIDGE

RUE HAUTE CHATEAU

RUE CHATEAU

⑧ ② ①

AVE. CESAR GEOFFRAY

R. L'EVECHE

③

R. DES FOURS

RIVER

RUE DE ROI

RUE CHARITE

QUAI MARECHAL FOCH

TO MALAUCENE & MONT VENTOUX

VILLE-HAUTE

CHATEAU

TRAIL

TO LE CRESTET ON FOOT

DCH

1 Hôtel le Beffroi
2 L'Evêché Chambres
3 Hôtel la Fête en Provence
4 Hôtel Burrhus
5 La Bartavelle Restaurant
6 Le Brin d'Olivier Rest.
7 Le Tournesol & La Lyriste Restaurants
8 Bistro du'O Restaurant
9 Café Universal
10 Bike Rental
11 Launderette
12 To Car Rental & Malaucène
13 Bus to Avignon/Orange
14 Bus from Avignon/Orange
15 To Séguret by bike or car

and a lone pedestrian street (but a disappointing main square, place Montfort). The car-free medieval hill town looms above, with meandering cobbled lanes, a dash of art galleries and cafés, and a ruined castle with a good view from its base. (Vaison la Romaine is also a good place to have your hair done, since there are more than 20 hairdressers in this small town.)

Orientation to Vaison la Romaine

The city is split in two by the Ouvèze River. The Roman Bridge connects the more modern lower town (Ville-Basse) with the hill-capping medieval upper town (Ville-Haute).

Tourist Information

The superb TI is in the lower city, between the two Roman ruin sites, at place du Chanoine Sautel (July–Aug Mon–Sat 9:00–19:00,

Sun 9:00–12:00; Sept–June Mon–Sat 9:00–12:00 & 14:00–17:45, Sun 9:00–12:00 except closed Sun Oct–April; tel. 04 90 36 02 11). Say *bonjour* to *charmante* and ever-so-patient Valerie—get bus schedules, ask about festivals and evening programs, and pick up information on walks from Vaison la Romaine. Ask for the English pamphlets on biking and hiking—they have maps and instructions for several bike and walking loops, ranging from easy half-day trips to all-day affairs.

Arrival in Vaison la Romaine

By Bus: The unmarked bus stop to Orange and Avignon is in front of the Cave la Romaine winery. Buses from Orange or Avignon drop you across the street (3–5/day, 45 min from Orange, 1.5 hours from Avignon). Tell the driver you want the stop for the *Office de Tourisme*. When you get off the bus, walk five minutes down avenue Général de Gaulle to reach the TI and recommended hotels.

By Car: Follow signs to *Centre-Ville*, then *Office de Tourisme*; park free across from the TI. Most parking is free in Vaison la Romaine.

Helpful Hints

Market Day: Sleep in Vaison la Romaine on Monday night, and you'll wake to an amazing Tuesday market. But be warned: Mondays are quiet during the day, as many shops close (but sights are open). If you spend a Monday night, avoid parking at market sites, or you won't find your car where you left it (if signs indicate *Stationnement Interdit le Mardi*, don't park there—ask your hotel where you can park).

Internet Access: Cybercafés come and go here—ask the TI for a recommendation. For free Wi-Fi, head to **Café Universal** on place Montfort.

Laundry: The self-service **Laverie la Lavandière** is on cours Taulignan, near avenue Victor Hugo (daily 8:00–22:00). The friendly owners, who work next door at the dry cleaners, will do your laundry while you sightsee—when you pick up your laundry, thank them with a small tip (dry cleaners open Mon–Sat 9:00–12:00 & 15:00–19:00, closed Sun).

Bike Rental: Try **Mag 2 Roues,** in the lower town on cours Taulignan (tel. 04 90 28 80 46).

Taxi: To get a taxi, call 04 90 36 00 04 or 06 22 28 24 49.

Car Rental: ADA has cheap rates (open daily, 24 avenue Jules Ferry, tel. 06 22 76 55 86). Wallgreen has a few cars for rent at **Vaison Pneus** (closed Sun, avenue Marcel Pagnol, tel. 04 90 28 73 54).

Local Guide: Let sincere and knowledgeable **Anna-Marie Melard** bring those Roman ruins to life for you (€55/80-min tour, tel. 04 90 36 50 48).

Cooking Classes: Charming **Barbara Schuerenberg** offers reasonably priced, easygoing cooking classes from her home in Vaison la Romaine (€60, includes lunch, tel. 04 90 35 68 43, www.cuisinedeprovence.com, barbara@cuisinedeprovence .com).

Sights in Vaison la Romaine

Roman Ruins—Ancient Vaison la Romaine had a treaty that gave it the preferred "federated" relationship with Rome (rather than simply being a colony). This, along with a healthy farming economy (olives and vineyards), made it a most prosperous place...as a close look at its sprawling ruins demonstrates. About 6,000 people called Vaison la Romaine home 2,000 years ago. When the barbarians arrived, the Romans were forced

out, and the townspeople fled into the hills (see the sidebar on page 166). Here's something to ponder: The town has only recently reached the same population it had during its Roman era.

Vaison la Romaine's Roman ruins are split by a modern road into two sites: Puymin and La Villasse. Each is well-presented

THE COTES DU RHONE

with some English information panels (less necessary if you use the audioguide), offering a good look at life during the Roman Empire. The Roman town extended all the way to the river, and its forum lies under place Montfort. What you can see is only a small fraction of the Roman town's extent—most is still buried under today's city.

Visit **Puymin** first. Nearest the entry are the scant but impressive ruins of a sprawling mansion. Find the faint remains of a col-

orful frescoed wall. Climb the hill to the good little museum (pick up your audioguide here; exhibits also explained in English loaner booklet). Behind the museum is a 6,000-seat theater that is well used today, with just enough seats for the whole town (of yesterday and today). Back across the modern road in **La Villasse,** you'll explore a "street of shops" and the foundations of more houses. You'll also see a few wells, used before Vaison's two aqueducts were built.

Cost and Hours: €8 Roman ruins combo-ticket includes both ruins, a helpful audioguide, and the cloister at the Notre-Dame de Nazareth Cathedral (see below); daily April–Sept 9:30–18:00, Oct–March 10:00–12:00 & 14:00–17:00.

Lower Town (Ville-Basse)—Vaison la Romaine's nondescript modern town stretches from its car-littered main square, place Montfort. The cafés grab the north side of the square, conveniently sheltered from the prevailing mistral wind, enjoying the generous shade of the ubiquitous plane *(platane)* trees (cut back each year to form a leafy canopy; see sidebar on page 251). A few blocks away, the stout **Notre-Dame de Nazareth Cathedral**—with an evocative cloister—is a good example of Provençal Romanesque (cloister entry-€1.50, or covered by €8 Roman ruins combo-ticket, daily 15:00–19:00). The pedestrian-only Grand Rue is a lively shopping street leading to the small river gorge and the Roman Bridge.

Roman Bridge—The Romans cut this sturdy, no-nonsense vault into the canyon rock 2,000 years ago, and it has survived ever since. Find the information panel at the new town end of the bridge. Until the 20th century, this was the only way to cross the Ouvèze River. The stone plaque on the wall *(Septembre 22-92...)* shows the high-water mark of the record flood that killed 30 people and washed away the valley's other bridges. The flood swept away the modern top of this bridge...but couldn't budge the 55-foot Roman arch.

Upper Town (Ville-Haute)—While there's nothing of particular importance to see in the fortified medieval old town atop the hill, the cobbled lanes and enchanting fountains make you want to break out a sketchpad. Vaison la Romaine had a prince-bishop since the fourth century. He came under attack by the Count of Toulouse in the 12th century. Anticipating a struggle, the prince-bishop abandoned the lower town and built a château on this rocky outcrop (about 1195). Over time, the rest of the townspeople followed, vacating the lower town and building their homes at the base of the château behind the upper town's fortified wall.

To reach the upper town, hike up from the Roman Bridge (passing memorials for both world wars) through the medieval gate, under the lone tower crowned by an 18th-century wrought-iron bell cage. The château is closed, but a steep, uneven trail to it rewards hikers with a fine view.

▲▲Market Day—In the 16th century, the pope gave Vaison la Romaine market-town status. Each Tuesday since then, the town has hosted a farmers market. Today merchants gather with gusto, turning the entire place into a festival of produce and Provençal products. This Tuesday-morning market is one of France's best, but it can challenge claustrophobes. Be warned that parking is a real headache unless you arrive early (see "Helpful Hints," earlier in this chapter; for tips on enjoying market day, see the Shopping chapter).

Wine-Tasting—Cave la Romaine, a five-minute walk up avenue Général de Gaulle from the TI, offers a variety of good-value wines from nearby villages in a pleasant, well-organized tasting room (daily 8:30–13:00 & 14:00–19:00, avenue St. Quenin, tel. 04 90 36 55 90, www.cave-la-romaine.com).

Hiking—The TI has good information on relatively easy hikes into the hills above Vaison la Romaine. It's about 75 minutes to the tiny hill town of Le Crestet, though views begin immediately. To find this trail, drive or walk past the upper town (with the castle just on your left), find the *chemin des Fontaines*, and stay the course as far as you like. Cars are not allowed on the road after about a mile. Consider taking a taxi to Le Crestet, and walking back (Le Crestet is described on page 168). The TI also has information on a loop hike from Vaison la Romaine to Crestet (a newer village below the older hillside town of Le Crestet)—it follows the same path to Le Crestet, with a different return route.

Biking—This area is not particularly flat, and if it's hot and windy, bike-riding is a dicey option. But if it's calm, the five-mile ride to cute little Villedieu (recommended restaurant described on page 177) is a delight. The bike route is signed along small roads; you'll find signs from Vaison la Romaine to Villedieu at the roundabout past Cave La Romaine toward Orange (see map on page 156). With a bit more energy, you can pedal beyond Villedieu on the lovely road to Mirabel (ask in Villedieu for directions—*oo ay mee-rah-bell?*) Or get a good map and connect the following villages for an enjoyable 11-mile loop ride: Vaison la Romaine, St. Romain-en-Viennois, Puyméras (with a recommended restaurant—see page 175), Faucon, and St. Marcellin-lès-Vaison. The TI and bike shop have good information on mountain-biking trails.

Swimming—For a fun river swim beneath a fine Roman bridge, drive or bike to the Ouvèze River near Entrechaux, and find the St. Michel Bridge (described on page 179).

Sleeping in Vaison la Romaine

Hotels in Vaison la Romaine are a good value. Those in the medieval upper town (Ville-Haute) are quieter, cozier, and cooler, but require a 15-minute walk to the TI and Roman ruins. If staying at one of the first three places, follow signs to *Cité Médiévale* and park just outside the upper village entry (driving into the Cité Médiévale itself is a challenge, with tiny lanes and nearly impossible parking). If you have a car, consider staying in one of the charming Côtes du Rhône villages near Vaison la Romaine (see "Sleeping Along the Côtes du Rhône," page 173).

$$$ Hôtel le Beffroi*** hides deep in the upper town, just above a demonstrative bell tower (you'll hear what I mean). It offers 16th-century red-tile-and-wood-beamed-cozy lodgings with nary a level surface. The rooms—split between two buildings a few doors apart—are Old World comfy, and some have views. You'll also find tasteful public spaces, a garden with view tables (light meals available in the summer), a small pool with more views, and animated Nathalie at the reception (standard Db-€95–115, superior

---

Sleep Code

(€1 = about $1.40, country code: 33)

S = Single, **D** = Double/Twin, **T** = Triple, **Q** = Quad, **b** = bathroom, **s** = shower only, ***** = French hotel rating system (0-4 stars). Unless otherwise noted, credit cards are accepted and English is spoken.

To help you sort easily through these listings, I've divided the rooms into three categories based on the price for a standard double room with bath:

$$$ Higher Priced—Most rooms €85 or more.
$$ Moderately Priced—Most rooms between €55–85.
$ Lower Priced—Most rooms €55 or less.

Db-€145, Tb-€170, rue de l'Evêché, tel. 04 90 36 04 71, fax 04 90 36 24 78, www.le-beffroi.com, info@le-beffroi.com). The hotel's restaurant offers *menus* from €28.

$$$ L'Evêché Chambres, almost next door to le Beffroi in the upper town (look for the ivy), is a five-room melt-in-your-chair B&B. The owners (the Verdiers) own the art boutique across the street, have an exquisite sense of interior design, and are passionate about books, making this place feel like a cross between a library and an art gallery (Sb-€75–90, standard Db-€85–100, Db suite-€115–140, the *solanum* suite is worth every euro, Tb-€120–160, Internet access and Wi-Fi, rue de l'Evêché, tel. 04 90 36 13 46, fax 04 90 36 32 43, http://eveche.free.fr, eveche@aol.com).

$$ Hôtel la Fête en Provence, conveniently located for drivers at the entry to the medieval upper town, has a variety of room shapes and sizes. All the rooms are chiffon-comfortable, and several have small kitchenettes. Rooms are located around a calming courtyard, and there's a pool and Jacuzzi next door (standard Db-€80, bigger Db with king-size bed and bath-€110, extra person-€15, Cité Médiévale, tel. & fax 04 90 36 36 43, www.hotellafete-provence .com, fete-en-provence@wanadoo.fr). Their apartments (€155) sleep up to six people, and come with a kitchenette and sitting area.

$ Hôtel Burrhus** is part art gallery, part funky hotel—and the best value in the lower town. It's a central, laid-back, go-with-the-flow place, with a broad terrace over the raucous place Montfort (the double-paned windows are effective, but for maximum quiet, request a back room). Its floor plan will confound even the ablest navigator. The bigger, newer rooms—with contemporary decor, bigger bathrooms, and air-conditioning—are worth the extra euros for most travelers (Db-€54–60, newer Db-€64–98, Qb apartment-€133, extra bed-€15, air-con in some rooms, free Internet access and Wi-Fi, 1 place Montfort, tel. 04 90 36 00 11, fax 04 90 36 39 05, www.burrhus.com, info@burrhus.com).

Eating in Vaison la Romaine

Vaison la Romaine offers a handful of excellent places—arrive by 19:30 or reserve ahead, particularly on weekends. And while you can eat very well on a moderate budget in Vaison, it's well worth venturing to nearby Côtes du Rhône villages to eat (see "Eating Along the Côtes du Rhône," page 175). Wherever you dine, begin with a fresh glass of Muscat from the nearby village of Beaumes de Venise.

La Bartavelle is a fine place to savor traditional French cuisine in the lower town. Owner Berangère (bear-ahn-zher) has put together a tourist-friendly mix-and-match menu of local options. You get access to the top-end selections even on the €22 bottom-end *menu*—just fewer courses. Be sure to reserve ahead (closed Mon, small terrace outside, air-con and pleasant interior, 12 place de Sus Auze, tel. 04 90 36 02 16).

Le Brin d'Olivier is the most romantic place I list, with soft lighting, hushed conversations, earth tones, and a menu that celebrates Provence (€29 *menu*, closed Wed, 4 rue du Ventoux, tel. 04 90 28 74 79).

Le Tournesol offers a good €18 dinner, with mostly Provençal dishes, rose walls, and friendly service. I love the *aubergine feuilleté* (eggplant puff pastry) and lamb with cheese. Show this book to get a free *kir* (daily, 30 cours Taulignan, tel. 04 90 36 09 18, owner Patrick speaks a little English).

La Lyriste, named for the loudest "singing" *cigale* (cicada), puts cuisine above decor. Marie serves what hubby Benoit cooks. Both are shy, yet proud of their restaurant. There's a fine *menu* for €19, but go for the slightly pricier *menus,* which are inventive and *très delectable* (closed Mon, indoor and outdoor seating, 45 cours Taulignan, tel. 04 90 36 04 67).

Bistro du'O, in the upper village, is the buzz of Vaison's yuppie crowd. Reserve ahead and you'll dine on soft leather chairs under soaring stone arches and enjoy mouthwatering cuisine that is creatively presented yet affordable. The lamb is terrific (*menus* from €29, closed Sun, rue du Château, tel. 04 90 41 72 90).

Hôtel le Beffroi's garden is just right for a light dinner in the summer (*menus* from €28, recommended earlier under "Sleeping in Vaison la Romaine").

Vaison la Romaine Connections

The most central bus stop is at Cave Vinicole.

From Vaison la Romaine by Bus to: Avignon (5/day during school year—called *période scolaire*, otherwise 3/day, 1.5 hrs; much faster to bus to Orange and train from there), **Orange** (3–5/day, 45 min), **Nyons** (2–3/day, 45 min), **Crestet** (lower village below Le Crestet, 2/day, 5 min), **Carpentras** (2/day, 45 min). Bus info: tel. 04 90 36 05 22.

The Best of the Côtes du Rhône Villages

Officially, the Côtes du Rhône vineyards follow the Rhône River from just south of Lyon to Avignon. Our focus is the southern section of the Côtes du Rhône, centering on the small area between Châteauneuf-du-Pape and Vaison la Romaine. This area is best toured by car or bike. My self-guided driving tour (see next page) starts in the village of Séguret, then returns to Vaison la Romaine and winds clockwise around the Dentelles de Montmirail, visiting the mountaintop village of Le Crestet, adorable little

THE CÔTES DU RHÔNE

Suzette, and the renowned wine villages of Beaumes de Venise and Gigondas. I've listed several wineries *(domaines)* along the way. Before you go, study up with "Provençal Wine-Tasting 101" on page 48. Even if wine isn't your thing, don't miss this scenic drive.

Planning Your Time

While seeing the Côtes du Rhône is possible as a day trip by car from Arles or Avignon, you'll have a more enjoyable and intimate experience if you sleep in one of the villages (my favorite accommodations are listed under "Sleeping Along the Côtes du Rhône" on page 173).

With a car, the best one-day plan is to take the driving tour described below (allow an entire day for the 80-mile round-trip from Avignon). Try to get the first two stops done before lunch (most wineries are closed 12:00–14:00), then complete the loop in the afternoon. Some wineries are closed on Sundays, holidays, and during the harvest (mid-Sept). This route is picnic-friendly, but there are few shops along the way—stock up before you leave.

Getting Around the Côtes du Rhône Villages

This area is clearly easiest if you have four wheels. Without a car, it's tougher, but a representative sampling is doable by **bike** (for ideas, see "Biking" on page 160) or by **bus** (3–5 buses/day from Avignon and Orange stop at several Côtes du Rhône villages; consider taking the bus one-way, then returning by taxi). For less effort and more expense, **Wine Safari Tours** is happy to follow this route (see "Tours of Provence," page 40).

Self-Guided Driving Tour

The Côtes du Rhône Wine Road

This tour introduces you to the characteristic best of the Côtes du Rhône wine road. While circling the rugged Dentelles de Montmirail mountain peaks, you'll experience all that's unique about this region: its natural beauty, glowing limestone villages, inviting wineries, and rolling hills of vineyards. As you drive, notice how some vineyards grow at angles—they're planted this way to compensate for the strong effect of the mistral wind.

This trip provides a crash course in Rhône Valley wine, an excuse to meet the locals who make the stuff, and breathtaking scenery—especially late in the day, when the famous Provençal sunlight causes colors to absolutely pop.

The many fine restaurants along the way are another highlight of the route. I've mentioned some of my favorites; you'll find much

Côtes du Rhône Driving Tour

5 MILES
10 KM

TO NYONS & GRIGNAN
D-94
MIRABEL
TO ARDECHE GORGES
D-94
D-7
VILLE-DIEU
D-938
PUYMERAS
FAUCON
TO BUIS LE BARONNIES
ROAIX
D-935
D-8
RASTEAU
CAIRANNE
D-69
BIKE LOOP
ENTRE-CHAUX
D-5
D-40
TO LE BRANTES
VAISON LA ROMAINE
SEGURET
D-88
PATH
DENTELLES DE MONTMIRAIL
LE CRESTET
D-13
MALAUCENE
SABLET
D-975
GIGONDAS
SUZETTE
D-90
D-974
TO MONT VENTOUX
TO ORANGE & AVIGNON
VACQUEYRAS
LAFARE
D-19
BEDOIN
D-974
LA ROQUE ALRIC
LE BARROUX
TO MONT VENTOUX
TO ORANGE & A-7
D-977
BEAUMES DE VENISE
D-7
D-938
D-974
D-950
CARPENTRAS
D-942
TO AVIGNON
D-942
D-49
D-938
TO ISLE-SUR-LA-SORGUE & LUBERON
DCH

❶ Séguret
❷ Domaine de Mourchon Winery
❸ Le Crestet
❹ La Col de la Chaîne Mountain Pass
❺ Suzette
❻ Domaine de Coyeux Winery
❼ Domaine de Durban Winery
❽ Gigondas

more detail about these under "Eating Along the Côtes du Rhône" on page 175.

Our tour starts just south of Vaison la Romaine in little Séguret. This town is best for a visit early or late, when it's quieter. (If you get a late start or prefer ending your tour here, begin the tour in Le Crestet—stop #3—and save the first two stops for last.)

• *From Vaison la Romaine, the easiest way to reach Séguret is to follow signs for* Orange, *then look for the turnoff to Séguret in a few minutes.*

The Life of a Hill Town in Provence

Heat-seeking northerners have made Provence's hill towns prosperous and worldly. But before the 1960s, nobody wanted to live in these sun-drenched, rock-top settings. Like lost ships in search of safe harbor, the people of long ago took refuge here only out of necessity.

When the Romans settled Provence (125 B.C.), they brought stability to the warring locals, and hill-towners descended en masse to the Roman cities (such as Arles, Orange, Nîmes, and Vaison la Romaine). There they enjoyed theaters, fresh water from aqueducts, and commercial goods brought via the Roman road that stretched from Spain to Italy (passing along the northern edge of the Luberon).

When Rome fell (A.D. 476), barbarians swept in to rape and pillage, forcing locals back up into the hills, where they'd stay for almost 1,000 years. These "Dark Ages" were when many of the villages we see today were established. Most grew up around castles, since peasants depended on their lord for security. The hill-towners gathered stones from nearby fields and built their homes side by side to form a defensive wall, terracing the hillsides to maximize the scarce arable land. They would gather inside heavy-stone Romanesque churches to pray for salvation. Medieval life was not easy behind those walls—there were barbarians, plagues, crop failures, droughts, thieves, wars, and the everyday battle with gravity.

As the Renaissance approached, and Provence came under the protection of an increasingly centralized French nation, barbarian invasions dwindled. Just when the hill-towners thought the coast was clear to relocate down below, France's religious wars (1500s) chased them back up. As Protestants and Catholics duked it out, hilltop villages prospered, welcoming refugees. Little Séguret (pop. 100 today) had almost 1,000 residents; the village of Mérindol (near Avignon) sprouted from nowhere; and Fort de Buoux (near Apt, nothing but ruins today) was an impregnable fortress (see page 215). The turmoil of the Revolution (1789) continued to make the above-the-fray hill towns desirable.

Over the next century, hill towns slept peacefully as the rest of France modernized. Most of the hill towns you'll visit housed

THE COTES DU RHONE

By bike, or for a more scenic drive, cross to the Cité Médiévale side of the river in Vaison la Romaine, then follow D-977 signs downriver to Séguret.

❶ Séguret

Blending into the hillside with a smattering of shops, two cafés, made-to-stroll lanes, and a natural spring, this hamlet is understandably popular. Séguret makes for a good coffee or dinner between 200 and 600 people and were self-sufficient, producing just what was needed (farmers, lawyers, and telemarketers were at equilibrium). Many town fountains and communal washrooms date from this time. Animals were everywhere, outnumbering humans four to one.

But 20th-century life down below required fewer stairs—and was closer to the convenience of trains, planes, and automobiles. So after World War I, down the hill-towners moved. To build in the flatlands, they pillaged the hill towns' stones, roof tiles, you name it, leaving those villages in ruin. By mid-century, most of these lovely villages became virtual ghost towns (in 1965, Le Crestet had but 15 residents—less than a third of its current, still-tiny population).

In recent years, hill towns have bounced back. Lavender production took off, and the government launched irrigation projects. But most of all, real estate boomed as Parisians, northern Europeans, and (to a lesser extent) North Americans discovered the rustic charm of hill-town life. They invested huge sums—far more than most locals could afford—to turn ancient stone structures into modern vacation homes (in many cases, buying several houses and combining them into one). Today's hill towns survive in part thanks to these outsiders' deep pockets.

Today, many villages have organizations to preserve their traditions and buildings (such as Les Amis de Séguret, or "Friends of Séguret"). Made up of older residents, groups like these raise money, sponsor festivals and dances, and even write collective histories of their villages. Many fear that younger folks won't have the motivation to carry on this tradition.

But hope springs eternal, as there may be a movement of locals back to these villages. Some northerners are finding hill-town life less romantic as their knee replacements fail. Meanwhile, the popularity of organic produce makes it financially viable for hill-town farmers with smaller plots to pursue their healthy dreams of living off the land. Finally, the Internet has allowed some hill-towners to live in remote villages and telecommute, rather than move into bigger cities. Could the cycle be restarting? Armed with their laptops, will hill-towners once again prosper when the next wave of barbarians comes?

stop (restaurants recommended on page 175).

Séguret's name comes from the Latin word *securitas* (meaning "secure"). The bulky entry arch came with a massive gate, which drilled in the message of the village's name. In the Middle Ages, Séguret was patrolled 24/7—they never took their *securitas* for granted. Walk through the arch. To appreciate how the homes' outer walls provided security in those days, drop down the first passage on your right (near the fountain). These exit passages, or *poternes,* were needed in periods of peace to allow the town to expand below.

Find Séguret's open washbasin *(lavoir),* a hotbed of social activity and gossip over the ages. The basins behind the fountain (now planted) were reserved for washing animals (which outnumbered residents in the Middle Ages); the larger ones (on the left) were for laundry only. Public washbasins like this were used right up until World War II. Farther on, the community bread oven *(four banal)* was used for festivals and celebrations. Rue Calade leads to the unusual 12th-century church for views (the circular village you see below is Sablet). This rock-sculpted church is usually closed, but it's worth a look from the outside. High above, a castle once protected Séguret, but all that's left today is a tower that you can barely make out (trails provide access). At Christmas, this entire village transforms itself into one big crèche scene—a Provençal tradition that has long since died out in other villages. To sleep well or have a fine meal with lavish views, land a room or a table at the recommended **La Table du Comtat,** just beyond the rock-sculpted church.

• *Signs near Séguret's parking will lead you up, up and away to our next stop, Domaine de Mourchon.*

❷ Domaine de Mourchon

This high-flying new winery has become the buzz of the Côtes du Rhône by blending state-of-the-art technology with traditional

winemaking methods (a dazzling ring of stainless-steel vats holds wines grown on land plowed by horses). The wines are winning the respect of international critics, yet the (Scottish) owners seem eager to help anyone understand Rhône Valley wines. Language is not an issue here, nor is a lack of stunning views. Free English tours of the vineyards are offered once a week (likely Wed at 17:00, check their website or call to verify; open daily 10:00–12:00 & 14:00–18:00, tel. 04 90 46 70 30, www.domainedemourchon.com).

• *Next, return to Vaison la Romaine and follow signs toward* Carpentras/Malaucène. *After passing through Crestet, you'll come to Le Crestet (on D-938). Look for signs leading up to* Le Village *and park at its entry.*

❸ Le Crestet

This village—founded after the fall of the Roman Empire, when people banded together in high places like this for protection from marauding barbarians—followed the usual hill-town evolution (see sidebar). The outer walls of the village did double duty as ramparts and house walls. The castle above (from about A.D. 850) provided a final safe haven when the village was attacked.

The Bishop of Vaison la Romaine was the first occupant, lending little Le Crestet a certain prestige. With about 500 residents in 1200, Le Crestet was a very important town in this region, reaching its zenith in the mid-1500s, when 660 people called it home. Le Crestet's gradual decline started when the bishop moved to Vaison la Romaine in the 1600s, though the population remained fairly stable until World War II. Today, about 35 people live within the walls year-round (about 55 during the summer).

Wander the peaceful lanes and appreciate the amount of work it took to put these stones in place. Notice the elaborate water channels. Le Crestet was served by 18 cisterns in the Middle Ages, and disputes over water were a common problem. The peaceful church (might be closed, €0.50 turns the lights on) has a beautiful stained-glass window behind the altar. Imagine hundreds of people living here, and animals roaming everywhere. Get to the top of town. The village's only business, the recommended café-restaurant **Le Panoramic,** has an upstairs terrace with a view that justifies the name...even if the food is overpriced and mediocre.

Walkers can return to Vaison la Romaine along a scenic footpath. The trail leaves from the very top of the village, at the upper, non-château end. Look for the brown sign, which indicates that it's eight kilometers (5 miles) to Vaison la Romaine, and—in a few steps—turn right, following the yellow sign that shows it's 5.1 kilometers (3 miles) to Vaison la Romaine.

• *Drivers should carry on and reconnect with the road below, following signs to* Malaucène. *As you near Malaucène, look for the huge boules courts separated by logs (on your left). Entering Malaucène, turn right on D-90 (direction: Suzette) just before the gas station. As you climb to the mountain pass, look for signs on the left to* La Col de la Chaîne *(Chain Pass). From this point on, the scenery gets better fast.*

❹ La Col de la Châine Mountain Pass

Get out of your car at the pass (about 1,500 feet) and enjoy the breezy views. Wander about. The peaks in the distance—thrusting up like the back of a stegosaurus or a bad haircut (you decide)—are the Dentelles de Montmirail, a small range running just nine miles basically north to south and reaching 2,400 feet in elevation. This region's land is constantly shifting. Those rocky tops were the result of a gradual uplifting of the land, then were blown bald by the angry mistral wind. Below, pine and oak trees mix with scotch broom, which blooms brilliant yellow in May and June. The village below the peaks is Suzette (you'll be there soon). The yellow-signed hiking trail leads to the castle-topped village of Le Barroux (3.5 miles, mostly downhill).

The scene is lovely and surprisingly undeveloped. You can thank the lack of water for the absence of more homes or farms in this area. Water is everything in this parched region, and if you don't have ready access to it, you can't build or cultivate the land. (Some farmers have drilled down as far as 1,300 feet to try to find water.) With no water at hand, farmers here lie awake at night worrying about fire. Hot summers, dry pines, and windy days make a scary recipe for fast-traveling fires.

Now turn around and face Mont Ventoux. Are there clouds in the horizon? You're looking into the eyes of the Alps (behind Ventoux), and those "foothills" help keep Provence sunny.

• *Time to push on. You'll pass countless yellow trail signs along this drive. (The Dentelles provide fertile ground for walking trails.) To sleep nearby, try La Ferme Dégoutaud, just ahead (described on page 175). With the medieval castle of Le Barroux topping the horizon in the distance (off to the left), drive on to little...*

❺ Suzette

Tiny Suzette floats on its hilltop, with a small 12th-century chapel, one café, a handful of residents, and the gaggle of houses where they live. Park in Suzette's lot, below, then find the big orientation board above the lot (Rome is 620 kilometers—385 miles—away). Look out to the broad shoulders of Mont Ventoux. At 6,000 feet, it always seems to have some clouds hanging around. If it's clear, the top looks like it's snow-covered; if you drive up there, you'll see it's actually white stone (see the Mont Ventoux drive, page 177). If it's very cloudy, the mountain takes on a dark, foreboding appearance.

Look to the village. A sign asks you to *Respectez son Calme* (respect its peace). Suzette's homes once lived in the shadow of an imposing castle, destroyed during the religious wars of the mid-1500s. The recommended **Les Coquelicots** café makes a good lunch or drink stop. Good picnic tables lie just past Suzette on our route. Back across the road from the orientation table is a tasting room for **Château Redortier** wines (English brochure and well-explained list of wines provided; skip their whites, but try the good rosés and reds).

• *If you're enjoying the views and can't get enough of this landscape, consider adding this 20-minute detour from Suzette: Drive down to Le Barroux, then loop back to D-90 via the rock-swirled village of La Roque Alric, and rejoin our route in La Fare.*

Otherwise, continue from Suzette in the direction of Beaumes de Venise. You'll drop down into the lush little village of La Fare. Here, joyriders can take another 20-minute detour into

---

Cicadas *(Cigales)*

In the countryside, listen for *les cigales*. They sing in the heat and are famous for announcing the arrival of summer. (Locals say their song also marks the coming of the tourists...and more money.) People here love these ugly, long-winged bugs, an integral part of Provençal life. You'll see souvenir cicadas made out of every material possible. If you look closely—they are well-camouflaged—you can find live specimens on tree trunks and branches. Cicadas live for about two years, all but the last two weeks of which are spent quietly underground as larvae. But when they go public, their chirping begins with each sunrise and goes nonstop until sunset.

---

the mountains by taking a sharp right on entering the village, following Dentelles de Montmirail signs. The Domaine de Cassan winery lies near the end of the road that also leads to the Col du Cayron hiking trail (to the village of Gigondas). Your partner could drop you off and meet you in Gigondas (it's a 1.5-hour walk over the pass).

But La Fare's best wine-tasting opportunity is back on our route just after leaving the village, at...

❻ Domaine de Coyeux

The private road winds up and up to this impossibly beautiful setting, with the best views of the Dentelles I've found. Olive trees

line the final approach, and *Le Caveau* signs lead to a modern tasting room (you may need to ring the buzzer). These wines have earned their excellent reputation (and are now available in the US). Start with their delectable Côtes du Rhône Villages red, and finish with their trademark dry and sweet Muscats (wines range from €7–13 per bottle, Mon–Sat 10:00–12:00 & 14:00–18:00, closed Sun except May–Aug, tel. 04 90 12 42 42, staff a tad formal, some English spoken). After tasting, take time to wander about the vineyards.

• *Drive on toward Beaumes de Venise. You'll soon pass the recommended* **Côté Vignes**, *a fine place for lunch or dinner. Next you'll drop out of the hills as you approach Beaumes de Venise. To find the next winery, keep right at the first* Centre-Ville *sign as the road bends left, then carefully track* Domaine de Durban *signs for three scenic miles to...*

THE CÔTES DU RHÔNE

❼ Domaine de Durban

Find the small tasting room and let your young hostess take your taste buds on a tour. This *domaine* produces appealing whites,

reds, and Muscats. Start with the 100 percent Viognier (€4.50 a bottle), then try their Viognier–Chardonnay blend. Their rosé is light and refreshing (and cheap). Their three reds are very different from each other: One is fruity, one is tannic (aged in oak), and one has some fruit and tannin. Finish with their popular Muscat de Venise (wines cost €4–10 per bottle, Mon–Sat 9:00–12:00 & 14:00–18:30, closed Sun, tel. 04 90 62 94 26). Picnics are not allowed, and the grass is off-limits, though strolling amid the gorgeous vineyards is OK.

• *Retrace your route to Beaumes de Venise, turn left at the bottom, then make a quick right and navigate through Beaumes de Venise, following signs for* Vacqueyras. *At a big roundabout, you'll pass Beaumes de Venise's massive cave coopérative, which represents many growers in this area (big selection, but too slick for my taste; daily 8:30–12:30 & 14:00–19:00). Continue following signs for* Vacqueyras *(a famous wine village with another cave coopérative), and then signs for* Gigondas *and* Vaison par la route touristique. *As you enter Gigondas, follow signs to the TI and park on or near the tree-shaded square.*

❽ Gigondas

This town produces some of the region's best reds and is ideally situated for hiking, mountain-biking, and driving into the mountains. The **TI** has a list of wineries, *chambres d'hôte*, and good hikes or drives (Mon–Sat 10:00–12:30 & 14:00–18:00, likely closed Sun, place du Portail, tel. 04 90 65 85 46, www.gigondas-dm.fr). The €2.50 *Chemins et Sentiers du Massif des Dentelles* hiking map is helpful, though not critical, since routes are well-signed. The blue route makes a good one-hour round-trip high above Gigondas to superb views (walk up the steep road from the Mairie next to the TI and follow blue markers toward the Dentelles). You can extend this hike into a three-hour loop. At the least, take a short walk through the village lanes above the TI—the church is an easy destination with good views over the heart of the Côtes du Rhône vineyards.

Several good tasting opportunities can be found on the main square. **Le Caveau de Gigondas** is best, where Sandra and Barbara await your visit with a large and free selection of tiny bottles for sampling, filled directly from the barrel (daily 10:00–12:00 & 14:00–18:30, 2 doors down from TI, tel. 04 90 65 82 29). Here you can compare wines from a variety of private producers in an intimate, low-key surrounding. The provided list of wines is helpful. A self-imposed gag rule (intended to keep staff from favoring the production of a single winery in this co-op showcase) makes it hard to get a strong recommendation here, so it's best to know what you want (see "French Wine Lingo," page 47).

You'll find a small grocery store and several eating options in the village. Diagonally across from the TI, the shaded red tables of **Du Verre à l'Assiette** ("From Glass to Plate") entice lunchtime eaters (also good interior ambience, €10 salads, €14 *plats*, daily, place du Village, tel. 04 90 12 36 64). To dine very well or sleep nearby, find the recommended **Hôtel les Florets**, a half-mile above town (closed Wed).

• From Gigondas, follow signs to the circular wine village of Sablet—with generally inexpensive yet tasty wines (the TI and wine cooperative share a space in the town center)—then past Séguret and back to Vaison la Romaine, where our tour ends.

If you haven't had your fill, consider adding on some...

Villages North of the Côtes du Rhône Drive

Cairanne, toward Orange from Vaison la Romaine, is a pleasant village producing fine wines with one of the best wine *coopératives* in this region. **Grignan,** 30 minutes north of Vaison la Romaine at the northern limit of Provence, is impressively set on a rocky spur and features one of Provence's grandest châteaux (French-only tours).

Sleeping Along the Côtes du Rhône

(€1 = about $1.40, country code: 33)
These accommodations are along the self-guided driving tour route described above. They offer a great opportunity for drivers who want to experience rural France and get better values.

Near Vaison la Romaine

These accommodations are within a 10-minute drive of Vaison la Romaine.

$$$ Domaine de Cabasse*** is a lovely spread flanked by vineyards at the foot of Séguret (with a walking path to the village). Winemaking is their primary business (tastings possible), though the hotel is well-run by its relaxed staff. The 13 rooms have retained a simple Old World feel. All the rooms have decks, and a big pool is at your disposal. From the entry gate—which opens automatically...and slowly—the place appears more formal than it is (Db-€125–140, breakfast-€12.50, Wi-Fi in lobby, on D-23 between Sablet and Séguret, tel. 04 90 46 91 12, fax 04 90 46 94 01, www.cabasse.fr, info@cabasse.fr). The restaurant offers a satisfying, though limited, €29 dinner *menu* served inside or out.

$$$ Hôtel Les Florets**, a half-mile above Gigondas, is surrounded by pine trees at the foothills of the Dentelles de Montmirail. It comes with a huge terrace that Van Gogh would have loved, thoughtfully designed rooms, and a fine restaurant (standard Db-€100–110, superior Db-€125–150, annex rooms are best, tel. 04 90 65 85 01, fax 04 90 65 83 80, www.hotel-lesflorets .com, accueil@hotel-lesflorets.com). For more details about the hotel's restaurant, see page 176.

$$$ Domaine des Tilleuls***, 10 minutes from Vaison la Romaine in workaday Malaucène, is a winning, well-priced refuge, and the most family-friendly place I list. (Welcoming owners Arnould and Dominique have three kids.) Its 20 country-modern rooms fill an old farmhouse overlooking lovely grounds with namesake linden trees *(tilleuls)*, a sandbox, toys, and a large pool. If you missed market day in Vaison la Romaine, sleep here Tuesday night and wake to a bustling market (Db-€84–100, Tb/Qb-€108–120, breakfast-€12, Wi-Fi, well-signed in Malaucène on the route to Mont Ventoux, tel. 04 90 65 22 31, fax 04 90 65 16 77, www.hotel -domainedestilleuls.com, info@hotel-domainedestilleuls.com).

$$ La Table du Comtat is ideal if you want to sleep in adorable little Séguret. Rooms are simple and traditional, and a fair value. Some have views; the terrace and restaurant are a serious draw (Db-€80–110, no air-con, tel. 04 90 46 91 49, www.table -comtat.fr, direction@table-comtat.fr).

$$ L'Ecole Buissonnière Chambres is run by an engaging Anglo-French team, Monique and John, who share their peace and quiet 10 minutes from Vaison la Romaine. This creatively restored farmhouse has three character-filled half-timbered rooms, and convivial public spaces. Getting to know John, who has lived all over the south of France and even worked as a *gardian* (cowboy) in the Camargue, is worth the price of the room; he's also generous with his knowledge of the area. The outdoor kitchen allows guests to picnic in high fashion in the tranquil garden (Db-€56–65, Tb-€75–79, Qb-€90–97, includes breakfast, cash only, Wi-Fi; between Villedieu and Buisson on D-75— leave Vaison following signs to *Villedieu*, then follow *Buisson* and turn left onto D-75; tel. 04 90 28 95 19, ecole.buissonniere@wanadoo .fr). Ask about their all-inclusive stay for groups of four to seven people (includes pickup at airport or train station, winery and region tour, and dinners).

Near Suzette
$$ La Ferme Dégoutaud, a 20-minute drive from Vaison la Romaine, is a splendidly situated, roomy, and utterly isolated *chambre d'hôte* about halfway between Malaucène and Suzette (well-signed, a mile down a dirt road). Animated Véronique (minimal English) rents three country-cozy rooms with many thoughtful touches, a view pool, table tennis, picnic-perfect tables, and a barbecue at your disposal (Db-€70, Tb-€80, Qb-€90, breakfast-€7, tel. & fax 04 90 62 99 29, www.degoutaud.fr, le.degoutaud@wanadoo.fr).

Eating Along the Côtes du Rhône

Drivers enjoy a wealth of country-Provençal dining opportunities in rustic settings, handy to many of the rural accommodations. Many of these eateries are described in my self-guided driving tour route explained above; I've listed them by distance from Vaison la Romaine (nearest to farthest). Most are within a 10-minute drive of Vaison la Romaine. All have some outdoor seating and should be considered for lunch or dinner.

La Girocedre is an enchanting place to eat lunch or dinner if you have a car and it's nice outside. Just three picturesque miles from Vaison la Romaine in adorable Puyméras, this place offers a complete country-Provençal package: outdoor tables placed just-so in a lush garden, warm interior decor, and real Provençal cuisine (€18 three-course lunch *menus,* €13–18 *plats,* à la carte ordering only at dinner, closed Mon, tel. 04 90 46 50 67).

Auberge d'Anaïs, at the end of a dirt road 10 minutes from Vaison la Romaine, is another find—and a true Provençal experience. Outdoor tables gather under cheery lights with grand views and reliable cuisine. Ask for a table *sur la terrasse* (€10 lunch *menu,* good three-course dinner *menus* from €17, closed Mon, tel. 04 90 36 20 06). From Vaison la Romaine, follow signs to *Carpentras,* then *St. Marcellin;* signs will guide you from there.

Le Panoramic, in hill-capping Le Crestet, serves average salads, pizzas, and *plats* for more than you should spend at what must be Provence's greatest view tables. Come for a drink and view, but if you're really hungry, eat elsewhere (open daily for lunch and dinner, tel. 04 90 28 76 42). Drivers should pass on the first parking lot in Le Crestet and keep climbing to park at place du Château. The restaurant is to your right as you face the view.

Domaine de Cabasse lets you dine surrounded by vineyards at a relaxed wine estate/hotel, though you must book ahead. Even with its limited-selection €29 *menu,* it more than merits the short drive from Vaison la Romaine (see hotel listing earlier).

Lavender

Whether or not you travel to Provence during the late-June and July lavender blossom, you'll see and smell examples of this particularly local product everywhere—in shops, on tables in restaurants, and in your hotel room. And if you come during lavender season, you'll experience one of Europe's great color events, where rich fields of purple lavender meet equally rich yellow fields of sunflowers. While lavender season is hot, you'll find the best fields in the cooler hills, since the flowers thrive at higher altitudes. The flowers are harvested in full bloom (beginning in mid-July), then distilled to extract the oils for making soaps and perfume. For a good explanation of this process, visit the Museum of Lavender in Coustellet (see page 206 in the next chapter).

While lavender seems like an indigenous part of the Provence scene, it wasn't cultivated here until about 1920, when it was imported by the local perfume-makers. Since lavender is not native to Provence, growing it successfully requires great care. Three kinds of lavender are grown in Provence: true lavender (traditionally used by perfumemakers), spike lavender, and lavandin (a cloned hybrid of the first two). Today, a majority of Provence lavender fields are lavandin—which is also mass-produced at factories, a trend that is threatening to put the true lavender grower out of business.

Some of the best lavender fields bloom near Vaison la Romaine. Lavender blooms later the higher you go; the ones described here are listed from lowest to highest elevations. For an impressive display, drive north of Vaison la Romaine and ramble the tiny road between Valréas and Vinsobres (D-190 and D-46). You'll see more beautiful fields along D-538 between Nyons and Dieulefit, and still more if you climb Mont Ventoux to Sault (described on the next page).

La Table du Comtat, in charming little Séguret, allows you to combine a village visit with a fine meal and finer views over vineyards and villages. Book a window table in advance, and come while there's still light (€20 lunch *menu*, €35 dinner *menu*, classic French cuisine, closed Tue evening and Wed, tel. 04 90 46 91 49).

Hôtel les Florets, in Gigondas, is a traditional, family-run place that's worth the drive. Dinners are a sumptuous blend of classic French cuisine and Provençal accents, served with class by English-speaking Thierry. The marvelous terrace makes your meal even more memorable (*menus* from €38, restaurant closed Wed, service can be slow; see hotel listing earlier).

La Maison Bleue, on Villedieu's adorable little square, is a pizza-and-salad place with great outdoor ambience. Skip it if the weather forces you inside (open for lunch and dinner, closed Wed, tel. 04 90 28 97 02).

Les Coquelicots, a tiny eatery surrounded by vines and views in minuscule Suzette, is a sweet spot. The food is scrumptious (owner/chef Frankie insists on fresh products), and the setting is memorable. Try the €14 *Assiette Provençale,* his omelets with herbs, or any of his grilled meats and fish (May–Sept usually closed Tue evening and all day Wed, Oct–April open weekends only, tel. 04 90 65 06 94).

Côté Vignes, off a short dirt road between Suzette and Beaumes de Venise, is a lighthearted wood-fired-everything place with outdoor tables flanked by fun interior dining. Young Corrine runs the restaurant with enthusiasm; try the Camembert cheese flambé with lettuce, potatoes, and fine ham (€9 salads and good pizza, *menus* from €17, closed Tue evening and Wed, tel. 04 90 65 07 16).

More Côtes du Rhône Drives

For further explorations of the Côtes du Rhône region, consider these fine options: a scenic mountaintop, an off-the-beaten-path countryside ramble, and an impressive gorge.

▲Mont Ventoux and Lavender

The drive to Mont Ventoux is worth ▲▲▲ if skies are crystal-clear, or in any weather between late June and the end of July, when the lavender blooms. It also provides a scenic connection between the Côtes du Rhône villages and the Luberon. Allow an hour to drive to the top of this 6,000-foot mountain, where you'll be greeted by cool temperatures, crowds of visitors, and acres of white stones.

Mont Ventoux is Provence's rooftop, with astonishing Pyrénées-to-Alps views—but only if it's really clear (which it usually isn't). But even under hazy skies, it's an interesting place. The top combines a barren and surreal lunar landscape with souvenirs, bikers, and hikers. All that chalky mess you see was once the bottom of a sea. Miles of poles stuck in the rock identify the route (the top is usually snowbound Dec–April). **Le Vendran** restaurant (near the old observatory and Air Force control tower) offers snacks and meals with commanding views. An orientation board is available on the opposite side of the mountaintop.

Between Mont Ventoux and the Luberon, you'll duck into and out of several climate zones and astonishingly diverse landscapes.

THE CÔTES DU RHÔNE

The scene alternates between limestone canyons, lush meadows, and wildflowers. Thirty minutes east of Mont Ventoux, lavender fields forever surround the rock-top village of **Sault** (pronounced "soh"), which produces 40 percent of France's lavender essence. Sault, a welcoming town in any season, goes unnoticed by most hurried travelers. It's a slow-down-and-smell-the-lavender kind of place, with a sociable "mountain market" on Wednesdays.

Getting to Mont Ventoux: To reach Mont Ventoux from Vaison la Romaine, go to Malaucène, then wind up D-974 for 40 minutes to the top (or start at cute little Bedoin, which has a local Monday market; from there, D-974 offers a longer, prettier route to the top). If continuing to Sault (a worthwhile detour when the lavender blooms) or on to the Luberon (worthwhile anytime—see next chapter), follow signs to *Sault*, then *Gordes*. The *Les Routes de la Lavande* brochure suggests driving and walking routes in the area (available online at www.routes-lavande.com or at Sault TI, tel. 04 90 64 01 21).

Drôme Provençale Loop Drive

This scenic drive works best if you have time to immerse yourself in the subtle pleasures of Provence. While you don't need to go out of your way to find lovely views and hill towns in Provence, this meander north into the Drôme Provençale gets you away from popular tourist areas and combines more great scenery on a big scale with overlooked towns and villages (see map on pages 150–151). This loop is best on Thursdays, when it's market day in Nyons; and good on Wednesdays, when it's market day in Buis les Barronies. If the wind is howling, the drive provides some relief, as you'll be in and out of gorges and protected by mountain slopes. Allow most of a day for this up-and-down, curve-filled drive, particularly if it's market day in Nyons.

From Vaison la Romaine, drive to **Nyons,** an attractive mid-size town set along a river and against the hills. Here you'll find a Roman bridge with views, an olive mill, a lavender distillery, a handful of walking streets, and an arcaded square—all with few tourists. Nyons is famous for its rollicking Thursday market (until 12:30) and for producing France's best olives—which you can taste at its well-organized **Coopérative** (daily 9:00–12:00 & 14:00–19:00, interesting museum about olives, on place Olivier de Serres, tel. 04 75 26 95 00).

From Nyons, head for the hills following signs to *Gap* on D-94, then follow signs to *St. Jalles* on D-64. Little **St. Jalles** hovers above the road, with a pretty Romanesque church (usually closed), two cafés (Café de Lavande overhangs the river, providing a fine backdrop for a drink, lunch, or a snack), and a small winery making crisp whites and easy-to-drink reds (Domaine de Rieu

Frais, Mon–Sat 10:00–12:00 & 14:00–18:00, closed Sun).

From St. Jalles, cross the bridge following D-108 and *Buis les Barronnies* signs, and start your ascent over the rocky mountains. Prepare for miles of curves, sensational views, and no guardrails. Drop down (er, drive down) and meet the Ouvèze River, then follow it into bustling **Buis les Barronnies** (with all the services, including many cafés and an attractive old town to stroll). Buis les Barronnies is the linden tree capital of France and hosts an earthy outdoor market on Wednesdays with produce and crafts.

From Buis les Barronnies, continue south on D-5 (notice the rock fin that crowns the town as you leave), then turn left toward Eygaliers on D-72. Follow this slow, serpentine road along the back side of Mont Ventoux and go all the way to the jewel of this trip: **Brantes,** one of Provence's most spectacularly located villages. Stop here for some fresh air and a look at the local pottery.

Finally, follow signs back to *Vaison la Romaine* along the faster, less curvy D-40. A few minutes before Vaison la Romaine, you'll pass through pleasing little Entrechaux. If you have energy for one more stop, take the short detour toward St. Marcellin at the roundabout just before entering Entrechaux, and follow *Vallée de l'Ouvèze* signs. You'll come to the Roman-era **St. Michel Bridge,** with good swimming and intriguing rock-cut channels the Romans used for mixing mortar (from lime and sand). Cross the narrow bridge and park on the other side.

▲Ardèche Gorges (Gorges de l'Ardèche)

These gorges, which wow visitors with abrupt chalky-white cliffs, follow the Ardèche River through immense canyons and thick forests. To reach the gorges from Vaison la Romaine, drive west 45 minutes, passing through Bollène and Pont Saint-Esprit to Vallon Pont d'Arc (the tourist hub of the Ardèche Gorges). From Vallon Pont d'Arc, you can canoe along the peaceful river through some of the canyon's most spectacular scenery and under the rock arch of Pont d'Arc (half-day, all-day, and 2-day trips possible; less appealing in summer, when the river is crowded and water levels are low), and learn about hiking trails that get you above it all (**TI** tel. 04 75 88 04 01, www.vallon-pont-darc.com). If continuing north toward Lyon, connect Privas and Aubenas, then head back via the autoroute. Endearing little **Balazuc**—a village north of the gorges, with narrow lanes, flowers, views, and a smattering of cafés and shops—makes a fine stop.

HILL TOWNS OF THE LUBERON

France's Answer to Italy's Tuscany

Just 30 miles east of Avignon, the Luberon region hides some of France's most captivating hill towns and sensuous landscapes. Those intrigued by Peter Mayle's books love joyriding through the region, connecting I-could-live-here villages, crumbled castles, and meditative abbeys. Mayle's bestselling *A Year in Provence* describes the ruddy local culture from an Englishman's perspective as he buys a stone farmhouse, fixes it up, and adopts the region as his new home. His book is a great read while you're here—or better yet, get it as an audio book and listen as you drive.

The Luberon terrain in general (much of which is a French regional natural park) is as appealing as its villages. Gnarled vineyards and wind-sculpted trees separate tidy stone structures from abandoned buildings—little more than rock piles—that seem to challenge city slickers to fix them up. Mountains of limestone bend along vast ridges, while colorful hot-air balloons survey the sun-drenched scene from above. The wind is an integral part of life here. The infamous mistral wind, finishing its long ride in from Siberia, hits like a hammer (see the *"Le Mistral"* sidebar on page 52).

Planning Your Time

There are no obligatory museums, monuments, or vineyards in the Luberon. Treat this area like a vacation from your vacation. Downshift your engine. Brake for the views, and get out of your car to take a walk. Get on a first-name basis with a village.

To enjoy the ambience of the Luberon, you'll want at least one night and a car (only Isle-sur-la-Sorgue—and, to a lesser extent, Lourmarin—are accessible by train or bus). Allow a half-day for Isle-sur-la-Sorgue if it's market day (less time if not). Add more time if you want to paddle the Sorgue River or pedal between villages (canoe trips and bike rental described on page 189). You'll also want a full day for the Luberon villages.

For the ultimate Luberon experience, drivers should base themselves in or near Roussillon. The village of Lourmarin works as a southern base for visiting Luberon sights, as well as Aix-en-Provence, Cassis, and Marseille. To lose the tourists, set up in St-Saturnin-lès-Apt or Saignon. If you lack wheels or prefer streams to hills and prefer a little more action, stay in Isle-sur-la-Sorgue, located within striking distance of Avignon and just outside the Luberon. Adequate train service from Avignon and Marseille, and some bus service, connect Isle-sur-la-Sorgue with the real world. Level terrain, tree-lined roads, and nearby villages make Isle-sur-la-Sorgue good for biking. Determined travelers can also take a bus from Avignon or Aix-en-Provence to reach Lourmarin.

Getting Around the Luberon

By Car: Luberon roads are scenic and narrow. With no major landmarks, it's easy to get lost in this area—and you will get lost, trust me—but getting lost is the point. Pick up the Michelin Local map #332 or #528 to navigate.

If connecting this region with the **Côtes du Rhône,** avoid driving through Carpentras (terrible traffic, confusing signage). If you're in a hurry, use the autoroute from Cavaillon and get off in Orange (if you plan to visit that town), or use the exit before Orange Centre (exit #22) to get to the villages. If time is not an issue, drive via Mont Ventoux—one of Provence's most spectacular routes (see page 177).

By Bus: Isle-sur-la-Sorgue is easy by bus from Avignon, with several daily trips and a central stop at the post office (6/day Mon–Sat, 3–4/day Sun, 45 min). Buses link Lourmarin with Avignon (3/day, 1.5 hrs) and Aix-en-Provence (3/day, 1.25 hrs with transfer in Pertuis), making it a workable village stop between these cities. Without a car or minivan tour, I'd skip the more famous hill towns of the Luberon.

By Train: Trains get you to Isle-sur-la-Sorgue (station called "L'Isle–Fontaine de Vaucluse") from Avignon (10/day on weekdays, 5/day on weekends, 30 min) or from Marseille (8/day, 1–2 hours). If you're day-tripping by train, check return times before leaving the station.

By Minivan Tour: Dutchman Mike Rijken, who runs **Wine Safari,** offers tours of this area, as do several other Avignon-based companies (see "Tours of Provence" on page 40).

By Bike: Hardy bikers can ride from Isle-sur-la-Sorgue to Gordes, then to Roussillon, connecting other villages in a full-day loop ride (30 miles round-trip to Roussillon and back, with lots of hills). Many appealing villages are closer to Isle-sur-la-Sorgue and offer easier biking options (see "Biking" on page 189).

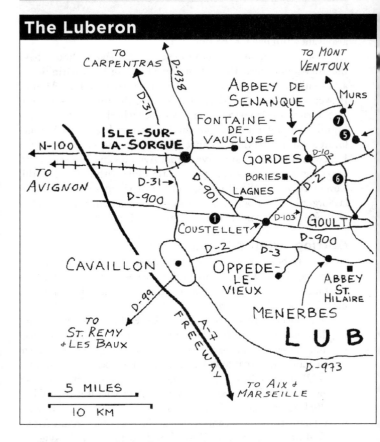

The Luberon

Luberon Area Market Days

Monday: Cavaillon (produce and antiques/flea market)

Tuesday: Gordes and Lacoste (both small)

Wednesday: Sault (produce and antiques/flea market)

Thursday: Roussillon (cute) and Isle-sur-la-Sorgue (good, but smaller than its Sunday market)

Friday: Lourmarin (very good) and Bonnieux (pretty good)

Saturday: Apt (huge produce and antiques/flea market)

Sunday: Isle-sur-la-Sorgue (granddaddy of them all, produce and antiques/flea market) and Coustellet (very good and less touristy)

TO MONT VENTOUX

D-943

ST-SATURNIN-LES-APT

JOUCAS
D-2

RUSTREL

ROUSSILLON

❾

D-22

LE COLORADO PROVENCAL

VIENS

LE CHENE

❸

D-943

APT

D-209

ST. MARTIN

D-190

❷

❹

ST. JULIEN BRIDGE

D-943

SAIGNON

D-900

TO GRAND CANYON DU VERDON

❿

BUOUX

FORT DE BUOUX

❽

BONNIEUX

LACOSTE

E   R   O   N

LOURMARIN

D-943

TO AIX & MARSEILLE

DCH

❶ Chambres Sous l'Olivier
❷ Le Clos des Cigales Hôtel
❸ Hôtel les Sables d'Ocre
❹ La Petite Ecole Rest.
❺ Hostellerie des Commandeurs
❻ La Ferme de la Huppe
❼ Le Mas du Loriot Hôtel
❽ Mas del Sol
❾ Mas Perréal
❿ Château de la Canorgue Winery

Isle-sur-la-Sorgue

This sturdy market town—literally, "Island on the Sorgue River"—sits within a split in its crisp, happy little river. It's a workaday town, with a gritty charm that feels refreshingly real after so many adorable villages. It also makes a good base for exploring the Luberon (15 minutes by car, doable by hardy bikers) and Avignon (30 min by car or train) and can work for exploring the Côtes du Rhône by car (allow an hour to Vaison la Romaine).

THE LUBERON

After the arid cities and villages elsewhere in Provence, the presence of water at every turn is a welcome change. In Isle-sur-la-Sorgue—called the "Venice of Provence"—the Sorgue River's extraordinarily clear and shallow flow divides like cells, producing water, water everywhere. The river is essential to the region's economy. The fresh spring water of the Sorgue's many branches has provided ample fish, nourishment for crops, and power for key industries for centuries. Today, antiques shops power the town's economy—every other shop seems to sell some kind of antique.

Orientation to Isle-sur-la-Sorgue

While Isle-sur-la-Sorgue is renowned for its market days (Sun and Thu), it's otherwise a pleasantly average town with no important sights and a steady trickle of tourism. It's calm at night and downright dead on Mondays. The town revolves around its river, the church square, and two pedestrian-only streets, rue de la République and rue Carnot.

Tourist Information
The TI has information on hiking, biking itineraries, and a line on rooms in private homes, all of which are outside the town (Mon–Sat 9:00–12:30 & 14:30–18:00, Sun 9:00–12:30, in town center next to church, tel. 04 90 38 04 78, www.oti-delasorgue.fr).

Arrival in Isle-sur-la-Sorgue
By Car: Traffic is a mess and parking is a headache on market days (all day Sunday and Thursday mornings). Circle the ring road and look for parking signs, or give up and find the pay lot behind the post office (PTT). There are several lots just west of the roundabout at Le Bassin (marked on the map on page 186). You'll also pass freestyle parking on roads leaving the city. Don't leave anything visible in your car.

By Train: Remember that the train station is called "L'Isle–Fontaine de Vaucluse." To reach my recommended hotels, walk straight out of the station and turn right on the ring road.

By Bus: The bus from Avignon drops you near the post office (PTT, ask driver for "*luh pay-tay-tay*"), a block from the recommended Hôtel les Névons.

Helpful Hints
Shop Hours: The antiques shops this town is famous for are open Saturday to Monday only.

Internet Access: Try **Taxiphone Internet Station,** across from the church and TI and a block down rue Danton at #3 (tel. 04 90 20 03 28).

Bookstore: You'll find a handful of English novels at **La Marque-Page de l'Isle,** where the pedestrian street rue de la République meets Notre-Dame des Anges church (Tue–Sat 7:00–12:30 & 15:00–19:00, Sun–Mon 7:00–12:30).

Laundry: It's just off the rue de la République, at 23 impasse de l'Hôtel de Palerme (daily 7:00–20:00).

Supermarket: A well-stocked **Spar** market is on the main ring road, near the Peugeot Car shop and the train station (Mon–Sat 8:30–12:30 & 15:00–19:00, Sun 15:00–19:00). A smaller **Casino** market is more central on pedestrian rue de la République (Tue–Sun 7:30–12:30 & 15:30–19:30, closed Mon).

Bike Rental: Christophe at **Isles 2 Roues,** by the train station, rents good bikes (€15/day, closed Sun–Mon, must show your passport, 10 avenue de la Gare, tel. 04 90 38 19 12).

Taxi: Call 06 84 64 32 67.

Public WC: There's a good WC in the parking lot between the post office (PTT) and the Hôtel les Névons.

Hiking: The TI has good information on area hikes; most trails are accessible by short drives, and you can use a taxi to get there.

Self-Guided Walk

Wandering Isle-sur-la-Sorgue

The town has crystal-clear water babbling under pedestrian bridges stuffed with flower boxes, and its old-time carousel is always spinning. For this walk, navigate by the town's splintered streams and nine mossy waterwheels, which, while still turning, power only memories of the town's wool and silk industries.

• *Start your tour at the church next to the TI—where all streets seem to converge—and make forays into the town from there. Go first to the church.*

Notre-Dame des Anges: This 12th-century church has a festive Baroque interior and seems overgrown for today's town. Walk in. The curls and swirls and gilded statues date from an era that was all about Louis XIV, the Sun King. This is propagandist architecture, designed to wow the faithful into compliance. (It was made possible thanks to profits generated from the town's river-powered industries.) When you enter a church like this, the heavens should open up and assure you that whoever built it had unearthly connections (daily 10:00–12:00 & 15:15–17:00, Mass on Sun at 10:30).

Outside the church, notice the buildings' faded facades around you, recalling their previous lives (Fabrique de Chausseures was a shoemaker; *meubles* means furniture). Admire Fauque Beyret's

THE LUBERON

THE LUBERON

Isle-sur-la-Sorgue

- ❶ La Prévôté Hôtel/Rest.
- ❷ Hôtel les Névons
- ❸ To Le Pont des Aubes, Chambres Sous l'Olivier & L'Ousteau de l'Isle Rest.
- ❹ Hôtel/Rest. les Terrasses du Bassin
- ❺ Le Caveau de la Tour de l'Isle Wine Bar & Casino Market
- ❻ Fromenterie Bakery & Bus from Avignon
- ❼ Bus to Avignon
- ❽ Café de France & La Marque-Page de l'Isle (Bookstore)
- ❾ Launderette
- ❿ Internet Station
- ⓫ Spar Market
- ⓬ Bike Rental
- ⓭ Delices de Luberon Shop
- ⓮ Riverfront Stroll to Partage des Eaux (Swimming)
- ⓯ Antique Toy & Doll Museum

Legend:
- → SELF-GUIDED WALK
- ✿ WATERWHEELS
- Ⓑ BUS STOP
- Ⓟ PARKING
- ⋔ VIEW

TRAIN STN.

antique facade—Isle-sur-la-Sorgue retains a connection to its past uncommon in this renovation-happy region.

• *Angling left in front of the church, wander down rue Danton to lose the crowds and find...*

Three Waterwheels: These big forgotten waterwheels have been in business here since the 1200s, when they were first used

for grinding flour. Paper, textile, silk, and woolen mills would later find their power from this river. At its peak, Isle-sur-la-Sorgue had 70 waterwheels like this, and in the 1800s, the town competed with Avignon as Provence's cloth-dyeing and textile center. Those stylish Provençal fabrics and patterns

you see for sale everywhere were made possible by this river.

• *Double back to the church, turn left under the arcade, then find the small stream just past the TI. Breakaway streams like this run under the town like subways run under Paris. Take a right on the first street after the stream; it leads under a long arch (along rue J. J. Rousseau). Follow this straight, and veer slightly right at place F. Buisson to the main river, then follow it left. You'll come to...*

Le Bassin: Literally translated as a "pond," this is where the Sorgue River enters the town and separates into many branches. Track as many branches as you can see (Frank Provost hides a big one), and then find the round lookout point for the best perspective (carefully placed lights make this a beautiful sight after dark). Fishing was the town's main industry until the waterwheels took over. In the 1300s, local fishermen provided the pope with his fresh-fish quota. They either trapped them in nets or speared them while standing on skinny, flat-bottomed boats. Several streets are named after the fish they caught—including rue de l'Aiguille (Eel Street) and rue des Ecrevisses (Crayfish Street).

The sound of the rushing water reminds us of the power that rivers can generate. With its source (a spring) a mere five miles away, the Sorgue River never floods and has a constant flow and temperature in all seasons. Despite its exposed location, Isle-sur-la-Sorgue prospered in the Middle Ages, thanks to the natural protection this river provided. Walls with big moats once ran along the river, but they were destroyed during the French Revolution.

• *Cross the busy roundabout, and walk to the orange **Delices de Luberon** store. Find the small tasting table with 12 scrumptious tapenades. Walk behind the store to find the river and take a refreshing...*

Riverfront Stroll: Follow the main river upstream, along the bike/pedestrian lane, as far as you like. The little road meanders about a mile, following the serene course of the river, past water-front homes and beneath swaying trees. It ends at the Hôtel le Pescador and a riverfront café. The wide and shallow Partage des Eaux, where the water divides before entering Isle-sur-la-Sorgue, is perfect for a cool swim on a hot day.

Sights in Isle-sur-la-Sorgue

▲▲**Market Days**—The town erupts into a carnival-like market frenzy each Sunday and Thursday, with hardy crafts and local produce. The Sunday market is astounding and famous for its antiques; the Thursday market is more intimate (see market tips in the Shopping chapter). Find a table across from the church at the Café de France and enjoy the scene.

Antique Toy and Doll Museum (Musée du Jouet et de la Poupée Ancienne)—The town's lone sight is a fun and funky toy museum with more than 300 dolls displayed in three small rooms (€3.50, kids-€1.50; July–Sept Mon–Sat 10:30–18:30, Sun 11:00–18:00; Oct–June Tue–Fri 13:00–18:00, Sat–Sun 11:00–17:00, closed Mon; 26 rue Carnot).

Near Isle-sur-la-Sorgue

Fontaine-de-Vaucluse—You'll read and hear a lot about this overrun village, impressively located at the source of the Sorgue River, where the medieval Italian poet Petrarch mourned for his love, Laura. The river seems to magically appear from nowhere (the actual source is a murky, green waterhole) and flows through the town past a lineup of cafés, souvenir shops, and wall-to-river tourists. While the setting is beautiful—with cliffs jutting to the sky and a ruined castle above—the trip is worth it only if the spring is flowing. *Sans* flowing spring, this is the most overrated sight in France. Ask your hotelier if the spring is active, and arrive early or late to avoid crowds. It's a good bike ride here from Isle-sur-la-Sorgue (about four miles).

Arriving by car, you'll pay €3 to park, and then walk about 20 minutes along the sparkling river to *la source* (the spring), located in a cave at the base of the cliff. (It's an uphill hike for the last part.) The spring itself is the very definition of anticlimactic, unless it's surging. At those times, it's among the most prolific water producers in the world, with a depth no one has yet been able to determine.

The path to the spring is lined with distractions. The only stops worth your time are the riverfront cafés—**Philip's** offers the best seats—and the **Moulin à Papier,** a reproduction of a 17th-century paper mill. Here, you'll see the value of harnessing the river's power. In the mill, a 22-foot-diameter paddle wheel turns five times a minute, driving hammers that pound paper for up to

36 hours (free, open daily 9:00–19:00). As you watch the hammers pound away, imagine Isle-sur-la-Sorgue's waterwheels and the industries they once powered. The shop inside sells paper in every size and shape.

Canoe Trips on the Sorgue—A better reason to travel to Fontaine-de-Vaucluse is to canoe down the river. A guide escorts small groups in canoes, starting in Fontaine-de-Vaucluse and ending in Isle-sur-la-Sorgue; you'll return to Fontaine-de-Vaucluse via shuttle bus (call for departure times; a shuttle bus will pick you up in Isle-sur-la-Sorgue). If you're really on vacation, take this five-mile, two-hour trip. **Kayaks Verts** is a family operation run by happy-go-lucky Michel, who speaks "small English" (€19/person, tel. 04 90 20 35 44).

Biking—Isle-sur-la-Sorgue is ideally situated for short biking forays into the mostly-level terrain. Pick up a biking itinerary at the TI. These towns make easy biking destinations from Isle-sur-la-Sorgue: Velleron (5 miles north, flat, a tiny version of Isle-sur-la-Sorgue with waterwheels, fountains, and an evening farmer's market Mon–Sat 18:00–20:00); Lagnes (3 miles east, a pretty and well-restored hill town with views from its ruined château); and Fontaine-de-Vaucluse (5 miles northeast, gently uphill, described on previous page). Allow 30 miles and many hills for the round-trip ride to Roussillon. (A bike-rental company in Isle-sur-la-Sorgue is listed under "Helpful Hints," earlier.)

Sleeping in Isle-sur-la-Sorgue

Pickings are slim for good sleeps in Isle-sur-la-Sorgue, though the few I've listed provide solid values.

$$$ La Prévôté*** has the town's highest-priced digs. Its five meticulously decorated rooms—located above a classy restaurant—are each decorated in earth tones, with high ceilings, a few exposed beams, and beautiful furnishings. Helpful Séverine manages the hotel while chef-hubby Jean-Marie controls the kitchen (standard Db-€130, larger Db-€150, suite Db-€180, no air-con or elevator, Internet access and Wi-Fi, rooftop deck with Jacuzzi, no parking, one block from the church at 4 rue J. J. Rousseau, tel. & fax 04 90 38 57 29, www.la-prevote.fr, contact@la-prevote.fr).

$$ Hôtel les Névons**, two blocks from the center (behind the post office), is concrete motel–modern outside, but a good value within. The staff is eager to please, and you have two wings to choose from: the new wing, with cavernous (by local standards) and well-appointed rooms; or the old wing, with more modest, cheaper (but fine) rooms. There are several family suites and a roof deck with 360-degree views around a small pool (old wing—Db-€60–65; new wing—huge Db-€70–80, Tb-€80–90,

THE LUBERON

Sleep Code

(€1 = about $1.40, country code: 33)
S = Single, **D** = Double/Twin, **T** = Triple, **Q** = Quad, **b** = bathroom,
s = shower only, * = French hotel rating system (0-4 stars).
Unless otherwise noted, credit cards are accepted and English
is spoken.

To help you sort easily through these listings, I've divided
the rooms into three categories based on the price for a
standard double room with bath:

$$$ Higher Priced—Most rooms €90 or more.
$$ Moderately Priced—Most rooms between €60-90.
$ Lower Priced—Most rooms €60 or less.

Qb-€95; air-con, Internet access, Wi-Fi in lobby, easy parking, 205 chemin des Névons, push and hold the gate button a bit on entry, tel. 04 90 20 72 00, fax 04 90 20 56 20, www.hotel-les-nevons .com, info@hotel-les-nevons.com).

$$ Le Pont des Aubes Chambres has two huggable rooms in an old green-shuttered farmhouse right on the river a mile from town. Borrow a bike or a canoe. From here, you can cross a tiny bridge and walk 15 minutes along the river into Isle-sur-la-Sorgue, or cross the street to the recommended L'Ousteau de l'Isle restaurant. Charming Martine speaks English, while husband Patrice speaks smiles (Db-€70, Tb-€85, 1-room apartments-€380/week, cash only, a mile from town toward Apt, next to Pain d'Antan Boulangerie at 189 route d'Apt, tel. & fax 04 90 38 13 75, http: //perso.wanadoo.fr/lepontdesaubes, patriceaubert@wanadoo.fr).

$ Hôtel les Terrasses du Bassin rents eight spotless rooms with designer touches over a good restaurant on Le Bassin, where the river waters separate before running through town. Several rooms look out over Le Bassin, a few have queen-size beds, and there's some traffic noise (Db-€52-62, Tb-€72, air-con planned, 2 avenue Charles de Gaulle, tel. 04 90 38 03 16, fax 04 90 38 65 61, www.lesterrassesdubassin.com, corinne@lesterrassesdu bassin.com).

Near Isle-sur-la-Sorgue

$$$ Chambres Sous l'Olivier, located five minutes east of Isle-sur-la-Sorgue, is well-situated for exploring the hill towns of the Luberon and Isle-sur-la-Sorgue. Its six lovely rooms are housed in a massive 150-year-old farmhouse with lounges that you and your entire soccer team could spread out in. Julien and Carole take care of your every need, and they'll cook you a full-blown

THE LUBERON

dinner with wine for €29 per person (Db-€90–135, Tb-€120, two-room Tb-€180, three-room suite for up to six people-€220, prices include breakfast; credit cards not accepted—pay with cash, euro travelers checks, or bank transfer; pool; route d'Apt, tel. 04 90 20 33 90, www.chambresdhotesprovence.com, souslolivier@orange .fr). It's below Isle-sur-la-Sorgue, about 25 minutes from Avignon toward Apt on D-900 (near Petit Palais—don't go to Lagnes by mistake). Look for signs 200 yards after the big sign to *le Mas du Grand Jonquier,* on the right.

Eating in Isle-sur-la-Sorgue

Inexpensive restaurants are easy to find in Isle-sur-la-Sorgue, but consistent quality is another story. The restaurants I list offer good value, but none of them is really "cheap." For inexpensive meals, troll the riverside cafés for today's catch. Dining on the river is a unique experience in this arid land famous for its hill towns, and shopping for the perfect table is half the fun. Riverside picnics work well here (the Fromenterie bakery, listed below, stocks mouthwatering quiche and more).

Begin your dinner with a glass of wine at the cozy **Le Caveau de la Tour de l'Isle** (the wine bar hides in the rear, Tue–Sun 9:30–12:30 & 15:30–20:00 except closed Sun afternoon, closed Mon, 12 rue de la République, tel. 04 90 20 70 25).

Les Terrasses du Bassin, a new player in town, shows great promise with moderate prices, good choices, and a cool riverfront location (terrace dining available). The hardworking owners are dedicated to providing a good value and welcoming service. Say hello to Max and come for a full meal or just a *plat* (€9 lunch salads and starters, €16 dinner *plats,* €25 dinner *menu,* closed Tue–Wed Oct–May, 2 avenue Charles de Gaulle, tel. 04 90 38 03 16).

La Prévôté is a place to really do it up. Its dining room is covered in wood beams, the outdoor patio is peaceful, and the ambience is country-classy but not stuffy. A branch of the Sorgue runs under the restaurant, visible through glass windows (*menus* from €40, save room for amazing cheese platter, closed Tue–Wed, 4 rue J. J. Rousseau, on narrow street that runs along left side of church as you face it, tel. 04 90 38 57 29).

L'Ousteau de l'Isle, a mile from the town center, dishes up regional cuisine with a modern twist and a friendly welcome. Skip the modern interior and ask for a table *sur la terrasse* (dinner *menus* from €28, lunch *menu* for €18, closed Tue–Wed, 147 chemin de Bosquet, tel. 04 90 20 81 36). From Isle-sur-la-Sorgue's center, follow signs toward *Apt,* and turn right at Pain d'Antan Boulangerie; or walk 20 minutes along the river and cross the small bridge to chemin de Bosquet.

THE LUBERON

The **Fromenterie** bakery next to the post office (PTT) sells decadent quiche, monster sandwiches, desserts, wine, and other drinks—in other words, everything you need to picnic (open daily until 20:00).

The Heart of the Luberon

A 15-minute drive east of Isle-sur-la-Sorgue brings you to this protected area, where canyons and ridgelines rule, and land developers take a back seat. Here, still-proud hill towns guard access to winsome valleys, while carefully managed vineyards (producing mostly inexpensive wines) play hopscotch with cherry groves, lavender fields, and cypress trees.

Peter Mayle's *A Year in Provence* nudged tourism in this area into overdrive. A visit to Mayle's quintessential Provence includes many of the popular villages and sights described in this chapter. While the hill towns can be seen as subtly different variations on the same theme, each has a distinct character. Look for differences: the color of shutters, the pattern of stones, the way flowers are planted, or the number of tourist boutiques. Every village has something to offer—it's up to you to discover and celebrate it.

Stay in or near Roussillon. By village standards, Roussillon is always lively, and it struggles to manage its popularity. When restaurant-hunting, read descriptions of the villages in this chapter—many good finds are embedded in the countryside. For aerial views high above this charmed land, consider a hot-air balloon trip (see page 198).

Planning Your Time

With a car and one full day, I'd linger in Roussillon in the morning, visit the St. Julien Bridge, then have lunch nearby in Lacoste or Bonnieux. After lunch, continue the joyride past Ménerbes to Oppède-le-Vieux, then return through Coustellet and Gordes. With a second full day, I'd start by climbing the Fort de Buoux, then lunch nearby. After lunch, continue to Saignon and Viens, then loop back via Le Colorado Provençal and St-Saturnin-lès-Apt.

I've described sights at each of the stops listed above, but you'll need to be selective—you can't see them all. Read through your options and choose the ones that appeal most. Slow down and get to know a few places well, rather than dashing between every stop you can cram in. The best sight is the dreamy landscape between the villages.

Roussillon

With all the trendy charm of Santa Fe on a hilltop, photogenic Roussillon requires serious camera and café time (and €3 for parking). Roussillon has been a protected village since 1943 and has benefited from a complete absence of modern development. An enormous deposit of ochre gives the earth and its buildings that distinctive red color and provided this village with its economic base until shortly after World War II. This place is popular; it's best to visit early or late in the day.

Orientation to Roussillon

Roussillon sits atop Mont Rouge (Red Mountain) at about 1,000 feet above sea level, and requires some uphill walking to reach. Exposed ochre cliffs form the village's southern limit.

Tourist Information

The little TI is in the center, across from the David restaurant. If in need of accommodations, leaf through their good binders describing area hotels and *chambres d'hôte*. Walkers should get info on trails from Roussillon to nearby villages (TI open April–Oct Mon–Sat 9:30–12:00 & 13:30–18:00, closed Sun except in summer; Nov–March Mon–Sat 14:00–17:30, closed Sun; tel. 04 90 05 60 25).

Arrival in Roussillon

Parking lots are available at every entry to the village. The closest two lots are on the northern edge (Parking Sablons, by the recommended Hôtel Rêves d'Ocres) and on the southern flank, closer to the ochre cliffs (Parking Pasquier). If you approach from Gordes or Joucas, you'll park at Sablons. If you're coming from D-900 and the south, you'll land at Pasquier (but don't park there on Wednesday night, because Thursday is Roussillon's market day). Leave nothing valuable showing in your car.

Helpful Hints

An ATM is next to the TI. Internet access and a modest selection of English books are available at the delightful **Librairie du Luberon** on the main square (daily 10:00–18:00, tel. 04 90 71 55 72; its nifty café is described later, under "Eating in Roussillon").

Roussillon

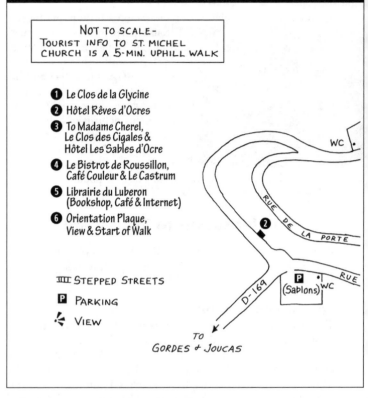

NOT TO SCALE –
TOURIST INFO TO ST. MICHEL
CHURCH IS A 5-MIN. UPHILL WALK

① Le Clos de la Glycine
② Hôtel Rêves d'Ocres
③ To Madame Cherel,
   Le Clos des Cigales &
   Hôtel Les Sables d'Ocre
④ Le Bistrot de Roussillon,
   Café Couleur & Le Castrum
⑤ Librairie du Luberon
   (Bookshop, Café & Internet)
⑥ Orientation Plaque,
   View & Start of Walk

▥ STEPPED STREETS
🅿 PARKING
⚐ VIEW

RUE DE LA PORTE

WC

D-169   🅿 (Sablons) WC   RUE

TO
GORDES & JOUCAS

Self-Guided Walk

Welcome to Roussillon

This quick walk will take you through Roussillon's village to its ochre cliffs.

• *To begin the walk, climb a few minutes from either parking lot (passing the Hollywood set–like square under the bell tower and the church) to the summit of...*

▲The Village

Find the orientation plaque and the dramatic viewpoint, often complete with a howling mistral. During the Middle Ages, a castle stood where you are, on the top of Red Mountain (Mont Rouge), and watched over the village below. While nothing remains of the castle today, the strategic advantage of this site is clear. Count how many villages you can identify, and then notice how little sprawl there is in the valley below. Because the Luberon is a natural reserve (Parc Naturel Régional du Luberon), development is strictly controlled.

A short stroll down leads to the church. Duck into the pretty 11th-century Church of St. Michel, and appreciate the natural air-

conditioning and the well-worn center aisle. The white interior tells you that the stone came from elsewhere, and the WWI memorial plaque over the side door suggests a village devastated by the war (over 40 died from little Roussillon).

On leaving the church, look across the way to the derelict building, a reminder of Roussillon's humble roots. After World War II, when the demand for ochre faded, this became a dusty, poor village. Adding to the town's economic woes, many residents

THE LUBERON

Boules (Pétanque)

The game of *boules*—also called *pétanque*—is the horse-shoes of Provence and the Riviera. It's played in every village, almost exclusively by men, on level dirt areas kept specifically for this purpose. It was invented here in the early 1900s, and today every French boy grows up playing *boules* with Papa and *Ton-Ton* (Uncle) Jean. It's a social-yet-serious sport, and end-lessly entertaining to watch—even more so if you understand the rules.

Boules is played with heavy metal balls (*boules,* about the size of baseballs) and a small wooden target ball (*le cochonnet,* about the size of a table tennis ball). Whoever gets his *boule* closest to the *cochonnet* wins. It's most com-monly played in teams of two, though individual competition and teams of three are not uncommon. (There are *boules* leagues and professional players who make little money but are national celebrities.) Most teams have two specialists, a *pointeur* and a *tireur*. The *pointeur* goes first and tries to lob his balls as close to the target as he can. The *tireur's* job is to blast away opponents' *boules*.

Here's the play-by-play: Each player gets three *boules.* A coin toss determines which team goes first. The starting team scratches a small circle in the dirt, in which players must stand (with both feet on the ground) when launching their *boules.* Next, the starting team tosses the *cochonnet* (about 6–10 yards)—that's the target. The *boule* must be tossed underhand, and can be rolled, thrown sky-high, or rocketed at its target. Most lob it like a slow pitch in softball, with lots of backspin. The starting team's *pointeur* shoots, then the other team's *pointeur* shoots until he gets closer. Once the second team lands a *boule* closer, the first team is back up. If the opposing team's *boule* is very near the *cochonnet,* the *tireur* will likely attempt to knock it away. If the team decides that they can lob one in closer, the *pointeur* shoots.

Once all *boules* have been launched, the tally is taken. This is where it gets tense, as the difference in distance often comes down to millimeters. Faces are drawn, lips are pursed, and eyes are squinted as teams try to sort through the who's-closer process. I've seen all kinds of measuring devices, from shoes to belts to tape measures. The team with the ball clos-est to the target receives one point, and the teams keep going until someone gets 13 points.

fled for an easier life below, with level streets and modern conveniences. Abandoned buildings like this presented a serious
problem (common throughout France)...until the tourists discovered Roussillon, and people began reinvesting in the village. This
building is still looking for a buyer.

• *Continue down to the village.*

Notice the clamped-iron beams that shore up old walls.
Examine the different hues of yellow and orange. These lime-
finished exteriors, called *chaux* (literally "limes"), need to be redone
about every 10 years. Locals choose their exact color...but in this
town of ochre, it's never white. The church tower that you walk
under once marked the entrance to the fortified town. Just before
dropping down to the square, turn right and find the gigantic
150-year-old grapevine that decorates Restaurant la Treille. This is
what you get when you don't prune.

Linger over *un café*, or—if it's later in the day—*un pastis*, in
what must be the most picturesque village square in Provence (place

de la Mairie). Watch the stream of
shoppers. Is anyone playing *boules*
at the opposite end? You could
paint the entire town without ever
leaving the red-and-orange corner
of your palette. Many do. While
Roussillon receives its share of
day-trippers, mornings and evenings are romantically peaceful
on this square. The Librairie du
Luberon bookshop on the square's corner deserves a visit; don't
miss its top-floor café.

• *With the cafés on your right, drop downhill past the lineup of shops and
turn right past the TI to find the parking lot just beyond. For centuries,
animals grazed here. It was later turned into a school playground.
When tourists outnumbered students, it became a parking lot. Walk past
the parking lot with the cliffs on your left and find the...*

▲▲Ochre Cliffs

Roussillon was Europe's capital for ochre production until World
War II. A stroll to the south end of town, beyond the upper parking lot, shows you why: Roussillon sits on the world's largest known
ochre deposit. A radiant orange path leads through the richly colored ochre canyon, explaining the hue of this village (€2.50, ask
about combo-tickets with the Ochre Conservatory—described
below; daily 9:00–17:00, until 19:00 in summer; beware—light-
colored clothing and orange powder don't mix).

Ochre is made of iron oxide and clay. When combined with
sand, it creates the yellowish-red pigments you see in the buildings

around you. While ochre is also produced in the US and Italy, the quality of France's ochre is considered *le best*.

The value of Roussillon's ochre cliffs was known even in Roman times. Once excavated, the clay ochre was rinsed with water to separate it from sand, then bricks of the stuff were dried and baked for deeper hues. The procedure for extracting the ochre did not change much over 2,000 years, until ochre mining became industrialized in the late 1700s. Used primarily for wallpaper and linoleum, ochre use reached its zenith just before World War II. (After that, cheaper substitutes took over.)

Sights near Roussillon

Ochre Conservatory (Conservatoire des Ocres et Pigments Appliqués)—If the ochre cliffs inspire you, visit this colorful, interesting exposition, about a half-mile below Roussillon toward Apt on D-104. Fifty-minute tours of a reconstructed ochre factory explain how ochre is converted from an ore to a pigment, from extraction to shipping (€6, ask about combo-ticket with ochre cliffs; tours usually daily at 11:00, 14:00, 15:00, and 16:00; tours are in French, but most guides will explain the basics in English, short English handout available, great gift shop, tel. 04 90 05 66 69, www.okhra.com).

Hot-Air Balloon Flight—Ply the calm morning air above the Luberon in a hot-air balloon. The Montgolfières–Luberon outfit has two flight options: the Four-Star Flight (€255, 1.5 hours in balloon, allow 3 hours total, includes picnic and champagne) and the economy-class Tourist Flight (€160, 45 min, includes glass of bubbly). For either flight, meet on the main road below Joucas at 7:00 (reserve a few days ahead, maximum 12 passengers, tel. 04 90 05 76 77, fax 04 90 05 74 39, www.montgolfiere-luberon.com).

Goult—Bigger than its sister hill towns, this surprisingly quiet village seems content to be away from the tourist path. Wander up the hill to the panoramic view and windmill, and consider its many good restaurants—where you won't have to compete with tourists for a table. **La Bartavelle** is the best in town and has reasonable prices. When it's warm, tables spill along a quiet alley. Reservations several days in advance are essential (*menus* from €40, closed Tue–Wed, rue du Cheval Blanc, tel. 04 90 72 33 72).

Sleeping in Roussillon

(€1 = about $1.40, country code: 33)
The TI posts a list of hotels and *chambres d'hôte*. Parking is free if you sleep in Roussillon—ask your hotelier where to park. The village offers three good-value accommodations—conveniently, one

for each price range.

$$$ Le Clos de la Glycine*** provides Roussillon's plushest accommodations, with nine gorgeous rooms located dead-center in the village (Db-€140–155, big Db-€180, loft suite with deck and view-€275, Wi-Fi, located at the refined restaurant David—so they prefer you pay for half-pension, across from the TI on place de la Poste, tel. 04 90 05 60 13, fax 04 90 05 75 80, www.luberon -hotel.com, le.clos.de.la.glycine@wanadoo.fr).

$$ Hôtel Rêves d'Ocres** is a solid two-star value, run by eager-to-help Sandrine and Yvan. It's ochre-colored, warm, and comfortable, with 16 mostly spacious and tastefully designed rooms—some with musty bathrooms. Eight smaller rooms have view terraces, but are *très* cozy. There's also a lovely lounge where you can stretch out (Sb-€56, Db without balcony-€76, Db with balcony-€82, Tb-€95, Qb-€115, meek air-con, Internet access, Wi-Fi, route de Gordes, tel. 04 90 05 60 50, fax 04 90 05 79 74, www.hotel-revesdocres.com, hotelrevesdocres@wanadoo.fr). Coming from Gordes and Joucas, it's the first building you pass in Roussillon.

$ Madame Cherel rents ramshackle rooms that are barely this side of a youth hostel. A shared view terrace and good reading materials are available, and the beds have firm mattresses (D-€45–49, family suite available, includes breakfast, cash only, 3 blocks from upper parking lot, between the gas station and school, La Burlière, tel. 04 90 05 71 71, mulhanc@hotmail.com). Chatty and sincere Cherel speaks English and is a wealth of regional travel tips.

Near Roussillon

The next two listings, for drivers only, are most easily found by turning north off D-900 at the *Roussillon/Les Huguets* sign. It's the second turn-off to Roussillon coming from Avignon. Joucas, St-Saturnin-lès-Apt, and Lacoste (all described later in this chapter) also have good beds near Roussillon.

$$$ Le Clos des Cigales, run by friendly Philippe, has five blue-shuttered, stylish bungalows. Two are doubles, three are two-room suites with tiny kitchenettes, and all have private patios facing a big pool. When you arrive, you'll understand the name—the cacophony from the *cigales* (cicadas) is deafening (Db-€88, Tb-€115, Qb-€135, includes breakfast, Wi-Fi, table tennis, hammock, 5 min from Roussillon towards Goult on D-104, tel. & fax 04 90 05 73 72, www.leclosdescigales.com, philippe.lherbeil @wanadoo.fr).

$$ Hôtel Les Sables d'Ocre** is a modern resort kind of place, with 22 motel-esque rooms, a big pool, the greenest grass around, air-conditioning, and fair rates (Db-€70, spring for the

Db with garden balcony-€84, Tb loft-€100–120, a half-mile after leaving Roussillon towards Apt at intersection of D-108 and D-104, tel. 04 90 05 55 55, fax 04 90 05 55 50, www.roussillon-hotel.com, sablesdocre@free.fr).

Eating in Roussillon

Choose ambience over cuisine if dining in Roussillon, and enjoy any of the eateries on the main square. It's a festive place, where children twirl while parents dine, and dogs and cats look longingly for leftovers. Restaurants change with the mistral here—what's good one year disappoints the next. Consider my suggestions and go with what looks best (or look over my recommendations in other Luberon villages). Look also at the hotels listed in Joucas (see page 202)—all offer quality cuisine at fair prices, just a few minutes' drive from Roussillon. The first three places listed next share the same square and offer similar values. One should always be open.

At **Le Bistrot de Roussillon,** David and Johan offer the most consistent value on the square, with excellent salads (try the *salad du bistrot*) and *plats* for the right price. There's a breezy terrace in back and a comfy interior (€15 for a filling salad and dessert, €22 three-course *menu*, €13 *plats*, daily, tel. 04 90 05 74 45).

Café Couleur and **Le Castrum** flank Le Bistrot de Roussillon, offering similar atmosphere and prices, but less-steady quality.

Librairie du Luberon, opposite the above-listed restaurants on the square, hides a slick top-floor café/*salon de thé* above its bookstore. Have lunch or a drink outside on the splendid terrace, or inside surrounded by books—for a price (€19 *plats*, café closed Mon).

Near Roussillon, in Le Chêne

The following is just one of many excellent eateries that lie a short drive from Roussillon; for others, don't miss the "Luberon Restaurants that Justify the Trip" sidebar.

La Petite Ecole is where locals go for fine cuisine at affordable prices. The perfect team—host Denis and chef Sophie—enthusiastically welcome travelers and locals into their nine-table restaurant (more tables outside). It's in an old schoolhouse with an unimpressive roadside location (but you won't care). This is a real experience—the food is fresh and very Provençal. Arrive when they open at 19:30 to score a table, or reserve ahead. There's an outdoor terrace, but I like the inside scene (€21 two-course *menus*, €29 three-course *menus*, cheaper at lunch, closed Tue–Wed, below Roussillon on D-900 in Le Chêne, tel. 04 32 52 16 41).

Luberon Restaurants that Justify the Trip

Many of the restaurants in the countryside around Roussillon are worth a detour. Use the list below as a quick reference, then flip to the full descriptions (page numbers noted) of those that sound most appealing. All of these are within a 20-minute drive from Roussillon. Remember that Isle-sur-la-Sorgue is a manageable 30-minute drive from Roussillon.

Ideal for Dinner

La Petite Ecole, in a converted schoolhouse in Le Chêne, is popular with locals for its reasonably priced Provençal cuisine (closed Tue–Wed; see page 200).

Hôtel des Voyageurs, located in St-Saturnin-lès-Apt, is another local favorite (closed all day Wed and Thu for lunch, 15-min drive from Roussillon; see page 212).

L'Auberge de la Loube is the ultimate country/Provençal experience. But, because it makes for a long after-dinner drive, many find it's best for lunch (closed Sun evening and all day Mon and Thu; see page 216).

Hostellerie des Commandeurs is inexpensive, traditional, friendly, and a solid value that's good for families (closed Wed, in Joucas—a 5-min drive from Roussillon; see page 202).

Le Fournil, in Bonnieux, has excellent food and a gorgeous terrace to match (closed for dinner Mon, closed for lunch Mon–Tue and Sat; see page 207).

Le Tenil, just below Le Fournil in Bonnieux, owns great Luberon views (closed Sun; see page 207).

Le Bistrot de Roussillon, on the village square with a terrace out back, has excellent salads and *plats* priced just right (open daily; see page 200).

Best Places to Lunch

Le Fournil in Bonnieux (with a good-value lunch *menu*), **Le Bistrot de Roussillon,** and **L'Auberge de la Loube** are all listed for dinner, above—but are also top lunch stops. Here are some others to consider:

Bar/Restaurant de France, in Lacoste, is an easygoing eatery with sensational view tables and good *plats*, omelets, and salads (daily, lunch only off-season; see page 209).

L'Auberge des Seguins is a corner of paradise awaiting those who survive the climb to Fort de Buoux (daily; see page 216).

Auberge du Presbytère, in the village of Saignon, offers a slow, tasty lunch by the fountain on one of Provence's most handsome squares (closed Wed; see page 214).

Le Petit Jardin Café, in remote Viens, offers an unpretentious lunch or dinner stop, with cozy interior tables, a garden terrace, and reasonable prices (closed Wed; see page 213).

Joucas

This understated, quiet, and largely overlooked village slumbers below the Gordes buzz. Vertical stone lanes with carefully arranged flow-

ers and well-restored homes play host to aspiring Claude Monets and a smattering of locals. There's not much to do or see here, except eat, sleep, and just be. Joucas has one tiny grocery, a view café, one pharmacy, a good kids' play area, and one good-value accommodation option. Sleep here for a central location and utter silence. For views, walk past the little fountain in the center and up the steep lanes as high as you want.

Several **hiking** trails leave from Joucas. Gordes and Roussillon are each three miles away, uphill. Even better, hikers can take the three-mile hike to the attractive village of Murs, with several cafés/restaurants, though it's easier in the other direction (yellow signs point the way from the top of the village). You don't have to go far to enjoy the natural beauty on this trail.

Sleeping and Eating in Joucas

$$ Hostellerie des Commandeurs**, run by soft Sophie, has modern, comfortable, and clean rooms in the village of Joucas. It's kid-friendly, with a big pool and a sports field/play area next door. Ask for a south-facing room *(coté sud)* for the best views, or a north-facing room *(coté nord)* if it's hot. All rooms have showers (Db-€62–65, extra bed-€16, small fridges, above park at village entrance, tel. 04 90 05 78 01, fax 04 90 05 74 47, www.lescommandeurs.com, hostellerie@lescommandeurs.com). The simple restaurant offers tasty cuisine at fair prices (three-course *menus* from €20, succulent lamb, memorable crème brûlée with lavender, restaurant closed Wed).

Near Joucas

$$$ La Ferme de la Huppe*** has a Gordes address, but it's closer physically and spiritually to Joucas. This small farmhouse-elegant haci-enda makes an excellent mini-splurge. Ten low-slung rooms gather on two levels behind the stylish pool. The decor is tasteful, understated, and rustic (small Db-€110, bigger Db-€140–170, much bigger Db-€200, includes good breakfast, small fridges, air-con,

Wi-Fi; between Joucas and Gordes on D-156 road to Goult, just off D-2; tel. 04 90 72 12 25, fax 04 90 72 25 39, www.lafermedela huppe.com, info@lafermedelahuppe.com). Dine poolside or in the smart dining room (€35 three-course *menu* or €20 *plats*).

$$$ Le Mas du Loriot is another worthwhile almost-in-Joucas value. Gentle owners Alain and Christine have carved the ideal escape out of an olive grove, with eight soothing rooms, private terraces, a generous pool, and home-cooked dinners—all at fair prices and with a view to remember (Db-€110–140, extra bed-€20, €30 four-course dinners available three nights a week—when half-pension is a smart idea, Internet access, on D-102 between Joucas and Murs, tel. 04 90 72 62 62, fax 04 90 72 62 54, www .masduloriot.com, hotel@masduloriot.com).

More Luberon Towns

Le Luberon is packed with appealing villages and beautiful scenery, but it has only a handful of must-see sights. I've grouped them by area to make your sightseeing planning easier (see the Luberon map at the beginning of this chapter). Busy D-900 slices like an arrow through the heart of the Luberon, dividing the region in half. The more popular and visited section lies above D-900 (with Roussillon and Gordes), while the villages to the south seem a bit less trampled.

The busiest sights are in and near Gordes; I've listed those first, to encourage you to avoid afternoon crowds. Beyond that, you're free to connect the stops however you please. Rambling the Luberon's spaghetti network of small roads is a joy, and getting lost comes with the territory—go with it. None of the sights listed below is must-see, but all are close to each other. Pick up a good map (Michelin Local map #332 and #528 work for me).

Gordes and Nearby Sights

Gordes

For the last 40 years, Gordes has been the most touristy and trendy town in the Luberon—creating gridlock and parking headaches (come early). In the 1960s, Gordes was a virtual ghost town of derelict buildings. But now it's thoroughly renovated and filled with people who live in a world without calluses. Many Parisian big shots and wealthy foreigners have purchased and restored older homes here, putting property values out of sight for locals.

Ponder a region that in the last 35 years has experienced such a dramatic change. Post-World War II, the Luberon was mired in poverty. By 1970, the Luberon had recovered but was still unknown to most travelers. Locals led simple lives and had few ambitions. Then came the theater festival in Avignon, bringing directors who wanted to re-create perfect Provençal villages on film. Parisians, Swiss, Brits, and a few Americans followed, willing to pay any price for their place in the Provençal sun. Property taxes increased—as did the cost of *une bière* at the corner café—and all too soon, villagers found themselves with few affordable options.

The village's setting is striking. As you approach Gordes, make a hard right at the impressive view of the place (you'll find some parking along the small road). Beyond here, the village has little of interest, except its many boutiques and its Tuesday market (which ends at 13:00). The town's 11th-century castle houses a mildly interesting collection of contemporary art.

There are two sights near Gordes—the Abbey Notre-Dame de Sénanque and the Village des Bories—both well-marked from Gordes and described below.

Near Gordes

Abbey Notre-Dame de Sénanque—This still-functioning and beautifully situated Cistercian abbey was built in 1148 as a

back-to-basics reaction to the excesses of Benedictine abbeys. The Cistercians strove to be separate from the world, and to recapture the simplicity, solitude, and poverty of the early Church. To succeed required industrious self-sufficiency—a skill that these monks had. Their movement spread and colonized Europe with a new form of Christianity. By 1200, there were more than 500 such monasteries and abbeys in Europe.

The abbey is best appreciated from the outside, and is worth the trip for its splendid and remote setting alone. Come early or late, stop at a pullout for a bird's-eye view as you descend, then wander the abbey's perimeter with fewer tourists. The abbey church (Eglise Abbatiale) is open and highlights the utter simplicity sought by these monks. The beautiful bookshop is worth a look as well (Cistercians know how to turn a profit). In late June through much of July, the lavender fields that surround the abbey make for breathtaking pictures and draw loads of visitors, making it more important to arrive early or late.

The abbey itself is only open for tours (in French only, English handout, about 6/day Mon–Sat, one hour, limited to 50 people,

so call ahead or check their website) and to attend Mass (Sun at 10:00, Mon at 8:30, Tue–Sat at 12:00). The tour covers Sénanque's church, the small cloisters, the refectory, and a *chauffoir* (small heated room where monks could copy books year-round). A small monastic community still resides here (€7 admission includes tour, open Mon–Sat 10:00–12:00 & 13:30–18:00, Sun 14:00–18:00, tel. 04 90 72 05 72, www.senanque .fr). For more on monasteries, see the "Medieval Monasteries" sidebar later in this chapter.

If your next destination is near Roussillon, Bonnieux, or Apt, leave the abbey opposite the way you arrived, following signs to *Gordes*, then *Roussillon*, then follow *Murs* and *Joucas*...and enjoy the ride.

Village des Bories—A lengthy stone-bordered dirt road sets the mood for this mildly entertaining open-air museum. The vertical stones you see on the walls as you approach the site were used as counterweights to keep these walls, built without mortar, intact. The "village" you tour is composed of dry-laid stone structures, proving that there has always been more stone than wood in this rugged region. Stone villages like this predated the Romans—some say by 2,000 years. This one was inhabited for 200 years (from about 1600 to 1800). *Bories* (dry-stone huts) can still be seen in fields throughout the Luberon; most are now used to store tools or hay. A look around these hills confirms the supply of building materials: The trees are small and gnarled (not good for construction), but white stone grows everywhere.

The Village des Bories is composed of five "hamlets." You'll duck into several homes and see animal pens, a community oven, and more (identified in English). Study the "beehive" stone-laying method and imagine the time it took to construct. The villagers had no scaffolds or support arches—just hammers and patience (€5.50, buy €4 booklet of English translations to learn more, daily June–Sept 9:00–20:00, Oct–May 9:00–17:30, tel. 04 90 72 04 39).

Bouillon Olive Mill and Museum of Glass (Moulin des Bouillons and Musée de l'Histoire du Verre)—This fun museum park is a true Back Door experience. Find an hour and fork it over to two charming women who will explain to you (in fine English) the mill and the museum. Start with Carole at the olive mill, which has been in use for more than 2,000 years. You'll learn about this ancient practice, including how olive oil and its products are made. The Roman remains are nice, but they take a back seat to the massive 400-year-old oak olive press.

Then wander with the chickens through a small park and modern sculpture garden to the solar-paneled, bunker-like Museum of Glass. Here, Béatrice will teach you about the historic importance of glass from Roman times to contemporary glassblowing. You'll learn about the medieval art of stained glass and see modern glass made by the museum's benefactor, Madame Frédérique Duran. The newest exhibit describes the use of glass to dispose of nuclear waste (€5 apiece for mill or museum, €7.50 for both, April–Oct Wed–Mon 10:00–12:00 & 14:00–18:00, closed Tue, by appointment in winter, tel. 04 90 72 22 11). It's well-signed between Gordes, Coustellet, and St. Pantaleon on D-148.

Museum of Lavender (Musée de la Lavande)—Located halfway between Gordes and Isle-sur-la-Sorgue in Coustellet, this surprisingly interesting museum does a fine job explaining the process of lavender production with interesting exhibits and good English information (via an audioguide, a film, and posted explanations at the exhibits). It's popular with tour groups, smells great inside, and offers the ultimate "if they made it with lavender, we sell it" gift shop (€6, daily May–Sept 9:00–19:00, Oct–April 9:00–13:00 & 14:00–18:00, in Coustellet just off D-900 toward Gordes, tel. 04 90 76 91 23). For more on this fragrant flower, see page 176.

Villages and Sights South of Roussillon

These villages and sights below Roussillon and D-900 feel less visited than places north of this busy road. You'll need a good half-day to visit them all (see the map on page 182 to get oriented). They work well in the order described below, with lunch in Bonnieux or Lacoste (see "Luberon Restaurants that Justify the Trip" sidebar, earlier in this chapter). The first sight is situated south of Roussillon, where D-108 crosses D-900.

St. Julien Bridge (Pont St. Julien)

This delicate three-arched bridge survives as a testimony to Roman engineers—and to the importance of this rural area 2,000 years ago. It's the only surviving bridge on what was the main road from northern Italy to Provence—the primary route used by Roman armies. The 215-foot-long Roman bridge was built from 27 B.C. to A.D. 14. Mortar had not yet been invented, so (as with Pont du Gard) stones were carefully set in place.

Amazingly, the bridge survives today, having outlived Roman marches, hundreds of floods, and decades of automobile traffic. A new bridge finally rerouted traffic from this beautiful structure in 2005.

Walk below the bridge. Notice how thin the layer of stone seems between the arch tops and the road. Those open niches weren't for statues, but instead allowed water to pass through when the river ran high. (At its current trickle, that's hard to fathom.) Walk under an arch and examine the pockmarks in the side—medieval thieves in search of free bronze stole the clamps.

Château de la Canorgue Winery

Well-signed halfway between the St. Julien Bridge and Bonnieux, this pretty winery makes even prettier wines at reasonable prices (average bottle is €10). They also make it easy for travelers, with a welcoming tasting room offering the full range of wines—from Viognier and Chardonnay whites to rosés and rich reds. Owner-in-waiting and winemaker Nathalie greets guests on weekdays. Compare the *Vendanges de Nathalie* with the *vin du pays* for a good contrast in reds (Mon–Sat 10:00–12:00 & 14:00–18:00, closed Sun, tel. 04 90 75 81 01).

Bonnieux

Spectacular from a distance, this town disappoints me up close. It lacks a pedestrian center, though the Friday-morning market briefly creates one. The main reason to visit here is to enjoy its excellent restaurants and views.

Eating in Bonnieux: The two Bonnieux eateries I list are next to the TI. Eat outside at the first place, and inside at the second.

Le Fournil has marvelous food, a postcard-perfect terrace, and

outdoor tables around a tranquil fountain. The interior is uninviting (unless you dig caves and modern decor), so book an outdoor table or skip it (€15 lunch *plats*, €42 dinner *menus;* closed for dinner Mon; closed for lunch Mon–Tue and Sat; tel. 04 90 75 83 62).

Le Tenil sits across from Le Fournil, with fabulous Luberon views and cuisine to match (€25–30 *menu*, closed Sun, book ahead for a window table, tel. 04 90 75 61 28).

Sleeping near Bonnieux: The country-elegant *chambre d'hôte* **\$\$\$ Mas del Sol,** ideally situated between Bonnieux and Lacoste, is ideal for connoisseurs of the Luberon. Young Lucine and Richard Massol rent five bright, spacious rooms that come with

THE LUBERON

Medieval Monasteries

France is littered with medieval monasteries, and Provence is no exception. Most have virtually no furnishings (they never had many), which leaves the visitor with little to reconstruct what life must have been like in these cold stone buildings a thousand years ago. A little history can help breathe life into these important yet underappreciated monuments.

After the fall of the Roman Empire, monasteries arose as refuges of peace and order in a chaotic world. While the pope got rich and famous playing power politics, monasteries worked to keep the focus on simplicity and poverty. Throughout the Middle Ages, monasteries were mediators between Man and God. In these peacefully remote abbeys, Europe's best minds struggled with the interpretation of God's words. Every sentence needed to be understood and applied. Answers were debated in universities and contemplated in monasteries.

St. Benedict established the Middle Ages' most influential monastic order (Benedictine) in Monte Cassino, Italy, in A.D. 529. He scheduled a rigorous program of monastic duties that combined manual labor with intellectual tasks. His movement spread north and took firm root in France, where the abbey of Cluny (Burgundy) eventually controlled more than 2,000 dependent abbeys and vied with the pope for control of the Church. Benedictine abbeys grew dot-com rich, and with wealth came excess (king-size beds and Wi-Fi). Monks lost sight of their purpose and became soft and corrupt. In the late 1100s, the determined and charismatic St. Bernard rallied the Cistercian order by going back to the original rule of St. Benedict. Cistercian abbeys thrived as centers of religious thought and exploration from the 13th through the 15th centuries.

views and a big breakfast. The setting is unbeatable, and the stylish pool and gardens will calm your nerves (Db-€100–140, tel. 04 90 75 94 80, www.mas-del-sol.com, emasdelsol@wanadoo.fr). From D-900, take the D-36 turnoff to Bonnieux and look for *Mas del Sol* signs after about four kilometers.

Lacoste

Little Lacoste slumbers across the valley from Bonnieux in the shadow of its looming castle. Climb through this photogenic village of arches and stone paths, passing American art students (from the Savannah College of Art and Design) showing their work. Support an American artist, learn about their art, and then keep climbing and climbing to the ruined castle base. The view of Bonnieux from the base of Lacoste's castle is as good as it gets.

The Marquis de Sade (1740–1814) lived in this castle for more than 30 years. Author of dirty novels, he was notorious for hosting

Cistercian abbots ran their abbeys like little kingdoms, doling out punishment and food to the monks, and tools to peasant farmers. Abbeys were occupied by two groups: the favored monks from aristocratic families (such as St. Bernard) and a larger group of lay brothers from peasant stock, who were given the heaviest labor and could join only the Sunday services.

Monks' days were broken into three activities: prayer, reading holy texts, and labor. Monks lived in silence and poverty with few amenities—meat was forbidden, as was cable TV. In summer, they ate two daily meals; in winter, just one. Monks slept together in a single room on threadbare mats covering solid-rock floors.

With their focus on work and discipline, Cistercian abbeys became leaders of the medieval industrial revolution. Among the few literate people in Europe, monks were keepers of technological knowledge—about clocks, waterwheels, accounting, foundries, gristmills, textiles, and agricultural techniques. Abbeys became economic engines that helped drive France out of its Middle Aged funk.

As France (and Europe) slowly got its act together in the late Middle Ages, cities reemerged as places to trade and thrive. Abbeys gradually lost their relevance in a brave new humanist world. Kings took over abbot selection, further degrading the abbeys' power, and Gutenberg's movable type made monks obsolete. The French Revolution closed the book on abbatial life, with troops occupying and destroying many abbeys. The still-functioning Abbey Notre-Dame de Sénanque, near Gordes, is a rare survivor.

orgies behind these walls, and for kidnapping peasants for scandalous purposes. He was eventually arrested and imprisoned for 30 years, and thanks to him, we have a word to describe his favorite hobby—sadism. Today, clothing designer Pierre Cardin is spending a fortune renovating the castle in lavish fashion, complete with a concert hall. Some locals whisper that he's the Marquis de Sade reincarnated. Could "Cardism" be next?

Eating in Lacoste: If it's time for lunch, find the **Bar/Restaurant de France**'s outdoor tables overlooking Bonnieux and savor the view (inexpensive, good omelets, daily, lunch only off-season, tel. 04 90 75 82 25).

Abbey St. Hilaire

A dirt road off D-103 between Lacoste and Ménerbes leads down to this long-forgotten and pint-size abbey. There's not much to see here—it's more about the experience. The tranquility and isolation sought by monks 800 years ago are still palpable in the simple church and modest cloisters. Once a Cistercian outpost for the bigger abbey at Sénanque, Abbey St. Hilaire is now owned by Carmelite Friars. The lone stone bench in front is picnic-ready, and a rugged WC is cut into the rock (across the courtyard). Leave nothing valuable in your car at this remote site.

Ménerbes

Ménerbes is (in)famous as the village that drew author Peter Mayle's attention to this region, but offers little of interest (unless you're into corkscrews). If you must explore Ménerbes, stash your car, then follow *Eglise* signs to the end of the village and find the heavy Romanesque church (closed and under renovation) and graveyard (good views in all directions). You're face-to-face with the Grand Luberon ridge. Notice the quarry carved into its side, where the stone for this village came from. Foodies can duck into the snazzy **Maison de la Truffe et du Vin,** which offers "truffle discovery workshops" (call for schedule, tel. 04 90 72 52 10). The **Corkscrew Museum** (Musée du Tire-Bouchon) lies a kilometer below Ménerbes and is worth a stop if you're a corkscrew enthusiast or want to taste their wines (Domaine de la Citadelle). They have 1,200 corkscrews on display in glass cases and a well-stocked gift shop (€4 for the "museum," includes tasting, daily 10:00–12:00 & 14:00–19:00, tel. 04 90 72 41 58).

Oppède-le-Vieux

This windy barnacle of a town clings with all its might to its hillside. There's one boutique, two cafés, and a dusty little square at

the base of a short, ankle-twisting climb to a pretty little church and ruined castle. This off-the-beaten-path fixer-upper of a village was completely abandoned in 1910, and today has a ghost town–like feel (it once housed 200 people). The inhabited village below has a rugged character and shows little inclination for boutiques and smart hotels. It's ideal for those looking to perish in Provence.

Plan your ascent to the castle. It's 20 minutes straight up, but the Luberon views justify the effort. (After making this walk, you'll understand why locals abandoned it for more-level terrain.) Small information panels provide a worthwhile background in English as you climb. Walk under the central arch of the building across from Le Petit Café and climb. After walking under the arch, look back to notice the handsome building it supports. At the fork, either way works—though the path to the right is easier. Find the little church terrace. From here, tiled rooftops paint a delightful picture with the grand panorama; the flat plain of the Rhône delta is visible off to the left. The colorful **Notre-Dame d'Alidon church** (1588) is generally open (9:30–18:30; depends on village volunteers who are eager to answer questions). There's been a church on this site for 1,000 years. Pick up the English text and imagine having to climb this distance at least every Sunday—for your entire life. Notice the pride locals have for their church: You'll see new gold-leaf accents and other efforts to spruce up the long-abandoned building. The steps to chapels on the right were necessary, thanks to the church's hillside setting. Wander above the church. Mountain goats can climb on what remains of the castle (pay attention—there are no rails).

Once you're back down, consider a light lunch or an overnight at **Le Petit Café** (cheap lunches with views of the castle ruins, simple but comfy Db-€60–70, big Db-€90, includes breakfast, Jacuzzi, sauna, rooftop terrace, tel. 04 90 76 74 01, www.lepetit cafe.fr, café open for dinner May-Oct but closed Thu).

Getting There: To find Oppède-le-Vieux from D-900, follow signs to *Oppède* and *Oppède le Village*, then *Oppède-le-Vieux*, and drive towards le Grand Luberon massif. You'll follow a long, one-way loop and be forced to park a few hundred yards from the village (unless you're sleeping there), for which you'll get to pay €3.

Villages and Sights East of Roussillon: La Provence Profonde

Provence is busy with tourists, but there are still plenty of characteristic and less-discovered places to explore. The area east of Roussillon feels quieter and less touristed—come here to get a sense of how most villages were before they became "destinations." Here are the key sights in the order that you'll pass them coming from Roussillon or Joucas. Allow a full day to complete this loop. If all you have is a half-day, head straight for the Fort de Buoux (see map on page 183).

St-Saturnin-lès-Apt

Most tourists pass by this pleasant town (with a lively Sunday market) on their way to more famous destinations. I couldn't find a souvenir shop. Ditch your car below the main entry to the town (just below the old city) and walk up the main drag past the Hôtel Hubert (rue de la République). You'll come to a striking church that's a fine example of Provençal Romanesque, with a tall, rounded spire (the interior is often closed). From here, find the ramp with

Le Château signs and climb. The ruined "château" grows right out of the rock, making it difficult to tell the man-made from the natural. Go left as you enter and hike as high as the sun allows with no shade—faded green dots guide you up. It's a scamperer's paradise, with views that rank among the best village-top vistas I found in Provence. The small chapel at the very top is closed, so there's no reason to climb all the way up. To get back down, find your way through the small opening to the little dam.

Sleeping and Eating in or near St-Saturnin-lès-Apt: For a warm welcome, stay at **$$$ Mas Perréal** just outside St-Saturnin-lès-Apt. American Kevin and his Parisian wife Elisabeth left no stone unturned as they restored their lovely farmhouse. Elisabeth teaches French—that's how Kevin met her—and still gives lessons (book in advance). This place features sumptuous rooms (each with its own terrace), a pool, 360-degree views (they own the vineyards and orchards around you), elaborate American-size breakfasts that change weekly, and no language barrier (Db-€120–130, includes big breakfast, tel. 04 90 75 46 31, fax 04 90 04 88 08, www.mas perreal.com, elisabeth-kevin@masperreal.com). Mas Perréal is off D-943, between St-Saturnin-lès-Apt and D-900. Coming from D-900, turn left at Moulin d'Huile d'Olive, continue 1.2 kilometers (three-quarters of a mile), cross one "major" road, then look for signs on your right.

$ Hôtel des Voyageurs*, with amiable owners Nadine and Alain (who speak no English), is a time-warp that has survived many Provençal trends without changing its look or product. The basic, budget accommodations gather around uneven floors and a frumpy upstairs terrace that only an artist could love (modest but fine Db-€52–60, big Db-€66). The Old World restaurant, with pink-and-rose tablecloths above vintage floor tiles,

serves traditional cuisine that locals adore (*menus* from €20, closed all day Wed and Thu for lunch, tel. 04 90 75 42 08, fax 04 90 75 50 58). It's at the base of the old village—look for signs.

Le Colorado Provençal

This park has ochre cliffs similar to Roussillon's, but they're spread over a larger area, with well-signed trails. If hiking through soft,

THE LUBERON

orange sand through Bryce Canyon–like rocks strikes your fancy, follow signs toward the village of *Rustrel*, the gateway to Le Colorado Provençal.

The park is located a kilometer below Rustrel off D-22, between Apt and Gignac. There are two parking lots. Skip the sprawling lot on D-22 with the big signs and snack stands—it's more expensive and leaves you 15 minutes from the trails. The less-expensive and more-convenient *Parking Municipal* at the trailhead is 200 yards toward Apt from the big parking lot (look for small signs to *Colorado Provençal* off D-22, allow €3.50 for parking). There's no entry fee to the park, which is always open, with parking attendants available from about 9:00 until 17:00 or 18:00.

For the best walk, cross the little footbridge and follow either the Cheminée de Fée or the Sahara trail. (Trails are color-coded and easy to follow, allow about 30–40 min for each with modest elevation gain; Cheminée de Fée is more impressive, but steeper.) Light-colored clothing is a bad choice. Signs remind you to please remain on the trails and not to climb the cliffs.

Viens

Located about 15 minutes uphill and east of Le Colorado Provençal (turn right when leaving Colorado), this village is where Luberon

locals go to get away. With a setting like this, it's surprising that modest Viens is not more developed. The panoramas are higher and more vast than around Roussillon (with some lavender fields), and the vegetation is more raw. Walk the streets of the old town (bigger than it first appears) and visit the few shops scattered about. Find the courtyard of the old château, then find the lone stone arch overlooking the view. This is how Gordes must have looked before it became chic.

Eating in Viens: **Le Petit Jardin Café,** just below the town's only phone booth, fits perfectly in this unpretentious town. Come for a drink and rub shoulders with locals (notice the photos on the walls); or better, have a meal and meet Madame and Monsieur Aubert. Dine in the small traditional interior, or outside on a garden terrace (*menu du jour*-€13 on weekdays, more elaborate €22 *menu* on weekends, lunch served 12:00–14:00, closed Wed, tel. 04

90 75 20 05). A small **grocery store** and a **bakery** are a few blocks past the café, toward St. Martin de Castillon.

To reach the next village (Saignon), follow signs to *St. Martin de Castillon*, then turn right on D-900 toward Apt.

Saignon

Sitting high atop a rock spur, this village looks down onto Apt, a city of only 11,500—which from here looks like a megalopolis after all these tiny villages. You can peek into the too-big-for-this-village Romanesque church (Notre-Dame de la Pitié) and admire its wood doors and tympanum, then follow *Le Rocher* signs through the village up to the "ship's prow." If you need to see it all, climb to the Le Rocher Bellevue for grand views over lavender fields (about three stories of stairs to the top). There's a handful of cafés, a cushy hotel (described below), and a grocery store in the linear village's center. Parking is best just above the town (hike or drive farther above town for sensational views over Saignon).

Sleeping and Eating in Saignon: **$$$ Auberge du Presbytère***** houses some of the most appealing rooms I list in Provence, on one of the region's most handsome little squares. This vine-strewn place is family-run, so expect kids underfoot. Three rooms come with private terraces, but all combine a homey feel with exquisite furnishings and bathrooms you can stretch out in (Db-€70–120, Tb/Qb loft-€150, massive studio with terrace-€200). The restaurant is what draws most to Saignon. Enjoy lunch fountain-side on the square, or eat inside at dinner (*plats* from €18, *menus* from €29, restaurant closed Wed; place de la Fontaine, tel. 04 90 74 11 50, fax 04 90 04 68 51, www.auberge-presbytere.com, reception@auberge-presbytere.com). Hotel guests may have pool privileges at another hotel in the village—ask.

BUOUX

Buoux (pronounced "boox"), a way-off-the-beaten-path village, is home to two memorable restaurants and Provence's without-a-doubt best ruined castle. A trip to this far-flung corner rewards with rocky canyons, acres of lavender, and few tourists. Start early and climb to the castle before the heat rises, then have a long, well-earned lunch nearby (see recommendations under "Eating in Buoux," later). If you liked Les Baux but weren't so fond of the crowds and don't need an audioguide, you'll love it here.

Buoux is south of Apt on D-113 between Saignon and Lourmarin. Ambitious travelers can combine a visit to Buoux with Lourmarin and Bonnieux.

THE LUBERON

Sights in Buoux

▲▲Fort de Buoux

The remains of this remote ridge-top castle are a playground for energetic lovers of crumbled ruins and grand views. You need good

legs and stable shoes to navigate the steep, uneven footing.

Floating like a cloud above the valleys below, the fort is easy to miss—it blends with the limestone rock cliffs that dominate the landscape. The long, rocky outcrop has been inhabited since prehistoric times. In the Middle Ages, it was home to hundreds of residents and a powerful castle that controlled a vast area. Like Les Baux, the fort was destroyed in the 1500s during the wars of religion (it was a Protestant base) and again in the 1600s by a paranoid King Louis XIII (see "The Life of a Hill Town in Provence" on page 166).

Madame la Caretaker lives in the flowery house where you buy your ticket (€3). Get the English map and start climbing. The map suggests a one-way route through the rocky ruins. You'll start with what's left of the village, then scramble around rock piles along the long outcrop to the castle remains, once home to hundreds of residents. You'll also climb around the remains of homes, a church, cisterns, and medieval storage silos.

The unforgettable highlight of this castle is a three-story stone spiral staircase. Cut into the cliffs, it leads back down to the base (follow the faded white arrows as you leave the ruins). The staircase is steep and has no handrails and big steps, so be very careful—or return the way you came.

Getting There: To reach the fort from Apt and the north, drive through Buoux, pass L'Auberge de la Loube, drop down, and follow signs to *Fort de Buoux* (and *L'Auberge des Seguins*). If coming from the south, follow signs to *Apt*, then *L'Aubgere des Seguins* and *Fort de Buoux*. Park in the dirt lot and walk about 15 minutes up a dirt road to the foot of the fort.

Sleeping in Buoux

$ L'Auberge des Seguins is a stone's throw from the parking area for the fort. It's a lush and simple Shangri-la kind of place at the end of the valley, with confident young Amélie (and hound Miette) in charge. The rambling old farm is purposefully unmanicured, as guests are encouraged to enjoy the natural beauty. The 28 rooms are simple, clean, and squirreled about the place:

THE LUBERON

Some require a dirt path to reach, and some are built into the rocky cliff. Kids love it (there's also a big pool, but it's not heated). This place is a very good value unless you need things just so (Db-€58, half-pension with good dinners-€58 per person, €37 per person if you sleep in the cool dorm rooms, tel. 04 90 74 16 37, www.aubergedesseguins.com, aubergedesseguins@gmail.com). See also "Eating in Buoux," next.

Eating in Buoux

L'Auberge de la Loube ("Inn of the Wolf") is up the road from the fort in Buoux village and delivers the ultimate in Provençal country-coziness. Plan to stay a while and enjoy the superb cuisine and setting (indoors or out) and eccentric owner, Monsieur Leporati. You'll understand why it was one of Peter Mayle's favorites. Call a day ahead to secure a table (allow €24 for lunch—more on Sun, €33 for dinner, cash only, reasonable wine list, closed Sun evening and all day Mon and Thu, tel. 04 90 74 19 58).

L'Auberge des Seguins (also listed under "Sleeping in Buoux") has a good restaurant and a small café with bar food and snacks. The choices are limited, but the produce is very fresh—manager Amélie brags that they only use the small refrigerator for ice cream (€7–15 lunch options, €25 dinner *menu*, indoor and outdoor seating, closed Mon for lunch).

Lourmarin

The southernmost Luberon village of Lourmarin has a fine Friday market, a beautiful Renaissance château on its fringe, and an enchanting town center. Lourmarin sits on a level plain and feels strangely peaceful and happy, away from the more-visited villages in the heart of the Luberon. This self-assured and lovely town accommodates a healthy (mostly French) tourist demand without feeling overrun. It's the best Luberon village to enjoy in the winter when other, better-known towns rattle about with few residents and little commercial activity.

Existentialist writer Albert Camus *(The Stranger)* lived in Lourmarin in the 1950s, lending it a certain fame that persists today. Author Peter Mayle moved here not long ago, adding to the village's cachet...and now you're here, too. Lourmarin makes a good base for touring the southern Luberon, Aix-en-Provence, and even Marseille and maybe Cassis. From here, you can tour big cities, beaches, and castles, returning every night to the comfort of your village.

Getting There: Three buses per day link Lourmarin to Avignon (1.5 hrs), and to Aix-en-Provence (1.25 hrs, bus to Pertuis leaves 3/day, transfer there to bus bound for Aix-en-Provence, 2/hr).

Orientation to Lourmarin

Tourist Information

The TI is located across from the soccer field and the château on avenue Philippe de Girard (Mon–Sat 10:00–12:30 & 15:00–18:00, closed Sun, tel. 04 90 68 10 77).

Theft Alert: There have been a rash of break-ins at car lots in Lourmarin. Park centrally, and leave nothing visible in your car.

Sights In Lourmarin

Château de Lourmarin—The impressive château looks across a grassy meadow at the village and offers a rare-in-this-region look inside a Renaissance châ-

teau. Tour the château on your own, with the help of its decent English handout and posted explanations. You'll see several well-furnished rooms, a fine kitchen, gorgeous exterior galleries, and a slick double spiral staircase in stone (€5.50, daily May–Sept 10:00–11:30 & 14:30–17:30, Oct–April until 16:00, tel. 04 90 68 15 23).

Friday Market—This little town erupts into a market frenzy every Friday until 13:00. Sleep here Thursday night and awake to the commotion, arrive early, or prepare for a good walk from your car.

Sleeping in Lourmarin

Try to sleep here on a Thursday, so you can awake to Friday's market. The good-value Villa St. Louis and Les Chambres de la Cordière sit across from each other at the very eastern end of the town center.

$$$ At Les Olivettes, Joseph and Elizabeth DeLiso rent five apartments just a five-minute walk from the village center. The apartments are well-furnished and very comfortable, with kitchens, living rooms, CD players, and Internet access. They are rentable by the week or half-week (one-bedroom unit-€430/3 nights, two-bedroom unit-€842/3 nights, credit cards OK, avenue Henri Bosco, tel. 04 90 68 03 52, www.olivettes.com, lourmarin @olivettes.com).

$$ Villa St. Louis is a splendid place. It's a cross between a museum, a fine old manor home, and a garage sale. The fun and slightly eccentric owner, Madame Bernadette, adds charm to a house packed with character. The dreamy backyard is ideal for a siesta (hammock provided) and picnics. The rooms are like Grandma's, and there's a common room with a fridge (Db-€65–75, includes breakfast, cash only, secure parking, loaner bikes, 35 rue de Henri Savournin, tel. 04 90 68 39 18, fax 04 90 68 10 07, www .villasaintlouis.com, villasaintlouis@wanadoo.fr).

$$ Les Chambres de la Cordière is a cool getaway. Owner Françoise's goal is to make you feel at home. Six cozy rooms are tucked into the village's oldest building (c. 1582), with a tiny court-yard and welcoming cats. Four rooms come with mini-kitchens; the two with full kitchens are usually rented only by the week (Db-€65–70, Tb-€85, Qb-€100, includes breakfast, cash only, rue Albert Camus, tel. & fax 04 90 68 03 32, www.cordiere.com, cordiereluberon@aol.com).

Eating in Lourmarin

All roads seem to converge on the postcard-perfect intersection near **Café de la Fontaine,** where you can enjoy a light meal or snack inside or out—or choose from several cafés. The following listings are within a block of this intersection.

Restaurant l'Antiquaire makes me feel as if I'm in an Impressionist painting, and it is *the* place to eat well in Lourmarin (indoor seating only, €32 *menu*, €40 bouillabaisse possible if ordered ahead, closed Sun–Mon, indoors only but air-con, a block up from Café de la Fontaine on 9 rue du Grand Pré, tel. 04 90 68 17 29).

Le Bistrot Lyonnais offers a change from the usual Provençal fare, with red-leather ambience in a cozy, shoebox-sized room, and hearty cuisine from Lyon (€15 *plats*, €26 *menu*, closed Sun and Thu, 2 avenue Philippe de Girard, tel. 04 90 68 29 74).

La Recreation, across the street, features a welcoming terrace and regional cuisine with vegetarian options (€16–20 *plats*, €26 *menus,* closed Wed except in summer, next to the TI on avenue Philippe de Girard, tel. 04 90 68 23 73).

MARSEILLE, CASSIS, AND AIX-EN-PROVENCE

In the rush to get between Avignon and the Riviera, most travelers zip through the eastern fringe of Provence. That's a shame, as this area offers compelling cities and a strikingly beautiful coastline, all in a tight package. I cover three different-as-night-and-day places, each worthy of a slice of your time. Marseille is an untouristy, semi-seedy-but-vibrant port city with 2,600 years of history. The nearby coastal village of Cassis offers the perfect antidote to the big city. And just inland, popular and polished Aix-en-Provence is the yin to Marseille's yang, with beautiful people to match its lovely architecture.

Marseille

Those who think of Marseille as the "Naples of France"—a big, gritty, dangerous port—missed the boat. Today's Marseille (mar-say),

while hardly pristine, is closer to the "Barcelona of France." It's a big, gritty port, *sans* question, but it has a distinct culture, a proud spirit, a new prosperity, and a populace determined to clean up its act. That's a tall order, but they're off to a fair start. Thousands of Marseille's historic buildings are undergoing a massive renovation program, and a new tramway system is up and running.

France's oldest (600 B.C.) and second-biggest city (and Europe's third-largest port) nurtures a history that goes back to ancient

MARSEILLE

Marseille, Cassis, and Aix-en-Provence

Greek times—and challenges you to find its charm. Marseille is a world apart from France's other leading cities (such as Paris and Lyon). It's amazing to think that Marseille has only one essential sight to visit (Notre-Dame de la Garde). The city itself is the museum, the streets are its paintings, and the happy-go-lucky residents provide its ambience.

You're likely to hear as much Arabic as French. The influence of immigrants is huge: More than 25 percent of the city's population came from countries in North Africa. These migrants have created residential ghettos where nary a word of French is uttered—infuriating anti-immigrant French people certain that this will be the destiny for the rest of "their" country (see sidebar on page 223).

Most tourists leave Marseille off their itinerary—it doesn't fit their idea of the French Riviera or of Provence. But it would be a shame to come to the south of France and not experience the region's leading city and namesake of the French national anthem. By train, it's made-to-order for a quick visit. And with the TGV line making it just a three-hour trip from Paris, this much-maligned city seems eager to put on a welcoming face.

Planning Your Time

For a stimulating four-hour tour of Marseille that covers the basics, walk from the train station down La Canebière, wander around the Old Port on quai du Port, climb to the La Charité Museum (ideal lunch café), find the cathedral, then return to the port and take the shuttle ferry across to the new town (with the best eating options). Finally, take a bus, tourist train, or taxi up to Notre-Dame de la Garde before returning to the station.

Orientation to Marseille

Marseille is huge, with 820,000 people—so keep it simple and focus on the area immediately around the Old Port (Vieux Port). A main boulevard (La Canebière) meets the colorful Old Port at a cluster of small (and skippable) museums and the TI. The characteristic Panier district is the old town, blanketing a hill that tumbles down to the port. The harborside is a lively, broad promenade lined with inviting eateries, amusements, and a morning fish

market. Everything described here (except Notre-Dame de la Garde) is within a 30-minute walk of the train station.

In 2009, the city unveiled both a smart new tramway line and a cheap public bike system called le Vélo (similar to Vélib' bikes in Paris)—though visitors won't find much use for either.

Tourist Information

The main TI is right at the **Old Port** (Mon–Sat 9:00–19:00, Sun 10:00–17:00, 4 La Canebière, tel. 04 91 13 89 00, www.marseille -tourisme.com). Pick up the good city map, the flier with a self-guided walk through the old town, and information on museums and the weekly walking tours.

Arrival in Marseille

By Train: St. Charles Station (Gare St. Charles) is busy, modern, and user-friendly. Many services are along or outside of track A, including a good cafeteria, WCs (€0.50), baggage storage (daily 8:15–21:00), and a quiet waiting area *(Salle d'Attente)*. Exiting by track A to Square Narvik, car rental and Hôtel Ibis are on your left, while access to the old city by foot is to the right. With your back to the tracks, turn right to find several cafés and sandwich shops (including McDonald's) and the exit that leads to the bus station (including airport buses).

To get from the train station to the Old Port, you can walk, take the Métro, or catch a taxi.

On **foot,** it's a 15-minute downhill gauntlet along grimy streets from the station to the Old Port. Leave the station through the exit at track A, veer right, and admire the view from atop the stairs (Toto, we're not in Cassis anymore). That's Notre-Dame de la Garde overlooking the city. Walk down the stairs and straight on boulevard d'Athènes, which becomes boulevard Dugommier. Turn right at McDonald's onto the grand boulevard, La Canebière, which leads directly to the port and the main TI.

By **Métro,** it's an easy subterranean trip from the train station to the Old Port: Go down the escalator opposite track E and buy a ticket (from the machines or inside the *Accueil* office, €1.80 ticket is good for one hour of travel on Métro and buses, all-day pass costs €4.70). Descend the long escalator, and take the blue line #1 (direction: La Timone) two stops to Vieux Port. Following *Sortie la Canebière* exit signs, you'll pop out at the TI (and smell the fish market). To return to the station from here, take the blue line #1 (direction: La Rose) two stops and get off at the stop called Gare SNCF.

If you take a **taxi,** allow €9 to the port and €11 to Notre-Dame de la Garde—though train station cabbies may refuse these short trips if business is hopping (tel. 04 91 02 20 20). Taxis along the port will take you on shorter rides.

By Car: Drivers who are good in big, crazy cities can navigate Marseille. Leaving the autoroute, signs to *Vieux Port, Centre-Ville,* and *Office du Tourisme* take you right to the Old Port. At the port, turn left and let the blue *P* signs direct you into an underground lot with 625 spaces (€5/3 hours, €14/24 hours). Locals claim pay lots are patrolled and safe.

By Plane: Marseille's airport (Aéroport Marseille–Provence), about 16 miles north of the city center, is small and easy to navigate (tel. 04 42 14 14 14, www.marseille.aeroport.fr). Frequent buses run

Vive la Différence

Marseille is one of Europe's greatest cultural melting pots. An important trading center since ancient times, Marseille has long been defined by the waves of immigrant peoples who have called this beautifully situated port home. Accessible by land and sea to North Africa, Spain, Italy, and Greece, Marseille once attracted Phoenicians, Greeks, and Romans. Today, Marseille houses France's largest concentration of immigrants: 200,000 of its more than 800,000 residents are Muslim; 80,000 are Jewish (Marseille has had a large Jewish population since the Jews were expelled from Spain in 1492); 80,000 are Armenian Orthodox (escaping Ottoman injustices); and there are 70,000 Comorans (from a group of islands in the Indian Ocean).

There's a spirit of cooperation among Marseille's immigrants, who understand that what benefits one group helps them all. While anti-Semitic and anti-government riots have disrupted other parts of France in recent years (Paris in particular), gritty Marseille has remained quiet. Unlike in Paris, immigrants in Marseille live in the city center, not the suburbs, so they are more visible (and hard to ignore). And while unemployment is high among immigrants, it is nowhere near as high as in Parisian suburbs. The commercial port, a thriving high-tech industry, and tourism (mostly from cruise ships) fuel Marseille's economy. The city has also invested mightily in jobs programs and city-center renovation projects that have benefited its lower-income residents.

Marseille engenders a strong sense of identity apart from France (and the French language) that unites this city's diverse population. Locals see themselves as *Marseillais* (mar-say-ay) first, and as French second (or third, after their native country). Locals' fierce pride is manifested in their passion for Olympique de Marseille, the city's soccer team. Since 1899, *Marseillais* have lived and died with the fate of their team. (A few years ago, I was here the day that 30,000 Marseille fans were boarding trains to Paris for the France finals.) The Olympique de Marseille has made a point of creating a team that looks like the city by recruiting players from North African countries (Zinédine Zidane is the most famous example). The strategy seems to have worked, as Marseille has won the French Cup more than any other team in France.

Immigrant populations are booming in cities throughout Europe, challenging local governments to accommodate them. Many would do well to study Marseille.

Marseille at a Glance

▲▲Notre-Dame de la Garde Marseille's landmark sight: a huge Romanesque-Byzantine basilica, towering above everything, with panoramic views. **Hours:** Daily in summer 7:00–20:00, until 19:00 in winter. See page 232.

▲Marine Museum Grandiose building with small exhibit on the city's maritime history. **Hours:** June–Sept Tue–Sun 10:00–18:00, Oct–May Tue–Sun 10:00–17:00, closed Mon. See page 227.

▲Old Port Economic heart of town, featuring lots of boats and a fish market, all protected by two impressive fortresses. **Hours:** Port—always open; fish market—daily until 13:00. See page 227.

▲La Charité Museum Housed in a beautiful building with Celtic, Greek, Roman, and Egyptian artifacts, plus temporary exhibits. **Hours:** June–Sept Tue–Sun 11:00–18:00, Oct–May Tue–Sun 10:00–17:00, closed Mon. See page 230.

Marseille History Museum Shows off the city's remarkable history with artifacts from Caesar to Louis XIV. **Hours:** Mon–Sat 12:00–19:00, closed Sun. See page 227.

Cathédrale de la Nouvelle Major Impressive striped cathedral with floor and wall mosaics. **Hours:** Daily 10:00–12:00 & 14:00–18:00. See page 231.

Arab Markets Taste of North Africa in downtown Marseille. **Hours:** Open long hours daily. See page 226.

Fashion Museum Sparse collection of dresses from the last half-century. **Hours:** June–Sept Tue–Sun 11:00–18:00, Oct–May Tue–Sun 10:00–17:00, closed Mon. See page 227.

Château d'If Island with fortress-turned-prison, featured in Alexandre Dumas' *The Count of Monte Cristo*. **Hours:** Boats depart daily from quai des Belges, usually on the hour 9:00–17:00. See page 233.

to Marseille's St. Charles train station (€9, 3/hr, 25 min) and to Aix-en-Provence (stops at Aix-en-Provence's TGV station or bus station, 2/hr, 30 min, www.rdt13.fr). A five-minute shuttle bus trip connects the airport to a nearby train station, called Vitrolles Aéroport. This station is most useful for its direct service to cities west of Marseille, including Arles, Avignon, and Nîmes. (You can also take a train from this station into Marseille, but the bus described above is easier and more frequent.) For destinations east of Marseille (such as Cassis, Nice, or Italy), take the bus to Marseille's Gare St. Charles and connect by train from there. If you need to sleep near the airport, consider Hôtel Louisiana (see page 234).

Helpful Hints

Pickpockets: As in any big city, thieves thrive in crowds and target tourists. Wear your money belt, and assume any commotion is a smokescreen for theft.

Car Rental: All the major companies are represented at St. Charles Station (see "Arrival in Marseille," earlier).

Bus #60 to the Basilica: This handy bus scoots you from the Old Port up to Notre-Dame de la Garde in 10 minutes for just €1.80 round-trip (ticket is good for one hour, pay driver, 3/hr). Ask the driver for the Notre-Dame de la Garde stop (where most are going). To return to the port, you can board the bus at this same stop.

Soccer Matches: *Le football* is to Marseille what American football is to Green Bay: Frenzied fans go crazy, and star-worship is always temporary. One of the best-ever soccer players was raised here: Zinédine Zidane (known to Americans mostly for his notorious head-butt of an opponent during the 2006 World Cup finals). If you're here during soccer season (end of July to mid-May), consider getting tickets to a match (every other Sat, tickets start at about €15, ask at the TI or at the **FNAC** store in La Centre Bourse behind the Marine Museum—see page 227). To get to the soccer stadium (Stade Vélodrome), take Métro line 2 (direction: Ste. Marguerite) to the stop called Point du Prado.

Tours in Marseille

Ask at the TI about occasional **walking tours** in English (usually Sat afternoons) and the two-hour **taxi tours** with recorded information in English (arranged through the TI, €66 for up to 4 people).

Le Petit Train's helpful little tourist trains with skimpy recorded information make two routes through town. Both leave at least hourly from the port (across from TI). The more interesting Notre-Dame de la Garde route (#1) saves you the 30-minute climb to the basilica's fantastic view, and runs along an appealing section of Marseille's waterfront (€7, allow 60 min round-trip, including 20 min to visit the church, runs daily, April–Oct usually every 20 min 10:00–13:00 & 14:00–18:30, March and Nov every 60 min, Dec–Feb 5/day, tel. 04 91 25 24 69). I'd skip the Vieux Marseille route (#2), which toots you through the Panier district—better done on foot (€6, 40 min, April–Oct only).

Le Grand Tour's double-decker buses with open seating up top offer a 16-stop, hop-on, hop-off route that is very similar to Le Petit Train's routes. The pricey buses depart from next to the Petit Train stop and run only once an hour, leaving you too long at most stops. Skip these buses (€18 for one-day pass).

Sights in Marseille

I've listed these sights in roughly the order that you come to them as you approach the Old Port on La Canebière. I've also included some commentary to help you connect the dots.

• *Start by the McDonald's at the corner of La Canebière and boulevard Dugommier.*

Along La Canebière

The boulevard La Canebière (pronounced "can o' bee-air") with its

new facelift—and classy tramway— is the celebrated main drag of Marseille. Strolling this stubby thoroughfare, you feel surrounded by a teeming and diverse city. Two blocks before the harbor, you'll find three museums and a stylish shopping district. The boulevard dead-ends at the Old Port's fish market and TI.

Arab Markets—Marseille's huge Moroccan, Algerian, and Tunisian populations give the city a special spice. For a taste of Africa, leave La Canebière by turning left at the second street onto rue Longue des Capucins and walk down a few blocks (to rue d'Aubagne). Suddenly you're immersed in an exotic and fragrant little medina filled with commotion—and no one's speaking French. Stop by **Soleil d'Egypte** and try a *bourek* wrap (apple and ground round) or better, try the *pastilla* wrap (chicken, almonds, onions, and egg)—each costs €2.50. Double back to La Canebière on rue d'Aubagne, stopping to pick up dessert (Tunisian pastries) at **La Carthage** bakery.

• *Continuing down La Canebière, the grand triumphal arch you see far to the right at cours Belsunce marks the gateway to the city of Aix-en-Provence. Next, the big building that seals the street to the left at rue Ferréol is Marseille's préfecture, or regional administration. Now, cross La Canebière and you'll come to the...*

Fashion Museum (Musée de la Mode)—The exhibits here are as skimpy as most of its dresses, with two rooms full of creative and colorful outfits from the 1950s to today (€3, June–Sept Tue–Sun 11:00–18:00, Oct–May Tue–Sun 10:00–17:00, closed Mon year-round, 11 La Canebière, in Espace Mode Mediterranée).

For more fashion, cross back over La Canebière, continue across place du Général de Gaulle (passing the merry-go-round), and find the tiny rue de la Tour, Marseille's self-proclaimed "rue de la Mode." It's lined with shops proudly displaying the latest fashions, mostly from local designers. Just beyond that is the 1920s Art Deco facade of Marseille's opera house.

• *Near the end of La Canebière, on the right side, find the tall and grandiose chamber of commerce building that houses the...*

▲**Marine Museum**—Step inside (free entry) and take in the grand 1860s interior. A relief on the ceiling shows great moments in Marseille's history and a large court with a United Nations of plaques, reminding locals how their commerce comes from trade around the world.

The small ground-floor exhibit on the city's maritime history starts (to the right as you enter) with an impressive portrait of Emperor Napoleon III (who called for the building's construction) and his wife. Sketches show the pomp surrounding its grand opening. The next room traces the growth of the city through charts of its harbor, and the following rooms display models of big ships over the centuries (€2, June–Sept Tue–Sun 10:00–18:00, Oct–May Tue–Sun 10:00–17:00, closed Mon year-round, tel. 04 91 39 33 33).

• *In La Centre Bourse, the modern shopping center behind the chamber of commerce, you'll find the...*

Marseille History Museum (Musée d'Histoire de Marseille)—Come here for a French-only introduction to Marseille's remarkable history, including the remains of an old Roman ship and bits of a Greek vessel—both found here (€2, no English, Mon–Sat 12:00–19:00, closed Sun, tel. 04 91 90 42 22, www.marseille.fr).

• *The TI is back across La Canebière, a short block down from the Marine Museum. After checking in at the TI, cross the big street and get close to the...*

Old Port (Vieux Port)

Protected by two impressive fortresses at its mouth, Marseille's Vieux Port has long been the economic heart of town. These citadels were built in the 17th century under Louis XIV, supposedly to protect the city. But locals figured the forts were

MARSEILLE

Marseille

VIEW
METRO STATION
PARKING
SELF-GUIDED WALK

CATHEDRALE DE LA NOUVELLE MAJOR

LA CHARITE MUSEUM

LE PANIER

WW II MEMORIAL

ST. JEAN FORT

ST. LAURENT

CITY HALL

OLD PORT

SHUTTLE BOATS

Vieux Port

BLVD. LIVON

ST. NICOLAS FORT

QUAI DE RIVE NEUVE

PLACE AUX HUILES

RUE NEUVE STE. CATH.

RUE SAINTE

BLVD. CORDERIE

END

TO NOTRE DAME GARDE

1 Mercure Grand Hôtel Beauvau & Hôtel Kyriad

2 Hôtel Ibis Marseille Gare St. Charles

3 Hôtel Relax

4 Place aux Huiles Eateries

5 Cours d'Estienne d'Orves Eateries

6 La Daurade & Other Rue Saint-Saëns Eateries

❼ Le Souk & Les Galinettes
  Chez Madie Restaurants

❽ La Charité Museum Café

❾ Arab Markets

❿ Le Petit Trains Departure
  Point & Taxi Stand

⓫ Bus #60 Stop & Boat
  Dock for Island &
  Calanques Cruises

⓬ McDonald's & Start of
  Self-Guided Walk

actually designed to keep an eye on Marseille—a city that was essentially autonomous until 1660, and a challenge to thoroughly incorporate into the growing kingdom of France.

Today, the serious shipping is away from the center, and the Old Port is the happy domain of pleasure craft. The fish market along quai des Belges (where you're standing) thrives each morning (unless the mistral wind kept the boats home the day before). The stalls are gone by 13:00, but the smells linger. Looking out from here, Le Panier (the old town) rises to your right. The harborfront below Le Panier was destroyed in 1943 by the Nazis, who didn't want a tangled refuge for resistance fighters so close to the harbor. Today, it's rebuilt as modern condos and trendy restaurants.

• *Walk around the right side of the port and find the small ferry dock (La Ligne du Ferry Boat) that crosses the port. You'll be back here soon. But for now, turn around and find the City Hall.*

Le Panier District (Old Town)

Until the mid-19th century, Marseille was just the hill-capping old town and its fortified port. Today, that old town is the best place to find the town's soul. The ornate **City Hall** (Hôtel de Ville) stands across from the three-masted sailboat and the little shuttle ferry. Its bust of Louis XIV overlooks the harbor. Rue de la Prison leads behind the City Hall and up the hill (where we're headed shortly). At the crest of the hill—the highest point in the old town—is the peaceful place des Moulins, named for the 15 windmills that used to spin and grind from this windy summit. (Today, only the towers of three remain.)

• *Walk up the broad stairway, passing the City Hall, turn left at the top, then track the brown signs up—and up some more—to Vieille Charité. As you walk, read the thoughtful English-information plaques (posted on iron stands at points of historic interest) and listen for the sounds of local life being played out, on the streets and in the rooms just above.*

▲**La Charité Museum (Centre de la Vieille Charité)**—Now a museum, this was once a poorhouse. In 1674, the French king decided that all the poor people on the streets were bad news. He built a huge triple-arcaded home to house a thousand needy subjects. In 1940, the famous architect Le Corbusier declared it a shame that such a fine building was so underappreciated. Today, the striking building—wonderfully renovated and beautiful in its arcaded simplicity—is used as a collection of art galleries surrounding a Pantheon-esque church. You can stroll around the courtyard for free. (Good WCs are in the far-left corner.)

The pediment of the church features the figure of Charity taking care of orphans (as the state did with this building). She's flanked by pelicans (symbolic of charity, for the way they were said to pick flesh from their own bosom to feed their hungry chicks, according to medieval legend). The ground floor outside the church houses temporary exhibits. Upstairs, you'll find rooms with interesting collections of Celtic (c. 300 B.C.), Greek, and Roman artifacts from this region. There's also a surprisingly good Egyptian collection, and masks from Africa and the South Pacific (€2–5 depending on exhibits, no English information, June–Sept Tue–Sun 11:00–18:00, Oct–May Tue–Sun 10:00–17:00, closed Mon year-round, idyllic restaurant/bar, tel. 04 91 14 58 80).

• *From La Charité, cross the small cobbled triangular square, turn right on rue du Petit Puits, and follow the street down, veering left, then right, to find...*

Cathédrale de la Nouvelle Major—Bam. This astonishing

striped cathedral seems lost out here, away from the action and above the nondescript cruise-ship port. The cathedral was built in the late 1800s to replace the old cathedral that the city had outgrown. It's more impressive from the outside, but worth a quick peek inside for its floor and wall mosaics over the nave (daily 10:00–12:00 & 14:00–18:00).

• *Return to the Old Port by walking up the tree-lined esplanade de la Tourette. Marseille's sprawling modern port is behind you and becomes visible as you climb.*

The Great Maritime Port of Marseille (GPMM)—The economy of Marseille is dominated by its modern commercial ports, which extend 30 miles west from here (a nearby canal links Marseille to inland France via the Rhône River, adding to the port's importance). Over 100 million tons of freight pass through this port each year (60 percent of which is petroleum), making this one of Europe's top three ports. Container traffic is significant, but is hampered by crippling strikes for which the left-leaning city is famous. By contrast, cruise-ship tourism has taken off in a big way, bringing more than 550,000 passengers to Marseille each year.

• *Keep walking. A brilliant view awaits you at the bend.*

View Terrace—Voilà! This is one of the best views of Marseille, with Notre-Dame de la Garde presiding above, and twin forts below protecting the entrance to the Old Port. The ugly, boxy building marked "Memorial" at the base of the fort (below and to your right) is a memorial to those lost during the Nazi occupation of the city in World War II. The small church to your left is the Church of St. Laurent, which once served as a parish church for sailors and fishermen—notice the lighthouse-like tower.

• *Continue down the steps back to the Old Port.*

From the Old Port to the New Town

Halfway along the promenade (quai du Port), at the City Hall, you'll see the fun little **shuttle boat** that ferries locals across the harbor to the new town (free, every 10 min 7:00–19:20, lunch break from about 12:00–13:15). Note the unusual two-way steering wheel as you sail. You'll dock in the new town—which, because of the 1943 bombings, is actually older than the "old" town along the harborfront.

Directly in front of the ferry landing, you'll find popular bars and brasseries, good for a quick meal or memorable drink. Wander in along place aux Huiles, make your way left, and find a smart pedestrian zone crammed with cafés and restaurants (see "Eating in Marseille," page 235).

• *Our walk is over. Don't miss a trip up to Notre-Dame de la Garde, described next.*

Overlooking the Old Port

▲▲**Notre-Dame de la Garde**—Crowning Marseille's highest point, 500 feet above the harbor, is the city's landmark sight.

This massive Neo-Romanesque–Byzantine basilica, built in the 1850s during the reign of Napoleon III, is a radiant collection of domes, gold, and mosaics. The monumental statue of Mary and the Baby Jesus towers above everything (Jesus' wrist alone is 42 inches around, and the statue weighs nine tons). While people come here mostly for the commanding city view, the interior will bowl you over (open daily in summer 7:00–20:00, until 19:00 in winter, cafeteria and WCs just below the view terrace). This hilltop has served as a lookout, as well as a place of worship, since ancient times. Climb to the highest lookout for an orientation table and the best views. Those islands straight ahead are the Iles du Frioul, including the island of If—where the

Count of Monte Cristo spent time (described below).

Getting There: To reach the church, you can hike 30 minutes straight up from the harbor. To save some sweat, catch a taxi (about €10), hop on bus #60, or ride the tourist train—all stop on the harborfront near the fish market (see map on page 228 and "Helpful Hints" on page 225).

Offshore Islands and Calanques

Château d'If—When King François I visited Marseille in the 16th century, he realized the potential strategic importance of a fort on the uninhabited island of If (one of the Islands of Frioul), just outside the harbor. His château was finished in 1531. The impregnable fortress, which never saw battle, became a prison—handy for locking up Protestants during the Counter-Reformation. Among its illustrious inmates was José Faria, a spiritualist priest who was the idol of Paris and whom Alexandre Dumas immortalized in *The Count of Monte Cristo.* Since 1890, the château has been open to the public. Tour boats take tourists to this French Alcatraz, where the required two-hour stay will leave you sensitive to the count's predicament. I'd bypass this prison (€10 round-trip, €5 château entry, 30-min trip, usually depart daily on the hour 9:00–17:00, get the latest at the TI).

Islands of Frioul (Iles du Frioul)—These islands, which offer a nature break from the big city with a few hiking paths and cafés, are another 15 minutes away (round-trip with Château d'If-€10, boats run daily on the half-hour 9:30–17:30, get the latest at the TI).

Calanques Cruises—For those who won't get to Cassis, **Croisières Marseille Calanques** offers day trips to the chalky, fjord-like *calanques* east of Marseille (€15/2 hours, €25/3 hours, tel. 08 25 13 68 00, www.croisieres-marseille-calanques.com). Boats depart from the Old Port across from the TI. To read up on *calanques*, see page 239.

Sleeping in Marseille

Stay in Marseille only if you want a true urban experience. Hotel values and ambience are better 20 minutes away in Cassis (see page 241).

$$$ Mercure Grand Hôtel Beauvau**** lets you buy away the gritty reality outside your door with business-class comfort (Db-€190, Db with port view-€270, rates are frequently reduced,

---

Sleep Code

(€1 = about $1.40, country code: 33)
S = Single, **D** = Double/Twin, **T** = Triple, **Q** = Quad, **b** = bathroom,
s = shower only, * = French hotel rating system (0–4 stars).
Unless otherwise noted, credit cards are accepted and English
is spoken.

To help you sort easily through these listings, I've divided
the rooms into three categories based on the price for a
standard double room with bath:

\$\$\$ Higher Priced—Most rooms €90 or more.
\$\$ Moderately Priced—Most rooms between €60–90.
\$ Lower Priced—Most rooms €60 or less.

Wi-Fi in little lobby, 4 rue Beauvau, tel. 04 91 54 91 00, fax 04 91
54 15 76, h1293@accor.com).

\$\$\$ Hôtel Ibis Marseille Gare St. Charles**, with 180 rooms
(which are often fully booked), is a worthwhile value because it's
right at the train station—on the left as you exit (Db-€85–95, €10
less on weekends, extra bed-€10, check for deals on their website,
air-con, elevator, Square Narvick, tel. 04 91 95 62 09, fax 04 91 50
68 42, www.ibishotel.com, h1390@accor.com).

\$\$\$ Hôtel Kyriad**, a block off the port behind the TI, is a
shade musty but offers relative quiet and livable comfort at good
rates (Db-€90, Db with king-size bed-€98, Tb-€110, air-con,
elevator, Wi-Fi, 6 rue Beauvau, tel. 04 91 33 02 33, fax 04 91 33 21
34, kyriad.vieux-port@wanadoo.fr).

\$\$ Hôtel Relax*, run by sweet Houria (pronounced "oo-
ree-ah," which means "Liberty" in Arabic—she's Algerian), her
husband Ali, and their son, feels more like a B&B and is a good
budget stay. Despite its downtown location, it has little traffic noise
and a lobby any poodle would love. Book this place way ahead.
Half the simple rooms overlook a classy square—worth requesting, as the back-side rooms can be gloomy (back-side Db-€62, Db
on square-€67, rooms have small bathrooms with step-up showers,
air-con, Wi-Fi, just 2 blocks off harbor on place de l'Opéra at 4 rue
Corneille, tel. 04 91 33 15 87, fax 04 91 55 63 57, www.hotelrelax.fr,
hotelrelax@free.fr).

Near the Airport: **\$ Hôtel Louisiana*** is cheap, near the air-
port, and has easy train connections to Marseille. If you have an
early flight, consider bedding down here. Rooms are small but
clean, and the restaurant serves affordable meals (Db-€50–65;
Impasse Pythagore, Z.I. de Couperigne, 13127 Vitrolles; tel. 04 42
15 09 30, www.hotel-louisiana.com).

Eating in Marseille

In the New Town: For the best combination of trendiness, variety, and a fun people scene, consider eating in the new town, on or near quai de Rive-Neuve (on the left side of the Old Port as you look out to sea). Look for place aux Huiles, cours d'Estienne d'Orves, and rue Saint-Saëns for a melting pot of international eateries ranging from giant salads and fresh seafood to crêpes, Vietnamese dishes, Belgian waffles, and Buffalo wings. Don't expect high cuisine here, but the ambience can't be beat. **La Daurade** is worth considering, with fresh seafood at fair prices served in a classy setting (€18 *menus*, €20 bouillabaisse, closed Wed, 36 rue Saint-Saëns, tel. 04 91 33 82 42).

Near the Old Port: For good views *en terrasse*, go to the other side of the port. Consider a real Moroccan dinner at **Le Souk** (€16 couscous and *tajine* dishes, €20 three-course *menu*, intimate and authentic interior, closed Mon, 100 quai du Port, tel. 04 91 91 29 29). If you must have bouillabaisse, try **Les Galinettes Chez Madie** (€26 *menu*, €35/person for bouillabaisse, closed Sun, 138 quai du Port, tel. 04 91 90 40 87).

Near La Charité: **La Charité Museum** has a lovely, quiet courtyard café (lunch only).

Marseille Connections

Marseille is well-served by TGV and local trains, and is the hub for many smaller stations in eastern Provence.

From Marseille by Train to: Cassis (20/day, 25 min), **Aix-en-Provence** Centre-Ville station (2/hr, 35 min), **Antibes** (16/day, 2.5 hrs), **Nice** (18/day, 2.5 hrs), **Arles** (20/day, 1–2 hrs), **Avignon TGV** (10/day, 1 hr), **Paris** (hourly, 3.25 hrs), **Isle-sur-la-Sorgue** (8/day, 1–2 hrs).

From Marseille's Train Station by Bus to: Marseille Airport (3/hr, 25 min), **Cassis** (8/day, 50 min), **Aix-en-Provence** (4/hr, 50 min).

From Marseille's Métro Castellane by Bus to: Cassis (10/day, 40 min).

Cassis

Crouching in awe of impossibly high cliffs, Cassis (kah-see) is an unpretentious port town that gives travelers a sunny time-out from their busy vacation. Two hours away from the fray of the Côte d'Azur, Cassis is a poor man's St-Tropez. Outdoor cafés line the small port on three sides, where boaters clean their crafts as they chat up café clients. Cassis is popular with the French and close enough to Marseille to be busy on weekends and all summer. Come to Cassis to dine portside, swim in the glimmering-clear water, and explore its rocky *calanques* (fjord-like inlets).

Orientation to Cassis

The Massif du Puget mountain hovers over little Cassis, with hills spilling down to the port. Cap Canaille cliff rises from the southeast, and the famous *calanques* inlets hide along the coast northwest of town. Hotels, restaurants, and boats line the attractive little port.

Tourist Information

The TI is in the modern building in the middle of the port among the boats (Mon–Sat 9:00–12:30 & 14:00–18:00, Sun 10:00–12:00, longer hours in summer, quai des Moulins, toll tel. 08 92 25 98 92—costs €0.34/min, www.cassis.fr, info@ot-cassis.com). If going to Marseille, pick up a map here.

Arrival in Cassis

By Train: Cassis' hills forced the train station to be built two miles away. It's a small station with limited hours (no baggage storage, ticket windows open Mon–Fri 6:15–12:45 & 13:45–20:45, Sat 9:30–12:45 & 13:45–18:10, closed Sun). If you need to buy tickets when the station is closed, use the machines (coins only).

Some weekday trains are met by **buses** making the 10-minute drive into town. The schedule is posted at the stop (€0.80; 3/hr Mon–Fri 6:45–8:45 & 16:25–21:15; 1/hr Mon–Fri 8:45–15:45 and Sat 8:10–13:20, last bus at 13:20 on Sat; no buses Sun). When you exit the bus, turn right on rue de l'Arène and walk downhill five minutes to reach the port.

A **taxi** into town costs about €10 with baggage and is worth the expense unless a bus is waiting. Taxis usually meet arriving trains; if not, call 04 42 01 78 96 (a pay phone is outside the train station). Otherwise, it's a 45-minute walk into town (turn left out of the station and follow signs).

By Bus: Regional buses (including those from Marseille) drop you off a five-minute walk from the port (turn right on avenue P. Lariche).

By Car: There are two exits from the autoroute for Cassis; the second (coming from Aix-en-Provence) costs €1 more in tolls but saves you 10 minutes, provides easy access to La Route des Crêtes (described later under "Sights in Cassis"), and offers memorable views.

The hills above Cassis make navigating here a challenge. Hotels are signed, though the blue signs can be tricky to follow, so pay attention. Hotel parking is minimal, and the traffic is worse the closer you get to the port. Outside of summer, drivers arriving by 10:00 can usually find curbside parking (about €1/hr, free 18:00–9:00); latecomers will probably need to park in one of the well-marked pay lots above the port (Parking de la Viguerie is closest but often full, and their *Abonnés* entrance is for locals only). If you are driving on weekends in May, June, and September, or any day in July and August, take advantage of the free parking with shuttle service from Parking les Gorguettes high above the town (well-signed).

Helpful Hints

Market Days: The market hops on Wednesdays and Fridays until 12:30 (on the streets around the Hôtel de Ville).

Beaches: Cassis' beaches are pebbly. The big beach behind the TI is sandier than others, though water shoes still help. You can rent a mattress with a towel (about €15/day) and pedal boats (about €10/hr). Underwater springs just off the Cassis shore make the water clean, clear, and a bit cooler than at other beaches.

Internet Access: Cassis Télécom is a few blocks from the port, across from Parking la Viguerie (Mon–Sat 9:00–12:00 & 15:00–18:30, until 19:00 July–Aug, closed Sun, 23 rue de la Viguerie, tel. 04 42 98 81 94).

Laundry: Walk up rue Victor Hugo, then find 9 rue Autheman (self-service or full-service, daily 9:00–19:30).

Grocery Store: The **Casino** market is next door to Hôtel le Liautaud (daily 8:30–12:30 & 15:30–19:00, Sun until 18:00).

Wine Tasting: Le Chai Cassidain is a wine bar that welcomes visitors with red-leather stools and a good selection of regional wines offered by the bottle or by the glass (daily 10:00–13:00 & 15:00–19:00 and often later, 4 blocks from port at 6 rue Séverin Icard, tel. 04 42 01 99 80).

Taxi: Call 04 42 01 78 96 or find the main taxi stand across from Hôtel Cassitel by the *boules* court.

Tourist Train: The little white *train touristique*, with commentary in French and English, will take you on a worthwhile 45-minute circuit out to the peninsula on the Port-Miou *calanque* and back (€6, March–Oct, afternoons only, catch it next to Hôtel Liautaud on the port, tel. 04 42 01 09 98).

CASSIS

Self-Guided Tour

Cassis Visual Tour from the Port

Find a friendly bench in front of Hôtel le Golfe—or, better, enjoy a drink at their café—and read this quick town intro.

Cassis was born more than 2,500 years ago (on the hill with the castle ruins, across the harbor). Ligurians, Phoenicians, maybe Greeks, certainly Romans, and plenty of barbarians all found this spot to their liking.

Parts of the castle date from the eighth century, and the **fortress walls** were constructed in the 13th century to defend against seaborne barbarian raids. The Michelin family recently sold the fortress to investors who wanted to turn it into a luxury hotel. Cassis' planning commission had other ideas.

In the 18th century, when things got safer, people moved their homes back to the waterfront. Since then, Cassis has made its living through fishing, quarrying its famous white stone, producing well-respected white wines—which, conveniently, pair well with the local seafood dishes, and *bien sûr*, with tourists like us.

With improvements in transportation following the end of World War II, tourism rose gradually in Cassis, though crowds are still sparse by Riviera standards. While foreigners overwhelm nearby resorts, Cassis is popular mostly with the French, and still feels unspoiled. The town's protected status limits the height of the buildings along the waterfront. Cassis' port is home to some nice boats...but they're chump change compared to the glitzier harbors farther east.

The big cliff towering above the castle hill is **Cap Canaille.** Europe's highest maritime cliff, it was sculpted by receding glaciers (wrap your brain around that concept), and today drops 1,200 feet straight down. You can—and should—drive or taxi along the top for staggering views (see "Above Cassis: La Route des Crêtes," page 241). Return to this bench at sunset, when the Cap glows a deep red.

If you can overcome your inertia, walk to your right, then veer left on top of the short wall in front of the public WCs. The rocky shore over your right shoulder looks cut away just for sunbathers. But Cassis was once an important **quarry,** and stones were sliced right out of this beach for easy transport to ships. The Statue of Liberty's base sits on this rock, and even today, Cassis stone remains highly valued throughout the world...but yesterday's quarrymen have been replaced by today's sunbathers.

Cassis

100 YARDS
100 METERS

TO TRAIN STATION, BUS STOP, D-1 & AUTOROUTE

TO PLAGE DU BESTOUAN (BEACH), CALANQUES ←

La Viguerie

ST. MICHEL

AVE. E. AGOSTINI

AVE. AUTHEMANN

R. CIOTAT

AVE. V. HUGO

CASINO

PORT

POST

QUAI ST PIERRE

BOAT TIX

RUE BARTH

RUE DE L'ARENE

TO CALANQUES

PLACE MONTMORIN

(BIG) BEACH

TO CAP CANAILLE →

DCH

B BUS STOP TO/FROM TRAIN STATION
T TAXI STAND
P PARKING

❶ Best Western Hôtel la Rade
❷ Hôtel le Golfe
❸ Hôtel le Clos des Arômes
❹ Hôtel Cassitel
❺ Hôtel Laurence
❻ To Mahogany Hôtel de la Plage & Le Jardin d'Emile Hôtel
❼ El Sol, L'Oustau de la Mar & Bar Canaille Restaurants
❽ Le 8 et Demi Café & Grand Marnier Crêpes
❾ Le Grand Large Restaurant

❿ L'Escalier Restaurant
⓫ La Girondole Restaurant
⓬ Le Chai Cassidain Wine Bar
⓭ Télécom Internet Café
⓮ Launderette
⓯ Casino Grocery
⓰ Tourist Train (Afternoon Only)
⓱ Motorboat Rental & WC
⓲ Pedal Boat Rental
⓳ Kayak Rental

Sights in Cassis

▲▲▲The Calanques

Calanques (kah-lahnk) are the narrow inlets created by the prickly extensions of cliffs that border the shore. Until you see the intimate beaches and exotic fjords of translucent blue water, it's hard to understand what all the excitement is about. You can hike, or cruise by boat or kayak, to many *calanques,* all of which are located along the 13 miles of coast between Cassis and Marseille. Bring water, sunscreen, and anything else you need for the day, as there's nary a baguette for sale. Don't dawdle—to limit crowds and because of fire hazards, the most popular *calanques* can be closed to visitors by 11:00 in high season (late June–mid-Sept) and on weekends. When they are "closed," the only way to see the *calanques* is by boat or kayak. The TI can give you plenty of advice about enjoying the *calanques*.

Boats offer trips of various lengths (3 *calanques*-€13, 2/hr, 45 min; 5 *calanques*-€15, 3/day, 65 min; 8–10 *calanques*-€16–20, 1–3/day, 2 hrs; tel. 04 42 01 90 83, www.calanques-cassis.com). The three-*calanques* tour seems most popular. Tickets are sold (and boats depart) from a small booth on the TI side of the port. *Prochain départ* means "next departure." Boats vary in size (some seat up to 100). On the opposite side of the port, in front of Hôtel le Golfe, Didier Crespi offers more personal cruises on his smaller boat *Le Calendal* (an old anchovy fishing boat, seats 12 max). His commentary is in French only, but he can give you the basics in English (3 *calanques*-€13, 60 min, drop by or call for the day's schedule, mobile 06 63 35 66 51).

Hardy souls can **hike** to three of the *calanques* (Port-Miou, Port-Pin, and d'En-Vau)—though shade is nonexistent, and maps lack detail (verify route as you go). For most, the best *calanque* by foot is Calanque Port-Pin, about an hour from Cassis (30 min after the linear, boat-lined Calanque Port-Miou). It's intimate and well-forested, with a small beach.

If you leave early, the most spectacular *calanque* to hang out at is **Calanque d'En-Vau.** In summer (late June–mid-Sept), access is strictly controlled, and this *calanque* is closed by 11:00. From Cassis, hiking is the most reliable option. At the TI, get a map and ask about the trail conditions. Start along the road behind the Hôtel le Golfe and walk past the Plage du Bestouan, continuing to the Calanque Port-Miou along the avenue des Calanques. You'll join the *GR (Grande Randonnée)* trail at the Port-Miou Calanque and walk with the sea to your left, following the Chemin du Petit Prince (indicated by red, white, and green markers painted on rocks, trees, and other landmarks).

To explore the *calanques* on your own, you have several options. You can rent a **kayak** (one-seater-€25/4 hours, two-seater-€40/4 hours, tel. 04 42 01 80 01 to reserve, at Quai St. Pierre on the beach in Cassis, or ask at TI about two other companies that rent from Port Miou). If the hiking trails are closed, this is the only way you'll be able to get to those *calanques* beaches. Small **motorboats** can be rented without a special boating license (€100/half-day, €140/day, €700 cash or credit-card imprint as deposit; at Loca'Bato office, a few steps away from Hôtel le Golfe; tel. 04 42 01 27 04). Other options include **kayak tours** (sunset tour-€30 per person, half-day tour-€35, full-day tour-€55, depart from nearby town of La Ciotat, advance reservations smart, tel. 06 12 95 20 12, www.provencekayakmer.fr) and **skippered boat rental** (up to 8 people, about €250/half-day, €440/day, ask at TI).

▲▲Above Cassis: La Route des Crêtes

If you have a car, or are willing to spring for a taxi (€30 for a 30-min trip, 4 people per taxi), you must take this remarkable drive. Ride straight up to the top of Cap Canaille and toward the next town, La Ciotat. It's a twisty road, providing access to numbingly high views over Cassis and the Mediterranean. From Cassis, follow signs to *La Ciotat/Toulon*, then *La Route des Crêtes*. The towns just east of Cassis (La Ciotat, Bandol, etc.) do not merit a detour. This road is occasionally closed (because of strong winds or road repair), though you can usually get partway up—before investing time and money in this trip, check at the TI.

Sleeping in Cassis

(€1 = about $1.40, country code: 33)
Cassis hotels are laid-back places with less polish but lower rates than those on the Riviera. Some close from November to March, but those that stay open offer good discounts. All are busy on weekend and summer nights, when many can come with late-night noise. Book early for sea views and bring earplugs. Most hotels have a few invaluable parking spots that you can reserve when booking your room.

Near the Port or in Town

$$$ Best Western Hôtel la Rade*** sits on a busy road above the northwest corner of the port, with good views from its lovely poolside deck. It rents small, simple, and overpriced rooms with questionable air-conditioning (Db-€120, bigger Db-€170, suites-€225–250, extra bed-€15, free Internet access and Wi-Fi, parking-€15, route des Calanques, 1 avenue de Dardanelles, tel. 04 42 01 02 97, fax 04 42 01 01 32, www.hotel-cassis.com, larade @hotel-cassis.com).

$$ Hôtel le Golfe**, over an easygoing (but not late-night) café, has good rates, air-conditioning, friendly English-speaking Michele at the desk, and the best views of the port. Half of its basic-but-cute little blue-and-yellow rooms come with port views and small balconies and are worth booking ahead (Db with view and some noise-€90–100, Db without view-€75–85, rates depend on time of year, extra bed-€18, 2 extra beds-€25, 3 parking spaces-€8/day, nearby garage-€10/day, 3 place Grand Carnot, tel. 04 42 01 00 21, fax 04 42 01 92 08, www.legolfe-cassis.fr, contact @legolfe-cassis.fr).

$$ Hôtel le Clos des Arômes** is for those who don't need to be right on the port and prefer a quieter retreat. This place has appealing ambience with public spaces you can stretch out in. *Très provençal*, it has a big courtyard terrace and a good restaurant. It's run by service-oriented and capable staff. The rooms have old furnishings, so-so beds, dim lighting, and no air-conditioning (some have ceiling fans), but the place works in spite of these things (standard Db-€75, bigger Db-€85, Tb/Qb-€95, Internet access and Wi-Fi, near Parking la Viguerie at 10 rue Abbé Paul Mouton, tel. 04 42 01 71 84, fax 04 42 01 31 76, www.le-clos-des-aromes .com, closdesaromes@orange.fr). They accept reservations by email, but prefer the phone.

$$ Hôtel Cassitel**, located on the harbor over a loud café (particularly noisy on weekends), has comfortable rooms with air-conditioning and Wi-Fi. The harborview rooms come with night noise (standard Db-€75–80, large Db-€90–100, extra bed-€13, parking garage-€12/day, place Clemenceau, tel. 04 42 01 83 44, fax 04 42 01 96 31, www.hotel-cassis.com, cassitel@hotel-cassis.com).

$ Hôtel Laurence** offers Cassis' best budget beds, in small but relatively clean, tasteful, and air-conditioned rooms. Some come with decks and views. You must call a few days ahead to confirm your reservation (Db-€48–68, Db with balcony-€67–80, Db with view terrace-€77–90, extra bed-€13, cash only, closed in winter, 2 blocks off the port beyond Hôtel Cassitel at 8 rue de l'Arène, tel. 04 42 01 88 78, fax 04 42 01 81 04, www.cassis-hotel-laurence .com, contact@cassis-hotel-laurence.com).

On the Plage du Bestouan

The next two hotels are a 10-minute walk from the port on the next beach west, the Plage du Bestouan. Easy parking makes them good for drivers.

$$$ Mahogany Hôtel de la Plage*** has a big, modern exterior, spacious lobby, and well-conceived rooms at acceptable rates (Db with decks and sea view or much bigger suite-like rooms without view-€155–175, suite with view Db-€200–230, includes breakfast, air-con, parking-€15, Plage du Bestouan, tel. 04 42 01 05 70, fax 04 42 01 34 82, www.hotelmahogany.com, info@hotel mahogany.com).

$$$ Le Jardin d'Emile** is a villa-hotel located below the Mahogany Hôtel de la Plage. It's a charming little refuge with rich colors inside and out, plush rooms, and a green garden. Six of the seven rooms have decks, and three have sea views (Db-€140, extra bed-€30, air-con, free and secure parking, Plage du Bestouan, tel. 04 42 01 80 55, fax 04 42 01 80 70, www.lejardindemile.fr, provence@lejardindemile.fr).

Eating in Cassis

Shop the lineup of tempting restaurants along the port, consider the recommended places below, and then decide for yourself. You can have a simple crêpe or go all-out for bouillabaisse with the same great view. Arrive by 19:30 for the view tables. Picnickers can enjoy a beggars' banquet at the benches at Hôtel le Golfe or on the beach (small grocery stores open until 19:00).

Dining Portside

The first three places offer €23–27 *menus* and are ideally situated side by side, allowing diners to comparison shop. I've enjoyed good meals at each of them.

El Sol is sharp and popular with discerning diners (closed Sun eve and all day Mon, 20 quai des Baux, tel. 04 42 01 76 10).

L'Oustau de la Mar is a good choice, with a loyal following, fair prices, and welcoming owner Dominique. Try the *dos de loup de mer à la crème d'olives*—a whitefish smothered in a delectable sauce (closed Thu, 20 quai des Baux, tel. 04 42 01 78 22).

Bar Canaille specializes in fresh seafood platters (open daily, 22 quai des Baux, tel. 04 42 01 72 36).

Le 8 et Demi serves crêpes, pizza, salads, and good Italian gelato on plastic tables with front-and-center portside views (closed Thu, 8 quai des Baux, tel. 04 42 01 94 63).

The **Grand Marnier crêpe stand** cooks delicious dessert crêpes to go—the Grand Marnier crêpe rules. This is ideal for strollers (next to recommended Le 8 et Demi restaurant).

Dining Away from the Port

Le Clos des Arômes, listed earlier under "Sleeping in Cassis," is the place to come for a refined, candlelit dinner. Dine on a lovely terrace and let Julien take care of your every need (€26 *menu*, closed Tue–Wed for lunch and all day Mon, tel. 04 42 01 71 84).

Le Grand Large owns the scenic beachfront next to the TI. Come here for a quiet drink before dinner, or to dine seaside rather than portside (€27 *menu*, open daily, Plage de Cassis, tel. 04 42 01 81 00).

L'Escalier is a simple eatery offering good value, just off the port and up a quiet alley (€19 *menu*, closed Thu, tel. 04 42 32 33 80).

La Girondole is an easy place for families, with inexpensive pizza and salads. It's a block off the port and popular with locals (open daily in summer, take-away also possible, closed Tue off-season, 1 rue Thérèse Rastit, tel. 04 42 01 13 39).

Cassis Connections

While the train station is two miles from the port, shuttle buses meet some trains on weekdays (plus a few on Sat morning, but none on Sun), and taxis are reasonable (about €10 into the center, tel. 04 42 01 78 96). For details, see "Arrival in Cassis," earlier. All destinations below require a transfer in Marseille.

From Cassis by Train to: Marseille (20/day, 25 min), **Aix-en-Provence** (12/day, 1.5 hrs), **Arles** (7/day, 2 hrs), **Avignon TGV** (7/day, 2 hrs), **Nice** (14/day, 3 hrs, transfer in Marseille or Toulon), **Paris** (7/day, 4 hrs).

Aix-en-Provence

Aix-en-Provence is famous for its outdoor markets, beautiful people, and ability to embrace the good life. It was that way when

the French king made the town his administrative capital of Provence, and it's that way today. For a tourist, Aix-en-Provence (the "Aix" is pronounced "X") is happily free of any obligatory turn-stiles. And there's not a single ancient sight to see. It's just a wealthy town filled with 140,000 people—most of whom, it seems, know how to live well and look good. Aix-en-Provence's 40,000 students (many from other countries) give the city a youthful energy and its well-deserved nickname, "Sex-en-Provence."

Orientation to Aix-en-Provence

With no "must" sights (unless you're a student), Aix works well as a day trip, and is best if you can come on days when the markets thrive (Tue, Thu, and Sat). The city can be seen in a 1.5-hour stroll from the TI or train station. Cours Mirabeau (the grand central boulevard) divides the stately, quiet Mazarin Quarter from the lively old town. In the old sections, lovely squares are laced together by fine pedestrian shopping lanes that lead to the cathedral.

Tourist Information

The TI anchors the west end of cours Mirabeau at La Rotonde traffic circle. You'll feel like you're taking out a loan here, with individual desks and chairs for each information agent. Get the walking-tour brochure *In the Footsteps of Cézanne*, with the best city-center map and a good overview of excursions in the area. The TI has other maps that cover areas beyond old Aix (Mon–Sat 8:30–19:00, Sun 10:00–13:00 & 14:00–18:00, longer hours in the summer, shorter hours in the winter, 2 place du Général de Gaulle, tel. 04 42 16 11 61, www.aixenprovencetourism.com). English **walking tours** of the old town are offered at 10:00 on Tuesdays, Thursdays, and Saturdays (€8, depart from the TI).

Arrival in Aix-en-Provence

By Train: Aix-en-Provence has two train stations: Centre-Ville, near the city center; and the faraway TGV station. Neither has baggage storage.

Arrival at the Centre-Ville Station: It's a breezy 10-minute stroll to the TI and pedestrian area (walk straight up avenue Victor Hugo, turn left at first intersection, still on Victor Hugo; TI is on the left when you reach La Rotonde, the big traffic circle).

Arrival at Aix-en-Provence TGV Station: Shuttle buses *(navettes)* connect the distant, futuristic TGV station with Aix-

en-Provence's city-center bus station, described below (€5, 3/hr, 20 min). From the tracks, follow signs for *Navette–Direction Aix Centre* to the end of the hall and downstairs (buses leave from an underpass below the tracks).

If you're headed from Aix's city center to the TGV station, the *navette* buses usually depart from stall #4 at the bus station (schedule posted). To find the TGV by car from Aix-en-Provence, get on the A-51 autoroute toward *Marseille,* get off at the first exit (Les Milles), and track signs for another 10 minutes.

By Bus: From the sidewalk bus station *(gare routière),* it's a 10-minute walk to the TI: Head uphill to the flowery roundabout and turn left toward the splashing fountain (La Rotonde, the big traffic circle by the TI).

By Car: The city is very well-signed (yellow for hotels, green for parking). First, follow signs to *Centre-Ville,* then the yellow signs to your hotel. If your hotel has parking, use it. Otherwise, once you've spotted your hotel sign, follow green signs to park in the first pay lot you see (I've noted the closest parking to each hotel under "Sleeping in Aix-en-Provence"). Day-trippers should look

Aix-en-Provence

TO CEZANNE'S STUDIO

NOTRE-DAME

BLVD.

St. SAUVEUR

BLVD. JEAN JAURES

FINISH

OLD

TO

MUSEUM OF OLD AIX

TO AVIGNON

11

12

Forum des Cardeurs

21

10

COURS SEXTIUS

R. LISSE DES CORD.

RUE CORD.

Post

18

City Hall

RICHELME SQUARE

5

D'ENT.

FOCH

JAUDE

TO LUBERON

BLVD. DE LA REPUBLIQUE

23

16

PLACE RAMUS

BERNAD.

15

20

13

NAZ.

BONAPARTE

R. VICT. LEYDET

R. ESP.

ESPARIAT

19

22

8

COURS

LA ROTONDE
(PLACE DE GAULLE)

Post

START

3

MAZARIN

VICTOR HUGO AVE.

GOYRAND

14

VILLARS

R. LAPIERRE

RUE GONTARD

CARDI-

1

HUGO

BLVD.

P

AVE. DES BELGES

R. DESPLACES

P

23

BUS STN.
& TGV SHUTTLE BUS

AVE. EUR.

TRAIN STATION

TO MARSEILLE, CASSIS & TGV STATION

AIX-EN-PROVENCE

1. Hôtel Cézanne
2. Grand Hôtel Negre Coste
3. Hôtel Saint Christophe
4. To Chambre d'Hôte Pavillon de la Torse
5. Hôtel le Manoir & Le Zinc d'Hugo Rest.
6. Hôtel Cardinal
7. Hôtel des Quatre Dauphins & Paradox Bookshop
8. Hôtel de France
9. Restaurants Aux Deux Garçons & Le Grillon
10. Le Papagayo Café & Juste en Face
11. Café l'Archevêché
12. La Médina de Fez Rest.
13. Restaurant le Formal
14. Le Passage Restaurant
15. Charlotte Restaurant
16. Le Bistro Latin Restaurant
17. La Brocherie Restaurant
18. Café de l'Unic
19. Monoprix (Groceries)
20. Launderettes (2)
21. Internet Café
22. Electric Minibus Stop
23. Car Rental (2)

200 YARDS
200 METERS

 SELF-GUIDED WALK

P PARKING

DCH

Aix-en-Provence History

Aix-en-Provence was founded in about 120 B.C. as a Roman military camp on the site of a thermal hot spring (in France, "Aix" refers to a city built over a hot spring). The Romans' mission: to defend the Greek merchants of Marseille against the local Celts. Strategically situated Aix-en-Provence was the first Roman base outside Italy—the first foreign holding of what would become a vast empire. (The region's name—Provence—comes from its status as the first Roman province.) But Rome eventually fell, and the barbarians destroyed Aix-en-Provence in the fourth century. Through the Dark Ages, Aix-en-Provence's Roman buildings were nibbled to nothing by people needing the pre-cut stone. No buildings from Roman Aix-en-Provence survive.

Aix-en-Provence was of no importance through the Middle Ages. Because the area was once owned by Barcelona, Provence has the same colors as Catalunya: gold and red. In 1481, the Count of Provence died. He was hairless (according to my guide). Without a hair, Provence was gobbled up by France. When Aix-en-Provence was made the district's administrative center, noble French families moved in, kicking off the city's beautiful age (belle époque). They built about 200 *hôtels particuliers* (private mansions)—many of which survive today, giving Aix-en-Provence its classy appearance. As you wander around the town, look up, peek in, and notice the stately architecture with its grandiose extra touches.

Aix-en-Provence thrived thanks to its aristocratic population. But when the Revolution made being rich dicey, Aix-en-Provence's aristocracy and clergy fled. Aix-en-Provence entered the next stage of its history as the "Sleeping Beauty city." Later in the 19th century, the town woke up and resumed its familiar, pretentious ways. In Aix-en-Provence, the custom of rich people being bobbed along in sedan chairs survived longer than anywhere else in France. After the Revolution, you couldn't have servants do it—but you could hire pallbearers in their off-hours to give you a lift. If ostentatiousness ever became the norm...it happened in Aix-en-Provence.

for the La Rotonde parking area (near the TI) or park in any pay lot near the old city. Allow €14 for 24 hours of parking.

Helpful Hints

Markets: Aix-en-Provence bubbles over with photogenic open-air morning markets in several of its squares: **Richelme** (produce daily), **Palace of Justice** (flea market Tue, Thu, and Sat), and **L'Hôtel de Ville** (flower market Tue, Thu, and Sat; book market on first Sun of each month). Most pack up at 13:00, except the book market, which runs all day. It's well worth planning your visit for a market day if at all possible.

Internet Access: Internet cafés are plentiful in this college town. Ask at your hotel, or try **ProGamers,** with the longest hours (Mon–Sat 10:00–24:00, Sun 14:00–22:00, 14 forum des Cardeurs, tel. 04 42 96 14 22).

English Bookstore: Located on the quiet side of Aix-en-Provence, the low-key **Paradox Bookshop** has a modest collection of adult and children's books, a good selection of tourist guides (Cassis, Arles, Avignon, and so on), and a small supply of American grocery staples like peanut butter. The owner, Ms. Graillon, carries my guidebooks, speaks fluent English, and is a good source for information (Mon–Sat 10:00–12:30 & 14:00–18:30, closed Sun, 15 rue du 4 Septembre, tel. 04 42 26 47 99).

Laundry: There's a launderette at 11 rue des Bernadines, and another at 3 rue Fernand Dol (both daily 8:00–19:00).

Supermarket: Monoprix, on cours Mirabeau two long blocks up from La Rotonde, has a grocery store in the basement (Mon–Sat 8:30–21:00, closed Sun).

Taxi: Call 04 42 27 71 11 or 06 16 23 82 39.

Car Rental: Hertz is across from the Centre-Ville train station (43 avenue Victor Hugo, tel. 04 42 27 91 32), and **Europcar** is near La Rotonde (55 boulevard de la République, tel. 08 25 89 69 76). All major companies have offices at the TGV station.

Local Guide: Caroline Bernard speaks great English and enjoys teaching visitors about the wonders of her city (bernardcaro @aol.com, or contact her through the TI).

Electric Minibus Joyride: For a mere €0.50, take an orientation ride on a *Diabline*—a six-seater electric-powered minibus. It leaves every 10 minutes from the La Rotonde fountain, opposite the TI (Mon–Sat 8:30–13:00 & 15:00–19:30, none on Sun, 40 min round-trip). You can also wave down the young drivers anywhere and hop on. There are two routes (A and B); ask the driver for a map when you board. Line A gives you a better overview of the city and runs a route similar to the self-guided walk described below. It also gets you near Cézanne's

Studio. Designed with local seniors in mind, the minibus provides a fun (and less glamorous) slice-of-life experience in Aix-en-Provence.

Petit Train: Rest your feet and discover Aix-en-Provence's historic center on a 50-minute tour on the little train, while listening to English commentary (€6, depart from La Rotonde fountain). Ask about the longer tours that cover Cézanne's steps.

Wine-Tasting: At **Wine in Provence**, just-happy-to-be-here Americans Hilary and Brian want to help you discover French wine in a fun, relaxed setting. Their dream is to show you a side of Provence that you wouldn't otherwise see—through the lens of French wines (2-hour tasting of 5–6 mostly Provençal wines-€50, 6-hour cooking and wine-tasting class-€150, tel. 06 47 30 77 31, www.wineinprovence.com, contact @wineinprovence.com).

Famous Local Product: You'll see signs at fancy bakeries advertising *calissons d'Aix*, the city's homemade pastry. They're made with almond paste—kind of like a marzipan cake—and make fine souvenirs.

Dark Sunglasses: You may want to pick up a pair of especially dark glasses to be more discreet when appreciating the beautiful people of Aix-en-Provence.

Self-Guided Walk

Welcome to Aix-en-Provence

I've listed these streets, squares, and sights in the order of a handy, lazy orientation stroll. This walk is highlighted on the map on page 246.

• *Start across from the TI, on cours Mirabeau near the small fountain.*

La Rotonde: In the 1600s, the roads from Paris and Marseille met just outside the Aix-en-Provence town wall at a huge roundabout called La Rotonde. From here, locals enjoyed a sweeping view of open countryside before entering the town. As time passed, Aix-en-Provence needed space more than fortifications. The wall was destroyed and replaced by a grand boulevard (cours Mirabeau). A modern grid-plan town, the Mazarin Quarter, arose across the boulevard from the medieval town (to the right as you look up cours Mirabeau). In 1860, to give residents water and shade, the town graced La Rotonde with a fountain and the boulevard with trees. Voilà: The modern core of Aix-en-Provence was created.

• *Saunter up cours Mirabeau.*

Cours Mirabeau: This "Champs-Elysées of Provence" divides the higgledy-piggledy old town and the stately Mazarin Quarter. Designed for the rich and famous to strut their fancy stuff, cours Mirabeau survives much as it was: a single lane for traffic and an

Plane Trees

Stately old plane trees line roads and provide canopies of shade for town squares all over southern France. These trees are a part of the local scene.

The plane tree is a hybrid of the Asian and American sycamores—created accidentally in a 16th-century Oxford botanical garden. The result was the perfect city tree: fast-growing, resistant to urban pollution, and hearty (it can survive with little water and lousy soil). The plane tree was imported to southern France in the 19th century to replace the traditional elm trees. Napoleon planted them along roads to give his soldiers shade for their long marches. Plane trees were used to leaf up grand boulevards as towns throughout France—including Aix-en-Provence—built their Champs-Elysées wannabes.

extravagant pedestrian promenade, shaded by plane trees (see sidebar) and lined by 17th- and 18th-century mansions for the nobility.

The street follows a plan based on fours: 440 meters long, 44 meters wide, plane trees (originally elms) four meters apart, and decorated by four fountains. The "mossy fountains," covered by 200 years of neglect, trickle with water from the thermal spa that gave Aix its first name. At the end of the boulevard, a statue celebrates the last count of Provence, under whose rule this region joined France.

Cours Mirabeau was designed for showing off. Today, it remains a place for *tendance* (trendiness)—or even *hyper-tendance*. Show your stuff and strut the broad sidewalk. Grab a seat in an upscale café and observe.

• *From the mossy fountain at rue du 4 Septembre, turn right into Aix-en-Provence's quiet side, the pleasing little place des Quatre Dauphins. This marks the center of the...*

Mazarin Quarter (Quartier Mazarin): Built in a grid plan during the reign of King Louis XIV, the Mazarin Quarter remains a peaceful, elegant residential neighborhood—although each of its mansions now houses several families rather than just one. Study the quarter's Baroque and Neoclassical architecture (from the 17th and 18th centuries). The square's Fountain of the Four Dolphins, inspired by Bernini's fountains in Rome, dates from an age when Italian culture set the Baroque standard across Europe.

Wander up rue Cardinale to the **Musée Granet,** which faces a handsome square and features Aix's home-grown artists (including a few paintings by Cézanne—see sidebar on page 254). The vertical St. Jean de Malte church sits across from the museum.

• *Return to the cours Mirabeau and pop into #53, the venerable...*

Aux Deux Garçons: This café, once frequented by Paul Cézanne, is now popular with the local mafia—don't take photos. Check out its beautiful circa-1790 interior. It's a fine place for a pricey drink or meal (recommended in "Eating in Aix-en-Provence"). The Cézanne family hat shop was next door (#55). Cézanne's dad must have been some hatter. He parlayed that successful business into a bank, then into greater wealth, setting up his son to be free to enjoy his artistic pursuits.

• *From here, we'll enter the lively Old Town, where pedestrian streets*

*are filled with strolling beauties and romantic street musicians. This is the place in Aix-en-Provence for shopping. Leave cours Mirabeau down the tiny passage Agard, 10 steps past Aux Deux Garçons. It leads to the **Palace of Justice Square**, which hosts a bustling flea market (Tue, Thu, and Sat mornings). If the market is on, dally awhile. Leave this square heading left along the first street you crossed to*

enter it. *The street you're on, rue Marius Reinaud, hosts the top designer shops in town. Pause several blocks down at the peaceful courtyard square called...*

Place d'Albertas: This sweet little square was created by the guy who lived across the street. He hated the medieval mess of buildings facing his mansion, so he drew up a harmonious facade with a fountain, and hired an architect to build his ideal vision and mask the ugly neighborhood. The neighbors got a nice new facade, and the rich guy got the view of his dreams. The long-overdue restoration of this once run-down square is under way, and making a remarkable difference.

• *From here, turn right on rue Aude, the main street of medieval Aix-en-Provence (which leads eventually to the cathedral). Notice how effectively the green bollards keep cars from parking in this virtual car-free zone. Notice also the side streets, with their traffic-barrier stumps that lower during delivery hours. Make your way to...*

Richelme Square (Place Richelme): This square hosts a lively market, as it has for centuries (daily 7:00–13:00). It's a quintessential Provençal scene—classic architecture, plane trees, farmers selling local produce, and a guy in the goat-cheese stall near the Bar de l'Horloge who looks just like Paul Cézanne—or Jerry Garcia, if that's more your style. (He's fully aware of his special good looks. Drop by for a sample and a photo if you like.) The cafés at the end of the square are ideal for market observation. **Café de l'Unic** draws a lively and young pre-dinner crowd.

• *One block uphill is the stately...*

L'Hôtel de Ville Square (Place de l'Hôtel de Ville): This square, also known as place de la Mairie, is marked by a Roman

column. Stand with your back to the column and face the Hôtel de Ville. The center niche of this 17th-century City Hall once featured a bust of Louis XIV. But since the Revolution, Marianne (the Lady of the Republic) has taken his place. As throughout Europe, the three flags represent the region (Provence), country (France), and the European Union. Provence's flag carries the red and yellow of Catalunya (the region in Spain centered on Barcelona) because the counts of Provence originated there. The coat of arms combines the Catalan flag and the French fleur-de-lis.

The 18th-century building on your left was once the town's corn exchange (today it's the local book exchange). Its glorious pediment features figures representing the two rivers of Provence: old man Rhône and madame Durance. While the Durance River floods frequently (here depicted overflowing its frame), it also brings fertility to the fields (hence the cornucopia).

Back toward the Hôtel de Ville (where you're heading), the 16th-century bell tower was built in part with stones scavenged from ancient Roman buildings—notice the white ones at the tower's base. The niche above the arch once displayed the bust of the king. Since the Revolution, it has housed a funerary urn that symbolically honors all who gave their lives for French liberty. Under the arch, a small plaque honors the American 3rd Division that liberated the town in 1944 (with the participation of French troops; Aix-en-Provence got through World War II relatively unscathed).

History aside, the square is a favorite part of the Aix-en-Provence experience for its colorful morning markets: flowers (Tue, Thu, and Sat) and old books (Sun). Each afternoon, café tables replace the market stalls.

• *Stroll under the bell tower and up rue Gaston de Saporta, to the yellow-bannered...*

Paul Cézanne in Aix-en-Provence

Post-Impressionist artist Paul Cézanne (1839–1906) loved Aix-en-Provence. He studied law at the university (opposite the cathedral), and produced most of his paintings in and around Aix-en-Provence—even though this conservative town didn't understand him or his art. Today the city fathers milk anything remotely related to his years here. But because the conservative curator of the town's leading art gallery, the Granet Museum, decreed "no Cézannes," you can see only a few of Cézanne's lesser original paintings in Aix-en-Provence. Bad curator.

Instead, fans of the artist will want to pick up the *In the Footsteps of Cézanne* self-guided-tour flier at the TI, and follow the bronze pavement markers around town.

Cézanne's **last studio** (Atelier Cézanne)—preserved as it was when he died—is open to the public. It's a 30-minute walk from the TI, or you can get there on electric minibus A (see "Helpful Hints," earlier). While there is no art here, his tools and personal belongings make it almost interesting for enthusiasts—I'd skip it. If you must go, it's best (and essential in high season) to reserve a visit time in advance at the TI or at www.aixenprovencetourism.com (€6, daily July–Aug 10:00–18:00, April–June and Sept 10:00–12:00 & 14:00–18:00, Oct–March until 17:00, 2 miles from TI at 9 avenue Cézanne, tel. 04 42 16 10 91, www.atelier-cezanne.com).

Museum of Old Aix-en-Provence (Musée du Vieil Aix): This museum fills a 17th-century mansion with a scant collection of artifacts. The building interior itself is of most interest. Pop in for a look at the grand staircase and fancy ceilings. The exhibits include lots of *santons*—painted clay figurines popular in old-time manger scenes (€4, pick up the English handout, April–Sept Tue–Sun 10:00–13:00 & 14:00–18:00, Oct–March until 17:00, closed Mon, 17 rue Gaston de Saporta, tel. 04 42 21 43 55).

• *A block farther uphill, facing the historic university building (where Cézanne studied) is the...*

Cathedral of the Holy Savior (Saint-Sauveur): This church was built atop the Roman forum—likely on the site of a pagan temple. As the cathedral grew with the city, its interior became a parade of architectural styles. The many-faceted interior is at once confusing and fascinating, with three distinct sections: Standing at the entrance, you face the Romanesque section; to the left are the

Gothic and then the Baroque sections. We'll visit each in turn.

In the **Romanesque section,** branching off to the right is the baptistery, with its early Christian (fourth-century) Roman font. It's big enough for immersion, which was the baptismal style in Roman times. Also notice that it's eight-sided, symbolizing eternity: one side more than the seven days it took God to create everything. The font is surrounded by ancient columns with original fourth-century capitals below a Renaissance cupola. Farther down is the door to the 12th-century cloister (visits on the half-hour except 12:00–14:00, or just open the outer door and peer through the iron gate). Beyond that, find the closet-sized architectural footprint of the original Christian chapel from the Roman era.

In the **Gothic section,** two organs flank the nave: One works, but the other is a prop, added for looks...an appropriately symmetrical Neoclassical touch, as was the style in the 18th century. The precious door (facing the street from this section) is carved of chestnut with a Gothic top (showing sibyls, or ancient female prophets) and Renaissance lower half (depicting prophets). Since it faces the street, it's covered by a second, protective door (viewable on request).

In the **Baroque section,** don't miss the finely detailed three-paneled altar painting of the burning bush (15th century, by Nicolas Froment).

• *Your tour is over. Walking back through town, drop by a designer bakery to try a* calisson, *Aix-en-Provence's local pastry (see "Helpful Hints," earlier). Or, for fewer calories and just as much fun, marvel at a town filled with people who seem to be living life very, very well.*

Sleeping in Aix-en-Provence

(€1 = about $1.40, country code: 33)
Hotel rooms, starting at about €60, are surprisingly reasonable in this highbrow city. Reserve ahead, particularly on weekends. Hotel stars have less meaning here. The best values are on the quiet side of cours Mirabeau in the Mazarin Quarter.

$$$ Hôtel Cézanne*, a block up from the Centre-Ville train station, is all about service with a smile. The lobby and 55 plush, spacious rooms are *très* modern, with every creature comfort (and cool faucets). This stylish place pampers guests with an efficient, English-speaking staff and amenities like a daily champagne "brunch" that includes French toast, omelets, and smoked salmon (€20, served until noon, try the French toast with honey) and free non-alcoholic drinks from your minibar (standard Db-€180, deluxe Db-€240, some king-size beds, air-con, elevator, free and easy Internet access and Wi-Fi, 40 avenue Victor Hugo, tel. 04 42 91 11 11, fax 04 42 91 11 10, www.hotelaix.com, hotelcezanne @hotelaix.com).

$$$ Grand Hôtel Negre Coste** occupies a privileged position at the center of cours Mirabeau. This once grand, now faded hotel houses traditional rooms and a formal staff, and may have rooms when others don't (Db-€105–115, big Db-€135, air-con, Internet access and Wi-Fi, private garage-€10, 33 cours Mirabeau, tel. 04 42 27 74 22, fax 04 42 26 80 93, www.hotelnegrecoste.com, contact@hotelnegrecoste.com).

$$$ Hôtel Saint Christophe**, a basic business hotel with fair-enough rates, is located behind the TI and above a swanky brasserie. It has 58 tight but well-equipped rooms, some with small terraces (Db-€90–100, mezzanine suite sleeps up to 4-€110–150, air-con, elevator, parking garage-€12, 2 avenue Victor Hugo, tel. 04 42 26 01 24, fax 04 42 38 53 17, www.hotel-saintchristophe.com, saintchristophe@francemarket.com).

$$$ Chambre d'Hôte Pavillon de la Torse is an upscale B&B that my readers gush about—for good reason. A lane of plane trees escorts you to a beautiful retreat in a park-like setting, with

a 25-meter lap pool surrounded by gardens that Louis would appreciate. In this lovingly renovated manor house, eager-to-help American Mary and Frenchman François offer every amenity. It's located just beyond the noise of the city on a large park (Db-€140–180, €20 less Nov–March; extra bed-€20 for kids who must be 5 or older, €40 for adults; 2-night minimum, includes breakfast, Internet access and Wi-Fi, easy parking, 15-min walk south of the old city at 69 cours Gambetta, tel. 04 42 26 10 52, www.latorse.com, contact@latorse.com).

$$ Hôtel le Manoir***, built on the heavy arches of a medieval monastery, is modest, peaceful, and central. The decor is strictly traditional and furnishings are worn, though the setting is ideal (small Db-€64, standard Db-€78–94, Tb-€85–94, Qb-€105, elevator, limited free parking, 8 rue d'Entrecasteaux, tel. 04 42 26 27 20, fax 04 42 27 17 97, www.hotelmanoir.com, infos@hotel manoir.com).

$$ Hôtel Cardinal** is a solid value on Aix-en-Provence's classy side, across cours Mirabeau from the pedestrian zone. It's a shy, rose-colored hotel with 29 traditionally furnished rooms and a hopelessly confusing floor plan (Sb-€60, Db-€70, cavernous Db suite in nearby annex-€110, elevator, air-con planned for 2010, Wi-Fi, closest parking is Mignet, 24 rue Cardinale, tel. 04 42 38 32 30, fax 04 42 26 39 05, www.hotel-cardinal-aix.com, hotel.cardinal@wanadoo.fr).

$$ Hôtel des Quatre Dauphins** is a small, appealing hotel in the quiet quarter with soft rooms, Old World decor, and good prices (Db-€70–85, bigger Db-€90–105, Tb-€120, air-con, Wi-Fi, closest parking is Mignet, 54 rue Roux Alphéran, tel. 04 42 38 16 19, fax 04 42 38 60 19, www.lesquatredauphins.fr, lesquatre dauphins@wanadoo.fr).

$$ Hôtel de France** couldn't be more central, in the thick of the pedestrian zone near La Rotonde roundabout. The place is frumpy, with some squishy beds, and it could use some upgrading—but I guess that keeps the prices acceptable. Rooms on the noisier street side are bigger than on the quieter courtyard side (Db-€80–105, extra bed-€24, air-con, elevator, use La Rotonde parking, 63 rue Espariat, tel. 04 42 27 90 15, fax 04 42 26 11 47, www.hoteldefrance-aix.com, hoteldefrance-aix@wanadoo.fr).

Eating in Aix-en-Provence

In Aix-en-Provence, you have dining options on squares, along a grand boulevard, or tucked into little restaurants on side streets. The squares are mostly for desserts and drinks (consider dining better elsewhere without the ambience, then heading to a square for dessert). Cours Mirabeau hosts the promenade scene, with plenty of eating options.

Along Cours Mirabeau
If you're interested in a delicious view more than delicious food, eat with style on cours Mirabeau.

Aux Deux Garçons has always been the place to see and be seen: a vintage brasserie with door-to-door waiters in aprons, a magnificent interior, and well-positioned outdoor tables with properly placed silverware on white tablecloths. It's busy at lunch but quiet for dinner (€20 *plats*, two-course *menus* from €28, open daily, 53 cours Mirabeau, tel. 04 42 26 00 51). Even if you're not eating here, pop in to see the decor (see page 252).

Le Grillon is a younger, more boisterous, and less pricey choice for dinner on cours Mirabeau (white tablecloths, €15 *plats*, €24 *menu*). Its bar is a hit with locals for the prime seating: front and center on the boulevard's strolling fashion show (open daily for lunch and dinner, corner of rue Clémenceau and cours Mirabeau, tel. 42 27 58 81).

On Aix-en-Provence's Squares
While Aix-en-Provence is blessed with many atmospheric squares, few come with real restaurants. To eat outdoors enjoying the ambience of a square, consider these options.

On Forum des Cardeurs: Just off L'Hôtel de Ville Square, the forum des Cardeurs is café-crammed. Browse the selection from top to bottom, then decide. **Le Papagayo** has a good selection of salads and a quiche of the day (big €14 salads, open daily for lunch and dinner, 22 forum des Cardeurs, tel. 04 42 23 98 35). **Juste en Face,** facing Papagayo, features grilled specialties and Mediterranean cuisine, specializing in North African *tajine* (€16 *plats*, open daily, 6 rue Verrerie, tel. 04 42 96 47 70).

On Place des Martyrs de la Resistance: A short block below the cathedral, this quiet square is good for a light meal. **Café l'Archevêché** is reasonable and understandably proud of its pizzas (lunch only except June–mid-Sept, tel. 04 42 21 43 57). For a change of pace, a few blocks away find **La Médina de Fez** for authentic Moroccan cuisine at fair prices (*menus* from €19, closed Mon, 35 rue Campra, tel. 04 42 21 68 58).

Closer to La Rotonde

Restaurant le Formal is the love child of Jean-Luc le Formal and Yvonne Kruithof, who cook and serve beautifully presented dishes in their small, stylish eatery. Weaving modern decor with heavy stone arches, this contemporary place features "inventive French nouveau cuisine" (€37 *menu*, lunch specials, reservations smart for dinner, Tue–Sat lunch from 12:00 and dinner from 19:30, closed Sun–Mon, 32 rue Espariat, tel. 04 42 27 08 31).

Le Zinc d'Hugo is a tiny and warm bistro with simple wood tables, a smoky grill, and an artsy feel, featuring fresh products from throughout France (*plats* from €15, closed Sun–Mon, 22 rue Lieutaud, tel. 04 42 27 69 69).

Le Passage, a dazzling eatery without a tourist in sight, caters to locals by combining a simple, modern menu with a love of wine. Trendy yet inviting, the spacious atrium has several floors (each with a different ambience), a wine bar, and a breezy backyard terrace. Monday nights have live jazz from 20:00. Its slogan, *le goût du plaisir* ("the taste of pleasure"), says it all (€20–35 *menus,* great prices from extensive list of fine French wines, daily 10:00–24:00, hiding out a block off La Rotonde at 10 rue Villars, tel. 04 42 37 09 00).

Charlotte is Aix's low-key, down-and-dirty diner, where locals come for a good meal at a good price in simple surroundings. The entrance is the epitome of low-profile (€19 three-course *menu* only, no à la carte, 32 rue des Bernadines, tel. 04 42 26 77 56).

Le Bistro Latin is a small, central place that's easy on English-only speakers. You can expect a sincere welcome and good regional cuisine at honest prices (€26 three-course *menu*, 18 rue de la Couronne, tel. 04 42 38 22 88).

In the Mazarin Quarter

La Brocherie dishes up French rather than Provençal cuisine. Its stone-rustic, indoors-only ambience is best for cooler days. This family-owned bistro—run by Messieurs Soudain and Tourville—is deep in the Mazarin Quarter and features food from the farm (it's about beef). Dig into the hearty self-service salad buffet (all you can eat, €12) and meats grilled over a wood fire (skip the fish options). The €20 *menu* includes the salad bar (closed Sun, indoor seating only, 5 rue Fernand Dol, tel. 04 42 38 33 21).

Aix-en-Provence Connections

Remember, Aix-en-Provence has both a TGV station and a Centre-Ville train station (see "Arrival in Aix-en-Provence," page 245). In some cases, destinations are served from both stations; I've listed the station with the best connection.

From Aix-en-Provence's Centre-Ville Station by Train to: Marseille (2/hr, 35 min), **Cassis** (12/day, 1.5 hrs, transfer in Marseille), **Arles** (10/day, 2 hrs, transfer in Marseille).

From Aix-en-Provence's TGV Station by Train to: Avignon TGV (10/day, 25 min), **Nice** (10/day, 3.5 hrs, usually change in Marseille), **Paris** (14/day, 3 hrs, may require transfer in Lyon).

From Aix-en-Provence by Bus to: Marseille (4/hr, 50 min), **Marseille airport** (2/hr, 30 min), **Lourmarin** (75 min total—bus to Pertuis leaves 2/hr, transfer there to Avignon-bound bus, 3/day).

THE FRENCH RIVIERA

La Côte d'Azur

A hundred years ago, celebrities from London to Moscow flocked to the French Riviera to socialize, gamble, and escape the dreary weather at home. Today, budget vacationers fill belle époque resorts at France's most sought-after fun-in-the-sun destination. This scenic strip is speckled with intriguing museums and heat-seeking Europeans.

The region got its nickname from turn-of-the-20th-century vacationing Brits, who simply extended the Italian Riviera west to France. Their original definition of the French Riviera only went as far as Nice, though the Riviera label has been stretched even farther westward since these Victorian Brits strolled their promenade. Today, this summer fun zone—which, for our purposes, runs from St-Tropez to the Italian border—is *La Côte d'Azur* to the French. All of my French Riviera destinations are on the sea, except for a few hill towns and the Gorges du Verdon.

This sunny sliver of land has been inhabited for more than 3,000 years. Ligurians were first, then Greeks, then Romans—who, as usual, had the greatest impact. After the fall of Rome, Nice became an important city in the Kingdom of Provence (along with Marseille and Arles). In the 14th century, Nice's leaders voted to throw their beach towel in with the Duke of Savoy's mountainous kingdom (also including several regions of northern Italy), which would later evolve into the Kingdom of Sardinia. It was not until 1860 that Nice (and Savoy) became a part of France—the result of a citywide vote made possible by Napoleon III and the King of Sardinia.

Nice has world-class museums, a splendid beachfront promenade, a seductive old town, and all the drawbacks of a major city (traffic, crime, pollution, and so on). The day-trip possibilities are easy and exciting: Monte Carlo welcomes everyone, with cash reg-

The French Riviera

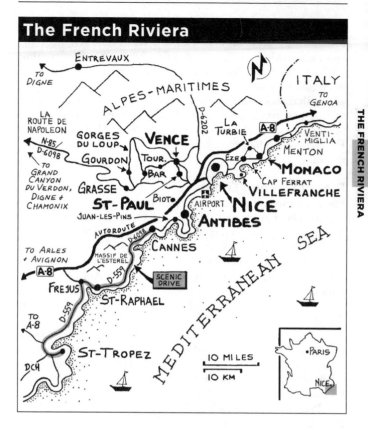

isters open; Antibes has a thriving port and silky sand beaches; and image-conscious Cannes is the Riviera's self-appointed queen, with an elegant veneer hiding...very little. Yacht-happy St-Tropez swims alone an hour west (halfway to Cassis and Marseille). The Riviera's overlooked interior transports travelers to a world apart, with cliff-hanging villages, impossibly steep canyons, and alpine scenery—a refreshing alternative to the beach scene.

Choose a Home Base

My favorite home bases are Nice, Antibes, and Villefranche-sur-Mer.

Nice is the region's capital and France's fifth-largest city. With convenient train and bus connections to most regional sights, this is the most practical base for train travelers. Urban Nice also has a full palette of museums (most of which are free), a beach scene that rocks, the best selection of hotels in all price ranges, and good nightlife options. A car is a headache in Nice, though it's easily stored at one of the many pricey parking garages.

Nearby **Antibes** is smaller, with a bustling center, a lively night scene, great sandy beaches, grand vistas, good walking trails, and a much-admired Picasso Museum. Antibes has frequent train service to Nice and Monaco, and quick connections by train or car to Grasse. It's also an easy place for drivers.

Villefranche-sur-Mer is the romantic's choice, with a serene setting and small-town warmth. It has finely ground pebble beaches, quick public transportation to Nice, Monaco, and Cap Ferrat, easy parking, and a smaller selection of hotels in most price ranges.

Planning Your Time

Ideally, allow a day and a half for Nice itself, an afternoon to explore inland hill towns, a day for Italian-esque Villefranche-sur-Mer and lovely Cap Ferrat, a day for Monaco and the Corniches, and—if time allows—a day for Antibes and Cannes. Consider using two different Riviera bases, and enjoy each for a couple of nights—Villefranche-sur-Mer pairs well with Antibes or Nice. And if you must do St-Tropez, visit it while traveling to or from destinations farther west (such as Cassis, Aix-en-Provence, and Arles) and avoid it on weekend afternoons, as well as all summer.

Monaco has a unique energy at night, and Antibes works well by day (good beaches and hiking) and by night (fine choice of restaurants and a lively after-hours scene). Hill town–loving naturalists should add a night or two inland to explore the charming hill-capping hamlets near Vence.

Priorities: Depending on the amount of time you have in the Riviera, spend it this way:

3 days:	Nice, Villefranche-sur-Mer with Cap Ferrat, and Monaco
5 days, add:	Antibes and maybe Cannes, and hill towns near Vence
7 days, add:	Grand Canyon du Verdon and St-Tropez

Helpful Hints

Medical Help: Riviera Medical Services has a list of English-speaking physicians for anywhere along the Riviera. They can help you make an appointment or call an ambulance (tel. 04 93 26 12 70, www.rivieramedical.com).

Sightseeing Schedules: On Mondays, the following sights are closed—the Modern and Contemporary Art Museum, Fine Arts Museum, and cours Saleya market in Nice, along with Antibes' Marché Provençal. On Tuesdays, the Chagall, Matisse, and Archaeological museums in Nice are closed.

Events: The Riviera is famous for staging major events. Unless you're actually taking part in the festivities, these events give you only room shortages and traffic jams. Here are the three biggies in 2010: **Nice Carnival** (Feb 12–28), **Grand Prix of Monaco** (May 20–23), and Festival de Cannes, better known as the **Cannes Film Festival** (May 12–23).

Getting Around the Riviera

By Train and Bus: Trains and buses do a good job of connecting places along the coast (with views along many sections), and buses provide reasonable service to some inland hill towns. The high-speed TGV trains stop in Cannes and Antibes, as well as in Nice and Marseille. Nice is well-connected to most sights on the Riviera (for details on all the connections, see "Getting Around the Riviera" in the Nice chapter, page 272). While trains are faster, buses are cheaper and more frequent to destinations near Nice. St-Tropez is remote, requiring a bus or boat connection. Details are provided under each destination's "Connections" section. For a scenic inland train ride, take the narrow-gauge train into the Alps (see page 285). Never board a train without a ticket or valid pass—fare inspectors don't accept any excuses, and the minimum fine is €70.

By Car: After Paris, this is France's second most challenging region to drive in. Beautifully distracting vistas (natural and human), loads of Sunday-driver tourists, and an overabundance of cars make for a dangerous combination; pay extra attention while driving down here. Parking can be tricky for the same reasons, so have patience and consider the bus or train. Have lots of coins ready for parking and for autoroute tolls.

The Riviera is awash with scenic roads. To sample some of the Riviera's best scenery, drivers should find the splendid coastal road between Cannes and Fréjus (D-6098 from Cannes/D-550 from Fréjus, old route N-98), which works well when connecting the Riviera with Provence. If it weren't for the Mediterranean sea below, you'd swear you were in Arizona (in Fréjus, follow signs to *Centre-Ville,* then *Cannes par la Bord de la Mer;* from Cannes, drive to the western end of town and follow *La Napoule* to reach the road). Drivers should also scour the three Corniches between Nice and Monaco (see page 334) and take my recommended inland hill-towns drive (on page 394). Farther inland, the Grand Canyon du Verdon patiently awaits, with breathtaking gorges and alpine scenery. But even if you have a car, consider the convenience that trains and buses offer for basic sightseeing between Monaco and Cannes.

By Boat: Trans Côte d'Azur offers boat service from Nice to Monaco or to St-Tropez from June into September, as well as between Cannes and St-Tropez (tel. 04 92 98 71 30, www.trans -cote-azur.com). For details, see "Getting Around the Riviera" in the Nice chapter (page 273).

THE FRENCH RIVIERA

The Riviera's Art Scene

The list of artists who have painted the Riviera reads like a Who's Who of 20th-century art. Pierre-Auguste Renoir, Henri Matisse, Marc Chagall, Georges Braque, Raoul Dufy, Fernand Léger, and Pablo Picasso all lived and worked here—and raved about the region's wonderful light. Their simple, semi-abstract, and—most importantly—colorful works reflect the Riviera. You'll experience the same land-scapes they painted in this bright, sun-drenched region, punctuated with views of the "azure sea." Try to imagine the Riviera with a fraction of the people and development you see today.

But the artists were mostly drawn to the uncomplicated lifestyle of fishermen and farm-ers that has reigned here since time began. As the artists grew older, they retired in the sun, turned their backs on modern art's "isms," and painted with the wide-eyed wonder of children, using bright primary colors, basic outlines, and simple subjects.

A dynamic concentration of well-organized modern- and contemporary-art museums (many described in this book) litter the Riviera, allowing art-lovers to appreciate these masters' works while immersed in the same sun and culture that inspired them. Many of the museums were designed to blend pieces with the surrounding views, gardens, and fountains, thus highlighting that modern art is not only stimulating, but sometimes simply beautiful.

Entire books have been written about the modern-art galleries of the Riviera. If you're a fan, do some studying before your visit to be sure you know about that far-out museum of your dreams. Even if you aren't usually turned on by modern art, take the opportunity to experience the region's brilliant display of it by visiting the Fondation Maeght in St-Paul-de-Vence, and the Chagall and Matisse museums in Nice.

The Riviera's Cuisine Scene

The Riviera adds a Mediterranean flair to the food of Provence. While many of the same dishes served in Provence are available throughout the Riviera (see "Provence's Cuisine Scene," page 44), there are differences, especially if you look for anything Italian or from the sea. The proximity to the water and historic ties to Italy are clear in this region's dishes.

La salade niçoise (nee-swahz) is where most Riviera meals start. A true specialty from Nice, this salad has many versions, though most include a base of green salad topped with green beans, boiled potatoes (sometimes rice), tomatoes (sometimes corn), anchovies, olives, hard-boiled eggs, and lots of tuna. Every café and restaurant adds its own twist to this filling dish that goes down well on sultry days.

For lunch on the go, look for a *pan bagnat* (like a *salade niçoise* stuffed into a hollowed-out soft roll). Other tasty bread treats include *pissaladière* (bread dough topped with onions, olives, and anchovies), *fougasse* (a spindly, lace-like bread sometimes flavored with nuts, herbs, olives, or ham), and *socca* (a thin chickpea crêpe, seasoned with pepper and olive oil and often served in a paper cone by street vendors).

Invented in Nice, ravioli and potato gnocchi can be found on menus everywhere (ravioli can be stuffed with a variety of fillings, but it's best with seafood). Thin-crust pizza and *pâtes fraîches* (fresh pasta) are generally a good value throughout the Riviera.

Bouillabaisse is the Riviera's most famous dish; look for it in any seafront village or city. It's a spicy fish stew based on recipes handed down from sailors in Marseille. It must contain at least four types of fresh fish, though most have five to twelve kinds. A true bouillabaisse never has shellfish. The fish—cooked in a tomato-based stock and flavored with saffron (and sometimes anise and orange)—is separated from the stock before serving. The cook then heightens the flavor of the stock by adding toasted croutons and a dollop of *rouille* sauce (a thickened reddish mayonnaise heady with garlic and spicy peppers). This dish often requires a minimum order of two even though it can cost up to €40–60 per person.

Those on a budget can enjoy other seafood soups and stews. Less pricey than bouillabaisse but equally good is the local *soupe de poisson* (fish soup). It's flavored like bouillabaisse, with anise and orange, and served with croutons and *rouille* sauce. For a less colorful but still tasty soup, look for *bourride,* a creamy fish concoction thickened with an aioli garlic sauce instead of the red *rouille;* or *baudroie,* a fishy soup cooked with vegetables and garlic.

The Riviera specializes in all sorts of fish and shellfish. Other options include *"fruits de mer,"* or platters of seafood (including tiny shellfish, from which you get the edible part only by sucking really hard), herb-infused mussels, stuffed sardines, squid (slowly simmered with tomatoes and herbs), and tuna *(thon)*. The popular *loup flambé au fenouil* is grilled sea bass, flavored with fennel and torched with *pastis* prior to serving.

Cheese and dessert dishes of the Riviera are indistinguishable from those in Provence. Refer to "Provence's Cuisine Scene" (page 44) for suggestions.

You're better off avoiding fixed-price *menus* at most places and just ordering a first course and a main course, or a main course and dessert. I prefer licking my dessert on an after-dinner waterfront stroll (works great in all three home bases I recommend).

Unfortunately, memorable restaurants that showcase the Riviera's cuisine are more difficult to find than in neighboring Provence. Because most visitors come more for the sun than the food, and because the clientele is predominantly international, many restaurants aim for the middle and are hard to tell apart. When dining on the Riviera, I look for views and ambience more than top-quality cuisine.

Wines of the Riviera

Do as everyone else does: Drink wines from Provence. Bandol (red) and cassis (white) are popular and from a region nearly on the Riviera. The only wines made in the Riviera are Bellet rosé and white, the latter often found in fish-shaped bottles. For more on Provençal wine, see page 46.

NICE

Nice (sounds like "niece"), with its spectacular Alps-to-Mediterranean surroundings, eternally entertaining seafront promenade, and intriguing museums, is an enjoyable big-city highlight of the Riviera. In its traffic-free old city, Italian and French flavors mix to create a spicy Mediterranean dressing. Nice may be nice, but it's hot and jammed in July and August—reserve ahead and get a room with air-conditioning *(une chambre avec climatisation)*. Everything you'll want to see in Nice is within walking distance, or a short bus or tram ride away.

Orientation to Nice

Nice revolves around its grand place Masséna, where pedestrian-friendly avenue Jean Médecin meets Old Nice and the Albert 1er

parkway. Most recommended sights and hotels are between the train station and the beach, near avenue Jean Médecin or boulevard Victor Hugo. It's a 20-minute walk (or a €10 taxi ride) from the train station to the beach, and a 20-minute walk along the promenade from the fancy Hôtel Negresco to the heart of Old Nice.

The new tramway is very handy. A 10-minute ride takes you through the center of the city, connecting the train station, place Masséna, Old Nice, the bus station, and the port (from nearby place Garibaldi). Notice how traffic signals favor the tram cars. The tram and city and regional buses cost only €1 per trip, making this one of the cheapest and easiest cities in France to get around in (see "Getting Around Nice," later).

Tourist Information

Nice's helpful TI has three locations: at the **airport** (in Terminal 1, daily 8:00–21:00, closed Sun off-season), next to the **train station** (usually busy; summer Mon–Sat 8:00–20:00, Sun 9:00–18:00; rest of year Mon–Sat 9:00–19:00, Sun 10:00–17:00), and facing the **beach** at 5 promenade des Anglais (usually quiet, daily 9:00–18:00, until 20:00 July–Aug, closed Sun off-season, tel. 08 92 70 74 07—costs €0.34/min, www.nicetourisme.com). Pick up the thorough *Practical Guide to Nice*, information on day trips (such as city maps of Antibes or Monaco, and details on boat excursions), and a free Nice map (or find a better one at your hotel).

Arrival in Nice

By Train: All trains stop at Nice's main station, Nice-Ville (baggage storage at the far right with your back to the tracks, lockers open daily 8:00–21:00, left luggage desk Mon–Sat 8:45–12:00 & 14:00–15:45, closed Sun). This is one busy station, and theft is a problem, so never leave your bags unattended.

Turn left out of the station to find a **TI** just a few steps away. Continue a few more blocks for the Gare Thiers **tram stop** (this will take you to place Masséna, the old city, bus station, and port). Board the tram heading toward the right, direction Pont Michel (see "Getting Around Nice," later). You'll find many recommended hotels a 10- to 20-minute walk down the same street (those listed under "Between Nice Etoile and the Sea," on page 291), though it's easier taking the tram to place Masséna and walking from there.

To walk to other recommended hotels (those listed under "Between the Train Station and Nice Etoile" and "Between Boulevard Victor Hugo and the Sea," on page 292), cross avenue Thiers in front of the station, go down the steps by Hôtel Interlaken, and continue walking down avenue Durante. Follow this same route for the fastest path to the beach—avenue Durante turns into rue des Congrès. You'll soon reach the heart of Nice's beachfront promenade.

For **taxis** or for **buses to the airport,** walk straight out of the train station. Taxis are in the first lane. Express airport bus #99 and the milk-run airport bus #23 are in the second lane. **Car rental** offices are to the right.

By Bus: Nice's bus station *(gare routière)* is sandwiched between boulevard Jean Jaurès and avenue Félix Faure, next to the old city. The station has no baggage storage. Cross boulevard Jean Jaurès to catch the tram or to enter teeming Old Nice. Cross avenue Félix Faure to get to my recommended hotels near Nice Etoile.

By Car: Driving into the city on the autoroute from the west, take the first Nice exit (for the airport—called Côte d'Azur,

Nice

NICE

1/4 MILE
400 METERS

— TRAM
P PARKING

C I M I E Z

MATISSE MUSEUM
ROMAN RUINS
ARCHAEOLOGICAL MUSEUM

BLVD. DE CIMIEZ
AVE. DES ARENES
DE CIMIEZ

CHAGALL MUSEUM

GARE DE SUD TRAIN STN.
TO ENTREVAUX

AVE. MALAUSSENA
AVE. COMBOUL
TUNNEL

RUSSIAN CATH.

FREEWAY
ELE-VATED
AVE. THIERS
RAIMBALDI
DESAMBROIS
TO ❶

GAMBETTA BLVD.
AVE. DURANTE
JEAN MEDECIN
NOTRE-DAME
P
DUBOUCHAGE
MODERN ART MUSEUM
RUE BARLA
TO ❷

TRAIN STN.

HUGO
CONGRES
BLVD.
PLACE MASSENA
BUS STN.
CASSINI
PLACE GARI-BALDI
TO ❸

TO ❻ R. DE FRANCE

MASSENA MUSEUM
RUE MASSENA
❺
❽
❶❶ ❶❷
AVE. FAURE
BLVD. JAURES
CASTLE HILL
QUAI DU LUNEL
PORT.

HOTEL NEGRESCO
❹
❶❶
OLD NICE
COURS SALEYA
ELEVATOR
❾

TO AIROPORT

PROMENADE DES ANGLAIS
QUAI D. ETATS-UNIS
❿
B E A C H E S
❼

TOURIST TRAIN PICK-UP
BELLANDA TOWER

TO ANTIBES, CANNES & VENCE

TO VILLEFRANCHE, MONACO & ITALY

DCH   M E D I T E R R A N E A N   S E A

❶ To High Corniche (sky-high route to Monaco)

❷ To Middle Corniche (middle route, best for Monaco & Eze-le-Village)

❸ To Low Corniche (low route to Villefranche-sur-Mer & Cap Ferrat)

❹ Start of "Welcome to the Riviera" Walk

❺ Start of "Old Nice" Walk

❻ To Fine Arts Museum

❼ World War II Monument

❽ US Consulate

❾ Trans Côte d'Azur Cruises

❿ Le Grand Tour Bus Departure Point & Albert I Park

⓫ Buses #15 & #22 Stops (3)

⓬ Bus #17 Stops (2)

Central) and follow signs for *Nice Centre* and *Promenade des Anglais*. (Be ready to cross three left lanes of traffic as soon as you get off the autoroute.) Try to avoid arriving at rush hour (usually Mon–Fri 8:00–9:30 & 17:00–19:30), when promenade des Anglais grinds to a halt. Hoteliers know where to park (allow €15–24/day). The parking garage at the Nice Etoile shopping center on avenue Jean Médecin is pricey but near many of the hotels listed in this chapter (ticket booth on third floor, about €20/day, €10–12 20:00–8:00). All on-street parking is metered (9:00–18:00 or 19:00), but usually free all day on Sunday.

By Plane: For information on Nice's handy airport, see "Nice Connections" at the end of this chapter.

Helpful Hints

NICE

Theft Alert: Nice has more than its share of pickpockets. Have nothing important on or around your waist, unless it's in a money belt tucked out of sight (thieves target fanny packs); don't leave anything visible in your car; be wary of scooters when standing at intersections; don't leave things unattended on the beach while swimming; and stick to main streets in Old Nice after dark.

US Consulate: You'll find it at 7 avenue Gustave V (tel. 04 93 88 89 55, fax 04 93 87 07 38, http://france.usembassy.gov/nice .html).

Canadian Consulate: It's at 2 place Franklin (tel. 04 93 92 93 22, fax 04 93 92 55 51).

Medical Help: Riviera Medical Services has a list of English-speaking physicians. They can help you make an appointment or call an ambulance (4 boulevard Maurice Maeterlinck, tel. 04 93 26 12 70, www.rivieramedical.com).

Museums: Some Nice museums (Chagall, Matisse, Archaeological) are closed Tuesdays, while others (Modern and Contemporary Art, Fine Arts) close on Mondays. City museums are free of charge—so all of the sights in this chapter (except the Chagall Museum and the Russian Cathedral) cost zilch to enter. Rainy-day options are a swinging deal here.

Internet Access: There's no shortage of places to get online in Nice—they're everywhere. Ask at your hotel, or just look up as you walk (keep your eye out for the @ symbol).

English Bookstore: The Cat's Whiskers has an eclectic selection of novels and regional travel books, including mine. Say *bonjour* to mellow owner Linda (Tue–Sat 10:00–12:00 & 14:00–19:00, closed Sun–Mon, 26–30 rue Lamartine—see map on page 288, tel. 04 93 80 02 66).

Laundry: You'll find launderettes everywhere in Nice—ask your hotelier for the nearest one. The self-service **Point Laverie**

is centrally located (daily 8:00–20:00, at the corner of rue Alberti and rue Pastorelli, next to Hôtel Vendôme—see map on page 288).

Grocery Store: The big **Monoprix** on avenue Jean Médecin and rue Biscarra has it all, including a deli counter, bakery, and cold drinks (closed Sun, see map on page 298). You'll also find many small grocery stores (some open Sun and/or until late hours) near my recommended hotels.

Renting a Bike (and Other Wheels): Roller Station rents bikes (*vélos*, €5/hr, €10/half-day, €15/day), rollerblades (*rollers*, €6/day), Razor-type scooters (*trotinettes*, €6/half-day, €9/day), and skateboards (€6/half-day, €9/day). You'll need to leave your ID as a deposit (daily 9:30–19:00, July–Aug until 20:00, next to yellow awnings of Pailin's Asian restaurant at 49 quai des Etats-Unis—see map on page 288, another location at 10 rue Cassini near place Garibaldi, tel. 04 93 62 99 05, owner Eric). If you need more power, try the electric-assisted bikes or scooters at **Energy Scoot** (2 rue St. Philippe, near the promenade des Anglais and avenue Gambetta, tel. 04 97 07 12 64).

Car Rental: Renting a car is easiest at Nice's airport, which has offices for all the major companies. You'll also find most companies represented at Nice's train station and near Albert 1er Park.

English Radio: Tune into Riviera-Radio at FM 106.5.

Views: For panoramic views, climb Castle Hill (see page 284), or take a one-hour boat trip (described later, under "Tours in Nice").

Rocky Beaches: To make life tolerable on the rocks, swimmers should buy a pair of the cheap plastic beach shoes sold at many shops (flip-flops fall off in the water). Try **Go Sport** on place Masséna at #13, which also sells cheap sunglasses (daily 10:00–19:00—see map on page 294).

Getting Around Nice

While you can walk to most attractions in Nice, smart travelers make good use of the buses and tram. Both are covered by the same single-ride €1 ticket (good for 74 min in one direction, including transfers between bus and tram; can't be used for a round-trip). An all-day pass is €4 (valid on local buses and trams, as well as buses to nearby destinations—see "Getting Around the Riviera," next page).

The **bus** is handy to reach the Chagall and Matisse museums and the Russian Cathedral. Make sure to validate your ticket in the machine just behind the driver—watch to see how locals do it.

Nice's new **tramway** makes an "L" along avenue Jean Médecin and boulevard Jean Jaurès. This handy tram is smooth and speedy; traffic signals detect when trams come and magically turn to green.

NICE

The tram connects the main train station (Gare Thiers stop), place Masséna (Masséna stop, a few blocks' walk from the sea), Old Nice (Opéra-Vieille Ville), the bus station (Cathédrale-Vieille Ville), and the Modern and Contemporary Art Museum and port (Place Garibaldi). It also comes within a few blocks of the Gare du Sud train station (Libération stop)—the departure point for the scenic Chemins de Fer de Provence trains (see page 285). Taking the tram in the direction of Pont Michel takes you from the train station toward the beach and bus station (direction Las Planas goes the other way). Buy tickets at the machines on the platforms (coins only, no credit cards, choose the English flag to change the display language, spin the round knob and push the green button to select your ticket, or press the red button to cancel). If you're having trouble, ask anyone for help. (Press the green button twice at the end to get your ticket.) Once you're on the tram, validate your ticket by inserting it into the top of the white box, then reclaiming it.

Taxis are handy for getting to Nice's outlying sights, and worth it if you're nowhere near a bus or tram stop (figure €10–12 from promenade des Anglais). They normally only pick up at taxi stands *(tête de station),* or you can call 04 93 13 78 78.

The hokey **tourist train** gets you up Castle Hill (see "Tours in Nice," later in this chapter).

Getting Around the Riviera

Nice is perfectly situated for exploring the Riviera by public transport. Monaco, Eze-le-Village, Villefranche-sur-Mer, Antibes, St-Paul-de-Vence, Grasse, and Cannes are all within a one-hour bus or train ride. Boats go from Nice to Monaco and St-Tropez. Fares are cheap, but you need to carry plenty of change to buy train tickets from machines at smaller, unstaffed stations and to buy bus tickets from drivers (who can't make change for large bills).

By Train: Speedy trains effortlessly link the Riviera's beachfront destinations—Cannes, Antibes, Nice, Villefranche-sur-Mer, Monaco, Menton, and the inland perfume town of Grasse (see sidebar for approximate travel times and one-way prices). There is no faster way to move about the Riviera than by train. All trains serving Nice arrive at and depart from the Nice-Ville station. Never board a train without a ticket or valid pass. Fare inspectors don't accept excuses, and you'll pay a fine of at least €70.

By Bus: At Nice's efficient bus station on boulevard Jean

Jaurès, you'll find several bus companies, WCs, and vending machines with sandwiches and drinks (but no baggage storage). If you want fresher food, head to one of the bakeries just across the street (toward Old Nice). I've listed general bus information below, but you can get timetables and prices from the English-speaking clerk at the information desk (Mon–Sat 6:30–20:00, closed Sun, tel. 04 93 85 61 81). Buy tickets from the driver.

Any one-way ride costs €1 (except on express airport buses)—whether you're riding 15 minutes to Villefranche-sur-Mer, 45 minutes to Monaco, or an hour to Antibes. This is simply an amazing deal. However, note that (aside from airport buses) you might be charged an extra €5 for bringing a big bag onto Riviera buses (though it's unclear how strictly this new rule will be enforced). Two private bus companies provide service to Riviera destinations: the more important Ligne d'Azur and the less convenient TAM. The same tickets work on buses for both companies (and for local buses and trams within Nice)—you can even transfer between the buses of the two different companies. The €1 single ticket (called "**Ticket Azur**"), available on all Ligne d'Azur buses, lets you take a one-way ride anywhere within the bus system (if you board a TAM bus and want to transfer, ask for a transfer: *un ticket correspondance*). The €4 all-day ticket (**Carte Journée**) is good on Nice's city buses and tramway, as well as on buses throughout the region. This all-day ticket only makes sense if you plan to take the bus to museums, use the tramway several times, or are going to the airport. Check schedules on their websites: Ligne d'Azur (www.lignedazur.com) and TAM (www.cg06.fr/transport/transports-tam.htm).

Since express buses to and from the airport (#98 and #99) require the €4 all-day ticket, savvy riders pack in other bus and/or tram rides on the day of their flight.

By Minivan Excursion: Sylvie Di Cristo offers lively full-day tours in her car or minivan throughout the French Riviera and up to the southern Alps. She loves to teach about this area's culture and history (€170/person for 2–3 people, €120/person for 4–6 people, 2-person minimum, mobile 06 09 88 83 83, www.azur-guides.net, sylvie.di.cristo@wanadoo.fr). The TI and most hotels have information on other minivan excursions from Nice (roughly €50–60/half-day, €80–110/day). **Med-Tour** is one of many tour operators (tel. 04 93 82 92 58, mobile 06 73 82 04 10, www.med-tour.com); **Tour Azur** is a bit pricier (tel. 04 93 44 88 77, www.tourazur.com); and **Revelation Tours** specializes in English excursions (tel. 04 93 53 69 85, www.revelation-tours.com). All companies also offer private tours by the day or half-day (check with them for their outrageous prices, about €90/hr).

By Boat: From June to mid-September, Trans Côte d'Azur

NICE

Public Transportation in the Nice Region

Many key Riviera destinations are connected by direct bus or train service from Nice, and some are served by both. Since bus fare is only €1, the pricier train is only a better choice when it saves you time (which it generally does). You make the call—both modes of transportation work well. All prices are one-way. Unless otherwise noted, the following bus frequencies are for Monday–Saturday (Sunday often has limited or no service).

Destination	Bus from Nice	Train from Nice
Villefranche-sur-Mer	4/hr daily, 15 min	2/hr, 10 min, €1.80
Cap Ferrat	about 2/hr daily, 30 min*	none
Monaco	4/hr Mon–Sat, 3/hr Sun, 45 min	2/hr, 20 min, €3.50
Menton	4/hr Mon–Sat, 3/hr Sun, 1 hr	2/hr, 25 min, €3.60
Antibes	2–4/hr, 1–1.5 hrs	2/hr, 15–30 min, €3.90
Cannes	2–4/hr, 1.5–1.75 hrs	2/hr, 30–40 min, €6
St-Paul-de-Vence	every 40 min, 45 min	none
Vence	every 40 min, 50 min	none
Grasse	every 40 min, 1.25 hr	1/hr, 1.25 hr, €7
Eze-le-Village	16/day, 25 min	none
La Turbie	4/day, 45 min	none

*A more-frequent bus to Cap Ferrat entails a longer walk. Buses also run from Monaco to Eze-le-Village and to La Turbie, allowing travelers to triangulate Nice, Monaco, and Eze-le-Village or La Turbie for a good all-day excursion—ending up back in Nice (see page 362 for details).

offers scenic trips from Nice to Monaco and Nice to St-Tropez. Boats leave in the morning and return in the evening, giving you all day to explore your destination. Drinks and WCs are available on board. Boats to **Monaco** depart at 9:30 and return at 18:00 (€30 round-trip, 45 min each way, June–Sept Tue, Thu, and Sat only). Boats to **St-Tropez** depart at 9:00 and return at 19:00 (€52 round-trip, 2.5 hrs each way; July–Aug Tue–Sun, no boats Mon; late June and early Sept Tue, Thu, and Sun only). Reservations are required for both boats, and tickets for St-Tropez often sell out, so book a few days ahead (tel. 04 92 98 71 30, www.trans-cote-azur

.com, croisieres@trans-cote-azur.com). The boats leave from Nice's port, bassin des Amiraux, just below Castle Hill—look for the blue ticket booth *(billeterie)* on quai de Lunel (see map on page 269). The same company also runs one-hour round-trip cruises along the coast to Cap Ferrat (see "Tours in Nice," next).

Tours in Nice

Bus Tour—Le Grand Tour Bus provides a 14-stop, hop-on, hop-off service on an open-deck bus with headphone commentary (2/hr, about 90 min for the full loop) that includes promenade des Anglais, old port, Cap de Nice, and the Chagall and Matisse museums on Cimiez Hill (€20/1-day pass, €23/2-day pass, cheaper for seniors and students, €10 for last tour of the day at about 18:00, some hotels offer small discounts, buy tickets on bus, main stop is near where promenade des Anglais and quai des Etats-Unis meet, across from plage Beau Rivage, tel. 04 92 29 17 00). This tour is a pricey way to get to the Chagall and Matisse museums, but it's an acceptable option if you also want a city overview. Check the schedule if you plan to use this bus to visit the Russian Cathedral, as it may be faster to walk.

Tourist Train—For €7 (or €3 for children under 9), you can spend 40 embarrassing minutes on the tourist train tooting along the promenade, through the old city, and up to Castle Hill. This is a sweat-free way to get to Castle Hill...but so is the elevator, which is much cheaper (every 30 min, daily 10:00–18:00, June–Aug until 19:00, recorded English commentary, meet train near Le Grand Tour Bus stop on quai des Etats-Unis, tel. 04 93 62 85 48).

▲Boat Cruise—Here's your chance to join the boat parade and see Nice from the water. On this one-hour, star-studded tour, you'll cruise in a comfortable yacht-size vessel to Cap Ferrat and past Villefranche-sur-Mer, then return to Nice with a final lap along promenade des Anglais. It's a scenic trip (the best views are from the seats on top), and worthwhile if you won't be hiking along the Cap Ferrat trails that provide similar views. French (and sometimes English-speaking) guides play Robin Leach, pointing out mansions owned by some pretty famous people, including Elton John (just as you leave Nice, it's the soft-yellow square-shaped place right on the water), Sean Connery (on the hill above Elton, with rounded arches and tower), and Microsoft mogul Paul Allen (in saddle of Cap Ferrat hill, above yellow-umbrella beach with sloping red-tile roof). They also like to point out the mansion where the Rolling Stones recorded *Exile on Main Street* (between Villefranche-sur-Mer and Cap Ferrat). I wonder if this gang ever hangs out together... (€15; May–Oct Tue–Sun 2/day, usually at 11:00 and 15:00, no boats Mon; March–April Tue–Wed, Fri, and Sun at 15:00; no boats Nov–Feb; call ahead to verify schedule, arrive 30 min early to get best seats, drinks and WCs available). For directions to the dock and contact information, see "Getting Around the Riviera—By Boat," earlier.

Walking Tours—The TI on promenade des Anglais organizes weekly walking tours of Old Nice in French and English (€12, May–Oct only, usually Sat morning at 9:30, 2.5 hours, reservations necessary, depart from TI, tel. 08 92 70 74 07).

Nice's cultural association (Centre du Patrimoine) offers incredibly cheap €5 on-demand walks on varying themes (in English, minimum 3 people). Call 04 92 00 41 90 or 06 76 98 67 82 a few days ahead to make a reservation. Most tours start at their office at 75 quai des Etats-Unis; look for the red plaque next to Musée des Ponchettes (see map on page 294).

Les Petits Farcis Cooking Tour and Classes—Canadian food-journalist-turned-Francophile Rosa Jackson is making a Mediterranean splash with her cooking classes in Old Nice. Her single-day classes include a morning trip to the open-air market for picking up ingredients, and an afternoon session, where you'll learn what to do with your purchases. She also offers a three-hour "Taste of Nice" food tour (food tour-€80, tour and class-€190, other options, mobile 06 81 67 41 22, www.petitsfarcis.com).

Local Guide—Lovely Pascale Rucker tailors excellent tours to your interests in and around Nice. Book in advance, though it's also worth a try on short notice (€140/half-day, €230/day, tel. & fax 04 93 87 77 89, mobile 06 16 24 29 52).

Sights in Nice

To bring culture to the masses, the city of Nice has nixed the entry fee to all municipal museums—so it's free to enter any of the sights listed below, except the Chagall Museum and the Russian Cathedral. Cool. The first two museums (Chagall and Matisse) are a long walk northeast of Nice's city center, and because they're on the same bus line (in the same direction), it makes sense to visit them on the same trip. From place Masséna, the Chagall Museum is a 30-minute walk, and the Matisse Museum is a 60-minute walk.

▲▲▲Chagall Museum (Musée National Marc Chagall)— Inspired by the Old Testament, modern artist Marc Chagall custom-painted works for this building, which he considered a "House of Brotherhood." In typical Chagall style, these paintings are lively, colorful, and simple (some might say simplistic). The museum is a can't-miss treat for Chagall fans, and a hit

Nice at a Glance

▲▲▲**Chagall Museum** The world's largest collection of Chagall's work, popular even with people who don't like modern art. **Hours:** Wed-Mon 10:00–17:00, May-Oct until 18:00, closed Tue. See page 276.

▲▲**Promenade des Anglais** Nice's four-mile sun-struck seafront promenade. **Hours:** Always open. See page 284.

▲▲**Old Nice** Charming old city offering enjoyable atmosphere and a look at Nice's French-Italian cultural blend. **Hours:** Always open. See page 284.

▲**Matisse Museum** A worthwhile collection of Henri Matisse's paintings. **Hours:** Wed-Mon 10:00–18:00, closed Tue. See page 278.

▲**Russian Cathedral** Finest Orthodox church outside of Russia. **Hours:** Mon-Sat 9:00–12:00 & 14:30–18:00, Sun 14:30–18:00, until 17:00 off-season. See page 283.

Fine Arts Museum Lush villa shows off impressive paintings by Monet, Sisley, Bonnard, and Raoul Dufy. **Hours:** Tue-Sun 10:00–18:00, closed Mon. See page 281.

Modern and Contemporary Art Museum Ultramodern museum with enjoyable collection from the 1960s–1970s, including Warhol and Lichtenstein. **Hours:** Tue-Sun 10:00–18:00, closed Mon. See page 281.

Molinard Perfume Museum Small museum tracing the history of perfume. **Hours:** Daily July-Aug 10:00–19:00, Sept-June 10:00–13:00 & 14:00–18:30, sometimes closed Mon off-season. See page 282.

Castle Hill Site of an ancient fort boasting great views—especially in early mornings and evenings. **Hours:** Park closes at 20:00 in summer, earlier off-season. Elevator runs daily 10:00–19:00, until 20:00 in summer. See page 284.

NICE

even for people who usually don't like modern art.

For a complete self-guided tour of the museum, and directions on how to get here, see the Chagall Museum Tour chapter.

Cost, Hours, Location: €6.50, €7.50 with special exhibits, free first Sun of the month (but crowded), open Wed–Mon 10:00–17:00, May–Oct until 18:00, closed Tue year-round, avenue

Henri Matisse
(1869–1954)

Here's an outline of Henri Matisse's busy life:

1880s and 1890s—At age 20, Matisse, a budding lawyer, is struck down with appendicitis. Bedridden for a year, he turns to painting as a healing escape from pain and boredom. After recovering, he studies art in Paris and produces dark-colored, realistic still lifes and landscapes. His work is exhibited at the Salons of 1896 and 1897.

1897–1905—Influenced by the Impressionists, he experiments with sunnier scenes and brighter colors. He travels to southern France, including Collioure (on the coast near Spain), and seeks still more light-filled scenes to paint. His experiments are influenced by Vincent van Gogh's bright, surrealistic colors and thick outlines, and by Paul Gauguin's primitive visions of a Tahitian paradise. From Paul Cézanne, he learns how to simplify objects into their basic geometric shapes. He also experiments (like Cézanne) with creating the illusion of 3-D not by traditional means, but by using contrasting colors for the foreground and background.

1905—Back in Paris, Matisse and his colleagues (André Derain and Maurice de Vlaminck) shock the art world with an exhibition of their experimental paintings. The thick outlines, simple forms, non-3-D scenes, and—most of all—bright, clashing, unrealistic colors seemed to be the work of "wild animals" *(fauves)*. Fauvism is hot, and Matisse is instantly famous. (Though notorious as a "wild animal," Matisse himself was a gentle, introspective man.)

1906–1910—After just a year, Fauvism is out, and African masks are in. This "primitive" art form inspires Matisse to simplify and distort his figures further, making them less realistic but more expressive.

1910–1917—Matisse creates his masterpiece paintings. Cubism is the rage, pioneered by Matisse's friend and rival for the World's Best Painter award, Pablo Picasso. Matisse dabbles in Cubism, simplifying forms, emphasizing outline, and muting his colors. But ultimately, it proves to be too austere and analytical for his

Docteur Ménard, tel. 04 93 53 87 20, www.musee-chagall.fr.

▲**Matisse Museum (Musée Matisse)**—This museum, worth ▲▲▲ for his fans, contains the world's largest collection of Henri Matisse paintings. It offers a painless introduction to the artist, whose style was shaped by Mediterranean light and by fellow Côte d'Azur artists Pablo Picasso and Pierre-Auguste Renoir. The collection is scattered through several rooms with a few worthwhile works, though it lacks a certain *je ne sais quoi* when compared to the Chagall Museum.

Cost, Hours, Location: Free, Wed–Mon 10:00–18:00, closed deeply sensory nature. The Cubist style is most evident in his sculpture.

1920s—Burned out from years of intense experimentation, Matisse moves to Nice (spending winters there from 1917, settling permanently in 1921). Luxuriating under the bright sun, he's reborn, and he paints colorful, sensual, highly decorative works. Harem concubines lounging in their sunny, flowery apartments epitomize the lush life.

1930s—A visit to Tahiti inspires more scenes of life as a sunny paradise. Increasingly, Matisse plays around with the lines of the figures he draws to create swirling arabesques and decorative patterns.

1940s—Duodenal cancer (in 1941) requires Matisse to undergo two operations and confines him to a wheelchair for the rest of his life. Working at an easel becomes a struggle for him, and he largely stops painting in 1941. But as World War II ends, Matisse emerges with renewed energy. Now in his 70s, he explores a new medium: paper cutouts pasted onto a watercolored surface (découpages on gouache-prepared surface). The medium plays to his strengths: The cutouts are essentially blocks of bright color (mostly blue) with a strong outline. Scissors in hand, Matisse says, "I draw straight into the color." (His doctor advises him to wear dark glasses to protect his weak eyes against the bright colors he chooses.) In 1947, Matisse's book *Jazz* is published, featuring the artist's joyful cutouts of simple figures. Like jazz music, the book is a celebration of artistic spontaneity. And like music in general, Matisse's works balance different tones and colors to create a mood.

1947–1951—Matisse's nurse becomes a Dominican nun in Vence. To thank her for her care, he spends his later years designing a chapel there. He oversees every aspect of the Chapel of the Rosary (Chapelle du Rosaire) at Vence, from the stained glass to the altar to the colors of the priest's robe (see page 399). Though Matisse is not a strong Christian, the church exudes his spirit of celebrating life and sums up his work.

1954—Matisse dies.

NICE

Tue, 164 avenue des Arènes de Cimiez, tel. 04 93 81 08 08, www .musee-matisse-nice.org. The museum is set in an olive grove amid the ruins of the Roman city of Cemenelum. Part of the ancient Roman city of Nice, Cemenelum was a military camp that housed as many as 20,000 people.

Getting to the Matisse Museum: It's a long uphill walk from the city center. Take the bus (details below) or a cab (about €12 from promenade des Anglais). Once here, walk into the park to find the pink villa. **Buses #15, #17,** and **#22** offer frequent service to the Matisse Museum from just off place Masséna on rue

Gioffredo (Masséna Guitry stop, a block east of the Galeries Lafayette department store—see map on page 272; €1 for the trip). **Bus #20** connects the port to the museum. On any bus, get off at the Arènes–Matisse bus stop. (For bus tips on leaving the museum, see the end of this listing.)

Background: Henri Matisse, the master of leaving things out, could suggest a woman's body with a single curvy line—letting the viewer's mind fill in the rest. Ignoring traditional 3-D perspective, he used simple dark outlines saturated with bright blocks of color to create recognizable but simplified scenes composed into a decorative pattern to express nature's serene beauty. You don't look "through" a Matisse canvas, like a window; you look "at" it, like wallpaper.

Matisse understood how colors and shapes affect us emotionally. He could create either shocking, clashing works (Fauvism) or geometrical, balanced, harmonious ones (later pieces). While other modern artists reveled in purely abstract design, Matisse (almost) always kept the subject matter at least vaguely recognizable. He used unreal colors and distorted lines not just to portray what an object looks like, but to express its inner nature (even inanimate objects). Meditating on his paintings helps you connect with nature—or so Matisse hoped.

As you tour the museum, look for Matisse's favorite motifs, including fruit, flowers, wallpaper, and sunny rooms—often with a window opening onto a sunny landscape. Another favorite subject is the odalisque (harem concubine), usually shown sprawled in a seductive pose and with a simplified, masklike face. You'll also see a few souvenirs from his travels, which influenced much of his work.

◆Self-Guided Tour: Enter the museum at park level from the door opposite the olive grove (not via the basement entry). Take one of the free museum handouts, which provide minimal English information on the collection. Drop down a few steps and find the two rooms at the far right (Rooms 9 and 10) that house paintings from Matisse's formative years as a student (1890s). Tour these rooms clockwise, noticing how quickly his work evolves: from dark still lifes (Room 9) to colorful Impressionist works to more abstract pieces, all in a matter of a few years. A beige banner describes his "discovery of light," which the Riviera (and his various travels to sun-soaked places like Morocco and Tahiti) brought to his art. Room 11 is devoted to Matisse's move to Nice. Find the photograph of his apartment on cours Saleya, which is described in my Old Nice Walk chapter.

Other rooms on this floor highlight Matisse's fascination with dance and the female body. You'll see many pencil and charcoal drawings, and a handful of bronze busts; he was fascinated by

NICE

sculpture. In Room 7, *The Acrobat*—painted only two years before Matisse's death—shows the artist at his minimalist best. Look for the orange-bearded 1905 portrait of Matisse by André Derain.

Now head up one flight of stairs, following the smaller steps halfway up to the right, and see sketches and models of his famous Chapel of the Rosary in nearby Vence (see page 399) and related religious works. On the same floor, find paper cutouts from his *Jazz* series, more bronze sculptures, various personal objects, and linen embroideries inspired by his travels to Polynesia.

The bookshop, WCs, and generally worthwhile temporary exhibits are in the basement levels. The wall-hanging near the bookshop—Matisse's colorful paper cutout *Flowers and Fruits*—shouts, "Riviera!"

Leaving the Museum: When leaving the museum, find the stop for buses #15 and #22 (frequent service downtown and stops en route at the Chagall Museum). Turn left out of the Matisse Museum and stay left, exiting the park at the Archeological Museum, then turn right. At the three-way roundabout, cross to the far left and find the downhill stop for buses #15 and #22. It's by the elegant apartment building with the oval portico (the stop is on boulevard de Cimiez, not avenue des Arènes de Cimiez—see map on page 269). The stop for buses #17 (to the city center) and #20 (to Nice's port) also face downhill, but are on avenue des Arènes de Cimiez.

Fine Arts Museum (Musée des Beaux-Arts)—Housed in a sumptuous Riviera villa with lovely gardens, this museum holds 6,000 works from the 17th to 20th centuries. Start on the first floor and work your way up to experience an impressive array of paintings by Monet, Sisley, Bonnard, and Raoul Dufy, as well as a few sculptures by Rodin and Carpeaux (free, Tue–Sun 10:00–18:00, closed Mon, 3 avenue des Baumettes, inconveniently located at the western end of Nice, take buses #12 or #23 from the train station or bus #38 from the bus station, tel. 04 92 15 28 28, www.musee -beaux-arts-nice.org).

Modern and Contemporary Art Museum (Musée d'Art Moderne et d'Art Contemporain)—This ultramodern museum features an explosively colorful, far-out, yet manageable permanent collection (on the second floor) of mostly American and European art from the 1960s and 1970s. The exhibits include a few works by Andy Warhol, Roy Lichtenstein, and Jean Tinguely, and small models of Christo's famous wrappings. Several of Niki de Saint Phalle's works are almost huggable. The temporary exhibits can be as appealing to modern-art–lovers as the permanent collection—ask the TI, or check their website for what's playing.

Cost, Hours, Location: Free, Tue–Sun 10:00–18:00, closed Mon, about a 15-minute walk from place Masséna, near bus station on promenade des Arts, tel. 04 93 62 61 62, www.mamac-nice.org.

Molinard Perfume Museum—The Molinard family has been making perfume in Grasse (about an hour's drive from Nice—see page 403) since 1849. Their Nice store has a small museum in the back that illustrates the story of their industry. Back when people believed water spread the plague (Louis XIV supposedly bathed less than once a year), doctors advised people to rub fragrances into their skin and then powder their body. Back then, perfume was a necessity of everyday life.

Tiny Room 1 shows photos of the local flowers used in perfume production. Room 2 explains the earliest (18th-century) production method. Petals would be laid on a bed of animal fat. After baking in the sun, the fat would absorb the essence of the flowers. Petals would be replaced daily for two months until the fat was saturated. Models and old photos show the later distillation process (660 pounds of lavender would produce only a quarter-gallon of essence). Perfume is "distilled like cognac and then aged like wine." The small bottles on the table in the corner demonstrate the role of the "blender" and the perfume mastermind called the "nose" (who knows best). Notice the photos of these lab-coat-wearing perfectionists. Of the 150 real "noses" in the world, more than 100 are French. You are welcome to enjoy the testing bottles.

Cost, Hours, Location: Free, daily July–Aug 10:00–19:00, Sept–June 10:00–13:00 & 14:00–18:30, sometimes closed Mon off-season, just between beach and place Masséna at 20 rue St. François de Paule, see map on page 294, tel. 04 93 62 90 50, www.molinard.com.

Other Nice Museums—Both of these museums are acceptable rainy-day options, and free of charge.

The **Archaeological Museum** (Musée Archéologique) displays various objects from the Romans' occupation of this region. It's convenient—just below the Matisse Museum—but has little of interest to anyone but ancient Rome aficionados. You also get access to the Roman bath ruins...which are, sadly, overgrown with weeds (free, very limited information in English, Wed–Mon 10:00–18:00, closed Tue, near Matisse Museum at 160 avenue des Arènes de Cimiez, tel. 04 93 81 59 57, www.musee-archeologique-nice.org).

The **Masséna Museum** (Musée Masséna), like Nice's main square, is named in honor of Jean-André Masséna, a commander during France's Revolutionary and Napoleonic Wars (for more on him, see page 309). This centrally located mansion is worth a gander for its lavish decor and lovely gardens alone (pick up your free ticket at the boutique just outside). The ground floor shows rotating exhibits (on my last visit, this floor was filled with photos of Barack Obama and his family). The upstairs floors offer a folk-museum-like look at Nice through the years, with antique posters, models of the old casino destroyed in World War II (La Jetée Promenade, described on page 306), many 18th- and 19th-century paintings (mostly by artists from Nice), and other collections relevant to the city's tumultuous history. Find the images of Nice before they covered the river that runs under place Masséna. You'll also come across some Napoleon paraphernalia; Josephine's cape and tiara are impressive, and I'd look good in Napoleon's vest. Check out the paintings of the Italian patriot and Nice favorite Giuseppe Garibaldi, as well as his burial sheet (free, daily 10:00–18:00, 35 promenade des Anglais, tel. 04 93 91 19 10).

▲**Russian Cathedral (Cathédrale Russe)**—Nice's Russian Orthodox church—claimed to be the finest outside Russia—is worth

a visit. Five hundred rich Russian families wintered in Nice in the late 19th century. Since they couldn't pray in a Catholic church, the community needed a worthy Orthodox house of worship. Czar Nicholas I's widow provided the land (which required tearing down her house), and Czar Nicholas II gave this church to the Russian community in 1912. (A few years later, Russian comrades who *didn't* winter on the Riviera assassinated him.) Here in the land of olives and anchovies, these proud onion domes seem odd. But, I imagine, so did those old Russians.

Step inside (pick up English info sheet). The one-room interior is filled with icons and candles, and the old Russian music adds to the ambience. The wall of icons (iconostasis) divides things between the spiritual world and the temporal world of the worshippers. Only the priest can walk between the two worlds, by using the "Royal Door." Take a close look at items lining the front (starting in the left corner). The angel with red boots and wings—the protector of the Romanov family—stands over a symbolic tomb of Christ. The tall black hammered-copper cross commemorates the massacre of Nicholas II and his family in 1918. Notice the Jesus icon to the right of the Royal Door. According to a priest here, as worshippers meditate, staring deep into the eyes of Jesus, they enter a lake where they find their soul. Surrounded by incense, chanting, and your entire community...it could happen. Farther to the right, the icon of the unhappy-looking Virgin and Child is decorated with semiprecious stones from the Ural Mountains. Artists worked a triangle into each iconic face—symbolic of the Trinity.

Cost, Hours, Location: €3, Mon–Sat 9:00–12:00 & 14:30–18:00, Sun 14:30–18:00, until 17:00 off-season, chanted services Sat at 17:30 or 18:00, Sun at 10:00, no tourist visits during services, no short shorts, 17 boulevard du Tzarewitch, tel. 04 93 96 88 02, www.acor-nice.com. The park around the church stays open at lunch and makes a fine setting for picnics.

Getting to the Russian Cathedral: From the train station, it's a 10-minute walk. Exit the station to the right onto avenue Thiers, turn right on avenue Gambetta, go under the freeway, and turn left following *Eglise Russe* signs. Or, from the station, take any bus heading west on avenue Thiers and get off at avenue Gambetta (then follow the above directions).

Castle Hill (Colline du Château)—Nice was first settled on this hill, which offers sweeping views over the city—best by far in the early morning or late in the day (park closes at 20:00 in summer, earlier off-season). You can get to the top by foot, by elevator (€0.70 one-way, €1.10 round-trip, runs daily 10:00–19:00, until 20:00 in summer, next to beachfront Hôtel Suisse), or by pricey tourist train (described under "Tours in Nice," earlier in this chapter). Up top, you'll find cafés and an extensive play area for kids.

For more on Castle Hill, see the Welcome to the Riviera Walk chapter.

NICE

Sights in Nice

In the City

▲▲Wandering Old Nice (Vieux Nice)—Offering an intriguing look at Nice's melding of French and Italian cultures, the old city is a fine place to meander with ice cream in hand. Enjoy its mix of belle époque buildings, bustling market squares, tempting shops, and colorful people.

For all the details on this neighborhood, see the Old Nice Walk chapter.

▲▲Strolling the Promenade des Anglais—Sauntering along

Nice's four-mile seafront promenade is a must. From the days when wealthy English tourists lined the seaside with grand hotels up to today, as a favorite spot for Europeans to enjoy some fun in the sun—this stretch is *the* place to be in Nice.

For a self-guided walk of this strip, see the Welcome to the Riviera Walk chapter.

▲▲Wheeling the Promenade—Get a bike and glide along the coast in both directions (about 30 min each way). Roller Station rents bikes, in-line skates, and mini-scooters (see "Helpful Hints," earlier in this chapter). Both of the following paths start along promenade des Anglais.

The path to the west stops just before the airport at perhaps the most scenic *boules* courts in France. Stop and watch the old-timers while away their afternoon tossing those shiny metal balls (see page 196).

Heading east, you'll round the hill—passing a scenic cape and the town's memorial to both world wars—to the harbor of Nice, with a chance to survey some fancy yachts. Pedal around the harbor and follow the coast past the Corsica ferry terminal (you'll need to carry your bike up a flight of steps). From there, the path leads to an appealing tree-lined residential district.

Relaxing at the Beach—Nice is where the masses kick back on the rocks. After settling into the smooth pebbles, you can play

beach volleyball, table tennis, or *boules* (see page 196); rent paddleboats, personal watercraft, or windsurfing equipment; explore ways to use your zoom lens as a telescope; or snooze on comfy beach beds with end tables. To rent a spot on the beach, compare rates, as prices vary—beaches on the east end of the bay are usually cheaper (mattress—*un transat*-€12–18, umbrella-€3–5, towel-€4). Some hotels have special deals with certain beaches for discounted rentals (check with your hotel for details). Consider lunch in your bathing suit (€12 salads and pizzas in bars and restaurants all along the beach). For a peaceful café au lait on the Med, stop here first thing in the morning before the crowds hit. *Plage Publique* signs explain the 15 beach no-nos (translated in English).

While Nice's beaches are traditionally rocky, a few years ago a small sandy area appeared toward the Italy end of the bay.

Near Nice

Narrow-Gauge Train into the Alps (Chemins de Fer de Provence)—Leave the tourists behind and take the scenic train-bus-train combination that runs between Nice and Digne through

canyons, along whitewater rivers, and through many tempting villages (Nice to Digne: 4/day, 3.5 hours, about €19, 25 percent discount with railpass, departs Nice from the South Station—Gare du Sud—about 10 blocks behind the main train station, two blocks from the Libération

tram stop, 4 rue Alfred Binet, tel. 04 97 03 80 80, www.train provence.com).

Start with an 8:50 departure and go as far as you want. Little **Entrevaux** is a good destination that feels forgotten and still stuck in its medieval shell (90 scenic minutes from Nice, about €10). Climb high to the citadel for great views. The train ends in **Digne-les-Bains,** where you can catch a mainline train (covered by railpasses) to other destinations—or better, take the bus (quick transfer if you get the 8:50 train from Nice, free with railpass) to **Veynes** (4/day, 90 min). From there you can catch the most scenic two-car train to **Grenoble** (5/day, 2 hours), then take a train to Annecy (arriving about 18:50).

To do the entire trip from Nice to Annecy in one day, you must start with the 8:50 departure, but I'd rather spend a night in one of the tiny villages en route. **$ Hôtel Beauséjour*** in little Annot, about two hours from Nice, makes a fun and reasonable getaway (Db-€65–70, tel. 04 92 83 21 08, www.francebeausejour .com). Further along, in remote Clelles, you'll find the **$ Hôtel Ferrat****, a basic family-run mountain hacienda at the base of Mont Aiguille, with a swimming pool and a good restaurant (Db-€56–65, tel. 04 76 34 42 70, fax 04 76 34 47 47, hotel.ferrat @wanadoo.fr).

Nightlife in Nice

Promenade des Anglais, cours Saleya, and rue Masséna are all worth an evening walk. Nice's bars play host to one of the Riviera's most happening late-night scenes, full of jazz, rock, and trolling singles. Most activity focuses on Old Nice, near place Rossetti and along rue Droite. **Distilleries Ideales** is a fine place to start or end your evening, with a lively international crowd and a fun interior (where rues de la Poissonnerie and Barillerie meet, happy hour 18:00–20:00). Just down the street, **Wayne's Bar** is a happening spot for the younger, English-speaking backpacker crowd (15 rue Préfecture). The plush bar at **Hôtel Negresco** is fancy-cigar old English.

Plan on a cover charge or expensive drinks when music is involved. If you're out very late, avoid walking alone. Nice is well-known for its lively after-dark action; for more relaxed and accessible nightlife, consider nearby Antibes (page 364).

Sleeping in Nice

Don't look for charm in Nice. Go for modern and clean, with a central location and, in summer, air-conditioning. The rates listed here are for April through October. Prices generally drop €15–30 from November through March, but go sky-high in 2010 during the Nice Carnival (Feb 12–28), the Cannes Film Festival

---

Sleep Code

(€1 = about $1.40, country code: 33)
S = Single, **D** = Double/Twin, **T** = Triple, **Q** = Quad, **b** = bathroom,
s = shower only, ***** = French hotel rating (0-4 stars). Hoteliers
speak English, have elevators, and accept credit cards unless
otherwise noted.

To help you sort easily through these listings, I've divided
the rooms into three categories based on the price for a
standard double room with bath:

$$$ Higher Priced—Most rooms €100 or more.
 $$ Moderately Priced—Most rooms between €70-100.
  $ Lower Priced—Most rooms €70 or less.

(May 12–23), and Monaco's Grand Prix (May 20–23). Between
the Grand Prix and the film festival, the second half of May is
very tight every year. June is convention month, and Nice is one
of Europe's top convention cities. Reserve early if visiting May
through August, especially during these times. For parking, ask
your hotelier (several have limited private parking), or see "Arrival
in Nice—By Car," on page 268.

I've divided my sleeping recommendations into three areas:
between the train station and Nice Etoile shopping center (easy
access to the train station and Old Nice via the sleek new tramway, 20-min walk to promenade des Anglais); between Nice Etoile
and the sea (east of avenue Jean Médecin, good access to Old Nice
and the sea at quai des Etats-Unis); and between boulevard Victor
Hugo and the sea (a somewhat classier area, offering better access
to the promenade des Anglais but longer walks to the train station
and Old Nice). I've also listed a hotel near the airport and a hostel
on the outskirts.

Between the Train Station and Nice Etoile

This area offers Nice's cheapest sleeps, though most hotels near
the station ghetto are overrun, overpriced, and loud. These are the
pleasant exceptions (most are near avenue Jean Médecin). They're
listed in order of proximity from the train station, going toward
the beach.

$$ Hôtel Ibis Nice Centre Gare**, 100 yards to the right as
you leave the station, gives those in need of train station access a
reliable refuge in this seedy area. It's modern, with two-star busi-
ness comfort (Db-€90–105, air-con, Wi-Fi, bar, café, 14 avenue
Thiers, tel. 04 93 88 85 85, fax 04 93 88 58 00, www.ibishotel.com,
h1396@accor.com).

Nice Hotels

1. Hôtel Ibis Nice Centre Gare
2. Hôtel la Belle Meunière
3. Hôtel Durante
4. Hôtel St. Georges
5. Auberge de Jeunesse les Camélias
6. B&B Nice Home Sweet Home
7. Hôtel Masséna
8. Hôtel Suisse
9. Hôtel Mercure Marché aux Fleurs
10. Hôtel Vendôme & Launderette
11. Hôtel Lafayette

NICE

TO CHAGALL & MATISSE MUSEUMS

|||| RUE MASSENA PEDEST. ZONE

■■■ TRAM W/ STOPS

¼ MILE

.5 KM

CIMIEZ

AVE DESAMBROIS

MODERN ART MUSEUM

RUE BARLA

DEVOLUY

DUBOUCHAGE

P. R. DE POSTES

DE CILLE

ST. JEAN

PLACE GARI-BALDI

PASTORELLI

HOTEL GIOFFREDO

R. CATH. SEGURANE

BLACAS

ALBERTI

GUBERNATIS

AVE PAROL.

BUS STN.

⑩

⑪

⑦

FELIX FAURE

JEAN JAURES

COLLET

DCH

AVE

BLVD. R. PREFECTURE

DROITE

ROS-SETTI

OLD NICE

⑫

R. ALEX MARI

ST. FRAN. PAULE

COURS SALEYA

CASTLE HILL

ELEVATOR

DES ETATS-UNIS

⑨

㉒

R. PONCH.

⑧

TO PORT LYMPIA

QUAI CAPEAU

E S R

SEA

⑫ Hôtel de la Mer
⑬ Hôtel Negresco
⑭ Hôtel le Royal
⑮ Hôtel Windsor
⑯ Hôtel les Cigales
⑰ Hôtels Splendid & Gounod

⑱ Hôtel Villa Victoria
⑲ To Villa Saint Exupéry
⑳ To Hôtel Ibis Nice Aéroport
㉑ Cat's Whiskers Bookstore
㉒ Bike Rental
㉓ Electric Bike & Scooter Rental

$ Hôtel la Belle Meunière*, in a fine old mansion built for Napoleon III's mistress, offers cheap beds and private rooms a block below the train station. Lively and youth hostel–esque, this well-kept place attracts budget-minded travelers of all ages with basic-but-adequate rooms and charismatic Mademoiselle Marie-Pierre presiding (in perfect English). Tables in the front yard greet guests and provide opportunities to meet other travelers (bunk in 4-bed dorm-€23 with private bath, €18 with shared bath, Db-€60, includes breakfast, Wi-Fi, laundry service, 21 avenue Durante, tel. 04 93 88 66 15, fax 04 93 82 51 76, www.bellemeuniere.com, hotel.belle.meuniere@cegetel.net).

$$$ At Hôtel Durante*, you know you're on the Mediterranean as soon as you enter the cheery, way-orange building with its rooms wrapped around a flowery courtyard. Run by smiling Nathalie, the hotel's rooms are good enough (mostly big beds) and the price is right enough (Ds-€72–80, bigger Db-€100–150, Tb-€130–170, air-con, Wi-Fi, 16 avenue Durante, tel. 04 93 88 84 40, fax 04 93 87 77 76, www.hotel-durante.com, info@hotel-durante.com).

$$$ Hôtel St. Georges*, five blocks from the station toward the sea, has a backyard garden, reasonably clean and comfortable high-ceilinged rooms, orange tones, blue halls, fair rates, and friendly Houssein at the reception (Sb-€80, Db-€100, Tb with 3 separate beds-€120, extra bed-€20, air-con, Wi-Fi, 7 avenue Georges Clemenceau, tel. 04 93 88 79 21, fax 04 93 16 22 85, www.hotelsaintgeorges.fr, contact@hotelsaintgeorges.fr).

$ Auberge de Jeunesse les Camélias is a laid-back youth hostel with a great location and modern facilities. Rooms accommodate between four and seven people in bunk beds (136 beds in all) and come with showers and sinks—WCs are down the hall. Reservations must be made via the website in advance or on the same day by phone. If you don't have a reservation, call by 10:00, or better, try to snag a bunk in person. The place is popular but worth a try for last-minute availability (€23/bed, one-time €15 extra charge without hostel membership, includes breakfast, rooms closed 11:00–15:00 but can leave bags, Internet access, laundry, kitchen, safes, bar, 3 rue Spitalieri, tel. 04 93 62 15 54, www.hihostels.com, nice-camelias@fuaj.org, Isabelle at the desk and Bernard at the helm).

$ B&B Nice Home Sweet Home is a great value. Gentle Genevieve (a.k.a. Jennifer) Levert rents out three large rooms and one small single in her home. Her rooms are simply decorated, with high ceilings, big windows, lots of light, and space to spread out. One room comes with private bath; otherwise, it's just like at home...down the hall (S-€31–38, D-€61–70, Db-€65–75, Tb-€74–84, Q-€80–90, includes breakfast, air-con units available in summer, no elevator, two floors up, washer/dryer-€5, kitchen access,

35 rue Rossini at intersection with rue Auber, tel. 06 19 66 03 63, www.nicehomesweethome.com, glevert@free.fr).

Between Nice Etoile and the Sea

These hotels are either on the sea or within an easy walk of it, and are the closest to Old Nice.

$$$ Hôtel Masséna*******, in a classy building a few blocks from place Masséna, is a stylish business hotel showcasing 100 rooms with every amenity at almost-reasonable rates (small Db-€120–150, larger Db-€140–190, still larger Db-€200–270, extra bed-€30, some non-smoking rooms, check website or call same day for special rates—prices drop when hotel is not full, reserve parking ahead-€25/day, 58 rue Giofreddo, tel. 04 92 47 88 88, fax 04 92 47 88 89, www.hotel-massena-nice.com, info@hotel-massena-nice.com).

$$$ Hôtel Suisse******, below Castle Hill, has Nice's best ocean and city views for the money, and is surprisingly quiet given the busy street below. Rooms are quite comfortable, the decor is classy, and the staff is professional. There's no reason to sleep here if you don't land a view, so I've listed prices only for view rooms—many of which have balconies (Db-€170–205, extra bed-€36, breakfast-€15, 15 quai Rauba Capeu, tel. 04 92 17 39 00, fax 04 93 85 30 70, www.hotels-ocre-azur.com, hotel.suisse@hotels-ocre-azur.com).

$$$ Hôtel Mercure Marché aux Fleurs****** is chain-hotel impersonal but ideally situated across from the sea and behind cours Saleya. Rooms are smallish yet tastefully designed (some with beds in a loft). Prices are reasonable, though rates vary by season (Db-€125–155, superior Db-€230, sea view-€50 extra, air-con, 91 quai des Etats-Unis, tel. 04 93 85 74 19, fax 04 93 13 90 94, h0962@accor.com). Don't confuse this Mercure with the six others in Nice.

$$$ Hôtel Vendôme****** gives you a whiff of the belle époque, with pink pastels, high ceilings, and grand staircases in a mansion set off the street. Its public spaces are delightful. The rooms are modern and come in all sizes; the best have balconies (on floors 4 and 5)—request *une chambre avec balcon* (Sb-€115, Db-€150, Tb-€165, air-con, Internet access and Wi-Fi, book ahead for limited parking-€12/day, 26 rue Pastorelli, tel. 04 93 62 00 77, fax 04 93 13 40 78, www.vendome-hotel-nice.com, contact@vendome-hotel-nice.com).

$$$ Hôtel Lafayette******, in a handy location a block behind the Galeries Lafayette department store, looks average from the outside. But inside it's comfortable and homey, with 18 well-designed, mostly spacious rooms, all one floor up from the street. It's family-run by Kirill, Tina, and toddler Victor. Rooms not overlooking rue de l'Hôtel des Postes are quieter and worth requesting (standard Db-€105–120, spacious Db-€115–130, extra bed-€24, coffee service in rooms, central air-con, no elevator, 32 rue de l'Hôtel des Postes, tel. 04 93 85 17 84, fax 04 93 80 47 56, www.hotellafayettenice.com, info@hotellafayettenice.com).

$$ Hôtel de la Mer** is a humble place with an enviable position between place Masséna and Old Nice (it's among the closest of my listings to the old town). This small, *très* traditional place is run by gracious Madame Ferry (Db-€80–100, bigger Db facing place Masséna-€120–130, Tb-€90–145, top prices are for July–Aug, air-con, Wi-Fi, 4 place Masséna, tel. 04 93 92 09 10, fax 04 93 85 00 64, www.hoteldelamernice.com, hotel.mer @wanadoo.fr).

Between Boulevard Victor Hugo and the Sea

These hotels are either on the beach or within walking distance, and closest to promenade des Anglais.

$$$ Hôtel Negresco** owns Nice's most prestigious address on promenade des Anglais and knows it. Still, it's the kind of place that, if you were to splurge just once in your life…. Rooms are opulent (see page 305 for further description), and tips are expected (viewless Db-€360, Db with sea view-€460–580, view suite-€770–1,900, breakfast-€35, Old World bar, 37 promenade des Anglais, tel. 04 93 16 64 00, fax 04 93 88 35 68, www.hotel-negresco-nice .com, reservations@hotel-negresco.com).

$$$ Hôtel le Royal** stands shoulder-to-shoulder on promenade des Anglais with the big boys (the Negresco, Concorde, and Westminster hotels). With 140 rooms, big lounges, and hallways that stretch forever, it feels a bit institutional. But the prices are reasonable considering the solid air-conditioned comfort and terrific location—and they sometimes have rooms when others don't (viewless Db-€125, Db with sea view-€155–175, bigger view room-€175–195 and worth it, extra person-€25, 23 promenade des Anglais, tel. 04 93 16 43 00, fax 04 93 16 43 02, www.hotel-royal-nice.cote.azur.fr, royal @vacancesbleues.com).

$$$ Hôtel Windsor** is a snazzy garden retreat that feels like a cross between a modern-art museum and a health spa. Some of the contemporary rooms, designed by modern artists, defy explanation. It has a full-service bar, a small outdoor swimming pool and gym (both free for guests), an €11 sauna, €55 massages, and full meal service in the cool, shaded garden area (standard Db-€125, bigger Db-€155, big Db with balcony-€180, extra bed-€20, rooms over garden worth the higher price, air-con, Internet access and Wi-Fi, 11 rue Dalpozzo, tel. 04 93 88 59 35, fax 04 93 88 94 57, www.hotelwindsornice.com, reservation@hotelwindsornice.com).

$$$ Hôtel les Cigales** is one of my favorites. It's a smart little pastel place with tasteful decor, 19 plush rooms (most with tub-showers), air-conditioning, and a nifty upstairs terrace, all well-managed by friendly Mr. Valentino, with Veronique and Elaine. Book directly through the hotel and show this book for a surprise treat on arrival (standard Db-€135–160, Tb-€160–180, free Wi-Fi, 16 rue Dalpozzo, tel. 04 97 03 10 70, fax 04 97 03 10 71, www.hotel-lescigales.com, info@hotel-lescigales.com).

$$$ Hôtel Splendid** is a worthwhile splurge if you miss your Marriott. The panoramic rooftop pool, Jacuzzi, bar, restaurant, and breakfast room almost justify the cost...but throw in solid rooms (four of the six floors are non-smoking), a free gym, spa services, and air-conditioning, and you're as good as home (Db-€230, deluxe Db with terrace-€275, suites-€360–410, check website for special deals, parking-€24/day, 50 boulevard Victor Hugo, tel. 04 93 16 41 00, fax 04 93 16 42 70, www.splendid-nice.com, info@splendid -nice.com).

$$$ Hôtel Gounod* is behind Hôtel Splendid, and because the two share the same owners, Gounod's guests are allowed free access to Splendid's pool, Jacuzzi, and other amenities. Don't let the lackluster lobby fool you. Most rooms are richly decorated, with high ceilings and air-conditioning (Db-€165, palatial 4-person suites-€260, parking-€15/day, 3 rue Gounod, tel. 04 93 16 42 00, fax 04 93 88 23 84, www.gounod-nice.com, info@gounod-nice .com).

$$$ Hôtel Villa Victoria* is managed by cheery Marlena, who welcomes travelers into this spotless, classy old building with a green awning and an open, attractive lobby overlooking a generous garden. Rooms are traditional and well-kept, with space to stretch out (streetside Db-€150, garden-side Db-€165, Tb-€165–185, suites-€160–210, breakfast-€15, air-con, minibar, Wi-Fi, parking-€15, 33 boulevard Victor Hugo, tel. 04 93 88 39 60, fax 04 93 88 07 98, www.villa-victoria.com, contact@villa-victoria.com).

Barely Beyond Nice

$ Villa Saint Exupéry, a service-oriented hostel, is a haven two miles north of the city center. Its amenities and 60 comfortable, spick-and-span rooms create a friendly climate for budget-minded travelers of any age. There are units for one, two, and up to six people. Many have private bathrooms and views of the Mediterranean—some come with balconies. You'll also find a laundry room, complete kitchen facilities, and a lively bar. There's easy Internet access with a wall of computers in the lobby and Wi-Fi in all the rooms (bed in dorm-€30/person, S-€70, Db-€80, Tb-€115, includes big breakfast, no curfew; take bus #23 from the airport or train station, or take the tram—direction: Las Planas—to the Compte de Falicon stop and walk 10 min; ask about free pickup at

Old Nice Hotels and Restaurants

NICE

- ❶ Hôtel Suisse
- ❷ Hôtel Mercure Marché aux Fleurs
- ❸ Hôtel de la Mer
- ❹ La Cambuse Rest.
- ❺ La Festival de la Moule
- ❻ Nissa Socca Rest.
- ❼ L'Univers Rest.
- ❽ Restaurant Castel
- ❾ Chez Palmyre Restaurant
- ❿ L'Acchiardo Rest.

P PARKING

★ PLACE ROSSETTI

VIEW

TRAM W/ STOPS

TO BUS STN & 3 CORNICHE ROADS

TO PLACE GARIBALDI

JAURES

BOUCHERIE

FRANCOIS

CEMETERY

RUE DROITE

LA LOGE

RUE ROSSETTI

STE. REPARATE

ST. JACQUES

JESUS

STE. REP.

VIEILLE

RUE

LESAGE

LA PREFECTURE

POISSON

SALEYA

MONTEE

CASTLE HILL

ETATS-

WC

RUE DES PONCHETTES

UNIS

PLAY FIELD

SEA

ELEVATOR & BELLANDA TOWER

NICE

⑪ Oliviera Shop/Rest.

⑫ Restaurant du Gesù

⑬ Lou Pilha Leva Restaurant

⑭ Fenocchio's Gelato (2)

⑮ Distilleries Ideales

⑯ Wayne's Bar

⑰ Bike Rental

⑱ Go Sport

⑲ Centre du Patrimoine (Walking Tours)

⑳ Start of "Old Nice Walk"

train station, 22 avenue Gravier, tel. 04 93 84 42 83, fax 04 92 09 82 94, www.vsaint.com, reservations@vsaint.com).

Closer to the Airport

$$ Hôtel Ibis Nice Aéroport** offers a handy port-in-the-storm outlet for those with early flights or just stopping in for a single night (Db-€78–93 when no special events in town, 359 promenade des Anglais, tel. 04 89 88 30 30, fax 04 93 21 19 43, www.ibisnice .com, reception@ibisnice.com).

Eating in Nice

Remember, you're in a resort. Seek ambience and fun, and lower your palate's standards. Italian is a low-risk and regional cuisine. The restaurants listed below are concentrated in neighborhoods close to my recommended hotels. Promenade des Anglais is ideal for picnic dinners on warm, languid evenings. Old Nice has the best and busiest dining atmosphere, while the Nice Etoile area is more local, convenient, and offers a good range of choices. To feast cheaply, eat on rue Droite in Old Nice, or explore the area around the train station. For a more peaceful meal, head for nearby Villefranche-sur-Mer (see page 331). For terribly touristy trolling, wander the wall-to-wall eateries lining rue Masséna. Yuck.

In Old Nice

Nice's dinner scene converges on cours Saleya (koor sah-lay-yuh), which is entertaining enough in itself to make the generally mediocre food a good deal. It's a fun, festive spot to compare tans and mussels. Even if you're eating elsewhere, wander through here in the evening. For locations, see the map on page 298.

La Cambuse is a small island of refinement for those who want to dine on cours Saleya—and the lone restaurant along here that doesn't try to reel in passersby. Pascal makes an effort to provide quality cuisine with attentive service (say *bonjour* to him). Split a starter like the filling *petits farcis niçois* (stuffed vegetables), then order your own *plat* (€14 starters, €18–24 *plats*, good indoor and outdoor seating, 5 cours Saleya, tel. 04 93 80 82 40).

La Festival de la Moule is a simple, touristy place that's all about mussels. For just €13, you get all-you-can-eat mussels and fries in a lively outdoor setting (across the square from la Cambuse, 20 cours Saleya, tel. 04 93 62 02 12).

Nissa Socca offers good, cheap Italian cuisine and a bubbly atmosphere in a small room a few blocks from cours Saleya. Indoor tables are usually steamy—arrive early to land a table outside (€10 pizza and pastas, €15–24 *menus*, Mon–Sat from 19:00, closed Thu lunch and all day Sun, a block off place Rossetti on rue Ste.

Réparate, tel. 04 93 80 18 35).

L'Univers, a block off place Masséna, earned a Michelin star while maintaining a warm ambience. Its elegant dining room is as relaxed as a "top" restaurant can be, from its casual decor to the tasteful dinnerware. When the artfully presented food arrives, you know this is high cuisine (€44 delicious four-course *menu,* cheaper *menus* possible on weekdays, closed Sun, indoor seating only, 53 boulevard Jean Jaurès, tel. 04 93 62 32 22).

Restaurant Castel is your best eat-on-the-beach option, thanks to its location at the very east end of Nice looking over the bay. Dining here, you almost expect Don Ho to grab a mic. You're right on the beach below Castle Hill, perfectly positioned to watch evening swimmers get in their last laps as the sky turns pink and city lights flicker on. The views are unforgettable even if the cuisine is not; you can even have lunch at your beach chair if you've rented one (€10/half-day, €14/day). Dinner here is best, so arrive before sunset and linger long enough to merit the few extra euros the place charges (€16 salads and pastas, €20–24 main courses, 8 quai des Etats-Unis, tel. 04 93 85 22 66).

Dining Cheap *à la Niçoise*

Try at least one of these five places—not just because they're terrific budget options, but primarily because they offer authentic *niçoise* cuisine.

Chez Palmyre, lost in a time warp, redefines humble. Your hostess-grandmother Madame Palmyre shuffles between her small kitchen and the seven-table dining room. The four-course *menu* is only €14, and the cuisine could not be more homemade (closed Sun, cash only, 5 rue Droite, tel. 04 93 85 72 32).

L'Acchiardo, hidden away in the heart of Old Nice, is a dark and homey eatery that does a good job mixing a loyal clientele with hungry tourists. Its simple, hearty *niçoise* cuisine is served for fair prices by gentle Monsieur Acchiardo. The small plaque under the menu outside says it's been run by father and son since 1927 (€7 starters, €14 *plats,* €5 desserts, cash only, closed Sat–Sun, indoor seating only, 38 rue Droite, tel. 04 93 85 51 16).

Oliviera venerates the French olive. This shop/restaurant sells a variety of oils, offers free tastings, and serves a menu of dishes paired with specific oils (think of a wine pairing). Welcoming owner Nadim, who speaks excellent English, knows all of his producers personally and provides "Olive Oil 101" explanations with his tastings (best if you buy something afterwards or have a meal). You'll learn how passionate he is about his products, and once you come to taste, you'll want to stay and eat (€14–22 main dishes, Tue–Sat 10:00–22:00, closed Sun–Mon, indoor seating only, 8 bis rue du Collet, tel. 04 93 13 06 45).

Nice Restaurants

1. Rue Biscarra Eateries
2. Bistrot les Viviers
3. L'Ovale Restaurant
4. La Maison de Marie Rest.
5. La Part des Anges Wine Bar
6. Il Vino Ino Rest. & Cave de L'Origine Wine Bar
7. Chantecler Restaurant
8. Voyageur Nissart Rest.

NICE

9 Restaurant d'Angleterre & Zen Rest.

10 Monoprix Grocery Store

11 Bus #98 to Airport

12 Buses #15 & #22 to Chagall & Matisse Museums & Bus #17 to Matisse Museum

13 Buses #99 & 23 to Airport

Restaurant du Gesù, a happy-go-lucky budget eatery, squeezes plastic tables into a slanting square deep in the old city (sailors accustomed to dining off-balance will feel right at home). Arrive early or join the mobs waiting for an outside table; better yet, have fun in the soccer-banner–draped interior. The *raviolis sauce daube* is popular (€10 pizzas and pastas, closed Sun, 1 place du Jésus, tel. 04 93 62 26 46).

Lou Pilha Leva delivers fun and cheap lunch or dinner options with *niçoise* specialties and outdoor-only benches that are swimming in pedestrians (open daily, located where rues de la Loge and Centrale meet in Old Nice).

And for Dessert...

Gelato-lovers should save room for the tempting ice-cream stands in Old Nice. **Fenocchio** is the city's favorite, with 86 flavors ranging from tomato to lavender to avocado—all of which are surprisingly good (daily until 23:30, two locations: on place Rossetti and on rue de la Poissonnerie).

Eating near Nice Etoile

If you're not up for eating in Old Nice, try one of these spots around the Nice Etoile shopping mall.

On rue Biscarra: An appealing lineup of cafés overflowing with outdoor tables stretches along the broad sidewalk on rue Biscarra (just east of avenue Jean Médecin behind Nice Etoile, all closed Sun). The street should be traffic-free by your visit, adding to its appeal. Come here to dine with locals away from the touristy areas. The following three places are all reasonable enough: **L'Authentic** has the most serious and creative food and comes with two memorable owners: burly Philippe and sleek Laurent (€22 two-course *menus,* €25 three-course *menus,* reasonable pasta dishes, 18 bis rue Biscarra, tel. 04 93 62 48 88). **Le 20 sur Vin** is a neighborhood favorite with a cozy, wine-bar-meets-café ambience and (*bien sûr*) good wines and basic bistro fare (tel. 04 93 92 93 20). And **Le Cenac** sells pizza and simple dishes.

Bistrot les Viviers attracts those who require attentive service and authentic *niçoise* cuisine. This classy splurge (€35 dinner *menus,* €17 lunch *menus*) offers two settings as different as night and day (with the same prices): a soft, formal restaurant and a relaxed *bistrot* next door. I'd reserve a table in the atmospheric *bistrot,* where some outdoor seating is available. Fish is the chef's forte (restaurant closed Sun, *bistrot* open daily, 5-min walk west of avenue Jean Médecin at 22 rue Alphonse Karr, tel. 04 93 16 00 48).

L'Ovale is a find. Named for the shape of a rugby ball, how this ever-so-local and rugby-loving café survives in a tourist mecca, I'll never know. It's a well-run and welcoming restaurant with quality food at respectable prices. Join the lively crowd and dine inside on big *plats* for €13. Consider their specialty, *cassoulet* (€36 for two people, though it's enough for three), or enjoy *la planche de charcuterie* as a meaty, filling first course (excellent €17 three-course *menu*, €12 monster salads, closed Sun, air-con, 29 rue Pastorelli, tel. 04 93 80 31 65). Effervescent Johanna keeps an eye on things.

La Maison de Marie is a surprisingly good-quality refuge off touristy rue Masséna, where most other restaurants serve mediocre food to tired travelers. Enter through a deep-red arch to a bougainvillea-draped courtyard, and enjoy the fair prices and good food that draw neighborhood regulars and out-of-towners alike. The interior tables are as appealing as those in the courtyard (*menus* from €22, look for the square red flag at 5 rue Masséna, tel. 04 93 82 15 93).

La Part des Anges, an atmospheric wine shop with a few tables in the back, serves good-but-limited meals and a large selection of wines (open daily for lunch, Fri–Sat only for dinner, reserve ahead, indoor seating only, 17 rue Gubernatis, tel. 04 93 62 69 80).

Near Promenade des Anglais

Il Vino Ino, a block from promenade des Anglais, has street appeal. This lively, reasonably priced eatery does Italian food only, amid cheery decor either indoors or out (€12 pastas and salads, €18 *plats*, closed Sun, 33 rue de la Buffa, tel. 04 93 87 94 25).

Cave de L'Origine is a warm, local spot run by kind Isabelle and Carlo. It's where you'll find a quality food shop (*épicerie*) and wine bar/*bistrot* serving a small selection. Carlo loves talking about his all-natural wines and other products. Stop by for a glass of wine, to peruse the shop, or better, to reserve a table for a meal (€10 starters, €19 *plats*, open Tue–Sat for lunch, Thu–Sat for dinner, reservations smart, indoor seating only; shop open Tue–Sat 10:00–20:00, closed Sun–Mon; 3 rue Dalpozzo, tel. 04 83 50 09 60).

Chantecler has Nice's most prestigious address—inside the Hôtel Negresco. This is everything a luxury restaurant should be: elegant, soft, and top-quality. If your trip is ending in Nice, call or email for reservations—you've earned this splurge (*menus* from €90, closed Mon–Tue, 37 promenade des Anglais, tel. 04 93 16 64 00, chantecler@hotel-negresco.com).

Near the Train Station

The first two places listed below are hardly undiscovered—they're listed in many other guidebooks—but they deserve their acclaim and merit a detour for budget-minded travelers. All three provide good indoor and outdoor seating.

Voyageur Nissart has blended good-value cuisine with cool Mediterranean ambience and friendly service since 1908. Alexis and Max could not be kinder hosts, making this a top option for those on a budget (€16 three-course *menus*, €7 fine *salade niçoise*, €10 *plats*, closed Mon, 19 rue d'Alsace-Lorraine, tel. 04 93 82 19 60).

Restaurant d'Angleterre is family-run and ideal for hungry travelers on a tight budget. For €16, you get a filling three-course dinner with tasty choices and sharp service (closed Sun–Mon, 25 rue d'Angleterre, tel. 04 93 88 64 49).

Zen contemplates thoughtfully next door, providing a Japanese break from French cuisine. Its friendly staff, pleasing decor, and tasty specialties draw a strong following (€16 three-course *menu*, €13 sushi, 27 rue d'Angleterre, tel. 04 93 82 41 20).

Nice Connections

For rough train, bus, and boat schedules from Nice to nearby towns, see "Getting Around the Riviera" on page 272. Note that most long-distance train connections to other French cities require a change in Marseille.

From Nice by Train to: Marseille (18/day, 2.5 hrs), **Cassis** (14/day, 3 hrs, transfer in Toulon or Marseille), **Arles** (11/day, 3.75–4.5 hrs, most require transfer in Marseille or Avignon), **Avignon** (20/day, most of which are via TGV, 4 hrs, most require transfer in Marseille), **Paris**' Gare de Lyon (10/day, 6 hrs, may require change; 11-hr night train goes to Paris' Gare d'Austerlitz), **Aix-en-Provence** TGV station (10/day, 3.5 hrs, may require transfer in Marseille or Toulon), **Chamonix** (4/day, 10 hrs, 3 transfers), **Beaune** (7/day, 7 hrs, 1–2 changes), **Munich** (4/day, 12–13 hrs with 2–4 transfers, night trains possible via Italy), **Interlaken** (6/day, 9–11 hrs, 2–5 transfers), **Florence** (6/day, 7–9 hrs, 1–3 transfers), **Milan** (7/day, 5–5.5 hrs, 4 with transfers), **Venice** (5/day, 8–9 hrs, all require transfers), **Barcelona** (2/day, 11–12 hrs).

Nice's Airport

Nice's easy-to-navigate airport (Aéroport de Nice Côte d'Azur) is on the Mediterranean, a 20–30-minute drive west of the city center. Planes leave about hourly to Paris (one-hour flight, about the same price as a train ticket, check www.easyjet.com for the cheapest flights to Paris' Orly airport). The two terminals (Terminal 1 and Terminal 2) are connected by frequent shuttle buses *(navettes)*. Both terminals have banks, ATMs, taxis, baggage storage, and buses to Nice. The TIs for Nice and Monaco are in Terminal 1 (tel. 08 20 42 33 33 or 04 89 88 98 28, www.nice.aeroport.fr).

Taxis into the center are expensive considering the short distance (figure €35 to Nice hotels and €55 to Villefranche-sur-Mer, 10 percent more from 19:00–7:00 and all day Sun). Taxis stop outside door *(Porte)* A-1 at Terminal 1 and outside *Porte* A-3 at

Terminal 2. Notorious for overcharging, Nice taxis are not always so nice. If your fare for a ride into town is much higher than €35 (or €40 at night or on Sun), refuse to pay the overage. If this doesn't work, tell the cabbie to call a *gendarme* (police officer). It's always a good idea to ask for a receipt *(reçu)*.

Airport shuttle vans work with some of my recommended hotels, but they only make sense when going *to* the airport, not when arriving on an international flight. Unlike taxis, shuttle vans offer a fixed price that doesn't rise on Sundays, early mornings, or evenings. Prices are best for groups (figure €25 for one person, and only a little more for additional people). **Nice Airport Shuttle** is one option (€25/one person, €32/two people, mobile 06 60 33 20 54, www.nice-airport-shuttle.com), or ask your hotelier for recommendations.

Three bus lines connect the airport with the city center, offering good alternatives to high-priced taxis. **Bus #99** (airport express) runs from both terminals to Nice's main train station (€4, 2/hr, 8:00–21:00, 30 min, drops you within a 10-min walk of many recommended hotels). To take this bus *to* the airport, catch it right in front of the train station (departs on the half-hour). If your hotel is within walking distance of the station, #99 is a breeze. **Bus #98** serves both terminals, and runs along promenade des Anglais to Nice's main bus station *(gare routière)*, which is near Old Nice (€4, 3/hr, from the airport 6:00–23:00, to the airport until 21:00, 30 min). The slower, cheaper local **bus #23** serves only Terminal 1, and makes every stop between the airport and train station (€1, 3/hr, 6:00–20:00, 40 min, direction: St. Maurice). For all buses, buy tickets in the information office just outside either terminal, or from the driver. To reach the bus information office and stops at Terminal 1, turn left after passing customs and exit the doors at the far end. Buses serving Terminal 2 stop across the street from the airport exit. If you take bus #98 or #99, hang on to your €4 ticket—it's good all day on any public bus and the tramway in Nice, and for buses between Nice and nearby towns (see page 274 for details). Note that if you take your big bag onto any non-airport bus, you may be charged an extra €5.

To get to **Villefranche-sur-Mer** from the airport, take bus #98 to Nice's bus station *(gare routière)*, then transfer to the Villefranche-sur-Mer bus (bus #100, use same ticket).

To reach **Antibes** and **Cannes,** take line #200 from Terminal 1 (€1, about 2/hr, 45 min to Antibes, 1 hr to Cannes—duration depends on traffic). Pricey express buses (line #110) run directly to **Monaco** from the airport (€18, hourly, 50 min), but you'll save money by transferring in Nice to a Monaco-bound bus.

WELCOME TO THE RIVIERA WALK

From the Promenade des Anglais to Castle Hill

This leisurely, level walk begins on the promenade des Anglais (near the landmark Hôtel Negresco) and ends on Castle Hill above Old Nice. While the entire walk is enjoyable at any time, the first half makes a fine pre- or post-dinner stroll. Timing your stroll to end up on Castle Hill (this walk's grand finale) at sunset is a smart move. Allow one hour at a promenade pace to reach the elevator up to Castle Hill. A quick visit to the Masséna Museum (free, daily 10:00–18:00, see page 282), next to the starting point of this walk, sets the Riviera stage for this stroll.

The Walk Begins

Promenade des Anglais

Welcome to the Riviera. There's something for everyone along this four-mile-long seafront circus. Watch the Europeans at play, admire the azure Mediterranean, anchor yourself on a blue seat, and prop your feet up on the made-to-order guardrail. Later in the day, come back to join the evening parade of tans along the promenade.

For now, stroll like the belle époque English aristocrats for whom the promenade was paved. The broad sidewalks of the promenade des Anglais ("walkway of the English") were financed by wealthy English tourists who wanted a safe place to stroll and admire the view. The walk was done in marble in 1822 for aristocrats who didn't want to dirty their shoes or smell the fishy gravel. This grand promenade leads to the old city and Castle Hill.

• *Start at the pink-domed...*

Hôtel Negresco

Nice's finest hotel is also a historic monument, offering up the city's most expensive beds (see page 292) and a free "museum"

interior (always open—provided you're dressed decently, absolutely no beach attire). March straight through the lobby (as if you're staying here) into the exquisite Salon Royal, a cozy place for a drink and a frequent host to art exhibits (opens at 11:00). The chandelier hanging from the Eiffel-built dome is made of 16,000 pieces of crystal. It was built in France for the Russian czar's Moscow palace...but because of the Bolshevik Revolution in 1917, he couldn't take delivery. Read the explanation of the bucolic dome scene, painted in 1913 for the hotel, then saunter around the perimeter coun-

terclockwise. If the bar door is open (after about 15:00), wander up the marble steps for a look. Further along, nip into the toilets for either an early 20th-century powder room or a Battle of Waterloo experience. The chairs nearby were typical of the age (cones of silence for an afternoon nap sitting up).

The hotel's Chantecler restaurant is one of the Riviera's best (allow €90 per person before drinks; described on page 301). A few years ago, it lost one of its Michelin stars, so you'll understand if the staff doesn't smile. In France, big-time chefs are like famous athletes: People know about them and talk about who's hot and who's not. Cooking is serious business—a few years ago, a famous Burgundian chef lost a star and committed suicide. On your way out, pop into the Salon Louis XIV (right of entry lobby as you leave), where the embarrassingly short Sun King models his red platform boots (English descriptions explain the room).

Once outside, turn left and walk past the bar to the back to see the hotel's original entrance (grander than today's)—in the 19th century, classy people stayed out of the sun, and any posh hotel that cared about its clientele would design its entry on the shady north side.

• *Cross the promenade des Anglais, and—before you begin your seaside promenade—grab a blue seat and gaze out to the...*

Bay of Angels (Baie des Anges)

Face the water. The body of Nice's patron saint, Réparate, was supposedly escorted into this bay by angels in the fourth century. To your right is where you might have been escorted into France—Nice's airport, built on a massive landfill. On that tip of land way beyond the runway is Cap d'Antibes. Until 1860, Antibes and Nice were in different countries—Antibes was French, but Nice was a protectorate of the Italian kingdom of Savoy-Piedmont, a.k.a. the Kingdom of Sardinia. (During that period, the Var River—just west of Nice—was the geographic border between these two peoples.) In 1850, the people here spoke Italian and ate pasta. As Italy was uniting, the region was given a choice: Join the new country of Italy or join good old France (which was enjoying good times under the rule of Napoleon III). The vast majority voted in 1860 to go French...and voilà!

The green hill to your left (Castle Hill) marks the end of this walk. Farther left lies Villefranche-sur-Mer (marked by the tower at land's end, and home to lots of millionaires), then Monaco (which you can't see, with more millionaires), then Italy (with lots of, uh, Italians). Behind you are the foothills of the Alps (Alpes Maritimes), which gather threatening clouds, ensuring that the Côte d'Azur enjoys sunshine more than 300 days each year. While half a million people live here, pollution is carefully treated—the water is routinely tested and very clean.

• *With the sea on your right, begin...*

Strolling the Promenade

The block next to Hôtel Negresco houses a lush park and the Masséna Museum of city history (described on page 282 and worth a short detour). Nearby sit two other belle époque establishments: the West End and Westminster hotels, both boasting English names to help those original guests feel at home (the West End is now part of the Best Western group...to help American guests feel at home). These hotels symbolize Nice's arrival as a tourist mecca a century ago, when the combination of leisure time and a stable economy allowed visitors to find the sun even in winter.

As you walk, be careful to avoid the green bike lane. You'll pass a number of separate beaches—some private, others public. In spite of the rocks, they're still a popular draw. You can rent gear—about €12–18 for a mattress (*transat*) and a *chaise longue,* €3–5 for an umbrella, and €4 for a towel—and kick back. You'll also pass several beach restaurants (a highly recommended experience). Some of these eateries serve breakfast, all serve lunch, some do dinner, and a few have beachy bars...
tailor-made for a break from this walk. A few promote package deals, including a lounge chair, umbrella, locker, and meal, all for about €26. Why all this gear rental? In Europe, most beach-going

families take planes or trains, since parking and gas are pricey (even worse than in the US) and traffic is awful. So, unlike my family's beach trips, they can't stuff chairs, coolers, and the like in the trunk of their car and park right near the beach.

Even a hundred years ago, there was sufficient tourism in Nice to justify building its first casino (a leisure activity imported from Venice). Part of an elegant casino, La Jetée Promenade, stood on those white-covered pilings just offshore, until the Germans destroyed it during World War II. The Masséna Museum has images and models of the elaborate building. While La Jetée Promenade is gone, you can still see the striking 1930s Art Nouveau facade of the Palais de la Méditerranée, a grand casino, hotel, and theater.

The unappealing Casino Ruhl is farther along (just before the park). Anyone can drop in for some one-armed-bandit fun, but to play the tables at night you'll need to dress up and bring your passport. Albert 1er Park is named for the Belgian king who enjoyed wintering here. While the English came first, the Belgians and Russians were also big fans of 19th-century Nice. That tall statue at the edge of the park commemorates the 100-year anniversary of Nice's union with France.

Continue along the promenade, past the park. You're now on quai des Etats-Unis ("quay of the United States"). This name was given as a tip-of-the-cap to the Americans for finally entering World War I in 1917. Five minutes past the Hôtel Suisse (brilliant views as you walk), there's a monumental war memorial sculpted out of the rock in honor of the thousands of local boys who died serving their country in World Wars I and II.

• *Take the elevator next to the Hôtel Suisse up to Castle Hill (elevator open daily 10:00–19:00, until 20:00 in summer, €0.70 one-way, €1.10 round-trip).*

Castle Hill (Colline du Château)

This hill—in an otherwise flat city center—offers sensational views over Nice, the port (to the east), the foothills of the Alps, and the Mediterranean. The views are best early or at sunset, or whenever the weather's really clear (park closes at 20:00 in summer, earlier off-season). Nice was founded on this hill. Its residents were crammed onto the hilltop until the 12th century, as it was too risky to live in the flatlands below. Today, you'll find a waterfall, a playground, two cafés (with fair prices), and a cemetery—but no castle—on Castle Hill.

• *Your tour is finished. Enjoy the vistas. To walk down to Old Nice, follow signs from just below the upper café to Vieille Ville (not Le Port), turn right at the cemetery, then look for the walkway down on your left. If you're planning a boat tour (one hour, see page 275 for details), follow the* Le Port *signs to the bassin des Amiraux.*

OLD NICE
WALK

*From Place Masséna to
Place Rossetti*

This self-guided walking tour gives a helpful introduction to Nice's bicultural heritage and most interesting neighborhoods. Allow about an hour at a leisurely pace for this level walk, including a stop for coffee and *socca* (chickpea crêpe). It's best done in the morning (while the outdoor market still thrives and the *socca*'s hot), and preferably not on a Sunday, when many shops are closed. Because this walk ends near the bus station, it works well on the way to an afternoon bus excursion (e.g., to Monaco, Villefranche-sur-Mer, Cap Ferrat, or the inland hill towns). This walk is also a joy at night, when fountains glow and pedestrians control the streets.

The Walk Begins

• *Start on avenue Jean Médecin near Galleries Lafayette department store. Look up avenue Jean Médecin, away from the sea.*

Avenue Jean Médecin
Nice's newly renovated "main street," once a nightmare of cars and delivery vehicles tangling with pedestrians, has been turned into a pedestrian nirvana. As you walk along this major street, notice how quiet it is. Now think of a major street like this in your city, teeming with vehicles; then imagine it without the cars and trucks. Bravo Nice. I used to avoid this street at all costs. Now I can't get enough of it.

• *Stroll toward place Masséna and drink in the Italianesque colors and street theater that surround you. Find a bench on the east side of place Masséna near the fountains.*

Place Masséna

This vast square pays tribute to Jean-André Masséna, a French military leader during the Revolutionary and Napoleonic Wars.

He's not just another pretty face in a long lineup of French military heroes, but is considered among the greatest commanders in history—anywhere, anytime. Napoleon thought of him as "the greatest name of my military Empire." No wonder this city is proud of him.

This grand *place* is Nice's focal point, where old meets new, and where the recently built tramway bends between the bus and train stations. The square's new black-and-white pavement feels like an elegant outdoor ballroom, with the sleek tram waltzing across its dance floor. The men you see on pedestals high above are recent modern-art additions that arrived with the new tram. If you're here after dark, you'll see that they are illuminated from the inside and slowly change colors. Somehow, it works.

There's no better place than place Masséna to appreciate the city's Italian heritage (standing here makes me feel as if I'm in Venice's St. Mark's Square). The rich colors of the buildings reflect the taste of previous Italian rulers, back when Nice's residents rooted for Italian soccer teams. The fountains are the product of more recent tastes—to save money, they only have high pressure after 17:00. The distant hills behind the fountains separate Nice from Villefranche-sur-Mer, and that Italianesque clock tower is barely beyond Nice's bus station.

Look across place Masséna and down a grassy parkway. You're standing on Nice's historic river, the Paillon. It's been covered since the late 1800s and runs under place Masséna, then under the parkway to the sea. For centuries, this river was Nice's natural defense to the north and west (the sea protected the south, and Castle Hill defended the east). Imagine the fortified wall that once ran along its length from the hills behind you to the sea.

With the arrival of tourism in the 1800s, Nice spread beyond the river to your right (where your hotel is probably located). The modern can't-miss-it sculpture in the parkway is meant to represent the "curve of the French Riviera"—whatever that means—but looks more like an answer to local skateboarders' prayers. The new tram is the first of three planned routes, and is Nice's first serious stab at managing its debilitating traffic problems.

Old Nice Walk

Old Nice Walk

- *Cross the square toward the Caisse d'Epargne Côte d'Azur bank, and walk between the curved buildings. Head down rue de l'Opéra, turning left on...*

Rue St. François de Paule

You've entered Old Nice. Peer into the **Alziari** olive-oil shop at #14 (on the right, Mon–Sat 8:30–12:00 & 14:00–1900, closed Sun). Dating from 1868, the shop produces top-quality stone-ground olive oil. The proud and charming owner, Gilles Piot, claims that stone wheels create less acidity (since metal grinding builds

1 Place Masséna
2 Rue St. François de Paule
3 Cours Saleya
4 Café les Ponchettes
5 Rue de la Poissonnerie
6 Rue Droite
7 Place Rossetti

OLD NICE WALK

up heat). Locals fill their own containers from the huge vats (the cheapest one is peanut oil, not olive oil). Consider a gift for the olive oil–lover on your list. (Some may want to backpedal one block to the **Molinard** perfume shop and museum before continuing—see page 282.)

A block down on the left (at #7), **Pâtisserie Auer**'s grand old storefront has changed little since the pastry shop opened in 1820 (closed Sun). The writing on the window says, "Since 1820 from father to son." The gold royal shields on the back wall remind shoppers that Queen Victoria fed her sweet tooth here.

Across the street is Nice's grand **opera house,** dating from the same era. Imagine this opulent jewel buried deep in the old town of Nice, back in the 19th century. With all the fancy big-city folks wintering here, this rough-edged town needed some high-class entertainment. The four statues on top represent theater, dance, music, and singing.

• *Continue on, sifting your way through souvenirs to the cours Saleya (koor sah-lay-yuh).*

Cours Saleya

Named for its broad exposure to the sun *(soleil)*, this commotion of color, sights, smells, and people has been **Nice's main market square** since the Middle Ages
(produce market held Tue–Sun until 13:00—on Mon, an antiques market takes center stage). Amazingly, part of this square was a parking lot until 1980, when the mayor of Nice had an underground garage built.

The first section is devoted to the Riviera's largest flower market (all day Tue–Sun and in operation since the 19th century). Here you'll find plants and flowers that grow effortlessly and ubiquitously in this climate, including the local favorites: carnations, roses, and jasmine. Fresh flowers are perhaps the best value in this otherwise pricey city.

The boisterous produce section trumpets the season with mushrooms, strawberries, white asparagus, zucchini flowers, and more—whatever's fresh gets top billing.

Place Pierre Gautier (also called Plassa dou Gouvernou—bilingual street signs include the old Niçoise language, an Italian dialect) is where the actual farmers set up stalls to sell their produce and herbs directly. For a great market overview, climb the steps by Le Grand Bleu restaurant; you may have to step over the trash sacks.

From your perch, look up to the **hill** that dominates to the east. The city of Nice was first settled up there by Greeks (circa 400 B.C.). In the Middle Ages, a massive castle stood there, with turrets, high walls, and soldiers at the ready. Over time, the city grew down to where you are now. With the river guarding one side and the sea the other, this mountain fortress seemed strong—until Louis XIV leveled it in 1706. Nice's medieval seawall ran along the line of two-story buildings where you're standing.

Now, look across place Pierre Gautier to the large "palace." The **Ducal Palace** was where the kings of Sardinia (the city's

Italian rulers until 1860) would reside when in Nice. Today, it's police headquarters.

Resume your stroll down the center of cours Saleya, stopping when you see La Cambuse restaurant on your left. In front, hovering over the black-barrel fire with the paella-like pan on top, is the self-proclaimed **Queen of the Market,** Thérèse (tehr-ehz). When she's not looking for a husband, Thérèse is cooking *socca,* Nice's chickpea crêpe specialty. Spend €2.50 for a wad of *socca* (careful— it's hot, but good). If she doesn't have a pan out, that means it's on its way (watch for the frequent scooter deliveries). Wait in line...or else it'll be all gone when you return.

• *Continue down cours Saleya. The fine golden building that seals the end of the square is where Henri Matisse spent 17 years with a brilliant view onto Nice's world. If you're in the mood, the **Café les Ponchettes** is perfectly positioned for a people-watching break. If not, turn left a block before the end of the square and head down...*

Rue de la Poissonnerie

Look up at the first building on your right. **Adam and Eve** are squaring off, each holding a zucchini-like gourd. This scene (post-apple) represents the annual rapprochement in Nice to make up for the sins of a too-much-fun Carnival (Mardi Gras). Residents of Nice have partied hard during Carnival for more than 700 years (Feb 12–28 in 2010).

Now, walk a few doors down to #6 (right side). That filthy **iron grille** above the door allows air to enter the building, but keeps out uninvited guests. You'll see lots of these open grilles in Old Nice. They were part of a clever system that sucked in cool air from the sea, circulating it through homes and blowing it out through vents in the roof.

A few steps away, check out the small **Baroque church** (Notre-Dame-de-l'Annonciation) dedicated to St. Rita, the patron saint of desperate causes. She holds a special place in locals' hearts, making this the most popular church in Nice.

• *Turn right on the next street, where you'll pass Old Nice's most happening café/bar **(Distilleries Ideales)**, with a lively happy hour (18:00–20:00) and a Pirates of the Caribbean–style interior. Now turn left on "Right" Street (rue Droite), and enter an area that feels like a Little Naples.*

Rue Droite

In the Middle Ages, this straight, skinny street provided the most direct route from wall to wall, or river to sea. Stop at **Espuno's bakery** (at place du Jésus, closed Mon–Tue) and say *bonjour* to the friendly folks. Thirty years ago, this baker was voted the best in France—the trophies you see were earned for bread-making, not bowling. His son now runs the place. Notice the firewood stacked by the oven. Try the house specialty, *tourta de bléa* (pastry stuffed with pine nuts, raisins, and white beets).

Farther along, at #28, Thérèse (whom you met earlier) cooks her *socca* in the wood-fired oven before she carts it to her barrel on cours Saleya. The balconies of the mansion in the next block mark the **Palais Lascaris** (1647, gorgeous at night), a rare souvenir from one of Nice's most prestigious families. It's worth popping inside for its Baroque Italian architecture, antique musical instruments, tapestries, and furniture (free, Wed–Mon 10:00–18:00, closed Tue). Look up and make faces back at the guys under the balconies.

• *Turn left on the rue de la Loge, then left again on rue Centrale, to reach...*

Place Rossetti

The most Italian of Nice's piazzas, place Rossetti feels more like Roma than Nice. This square comes alive after dark. Fenocchio is popular for its many gelato flavors.

Walk to the fountain and stare back at the church. This is the **Cathedral of St. Réparate**—an unassuming building for a major city's cathedral. It was relocated here in the 1500s, when Castle Hill was temporarily converted to military-only. The name comes from Nice's patron saint, a teenage virgin named Réparate whose martyred body floated to Nice in the fourth century accompanied by angels (remember the Bay of Angels?). The interior of the cathedral gushes Baroque, a response to the Protestant Reformation. With the Catholic Church's Counter-Reformation, the theatrical energy of churches was cranked up—with re-energized, high-powered saints and eye-popping decor.

• *Our tour is over. If you're re-energized, take a walk up **Castle Hill**. To get there, cross place Rossetti and follow the lane leading uphill (see Castle Hill description in the Welcome to the Riviera Walk chapter). If it's early enough and you're up for a day trip, take a left outside the church and you'll eventually arrive at the bus station.*

CHAGALL MUSEUM TOUR

Musée Chagall

Even if you're suspicious of modern art, this museum—with the world's largest collection of Marc Chagall's work in captivity—is a delight. After World War II, Chagall returned from the United States to settle in Vence, not far from Nice. Between 1954 and 1967, he painted a cycle of 17 large murals designed for, and donated to, this museum. These paintings, inspired by the biblical books of Genesis, Exodus, and the Song of Songs, make up the "nave," or core, of what Chagall called the "House of Brotherhood."

Orientation

Cost: €6.50, €7.50 with special exhibits, free first Sun of the month (but crowded).

Hours: Wed–Mon 10:00–17:00, May–Oct until 18:00, closed Tue year-round.

Getting There: You can reach the museum, located on avenue Docteur Ménard, by bus or on foot.

Buses #15 and #22 serve the Chagall Museum from the Masséna Guitry stop, near place Masséna (5/hr Mon–Sat, 3/hr Sun, €1; stop faces eastbound on rue Gioffredo, a block east of Galeries Lafayette department store—see map on page 269). The museum's bus stop (called Musée Chagall, shown on the bus shelter) is on boulevard de Cimiez (walk uphill from the stop to find the museum).

To **walk** from central Nice to the Chagall Museum, go to the train-station end of avenue Jean Médecin and turn right onto boulevard Raimbaldi. Walk four long blocks along the elevated road, then turn left onto avenue Raymond Comboul, and follow *Musée Chagall* signs.

Information: While Chagall would suggest that you explore his works without help, the €3 museum guidebook, called *The Biblical Message*, is useful in explaining the symbolism. The free *Plan du Musée* helps locate the rooms, though you can do without, as the museum is pretty simple. Tel. 04 93 53 87 20, www.musee-chagall.fr.

Leaving the Museum: To take buses #15 or #22 back to downtown Nice, turn right out of the museum, then make another right down boulevard de Cimiez, and catch the bus heading downhill. To continue on to the Matisse Museum, catch buses #15 or #22 using the uphill stop, located across the street.

To walk to the train station from the museum, turn left out of the museum, then left again on the street behind it. Take the ramps and staircases down on your left, turn left at the bottom, cross under the freeway, then turn right to reach the station.

Taxis usually wait outside the museum.

Length of This Tour: Allow one hour.

Cuisine Art and WCs: An idyllic café (€10 salads and *plats*) awaits in the corner of the garden. A spick-and-span WC is next to the ticket desk (there's one inside, too).

The Tour Begins

This small museum consists of six rooms: two rooms with the 17 large murals, two rooms for special exhibits, an auditorium with stained-glass windows, and a mosaic-lined pond (viewed from inside). In the main hall, you'll find the core of the collection (Genesis and Exodus scenes). The adjacent octagonal room houses five paintings—the Song of Songs room.

• *Buy your ticket, pass through the garden, and enter the museum at the baggage-check counter (daypacks must be checked). Turn right into the first room and find...*

Old Testament Scenes

Each painting is a lighter-than-air collage of images that draw from Chagall's Russian folk-village youth, his Jewish heritage, biblical themes, and his feeling that he existed somewhere between heaven and earth. He believed that the Bible was a synonym for nature, and that color and biblical themes were key ingredients for understanding God's love for his creation. Chagall's brilliant blues and reds celebrate nature, as do his spiritual and folk themes. Notice the focus on couples. To Chagall, humans loving each other mirrored God's love of creation.

The paintings are described below in the order you should see them, going counterclockwise around the room (some paintings might be on loan to other museums). Look for posted explanations of each work in English.

Chagall Museum

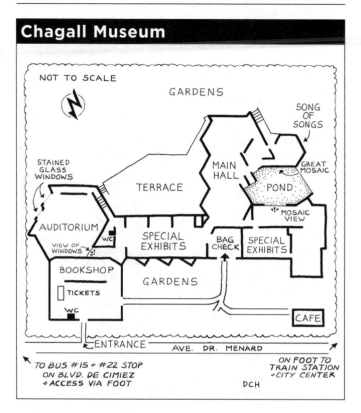

NOT TO SCALE

GARDENS

SONG OF SONGS

STAINED GLASS WINDOWS

MAIN HALL

GREAT MOSAIC

TERRACE

POND

MOSAIC VIEW

AUDITORIUM

WC

SPECIAL EXHIBITS

BAG CHECK

SPECIAL EXHIBITS

VIEW OF WINDOWS

BOOKSHOP

GARDENS

TICKETS

WC

CAFE

ENTRANCE   AVE. DR. MENARD

TO BUS #15 + #22 STOP ON BLVD. DE CIMIEZ + ACCESS VIA FOOT

ON FOOT TO TRAIN STATION + CITY CENTER

DCH

Abraham and the Three Angels

In the heat of the day, Abraham looked up and saw three men. He said, "Let a little food and water be brought, so you can be refreshed..." (Genesis 18:1–5)

Abraham refreshes God's angels on this red-hot day, and in return, they promise Abraham a son (in the bubble, at right), thus making him the father of the future Israelite nation.

The Sacrifice of Isaac

Abraham bound his son Isaac and laid him on the altar. Then he took the knife to slay his son. But the angel of the Lord called out to him from heaven, "Abraham!" (Genesis 22:9–11)

Tested by God, Abraham prepares to kill his only son, but the angel stops him in time. Notice that Isaac is posed exactly as Adam is in The Creation (described below). Abraham's sacrifice echoes three others: the sacrifice all men must make (i.e., Adam, the everyman), the sacrifice of atonement (the goat tied to a tree at left), and even God's sacrifice of his own son (Christ carrying the cross, upper right).

Chagall's Style

Chagall uses a deceptively simple, almost childlike style to paint a world that's hidden to the eye—the magical, mystical world below the surface. Here are some of his techniques:

- **Deep, radiant colors,** inspired by Expressionism and Fauvism (an art movement pioneered by Matisse and other French painters).
- **Personal imagery,** particularly from his childhood in Russia— smiling barnyard animals, fiddlers on the roof, flower bouquets, huts, and blissful sweethearts.

- **A Hasidic Jewish perspective,** the idea that God is everywhere, appearing in everyday things like nature, animals, and humdrum activities.
- **A fragmented Cubist style,** multifaceted and multidimensional, a perfect style to capture the multifaceted, multidimensional complexity of God's creation.
- **Overlapping images,** like double-exposure photography, with faint imagery that bleeds through, suggesting there's more to life under the surface.
- **Stained-glass-esque technique** of dark, deep, earthy, "potent" colors, and simplified, iconic, symbolic figures.
- **Gravity-defying compositions,** with lovers, animals, and angels twirling blissfully in midair.
- **Happy, not tragic mood** depicting a world of personal joy, despite the violence and turmoil of world wars and revolution.
- **Childlike simplicity,** drawn with simple, heavy outlines, filled in with Crayola colors that often spill over the lines. Major characters in a scene are bigger than the lesser characters. The grinning barnyard animals, the bright colors, the magical events presented as literal truth...Was Chagall a lightweight? Or a lighter-than-air-weight?

The Creation

God said, "Let us make man in our image, in our likeness..." (Genesis 1:26)

A pure-white angel descends through the blue sky and carries a still-sleeping Adam from radiant red-yellow heaven to earth. Heaven is a whirling dervish of activity, spinning out all the events of future history, from the tablets of the Ten Commandments to the Crucifixion—an overture of many images that we'll see in later paintings. (Though not a Christian, Chagall saw the Crucifixion as a universal symbol of man's suffering.)

Moses Receives the Ten Commandments

The Lord gave him the two tablets of the Law, the tablets of stone inscribed by the finger of God... (Exodus 31:18)

An astonished Moses is tractor-beamed toward heaven, where God reaches out from a cloud to hand him the Ten Commandments. While Moses tilts one way, Mount Sinai slants the other, leading our eye up to the left, where a golden calf is being worshipped by the wayward Children of Israel. But down to the right, Aaron and the menorah assure us that Moses will set things right. In this radiant final panel, the Jewish tradition—after a long struggle—is finally established.

Driven from Paradise

So God banished him from the Garden of Eden...and placed cherubim and a flaming sword to guard the way... (Genesis 3:23–24)

An angel drives them out with a fire hose of blue (there's Adam still cradling his flaming-red coq), while a sparkling yellow sword prevents them from ever returning. Deep in the green colors, we get glimpses of the future—Eve giving birth (lower-right corner) and the yellow sacrificial goat of atonement (top right).

Paradise

God put him in the Garden of Eden...and said, "You must not eat from the tree of the knowledge of good and evil..." (Genesis 2:15–17)

Paradise is a rich, earth-as-seen-from-space pool of blue, green, and white. Amoebic, still-evolving animals float around Adam (celibately practicing yoga) and Eve (with lusty-red hair). On the right, an angel guards the tempting tree, but Eve offers an apple, and Adam reaches around to sample the forbidden fruit.

The Rainbow

God said, "I have set my rainbow in the clouds as a sign of the covenant between me and the earth." (Genesis 9:13)

A flaming angel sets the rainbow in the sky, while Noah rests beneath it and his family offers a sacrifice of thanks. The pure-white rainbow's missing colors are found radiating from the features of the survivors.

Jacob's Ladder

He had a dream in which he saw a ladder resting on the earth with its top reaching to heaven, and the angels of God were ascending and descending on it... (Genesis 28:12)

In the left half, Jacob (Abraham's grandson) slumps asleep and dreams of a ladder between heaven and earth. On the right, a spinning angel with a menorah represents how heaven and earth are bridged by the rituals of the Jewish tradition.

CHAGALL MUSEUM

Marc Chagall
(1887–1985)

1887–1910: Russia

Chagall is born in the small town of Vitebsk, Belarus. He's the oldest of nine children in a traditional Russian, Hasidic Jewish family. He studies realistic art in his hometown. In St. Petersburg, he is first exposed to the Modernist work of Paul Cézanne and the Fauves.

1910–1914: Paris

A patron finances a four-year stay in Paris. Chagall hobnobs with the avant-garde and learns technique from the Cubists, but he never abandons painting recognizable figures or his own personal fantasies. (Some say his relative poverty forced him to paint over used canvases, which gave him the idea of overlapping images that bleed through. Hmm.)

1914–1922: Russia

Returning to his hometown, Chagall marries Bella Rosenfeld (1915), whose love will inspire him for decades. He paints happy scenes despite the turmoil of wars and the Communist Revolution. Moving to Moscow (1920), he paints his first large-scale works, sets for the New Jewish Theatre. These would inspire many of his later large-scale works.

1923–1941: France and Palestine

Chagall returns to France. In 1931, he travels to Palestine, where the bright sun and his Jewish roots inspire a series of gouaches (opaque watercolor paintings). These gouaches would later inspire 105 etchings to illustrate the Bible (1931–1952), which would eventually influence the 17 large canvases of biblical scenes in the Chagall Museum (1954–1967).

1941–1947: United States/World War II

Fearing persecution for his Jewish faith, Chagall emigrates to New York, where he spends the war years. The Crucifixion starts to appear in his paintings—not as a Christian symbol, but as a representation of the violence mankind perpetrates on itself. In 1947, his beloved Bella dies, and he stops painting for months.

1947–1985: South of France

After the war, Chagall returns to France, eventually settling in St-Paul-de-Vence. In 1952, he remarries. His new love, Valentina Brodsky, plus the southern sunshine, bring Chagall a revived creativity—he is extremely prolific for the rest of his life. He experiments with new techniques and media—ceramics, sculpture, book illustrations, tapestry, and mosaic. In 1956, he's commissioned for his first stained-glass project. Eventually he does windows for cathedrals in Metz and Reims, and a synagogue in Jerusalem (1960). The Chagall Museum opens in 1973.

CHAGALL MUSEUM

Jacob Wrestles with an Angel

So Jacob wrestled with him till daybreak. Jacob said, "I will not let you go unless you bless me..." (Genesis 32: 24, 26)

Jacob holds on while the angel blesses him with descendants (the Children of Israel) and sends out rays from his hands, creating, among others, Joseph (stripped of his bright-red coat and sold into slavery by his brothers).

Noah's Ark

Then he sent out a dove to see if the water had receded... (Genesis 8:8)

Adam and Eve's descendants have become so wicked that God destroys the earth with a flood, engulfing the sad crowd on the right. Only righteous Noah (center), his family (lower right), and the animals (including our yellow goat) are spared inside an ark. Here Noah opens the ark's window and sends out a dove to test the waters.

Moses Brings Water from the Rock

The Lord said, "Strike the rock, and water will come out of it for the people to drink..." (Exodus 17:5–6)

In the brown desert, Moses nourishes his thirsty people with water miraculously spouting from a rock. From the (red-yellow) divine source, it rains down actual (blue) water, but also a gush of spiritual yellow light.

Moses and the Burning Bush

The angel of the Lord appeared to him in flames of fire from within a bush... (Exodus 3:2)

Horned Moses—Chagall depicts him according to a medieval tradition—kneels awestruck before the burning bush, the event that calls him to God's service. On the left, we see Moses after the call, his face radiant, leading the Israelites out of captivity across the Red Sea, while Pharaoh's men drown (lower half of Moses' robe). The Ten Commandments loom ahead.

• *Return to* Moses Receives the Ten Commandments *and walk past it into a stained-glass window on your way to the octagonal room.*

Song of Songs

Chagall wrote, "I've been fascinated by the Bible ever since my earliest childhood. I have always thought of it as the most extraordinary source of poetic inspiration imaginable. As far as I am concerned, perfection in art and in life has its source in the Bible, and exercises in the mechanics of the merely rational are fruitless. In art as well as in life, anything is possible, provided there is love."

Chagall enjoyed the love of two women in his long life—his first wife, Bella, then Valentina, who gave him a second wind as

Song of Songs

Song of Solomon 7:11
Come, my lover, let us go to the countryside, let us spend the night in the villages.

Song of Solomon 5:2
I slept but my heart was awake.

Song of Solomon 2:17
Until the day breaks and the shadows flee, turn, my lover, and be like a gazelle or like a young stag on the rugged hills.

Song of Solomon 3:4
I held him and would not let him go.

Song of Solomon 7:7
Your stature is like that of the palm, and your breasts like clusters of fruit.

he was painting these late works. Chagall was one of the few "serious" 20th-century artists to portray unabashed love. Where the Bible uses the metaphor of earthly, physical, sexual love to describe God's love for humans, Chagall uses unearthly colors and a mystical ambience to celebrate human love. These red-toned canvases are hard to interpret on a literal level, but they capture the rosy spirit of a man in love with life. The sidebar above reflects the order of the verses displayed in the painting.

• *Head back toward the entry and turn left just before leaving the main hall and visit...*

The Pond

The great mosaic reflected in the pond evokes the prophet Elijah in his chariot of fire (from the Second Book of Kings)—with Chagall's own addition of the 12 signs of the zodiac, which he used to symbolize Time.

• *Back at the entry, turn right and pass through the exhibition room with temporary displays. At the end, you'll find...*

The Auditorium

This room is worth a peaceful moment to enjoy three Chagall stained-glass windows: the creation of light, elements, and planets (a visual big bang that's four "days" wide); the creation of animals, plants, man and woman, and the ordering of the solar system (two "days" wide, complete with fish and birds still figuring out where they belong); and the day of rest, with angels singing to the glory of God (the narrowest—only one "day" wide). If you like these windows, make sure to visit the cathedral in Reims on a future trip.

CHAGALL MUSEUM

VILLEFRANCHE-SUR-MER, CAP FERRAT, AND EZE-LE-VILLAGE

Between Nice and Monaco lies the Riviera's richest stretch of real estate, paved with famously scenic roads (called the Three Corniches), worthwhile stops, million-dollar vistas, and sea-splashed walking trails. Fifteen minutes from Nice, little Villefranche-sur-Mer stares across the bay to woodsy and exclusive Cap Ferrat. The eagle's-nest Eze-le-Village and the Corniche-topping La Trophée des Alpes (in La Turbie) survey the scene from high above.

Villefranche-sur-Mer

In the glitzy world of the Riviera, Villefranche-sur-Mer offers travelers an easygoing slice of small-town Mediterranean life.

From here, convenient day trips allow you to gamble in style in Monaco, saunter the promenade des Anglais in Nice, or drink in immense views from Eze-le-Village. Villefranche-sur-Mer feels Italian, with soft-orange buildings; steep, narrow streets spilling into the sea; and pasta on most menus. Luxury sailing yachts glisten in the bay—an inspiration to those lazing along the harborfront to start saving when their trips are over. Cruise ships make occasional calls to Villefranche-sur-Mer's famously deep harbor, creating periodic rush hours of frenetic shoppers and happy boutique owners. Sand-pebble beaches, a handful of

Between Nice and Monaco

- **1** Low Corniche Road
  (*Basse Corniche*
  or Corniche Inférieure
  & Bus #100 Route)
- **2** Middle Corniche Road
  (*Moyenne Corniche*)
- **3** Great or High Corniche Road
  (*Grande Corniche*)

interesting sights, and quick access to Cap Ferrat keep other visitors just busy enough.

Originally a Roman port, Villefranche-sur-Mer was overtaken by fifth-century barbarians. Villagers fled into the hills, where they stayed and farmed their olives. In 1295, the Duke of Provence—like many in coastal Europe—was threatened by the Saracen Turks. He asked the hillside olive farmers to move down to the water and establish a front line against the invaders, thus denying the enemy a base from which to attack Nice. In return for tax-free status, they stopped farming, took up fishing, and established *Ville-* (town) *franche* (without taxes). Since there were many such towns, this one was specifically "Tax-free town on the sea" *(sur Mer)*. In about 1560, the Duke of Savoy built an immense, sprawling citadel in the town (which you can still tour). And today, while the town has an international following (including Tina Turner), two-thirds of its 8,000 people call it their primary residence. That makes Villefranche-sur-Mer feel more like a real community than many neighboring Riviera towns.

Orientation to Villefranche-sur-Mer

Tourist Information

The TI is in the park named jardin François Binon, below the main bus stop, labeled Octroi (July–Aug daily 9:00–19:00; Sept–June Mon–Sat 9:00–12:00 & 14:00–18:00, closed Sun; a 20-min walk or €10 taxi from train station, tel. 04 93 01 73 68, www.villefranche -sur-mer.com). Pick up schedules for buses #81 to Cap Ferrat and #83 to Eze-le-Village (via an easy transfer). Also ask for the brochure detailing a self-guided walking tour of Villefranche-sur- Mer and information on boat rides (usually mid-June–Sept). If you plan to visit Cap Ferrat, you could ask for the simple brochure-map showing the walks around this peninsula and information on the Villa Ephrussi de Rothschild's gardens, though my map and directions are sufficient (see "Cap Ferrat," later in this chapter).

Arrival in Villefranche-sur-Mer

By Bus: Buses #81 and #100 share the same stops in Villefranche-sur-Mer (see "Villefranche-sur-Mer Connections," later in this chapter). The most central stop is Octroi, near the jardin François Binon and just above the TI. From this stop, the old town is downhill to the left. Since bus #100 runs more often, it's usually the better choice when coming from Nice to Villefranche. When going from Villefranche to Nice, take the first bus that comes.

By Plane: Allow an hour from Nice's airport to Villefranche-sur-Mer. Take express bus #98 from Nice's airport to its bus station (€4, 3/hr, 30 min), then transfer to bus #100 or #81 to Villefranche-sur-Mer (4/hr on #100, 3/hr Sun; about 2/hr on #81; 15 min). One €4 ticket covers the whole trip.

By Train: Not all trains stop in Villefranche-sur-Mer. Make sure your train does, or transfer in Nice or Monaco (depending on your direction). Villefranche-sur-Mer's train station is a 15-minute walk along the water from the old town and many of the hotels listed in this chapter. Find your way down toward the water, and turn right to walk into town. Taxis to my recommended hotels cost €10, but they don't wait here and prefer longer rides; call instead, and pray the phone is working (see "Helpful Hints," later, for taxi telephone numbers).

By Car: From Nice's port, follow signs for *Menton, Monaco,* and *Basse Corniche.* In Villefranche-sur-Mer, turn right at the TI (first signal after Hôtel la Flore) for parking and hotels. For a quick visit to the TI, park at the pay lot just below the TI. A bit farther down, you'll find free parking in the moat areas within the boundaries of the citadel—better for longer visits and well-signed from main road *(Parking Fossés).* There's a more-secure pay lot on the water across from Hôtel Welcome, and some hotels also have their own parking.

Helpful Hints

Market Day: An antiques market enlivens Villefranche-sur-Mer on Sundays (on place Amélie Pollonnais by Hôtel Welcome and in jardin François Binon by the TI). On Saturday

Villefranche-sur-Mer

1. Hôtel Welcome & Souris Gourmande Rest.
2. Hôtel Villa Vauban
3. Hôtel la Flore
4. To Hôtel la Fiancée du Pirate & Minibus Route
5. Hôtel de la Darse
6. Le Cosmo Bistrot/Brasserie
7. La Grignotière Restaurant
8. La Serre Restaurant
9. Le Roxy Restaurant
10. La Mère Germaine Rest.
11. Casino Grocery
12. Internet: Chez Net Bar & L'Ex Café
13. Boat Rides & Electric Bike Rental
14. Launderette
15. Octroi Bus Stop (from Nice; to Monaco & Cap Ferrat)
16. Octroi Bus Stop (to Nice; from Monaco & Cap Ferrat)

mornings, a small food market sets up near the TI (only in jardin François Binon). A small trinkets market springs to action on place Amélie Pollonnais whenever cruise ships grace the harbor.

Last Call: While Villefranche-sur-Mer makes a great base for day trips, the last bus back from Nice or Monaco is at about 20:00. After that, take the train or a cab.

Internet Access: Two options sit side by side on place du Marché. **Chez Net,** an "Australian International Sports Bar Internet Café," has American keyboards but no printers, while **L'Ex Café** has printers but only French keyboards. Both are open daily, have Wi-Fi, and let you enjoy a late-night drink while surfing the Internet.

Laundry: The town has two launderettes—both owned by Laura and located just below the main road on avenue Sadi Carnot. At the upper *pressing moderne,* Laura does your wash for you— for a price (Tue–Sun 9:00–12:30 & 15:00–18:30, closes Sat at 17:00, closed Mon, next to Hôtel Royal Riviera, tel. 04 93 01 73 71). The lower *laverie* is self-service only (daily 7:00–20:00, opposite 6 avenue Sadi Carnot).

Electric Bike Rental: If you plan to explore Cap Ferrat but don't feel like walking, consider renting an electric bike from **Eco-Loc.** The adventurous can also try this as an alternative to taking the bus to Nice or Eze-le-Village. You get about 25 miles on a fully charged battery (less on hilly terrain—after that you're pedaling; €7/hr, €20/4 hrs, €30/day, April–Sept daily 9:00–17:30, deposit and ID required, best to call for reservations 24 hrs in advance; helmets, locks, baskets, and child seats available; on the port next to Café Calypso, mobile 06 63 91 16 77).

Taxi: For a reliable taxi in Villefranche-sur-Mer, call or email **Didier** (mobile 06 15 15 39 15, taxididier.villefranchesurmer @orange.fr). If he's busy, beware of taxi drivers who overcharge—the normal weekday, daytime rate to central Nice is about €35; to the airport, figure €50–60; one-way to Cap Ferrat is about €20 and to Eze-le-Village is about €35. The five-minute trip from the waterfront up to the main street level (to bus stops on the Low Corniche) should be less than €10. Ask your driver to write down the price before you get in, and get a receipt when you pay (mobile 06 09 33 36 12 or 06 39 32 54 09).

Minibus: Little **minibus #80** will save you the sweat of going from the harbor up the hill, but it only runs once per hour (daily 7:00–19:00, €1). It travels from the port to the top of the hill, stopping near La Fiancée du Pirate (see "Sleeping in Villefranche-sur-Mer," below) before going over the hill to the outlying suburban Nice Riquier train station (only convenient if you're already on minibus, must transfer to train to downtown Nice).

Tourist Train: Skip the useless white **Petit Train** that goes nowhere interesting and costs €6 for a 20-minute ride.

Sports Fans: Lively *boules* action takes place each evening just below the TI and the huge soccer field (see page 196).

Sights in Villefranche-sur-Mer

The Harbor—Browse Villefranche-sur-Mer's minuscule harbor. While the town was once an important fishing community, only eight families still fish here to make money. Wander behind the Gare Maritime, gaze out to sea, and marvel at the beautiful sailing yachts that call this bay home. (You might see well-coiffed captains being ferried in by dutiful mates to pick up their statuesque call girls.) Local guides keep a list of the world's 100 biggest yachts and talk about some of them as if they're part of the neighborhood.

Looking far to the right, that last apartment building on the sea was the headquarters for the US Navy's Sixth Fleet following World War II and remained so until 1966, when de Gaulle pulled France out of the military wing of NATO. (The Sixth Fleet has been based in Naples ever since.) A wall plaque at the bottom of rue de l'Eglise commemorates the US Navy's presence in Villefranche.

Parallel to the beach and about a block inland, you can walk the mysterious rue Obscura—a covered lane running 400 feet along the medieval rampart. This street served as an air-raid shelter during World War II.

Chapel of St. Pierre (Chapelle Cocteau)—This chapel, decorated by artist Jean Cocteau, is the town's cultural highlight. Cocteau was a Parisian transplant who adored little Villefranche-sur-Mer and whose career was distinguished by his work as an artist, poet, novelist, playwright, and filmmaker. Influenced by his pals Marcel Proust, André Gide, Edith Piaf, and Pablo Picasso, Cocteau was a leader among 20th-century avant-garde intellectuals. At the door, a woman passionate about Cocteau's art collects a €2.50 donation for a fishermen's charity. She then sets you free to enjoy the chapel's small but intriguing interior—she's happy to give some explanations if you ask.

In 1955, Jean Cocteau covered the barrel-vaulted chapel with heavy black lines and pastels. Each of Cocteau's surrealist works—the Roma (Gypsies) of Stes-Maries-de-la-Mer who dance and sing to honor the Virgin, girls wearing traditional outfits, and three scenes from the life of St. Peter—are explained in English. Is that Villefranche-sur-Mer's citadel in the scene above the altar? (Tue–Sun 10:00–12:00 & 15:00–19:00, closed Mon and when fisherwoman is tired, below Hôtel Welcome).

Citadel—The town's mammoth castle was built in the 1500s by the Duke of Savoy to defend against the French. When the region joined France in 1860, it became just a barracks. In the 20th century, the city had no military use for the space, and started using the citadel to house its police station, City Hall, a summer outdoor theater, and two art galleries. There's still only one, fortified entry to this huge complex.

St. Michael's Church—The town church features an 18th-century organ and a fine crucifix—carved, they say, from a fig tree by a galley slave in the 1600s.

Boat Rides (Promenades en Mer)—These little cruises, with English handouts, are offered sporadically, usually on Wednesdays and Fridays (€11 for 1-hour cruise around Cap Ferrat, €16 for 2-hour cruise as far as Monaco—but doesn't actually stop there, 5/week July–Aug, 1/week June and Sept, none off-season, boats depart from the harbor across from Hôtel Welcome, call to confirm the ever-changing schedule, reservations a must, tel. 04 93 76 65 65, www.amv-sirenes.com).

You can be your own skipper and rent a motor boat at **Dark Pelican** (€60/4 hrs, €110/9 hrs, deposit required, on the harbor at the Gare Maritime, tel. 04 93 01 76 54, www.darkpelican.com).

Seafront Walks—A seaside walkway originally used by customs agents to patrol the harbor leads under the citadel and connects the old town with the interesting workaday harbor (port de la Darse). At the port, you'll find a few cafés, France's Institute of Oceanography (an outpost for the University of Paris oceanographic studies), and an 18th-century dry dock. This scenic walk turns downright romantic after dark—if you're sleeping elsewhere, take an ice-cream-licking stroll here. You can also wander along Villefranche-sur-Mer's waterfront and continue beyond the train station for postcard-perfect views back to Villefranche-sur-Mer (ideal in the morning—go before breakfast). You'll come to a quieter beach with good picnic benches. You can even extend your walk to Cap Ferrat (see "Getting to Cap Ferrat," page 336).

Sleeping in Villefranche-sur-Mer

You have a handful of good hotels to choose from in Villefranche-sur-Mer. The ones I list have sea views from at least half of their rooms—well worth paying extra for.

$$$ Hôtel Welcome*** easily has the best location in Villefranche-sur-Mer, anchored right on the water in the old town, with all 32 balconied rooms overlooking the harbor. The lobby opens to the water, and the stylish wine bar lowers my pulse. You'll pay top price for all the comforts in this smart hotel. Skip the claustrophobic sixth-floor rooms (Sb-€99, "comfort" Db-€196, bigger "superior" Db-€230, suites-€340–380, extra bed-€35, air-con, elevator, parking garage-€17–25/day, 3 quai Amiral Courbet, tel. 04 93 76 27 62, fax 04 93 76 27 66, www.welcomehotel.com, resa@welcomehotel.com).

$$$ Hôtel Villa Vauban*** is a small villa two blocks below the TI, with nine simple and huggable rooms. Many have balconies and sea views, and most come with Old World bathrooms. The cheaper rooms on the lower level are a tad musty. Amiable British expat Alan Powers adds a personal touch that's rare in this area, making the place feel more like an intimate B&B (Db with small view-€95–130, Db with big sea view-€125–170, Db suite with sea view-€140–190, air-con, Wi-Fi, 11 avenue Général de Gaulle, tel. & fax 04 93 55 94 51, www.hotelvillavauban.com, info@hotelvillavauban.com).

$$$ Hôtel la Flore*** is suitable if your idea of sightseeing is to enjoy the view from your spacious bedroom deck (most rooms have one) or the pool. The free parking couldn't be easier, the staff is a tad formal, and it's a 10-minute uphill walk from the old town (Db with no view-€85–135, Db with view and deck-€135–150, larger Db for up to five people with even better view and bigger deck-€170–210, Db mini-suite-€220, Qb loft with huge terrace-€220, extra bed-€34, 10–15 percent cheaper Oct–March, air-con, elevator; just off main road high above harbor—go 2 blocks from TI toward Nice, near the bus stop to Nice and Monaco at 5 boulevard Princesse Grace de Monaco; tel. 04 93 76 30 30, fax 04 93 76 99 99, www.hotel-la-flore.fr, hotel-la-flore@wanadoo.fr).

$$ Hôtel la Fiancée du Pirate is only feasible if you have a car, as it's high up in Villefranche-sur-Mer on the Middle Corniche (parking is no problem). Don't let the streetside appearance deter you. Friendly Eric and Laurence offer 15 bright and comfortable rooms, along with a pool, Jacuzzi, lush garden, roomy lounge area, and breakfast terrace with partial views of Cap Ferrat and the sea. Choose between rooms in the main building (Db-€100–120, Tb/Qb-€140–170), or view rooms on the garden patio (standard Db-€85–105, Tb/Qb-€115–135). From June to September, they

Sleep Code

(€1 = about $1.40, country code: 33)
S = Single, **D** = Double/Twin, **T** = Triple, **Q** = Quad, **b** = bathroom, **s** = shower only, * = French hotel rating (0–4 stars). Unless otherwise noted, credit cards are accepted and English is spoken.

To help you sort easily through these listings, I've divided the rooms into three categories based on the price for a standard double room with bath:

$$$ Higher Priced—Most rooms €120 or more.
$$ Moderately Priced—Most rooms between €80–120.
$ Lower Priced—Most rooms €80 or less.

require a three-night minimum stay and offer lunch, salads, and snacks by the pool (air-con, Wi-Fi, 8 boulevard de la Corne d'Or, Moyenne Corniche N7, tel. 04 93 76 67 40, fax 04 93 76 91 04, www.fianceedupirate.com, info@fianceedupirate.com).

$ Hôtel de la Darse** is a shy and unassuming little hotel with a pleasing terrace, burrowed in the shadow of its highbrow neighbors. This low-profile alternative on the water at Villefranche-sur-Mer's old port is a great budget option. It's less central—figure 5 or 10 minutes of level walking to the harbor, but a steep 10-minute walk up to the main road and buses. Most of the 20 rooms have been renovated, and the ones facing the sea are worth the extra few euros for their million-dollar-view balconies (view Db-€87, view Tb-€100, Qb-€113, most with air-con and some noise on weekend nights, book well ahead for these). Rooms on the quieter garden side are sharp and have air-con but no view (Sb-€63, Db-€72; extra bed-€10, up to 4 floors, no elevator, good-value breakfast, from TI walk or drive down avenue Général de Gaulle to the old Port de la Darse, parking usually available nearby, tel. 04 93 01 72 54, fax 04 93 01 84 37, www.hotel-dela-darse-villefranche-sur-mer.cote .azur.fr, hoteldeladarse@wanadoo.fr).

Eating in Villefranche-sur-Mer

Comparison-shopping is half the fun of dining in Villefranche-sur-Mer. Make an event out of a pre-dinner stroll through the old city. Check what looks good on the lively place Amélie Pollonnais (next to the Hôtel Welcome), saunter the string of pricey candlelit places lining the waterfront, and consider the smaller, wallet-friendlier eateries embedded in the old city's walking streets. I like eating along the tiny lanes of the old city and on place Amélie

Pollonnais, where the whole village seems to converge at night. Arm yourself with a gelato from the ice cream shop a few doors down from Chapel of St. Pierre (Cocteau's chapel), and enjoy a floodlit, post-dinner stroll.

Le Cosmo Bistrot/Brasserie takes center stage on place Amélie Pollonnais with a great setting—a few tables have views to the harbor and to Cocteau chapel's facade (after some wine, Cocteau pops). Manager Arnaud runs a tight-but-friendly ship and offers well-presented and tasty meals with good wines (I love their red Bandol). Ask for the daily suggestions and consider the €11 *omelette niçoise* (€12–14 fine salads and pastas, €16–21 *plats*, open daily, place Amélie Pollonnais, tel. 04 93 01 84 05).

Disappear into Villefranche-sur-Mer's walking streets and find cute little **La Grignotière,** serving generous and delicious €18 *plats*, and plenty of other options. The mixed seafood grill is a smart order, as is the spaghetti and *gambas* (shrimp). They also offer a hearty €30 *menu*, but good luck finding room for it. Gregarious Michel speaks English fluently and runs the place with his sidekick Bridget. Dining is primarily inside, making this a good choice for cooler days (daily May–Oct, closed Wed Nov–April, 3 rue Poilu, tel. 04 93 76 79 83).

La Serre, nestled below the church in the old town, is a simple place with a hardworking owner. Sylvie serves well-priced meals to a loyal local clientele, always with a smile. Choose from the many pizzas (all named after US states and €10 or less), salads, and meats; or try the good-value, €17 three-course *menu* (open daily, cheap house wine, 16 rue du May, tel. 04 93 76 79 91).

Le Roxy is a top budget option with tasty and filling *plats* for €11. It's unromantically located on the main road just above the TI, with a down-to-earth setting and hardworking Monique and chef-hubbie Bebert at your service. They make excellent pizza (€8.50), good salads, a filling mixed-seafood grill (€12), and a killer *soup de poisson* (€11, not served in the heat of summer). Ask for seconds and don't be in a hurry—everything is made fresh once you order (closed Mon–Tue, 2 avenue de Grande Bretagne, tel. 04 93 76 71 80).

La Mère Germaine, right on the harbor, is the only place in town classy enough to lure a yachter ashore. It's dressy, with formal service and a price list to match. The name commemorates the current owner's grandmother, who fed hungry GIs during World War II. Try the bouillabaisse, served with panache (€70/person with 2-person minimum, ask about the less-expensive but ample mini-version, €41 *menu*, open daily, reserve harborfront table, tel. 04 93 01 71 39).

Souris Gourmande ("Gourmet Mouse") is handy for a made-to-order sandwich, either to take away or to eat there. Be patient and get to know your chef, Albert (€5 sandwiches, daily 11:30–19:30, closed Fri in winter, at base of steps behind Hôtel Welcome). Sandwich in hand, you'll find plenty of great places to enjoy a harborside sit.

There's a handy **Casino market/grocery store** a few blocks above Hôtel Welcome at 12 rue Poilu (Thu–Tue 7:30–13:00 & 15:00–19:30, Wed 7:30–13:00 only).

For Drivers: If you have a car and are staying a few nights, consider the short drive up to Eze-le-Village or, better still, La Turbie. If it's summer (June–Sept), the best option of all is to go across to Cap Ferrat's plage de Passable for a before-dinner drink or a dinner you won't soon forget (recommendations listed under each destination later in this chapter).

Villefranche-sur-Mer Connections

The last bus leaves Nice for Villefranche-sur-Mer at about 19:45; the last bus from Villefranche-sur-Mer to Nice departs at about 20:50; and trains runs later (until 24:00). Never board a train without a ticket or valid pass—inspectors don't accept excuses. The minimum fine is €70.

From Villefranche-sur-Mer by Bus to: Beaulieu-sur-Mer (#81, about 2/hr daily, 10 min; or #100, 4/hr Mon–Sat, 3/hr Sun, 10 min), **Monaco** (#100, 4/hr Mon–Sat, 3/hr Sun, 25 min), **Nice** (#100, 4/hr Mon–Sat, 3/hr Sun, 15 min; or #81, about 2/hr daily, 15 min). Remember, all buses in this area cost €1 per ride, regardless of your destination (buy from driver). A ticket is good for 74 minutes in one direction and is good for transfers but not round-trips. In Villefranche-sur-Mer, all bus stops are along the main drag; the most convenient is the Octroi stop, just above the TI.

By Train to: Monaco (2/hr, 10 min), **Nice** (2/hr, 10 min), **Antibes** (2/hr, 40 min).

To Cap Ferrat: To get to Cap Ferrat by bus, you have two choices. The first option is **bus #81,** which follows a circular route from Nice to Villefranche-sur-Mer, through Beaulieu-sur-Mer, then to all the Cap Ferrat stops and back (about 2/hr daily until 19:30, 10 min). The more-frequent **bus #100** connects Nice and Monaco, stopping at Villefranche-sur-Mer (4/hr Mon–Sat, 3/hr Sun, 10 min, runs daily 6:00–20:00) and at the edge of Cap Ferrat (longer walk to Cap Ferrat sights than #81). A **taxi** to Cap Ferrat costs about €20. It's a 50-minute **walk** to the Cap (see "Getting to Cap Ferrat," page 336).

The Three Corniches

Nice, Villefranche-sur-Mer, and Monaco are linked by three coastal routes: the Low, Middle, and High Corniches. The roads are nicknamed after the decorative frieze that runs along the top of a building (cornice). Each Corniche offers sensational views and a different perspective on this exotic strip of land. You can find the three routes from Nice by driving up boulevard Jean Jaurès past the bus station *(gare routière)*. For the Low Corniche, follow signs to N-98 *(Monaco par la Basse Corniche)*, which leads past Nice's port. Shortly after the turnoff to the Low Corniche, you'll see signs for N-7 *(Moyenne Corniche)* leading to the Middle Corniche. Signs for the High *(Grande)* Corniche appear a bit after that; follow D-2564 to Col des 4 Chemins and the Grande Corniche.

Low Corniche: The Basse Corniche (also called "Corniche Inférieure") strings ports, beaches, and villages together for a traffic-filled ground-floor view. It was built in the 1860s (along with the train line) to bring people to the casino in Monte Carlo. When this Low Corniche was finished, many hill-town villagers descended to the shore and started the communities that line the sea today. Before 1860, the population of the coast between Villefranche-sur-Mer and Monte Carlo was zero. Think about that as you make the trip today.

Middle Corniche: The Moyenne Corniche is higher, quieter, and far more impressive. It runs through Eze-le-Village (described in this chapter) and provides breathtaking views over the Mediterranean, with several scenic pullouts. (The ones above Villefranche-sur-Mer are particularly stunning.)

High Corniche: Napoleon's crowning road-construction achievement, the Grande Corniche caps the cliffs with staggering views from almost 1,600 feet above the sea. It is actually the Via Aurelia, used by the Romans to conquer the West.

Villas: Driving from Villefranche-sur-Mer to Monaco, you'll come upon impressive villas. A particularly grand entry leads to the sprawling estate built by King Leopold II of Belgium in the 1920s. Those driving up to the Middle Corniche from Villefranche-sur-Mer can look down on this yellow mansion and its lush garden, which fill an entire hilltop. This estate was later owned by the Agnelli family (of Fiat fame and fortune), and then by the Safra family (American bankers).

The Best Route: For a ▲▲▲ route, **drivers** should take the Middle Corniche from Nice or Villefranche-sur-Mer to Eze-le-Village; from there, follow signs to the Grande Corniche and La Turbie (La Trophée des Alpes), then finish by dropping down into Monaco. **Buses** travel each route; the higher the Corniche, the less frequent the buses (4/hr on Low, roughly 5–6/day on Middle and

High; get details at Nice's bus station). There are no buses between Eze-le-Village and La Turbie, though buses do connect Nice and Monaco with La Turbie.

Self-Guided Bus Tour: If traveling by bus, be sure to follow my self-guided bus tour commentary at the end of this chapter.

The following villages and sights are listed from west to east, in order of how you'll reach them when going from Villefranche-sur-Mer to Monaco.

Cap Ferrat

This exclusive peninsula, rated ▲▲, decorates Villefranche-sur-Mer's bay views. Cap Ferrat is a peaceful eddy off the busy Nice–Monaco route (Low Corniche). You could spend a fine day on this peninsula, wandering the sleepy port village of St. Jean-Cap-Ferrat (a.k.a. St. Jean), touring the Villa Ephrussi de Rothschild mansion and gardens and the nearby Villa Kérylos, and walking on sections of the beautiful trails that follow the coast. If you have a house here, former Microsoft mogul Paul Allen is your neighbor.

Tourist Information: The main TI is between the port and Villa Ephrussi (Mon–Fri 9:00–16:00, closed Sat–Sun, 59 avenue Denis Séméria, bus #81 stops here at *Office du Tourisme*). A smaller TI is in the village of St. Jean-Cap-Ferrat (hours vary but generally Tue–Sat 11:00–18:00, closed Sun–Mon, 5 avenue Denis Séméria). The two TIs share a phone number and email address (tel. 04 93 76 08 90, office-tourisme@saintjeancapferrat.fr).

Planning Your Time

Here's how I'd spend a day on the Cap: From Nice or Villefranche-sur-Mer, take the bus (#81 or #100—see below) to a stop near the Villa Ephrussi, then visit the villa. Walk 30 minutes, mostly downhill, to St. Jean-Cap-Ferrat for lunch (many options, including grocery shops for picnic supplies) and poke about the village. Consider the 45-minute walk on the plage de Paloma trail (ideal for picnics). After lunch, follow a beautiful 30-minute trail to Villa Kérylos in Beaulieu-sur-Mer and tour that villa. Return to Villefranche-sur-Mer, Nice, or points beyond by train or bus. Details for all aspects of this day are provided below. (Skip the drive on the loop road around Cap Ferrat's peninsula.)

You can add Eze-le-Village to this day if you skip the small town of St. Jean-Cap-Ferrat and walk directly from the Villa Rothschild to the Villa Kérylos. Take bus #100 (direction: Monaco) from the stop near Villa Kérylos and get off at the Gare d'Eze stop, where you meet the #83 bus that shuttles up and up to the village (one €1 ticket covers both buses, get #83 schedule at a TI or check online at www.lignedazur.com).

Getting to Cap Ferrat

From Nice: From Nice, **bus #81** runs to all key Cap Ferrat stops (daily, about 2/hr until 19:30, 30 min to Villa Ephrussi de Rothschild—get off at Passable stop, schedules at bus station or at TI). The more frequent (4/hr Mon–Sat, 3/hr Sun) **bus #100** to Monaco drops you at Cap Ferrat's edge (stops Ange Gardien or Pont St. Jean), and from there, you can walk 20 minutes to Villa Ephrussi de Rothschild (after crossing over main road from bus stop, look for the center alleyway—chemin des Moulins—running straight up the Cap, turn left at the end, then keep right). By **car,** take the Low Corniche through Villefranche-sur-Mer.

From Villefranche: It's quick by **car** (Low Corniche) or **taxi** (allow €20 one-way), and easy by **bus** (#81 and #100). Both buses run from the main bus stop above Villefranche-sur-Mer's TI (marked Octroi). Bus #81 runs about twice an hour (daily until 19:30, 10 min, get a schedule from the TI, times listed for *Direction Le Port/Cap Ferrat* are when bus leaves Nice's *gare routière*—allow about 10 min after that to reach Villefranche-sur-Mer). The return bus (direction: Nice) begins in St. Jean-Cap-Ferrat village. Bus #100 to Monaco has more frequent service (4/hr Mon–Sat, 3/hr Sun, daily 6:00–20:00), but drops you at the edge of Cap Ferrat (see "From Nice," above).

You can also **walk** 50 minutes from Villefranche-sur-Mer to Cap Ferrat: Go past the train station along the beach, then climb the steps at the far end of the beach. Continue straight past the mansions (with ornate gates) and take the first right on avenue de Grasseuil. You'll see signs to the Villa Ephrussi de Rothschild, then to Cap Ferrat's port.

Sights on Cap Ferrat

▲**Villa Ephrussi de Rothschild**—In what seems like the ultimate in Riviera extravagance, Venice, Versailles, and the Côte d'Azur come together in the pastel-pink Villa Ephrussi. Rising above Cap Ferrat, this 1905 mansion has views west to Villefranche-sur-Mer and east to Beaulieu-sur-Mer.

Start with the well-furnished belle époque **interior** (helpful English handout provided). Upstairs, an 18-minute film (with English subtitles) gives good background on the life of rich and eccentric Beatrice, Baroness de Rothschild, the French woman from an important banking family who built and furnished the place. As you stroll through the halls, you'll pass rooms with royal furnishings and personal possessions, including her bathroom case for cruises. A fancy tearoom serves drinks and lunch with a view (11:00–17:30).

Cap Ferrat

TO
VILLEFRANCHE
& NICE

TO MONACO &
EZE-LE-VILLAGE

Bus #100
(NICE-TO-MONACO)
Stops

LOW CORNICHE

BEAULIEU

LOW CORNICHE

AVE MONNET

"ANGE
GARDIEN"
STOP

VILLA
KERYLOS

AVE. DE GRASSEUIL

DENIS SEM

DURANDY

VILLA EPHRUSSI
DE ROTHSCHILD

PLAGE DE
PASSABLE

CHEMIN DU ROY

ST. JEAN-
CAP-FERRAT
VILLAGE

ALB 1

PLAGE
PALOMA

BLVD. DE GAULLE

AVE. BELLEVUE

BLVD. DE GAULLE

LIGHTHOUSE

Ⓑ Bus #81 Stops
🅿 Parking
— Roads
- - - Trails
🏖 Beach

HOTELS
❶ Hôtel Brise Marine
❷ Hôtel Oursin & TI
❸ Hôtel/Rest. la Frégate
❹ Hôtel Royal Riviera

TRAILS
❺ St. Jean-Cap-Ferrat to
Beaulieu-sur-Mer (30 min)
❻ Plage de Paloma Loop (45 min)
❼ St. Jean-Cap-Ferrat to
Plage de Passable (2-3 hrs)

But the gorgeous **gardens** are why most come here. Designed in the shape of a ship, the gardens were motivated by Beatrice's many ocean-liner trips. Her small army of gardeners even dressed like sailors. Behind the mansion, stroll through the seven lush gardens re-created from locations all over the world. The sea views from here are amazing. Don't miss the Alhambra-like Spanish gardens, the rose garden at the far end, and the view back to the house from the "Temple of Love" gazebo.

Cost, Hours, Information: Palace and gardens-€10, skippable tour of upstairs-€3 extra, combo-ticket with Villa Kérylos-€15—valid for one week; mid-Feb–Oct daily 10:00–18:00, July–Aug until 19:00; Nov–mid-Feb Mon–Fri 14:00–18:00, Sat–Sun 10:00–18:00; tel. 04 93 01 33 09, www.villa-ephrussi.com. Kids will enjoy the free treasure-hunt booklet. Parking is tricky; there's a small turnaround at the top. The nearest bus stop is Passable (only via bus #81, 10-min walk uphill to the villa).

Walks from Villa Ephrussi: It's a lovely 30-minute stroll, mostly downhill, from Villa Ephrussi to the Villa Kérylos in Beaulieu-sur-Mer (described on page 341) or to the port of St. Jean-Cap-Ferrat. To get to either, make a hard left at the stop sign below the Villa Ephrussi and follow signs along a small road toward the Hôtel Royal Riviera on avenue Henri Honoré (see map on page 337). When the road comes to a T, keep going straight, passing a green gate down a pedestrian path, which ends at a trail—go left to reach Villa Kérylos, or head right to get to St. Jean-Cap-Ferrat (be careful to follow the path left at the Villa Sonja Rello). It's about 15 minutes to either destination once you join this path. To get to plage de Passable, turn left along the main road just below Villa Ephrussi and find signs in 50 yards (5 min down, at least 10 min back up).

Plage de Passable—This pleasant beach, located below Villa Ephrussi, comes with great views of Villefranche-sur-Mer and a rough, pebbly surface. It's a peaceful beach, popular with families. Half is public (free, with shower), and the other half is run by a small restaurant (€22 includes changing locker, lounge chair, and shower; reserve ahead in summer or on weekends as this is a prime spot, kayak rental available, tel. 04 93 76 06 17). If ever you were to do the French Riviera rent-a-beach ritual, this is the place.

To park near the beach, follow signs past it, and go around the bend to a surprise lot. If it's full, follow signs over the hill and around to Lido Parking, a few steps from plage de Passable (€6/day).

For me, the best reason to come here is for dinner. Beg, borrow, or steal a way here to arrive before sunset, then watch as darkness descends and lights flicker over Villefranche-sur-Mer's heavenly setting. At **Restaurant de la Plage Passable,** enjoy a surprisingly elegant dining experience to the sounds of children still at play on the beach. Notice the streetlights that illuminate the path of the Low and Middle Corniches (€16 starters, €20–27 *plats*, open daily late June–Sept, until 20:00 in good weather April–May and Oct only, tel. 04 93 76 06 17).

St. Jean-Cap-Ferrat—This quiet village port (also called St. Jean) lies in Cap Ferrat's center, yet off most tourist itineraries.

St. Jean houses yachts, boardwalks, views, and boutiques packaged in a "take your time, darling" atmosphere. It's a few miles off the busy Nice-to-Monaco road—convenient for drivers, yet it feels overlooked. A string of restaurants line the port, with just enough visitors to keep them in business, and there's a small TI in the village center (see "Tourist Information," earlier). St. Jean is especially peaceful at night.

The bus stop back to Villefranche-sur-Mer is a block above the port (sea side of street) near Hôtel la Frégate (if you need a taxi, call 04 93 76 86 00). The hiking trail to Beaulieu-sur-Mer (with access to Villa Ephrussi) begins farther up this road just after the Mairie (trail veers down to the right). It's just after the beach, to the left of the port as you look out to the water (see below).

▲▲Walks Around Cap Ferrat—The Cap is perfect for a walk, as you'll find well-maintained foot trails covering most of its

length. Depending on how much time you have, there are three easy, mostly level options (30 min, 45 min, or 2–3 hours). The TIs in Villefranche-sur-Mer and St. Jean-Cap-Ferrat have maps of Cap Ferrat with walking paths marked, or you can use this book's

directions (below) and map (page 337). During segments of all of the hikes, you can make out the three Corniche roads cut into the side of the massive cliffs.

Between St. Jean-Cap-Ferrat and Beaulieu-sur-Mer (30 minutes): A level walk takes you past sumptuous villas, great views, and fun swimming opportunities. To reach the trail from St. Jean-Cap-Ferrat's port, walk along the harbor with the water on your right, and work your way past the beach. Head up the steps to promenade Maurice Rouvier and continue; before long, you'll see smashing views of the whitewashed Villa Kérylos (and you might be able to make out the hill town of Eze-le-Village

CAP FERRAT

crowning the last peak on the right across the bay). To get from Beaulieu-sur-Mer to St. Jean-Cap-Ferrat, start walking at Villa Kérylos (with the sea on your left) toward the Hôtel Royal Riviera, and find the trail (be careful to stay left at the Villa Sonja Rello about halfway down). You can also reach this trail by walking 10 minutes downhill from the Villa Ephrussi (described above).

Plage de Paloma Loop Trail (45 minutes): Just east of St. Jean's port, a sea-soaked, view-loaded trail gives a terrific sampling of Cap Ferrat's beauty for a modest effort. From the port, walk or drive about a quarter-mile east (with the port on your left, passing Hôtel La Voile d'Or); you'll find the trailhead where the road comes to a T—look for a *Plage Paloma* sign. (Parking is available at the port or on streets near plage de Paloma.) Cross the small dirt park to start the trail, and do this walk counterclockwise. The trail is level and paved, yet uneven enough that good shoes are helpful. Plunk your picnic on one of the benches along the trail, or eat at the café on plage de Paloma at the end of the walk (sandwiches and salads). If time is tight, walk up the road toward *Plage Paloma* signs and find the trail for great views.

Plage de Passable to St. Jean-Cap-Ferrat (2–3 hours): For a longer hike that circles the Cap, follow the signs below Villa Ephrussi marked *Plage Passable* (10 min downhill on foot from the villa, parking available near the trailhead). Walk down to the beach (you'll find a good café that's ideal for lunch), turn left, and cross the beach. Go along a paved road behind a big apartment building, and after about 300 feet, take the steps down to the trail *(Sentier Littoral)*. Near the end of the trail, you'll pass by the port of St. Jean-Cap-Ferrat, where you have three options: take bus #81 back to Villefranche-sur-Mer, walk back to the Villa Ephrussi and plage de Passable via the shorter inland route (reverse the directions under "Walks from Villa Ephrussi," earlier), or continue on to Beaulieu-sur-Mer and take a bus to Monaco or Nice.

Sleeping on Cap Ferrat

In St. Jean-Cap-Ferrat
(€1 = about $1.40, country code: 33)

This sleepy village offers surprisingly good values, probably because it's off the main route (and less convenient if you don't have a car).

$$$ Hôtel Brise Marine***, flanked by tall palm trees and graced with gardens and a view terrace, is a peaceful retreat. Run by a gentle mother-son team, this aged mansion—with faded, Old World character—feels lost in a time warp. Many of its spacious rooms come with sensational views, and some have small balconies (view Db with balcony-€182, view Db without balcony-€155, breakfast-€14, air-con, Wi-Fi, minibar, secure parking-€14, ideally located between the port and plage de Paloma at 58 avenue Jean Mermoz, tel. 04 93 76 04 36, fax 04 93 76 11 49, www.hotel-brise marine.com, info@hotel-brisemarine.com).

$$ Hôtel Oursin** is central to the port, with 14 respectably priced and surprisingly well-appointed rooms all on one floor. Run by mother-and-son team Chantal and Aubrey, it's a welcoming, humble place with white walls, and feels more like a B&B than a hotel (smaller Db without air-con-€80, bigger Db with air-con and new bathroom-€105, larger Db with port views-€120, €20 less Oct–April, 1 avenue Denis Séméria, tel. & fax 04 93 76 12 55, www.hoteloursin.com, reception@hoteloursin.com).

$ Hôtel/Restaurant la Frégate, a simple, family-run place, overlooks the port with 10 spotless, no-frill rooms. Some have good views, while others overlook the garden courtyard (Db-€54–69 with no air-con and no view, Db–€86 with air-con and view, reserved owners, 11 avenue Denis Séméria, tel. 04 93 76 04 51, fax 04 93 76 14 93).

Near Cap Ferrat: Beaulieu-sur-Mer

This town, right on the Low Corniche road (just after Cap Ferrat), is busy with traffic. It's a good place to pick up the hiking trail to

St. Jean-Cap-Ferrat (described earlier), and to visit the unusual **Villa Kérylos.** In 1902, an eccentric millionaire modeled his new mansion after a Greek villa from the island of Delos from about 200 B.C. No expense was spared in re-creating this Greek fantasy, from the floor mosaics to Carrara marble columns to exquisite wood furnishings. The rain-powered shower is fun, and the included audioguide will increase your Greek IQ. The ceramics workshop—open only high season and weekend afternoons—offers a chance to test your talents (€9, combo-ticket with Villa Ephrussi de Rothschild-€15—valid for one week; mid-Feb–Oct daily 10:00–18:00, July–Aug until 19:00; Nov–mid-Feb Mon–Fri 14:00–18:00, Sat–Sun 10:00–18:00; tel. 04 93 01 47 29, www.villa-kerylos.com).

CAP FERRAT

Getting to and from Villa Kérylos

Drivers should park near the casino in Beaulieu-sur-Mer, not on the villa's access road. The Monaco–Nice bus #100 (4/hr Mon–Sat, 3/hr Sun, 20 min from Nice or Monaco) drops you at the Eglise stop at the Hôtel Metropole in Beaulieu (turn right off the bus and find signs to the Villa Kérylos). Trains (2/hr, 10 min from Nice or

Monaco) leave you a 10-minute walk away: Turn left out of the train station and left again down the main drag. Walk to the end, turn right, then find signs to Villa Kérylos. The walking trail from Villa Kérylos to Cap Ferrat and the Villa Ephrussi de Rothschild begins on the other side of the bay, below Hôtel Royal Riviera.

Eze-le-Village

Floating high above the sea, flowery and flawless Eze-le-Village (don't confuse it with the seafront town of Eze-Bord-de-Mer) is entirely consumed by tourism. This *village d'art et de gastronomie* (as it calls itself) nurtures perfume out- lets, upscale boutiques, steep cob- bled lanes, and magnificent views (best from the terrace at Château d'Eza). Touristy as this place cer- tainly Eze, its stony state of pres- ervation and magnificent hilltop setting over the Mediterranean

justify a visit. Day-tripping by bus to Eze-le-Village from Nice, Monaco, or Villefranche-sur-Mer works well, provided you know the bus schedules (ask at TIs or check www.lignedazur.com; Villefranche-sur-Mer requires a transfer).

Getting to Eze-le-Village: There are two Ezes: Eze-le-Village (the spectacular hill town) and Eze-Bord-de-Mer (a modern beach

resort far below Eze-le-Village). Eze-le-Village is about 20 minutes east of Villefranche-sur-Mer on the Middle Corniche. From Nice, two bus lines (#82 and #112) provide 16 buses per day to Eze-le-Village (eight on Sun, 25 min, €1). From Nice, Villefranche, or Monaco, you can also take the train or the Nice– Monaco bus to Eze-Bord-de-Mer, getting off at the Gare d'Eze stop. From here, take the #83 shuttle bus straight up to Eze-le-Village (€1, 8/ day, daily 9:45–18:00)—but find out the bus #83 schedule at a TI before you go, as service is infrequent. The schedule is also posted at the stop. To connect Eze-le-Village directly with Monte Carlo in Monaco, take bus #112 (7/day Mon–Sat, none on Sun, 25 min). There are no direct buses from Villefranche-sur-Mer to Eze-le- Village, and there are no buses between La Turbie (La Trophée des Alpes) and Eze-le-Village.

EZE-LE-VILLAGE

You can also take a taxi between the two Ezes (allow €22 one-way, mobile 06 09 84 17 84).

Orientation to Eze-le-Village

Bus stops and parking lots weld the town to the highway (Middle Corniche) that passes under its lowest wall. Eze-le-Village's main parking lot is a block below the town's entry. The bus stop to Nice is just across the road from the parking lot, and the stop to Eze-Bord-de-Mer is on the parking lot side of the main road, near the Casino Market. The helpful **TI** is in the lot's far corner (TI open April–Oct daily 9:00–19:00; Nov–March Mon–Sat 9:00–18:30, closed Sun; place de Gaulle, tel. 04 93 41 26 00, www.eze-riviera.com). English-language tours of the village and gardens are available for a small fee—it's best to call the TI to arrange in advance. Public WCs are located just behind the TI and in the village behind the church.

Self-Guided Walk

Welcome to Eze-le-Village

• *From the TI and parking lot, wander uphill into the town. You'll pass an exclusive hotel and the start of a steep trail down to the beach marked Eze/Mer. (For a panoramic view and ideal picnic perch, walk 60 steps down this path; descending 1,300 view-filled feet in about 1.25 hours on this trail would bring you to the beach below at Eze-Bord-de-Mer.) Continuing up, enter...*

Place du Centenaire: In this square, a stone plaque celebrates the 100th anniversary of the 1860 plebiscite, the time when all 133 Eze residents voted to leave the Italian Duchy of Savoy and join France. Vive la France! A town map here helps you get oriented.

• *Now pass through the once-formidable town gate (designed to keep the Ottomans out) and climb into the 14th-century village. You'll find occasional English information plaques on walls in the old city. Wandering the narrow lanes—ever uphill—you'll come to the...*

Château Eza: This was the winter getaway of the Swedish royal family from 1923 until 1953; today, it's a hotel. The château's tearoom (Salon de Thé), on a cliff overlooking the jagged Riviera and sea, offers the most scenic coffee or beer break you'll ever enjoy—for a price. The sensational view terrace is also home to an expensive-but-sensational restaurant. Reserve well ahead for dinner (menus from €105, €50 lunches, open daily, rooms for Db-€350–700, tel. 04 93 41 12 24, www.chateaueza.com, info@chateaueza.com).

• *Eventually the town ends at its hilltop castle ruins—now blanketed by the...*

Jardins d'Eze: Here, you'll find a prickly festival of cactus. Since 1949, these ruins have been home to 400 different plants 1,300 feet above the sea (€5, open daily, hours change frequently but usually May–Sept 9:00–19:00, Oct–April until dusk, well-described in English, tel. 04 93 41 10 30). At the top, you'll be treated to a commanding 360-degree view, with a helpful table d'orientation. On a crystal-clear day, you can see Corsica. The castle was demolished by Louis XIV in 1706. Louis destroyed castles like this all over Europe (most notably along the Rhine), because he didn't want to risk having to do battle with rebellious nobles inside them at some future date.

• *As you descend, drop by the...*

Eze Church: While built during Napoleonic times, it has an uncharacteristic Baroque fanciness—a reminder that 300 years of Savoy rule left the townsfolk with an Italian savoir faire and a sensibility for decor.

Sights in Eze-le-Village

Perfume Factory Fragonard—This factory, with its huge tour-bus parking lot, lies on the Middle Corniche, 350 feet below Eze-le-Village. Designed for tour groups, it cranks them through all day long. If you've never seen mass tourism in action, this place will open your eyes. (The gravel is littered with the color-coded F stickers that each tourist wears so that the salespeople know which guide gets the kickback.) Drop in for a free tour, which can last anywhere from 20 to 40 minutes depending on the walking ability of the group (daily 9:00–18:00, but best Mon–Fri 9:00–11:00 & 14:00–15:30, when the "factory" actually has people working, tel. 04 93 41 05 05). You'll see how the perfume and scented soaps are made and bottled before you're herded into the gift shop.

For a more personal and intimate look at perfume, cross the main road in Eze-le-Village to visit the **Gallimard** shop. Take a perfume tour and let the lovely ladies show you their scents.

Eating in Eze-le-Village

To enjoy Eze-le-Village in relative peace, visit at sunset and stay for dinner. There's a handy **Casino** market at the foot of the village by the bus stop, and a sensational picnic spot at the beginning of the beach trail (described above). You'll dine well at the stone-elegant **Le Troubador** (€40 *menu*, closed Sun–Mon, 4 rue du Brec, tel. 04 93 41 19 03), or for less, at the basic **Nid de l'Aigle** ("Eagle's Nest," at entry to the Jardins d'Eze, open Thu–Tue for lunch, April–Oct also open for dinner Fri–Mon, tel. 04 93 41 19 08).

La Trophée des Alpes

High above Monaco, on the Grande (High) Corniche in the over-looked village of La Turbie, lies one of this region's most evoca-tive historic sights (with dramatic views over the entire country of Monaco as a bonus). This massive Roman monument, rated ▲▲, commemorates Augustus Caesar's conquest of the Alps and its 44 hostile tribes. It's exciting to think that, in a way, La Trophée des Alpes celebrates a victory that kicked off the Pax Romana—joining Gaul and Germania, freeing up the main artery of the Roman Empire, and lacing together Spain and Italy.

Walk around the monument and notice how the Romans built a fine, quarried-stone exterior, filled in with rubble and coarse con-crete. Flanked by the vanquished in chains, the towering inscrip-tion tells the story: It was erected "by the senate and the people to honor the emperor." The monument was restored in the 1930s and 1940s with money from the Tuck family of New Hampshire.

The one-room **museum** shows a reconstruction and transla-tion of the dramatic inscription, which lists all the feisty alpine tribes that put up such a fight (€5; July–Sept Tue–Sun 9:30–19:00, Mon 9:30–17:00; April–June Tue–Sun 9:30–18:00, Mon 9:30–17:00; Oct–March daily 9:30–17:00; tel. 04 93 41 20 84). Escorts from the museum take people up to the monument, but it's not worth waiting for.

The sweet old village of **La Turbie** sees almost no tourists, but it has plenty of cafés and restaurants at its doorstep. To stroll the old village, park in the main lot on place Neuve (follow *Monaco* signs one block from the main road), then walk behind the post office and find brick footpaths—they lead through a village with nary a shop. To eat very well, try **La Terrasse,** the Riviera's most welcoming restaurant (I'm not kidding), where tables gather under sun shades, the sea lies miles below, and clients seem oblivious to the incredible setting. Let Helen, Jacques, and Annette tempt you to return for dinner at sunset, and book ahead for a table with a view (daily, near the PTT/post office at the main parking lot, 17 place Neuve, tel. 04 93 41 21 84).

Getting to and from La Trophée des Alpes (in La Turbie): By **car,** take the High Corniche to La Turbie, ideally from Eze-le-Village (La Turbie is 10 min east of, and above, Eze-le-Village), then look for signs to *La Trophée des Alpes.* Once in La Turbie, you can park in the lot in the center of town (place Neuve, follow *Monaco* signs for a short block) and walk from there (walk 5 min around the old village, with the village on your right); or drive to the site by turning right in front of La Régence Café. Those coming from farther afield can take the efficient A-8 to the La Turbie exit. To reach Eze-le-Village from La Turbie, follow signs to Nice, and then look for signs to Eze-le-Village.

You can also get here by **bus #116** from Nice (4/day, 45 min, €1, last bus returns to Nice at about 18:00) or **bus #114** from Monaco (6/day, 3/day Sat morning only, none on Sun, 20 min, €1). The bus stop is across from the PTT/post office on place Neuve (to reach La Trophée des Alps, walk around the old village, with the village on your right—5 min).

Quickie Riviera Bus Tour from Nice to Monaco

Don't have a car? You can still enjoy the trip from Nice to Monaco (and on to Menton, described on page 362). While most travelers see the Riviera from their train window as they zoom along the coast, the public bus affords a far better view of the crags, dreamy villas, and much-loved beaches that make it Europe's coast with the most.

This tour works best if you take the bus from Nice, ride the entire Nice–Monaco–Menton route (60 scenic minutes), enjoy Menton, then see Monaco (or you may find time for another stop) on the way back to Nice. To minimize bus and sightseeing crowds, time it so that you're on the bus by 9:00—but beware: Monte Carlo's casino does not open until 14:00 most days. Alternatively, come for late-afternoon sightseeing and stay into the evening.

Riding the bus couldn't be easier. Bus #100 runs four times an hour along the Low Corniche (daily 6:00–20:00, 3/hr on Sun, departs from Nice bus station). One simple €1 ticket (buy from the driver) is good for 74 minutes, no matter how far you go. Since bus fares are cheap, consider hopping on and off at great view-points (the next bus will be by soon). Riding from Nice toward Monaco, grab a seat on the right-hand side. All stops have names (usually posted on the shelter or bus stop sign)—I'll identify the ones that matter along this route. Keep your eyes peeled for town names and bus stops as we go. Your driver is a retired Formula 1 racer.

It's easiest to get a good seat if you board the bus in Nice's bus station (or if you go by 9:00). If there's a long line, you could wait for the next bus to be assured of a view seat (buses start from here and run every 15 min). At the Nice bus station, TV monitors list the platform, destination, and time for the next departure. You're looking for bus #100 to *destination: Monaco/Menton* (most likely from stall 17). Pay the driver as you get on, and be assertive with the crowds trying to board.

Self-Guided Bus Tour

This Nice-to-Monaco route along the Low Corniche was inaugurated with the opening of the Monte Carlo Casino in 1863. It was designed to provide easy and safe access from Nice (and the rest of France) to the gambling fun in Monaco. Here's what you'll see along the way:

In Nice: Shortly after the bus pulls out, you'll get a quick glimpse of Nice's snazzy Museum of Modern Art before passing through place Garibaldi (easy transfer to the tram on your way back), with its statue of Giuseppe Garibaldi (one of the men credited with uniting Italy in the 1860s) at the center.

Nice Harbor: This harbor was built in the 1700s. Before then, boats littered Nice's beach. You'll see some yachts, an occasional cruise ship, and the daily ferry to Corsica. If you get on or off here on your return, it's a pleasant 30-minute walk around the point to or from the promenade des Anglais.

From Nice to Villefranche-sur-Mer: As you scenically glide away from Nice, look back for views of the harbor, Castle Hill, and the sweeping Bay of Angels (consider hopping off here for photos). Imagine the views from the homes below. That soft, yellow, rounded tower ahead near the top of the hill is part of Sean Connery's property.

You'll soon pass the now-closed Hôtel Maerterlinck, one of several luxury hotels to go belly-up in recent years (now slated for condo-conversion). Next, you'll come to the yacht-studded bay of Villefranche-sur-Mer and the peninsula called Cap Ferrat—playground of the rich and famous, marked by its lighthouse on the point just across the bay. This bay is a rare natural harbor along the Riviera. Since it's deeper than Nice's, it hosts the huge cruise ships.

Villefranche-sur-Mer and Cap Ferrat: To see Villefranche-sur-Mer, one of the most charming towns along the Riviera, get off at the stop labeled Octroi (for more on Villefranche, see the beginning of this chapter).

After passing through Villefranche-sur-Mer, keep an eye out as the road arcs to the right (the Rolling Stones recorded *Exile on Main Street* just below in 1971—look for a pink place hidden by trees). You'll see sensational views over Villefranche-sur-Mer. At Cap Ferrat, the Baroness Rothschild's pink Villa Ephrussi, with its red-tiled roof, breaks the horizon. A little farther to the right is Baron Paul Allen's home (with a sloping red-tiled roof).

Consider stopping off to take a picture along this stretch, and combining your photo op with a stroll to nearby Cap Ferrat. For a Cap Ferrat adventure, hop out at the stop marked *Pont St. Jean* (just after the Total station). Cross the main road and find the walkway that runs up the center of the Cap (see "Getting to Cap Ferrat," earlier in the chapter, for details).

Beaulieu-sur-Mer: To visit the Villa Kérylos, get off at the Eglise stop, in front of the Hôtel Metropole. Just after the town of Beaulieu-sur-Mer, the cliffs create a microclimate and a zone nicknamed "Little Africa." (The bus stop is labeled Petite Afrique.) Exotic vegetation (including the only bananas on the Riviera) grows among private, elegant villas that made Beaulieu-sur-Mer *the* place to be in the 19th century.

Eze-Bord-de-Mer and Cap d'Ail: A few minutes after leaving Beaulieu-sur-Mer, be ready for scant, short-lived views way up to the fortified town of Eze-le-Village (when you round a big bend going left), which towers high above the little hamlet of Eze-Bord-de-Mer. To reach Eze-le-Village, the #83 shuttle bus makes the climb from the Gare d'Eze stop in Eze-Bord-de-Mer (daily, 8/day, shares the same eastbound stop used by bus #100).

Passing through a tunnel, you emerge at Cap d'Ail. The huge, deep yellow hospital-like building nearby was once a luxury hotel popular with the Russian aristocracy. Now it's occupied by private condos. At the first stop after the big yellow building (labeled Cap d'Ail), look above at the switchbacks halfway up the barren hillside. It was at the bend connecting these two switchbacks that Princess Grace Kelly (the former American movie star) was killed in a car crash in 1982. You can get off here and walk a lovely beach trail that will take you to Monaco in 30 minutes.

Monaco (three bus stops): Cap d'Ail borders Monaco—you're now leaving France. On your right, just before the castle-topped hill (Monaco-Ville, a.k.a. Le Rocher), is Monaco's Fontvieille district, featuring tall apartments all built on land reclaimed from the Mediterranean. The first Monaco stop (Place d'Armes) is the best one to use for visiting the palace and other old-town sights in Monaco-Ville.

If you stay on the bus, you'll pass through the tunnel, then emerge to follow the road that Grand Prix drivers race along. In late May, you'll see blue bleachers and barriers set up for the big race.

You'll pass the second Monaco stop (Stade Nautique), then enjoy the harbor and city views as you climb to the last Monaco stop (Casino). Get off here for a peek at the gambling action (a plush, terraced garden leads down to the casino) and an easy walk back into Monte Carlo. For information on Monaco, see the next chapter. If you stay on the bus for a few more minutes, you'll be back in France, and in 15 more minutes you'll reach the end of the line, **Menton** (described on page 362).

Bonne route!

MONACO

Despite overdevelopment, high prices, and wall-to-wall daytime tourists, Monaco is a Riviera must. Monaco is on the go. Since 1929, cars have raced around the port and in front of the casino in one of the world's most famous auto races, the Grand Prix de Monaco (May 20–23 in 2010; see sidebar later in this chapter). The modern breakwater—constructed elsewhere and towed in by sea—enables big cruise ships to dock here. The district of Fontvieille, reclaimed from the sea, bristles with luxury high-rise condos. But don't look for anything too deep in this glittering tax haven. Two-thirds of its 30,000 residents live here because there's no income tax—leaving fewer than 10,000 true Monegasques.

This minuscule principality (0.75 square mile) borders only France and the Mediterranean. The country has always been tiny, but it used to be...less tiny. In an 1860 plebiscite, Monaco lost two-thirds of its territory when the region of Menton voted to join France. To compensate, France suggested that Monaco build a fancy casino and promised to connect it to the world with a road (the Low Corniche) and a train line. This started a high-class tourist boom that has yet to let up.

While "independent," Monaco is run as a piece of France. A French civil servant appointed by the French president—with

the blessing of Monaco's prince—serves as state minister and manages the place. Monaco's phone system, electricity, water, and so on, are all French.

The death of Prince Rainier in 2005 ended his 56-year career of enlightened rule. Today, Monaco is ruled by Prince Rainier's unassuming son, Prince Albert Alexandre Louis Pierre, Marquis of Baux. At 50-some years old, Prince Albert is considered Europe's most eligible bachelor—though he has admitted to fathering two children out of wedlock. He's a bobsled enthusiast and avid environmentalist who seems determined to clean up Monaco's tarnished tax-haven, money-laundering image. (Monaco is infamously known as a "sunny place for shady people.")

Monaco is big business, and Prince Albert is its CEO. While its famous casino contributes only 5 percent of the state's revenue, its 43 banks—which offer an attractive way to hide your money—are hugely profitable. The prince also makes money with a value-added tax (19.6 percent, the same as in France), plus real estate and corporate taxes.

The glamorous romance and marriage of the American actress Grace Kelly to Prince Rainier added to Monaco's fairy-tale mystique. Grace Kelly (Prince Albert's mother) first came to Monaco to star in the 1955 Hitchcock movie *To Catch a Thief*, in which she was filmed racing along the Corniches. Later, she married the prince and adopted the country. Tragically, Monaco's much-loved Princess Grace died in a car wreck on that same Corniche in 1982. She was just 52 years old.

Monaco is a special place...there are more people in Monaco's philharmonic orchestra (about 100) than in its army (about 80 guards). The princedom is well-guarded, with police and cameras on every corner. (They say you could win a million dollars at the casino and walk to the train station in the wee hours without a worry...and I believe it.) Stamps are so few that they increase in value almost as soon as they're printed. And collectors snapped up the rare Monaco versions of euro coins (with Prince Rainier's portrait) so quickly that many locals have never even seen one.

Orientation to Monaco

The principality of Monaco consists of three distinct tourist areas: Monaco-Ville, Monte Carlo, and La Condamine. Monaco-Ville fills the rock high above everything else and is referred to by locals as Le Rocher ("The Rock"). This is the oldest section, home to the Prince's Palace and all the sights except the casino. Monte Carlo is the area around the casino (allow 40 minutes on foot from Monaco-Ville). La Condamine is the

MONACO

port (which divides Monaco-Ville and Monte Carlo). From here, it's a 15-minute walk up to the Prince's Palace or to the casino. Local buses shave time off this commute (see "Getting Around Monaco," later). A fourth, less-interesting area, Fontvieille, forms the west end of Monaco and was reclaimed from the sea by Prince Rainier in the 1970s.

Tourist Information

The main TI is at the top of the park, above the casino (Mon-Sat 9:00–19:00, Sun 10:00–12:00, 2 boulevard des Moulins, tel. 00-377/92 16 61 16 or 00-377/92 16 61 66, www.visitmonaco.com). From June to September, you might find information kiosks in the Monaco-Ville parking garage and on the port. There is also a TI desk for Monaco in Terminal 1 of Nice's airport.

Arrival in Monaco

By Bus from Nice and Villefranche-sur-Mer: See my "Quickie Riviera Bus Tour from Nice to Monaco" on page 346 to plan your route and for tips. Bus riders need to pay attention, since stops are not announced. Cap d'Ail is the town before Monaco, so be on the lookout after that (the last stop before Monaco is called Cimitière). You'll enter Monaco by passing the modern high-rises of the Fontvieille district. When you see the rocky outcrop of old Monaco, be ready to get off.

There are three stops in Monaco. Listed in order from Nice, they are: Place d'Armes (in front of a tunnel at the base of Monaco-Ville's rock), Stade Nautique (center on the port), and Casino (near the casino on avenue d'Ostende). The Place d'Armes stop is the best starting point. From there, you can walk up to Monaco-Ville and the palace (10 min straight up), or catch a local bus (line #1 or #2, details below). To reach the bus stop and steps up to Monaco-Ville, cross the street right in front of the tunnel and walk with the rock on your right for about 200 feet (good WCs at bus stop). If you prefer starting at the Casino stop, walk past Häagen-Dazs and turn right to find the casino.

For directions on returning to Nice by bus, see "Monaco Connections," near the end of this chapter.

By Train from Nice: This loooooong underground train station is in central Monaco, about a 15-minute walk to the casino or to the port, and about 25 minutes to the palace. The station has no baggage storage.

The TI and ticket windows are up the escalator at the Italy end of the station. There are four exits: three from the train platform level (one at each end and one in the middle), and one from above the platforms. To walk to the casino, use this upper exit (go up the escalator and pass the TI, then go up the elevator, then up another

Monaco

TO MENTON

N

BLVD. MOULINS

AVE. SPEL.

PARK

PLACE DU CASINO

LOEWS CASINO

CASINO

T ACCESS TO TRAIN STATION

P PARKING

B LOCAL BUS STOP

VIEW

MEDITERRANEAN SEA

PALAIS DES CONGRES & P "LE CASINO"

MONTE CARLO

MONACO-VILLE

MONTE CARLO STORY & P "LE PALAIS"

COUSTEAU AQUARIUM

BOTANICAL GARDEN

❶ Hôtel de France

❷ Boulangerie

❸ Huit et Demi Restaurant

❹ Palace Square Start of Self-Guided Walk

❺ Bus #100 to Nice: Place d'Armes Stop

❻ Bus #100 from Nice: Place d'Armes Stop

❼ Bus #100 to/from Nice: Stade Nautique Stop

❽ Bus #100 to Nice: Casino Stop

❾ Bus #100 from Nice: Casino Stop

❿ Bus #112 to Eze-le-Village & #114 to La Turbie

MONACO

escalator, exit the station, turn left on boulevard de la Princesse Charlotte, and turn right after about 5 blocks when you see the pedestrian *Casino* sign; allow 10 min).

To reach Monaco-Ville and the palace from the station, take the platform-level exit at the Nice end of the tracks (signed *Sortie Fontvieille/Monaco Ville*), which leads through a long tunnel (TI annex at end open during high season) to the foot of Monaco-Ville; turn left at the end of the walkway and hike 15 minutes up to the palace, or take the bus (#1 or #2). To reach Monaco's port, take the mid-platform exit, closer to the Italy end of the tracks (follow *Sortie la Condamine* signs down the steps and escalators, then follow *Accès Port* signs). It's a 25-minute walk from the port to the palace (to your right) or 15 minutes to the casino (to your left), or a short trip via buses #1 or #2. Avoid the exit through the glass doors at the extreme Italy end of the station.

If you plan to return to Nice by train after 20:30, when ticket windows close, buy your return tickets now or be sure to have about €4 in coins (since the ticket machines only take coins).

To take the short-but-sweet coastal **walking path** into Monaco's Fontvieille district, get off the train at Cap d'Ail, which is one stop before Monaco. Turn left out of the little station and walk 50 yards up the road, then turn left again, going downstairs and under the tracks. Turn left onto the coastal trail, and hike the 20 minutes to Fontvieille. You'll end up at Pointe des Douaniers. Once there, it's a 20-minute uphill hike to Monaco's sights (or hop on bus #100).

By Car: Follow *Centre-Ville* signs into Monaco, then watch for the red-letter signs to parking garages at *Le Casino* (for Monte Carlo) or *Le Palais* (for Monaco-Ville). The first hour of parking is free (about €4 next hr, €7/3 hrs).

Helpful Hints

Telephone Tip: To call Monaco from France, dial 00, then 377 (Monaco's country code) and the eight-digit number. Within Monaco, simply dial the eight-digit number.

Minivan Tours from Nice: Several companies offer daytime and nighttime tours of Monaco, allowing you freedom to gamble without worrying about catching the last train or bus home (see "Getting Around the Riviera," page 272).

Loop Trip by Bus: From Nice or Villefranche-sur-Mer, you can visit Monaco by bus, then take a bus from Monaco directly to Eze-le-Village (#112, no Sun bus) or La Turbie (#114, no Sun bus) and return home from there. See "Monaco Connections," near the end of this chapter for details.

MONACO

Getting Around Monaco

By Local Bus: Buses #1 and #2 link all areas (single ticket-€1, 10 tickets-€6, day pass-€3, pay driver, 10/hr, fewer on Sun, buses run until 21:00). You can split a 10-ride ticket with your travel partners. Most people need just two rides in Monaco.

By Tourist Train: "Monaco Tour" tourist trains begin at the aquarium and pass by the port, casino, and palace (€7, 2/hr, 10:30–18:00 in summer, 11:00–17:00 in winter depending on weather, 30 min, recorded English commentary).

By Taxi: If you've lost track of time at the casino, you can call the 24-hour taxi service (tel. 08 20 20 98 98)...provided you still have enough money to pay for the cab home.

Self-Guided Walk

Welcome to Monaco-Ville

All of Monaco's sights (except the casino) are in Monaco-Ville, packed within a few Disney-esque blocks. This walk makes a tidy loop around Monaco-Ville.

• *To get from anywhere in Monaco to the palace square (Monaco-Ville's sightseeing center, home of the palace and the Napoleon Collection), take bus #1 or #2 to place de la Visitation (end of the line). Turn right as you step off the bus and walk five minutes straight down either street leading from the end of the little square (the one on the left goes right past the post office, if you want Monaco stamps). If you're walking up from the port, the well-marked lane leads directly to the palace.*

Palace Square (Place du Palais): This square is the best place to get oriented to Monaco. Facing the palace, go to the right and

look out over the city (er...principality). This rock gave birth to the little pastel Hong Kong look-alike in 1215, and it's managed to remain an independent country for most of its nearly 800 years. Looking beyond the glitzy port, notice the faded green roof above and to the right: It belongs to the casino that put Monaco on the map. The famous Grand Prix runs along the port, and then up the ramp to the casino. And Italy is so close, you can almost smell the pesto. Just beyond the casino is France again (which flanks Monaco on both sides)—you could walk one-way from France to France, passing through Monaco in about 60 minutes.

The curious statue of a woman with a fishing net is dedicated to **Prince Albert I**'s glorious reign (1889–1922). Albert was a

Monaco at a Glance

▲**Casino of Monte Carlo** Classy casino that saved Monaco's economy. **Hours:** Slots and some gaming rooms—open Sept-June Mon-Fri at 14:00, Sat-Sun at 12:00, July-Aug daily at 12:00; elegant game rooms—some open Mon-Fri at 16:00 and Sat-Sun at 15:00, others at 21:00 or 22:00. Must have passport and adhere to dress code.

Prince's Palace Prince Albert's extravagant residence. **Hours:** April-Oct daily 9:30-18:00, closed Nov-March.

Napoleon Collection The prince's private collection of Napoleonic stuff, from medals, swords, and guns, to his cool *chapeau*. **Hours:** Same as Prince's Palace.

Changing of the Guard Big ceremony for a tiny nation. **Hours:** Daily at 11:55 on the palace square.

Cathedral of Monaco Final resting place for Princess Grace and Prince Rainier. **Hours:** Daily 8:30-18:45, until 18:00 in winter.

Cousteau Aquarium Jacques Cousteau's cliff-hugging aquarium. **Hours:** Daily July-Aug 9:30-19:30, April-June and Sept 9:30-19:00, Oct-March 10:00-18:00.

***Monte Carlo Story* Film** Informative 35-minute film describing Monaco's sexy history. **Hours:** Showings usually at 10:00, 11:00, 14:00, 15:00, 16:00, and 17:00; closed Dec.

Jardin Exotique Cliffside botanical garden mixing thousands of cacti and fantastic views. **Hours:** Daily mid-May-mid-Sept 9:00-19:00, mid-Sept-mid-May 9:00-18:00 or dusk.

Renaissance man with many skills and interests. He had a Jacques Cousteau–like fascination with the sea (and built Monaco's famous aquarium), and was a determined pacifist who made many attempts to dissuade Germany's Kaiser Wilhelm II from becoming involved in World War I.

• *Now walk toward the palace and find the statue of the monk grasping a sword.*

Meet **François Grimaldi,** a renegade Italian dressed as a monk, who captured Monaco in 1297 and began the dynasty that still rules the principality. Prince Albert is his great-great-great... grandson, which gives Monaco's royal family the distinction of being the longest-lasting dynasty in Europe.

• *Walk to the opposite side of the square.*

At the Louis XIV cannonballs, look down to Monaco's new-est area, the reclaimed-from-the-sea **Fontvieille** district, which has seen much of Monaco's post–World War II growth (residential and commercial—notice the lushly planted building tops). Prince Rainier continued—some say, was obsessed with—Monaco's economic growth, creating landfills (topped with apartments, such as Fontvieille), flashy ports, more beaches, and the new rail station. Today, thanks to Prince Rainier's efforts, tiny Monaco is a member of the United Nations. (If you have kids, there's a nifty play area just below on the left.)

You can buy Monaco stamps (popular collectibles, or use them to mail something from here) at the post office (PTT) a few blocks down rue Comte Félix Gastaldi.

•Backpedal a few steps to the...

Prince's Palace (Palais Princier): A medieval castle sat where Monaco's palace is today. Its strategic setting has had a lot to do with Monaco's ability to resist attackers. Today, Prince Albert lives in the palace while Princesses Stephanie and Caroline live just down the main street. The palace guards protect the prince 24/7 and still stage a **Changing of the Guard** ceremony with all the pageantry of an important nation (daily at 11:55, fun to watch but jam-packed). Audioguide tours take you through part of the prince's lavish palace in 30 minutes. The rooms are well-furnished and impressive, but interesting only if you haven't seen a château lately (€8 combo-ticket includes audioguide and the Napoleon Collection, April–Oct daily 9:30–18:00, last entry 30 min before closing, closed Nov–March, tel. 00-377/93 25 18 31).

• Next to the palace entry is the...

Napoleon Collection: Napoleon occupied Monaco after the French Revolution. This is the prince's private collection of items Napoleon left behind: military medals, swords, guns, letters, and, most interesting, his hat. I found this collection more appealing than the palace (€4 includes audioguide, €8 combo-ticket includes Prince's Palace, same hours as palace).

• With your back to the palace, leave the square through the arch to the right (under the most beautiful police station I've ever seen) and find the...

Cathedral of Monaco (Cathédrale de Monaco): The somber but beautifully lit cathedral, rebuilt in 1878 to show that Monaco cared for more than just its new casino, is where centuries of Grimaldis are buried. Circle slowly behind the altar (counterclockwise). The second tomb is that of Albert I, who did much to put Monaco

Le Grand Prix Automobile de Monaco

Each May, the Grand Prix de Monaco (May 20–23 in 2010) focuses the world's attention on this little country. The race started as an enthusiasts' car rally by the Automobile Club of Monaco (and is still run by the same group, more than 80 years later). To this day, drivers consider this one of the most important races on their circuits.

By Grand Prix standards, it's an unusual course, running through the streets of this tiny principality, sardined between mountains and sea. The hilly landscape means that the streets are narrow, with tight curves, steep climbs, and extremely short straightaways. Each lap is about two miles, beginning and ending at the port. Cars climb along the sea from the port, pass in front of the casino, race through the commercial district, and do a few dandy turns back to the port. The race lasts 78 laps, and whoever is still rolling at the end wins (most don't finish).

The Formula 1 cars look like overgrown toys that kids might pedal up and down their neighborhood street (if you're here a week or so before the race, feel free to browse the parking structure below Monaco-Ville, where many race cars are kept). Time trials to establish pole position begin three days before the race, which is always on a Sunday. In 2010, the time trials take place on May 20, 21, and 22, and the race itself is on May 23. More than 150,000 people attend the gala event; like the nearby film festival in Cannes, it's an excuse for yacht parties, splurges in fine restaurants, and staying at four-star hotels (notorious for raising their rates during this event).

on the world stage. The second-to-last tomb—inscribed *"Gratia Patricia, MCMLXXXII"*—is where Princess Grace was buried in 1982. Prince Rainier's tomb lies next to Princess Grace's (daily 8:30–18:45, until 18:00 in winter).

• *As you leave the cathedral, find the 1956 wedding photo of Princess Grace and Prince Rainier (keep an eye out for other photos of the couple as you walk), then walk left through the immaculately maintained Jardin Botanique, with more fine views. Find the...*

Cousteau Aquarium (Musée Océanographique): Prince Albert I built this impressive, cliff-hanging aquarium in 1910 as a monument to his enthusiasm for things from the sea. As 2010 marks its 100th anniversary, expect special exhibits and activities; a major exhibit on the biodiversity of the Mediterranean is planned. The aquarium, which Captain Jacques Cousteau directed for 32 years, has 2,000 different specimens, representing 250 species. The bottom floor features Mediterranean fish and colorful tropical species (all nicely described in English). My favorite was the zebra lionfish, though I'm keen on eels too. Rotating exhibits occupy the entry floor. Upstairs, the fancy Albert I Hall houses a museum (included in entry fee, very little English information) and features ship models, whale skeletons, oceanographic instruments and tools, and scenes of Albert and his beachcombers hard at work. Find the display on Christopher Columbus with English explanations. Don't miss the elevator to the rooftop terrace view, where you'll also find convenient WCs and a reasonable café (€13.50, kids-€8, daily July–Aug 9:30–19:30, April–June and Sept 9:30–19:00, Oct–March 10:00–18:00; down the steps from Monaco-Ville bus stop, at the opposite end of Monaco-Ville from the palace; tel. 00-377/93 15 36 00, www.oceano.mc).

• *The red-brick steps, across from the aquarium to the right, lead up to buses #1 and #2, both of which run to the port, the casino, and the train station. To walk back to the palace and through the old city, turn left at the top of the brick steps. For a brief movie break, take the escalator to the right of the aquarium as you leave it and drop into the parking garage, then take the elevator down and find the...*

Monte Carlo Story: This informative 35-minute film gives an entertaining account of Monaco's history and offers a comfortable, soft-chair break from all that walking (€7, headphone commentary in English; daily showings usually on the hour at 10:00, 11:00, 14:00, 15:00, 16:00, and 17:00; closed Dec, you can join frequent extra showings for groups on summer mornings, tel. 00-377/93 25 32 33).

Sights in Monaco

Above Monaco-Ville

Jardin Exotique—This cliffside municipal garden, located above Monaco-Ville, has eye-popping views from France to Italy. It's a fascinating home to more than a thousand species of cacti (some giant) and other succulent plants, but probably worth the entry only for view-loving botanists (some posted English explanations provided). Your ticket includes entry to a skippable natural cave and an anthropological museum, as well as a not-to-be-missed view snack bar/café (€7, daily mid-May–mid-Sept 9:00–19:00, mid-Sept–mid-May 9:00–18:00 or until dusk, tel. 00-377/93 15 29 80). Bus #2 runs here from any stop in Monaco, and makes for a worthwhile mini tour of the country, even if you don't visit the gardens. You can get similar views over Monaco for free from behind the souvenir stand at the Jardin's bus stop; or, for even grander vistas, cross the street and hike toward La Turbie.

In Monte Carlo

▲**Casino**—Monte Carlo, which means "Charles' Hill" in Spanish, is named for the local prince who presided over Monaco's 19th-century makeover. Begin your visit opposite Europe's most famous casino, in the park above the pedestrian-unfriendly traffic circle. In the mid-1800s, olive groves stood here. Then, with the construction of the casino, spas, and easy road and train access, one of Europe's poorest countries was on the Grand Tour map—*the* place for the vacationing aristocracy to play. Today, Monaco has the world's highest per-capita income.

The casino is intended to make the wealthy feel comfortable while losing money. Charles Garnier designed the place (with an opera house inside) in 1878, in part to thank the prince for his financial help in completing Paris' Opéra Garnier (which the architect also designed). The central doors provide access to slot machines, private gaming rooms, and the opera house. The private gaming rooms occupy the left wing of the building.

Count the counts and Rolls-Royces in front of Hôtel de Paris (built at the same time, visitors allowed but not with shorts on, www.montecarloresort.com), then strut inside past the slots to the sumptuous atrium. This is the lobby for the opera house (open only for performances). There's a model of the opera at the end of the room, and marble WCs on the right. If you're over 21, you can try your luck at the one-armed bandits (push button on slot machines to claim your winnings). If it's before 20:00, shorts are allowed at the slots, though you'll need decent attire to go any farther. After 20:00, shorts are off-limits everywhere.

The scene, flooded with camera-toting tourists during the day, is great at night—and downright James Bond–like in the private rooms. The park behind the casino offers a peaceful café and a good view of the building's rear facade and of Monaco-Ville.

If paying an entrance fee to lose money is not your idea of fun, you can access all games for free in the new, plebeian, American-style Loews Casino, adjacent to the old casino.

Cost and Hours: The slot machines and the first gaming rooms *(salons européens)* open Sept–June Mon–Fri at 14:00 and Sat–Sun at 12:00; July–Aug daily at 12:00. Slots are free, but you'll pay €10 to enter *les salons européens*. Most of the glamorous private game rooms open Mon–Fri at 16:00 and Sat–Sun at 15:00, though some don't open until 21:00 or 22:00. Here you can rub elbows with high rollers—provided you're 18 or older (bring your passport for proof) and properly attired (tie and jacket for men, dress standards for women are far more relaxed—only tennis shoes are a definite no-no). Men might be able to rent a tie and jacket at a nearby store (ask at the TI or casino before you go, casino tel. 00-377/92 16 20 00, www.montecarlocasinos.com).

Take the Money and Run: The return bus stop to Nice is at the top of the park, above the casino on avenue de la Costa (under the arcade to the left). To return to the train station from the casino, walk up the parkway in front of the casino, turn left on boulevard des Moulins (becomes avenue de la Costa), and walk through the posh mall at the bus stop. Find the rear escalator, climb a few steps, and turn left on boulevard de la Princesse Charlotte. You'll walk about 10 minutes, passing a Novotel (the entrance to the train station is at the Parking de la Gare). Once in the building, escalate, then elevate down to the station.

Sleeping and Eating in Monaco

(€1 = about $1.40, country code: 377)
$$ Hôtel de France, run by friendly Sylvie, is centrally located, spotlessly maintained, reasonably priced, and perfectly pleasant (Db-€90–115, Tb-€110–140, includes breakfast, no air-con, Wi-Fi, 6 rue de la Turbie, near west exit from train station, tel. 00-377/93 30 24 64, fax 00-377/92 16 13 34, www.monte-carlo.mc/france, hotel-france@monte-carlo.mc).

Several cafés serve basic, inexpensive fare (day and night) on the port. I prefer the eateries that line the flowery and traffic-free rue de la Princesse Caroline, which runs between rue Grimaldi and the port. The best this street has to offer is **Huit et Demi**. It has a white-tablecloth-meets-director's-chair ambience, mostly outdoor tables, and cuisine worth returning for (€13 salads, €15 pizzas, €18–24 *plats*, closed Sat for lunch and all day Sun, 7 rue de la Princesse Caroline, tel. 00-377/93 50 97 02).

In Monaco-Ville, you'll find incredible *pan bagnat* (*salade niçoise* sandwich), quiche, and sandwiches at the yellow-bannered **Boulangerie,** a block off Palace Square (open daily until 19:00, 8 rue Basse). Try the local *barbajuan* (a spring roll-size beignet with wheat, rice, and parmesan), or the focaccia sandwich (salted bread with herbs, mozzarella, basil, and tomatoes, all drenched in olive oil). For dessert, order the *fougasse monégasque* (a soft-bread pastry topped with sliced almonds and anise candies). Monaco-Ville has many pizzerias, crêperies, and sandwich stands, but the neighborhood is dead at night. If you're here in the evening, eat near the port.

MONACO

Monaco Connections

From Monaco by Train to: Nice (2/hr, 20 min, €3.50), **Villefranche-sur-Mer** (2/hr, 10 min), **Antibes** (2/hr, 45–60 min).

By Bus to: Nice (#100, 4/hr Mon–Sat, 3/hr Sun, 45 min, €1), **Nice Airport** (#110 express on the freeway, hourly, 50 min, €18), **Villefranche-sur-Mer** (#100, 4/hr Mon–Sat, 3/hr Sun, 25 min, €1), **Eze-le-Village** (#112, 7/day Mon–Sat, none on Sun, 25 min), **La Turbie** (#114, 6/day Mon–Fri, 3/day Sat morning only, none on Sun, 20 min), **Menton** (#100, 4/hr Mon–Sat, 3/hr Sun, 15 min).

The Monaco-to-Nice bus (#100) is not identified at every stop—verify with a local by asking, *"Direction Nice?"* There's a handy stop below Monaco-Ville at place d'Armes (on the main road to Nice in front of the Brasserie Monte Carlo). Another is a few blocks above the casino on avenue de la Costa (under the arcade to the left of Barclays Bank).

Buses #112 (to Eze-le-Village) and #114 (to La Turbie) depart Monaco from place de la Crémaillère, one block above the main TI and casino park. Walk up rue Iris with Barclays Bank to your left, curve right, and find the bus shelter across the street by the Costa à la Crémaillère café. Bus numbers for these routes are not posted, but this is the stop.

Last Call: The last bus leaves Monaco for Villefranche-sur-Mer and Nice at about 20:00; the last train leaves Monaco for Villefranche-sur-Mer and Nice at about 23:30. If you plan to leave Monaco by train after 20:30, buy your tickets in advance (since the window will be closed), or bring enough coins for the machines.

Near Monaco: Menton

If you wish the Riviera were less glitzy and more like a place where humble locals take their families to lick ice cream and make sand castles, visit Menton (15 minutes by bus beyond Monaco). Menton feels like a poor man's Nice. It's unrefined and unpretentious, with lower prices, fewer rentable umbrellas, and lots of Italians day-tripping in from just over the border (five miles away). There's not an American in sight.

The Menton beach, while a bit rough, is a joy. An inviting promenade lines the beach, and seaside cafés serve light meals and salads (much cheaper than in Nice). A snooze or stroll here is a fine Riviera experience. From the promenade, a pedestrian street leads through town. Small squares are alive with jazz bands playing crowd-pleasers under palm trees.

Stepping into the old town—which blankets a hill capped by a fascinating cemetery—you're immersed in a pastel-painted, yet dark and tangled Old World scene with (strangely) almost no commerce. A few elegant restaurants dig in at the base of the towering centuries-old apartment flats. The richly decorated Baroque St. Michael's Church (midway up the hill) is a reminder that, until 1860, Menton was a thriving part of the larger state of Monaco. Climbing past sun-grabbing flower boxes and people who don't get out much anymore, the steep stepped lanes finally deposit you at the ornate gate of a grand cemetery that fills the old castle walls. Explore the cemetery, which is the final resting place of many aristocratic Russians (buried here in the early 1900s) and offers breathtaking Mediterranean views.

Getting to Menton: While trains serve Menton regularly, the station is a 15-minute walk from the action. Buses are more convenient, as they drop visitors right on the beach promenade (#100, 4/hr Mon–Sat, 3/hr Sun, 1 hr from Nice, 15 min past Monaco, €1; see my self-guided bus tour on page 347).

ANTIBES, CANNES, AND ST-TROPEZ

The Riviera opens up west of Nice with bigger, sandier beaches and an overabundance of tasteless beachfront development. Ancient Antibes and superficial Cannes buck the blue-collar high-rise trend, each with thriving centers busy with pedestrians and yachts. Trendy St-Tropez, a scenic 1.5-hour drive from Antibes, marks the western edge of the French Riviera.

Antibes

Antibes has a down-to-earth, easygoing ambience that's rare in this area. Its old town is a maze of narrow streets and red-tile roofs rising above the blue Med, protected by twin medieval towers and wrapped in extensive ramparts. Visitors making the short trip from Nice browse Europe's biggest yacht harbor, snooze on a sandy beach, loiter through an enjoyable old town, and hike along a sea-swept trail. The town's cultural claim to fame, the Picasso Museum, shows off its great collection in a fine old building.

Though much smaller than Nice, Antibes has a history that dates back just as far. Both towns were founded by Greek traders in the fifth century B.C. To the Greeks, Antibes was "Antipolis"—the town *(polis)* opposite *(anti)* Nice. For the next several centuries, Antibes remained in the shadow of its neighbor. By the turn of the 20th century, the town was a military base—so the rich and famous partied elsewhere. But when the army checked out after World War I, Antibes was "discovered" and enjoyed a particularly roaring '20s—with the help of party animals like Rudolph Valentino and the rowdy (yet very silent) Charlie Chaplin. Fun-seekers even invented water-skiing right here in the 1920s.

Orientation to Antibes

Antibes' old town lies between the port and boulevard Albert 1er and avenue Robert Soleau. Place Nationale is the old town's hub

of activity. The restaurant-lined rue Aubernon connects the port and the old town. Stroll along the sea between the old port and place Albert 1er (where boulevard Albert 1er meets the water). The best beaches lie just beyond place Albert 1er, and the path is beautiful. Good play areas for children

are along this path and on place des Martyrs de la Résistance (close to recommended Hôtel Relais du Postillon).

Tourist Information

Antibes has two TIs. The most convenient is in the old town, just inside the walls at 32 boulevard d'Aguillon (Mon–Sat 10:00–12:00 & 13:30–18:00, closed Sun, tel. 04 93 34 65 65). The *Maison de Tourisme* is in the newer city, where the fountains squirt at 11 place Général de Gaulle (where boulevard Albert 1er and rue de la République meet; July–Aug daily 9:00–19:00; Sept–June Mon–Sat 9:00–12:30 & 13:30–18:00, Sun 9:00–12:00; tel. 04 97 23 11 11, www.antibesjuanlespins.com). At either TI, pick up the excellent city map and the self-guided walking tour of old Antibes, and get details on the hikes described below. The Nice TI has Antibes maps—plan ahead.

Arrival in Antibes

By Train: To get to the port, the old town, and the Picasso Museum (15–20-min walk), cross the street in front of the station, skirting left of the Piranha Café, and follow avenue de la Libération downhill as it bends left. At the end of the street, the port will be in front of you and the old town to the right.

To walk directly to my hotels and to the main TI in the modern city (10-min walk to TI), exit right from the station on avenue Robert Soleau; follow *Centre-Ville* and *Office du Tourisme* signs to place Général de Gaulle.

The last train back to Nice leaves at about midnight.

By Bus: Slow bus #200 stops a few blocks from the TI (turn right as you leave the TI to find the stops just off boulevard Dugommier: buses from Nice and to Cannes stop on avenue Aristide Briand; buses to Nice and from Cannes stop on boulevard Gustave Chancel). Buses from other destinations use the bus station at the edge of the old town on place Guynemer, a block

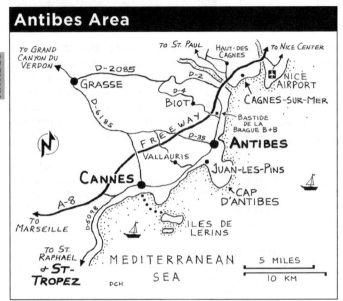

Antibes Area

to Grand Canyon du Verdon
to St. Paul
Haut-des Cagnes
to Nice Center
D-2085
GRASSE
D-2
D-4
BIOT
NICE AIRPORT
CAGNES-SUR-MER
D-6185
BASTIDE DE LA BRAGUE B+B
FREEWAY
D-35
ANTIBES
N
VALLAURIS
JUAN-LES-PINS
CANNES
CAP D'ANTIBES
A-8
D-6098
to Marseille
ILES DE LERINS
to St. Raphael + St-Tropez
MEDITERRANEAN SEA
5 MILES
10 KM
DCH

below the old town TI (info desk open Mon–Sat 8:30–12:00 & 14:30–17:30, closed Sun).

By Car: Day-trippers follow signs to *Centre-Ville*, then *Port Vauban*, and park near the old town walls (first 30 min free, then about €2.50/hr). Walk into the old town through the last arch on the right.

If you're sleeping here, follow *Centre-Ville* signs, then signs to your hotel, and get advice from your hotelier on where to park. (Most have free parking.) The most appealing hotels in Antibes are easiest by car. Antibes works well for drivers; compared to Nice, parking is easy, it's a breeze to navigate, and it's a convenient springboard for the Inland Riviera. Pay parking is usually available at Antibes' train station, so drivers can ditch their cars and day-trip from Antibes by train.

Helpful Hints

Monday, Monday: Avoid Antibes on Mondays, when all sights are closed.

Internet Access: The TI keeps an updated list of Internet cafés.

English Bookstore: Heidi's English Bookshop has a welcoming vibe and a great selection of new and used books, including my guidebooks (daily May–Sept 10:00–19:00, Oct–April 11:00–18:00, 24 rue Aubernon).

Laundry: Smiling **Madame Hallepau** will do your laundry while you swim. Her launderette is above the market hall on rue de la Pompe (Mon–Fri 8:30–12:00 & 15:00–18:30, closed Sat–Sun).

Grocery Store: Picnickers will appreciate the **Casino market** (daily until 22:00 in summer, until 21:00 off-season, where rue Sade meets place Nationale).

Taxi: Call 08 25 56 07 07 or 04 93 67 67 67.

Electric Bike and Scooter Rental: Energy Scoot has what you need to scoot along in style (88 boulevard Wilson, tel. 04 93 61 83 98, www.energy-scoot.fr).

Car Rental: The big-name agencies have offices in Antibes—the most central are **Avis** (32 boulevard Albert 1er, tel. 04 93 34 65 15) and **Hertz** (across from the train station at 46 avenue Robert Soleau, tel. 04 93 61 18 15). **Europcar** is less central, at 106 route de Grasse (tel. 04 93 34 79 79). These offices are closed 12:00-14:00 and Sundays.

Airport Bus: Bus #200 runs from near the main TI to Nice's airport (2–3/hr, about 45 min depending on traffic; to find the bus stop, see "Arrival in Antibes," earlier).

Getting Around Antibes

While most sights and activities are walkable, **bus #2** provides handy access to the best beaches, the path to La Phare de la Garoupe, and the Cap d'Antibes trail (all described later in this chapter). It runs from the bus station down boulevard Albert 1er, with stops every few blocks. You get three hours of travel for €1 (daily 7:00–19:00, about 2/hr, www.envibus.fr). Pick up a schedule for return times for this and other regional buses at the bus station.

A **tourist train** offers circuits around old Antibes, the port, the ramparts, and to Juan-les-Pins (€7, departs from place de la Poste, mobile 06 03 35 61 35).

Self-Guided Walk

Welcome to Antibes

This 40-minute amble will help you get your bearings, and works well day or night. Begin at the old port (Vieux Port) at the end of

avenue de Verdun (parking right there). You're standing across the street from an arch leading into the old town. Locals claim that this is Europe's first and biggest pleasure-boat harbor, with 1,600 stalls, and is the model for many others. That old four-pointed structure crowning the opposite

Antibes

1 To Hôtel Pension le Mas Djoliba
2 To Hôtels La Jabotte, Beau Site & Restaurant de Bacon
3 To Bastide de la Brague
4 Modern Hôtel
5 Hôtel Relais du Postillon
6 Hôtel le Cameo
7 La Marmite Restaurant
8 L'Aubergine Restaurant
9 Le Broc en Bouche Restaurant
10 Le Vauban Restaurant
11 Le Brulot & Le Brulot Pasta
12 Les Vieux Murs Restaurant
13 Casino Grocery
14 Heidi's English Bookshop
15 Launderette
16 Bus #200 from Nice & to Cannes
17 Bus #200 from Cannes to Nice/Nice Airport
18 Avis Car Rental
19 Hertz Car Rental
20 Europcar Car Rental
21 Electric Bike Rental

→ SELF-GUIDED WALK
P PARKING
→ ONE-WAY STREET

200 YARDS
200 METERS

end of the port is **Fort Carré** (described later in this chapter), which protected Antibes from foreigners for more than 500 years.

The pathetic remains of a once-hearty **fishing fleet** are moored in front of you. The Mediterranean is pretty much fished out. Most of the seafood you'll eat here comes from fish farms or the Atlantic.

Pass the sorry fleet with the port on your left and find the entry to the shell-shaped **plage de la Gravette,** a normally quiet public beach tucked right in the middle of old Antibes. Wander up the ramp to the round lookout to better appreciate the scale of the ramparts that protected this town. Because Antibes was the last fort before the Italian border, the French king made sure the ramparts were strong and well-defended—this must have been some tower. The

twin towers crowning the old town are the church's bell tower and the tower topping Château Grimaldi (today's Picasso Museum). Forested Cap d'Antibes is the point of land in the distance, with a terrific sea-soaked walking trail (see "Cap d'Antibes Hike," later in this chapter).

Backtrack and enter Antibes' **old town** through the arch under the rampart. Today, the town is the haunt of a large community of English, Irish, and Aussie boaters who help crew those giant yachts in Antibes' port. (That helps explain the Irish pubs and English bookstores.) Continue straight and uphill (halfway up on the right,

you'll pass rue Clemenceau, which leads to the heart of the old town), and you'll arrive at Antibes' **market hall** (Tue–Sun until 13:00, closed Mon except June–Aug). Like many other places in Antibes, this hall does double duty...it's filled with café tables at night.

Go left where the market starts (rue Chessel) and find Antibes' pretty pastel **Church of the Immaculate Conception,** built on the site of a Greek temple (worth a peek inside). A church has stood on this site since the 12th century. This one served as the area's cathedral until the mid-1200s. The stone bell tower stands apart from the church and predates it by 600 years, when it was part of the city's defenses. Those heavy stones were pillaged from Antibes' Roman monuments.

Looming above the church on prime real estate is the white-stone **Château Grimaldi,** where you'll find Antibes' prized **Picasso Museum** (described below, under "Sights in Antibes"). This site has been home to the acropolis of the Greek city of Antipolis, a Roman fort, and a medieval bishop's palace (once connected to the cathedral below). The château was the residence of the Grimaldi family (who still rule Monaco). Its proximity to the cathedral symbolized the sometimes too-cozy relationship between society's two dominant landowning classes: the Church and the nobility. (In 1789, the French Revolution changed all that.)

Find your way to the water and, heading right, follow the ramparts and views to the **History and Archaeology Museum.** From the terrace above the museum, you'll get a clear view of **Cap d'Antibes,** crowned by its lighthouse and studded with mansions (see "Cap d'Antibes Hike," later in this chapter). The Cap was long the refuge of Antibes' rich and famous, and a favorite haunt of F. Scott Fitzgerald and Ernest Hemingway. After a quick tour of the museum (described later), continue hugging the shore past place Albert 1er until you see the views back to old Antibes. Benches and soft sand await (a few copies of famous artists' paintings of Antibes are placed on bronze displays along the beach walkway). You're on your own from here—energetic walkers can continue to the view from the Phare de la Garoupe (see page 374); others can return to old Antibes and poke around in its peaceful back lanes.

Sights in Antibes

▲▲**Picasso Museum (Musée Picasso)**—Sitting serenely where the old town meets the sea, this compact three-floor museum offers a top collection of Picasso's paintings, sketches, and ceram-

ics. Picasso lived in this castle for four months in 1946, when he cranked out an amazing amount of art. Elated by the end of World War II, his works show a celebration of color and a rediscovery of light after France's long nightmare of war. Picasso was also inspired by his young and lovely companion, Françoise Gilot (with whom he would father two children). The resulting collection (donated by Picasso) put Antibes on the tourist map. You'll see many of his ceramics: plates with faces, bird-shaped vases, woman-shaped bottles, bull-shaped statues, and colorful tiles.

Cost and Hours: €6; mid-June–mid-Sept Tue–Sun 10:00–18:00, some summer evenings until 20:00; mid-Sept–mid-June Tue–Sun 10:00–12:00 & 14:00–18:00; closed Mon year-round, last entry 30 min before closing, tel. 04 92 90 54 20, www.antibes-juanlespins.com/eng/culture/musees.

➲ **Self-Guided Tour:** After entering, stroll outside for the view and appreciate Picasso's working environment (and wonder why he only spent four months here). The museum's interior is a soft, white world of arches and walls with ample natural light—making it a fine space for exhibiting art. The ground floor houses a permanent collection of 20th-century works by other Antibes residents and key contributors to the museum's founding, Hans Hartung and his partner, Anna-Eva Bergmann. Their work blends well with what you'll see by Picasso. The first floor up holds a small collection of pieces by Nicolas de Staël and exhibits of other modern artists that change annually.

The highlight for most is the top floor, where you'll find the permanent collection of Picasso's works, including his lively, frolicking *La Joie de Vivre* painting (from 1946). This large (4 feet by 8 feet) Greek bacchanal sums up the newfound freedom in a newly liberated France and sets the tone for the rest of the collection. You'll also see paintings with mythological figures and stories, including *Ulysses and the Sirens* and *Satyr, Faun, and Centaur with Trident*. There are also several Cubist-style nudes *(nus couchés)* and the *Antipolis Suite*—a series of 25 (mostly reclining) nudes, very simplified and stripped-down in style. These works demonstrate Picasso's cartoonist and caricaturist skills.

Don't miss the large collection of his ceramic creations. Inspired by a visit to a ceramics factory in nearby Vallauris, Picasso was smitten by the texture of soft clay and devoted a great deal of time to exploring this medium—producing over 2,000 pieces in one year.

History and Archaeology Museum (Musée d'Histoire et d'Archéologie)—More than 2,000 years ago, Antibes was the center of a thriving maritime culture. It became an important Roman city, featuring many of the hallmarks of Roman civilization—aqueducts, theaters, baths, and so on. This museum—the only place to get a sense of the city's ancient roots—displays Greek, Roman, and Etruscan odds and ends in two easy-to-visit rooms (no English descriptions, though the small museum brochure offers some background in English). Your visit starts at an 1894 model of Antibes and continues past displays of Roman coins, cups, plates, and scads of amphorae. The curious, long, lead pipe connected to a center box was used as a bilge pump; nearby is a good display of Roman anchors (€3, Tue–Sun 10:00–13:00 & 14:00–17:00, closed Mon, on the water between Picasso Museum and place Albert 1er, tel. 04 93 34 00 39, www.antibes-juanlespins .com/eng/culture/musees).

▲Market Hall (Marché Provençal)—The daily market bustles under a 19th-century canopy, with flowers, produce, Provençal products, and beach accessories (in the old town, behind Picasso Museum on cours Masséna). The market wears many hats: produce daily until 13:00, handicrafts Thursday through Sunday in the afternoon, and fun outdoor dining in the evenings (market closed Mon Sept–May).

Other Markets and Squares—Antibes' lively antiques/flea market fills place Nationale and place Audiberti (next to the port) on Thursdays and Saturdays (7:00–18:00). Its clothing market winds through the streets around the post office (rue Lacan) on Thursdays (9:00–18:00). Place Général de Gaulle, a pleasing, palm-studded, and fountain-flowing square in Antibes' modern city, is the trendy place to be seen.

Fort Carré—This impressively situated citadel, dating from 1487, was the last fort inside France. It protected Antibes from Nice, which until 1860 was part of Italy. You can tour this unusual four-pointed fort for the fantastic views, but there's little to see inside (€3, includes tour, Tue–Sun June–Sept 10:00–18:00, Oct–May 10:00–16:30, closed Mon).

It's a pleasant 30-minute portside walk from the old town to the fort (or taxi there and walk back). By foot or car, follow avenue du 11 Novembre around the port, and stay on the main road (walkers can follow the path by sports fields); drivers can park for free just after the soccer field. A signed dirt path leads to Fort Carré. Keep following the green-lettered *Le Fort/Sens de la Visite* signs.

▲Beaches (*Plages*)—The best beaches stretch between Antibes' port and Cap d'Antibes. The first you'll cross is the plage Publique (no rentals required). Next are the groomed plages de la Salis

and du Ponteil, with mattress, umbrella, and towel rental. All are busy but manageable in summer and on weekends, with cheap snack stands and exceptional views of the old town. The closest beach to the old town is at the port (plage de la Gravette), which seems calm in any season.

ANTIBES

Walks and Hikes

From place Albert 1er (where boulevard Albert 1er meets the beach), you get a good view of plage de la Salis and Cap d'Antibes. That tower on the hill is your destination for the first walk described below. The longer "Cap d'Antibes Hike" begins on the next beach, just over that hill.

▲▲Chapelle et Phare de la Garoupe—The territorial views—good at sunset, best at sunrise, skippable if hazy—from this viewpoint more than merit the 20-minute uphill climb from the plage de la Salis (a few blocks after Maupassant Apartments, where the road curves left, follow signs and the rough, cobbled chemin du Calvaire up to lighthouse tower). An orientation table explains that you can see from Nice to Cannes and up to the Alps. Take bus #2 to the plage de la Salis stop and find the trail a block ahead. By car, follow signs for *Cap d'Antibes,* then look for *Chapelle et Phare de la Garoupe* signs.

▲Cap d'Antibes Hike (Sentier Touristique Piétonnier de Tirepoil)—At the end of the mattress-ridden plage de la Garoupe (over the hill from Phare de la Garoupe lighthouse) lies a remark-

able trail around the tip of Cap d'Antibes. The beautiful path undulates above a splintered coastline splashed by turquoise water and peppered with exclusive mansions. You'll walk for two miles, then head inland along small streets, ending at the recommended Hôtel Beau-Site (and bus stop). You can walk as far as you'd like and then double back, or do the whole loop (allow 2.5 hours at most, use the TI's Antibes map). Bring good shoes, as the walkway is uneven and slippery in places. Sundays are busiest.

To get to the trail from Antibes, take bus #2 from the bus station or along boulevard Albert 1er for about 15 minutes to the La Fontaine stop at Hôtel Beau-Site (return stop is 50 yards away on opposite side, get return times at station). Walk 10 minutes down to plage de la Garoupe and start from there. By car, follow signs to *Cap d'Antibes,* then *plage de la Garoupe,* and park there. The trail begins at the far-right end of plage de la Garoupe.

Near Antibes

Juan-les-Pins—This soulless village, across the Cap d'Antibes isthmus from Antibes, is where the action is in the evenings. It's a modern beach resort with good beaches, plenty of lively bars and restaurants, and a popular jazz festival in July. Buses, trains, and even a tourist train (see "Getting Around Antibes," earlier in this chapter) make the 10-minute trip to and from Antibes constantly.

Marineland and Parc de la Mer—A few backstrokes from Antibes, Parc de la Mer is a world of waterslides, miniature golf, exhibits, and more. Marineland anchors this sea-park extravaganza with French-language shows featuring dolphins, sea lions, and killer whales (Marineland only—€38, kids-€28, €2 more in July–Aug and €6 less in winter; Aquasplash waterslide park—€24, kids-€20, closed in winter; the whole shebang—€44, kids-€35; various combo-tickets available for Aquasplash waterslides, miniature golf, and other attractions; daily 10:00–19:00, until 22:00 July–Aug, tel. 04 93 33 49 49, www.marineland.fr).

Getting There: The park is a short walk from the train station in nearby Biot (5 min from Antibes) and about 15 minutes from Antibes' bus station on buses #200 or #7. By car, the park is signed from RN-7, several miles from Antibes toward Nice.

Renoir Museum (Musée Renoir)—Halfway between Antibes and Nice, above Cagnes-sur-Mer, Pierre Auguste Renoir found his Giverny. This is where the artist spent the last 12 years of his life (1907–1919) tending his gardens, painting, and even dabbling in sculpture (despite suffering from rheumatoid arthritis). His home has been converted into a small museum, where visitors get a very personal look into Renoir's

later years. You'll see his studio, wheelchair, and bedroom, stroll in his gardens, and enjoy several of his and other artists' paintings of people and places around Cagnes-sur-Mer. It's a pleasant place and a must-see for his fans (€3, May–Sept Wed–Mon 10:00–12:00 & 14:00–18:00, closed Tue, Oct–April closes at 17:00, chemin des Collettes, tel. 04 93 20 61 07, www.cagnes-tourisme.com).

Getting There: Take bus #200 to Cagnes-sur-Mer (ask the driver for stop closest to the museum: *Musée Renoir? Quel arrêt?*, mew-zay reh-nwah kehl ah-reh), then walk uphill 15 minutes to the museum. The train stops downhill from the museum as well (40-min uphill walk to the museum—take a cab). Drivers go to Cagnes-sur-Mer, then follow brown *Musée Renoir* signs.

More Day Trips from Antibes—Antibes is halfway between Nice and Cannes (easy train and bus service to both), and close to the artsy pottery and glassblowing village of **Biot,** home of the Fernand Léger Museum as well as the Parc de la Mer (mentioned above; Biot easy to reach on frequent bus #200). The best parking is just above the town, allowing direct access to its pretty pedestrian street.

Another pottery center, **Vallauris,** is a striking hill town and a must for lovers of blown glass. Picasso fans will enjoy his murals in the Chapel of War and Peace (bus #5 from Antibes bus station, bus #200 from near the main TI, or go by train to Golfe-Juan-Vallauris—3/hr, 6 min, get details at local TIs).

Sleeping in Antibes

My favorite Antibes hotels require a car or taxi. Pickings are slim when it comes to centrally located hotels in this city, where restaurants are a dime a dozen but hotels play hard to get.

Outside the Town Center

$$$ Hôtel Pension le Mas Djoliba* ** is a good splurge, better for drivers (15–20-min walk from the beach and old Antibes, and a 25-min walk from the train station). Reserve early for this tranquil, bird-chirping, flower-filled manor house where no two rooms are the same. From May to September, they definitely prefer (but won't insist) that you dine here. It's hard to pass up once you see the setting—after a busy day of sightseeing, dinner by the pool is a treat. The bigger rooms are well worth the small additional cost (Db-€120–180, Db with breakfast and dinner-€170–250; several good family rooms-€190–260, figure €90 per person with breakfast and dinner; air-con, Wi-Fi, cool *boules* court and loaner balls, 29 avenue de Provence; from boulevard Albert 1er, look for blue signs as you approach the beach and turn right up avenue Gaston Bourgeois; tel. 04 93 34 02 48, fax 04 93 34 05 81, www.hotel-djoliba.com, contact@hotel-djoliba.com).

$$$ Hôtel La Jabotte ** defies the rules. Hidden along an ignored alley a block from the famous beaches and a 15-minute walk from the old town, this cozy place is run by owners who care. Yves, Claude, and dog Tommy have turned a small beach villa into a boutique hotel with personality: The colors are rich, the decor shows a personal touch, and most rooms have individual terraces facing a small, central garden where you'll get to know your neighbor (Db-€108–121, includes good breakfast and a few parking spots, no air-con, Wi-Fi, 13 avenue Max Maurey, take the third right after passing the big Hôtel Josse, tel. 04 93 61 45 89, fax 04 93 61 07 04, www.jabotte.com, info@jabotte.com).

$$ Hôtel Beau Site* ** is my only listing on Cap d'Antibes, a 10-minute drive from the old town (look for the blue sign). It's a terrific value if you want to get away...but not *too* far away. (But if you don't have a car, you'll feel isolated.) This place is a sanctuary, with sweet Nathalie in charge, a pool, a comfy patio garden, and easy parking. Eleven rooms have balconies (standard Db-€90,

Sleep Code

(€1 = about $1.40, country code: 33)
S = Single, **D** = Double/Twin, **T** = Triple, **Q** = Quad, **b** = bathroom, **s** = shower only, ***** = French hotel rating (0–4 stars). Unless otherwise noted, credit cards are accepted and English is spoken.

To help you sort easily through these listings, I've divided the rooms into three categories based on the price for a standard double room with bath:

$$$ Higher Priced—Most rooms €100 or more.
$$ Moderately Priced—Most rooms between €70–100.
$ Lower Priced—Most rooms €70 or less.

bigger Db-€125, even bigger Db-€160, family rooms-€175–230, extra bed-€25; huge breakfast-€12.50, continental breakfast-€6.50, air-con, Wi-Fi, bikes available, 141 boulevard Kennedy, tel. 04 93 61 53 43, fax 04 93 67 78 16, www.hotelbeausite.net, hbeausit @club-internet.fr). From the hotel, it's a 10-minute walk down to the plage de la Garoupe and a nearby hiking trail (described earlier, under "Walks and Hikes").

$$ Bastide de la Brague is an easygoing seven-room bed-and-breakfast hacienda in no-man's-land, up a dirt road above Marineland (10-min drive east of Antibes). But the place is a find as it's central to Riviera sights and run by a fun-loving family (wife Isabelle, who speaks English, hubby Franck, and Mama). Rooms are quite comfortable, air-conditioned, and affordable; several are made for families. Request the €22 home-cooked dinner and you'll get the works—from apéritif to coffee and everything in between (costs less for kids). There's enough space to stretch out, and they adore families (Db-€75–95, Tb/Qb-€95–115, includes breakfast, 55 avenue No. 6, Antibes 06600, tel. 04 93 65 73 78, www.bbchambre antibes.com, bb06@wanadoo.fr). Ask about their reasonably priced cooking lessons for small groups. Franck is happy to take guests on a private boat tour of the coast (allow €40 per person for all afternoon, 4 people minimum). From Antibes, follow signs that read *Nice par Bord de la Mer*, turn left toward Brague and Marineland, then right at the roundabout (toward Groules), then take the first left and follow signs.

In the Town Center

$$ Modern Hôtel**, in the pedestrian zone near the bus station, is a solid value for budget-conscious travelers. The 17 standard-size rooms—each with air-conditioning, bright decor, and Wi-Fi—are simple, spick-and-span, and well-run by Laurence (Sb-€60–70, Db-€68–88, 1 rue Fourmillière, tel. 04 92 90 59 05, fax 04 92 90 59 06, www.modernhotel06.com, modern-hotel@wanadoo.fr).

$$ Hôtel Relais du Postillon** is a mellow place on a central square above a peaceful café. Gregory and Johanna rent 3 cheap true singles and 12 well-designed doubles with small balconies, but no air-conditioning (Sb-€48, Db-€74–98, price varies by room size, most have tight bathrooms, Wi-Fi, 8 rue Championnet, tel. 04 93 34 20 77, fax 04 93 34 61 24, www.relaisdupostillon.com, relais@relaisdupostillon.com).

$ Hôtel le Cameo** is a busy café that rents a few basic rooms upstairs for needy travelers. All open onto the boisterous place Nationale, which means you don't sleep until the restaurant sleeps (Ds-€66, Db-€66–76, Tb-€66–78, Qb-€82, 5 place Nationale, tel. 04 93 34 24 17, fax 04 93 34 35 80, no English spoken).

Eating in Antibes

Antibes is a fun place to dine out. You can eat on a budget, enjoy a fine meal at an acceptable price, or join the party just inside the walls on boulevard d'Aguillon, under the festive Marché Provençal, or on place Nationale (all filled with tables and tourists—I prefer the Marché Provençal). The options are endless. Take a walk and judge for yourself, and be tempted by these good suggestions. Romantics should picnic at the beach (the **Casino market** is open late; see "Helpful Hints" on page 367). Everyone should stroll along the ramparts after dinner.

La Marmite offers diners an honest, unpretentious budget value in old Antibes, with eight tables, helpful service, and delicious seafood choices (*menus* from €16, closed Mon, 20 rue James Close, tel. 04 93 34 56 79).

L'Aubergine delivers fine cuisine at fair prices—including good vegetarian options—served in an intimate room rich with color. Arrive early to get a table (€32 bouillabaisse, *menus* from €23, opens at 18:30, closed Wed, 7 rue Sade, tel. 04 93 34 55 93).

Le Broc en Bouche has three personalities: It's a cozy wine bar, a bistro, and a collector's shop. Come early to get a seat at this cool little place and enjoy well-prepared dishes from a selective list (€23 *plats*, closed Tue–Wed, 8 rue des Palmiers, tel. 04 93 34 75 60).

Le Vauban is run by a young couple who draw a local following with their handsome interior, smart tableware, and reliable cuisine at fair prices (€27 three-course *menu*, closed Tue, 7 bis rue Thiers, tel. 04 93 34 33 05).

Le Brulot is an Antibes institution with two restaurants—Le Brulot and Le Brulot Pasta—that sit almost side by side a short block below Marché Provençal on rue Frédéric Isnard. Join locals at the very popular **Le Brulot,** known for its Provençal cuisine and meats cooked on an open fire. It's a small place, overflowing onto the street, with a few outside tables and a dining room below. Try the aioli (€19 *menus,* closed Sun, at #2, tel. 04 93 34 17 76). **Le Brulot Pasta** is family-friendly and goes Italian with excellent pizza (the €11 *printanière* is tasty and huge) and big portions of pasta, served in air-conditioned comfort under stone arches (daily, at #3, tel. 04 93 34 19 19).

Les Vieux Murs is *the* place to splurge in Antibes for regional specialties. Its candlelit, red-toned, *très romantique* interior overlooks the sea, and the outside tables are worth booking ahead—but pass on the upstairs room (€46 dinner *menu,* €30 lunch *menu,* open daily June–mid-Sept, closed Mon off-season, valet parking available, along ramparts beyond Picasso Museum at 25 promenade de l'Amiral de Grasse, tel. 04 93 34 06 73).

Restaurant de Bacon is the locals' pick as Antibes' best restaurant, thanks to its top-notch bouillabaisse and views of Antibes. Located on Cap d'Antibes, past the plage de la Salis, it's simple from the outside (no sign), but lovely on the inside, and made for seafood-lovers (*menus* from €50, allow €70 for bouillabaisse, closed Mon–Tue and Oct–Feb, boulevard de Bacon, tel. 04 93 61 50 02).

Antibes Connections

From Antibes by Train: TGV and local trains serve Antibes' little station. Trains go to **Cannes** (2/hr, 15 min), **Nice** (2/hr, 15–30 min, €3.90), **Grasse** (1/hr, 40 min), **Villefranche-sur-Mer** (2/hr, 40 min), **Monaco** (2/hr, 45–60 min), and **Marseille** (16/day, 2.5 hrs).

By Bus: Handy bus #200 ties everything together, but runs at a snail's pace when traffic is bad (Mon–Sat 4/hr, Sun 2–3/hr, any ride costs €1). This bus goes west to **Cannes** (35 min); and east to **Biot** (15 min—or take bus #7, below), **Cagnes-sur-Mer** (and its Renoir Museum, 25 min), and **Nice** (1–1.5 hrs). Some eastbound buses also stop at **Nice Airport** (2–3/hr, 45 min). Bus #7 runs from Antibes' bus station to **Biot** (14/day Mon–Sat, none Sun, 15 min).

Cannes

Cannes (pronounced "can"), famous for its film festival, is the sister city of Beverly Hills. That says it all. When I asked the

TI for a list of museums and sights, they just smiled. Cannes—with big, exclusive hotels lining mostly private stretches of perfect, sandy beach—is for strolling, shopping, dreaming of meeting a movie star, and lounging on the seafront. Cannes has little that's unique to offer the traveler...except a mostly off-limits film festival and quick access to two undeveloped islands. You can buy an ice-cream cone at the train station and see everything before you've had your last lick. Money is what Cannes has always been about—wealthy people come here to make the scene, so there's always enough *scandale* to go around. The king of Saudi Arabia purchased a serious slice of waterfront just east of town and built his compound with no regard to local zoning regulations. Money talks on the Riviera...and always has.

Orientation to Cannes

Don't sleep or drive in Cannes. Day-trip in by train or bus. It's a breeze, as trains and buses run frequently along the Riviera, and they all stop in Cannes (train is faster, bus is cheaper; for details, see "Cannes Connections," page 384). Buses arrive next to the train station. If you must drive, store your car at the parking garage next to the train station.

Turn left out of the train station (baggage storage available 8:30–20:30), find the busy **TI**, and pick up the nifty little city map (Mon–Sat 9:00–13:00 & 14:00–18:00, closed Sun, tel. 04 93 99 19 77, www.cannes.fr). On Sundays, when the train station TI is closed, drop by the glamorously quiet main TI, in the film festival building at 1 boulevard de la Croisette (daily 9:00–19:00).

Self-Guided Walk

Do the Cannes Cancan

This self-guided walking tour will take you to Cannes' sights in a level, one-hour walk at a movie-star pace. Well-kept WCs are available in the lobbies of any large hotel you pass.

• *From the train station TI, cross the street (veering slightly left) and walk for five unimpressive minutes down rue des Serbes to the beachfront. Cross the busy boulevard de la Croisette and make your way past snack stands to the sea. Find the round lookout and get familiar with...*

The Lay of the Land: Cannes feels different from its neighbors to the east. You won't find the distinctive pastel oranges

and pinks of Old Nice and Villefranche-sur-Mer. Cannes was never part of Italy—and through its architecture and cuisine, it shows.

Face the water. The land jutting into the sea on your left is actually two islands, St. Honorat and Ste. Marguerite. **St. Honorat** has been the property of monks for over 500 years; today its abbey, vineyards, trails, and gardens can be visited by peace-seeking travelers. **Ste. Marguerite,** which can also be visited, is famous for the stone prison that housed the 17th-century Man in the Iron Mask (whose true identity remains unknown).

Now look to your right. Those striking mountains sweeping down to the sea are the Massif de l'Esterel. Their red-rock outcrops oversee spectacular car and train routes (see page 263). Closer in, the hill with the medieval tower caps Cannes' old town (Le Suquet). This hilltop offers grand views, but little else. Below the old town, the port welcomes yachts of all sizes...provided they're big.

Face inland. On the left, find the modern, rust-colored building that's home to the famous film festival (we'll visit there soon). Back the other way, gaze up the boulevard. That classy building with twin black-domed roofs is Hôtel Carlton, our eventual target and as far as we'll go together in that direction.

• *Continue with the sea on your right and stroll the...*

Promenade (La Croisette): You're walking along boulevard de la Croisette—Cannes'
famed two-mile-long prom-
enade. First popular with
kings who wintered here
after Napoleon fell, the elite
parade was later joined by
British aristocracy. Today,
boulevard de la Croisette is
fronted by some of the most

expensive apartments and hotels in Europe. Appreciate the blue boxes that help keep La Croisette poodle-poop-free.

• *Stop when you get to...*

Hôtel Carlton: This is the most famous address on boulevard de la Croisette (allow €800–€5,500 for a night). Face the beach. The iconic Cannes experience is to slip out of your luxury hotel (preferably this one), into a robe (ideally, monogrammed with your initials), and onto the beach—or better yet, onto the pier (this avoids getting irritating sand on your carefully oiled skin). While you may not be doing the "fancy hotel and

monogrammed robe" ritual on this Cannes excursion, you can—for about €18—rent a chair and umbrella and pretend you're tanning for a red-carpet premiere. Cannes does have a few token public beaches, but most beaches are private and run by hotels like the Carlton. You could save money by sunning among the common folk, but the real Cannes way to flee the rabble and paparazzi is to rent a spot on a private beach (best to reserve ahead in July–Aug).

Cross over and wander into the hotel—you're welcome to browse (except during the festival). Ask for a hotel brochure, verify room rates, check for availability, then find the swanky Bar des Célébrités. Imagine the scene here during the film festival (see anyone famous?). A surprisingly affordable café (considering the cost of a room) lies just beyond.

• *You can continue your stroll down La Croisette, but I'm doubling back to the dull orange building that is Cannes'...*

Film Festival Hall: Cannes' film festival (Festival de Cannes), staged since 1939, completes the "Big Three" of Riviera

events (with Monaco's Grand Prix and Nice's Carnival). The hall where the festival takes place—a busy-but-nondescript convention center—sits like a plump movie star on the beach. You'll recognize the formal grand entryway—but the red carpet won't be draped for your visit. Find the famous (Hollywood-style) handprints in the sidewalk all around. To get inside during the festival, you have to be a star (or a photographer—some 3,000 paparazzi attend the gala event, and most bring their own ladders to get above the crowds). While off-limits to us, the festival

Handy Cannes and St-Tropez Phrases

Where is a movie star?	*Où est une vedette?*
I am a movie star.	*Je suis une vedette.*
I am rich and single.	*Je suis riche et célibataire.*
Are you rich and single?	*Etes-vous riche et célibataire?*
Are those real?	*Ils sont des vrais?*
How long is your yacht?	*Quelle est la longeur de votre yacht?*
How much did that cost?	*Combien coûtait-il?*
You can always dream...	*On peut toujours rêver...*

is all that matters around here—and worth a day trip if you're here while it's on. The town buzzes with mega-star energy, press passes, and revealing dresses. Locals claim that it's the world's third-biggest media event, after the Olympics and the World Cup (soccer). The festival prize is the Palme d'Or (like the Oscar for Best Picture). The French press can't cover the event enough, and the average Jean in France follows it as Joe would the World Series in the States. In 2008, the French surprised everyone by winning the prize for the first time in 21 years, for the unhyped, realistic drama *Entre les Murs (The Class*, about a teacher's struggles in a Paris middle school). In 2009, the prize went to the Austrian film *The White Ribbon*, director Michael Haneke's black-and-white depiction of the violent nature of a repressed village in pre-WWI Germany. The 2010 festival runs May 12–23.

• *Around the other side of the festival hall is the port, or Gare Maritime.*

The Port and Old Town (Le Suquet): The big-boy yachts line up closest to the Film Festival Hall. After seeing this yacht frenzy, everything else looks like a dinghy. Boat service to St-Tropez and the nearby islands of St. Honorat and Ste. Marguerite depart from the far side of the port (at quai Laubeuf; see "Sights in Cannes," below, for boat info). Cannes' oldest neighborhood, Le Suquet, is a 15-minute walk above the port, with little of interest except the panoramic views from its ancient church, Notre-Dame-de-l'Espérance (Our Lady of Hope).

• *Cue music. Roll end credits. Our film is over. For further exploration, between Le Suquet and the train station you'll find Cannes' underbelly—narrow lanes with inexpensive cafés and shops that regular folks can afford.*

Sights in Cannes

Shopping—Cannes is made for window-shopping (the best streets are between the station and the waterfront). Stroll down rue d'Antibes for the trendiest boutiques. Rue Meynadier anchors a pedestrian zone with more affordable shops closer to the port. To bring home a real surprise, consider cosmetic surgery. Cannes is well-known as *the* place on the Riviera to have your face (or other parts) realigned.

Excursions to St. Honorat and Ste. Marguerite Islands— Boats ferry tourists 15 minutes to these twin islands just off

Cannes' shore (about hourly 9:00–18:00, €12 round-trip). Both islands offer a refreshing change from the frenetic mainland, with almost no development, good swimming, and peaceful walking paths. On Ste. Marguerite, you can visit the castle and cell where the mysterious Man in the Iron Mask was imprisoned. On St. Honorat, you can visit the abbey where monks still live and pray.

Yachters' Itinerary—If you're visiting Cannes on your private yacht, here's a suggested itinerary:

1. Take in the Festival de Cannes and the accompanying social scene. Organize an evening party on your boat.

2. Motor over to Monte Carlo for the Grand Prix, scheduled— conveniently for yachters—just after the film festival.

3. Drop by Porto Chervo on Sardinia, one of the few places in the world where your yacht is "just average."

4. Head west to Ibiza and Marbella in Spain, where your friends are moored for the big party scene.

Eating in Cannes

For a tasty, easy lunch in Cannes, consider **Fournil St. Nicholas.** You'll get mouthwatering quiche and sandwiches and exquisite salads at affordable prices (leaving the train station, turn right and walk a few blocks to 5 rue Venizelos, tel. 04 93 38 81 12).

Cannes Connections

TGV and local trains serve Cannes' station. Buses stop next to the train station.

From Cannes by Train to: Antibes (2/hr, 15 min), **Nice** (2/hr, 30–40 min, €6), **Grasse** (roughly 1/hr, 30 min).

By Bus: Bus #200 heads east from Cannes along the Riviera (Mon–Sat 4/hr, Sun 2–3/hr, €1 for any destination), stopping at **Antibes** (35 min), **Nice Airport** (only about half of buses stop here, roughly 2/hr, 1–1.25 hrs), and **Nice** (1.5–1.75 hrs). Trip duration depends on traffic.

By Boat: Trans Côte d'Azur runs boat excursions from Cannes to **St-Tropez** (€42 round-trip, 75 min each way; July–mid-Sept daily 2/day; June and late Sept 1/day Tue, Thu, and Sat–Sun only; no service Oct–May; tel. 04 92 98 71 30, fax 04 92 00 42 31, www.trans-cote-azur.com). This boat trip is popular—book a few days ahead from June to September.

St-Tropez

St-Tropez is a busy, charming, and traffic-free port town smothered with fashion boutiques, elegant restaurants, and luxury

boats. If you came here for history or quaintness, you caught the wrong yacht. But if you have more money than you know what to do with, you're home. There are 5,700 year-round residents... and more than 100,000 visitors daily in the summer. Come in the winter if you can.

As with many seaside villages in southern France, the pastel beauty of St-Tropez was first discovered by artists. Paul Signac introduced several of his friends to St-Tropez in the late 1800s, giving the village its first notoriety. But it wasn't until Brigitte Bardot made the scene here in the 1956 film ...*And God Created Woman* that St-Tropez became synonymous with Riviera glamour. Since then, it's the first place that comes to mind when people think of the jet set luxuriating on Mediterranean beaches. For many, the French Riviera begins here and runs east to Menton, on the Italian border.

In St-Tropez, the village itself is the attraction, as the nearest big beach is miles away. Wander the harborfront, where fancy yachts moor stern-in, their carefully coiffed captains and first mates enjoying *pu-pus* for happy hour—they're seeing and being seen. Take time to stroll the back streets while nibbling a chocolate-and-Grand Marnier crêpe.

Orientation to St-Tropez

St-Tropez lies between its famous port and the hilltop Citadelle (with great views). The network of lanes between the port and Citadelle are strollable in a Carmel-by-the-Sea sort of way.

Tourist Information

The TI is starboard on the port (to you landlubbers, that's to the right as you face the sea), where quai Suffren and quai Jean Jaurès meet (daily April–Oct 9:30–12:30 & 14:00–19:00, July–Aug until 20:00, Nov–March until 18:00, tel. 08 92 68 48 28, www.ot-saint -tropez.com). Pick up their good, free walking-tour in English (usually inserted into a larger tourist brochure), ask about events in town, and get maps and bus information if you plan to hike along the coast.

Arrival in St-Tropez

For bus and boat details, see "St. Tropez Connections," at the end of this chapter.

By Bus: Buses leave you a few minutes' walk to the port, near the parking lot—Parking du Vieux Port—on avenue Général de Gaulle.

By Boat: Boats from St. Raphael deposit you by the Parking du Vieux Port, a five-minute walk to the port.

By Car: Prepare for traffic in any season—worse on weekends (forget driving on Sunday afternoons), always ugly during summer, and downright impossible between St-Tropez and St. Maxime on weekends. You can avoid this bottleneck by taking the autoroute to Le Luc, and following the windy D-558 to St-Tropez from here (via La Garde-Freinet and Port Grimaud).

The last few miles to St-Tropez are along a too-long, two-lane road with one way in, one way out, and too many people going exactly where you're going. There are two main parking lots (both about €2.50/hr): Parking des Lices (near all recommended hotels) and Parking du Vieux Port (best for day-trippers).

Self-Guided Walk

Welcome to St-Tropez

This quick, scenic walk is best done with the TI's walking-tour brochure.

• Begin at the round tower (Bureau du Port) at the port's vessel entry, by the Parking du Vieux Port.

Climb the steps for a fine **view.** Check out the massive crane—it's used to pull yachts that are bigger than my house out of the water for off-season maintenance. Moorage fees for the bigger yachts run €2,000 per day.

Walk along the port, and notice the busy deckhands (hustling before their captains arrive) and the artists competing for room to showcase their work. Saunter around to the opposite corner of the port, and work your way to the TI.

The red-tabled café **(Le Sénéquier)** by the TI is one of the town's most venerated, and has long attracted celebrities, including Jean-Paul Sartre. High-end cafés and restaurants line the port from here to the jetty—it doesn't seem to matter that you can't see the sea for the big yachts. See if you recognize anyone famous, and by all means, stop to wiggle your toes in the gleaming white sandy floor of Joseph l'Escale's restaurant.

Find the bulky round **tower** at the port's end with views across the bay—to St. Maxime and out to sea. A plaque honors the American, British, and French troops who liberated Provence on August 15, 1944.

Climb the jetty for great views over St-Tropez's port, then wander past the round tower to a walking path that leads around the town to small beaches and swimming opportunities. Notice how clear the water is, and how the homes seem at one with the sea. From here, you can continue along the shore, or walk up to the Citadelle for more views (see below). The small lanes below the Citadelle are St-Tropez's most appealing. Work your way to the big **place des Lices** (good cafés) and see if anyone is playing *pétanque*.

Sights in St-Tropez

In the Village

Window-shopping, people-watching, tan maintenance, and savoring slow meals fill people's days, weeks, and in some cases, lives. Here, one dresses up, sizes up one another's yachts, and trolls for a partner. While the only models you'll see are in the shop windows, Brigitte Bardot—who turns 76 in 2010—still hangs out on a bench in front of the TI signing autographs (Thu 15:00–17:30).

Museum of the Annonciade (Musée de l'Annonciade)—Though generally ignored, this museum houses an enchanting collection of works from the Post-Impressionist and Fauvist artists who decorated St-Tropez before Brigitte. Almost all canvases feature St-Tropez sights and landscapes. You'll see colorful paintings by Paul Signac, Henri Matisse, Georges Braque, Pierre Bonnard, Maurice de Vlaminck, and more. Gaze out the windows and notice how the port has changed since they were here (€5, Wed–Mon 10:00–12:00 & 14:00–18:00, closed Tue and in Nov, place Grammont, tel. 04 94 17 84 10).

St-Tropez

La Citadelle—This old fortress offers little but peacocks, occasional special exhibits (inquire at TI), and views over St-Tropez from its high walls. Good views are free from just outside its walls (€4, daily 10:00–12:00 & 13:00–17:30, closed in Nov, longer hours and more expensive during special exhibits, tel. 04 94 97 59 43).

Coastal Hike—The scenic Sentier du Littoral path, originally patrolled by customs agents, runs past the Citadelle for 12 miles along the coast and is marked with yellow dashes on the

ST-TROPEZ

SEA

TOUR DE PORTALET

TOUR VIEILLE

LA GLAYE

WC.

SAILORS' CEMETERY

R. FOUR

PONCHE

RUE

CAVAILLON

TO BEACHES

CITADELLE

STATUE

PLACE DES LICES

200 YARDS

200 METERS

DCH

pavement, walls, and trees. Leave St-Tropez along the road below the Citadelle, pass the Sailors' Cemetery, and you'll join the path before long. If you're really into this, take the 20-minute bus (*la navette*) from place des Lices in St-Tropez to the Capon/Pinet stop and walk three hours back to St-Tropez (bus only runs 2/day, taxi also works, get details at TI).

Boat Excursions—Several companies offer mildly interesting tours of the bay (paralleling the Sentier du Littoral described above). Le Brigantin has reliable outings in comfortable wooden vessels with personalized English commentary. You'll learn a smidgen about St-Tropez's history and a lot about villas of the rich and famous. Conrad Hilton and John Grisham both have little bungalows, and you'll sail right past Brigitte Bardot's surprisingly modest-looking home. Redhead Victoria (from Britain) staffs the information desk on the quai Suffren and can explain the trip (€10, kids age 5–10–€5, 4/day, tel. 04 94 54 40 61).

Boules—The vast *pétanque* (*boules*) court on place des Lices is worth your attention. Have a drink at the recommended Le Café and take in the action. Study up on the sport (see page 196) and root for your hero.

Near St-Tropez

Port Grimaud—While more modern than St-Tropez, Port Grimaud (located a few miles toward St. Maxime) is no less attractive or upscale. This "Venice of Provence" was reclaimed from a murky lagoon about 40 years ago, and is now lined with four miles of canals, lovely homes, and moorage for thousands of yachts. It's a fascinating look at what clever minds can produce from a swamp. Park at the lot across from the town entry (TI next to the parking lot, tel. 04 94 56 02 01), and cross the barrier and bridge into a beautiful world of privilege. Climb the church bell tower for a good panorama.

Sleeping in St-Tropez

(€1 = about $1.40, country code: 33)

Though everything seems pricey in this golden town, I've uncovered a few jewels. Sleep only in the town center, as traffic makes coming and going a royal headache. High season in St-Tropez runs from June through September, and weekends are busy year-round.

$$$ Hôtel La Ponche**** offers a warm welcome and the most central, luxurious beds I could find (Db-€250–400, Db with top-floor deck and sea view-€450–600, breakfast-€19, Wi-Fi, parking-€23, near the sea, several blocks behind the TI at 3 rue des Remparts, tel. 04 94 97 02 53, fax 04 94 97 78 61, www.laponche .com, hotel@laponche.com).

$$$ Hôtel les Palmiers*** is a relaxed place with a lush garden, a bar/lounge, and good rooms at normal three-star rates. It's on place des Lices, so parking is easy (standard Db-€90–115, bigger Db-€120–160, air-con, off place des Lices at 26 boulevard Vasserot, tel. 04 94 97 01 61, www.hotel-les-palmiers.com, info @hotel-les-palmiers.com).

$$ Hôtel le Colombier**, little and adorable, is on a quiet street. Its 11 soft and comfortable rooms enclose a small, sweet garden-patio. This is a terrific value (Db-€75–95, bigger Db with air-con-€132–160, Tb/Qb-€175–205, easy parking nearby, follow *Parking des Lices* signs and look for hotel signs on left, impasse des Conquêtes, tel. 04 94 97 05 31, fax 04 94 97 32 57).

$$ Hôtel Lou Cagnard** looks average from the outside. But enter the courtyard garden and you'll find a pretty, well-managed, and shockingly reasonable hotel (Ds-€69, bigger Db-€90–135, higher prices are for garden-side and larger rooms, one-week minimum June–Sept, air-con, free parking, follow signs to *Parking des Lices* and you'll pass the hotel, 18 avenue Paul Roussel, tel. 04 94 97 04 24, fax 04 94 97 09 44, www.hotel-lou-cagnard.com).

Eating in St-Tropez

There are several grocery stores in the old city. The **Casino market** is a block off the port, up rue V. Laugier.

Start or end your evening with St-Tropez's best port-view seats on the small deck at **Hôtel Sube's** bar on quai Suffren, near the TI (drinks only, fine interior).

Dining on place des Lices is a great opportunity to watch *pétanque* matches, with several appealing eateries to choose from. **Le Café** has long been the place to park your beret on this square, and serves surprisingly good cuisine. Stroll inside past the soft chairs and old wooden floor, and find one of the best zinc counters in France, complete with an atmospheric bar (daily, €30 *menus*, €18 *plats*, tel. 04 94 97 44 69). **Café des Arts,** at the end of the square, has good ambience inside and out, and serves pizza, salads, and *plats* for €10–15 (daily, tel. 04 94 97 02 25).

Christophe Leroy's **La Table du Marché,** just off place des Lices, is an inviting pastry shop/deli/restaurant. Delectable *menus* from €30 feature gourmet pasta, seafood, and meat dishes—and include a glass of wine (daily, 38 rue Georges Clemenceau, tel. 04 94 97 85 20).

Elsewhere in St-Tropez, **L'Auberge des Maures** has a rich, lively decor, indoor and outdoor tables, and a welcoming staff. It's a good place to go for quality Provençal cuisine (€50 *menu*, daily, 4 rue du Docteur Boutin, tel. 04 94 97 01 50).

St. Tropez Connections

From St-Tropez by Public Transportation: With no trains to St-Tropez, buses and boats are your only options. **Buses** serve St-Tropez from St-Raphaël's train station to the east (almost hourly, 80 min) and from Toulon to the west (7/day, 2 hrs). **Boats** make the one-hour trip from St-Raphaël to St-Tropez twice daily (€13 one-way, €24 round-trip, departs St-Raphaël at 9:30 and 14:30, departs St-Tropez at 10:30 and 17:15, tel. 04 94 95 17 46, www.bateauxsaintraphael.com, or call the TI). For boats connecting St-Tropez with Nice, see page 274; with Cannes, page 385.

INLAND RIVIERA

St-Paul-de-Vence
• Vence • Grasse
• Grand Canyon du Verdon

For a verdant, rocky, fresh escape from the beaches, head inland and upward. Some of France's most perfectly perched hill towns and splendid scenery hang overlooked in this region that's more famous for beaches and bikinis. A short car or bus ride away from the Mediterranean reaps big rewards: lush forests, deep canyons, and swirling hilltop villages. A longer drive (though still doable as a day trip) brings you to Europe's greatest canyon, the Grand Canyon du Verdon.

Getting Around the Inland Riviera

By Car: Driving is the most flexible way to tour this area (particularly in the off-season)—though summer and weekend traffic and parking challenges will test your patience. A one-day car rental is worth considering (see the "Helpful Hints" sections in the Nice and Antibes chapters). I describe the best route below.

By Bus: Buses get you to many of the places in this chapter. Vence, St-Paul-de-Vence, and Grasse are well-served by bus from Nice about every 40 minutes, and Grasse has train service from Nice, Antibes, and Cannes (see "Getting Around the Riviera" on page 272). Buses to Tourrettes-sur-Loup, Le Bar-sur-Loup, and Grasse leave from Vence daily except Sunday (7/day, 15 min to Tourrettes-sur-Loup, 35 min to Le Bar-sur-Loup, 50 min to Grasse, tel. 04 93 42 40 79, www.cg06.fr/transport/transports -tam.html). Buses do not serve the Gorges du Loup, the village of Gourdon, or the Gorges du Verdon.

Self-Guided Driving Tour

The Inland Riviera:
From St-Paul-de-Vence to Grasse

This splendid loop drive connects St-Paul-de-Vence, Vence, Tourrettes-sur-Loup, and Grasse (all described below, in that order). It's best done by car as a day trip from the Nice/Antibes area (allow all day), though it could be done en route to the Gorges du Verdon (the most impressive part of the Grand Canyon du Verdon area, described later in this chapter). Some of the villages on this loop can be linked by bus, but a car is essential to do the loop as described. Each of the stops is only minutes away from the next by car or bus, but allow 45 minutes to drive from Nice to the first stop, St-Paul-de-Vence. Start early if you want to see St-Paul-de-Vence without the mobs (have breakfast at St-Paul-de-Vence's recommended Café de la Place). If you won't be visiting the Gorges du Verdon (or if you care more about nature than art), take the exceptionally beautiful long way around from Vence to Gourdon (see "Alternate Route," page 396), and skip Tourrettes-sur-Loup and the Gorges du Loup (you won't miss them, trust *moi*). All of the bolded stops below are explained in detail later in this chapter.

Let's get started. Begin your day by leaving Nice along the promenade des Anglais and heading toward Cannes and Antibes. Follow *Grasse* signs, then *Vence* and *St-Paul-de-Vence* signs. On this route, you'll pass the tempting Renoir Museum in Cagnes-sur-Mer (described on page 375). Continue following *St-Paul-de-Vence* signs into the village, and park as close to the center as you can. After sampling **St-Paul-de-Vence,** visit the **Fondation Maeght** just above the town (park at the museum for free, or walk 20 min up from St-Paul-de-Vence, following blue signs).

After completing your course in contemporary art, find artsy **Vence,** a few miles away, with many good lunch options. From Vence, visit Matisse's famous **Chapel of the Rosary** (limited opening hours—see page 399; best views of Vence are a mile beyond the chapel, where there's a turnaround).

Next, head for slippery-sloped **Tourrettes-sur-Loup** (poorly signed from Vence, follow D-2210)—or skip Tourrettes-sur-Loup and follow the "Alternate Route" described later. From Tourrettes-sur-Loup, follow signs for *Pont-du-Loup* (fine views of Tourrettes-sur-Loup a mile after leaving). Before long, you'll see views of **Le Bar-sur-Loup,** clinging to its hillside in the distance. When you arrive at the junction of the roads to Gourdon and Le Bar-sur-Loup, look way up to your destination—the tiny soaring village of Gourdon. Sugar addicts can detour quickly down to **Pont-du-Loup** and visit the small candied-fruit factory

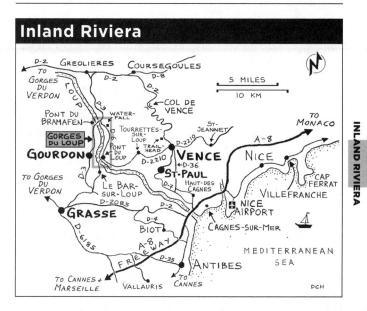

Inland Riviera

of **Confiseries Florian.** Follow *Gourdon* and *Gorges du Loup* signs to the right and climb into the teeth of a rocky canyon, the **Gorges du Loup.** It's a mostly second-gear road that winds between intimidating rock faces above a surging stream. (Buses cannot enter the Gorges du Loup, so non-drivers must continue on directly to Grasse.) Several miles into the gorge, you can visit the Cascades du Saut du Loup, which may have you thinking you've made a wrong turn into Hawaii (€1, easy walk down).

The drive passes all too quickly to where the road hooks back, crossing Pont du Bramafen, and up toward Gourdon. Climb above the canyon you just drove through and watch the world below miniaturize. At the top, the village of **Gourdon,** known as the "Eagle's Nest" (2,400 feet), waits for tourists with shops, good lunch options, and grand panoramas.

From Gourdon, slide downhill—passing stone quarries—toward **Grasse.** Enjoy sensational views down to (literally) over-

looked Le Bar-sur-Loup. Follow signs to *Grasse,* then *Centre-Ville,* and park at the first underground lot you come to (by the Grasse bus station). After improving your body odor in Grasse, return to your Riviera home base (allow 45 minutes to Nice, via Cannes and the autoroute), or continue to the Gorges du Verdon.

Alternate Route: If you won't be visiting the Gorges du Verdon, consider this delicious detour, which takes you a bit farther inland (ideal if staying in Vence): Follow the route described above until Vence and complete your sightseeing there, then find D-2 just before the bridge that leads to St-Jeannet, and follow signs for *Col de Vence* (the Vence pass). This road switches up and up beyond the tree line into a stones-only landscape to the pass in about 15 minutes. Great views over Vence begin a few minutes after leaving the town. (For a 45-minute uphill hike to great views over Vence and the Riviera, pass the Château St-Martin, drive another kilometer, then look for the brown trailhead sign to *Baous des Blancs*.) From the pass (3,000 feet), continue on D-2, trading rocky slabs for lush forests, pastures, and vast canyons. You'll pass the postcard-perfect village of Coursegoules (worth a photo but not a detour), then follow signs to *Gréolières*. At a roundabout just before Gréolières you'll find D-3, which leads to Nice, Gorges du Loup, and Gourdon. But first, continue a few minutes past Gréolières to the pullout barely above the village, with stirring views over the village and its ruined castle. Consider a coffee break in Gréolières before backtracking to the roundabout, following signs to *Gourdon*. After visiting Gourdon, you can continue to Grasse, or return to Nice.

St-Paul-de-Vence

The most famous of Riviera hill towns, and the most-visited village in France, feels that way—like an overrun and over-restored artist-shopping-mall. Its attraction is understandable, as every cobble and flower seems *just-so*, and the setting is memorable. Avoid visiting between 11:00 and 18:00, particularly on weekends. Arriving early will make it easier to find a parking space near the village (cars are not allowed inside St-Paul). Consider skipping breakfast at your hotel and instead eating at the local hangout, **Café de la Place,** where you can watch as waves of tourists crash into the town.

The **TI,** just through the gate into the old city on rue Grande, has maps with minimal explanations of key buildings (daily 10:00–18:00, tel. 04 93 32 86 95, www.saint-pauldevence.com). If the traffic-free lane leading to the old city is jammed, take the road that veers up and left just after the Café de la Place, and enter the town through its side door. Meander deep into St-Paul-de-Vence's quieter streets to find the panoramic views. See if you can find the hill town of Vence at the foot of an impressive mountain.

Fondation Maeght

This inviting, pricey, and far-out private museum is situated a steep walk or short drive above St-Paul-de-Vence. Fondation Maeght (fohn-dah-shown mahg) offers an excellent introduction to modern Mediterranean art by gathering many of the Riviera's most famous artists under one roof. The founder, Aimé Maeght, long envisioned the perfect exhibition space for the artists he supported and befriended as an art dealer. He purchased this arid hilltop, planted more than 35,000 plants, and hired an architect (José Luis Sert) with the same vision.

A sweeping lawn laced with amusing sculptures and bending pine trees greets visitors. On the right, a chapel designed by Georges Braque—in memory of the Maeghts' young son, who died of leukemia—features a moving purple stained-glass work over the altar. The unusual museum building is purposefully low-profile, to let its world-class modern-art collection take center stage. Works by Fernand Léger, Joan Miró, Alexander Calder, Georges Braque, and Marc Chagall are thoughtfully arranged in well-lit rooms. The backyard of the museum has views, a Gaudí-esque sculpture labyrinth by Miró, and a courtyard filled with the wispy

works of Alberto Giacometti. The only permanent collection in the museum consists of the sculptures, though the museum tries to keep a good selection of paintings by the famous artists here year-round. For a review of modern art, see "The Riviera's Art Scene" on page 264. There's also a great gift shop and cafeteria.

Cost and Hours: €11, €2.50 to take photos, daily July–Sept 10:00–19:00, Oct–June 10:00–18:00, tel. 04 93 32 81 63, www.fondation-maeght.com.

Getting There: The museum is a steep uphill-but-doable 20-minute walk from St-Paul-de-Vence and the bus stop. Blue signs indicate the way (parking is available at the top, though the lot can be full).

Vence

Vence is a well-discovered yet appealing town set well above the Riviera. While growth has sprawled well beyond Vence's old walls, and cars jam its roundabouts, the mountains are front and center and the breeze is fresh in this engaging town that bubbles with workaday life and ample tourist activity. Vence is best at night and makes a handy base for travelers wanting the best of both worlds: a hill-town refuge near the sea. Some enjoy the Gorges du Verdon as a day trip from Vence (see the route described under "Le Grand Canyon du Verdon," later in this chapter).

Orientation to Vence

Tourist Information

Vence's fully loaded and eager-to-help TI faces the main square at 8 place du Grand Jardin. They have bus schedules, brochures on the cathedral, and a city map with a well-devised self-guided walking tour (25 stops, incorporates informative wall plaques). They also publish a list of Vence art galleries with English descriptions of the collections. To properly engage you in French culture, the TI has information on French-language classes, and—even better—*pétanque* instruction with *boules* to rent for €3 per person (TI open June–Sept Mon–Sat 9:00–19:00, Sun 10:00–18:00; Oct–May Mon–Sat 9:00–18:00, closed Sun; tel. 04 93 58 06 38, www.ville-vence.fr).

Market day in the *cité historique* (old town) is on Tuesday and Friday mornings on place Clemenceau. There's a big all-day antiques market on place du Grand Jardin every Wednesday.

Arrival in Vence

By Bus: The bus stop is on place du Grand Jardin, next to the TI (schedules are posted in the window of the travel agency by the bus stop).

By Car: Follow signs to *cité historique,* and park where you can. A central pay lot is under place du Grand Jardin, across from the TI.

Sights in Vence

Explore the narrow lanes of the old town using the TI's worth-while self-guided tour map. Connect the picturesque streets, enjoy a drink on a quiet square, inspect an art gallery, and find the small 11th-century cathedral with its colorful Chagall mosaic of Moses (for background, see the Chagall Museum Tour chapter). If you're here later in the day, enjoy the *boules* action across from the TI (rent a set from the TI and join in).

Château de Villeneuve—This 17th-century mansion, adjoining an imposing 12th-century watchtower, bills itself as "one of the Riviera's high temples of modern art," with a rotating collection. Check with the TI to see what's playing in the temple (€5, Tue–Sun 10:00–12:30 & 14:00–18:00, closed Mon, tel. 04 93 58 15 78).

▲Chapel of the Rosary (Chapelle du Rosaire)—The chapel, a short drive or 20-minute walk from town, was designed by an

elderly and ailing Henri Matisse in thanks to the Dominican sister who had taken care of him (he was 81 when the chapel was completed—see the timeline of Matisse's life on page 278). The modest chapel is a simple collection of white walls laced with yellow, green, and blue stained-glass windows and charcoal black-on-white tile sketches. The sunlight filters through the glass and does a cheery dance across the sketches. While the chapel is the ultimate pilgrimage for serious Matisse fans, the experience may underwhelm others. (If you've taken my self-guided tour of the Matisse

Museum in Nice, you'll remember that he was the master of leaving things out.) Decide for yourself if Matisse met the goal he set himself: "Creating a religious space in an enclosed area of reduced proportions and to give it, solely by the play of colors and lines, the dimension of infinity."

Cost and Hours: €3, Mon, Wed, and Sat 14:00–17:30, Tue and Thu 10:00–11:30 & 14:00–17:30, Sun only open for Mass at 10:00 followed by tour of chapel, closed Fri and mid-Nov–mid-Dec, 466 avenue Henri Matisse, tel. 04 93 58 03 26, http://pagesperso-orange.fr/maison.lacordaire.

Getting There: To reach the chapel from the Vence TI, turn right out of the TI and walk or drive down avenue Henri Isnard, then right on avenue Henri Matisse, following signs to *St-Jeannet* (allow 20 min).

Sleeping in Vence

In the Old Town

Hôtel Miramar is a 10-minute walk above the old town. Both of the latter two places are a short walk from the TI, next to the

Sleep Code

(€1 = about $1.40, country code: 33)

S = Single, **D** = Double/Twin, **T** = Triple, **Q** = Quad, **b** = bathroom, **s** = shower only, * = French hotel rating (0–4 stars). Credit cards are accepted and English is spoken unless otherwise noted.

To help you sort easily through these listings, I've divided the rooms into three categories based on the price for a standard double room with bath:

$$$ Higher Priced—Most rooms €100 or more.
$$ Moderately Priced—Most rooms between €70–100.
$ Lower Priced—Most rooms €70 or less.

Château de Villeneuve; to reach them, turn right out of the TI, then right again, then left.

$$$ Hôtel Miramar*** is a laid-back 18-room Mediterranean villa perched on a ledge with grand panoramas. Friendly owner Daniel welcomes you into this refuge, which he's filled with many personal touches. The Old World rooms come in soothing colors, with firm beds and worn furnishings. The pool and view terrace could make you late for dinner, or seduce you into skipping it altogether—picnics are allowed (standard Db-€90–125, Db with balcony-€120–135, Db with great view and balcony-€160, family suite-€185, some rooms have air-con, most don't need it, bar, table tennis, parking, turn left out of the TI and follow the brown signs to 167 avenue Bougearel, tel. 04 93 58 01 32, fax 04 93 58 20 22, www.hotel-miramar-vence.com, contact@hotel-miramar-vence.com).

$$$ La Maison du Frêne is an art-packed B&B with four sumptuous rooms located behind the TI. Energetic Thierry combines his passion for contemporary art and hosting travelers in his lovingly restored manor house (Db-€140–180, higher price is for peak times, includes breakfast, air-con, Wi-Fi, 1 place du Frêne, tel. 04 93 24 37 83, www.lamaisondufrene.com, contact@lamaisondufrene.com).

$$ L'Auberge des Seigneurs*** is a shy little place just inside the old town. Its six simple yet character-filled rooms—above a cozy restaurant—have wood furnishings, red-tile floors, and good-enough bathrooms (spacious Sb-€65, Db-€85–100, place du Frêne, tel. 04 93 58 04 24, fax 04 93 24 08 01, www.auberge-seigneurs.com, sandrine.rodi@wanadoo.fr).

Near Vence, in St-Jeannet

To melt into the Inland Riviera's quiet side, drive 15 minutes from Vence to the remarkably situated, no-tourist-in-sight hill town of

INLAND RIVIERA

St-Jeannet. Views are endless and everywhere. It's so quiet, it's hard to believe that the beach is only 10 miles away. But the best reason to visit St-Jeannet is to stay at **$$ The Frog's House,** where Benôit and Corinne will eagerly welcome you to this region, which they are both mad about. This young couple offers a full menu of good rooms, fine meals, cooking lessons, hikes in the area, and day trips to popular destinations. If you don't have wheels, they'll happily pick you up at the train station or airport. The hotel is freshly renovated, so everything feels new. Rooms are small but sharp (Db-€76, Db with balcony-€89, includes breakfast, dinners-€25–35, tel. 04 93 58 98 05, mobile 06 28 06 80 28, www.thefrogshouse.com, info@thefrogshouse.com). There's a parking lot in the center of St-Jeannet, a few blocks from their small hotel.

Eating in Vence

Tempting outdoor eateries litter the old town; they all look good to me. Embedded lights in the old-town cobbles light the way after dark.

On place Clemenceau: These two restaurants serve tasty Provençal cuisine a few doors apart on the charming place Clemenceau: **La Cassolette,** at #10, is an intimate place with reasonable prices and a romantic terrace across from the floodlit church (€28 *menus,* €14–17 *plats,* closed Thu, tel. 04 93 58 84 15). **Les Agapes,** at #4, offers limited outdoor seating, a lovely upstairs dining room, and a menu that stays fresh with each season (€24 and €30 *menus,* closed Sun-Mon, tel. 04 93 58 50 64).

At nearby **La Peyra,** enjoy a relaxed dinner salad or pasta dish outdoors to the sound of the town's main fountain (€15 "maxi salads" and *plats,* daily, 13 place du Peyra, tel. 04 93 58 67 63).

L'Auberge des Seigneurs feels more alpine than Mediterranean, and is good for a cooler day, when you can sit by the fire and watch your meat being cooked. The choices are limited and filling. Sandrine will help you decide (*menus* from €32, closed Sun–Mon; also recommended under "Sleeping in Vence," earlier).

Near Vence: For a very personal experience, reserve ahead for a meal with Benôit and Corinne at **The Frog's House,** their small hotel in St-Jeannet. You'll dine in their grand kitchen and learn about local produce and recipes (€25–35 for dinner with wine and the works, see listing under "Sleeping in Vence," above).

Hill Towns and Sights
Between Vence and Grasse

The sights listed below are connected by the Inland Riviera self-guided driving tour described earlier in this chapter.

Shortcut from Vence to the Gorges du Verdon—To save time and add scenery, skip the town of Grasse and take D-2 from Vence following Col de Vence (Vence pass), and climb above the tree line. Follow D-2 up and over, passing the photogenic villages of Coursegoules and Gréolières, and continue west following signs to *Thorenc*, *Valderoure*, and *Grasse*, to where the road eventually meets D-6085 (old N-85). From here, turn left, then shortly after follow signs to the right to *Draguignan* and *Gorges du Verdon*, and join the route described under "Le Grand Canyon du Verdon."

Tourrettes-sur-Loup—This picturesque town, hemmed in by forests, looks ready to skid down its abrupt hill. Tourrettes-sur-Loup is small, with no sprawl. Known as the *Cité des Violettes*, the village produces more violets than anywhere else in France, most of which get shipped off to end up in bottles that make you smell nice.

Park in the lot at the village center and stroll the lanes. You'll still find a smattering of arts and crafts, though much less than in the "Vence towns." Plunge deep to find good views, as well as **Tom's Ice Cream** (afternoons only, closed Mon) and a few places to eat. Wednesday is market day (on place de la Libération). Views of Tourrettes-sur-Loup await a minute away on the drive to Pont-du-Loup.

Confiseries Florian—The candied-fruit factory hides between trees down in Pont-du-Loup (though their big, bright sign is hard to miss). Ten-minute tours of their factory leave regularly, covering the candied-fruit process and explaining the use of flower petals (like violets and jasmine) in their products. Everything they make is fruit-filled—even their chocolate (with oranges). The tour ends with a tasting of the *confiture* in the dazzling gift shop (tours are free, request a tour with English commentary, daily 9:00–12:00 & 14:00–18:00, gift shop stays open during lunch, tel. 04 93 59 32 91, www.confiserieflorian.com).

Gorges du Loup—The Inland Riviera is crawling with spectacular canyons only miles from the sea. Slotted between Grasse and Vence, the Gorges du Loup is the easiest gorge to reach and works in well with a day trip from the Nice area. You can drive about five miles right up into the canyon (on D-6), passing waterfalls and sheer rock walls, then return on the gorge's rooftop (on D-3) to the "Eagle's Nest" village of Gourdon for magnificent vistas and a complete change of scenery.

Gourdon—This 2,400-foot-high, cliff-topping hamlet features grassy picnic areas, a short lineup of tourist shops, and a few good lunch options. The village's most famous building is its château, which is best enjoyed from the outside (infrequent, French-only tours of the interior). A well-marked trail (Chemin du Paradis) leads down the cliffs to Le Bar-sur-Loup (1 hour)—now *that's* steep. The far side of the village features fabulous vistas, a tiny Romanesque church, and two options for lunch with a view...

Eating in Gourdon: **La Taverne Provençale** boasts a popular spread of outdoor tables overlooking the grandeur (€10–12 omelets and pasta dishes, €18 *menu,* lunch only, daily, place de l'Eglise, tel. 04 93 09 68

22). Just below is the most appropriately named restaurant in France, **Le Nid de l'Aigle** ("The Eagle's Nest"), which tempts travelers with fine cuisine and an equally remarkable setting with interior and exterior seating (€20 lunch *menu,* €30 dinner *menu;* July–mid-Sept daily lunch and dinner; mid-Sept–June Wed–Sun lunch only, Sat lunch and dinner, closed Mon–Tue; tel. 04 93 77 52 02).

Le Bar-sur-Loup—This town is the yin to St-Paul-de-Vence's yang: It has almost no tourist shops and little to do except wander the peaceful brick-lined lanes and enjoy the view. Park at the lot by the Hôtel de Ville and Syndicat d'Initiative (TI).

Grasse

Both the historic and contemporary capital of perfume, Grasse offers a contrast to the dolled-up hill towns above the Riviera. While famous for its pricey product, Grasse's urban center is a gritty yet intriguing collection of walking lanes, peek-a-boo squares, and vertical staircases. The place feels in need of a facelift, and refreshingly real. Its historic alliance with Genoa explains the Italian-esque look of the old city. Still, the only good reasons to visit Grasse are if you care about perfume, or if you're heading to or from the Gorges du Verdon.

Orientation to Grasse

Tourist Information

All sights in Grasse cluster near the main TI in the Palais du Congrès on cours Honoré Cresp, also referred to as place du Cours (July–Sept Mon–Sat 9:00–19:00, Sun 9:00–12:30 & 14:00–18:00; Oct–June Mon–Sat 9:00–12:30 & 14:00–18:00, closed Sun; tel. 04 93 36 66 66, www.grasse.fr, free cold water fountain). There's a branch TI (Grasse Espace Accueil) on place de la Foux near the bus station. At either TI, pick up an English map with a self-guided tour of the old city (handy information plaques). If heading to the Gorges du Verdon, get specifics here.

Arrival in Grasse

By Train: Fifteen trains a day connect Grasse with Nice (1.25 hr), Antibes (40 min), and Cannes (30 min). Free *navette* shuttle buses (3/hr) take you from the train station up and up to the bus station.

By Bus: Buses run directly to Cannes in 40 minutes and to Nice in 75 minutes. From the bus station on place de la Buanderie, it's a five-minute walk to the sights (walk one block up to boulevard du Jeu de Ballon, turn left, and take the pleasant stroll downhill to cours Honoré Cresp).

By Car: Grasse's size, hilly terrain, and inconsistent signage make it confusing for drivers. Those coming from Nice (via A-8), Antibes, and Cannes should follow signs to *Centre-Ville* and *Office du Tourisme* (follow *Peymeinade* signs if you lose *Centre-Ville* signs). Soon after passing the golden Fragonard perfume boutique, turn left into the Parking Honoré Cresp. This parking lot's *Sortie Parfumerie* leads directly to the Fragonard perfume tour. Those arriving from Vence, Gourdon, and the Gorges du Verdon should follow signs to *Centre-Ville* until Hôtel le Napoleon. Make a hard left after the hotel, then a quick right, and park at the lot next to the bus station *(gare routière)*. Then follow the walking directions from the bus station described above.

Sights in Grasse

Fragonard Perfume—This well-run, functioning factory, located dead-center in Grasse, provides frequent, fragrant, informative 20-minute tours and an interesting "museum" to explore while you wait. Pick up the English brochure describing what's in the museum cases, then drop down to where the tour begins. On your tour, you'll learn that the difference between perfume, eau de toilette, and cologne is only a matter of perfume-percentages. You'll also learn how the product is made today, as well as how they used to do it (by pressing flowers in animal fat). The tour ends

Fragrant Grasse

Grasse has been at the center of the fragrance industry since the 1500s, when it was known for its scented leather gloves. The cultivation of aromatic plants around Grasse slowly evolved to produce ingredients for soaps and perfumes, and by the 1800s, Grasse was recognized as the center for perfume (thanks largely to its flower-friendly climate), making it a wealthy city.

It can take a ton of carefully picked petals (like jasmine)—that's about 10,000 flowers—to make about two pounds of essence. A damaged flower petal is bad news. Today, perfumes are made from as many as 500 different scents; most are imported to Grasse from countries around the world. The "blender" of these scents and the perfume mastermind is called the "nose" (who knows best). The five master "noses" who work here must study their profession longer than a doctor goes to med school (seven years). They've had to show that they had the gift before entering "nose school" (in Versailles), and they cannot drink alcohol, ever.

Skip the outlying perfumeries with French-only tours. Only 3 factories out of 40 open their doors to visitors, and only one is worth visiting: Fragonard Perfume in Grasse.

with a whiff in the elegant gift shop (daily 9:00–18:00 or 18:30, last tour at 17:00 or 18:00, just off cours Honoré Cresp at 20 boulevard Fragonard, tel. 04 93 36 44 65, www.fragonard.com).

The same company runs a two-room **museum** (Musée Provençal du Costume et du Bijou) displaying traditional dresses and jewelry (free, daily 10:00–13:00 & 14:00–18:00, a block above the *parfumerie* on the pedestrian street at 2 rue Jean Ossola). Upon leaving, you'll be given a card to be exchanged for a free gift at a shop next door.

Villa Jean-Honoré Fragonard—The home of the 18th-century Baroque painter of swirling big bodies (whose father started the smelly business) houses a good collection of his paintings and reproductions (€3, excellent English handout; June–Sept daily 10:00–18:30; Oct–May Wed–Mon 10:00–12:30 & 14:00–18:30, closed Tue; turn left out of Fragonard Perfume and walk downhill to 23 boulevard Fragonard).

International Museum of Perfume (Musée International de la Parfumerie)—This city museum is the pride of Grasse, offering a thorough examination of the history and production of perfume (€3; June–Sept daily 10:00–19:00, Thu until 21:00; Oct–May Wed–Mon 11:00–18:00, closed Tue; English explanations throughout, helpful audioguide, between the main TI and the Fragonard factory at 2 boulevard du Jeu de Ballon, tel. 04 97 05 58 00, http://boutique.museesdegrasse.com).

Old Grasse—Just above the Fragonard Perfume museum, rue Jean Ossola leads into the labyrinth of ancient streets that form an intriguing, if unpolished, pedestrian area. Follow the TI's self-guided tour with your map (takes an hour at a speedy pace), or just wander and read the beige information plaques when you see them. To get a good taste of old Grasse, stroll up rue Jean Ossola, then turn right down rue Gazan to find the Romanesque cathedral (worth peering into for its tree trunk–like columns and austere decor). Next, drop down to place de l'Eveché (a *molto italiano* square two blocks downhill behind the cathedral, has good lunch options), then climb back up to the town's main square, place aux Aires (with more good eating options).

Le Grand Canyon du Verdon

Two hours north of Nice and three hours east of Avignon lies the Parc Naturel Régional du Verdon (a.k.a. Gorges du Verdon). This immense area of natural beauty is worth ▲▲▲...even to Arizonans.

Planning Your Time
The Grand Canyon du Verdon, Europe's greatest canyon, offers a dilly of a detour between Provence and the Riviera (figure seven hours with modest canyon time between Nice and the Luberon or Aix-en-Provence; see my self-guided driving tour of the Inland Riviera earlier in this chapter). You can reach the canyon on a long round-trip drive from the Nice area if you leave early (easier if staying in Vence or Antibes). Some visitors prefer to stop and smell the canyon, overnighting en route (suggestions later in this chapter).

Here are some rough driving times: Riviera to Grasse—1 hour, Grasse to Balcon de la Mescla—1 hour, Balcon de la Mescla to Aiguines—1 hour, Aiguines to Manosque (en route to Provence)—1 hour.

Orientation to
Le Grand Canyon du Verdon

The Park Naturel Régional du Verdon, far more than just its famous canyon, is an extensive area mixing alpine scenery with misty villages, meandering streams, and seas of gentle meadows. The canyon is the heart of the park, where overpowering slabs of

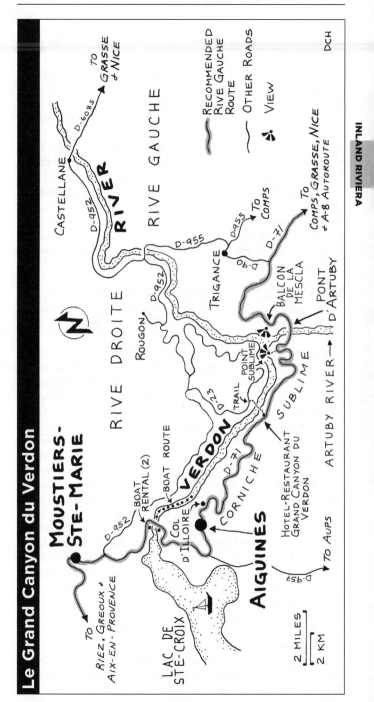

Le Grand Canyon du Verdon

MOUSTIERS-STE-MARIE

To
RIEZ, GREOUX +
AIX-EN-PROVENCE

RIVE DROITE

CASTELLANE

RIVE GAUCHE

VERDON RIVER

D-6085 TO GRASSE + NICE

D-952

D-952

ROUGON

D-23

TRAIL

POINT SUBLIME

D-955

TRIGANCE

D-71

D-90

D-955 To COMPS

To COMPS, GRASSE, NICE + A-8 AUTOROUTE

BALCON DE LA MESCLA

PONT D'ARTUBY

CORNICHE SUBLIME

ARTUBY RIVER

BOAT RENTAL (2)

BOAT ROUTE

COL D'ILLOIRE

D-71

D-952

AIGUINES

HOTEL-RESTAURANT GRAND CANYON DU VERDON

TO AUPS

D-957

LAC DE STE-CROIX

RECOMMENDED RIVE GAUCHE ROUTE

OTHER ROADS

VIEW

DCH

INLAND RIVIERA

2 MILES
2 KM

N

white and salmon-colored limestone plunge impossible distances to a snaking turquoise river below. You need a car, ample time, and a lack of vertigo to appreciate this area. If traveling in summer or on holiday weekends, go really early or skip it. Fill your tank before leaving Grasse or Moustiers-Ste-Marie, as gas is scarce. Roads crawl along the length of the canyon on both sides *(Rive Gauche and Rive Droite)*; the *Rive Gauche* (left bank) works best for most, though both are spectacular.

The Grand Canyon du Verdon is located between the villages of Moustiers-Ste-Marie and Aiguines to the west and Castellane to the east. The most scenic driving segments are along the right (north) bank between Moustiers-Ste-Marie and the Point Sublime overlook, and along the left (south) bank between Aiguines and the Balcon de la Mescla. (Thrill-seekers head for the Castellane area, where the whitewater rafting, climbing, and serious hiking trails are best.) Picnickers will find endless choices for the perfect lunch stop.

The Rive Gauche (Left Bank) Route

For drivers connecting the canyon with Provence or the Riviera, the left bank offers the most accessible and most scenic tour of the gorges.

Approaching from the Riviera: The most direct route from the Riviera follows D-6185 (old N-85), which starts near Cannes (A-8 autoroute from Nice to Cannes saves time) and passes through Grasse, changing to D-6085 and continuing north toward Digne and Castellane. You'll turn left off D-6085 about 20 kilometers before Castellane, following signs to the *Gorges du Verdon* and *Draguignan* (there's a fine medieval bridge just north of the road, about 3 kilometers before Comps-sur-Artuby, signed *La Souche*). Turn right at Comps-sur-Artuby, following signs to *Gorges du Verdon, Rive Gauche* (not *Rive Droite*). You'll reach the canyon rim at the Balcon de la Mescla and follow it for about 60 serpentine minutes (including stops) to the village of Aiguines (good overnight stop, described later in this chapter). Those continuing to Provençal destinations will go on to Moustiers-Ste-Marie (described later in this chapter), then Riez, then Gréoux-les-Bains. From Gréoux-les-Bains, follow signs for *Manosque*, then *Apt* for Luberon and Avignon; or use A-51 south to reach Aix-en-Provence, Cassis, Marseille, or Arles. Those making a day trip from Nice should return from Aiguines, following signs indicating *Aups* (D-957), then *Draguignan*, then *Nice* via A-8.

Approaching from Provence: All roads pass through Gréoux-les-Bains, which is about an hour northeast of Aix-en-Provence. Those coming from Cassis, Aix-en-Provence, and Arles will find A-51 north the fastest path; those coming from the Luberon and Avignon should take D-900 via Apt (turns into D-4100), then follow signs for *Manosque*. From Gréoux-les-Bains, follow signs to *Riez*, *Moustiers-Ste-Marie*, and *Aiguines* before entering the Grand Canyon du Verdon *(Rive Gauche)*. Leave the canyon after the Balcon de la Mescla, following signs for *Comps-sur-Artuby* (and *Draguignan* for a short distance), then *Grasse* and *Nice* for the Riviera. The fastest way from Grasse to Nice is via Cannes and A-8.

Self-Guided Driving Tour

Le Grand Canyon du Verdon: Rive Gauche (Left Bank)

At their deepest points, the gorges drop 2,200 feet to the river that carved them. At the bottom, the canyons can narrow to 26 feet across, while at the top, the canyon walls can spread as far as 4,700 feet apart.

You'll drive at an escargot's pace, navigating hairpin turns along the Corniche Sublime while enjoying constant views of rocky masses and vanishing-point views up the canyon. Hikes into the canyon are too long and too steep for most (but for hikers, I've described one good hike on this drive). Most travelers are better off walking along the road for a bit, or, even more sublime, walking along sections of small dirt roads that lead away from the asphalt (several to choose from; two are described below). There are many small pullouts along the route, so stop frequently and get out of that car to allow the driver a look at the views.

Here are the highlights along the route, from east to west:

The **Balcon de la Mescla** is the first pullout that drivers reach as they approach from Nice (and the last viewpoint for travelers coming from Provence). The lookout on the lower side of the gift shop/café is best (you'll find a good selection of maps and books in the friendly shop).

A little beyond, you can amble across Europe's highest bridge, **Pont d'Artuby,** and imagine working on its construction crew *(non, merci)*. About one kilometer west of the bridge, you'll find a grassy pullout (north side) with a short two-track dirt road that allows walkers to get away from the noise of the road and experience the gorges more peacefully (stash your car and follow the dirt path on foot—it's about 100 yards to the rocky edge of the canyon). You'll find an even better dirt-road option about two kilometers farther west (look for a pullout on the north side of the road) with sensational views down to the river and acres of limestone to scramble over.

About halfway through the canyon is the **Hôtel-Restaurant Grand Canyon du Verdon,** clinging to its cliff like a baby to its mother. This concrete, funky place looks slapped together, but the café terrace has a table for you with stupendous views (drinks, snacks, and meals available at fair prices; see also "Sleeping and Eating near the Grand Canyon du Verdon," later).

A stone's throw below the hotel is your best option for a sturdy **hike:** A posted trail leads all the way down to the river (parking available by the trailhead). It's a steep, challenging, and visually interesting 30 minutes down to the Passerelle de l'Estellie, and at least twice that long back up (good shoes and strong ankles are essential, as the rocky trail can be slippery). Once down, you can explore along the river, or cross the foot-bridge and prowl the right bank. Do this hike earlier in the day—in the afternoon, the high canyon walls can make dark-ness set in quickly. Once back up, celebrate with a drink on the hotel's terrace café.

Back along the main road, the **Col d'Illioure**—the last pass before leaving the canyon—provides sweeping views from the western portal. A large pullout allows parking where you'll find a few picnic tables scattered above and some good rock-scampering just below.

Just west of the canyon, the small village of **Aiguines** squats below waves of limestone and overlooks the long turquoise Lac de Ste-Croix. This unspoiled village has a handful of shops, hotels, and cafés (see "Sleeping and Eating near the Grand Canyon du Verdon," later). It's an outdoorsy, popular-with-hikers place that most canyon visitors cruise right through. Detour onto the grounds of the 15th- century château for the view over Aiguines (with picnic benches and a fun play area for kids). The château interior is closed to the public. Aiguines' **TI** is on the main drag (Mon–Fri 9:30–12:30 & 14:00–17:30, closed Sat–Sun, allée des Tilleuls, tel. 04 94 70 21 64, www.aiguines.com).

For more views over Aiguines and the lake, stroll up to the small **Chapelle St. Pierre** at the northern edge of town and find the orientation table. From here, you can walk along up the small road five minutes to the campground café, with nice tables on its broad view terrace (ideal for a pre-dinner drink or morning coffee).

Barely more than 30 years old, the man-made **Lac de Ste-Croix** is about six miles long and is the last stop for water flow-ing out of the Gorges du Verdon. For a fun lake/river experience, rent a canoe or paddle boat at either side of the low bridge half-way between Moustiers and Aiguines. You can paddle under the bridge, then follow the brilliant turquoise inlet upstream as far as 2.5 miles, tracing the river's route up the gorge on its final journey to the lake (€10/hour for paddle boat or canoe, figure 2 hours for a good trip).

Moustiers-Ste-Marie is another pretty Provençal face lined with boutiques—though this one comes with an impressive setting straddling a small stream at the base of the limestone cliffs of the Gorges du Verdon. The town is slammed with tourists clambering for the locally famous china and the usual Provençal kitsch. The **TI** is in the center, next to the church (daily 10:00–12:30 & 14:00–18:00, place de l'Eglise, tel. 04 92 74 67 84, www.moustiers.fr). For hotel and restaurant recommendations here, see below.

You can escape some of the crowds by climbing 30 minutes on a steep, ankle-twisting path to the **Chapelle Notre-Dame de Beauvoir**—a simple chapel that has attracted pilgrims for centuries. A notebook in the chapel allows travelers to pen a request for a miracle for a loved one. For most, the chapel does not warrant the effort, though you'll get fine views over the village by walking a short way up the path.

Sleeping and Eating near the Grand Canyon du Verdon

(€1 = about $1.40, country code: 33)
These are listed in the order you'll reach them on the self-guided driving tour. Notice that—unlike in the rest of this book—some hotel rates in this remote area are per person and for half-pension (including breakfast and dinner).

Midway Through the Canyon
$$$ Hôtel-Restaurant Grand Canyon du Verdon** has a funky structure that must have been grandfathered-in to own such an unbelievable location—2,500 feet high on the Corniche Sublime (described on the self-guided driving tour above). In addition to its incredible view terrace, the hotel rents 15 alpine-feeling, modern, basic rooms, half on the canyon and a few with view decks (open mid-April–mid-Oct, canyon-side Db or Tb-€68/person, non-canyon-side Db-€62/person, prices include a good-enough dinner and breakfast, tel. 04 94 76 91 31, fax 04 94 76 92 29, www.hotel-canyon-verdon.com, hotel.gd.canyon.verdon@wanadoo.fr).

In Aiguines

$$ Hôtel du Vieux-Château, which has been in business for 200 years, is Aiguines' most characteristic hotel. Run by Frédéric and his energetic mama, the hotel's 10 snug rooms are red-tiled, spotless, and cool, as there's little direct light (Db-€72–84, or about €60/person for half-pension, cozy restaurant open daily with simple, hearty fare and good soups, place de la Fontaine, tel. 04 94 70 22 95, fax 04 94 84 22 36, www.hotelvieuxchateau.fr, contact @hotelvieuxchateau.fr).

$$ Hôtel Altitude 823, just below, offers more predictable comfort with a bit less character at similar rates (€50–60 per person for half-pension, tel. 04 98 10 22 17, fax 04 98 10 22 16, www.altitude823-verdon.com, altitude823@laposte.net).

In Moustiers-Ste-Mar

$$ La Bonne Auberge offers no-frills rooms but a nice pool at the southern edge of the old town (Db-€65–85, extra bed-€15, garage-€5, route de Castellane, tel. 04 92 74 66 18, fax 04 92 74 65 11, www.bonne-auberge-moustiers.com, labonneauberge@club -internet.fr, closed Nov–March).

$ At Restaurant/Chambres Clerissy, Sophie offers a great value and a warm welcome with four spacious and spotless rooms. It's good for families (Db-€47, Tb-€57, breakfast-€5, cash only, place du Chevalier de Blacas, in the village center across from the left transept of the church, mobile 06 33 34 06 95, tel. & fax 04 92 74 62 67, www.clerissy.fr, contact@clerissy.fr).

Eating: There is no shortage of dining options in Moustiers-Ste-Marie. The simple **Restaurant Clerissy** (whose rooms are listed above) offers inexpensive and simple meals (crêpes and pizza) and appealing indoor and outdoor tables. **Côté Jardin** is a haven of quiet a few steps south of the old town, with a pleasing garden setting and good cuisine at fair prices (*menus* from €23, closed Mon–Tue, tel. 04 92 74 68 91).

TRAVELING WITH CHILDREN

With relatively few must-see museums, plenty of outdoor activities, and cooperative weather, Provence and the French Riviera are practically made for kids. This part of France has beaches, fun canoeing on safe rivers, good biking, Roman ruins to scramble over, abundant sunshine, and swimming pools everywhere. Teenagers love the seaside resorts (Cassis is best) and enjoy the hustle and bustle of cities like Avignon, Arles, Aix-en-Provence, and Nice. Younger kids tend to prefer the rural areas, which offer more swimming pools, open spaces, and parks.

To make your trip fun for everyone in the family, mix heavy-duty sights with kids' activities, like playing miniature golf or *boules*, renting bikes or canoes, and riding the little tourist trains popular in many towns. Kids also like audioguides, available at important sights in many cities. And if you're in France near Bastille Day, remember that firecracker stands pop up everywhere on the days leading up to July 14. Putting on their own fireworks show can be a highlight for teenagers.

Minimize hotel changes by planning three-day stops. Aim for hotels with restaurants, so older kids can go back to the room while you finish a pleasant dinner.

We've listed swimming pools in many places, but be warned: Public pools in France commonly require a small, Speedo-like bathing suit for boys and men (American-style swim trunks won't do)—though they usually have these little suits to loan. At hotel pools, any type of swimsuit will do.

For breakfast, croissants are a hit, though a good *pain au chocolat* (croissant with chocolate bits) will be appreciated even more. Hot chocolate, fruit, and yogurt are usually available. For lunch and dinner, it's easy to find fast-food places and restaurants with kids' menus, but it's more fun to find *crêperies*, which have a wide variety of fillings for both savory and dessert crêpes. For food emergencies, we travel with a plastic container of peanut butter brought from home and smuggle small amounts of jam from breakfast.

Kids homesick for friends can keep in touch with cheap international phone cards and email. Hotel Internet access and cyber-cafés are a godsend for parents with teenagers. Readily available Wi-Fi makes bringing a laptop worthwhile. Some parents find buying a French mobile phone—or roaming with an American mobile phone—a helpful investment; adults can stay connected to teenagers while allowing them maximum independence (see page 437). If you and your teenager both have mobile phones that work in Europe, sending each other text messages can be a relatively inexpensive way to keep in touch (much cheaper than actual phone calls).

Kids like the French adventure comics Astérix and Tintin (both available in English, sold in bigger bookstores with English sections).

It's fun to take kids to movies (even if not in English) just to see how theaters work elsewhere. Movies shown in their original language—usually with subtitles—are listed as *v.o.* at the box office. (One showing could be *v.o.* and the next could be dubbed in French, labeled *v.f.*) *Dessin animé* means "cartoon." While many live-action movies can be found in their original language with French subtitles, cartoons and kids' movies (intended for an audience that doesn't read so well yet) are almost always dubbed.

You'll find old-style merry-go-rounds in many cities, perfect for younger travelers (my daughter's goal was to ride a merry-go-round in every town...she came close). I've also identified parks with play areas when possible. Visits to local goat cheese-makers in early spring yield good kid rewards (look for *fromage fermier de chèvre* signs along the country roads). Goats are social animals and goat cheese-makers will usually let your child hold or pet one. You can also pick up some superb fresh cheese for your picnic.

The best thing we did on a recent trip was buy a set of *boules* (a.k.a. *pétanque*, a form of outdoor bowling—for the rules, see sidebar on page 196). We'd play *boules* before dinner, side by side with real players on the village court. Get your *boules de pétanque* at sporting-goods stores or larger department stores. Since they're heavy, buy a set only if you'll be driving. The *boules* also make fun, if weighty, souvenirs, and are just as enjoyable to play back at home.

Swap babysitting duties with your partner if one of you wants to take in an extra sight. And for memories that will last long after the trip, keep a family journal. Pack a small diary and a glue stick. While relaxing at a café over a *citron pressé* (lemonade), take turns writing about the day's events and include mementos such as ticket stubs from museums, postcards, or stalks of lavender.

Before You Go

Get your kids into the spirit ahead of time using these tips:

- Pick up books at the library and rent videos. Watch or read the Madeline stories by Ludwig Bemelmans, *The Hunchback of Notre-Dame* by Victor Hugo, *The Three Musketeers* by Alexandre Dumas, or Dumas' *The Man in the Iron Mask. Anni's Diary of France,* by Anni Axworthy, is a fun, picture-filled book about a young girl's trip; it could inspire your children. *How Would You Survive in the Middle Ages?,* by Fiona MacDonald, is an appealing "guide" for kids. Serious kid-historians will devour *The Kingfisher History Encyclopedia.* For a fantastical visit to Avignon in the days of the pope, *The Lady and the Squire* by former Monty Python Terry Jones is a fun read. If your children are interested in art, get your hands on *The History of Art for Young People* by Anthony Janson and *Discovering Great Artists: Hands-On Art for Children in the Styles of the Great Masters* by MaryAnn Kohl. (Also see the recommended books and movies list, which includes some good choices for teenagers, in this book's appendix.)
- Involve your kids in trip planning. Have them read about the places that you may include in your itinerary (even the hotels you're considering), and let them help in your decisions.
- Hotel selection is critical. In my recommendations, I've iden- tified hotels that seem particularly kid-friendly (pools, table tennis, grassy areas, easygoing owners, etc.). If you're staying for a week or more in one place, rent a *gîte* (see "*Gîtes* and Apartments," page 26).

What to Bring

- Children's books are scarce and expensive in France. Our chil- dren read much more when traveling in Europe than while at home, so don't skimp here (see list above).
- Bring peanut butter (hard to find in France)...or help your kids acquire a taste for Nutella, the tasty hazelnut-chocolate spread available everywhere. Look for organic (*bio*) stores in cities where you can find *Chocolade,* a less-sugary version of Nutella, and numerous nut butters.
- Choose items that are small and convenient for use on planes, trains, and in your hotel room: a small laptop computer, com- pact travel games, a deck of cards, a handheld video game, and drawing and coloring supplies. Consider bringing your own drawing paper, which is surprisingly expensive in Europe.
- For younger kids, Legos are easily packed and practical (it's

CHILDREN

also fun to purchase kits in Europe, where the Legos are sometimes different from those in the US).

- Budding fashionistas might enjoy traveling with—and buying new outfits for—a Corelle doll or another 16-inch doll. The French have wonderful doll clothes, with a much wider selection than typically found in the US.

- Benadryl does miracles in keeping ears and noses open during flights—with the added benefit of sleepiness for most children. I gave my kids Benadryl before bed for the first two nights in Europe, and they rarely had serious jet-lag issues.

- For traveling with infants, car-rental agencies usually have car seats for a small price, though you must reserve one ahead of time. And while most hotels have some sort of crib, I brought a portable crib and did not regret it.

- Cameras (even disposable ones) are a great investment to get your kids involved.

- For longer drives, audio books can be fun for the whole family (if carefully chosen). I recommend Peter Mayle's *A Year in Provence,* available on CD (or put it on your MP3 player/ iPod).

Planning Your Time

- Lower your sightseeing ambitions and prepare to savor fewer places for longer periods. Plan longer stays at fewer stops— you won't regret it.

- Don't overdo it. Tackle one key sight each day and mix in a healthy dose of fun activities.

- Follow this book's crowd-beating tips to a T. Kids despise long lines more than you do.

- Eat dinner early (19:00–19:30 at restaurants, earlier at cafés). Skip romantic eateries. Try relaxed cafés (or fast-food restaurants) where kids can move around without bothering others. Picnics work well.

- The best and cheapest toy selections are in the department stores, like Monoprix and Galeries Lafayette.

- Let kids help choose daily activities, lead you through ancient sights, and so on.

- Keep an eye out for *mini-golfs* (miniature golf).

Top Kid-Friendly Sights and Activities

These are listed in no particular order:

- Pont du Gard. An entire wing of the museum is dedicated to kids, who can also swim or take a canoe trip on the river. See page 138.

- Cassis. Boat trip to the *calanques* or the port and beaches for teenagers. See page 239.

- Changing of the Guard in Monaco (11:55 daily). See page 357.
- Cousteau Aquarium in Monaco. See page 358.
- Pedal boats on the Mediterranean (page 285) and into the Gorges du Verdon (page 410).
- Biking through vineyards to small villages, from Vaison la Romaine. See page 160.
- Les Baux's castle ruins, with medieval weaponry and great walls to climb. See page 83.
- Canoeing on the Ardèche River (page 179), the Sorgue River (page 189), or into the Gorges du Verdon (page 410).
- Boat trips from Nice (page 275), Villefranche-sur-Mer (page 329), or St-Tropez (page 389).
- Biking or in-line skating on the promenade des Anglais in Nice (page 284).
- Marineland near Antibes (page 375).
- Little tourist trains (in nearly every city).

Honorable mention goes to Arles' Ancient History Museum (see page 57), horseback riding and public beaches in the Camargue (page 95), Roman arenas in Nîmes (page 129) and Arles (page 64), Cathédrale d'Images near Les Baux (page 86), the beaches of Antibes (page 373), and the narrow-gauge train ride from Nice (see page 285).

CHILDREN

SHOPPING

Provence and the Riviera offer France's best shopping outside of Paris, with a great range of reasonably priced items ideal for souvenirs and gifts. And if approached thoughtfully, shopping in the south of France can be a culturally enlightening experience. There's no better way to mix serious shopping business with travel pleasure than at the weekly markets *(marchés)* in towns and villages throughout the region. These traditional market days are far more than fresh produce and fish; in many cases, about half the market is devoted to durable goods (like baskets, tablecloths, pottery, and local fabrics)—*très* handy for gift-scavenging travelers. If you miss market day, most Provençal towns have more than enough small shops that sell local products—and more than enough kitschy souvenirs. (They're often selling the same items you can find more cheaply at weekly markets.) If you crave French fashion, the cities described in this book have unlimited boutique shopping for clothing.

In this chapter, you'll find information on shopping for souvenirs, navigating market days, and browsing boutiques. For information on VAT refunds and customs regulations, see page 17. For a comparison of French clothing sizes to US sizes, see page 466.

What to Buy

Here's a shopping list of locally made goods in Provence and the Riviera. You'll find most of these items in tourist-oriented boutiques, though many of them can be had for less on market days. If you buy more expensive, nonperishable goods, most stores will work with you to send them home.

- **Jams** *(confiture)* containing lush and often exotic fruits, such as *fruits de passion* (passion fruit), *figues* (figs), and *pastèque* or *citre* (different types of watermelon).

- **Honey** *(miel),* particularly lavender *(lavande)* or rosemary *(romarin).* Stronger palates should try the chestnut *(châtaigne)* or even oak-flavored *(chêne)* honey.
- Tins of **tapenade** (olive paste) and all kinds of olives: black, green, and pricked with garlic or anchovies.
- **Olive-wood products** such as utensils and bowls. Olives are not just for nibbling; in Provence, the entire tree is used.
- Canned **pâtés,** including the buttery, rich *foie gras* (its "home" is Périgord, but you'll also find it in the markets of Provence). Canned goose, duck, and pork pâté can be imported to the US, but not beef.
- Packets of **herbs** (including the famous *herbes de Provence*), **salt** from the Camargue (look for *Fleur de Sel* for the best, and use sparingly), and bottles or tins of **olive oil** from local trees (Nyons is France's olive capital, though Les Baux is rightly proud of its olives as well). Most of these items can be found in attractive packaging that can be saved and enjoyed long after the product itself is gone.
- Sweets, including the famous *nougat de Montélimar* (a rich, chewy confection made with nuts and honey and sometimes flavored with lavender or other fragrances), *calissons* (orange-and-almond-flavored candy, shaped like the nut and originally from Aix-en-Provence), and **chocolates** from the Provençal producer Puyricard.
- **Soaps and lotions,** particularly those "perfumed" with local plants such as lavender *(lavande),* rosemary *(romarin),* or linden *(tilleul).* You'll also find colorful **sachets** containing the same fragrances.
- Brightly colored **table linens.** Souleiado and Les Olivades are the most famous local manufacturers, but good-quality knockoffs can be found in most any market or store.
- Local **pottery** (*poterie; faïence* is hand-painted *poterie*). Terre Provence is a well-known (and pricey) brand, but many other producers offer excellent quality, usually for less. Serious potters can plan ahead to visit a pottery fair featuring the best of the regions' potters (calendar at http://artceramistes.free.fr/marches/Provence/index.htm).
- *Santons,* the tiny, brightly adorned clay or wood Provençal figurines. Originally designed for traditional Christmas crèche scenes, today's *santons* ("little saints") represent all walks of life—from the local *boulanger* to the woman sewing bright Provençal cloth to the village doctor. The most famous *santon* makers are in Séguret and Aubagne. All *santon* makers belong to the *santon*-maker guild (think medieval stonecutters or woodworkers), and each *santon* is handmade and signed.

Market Day *(Jour du Marché)*

Market days are a big deal throughout France, and in no other region are they more celebrated than in Provence and the Riviera.

Markets have been a central feature of life in rural areas since the Middle Ages. No single event better symbolizes the French preoccupation with fresh products, and their strong ties to the small farmer, than the weekly market. Many locals mark their calendars with the arrival of the new season's produce.

Provence is a Mediterranean melting pot, where Italy, Spain, and North Africa intersect with France to do business. Notice the ethnic mix of the vendors (and the products they sell). Spices from Morocco and Tunisia, fresh pasta from Italy, saffron from Spain, and tapenade from Provence compete for your attention at Provence's *marchés*.

There are two kinds of weekly open-air markets: *les marchés* and *les marchés brocantes*.

Les marchés are more general in scope, more common, and more colorful, featuring products from local farmers and artisans. These markets can offer a mind-boggling array of choices, from the perishable (produce, meats, cheeses, breads, and pastries) to the nonperishable (kitchen wares, inexpensive clothing, brightly colored linens, and pottery).

Les marchés brocantes specialize in quasi-antiques and flea-market bric-a-brac. *Brocantes* markets began in the Middle Ages, when middlemen would gather to set up small stalls and sell old, flea-infested clothes and discarded possessions of the wealthy at bargain prices to eager peasants. Buyers were allowed to *rummage* through piles of aristocratic garbage.

Many *marchés* have good selections of produce and some *brocantes*. The best of all market worlds may rest in the picturesque town of Isle-sur-la-Sorgue, where, on Sunday mornings, a brilliant food *marché* tangles with an active flea market and a good selection of antiques.

I've listed days and locations for both market types throughout this book. Notice the signs as you enter towns indicating the *jours du marché* (essential information to any civilized soul, and a reminder not to park on the streets the night before—be on the lookout for *stationnement interdit* signs that mark "no parking" areas). Most *marchés* take place once a week in the town's main square, and, if large enough, they spill into nearby streets.

Usually, the bigger the market, the greater the overall selection, particularly for nonperishable goods. Bigger towns (like Arles) may have two weekly markets, one a bit larger than the other, with more nonperishable goods; in other towns (including Isle-sur-la-Sorgue), the second weekly market may simply be a smaller version of the main market day. The biggest market days are usually on weekends, so that everyone can go. In the largest cities (such as Avignon and Nîmes), modern market halls have been established with produce stands and meat counters selling fresh goods daily.

Market day is as important socially as commercially—it's a weekly chance for locals to resume friendships and get the current gossip. Here, neighbors can catch up on Henri's barn renovation, see photos of Jacqueline's new grandchild, and relax over *un café*. Dogs are tethered to café tables while friends exchange kisses. Tether yourself to a table and observe: three cheek-kisses for good friends (left-right-left), a fourth for friends you haven't seen in a while. (The appropriate number of kisses varies by region—Paris, Lyon, and Provence each have separate standards.)

Markets begin at about 8:00, with setup commencing in the predawn hours (for some, a reason not to stay in a main-square hotel the night before market day). They usually end by 13:00. Most perishable items are sold directly from the producers—no middlemen, no Visa cards, just really fresh produce (*du pays* means "grown locally"). Sometimes you'll meet a widow selling a dozen eggs, two rabbits, and a wad of herbs tied with string. But most vendors follow a weekly circuit of markets they feel works best for them, showing up in the same spot every week, year in and year out. At a favorite market, my family has done business with the same olive vendor and "cookie man" for 18 years.

It's bad form to be in a hurry on market day. Allow the crowd to set your pace. Observe the interaction between vendor and client. Notice the joy they can find in chatting each other up. Wares are displayed with pride. Generally the rule is "don't touch"—instead, point and let them serve you. If self-serve is the norm, the seller will hand you a bag. Remember, they use metric weight. Ask for *un kilo* (about 2 pounds), *un demi-kilo* (about 1 pound—also called *une livre*), or *un quart-kilo* (pronounced "car-kilo," about half a pound). Many vendors speak enough English to assist you in your selection. Your total price will be hand-tallied on small scraps of paper and given to you. Vendors are normally honest. If you're struggling to find the correct change, just hold out your hand and they will take only what is needed. (Still, you're wise to double-check the amount you just paid for that olive tree.)

At the root of a good market experience is a sturdy shopping basket or bag. Find the vendor selling baskets and other wicker items and go local (*osier* is the French name for wicker, *cade* is the Provençal name—from the basket-making Luberon village of

Key Shopping Phrases

English	French	Pronounced
Just looking.	*Je regarde.*	zhuh ruh-garde
How much is it?	*Combien?*	kohm-bee-ehn
Too big/small/ expensive	*Trop grand/ petit/cher*	troh grahn/ puh-tee/sher
May I try it on?	*Je peux l'essayer?*	zhuh puh luh-say-yay
Can I see more?	*Puis-je en voir d'autres?*	pweezh ehn vwahr doh-truh
I'll think about it.	*Je vais y penser.*	zhuh vayz-ee pahn-say
I'd like this.	*Je voudrais ça.*	zhuh voo-dray sah
on sale	*solde*	sold-ay
discounted price	*prix réduit*	pree ray-dwee
big discounts	*prix choc*	pree shock

SHOPPING

Cadenet); you can also find plastic and nylon versions. Most baskets are inexpensive, make for fun and colorful souvenirs, and can come in handy for odd-shaped or breakable carry-ons for the plane trip home. With basket in hand, shop for your heaviest items first. (You don't want to put a kilo of fresh apples on top of the bread you bought for your picnic.)

Markets change seasonally. In April and May, look for asparagus (green, purple, or the prized white—after being cooked, these are dipped in vinegar or homemade mayonnaise and eaten by hand). In late spring, shop for strawberries, including the best: *fraises des bois* (wild strawberries). Almost equally prized are the strawberries called *gariguettes* and *maras des bois*. Soon after, you'll see cherries and other stone fruits, plus the famously sweet Cavaillon melons (resembling tiny cantaloupes, often served cut in half with a spoonful or two of the sweet Rhône white wine Beaumes de Venise). Don't worry if these are split open—the abundance of sugar and sunshine are the cause, and the *fendus* are considered the sweetest. In late June and early September, watch for figs *(figues)*. From July through September, essential vegetables for the Provençal dish ratatouille—including eggplant, tomatoes, zucchinis, and peppers—come straight from the open fields. In the fall, you'll see stands selling game birds, other beasts of the hunt, and a glorious array of wild mushrooms.

After November and throughout the winter, look for little (or big, depending on your wallet size) black truffles. Truffles preserved and sealed in jars can safely be brought back to the United States. The Luberon is one of Provence's largest truffle-producing areas. The town of Carpentras hosts a truffles-only market on Friday mornings in winter, off the main roundabout in front of a café. Listen carefully and you might hear the Provençal language being spoken between some vendors and buyers. Richerenches, Northern Provence's truffle capital, holds its own winter truffle market; during its annual truffle-themed Mass, many parishioners would give a truffle as a small offering, instead of money.

For more immediate consumption, look for local cheeses (cow, called *vache*; sheep or ewe, called *brebis*; or the Provençal favorite: goat cheese, or *chèvre*, named *picodons*). Cheeses range from very fresh (aged one day) to aged for weeks. The older the cheese, the more dried and shrunken. Some may even be speckled with edible mold. Cheeses come in many shapes (round, logs, pyramids) and various sizes (from single-bite mouthfuls to wheels that will feed you for several meals). Some are sprinkled with herbs or spices. Others are more adorned, such as those rolled in ash *(à la cendre)* or wrapped in leaves *(banon)*. Watch for the locally produced *banon de banon*, a goat cheese soaked in *eau-de-vie* (the highly alcoholic "water of life"), then wrapped in chestnut leaves and tied with string—*ooh la la*.

Next, move on to the sausages (many also rolled in herbs or spices). Samples are usually free—try the *sanglier* (boar). Be on the lookout for locally produced wines or ciders (free tastings are standard) and find samples of *foie gras* (available in take-it-home tins), good with the sweet white wine of Beaumes de Venise. These items make perfect picnic fare when teamed with a crusty baguette.

Throughout Provence, you'll see vendors selling paella made *sur place* (on the spot) in huge traditional round pans. Paella varies by area and by chef, but most recipes include the traditional ingredients of fresh shellfish, chicken, and sausages mixed into saffron-infused rice. And throughout France, you'll see vans selling sizzling, spit-roasted chicken (perfectly bagged for carrying-out) or pizza (made to your liking on the spot). *Bon appétit!*

Clothing Boutiques

Those preferring fashion over food will be pleased to learn that they don't have to go to Paris to enjoy the latest trends. The stylish boutiques lining the shopping streets of Avignon, Nîmes, Aix-en-Provence, St. Rémy, Uzès, and Nice offer more than sufficient selection and style for the fashion-conscious. The expression for window-shopping in French is *faire du lèche-vitrines* (literally, "window-licking"). While hardly as freewheeling and relaxed as *les marchés,* you're a long way from the intimidating clerks of Paris. Still, they play by a different set of rules in France, and the better knowledge you have of the rules, the better player you'll be. While many shopkeepers speak some English, an effort to speak even a minimum of French earns better service. These tips should get you off on the right track:

- In small stores, always say, *"Bonjour, Madame or Mademoiselle or Monsieur"* when entering. For extra credit, apologize for bothering the clerk: *"Excusez-moi de vous déranger."* And remember to say, *"Au revoir, Madame/Mademoiselle/Monsieur"* when leaving.
- Except in department stores, it's not normal for the customer to handle clothing. Ask first before you pick up an item: *"Pourrais-je voir de plus près?"* (poo-ray-zhuh vwahr duh ploo pray; "May I see this closer?").
- For clothing-size comparisons between the US and France, see page 466 in the appendix.
- Forget returns (and don't count on exchanges).
- The customer is not always right; in fact, some clerks figure they're doing you a favor by waiting on you.
- Saturdays are busiest.
- Observe French shoppers, then imitate.

SHOPPING

FRANCE: PAST AND PRESENT

French History in an Escargot Shell

About the time of Christ, Romans "Latinized" the land of the Gauls. With the fifth-century A.D. fall of Rome, the barbarian Franks and Burgundians invaded. Today's France evolved from this unique mix of Latin and Celtic cultures.

While France wallowed with the rest of Europe in medieval darkness, it got a head start in its development as a nation-state. In 507, Clovis established Paris as the capital of his Christian Merovingian dynasty. Clovis and the Franks would eventually become Louis and the French. Charles Martel stopped the spread of Islam by beating the Spanish Moors at the Battle of Poitiers. And Charlemagne, the most important of the "Dark Age" Frankish kings, was crowned Holy Roman Emperor by the pope in 800. Charles the Great presided over the "Carolingian Renaissance" and effectively ruled an empire that was vast for its time.

The Treaty of Verdun (843), which divided Charlemagne's empire among his grandsons, marks what could be considered the birth of Europe. For the first time, a treaty was signed in vernacular languages (French and German), rather than in Latin. This split established a Franco-Germanic divide and heralded an age of fragmentation. While petty princes took the reigns, the Frankish king ruled only Ile de France, a small region around Paris.

Vikings, or Norsemen, settled in what became Normandy. Later, in 1066, these "Normans" invaded England. The Norman king, William the Conqueror, consolidated his English domain, accelerating the formation of modern England. But his rule also muddied the political waters between England and France, kicking off a centuries-long struggle between the two nations.

In the 12th century, Eleanor of Aquitaine (a separate country in southwest France) married Louis VII, king of France,

Top French Notables in History

Madame and Monsieur Cro-Magnon: Prehistoric hunter-gatherers who moved to France (c. 30,000 B.C.), painted cave walls at Lascaux and Font-de-Gaume, and eventually settled down as farmers (c. 10,000 B.C.).

Vercingétorix (72–46 B.C.): This long-haired warrior rallied the Gauls against Julius Caesar's invading Roman legions (52 B.C.). Defeated by Caesar, France fell under Roman domination, resulting in 500 years of peace and prosperity. During that time, the Romans established cities, built roads, taught in Latin, and converted people to Christianity.

Charlemagne (A.D. 742–814): For Christmas in A.D. 800, the pope gave King Charlemagne the title of Emperor, thus uniting much of Europe under the leadership of the Franks ("France"). Charlemagne stabilized France amid centuries of barbarian invasions. After his death, the empire was split, carving the outlines of modern France and Germany.

Eleanor of Aquitaine (c. 1122–1204): The beautiful, sophisticated ex-wife of the King of France married the King of England, creating an uneasy union between the two countries. During her lifetime, French culture was spread across Europe by roving troubadours, theological scholars, and skilled architects pioneering "the French style"—Gothic.

Joan of Arc (1412–1431): When France and England fought the Hundred Years' War to settle who would rule (1337–1453), teenager Joan of Arc—guided by voices in her head—rallied the French troops. Though Joan was captured and burned as a heretic, the French eventually drove England out of their country for good, establishing the current borders. Over the centuries, the church upgraded Joan's status from heretic to saint (canonized in 1920).

François I (1494–1547): This Renaissance king ruled a united, modern nation, making it a cultural center that hosted the Italian Leonardo da Vinci. François set the tone for future absolute monarchs, punctuating his commands with the phrase, "For such is our pleasure."

Louis XIV (1638–1715): Charismatic and cunning, the "Sun King" ruled Europe's richest, most populous, most powerful nation-state. Every educated European spoke French, dressed in Louis-style leotards and powdered wigs, and built Versailles-like palaces. Though Louis ruled as an absolute monarch (distracting the nobility with courtly games), his reign also fostered the arts and philosophy, sowing the seeds of democracy and revolution.

Marie Antoinette (1755–1793): As the wife of Louis XVI, she came to symbolize (probably unfairly) the decadence of France's ruling class. When Revolution broke out (1789), she was arrested, imprisoned, and executed—one of thousands who were guillotined on Paris' place de la Concorde as an enemy of the people.

Napoleon Bonaparte (1769–1821): This daring young military man became a hero during the Revolution, fighting Europe's royalty. He went on to conquer much of the Continent, become leader of France, and eventually rule as a dictator with the title of Emperor. In 1815, an allied Europe defeated and exiled Napoleon, reinstating the French monarchy—though future kings (including Napoleon's nephew, who ruled as Napoleon III) were subject to democratic constraints.

Claude Monet (1840–1926): Monet's Impressionist paintings captured the soft-focus beauty of the belle époque—middle-class men and women enjoying drinks in cafés, walks in gardens, and picnics along the Seine. At the turn of the 20th century, French culture reigned supreme while its economic and political clout was fading, soon to be shattered by the violence of World War I.

Charles de Gaulle (1890–1970): A career-military man, de Gaulle helped France survive occupation by Nazi Germany during World War II with his rousing radio broadcasts and unbending faith in France. As president, he led the country through its postwar rebuilding, divisive wars in Vietnam and Algeria (trying to preserve France's colonial empire), and turbulent student riots in the 1960s.

Contemporary French: Which recent French people will history remember? President François Mitterand (1916–1996), the driving force behind La Grande Arche and Opéra Bastille? Marcel Marceau (1923–2007), white-faced mime? Chef Paul Bocuse (b. 1926), inventor of *nouvelle cuisine?* Brigitte Bardot (b. 1934), film actress, crusader for animal rights, and popularizer of the bikini? Yves Saint Laurent (1936–2008), one of the world's greatest fashion designers? Jean-Marie Le Pen (b. 1928), founder of the far-right Front National party, with staunch anti-immigration policies? Bernard Kouchner (b. 1939), co-founder of Doctors without Borders and minister of foreign affairs under President Sarkozy? Or Zinédine Zidane (b. 1972), France's greatest soccer player ever, whose Algerian roots helped raise the status of Arabs in France?

bringing Aquitaine under French rule. They divorced, and she married Henry of Normandy, soon to be Henry II of England. This marital union gave England control of a huge swath of land, from the English Channel to the Pyrénées. For 300 years, France and England would struggle for control of Aquitaine. Any enemy of the French king would find a natural ally in the English king.

In 1328, the French king Charles IV died without a son. The English king (Edward III), Charles IV's nephew, was interested in the throne, but the French resisted. This quandary pitted France, the biggest and richest country in Europe, against England, which had the largest army. They fought from 1337 to 1453 in what was modestly called the Hundred Years' War.

Regional powers from within France actually sided with England. Burgundy took Paris, captured the royal family, and recognized the English king as heir to the French throne. England controlled France from the Loire north, and things looked bleak for the French king.

Enter Joan of Arc, a 16-year-old peasant girl driven by religious voices. France's national heroine left home to support Charles VII, the dauphin (boy prince, heir to the throne but too young to rule). Joan rallied the French, ultimately inspiring them to throw out the English. In 1430, Joan was captured by the Burgundians, who sold her to the English, who convicted her of heresy and burned her at the stake in Rouen. But the inspiration of Joan of Arc lived on, and by 1453, English holdings on the Continent had dwindled to the port of Calais.

By 1500, a strong, centralized France had emerged, with borders similar to those today. Its kings (from the Renaissance François I through the Henrys and all those Louises) were model divine monarchs, setting the standard for absolute rule in Europe.

Outrage over the power plays and spending sprees of the kings—coupled with the modern thinking of the Enlightenment (whose leaders were the French *philosophes*)—led to the French Revolution (1789). In France, it was the end of the *ancien régime*, as well as its notion that some are born to rule, while others are born to be ruled.

The excesses of the Revolution in turn led to the rise of Napoleon, who ruled the French empire as a dictator. Eventually, *his* excesses ushered him into a South Atlantic exile, and the French settled on a compromise role for their leader. The modern French king was himself ruled by a constitution. Rather than dress in leotards and powdered wigs, he went to work in a suit with a briefcase.

The 20th century spelled the end of France's reign as a military and political superpower. Devastating wars with Germany in 1870, 1914, and 1940—and the loss of her colonial holdings—left France with not quite enough land, people, or production to be a top player on a global scale. But the 21st century may see France rise again: Paris is again the cultural capital of Europe, and France—under the EU banner—is leading the push to unify Europe as a single economic power. And when Europe is a superpower, Paris may yet be its capital.

Contemporary Politics in France

Today, the key political issues in France (like everywhere) mainly revolve around the economy. Although France has suffered less than the US (financial institutions didn't get involved in risky home loans, and the French are less invested in the stock market), the country still has its share of problems. Unemployment is high (about 10 percent), and taxes are higher (about 44 percent of the Gross Domestic Product). Other concerns include the steadily increasing percentage of ethnic minorities (close to 10 percent of France's population is of North African descent), the extent of the European Union's power, and the need to balance workers' cushy benefits with having to compete in a global marketplace. The challenge for the leadership is to address these issues while maintaining the level of social services that the French expect from their government.

France is part of the 27-member European Union (a kind of "United States of Europe") that has successfully dissolved borders and implemented a single currency, the euro. While the government has been decidedly pro-EU, the people are more skeptical. In 2005, they voted against ratifying an EU constitution that would have increased the union's political powers. Many citizens fear that a more-powerful EU could ultimately infringe upon job security and social benefits (a huge issue in France).

French national politics are complex but fascinating. The country has seven major political parties and several smaller ones. From left to right, the major parties include the New Anticapitalist Party (Nouveau Parti AntiCapitaliste, NPA); the more–moderate, reformed Communists (Parti Communiste Français, PCF); the environmental party (Les Verts, "The Greens"); the middle-of-the-road Socialists (Parti Socialiste, PS); the centrist MoDem party (Mouvement Démocrate); the center-right Popular Movement (Union pour un Mouvement Populaire, UMP); and the racist, isolationist Front National (FN). In general, the two parties with the most support are the UMP and the Socialists. In the 2007 presidential election, the top two candidates came from these parties (current President Nicolas Sarkozy is a member of the UMP). But unlike in the US, informal coalitions are generally necessary for any party to "rule."

Trouble in Paradise:
Population Growth in Southern France

Amid the breezy, sun-kissed beaches, cities, and villages of Provence and the French Riviera, tension is brewing. The south of France has become a melting pot of people in search of their Provençal paradise. While some say the influx into this region has invigorated the culture, many residents are feeling growing pains. Two major trends are fueling the population boom in the south: northern Europeans looking for their place in the sun and North African immigrants looking for a better life in France.

Cheap flights and lightning-fast train service have enabled northern Europeans to experience the south of France as a weekend getaway...and a growing number are choosing to stay. Thanks to its sunny climate, relatively inexpensive homes (with pools), and plentiful transportation options, this region is an understandably big draw. Unfortunately, as wealthy northerners pick off local homes and inflate prices, the average Jean is losing out.

Immigration, particularly from North Africa, is another cause of the population boom. With the historic loss of able-bodied men from World Wars I and II, and native-French birth rates unable to replace those losses, France looked across the Mediterranean to its old colonies for cheap sources of manual labor. When these workers came, they brought their families, who stayed in France and had large families of their own. Today, France has Europe's largest Muslim population.

Five million North Africans legally reside in France (close to 10 percent of the population)—and many more live here illegally. More than 100,000 illegal immigrants arrive in France each year, about half of whom are North African. Most live in the south (more than a quarter of Marseille's population is North African). This concentration of immigrants among a very Catholic French population (Muslims outnumber Protestants 2 to 1), combined with high unemployment (15–20 percent compared to a national average of 10 percent), has led to the rise of racist politics. This anti-immigrant movement has been spearheaded by the Front National party, which wants to keep "France for the French." Its leader, Jean-Marie Le Pen, has referred to the increasing numbers of North Africans in France as "the silent invasion." The Front National generally receives about 20 percent of this region's vote in national elections.

The Front National party, led by Jean-Marie Le Pen, campaigns on a "France for the French" platform, which calls for the expulsion of ethnic minorities, restoration of the French franc, and broader police powers. In the fall of 2005, tensions mounted when disadvantaged youths (many of North African descent) rioted in the Parisian suburbs, protesting discrimination. The Front Nationalists have a staunch voter base of about 13 percent nationally, but rising unemployment and globalization worries have increased its following, allowing Le Pen to nudge the political agenda to the right.

On the left, the once-powerful Communists (PCF) tend to draw only about five percent of the popular vote, forcing them to be flexible and work with the less-radical Socialists and Greens. The popularity of the left-wing parties often rises when the economy is strong and falls when it's weak.

The French president is elected every five years by popular vote. Over the past 12 years, the right has been more successful in marshaling its supporters than the left: Both Sarkozy (elected in 2007) and previous president, Jacques Chirac (who served two terms), are conservatives. France also has a prime minister—a very powerful position when the president's party loses its majority in parliament (Assemblée Nationale). The prime minister (currently François Fillon) is chosen by the president and confirmed by the parliament. With seven major parties, a single majority is rare, so it takes a coalition to confirm a prime minister.

Sarkozy is pro-American (though he doesn't speak English) and pro–EU. He is tough on both crime and unchecked immigration. His solution to a sluggish economy involves a tough-love, carrot-and-stick approach—limiting the power of unions and cutting workers' benefits while offering tax incentives to those who work overtime (above the current 35–39-hour workweek). His policies are generating predictable resistance from unions: Expect at least one major strike somewhere in France during your trip.

More French eyebrows have been raised by Sarkozy's personal life. Within a year of becoming president, he divorced his wife of 11 years and married sexy Italian model-turned-singer Carla Bruni (who has been linked romantically with Mick Jagger and Eric Clapton). Sarkozy likes to jog, and he even wears sweats when relaxing *(quelle horreur!)*. The press has nicknamed Sarkozy "Président Bling-Bling" for his love of shiny things (such as Ray-Ban sunglasses, expensive watches, and yachts) and a jet-set lifestyle that often finds him consorting with celebrities.

PAST AND PRESENT

APPENDIX

Contents

Tourist Information

The French national tourist office **in the US** is a wealth of information. Before your trip, scan their website: www.franceguide.com. You can contact them to briefly describe your trip and request any information (such as city maps and schedules of upcoming festivals). To ask questions and request tourist materials (for a small shipping fee), email info.us@franceguide.com or call 514/288-1904. You can download many brochures free of charge at their website.

In France, your best first stop in a new city is generally the tourist information office (remember that these are abbreviated as **TI** in this book). Throughout Provence and the French Riviera, you'll find TIs are well organized, with English-speaking staff. A TI is a great place to get a city map, advice on public transportation (including bus and train schedules), information on special events, and recommendations for nightlife. Most TIs will help you find a room by calling hotels (for free or for a small fee) or by giving you a complete listing of available bed-and-breakfasts. Towns with a lot of tourism generally have English-speaking guides available for private hire (about $140 for a 2-hour guided town walk). Many TIs have information on the entire country or at least the region, so try to pick up maps for towns you'll be visiting later in your trip. If you're arriving in town after the office closes, call ahead or pick up a map in a neighboring town.

The French call TIs by different names. *Office de Tourisme* and *Bureau de Tourisme* are used in cities, while *Syndicat d'Initiative* or *Information Touristique* are used in small towns. Also look for *Accueil* signs in airports and at popular sights. These information booths are staffed with seasonal helpers who provide tourists with limited, though generally sufficient, information. Smaller TIs are often closed from 12:00 to 14:00.

Communicating

The Language Barrier and that French Attitude

You've no doubt heard that the French are "mean and cold and refuse to speak English." This is an out-of-date preconception left over from the days of Charles de Gaulle—and it's especially incorrect in this region. In these southern lands kissed by the sun and sea, you'll find your hosts more jovial and easygoing (like their Italian neighbors) than in the more serious north. Still, be reasonable in your expectations: Waiters are paid to be efficient, not chatty. And Provençal postal clerks are every bit as speedy, cheery, and multilingual as ours are back home.

The biggest mistake most Americans make when traveling to France is trying to do too much with limited time. This approach is a mistake in the bustling north, and a virtual sin in the laid-back south. Hurried, impatient travelers who miss the subtle pleasures of people-watching from a sun-dappled café often misinterpret French attitudes. By slowing your pace and making an effort to understand French culture by living it, you're far more likely to have a richer experience. With the five weeks of paid vacation and 35-hour work week that many French workers consider as nonnegotiable rights, your hosts can't comprehend why anyone would rush through their vacation.

The French take great pride in their customs, clinging to their belief in cultural superiority despite the fact that they're no longer a world superpower. Let's face it: It's tough to keep on smiling when you've been crushed by a Big Mac, Mickey Moused by Disney, and drowned in instant coffee. Your hosts are cold only if you decide to see them that way. Polite and formal, the French respect the fine points of culture and tradition. Here, strolling down the street with a big grin on your face and saying hello to strangers is a sign

APPENDIX

of senility, not friendliness (seriously). They think that Americans, while friendly, are hesitant to pursue more serious friendships. Recognize sincerity and look for kindness. Give them the benefit of the doubt.

French communication difficulties are exaggerated. To hurdle the language barrier, bring a small English/French dictionary, a phrase book (look for mine, which contains a dictionary and menu decoder), a menu reader (if you're a gourmet eater), and a good supply of patience (you can also use the French Survival Phrases—later in this chapter). In transactions, a small notepad and pen minimize misunderstandings about prices; have vendors write the price down.

Though many French people—especially those in the tourist trade, and in big cities—speak English, you'll get better treatment if you learn and use the French pleasantries. If you learn only five phrases, choose these: *bonjour* (good day), *pardon* (pardon me), *s'il vous plaît* (please), *merci* (thank you), and *au revoir* (good-bye). The French value politeness. Begin every encounter with *"Bonjour* (or *S'il vous plaît*), *madame* or *monsieur"* and end every encounter with *"Au revoir, madame* or *monsieur."*

The French are language perfectionists—they take their language (and other languages) seriously. Often they speak more English than they let on. This isn't a tourist-baiting tactic, but timidity on their part about speaking another language less than fluently. Start any conversation with, *"Bonjour, madame* or *monsieur. Parlez-vous anglais?"* and hope they speak more English than you speak French.

Telephones

Smart travelers use the telephone to reserve or reconfirm rooms, get tourist information, reserve restaurants, confirm tour times, or phone home. When spelling out your name on the phone, you'll find that some letters are pronounced differently in French: *a* is pronounced "ah," *e* is pronounced "eh," and *i* is pronounced "ee." To avoid confusion, say "*a*, Anne," "*e*, euro," and "*i*, Isabelle."

Generally the easiest, cheapest way to call home is to use an international phone card purchased in France. This section covers dialing instructions, phone cards, and types of phones.

How to Dial

Calling from the US to France, or vice versa, is simple—once you break the code. The European Calling Chart later in this chapter will walk you through it.

Dialing Domestically Within France

France has a direct-dial 10-digit phone system (no area codes). To make domestic calls anywhere within France, just dial the number.

For example, the number of one of my recommended hotels in Nice is 04 97 03 10 70. That's the number you dial whether you're calling it from across the street or across the country.

Dialing Internationally to or from France

If you want to make an international call, follow these steps:

1. Dial the international access code (00 if you're calling from Europe, 011 from the US or Canada).

2. Dial the country code of the country you're calling (see European Calling Chart in this chapter).

3. Dial the local number. If you're calling France, drop the initial zero of the phone number (the calling chart lists specifics per country).

Calling from the US to France: To call from the US to a recommended Nice hotel, dial 011 (the US international access code), 33 (France's country code), then 4 97 03 10 70 (the hotel's number without its initial zero).

Calling from France to the US: To call from Nice to my office in Edmonds, Washington, I dial 00 (Europe's international access code), 1 (the US country code), 425 (Edmonds' area code), and 771-8303.

Note: You might see a + in front of a European number. When dialing the number, replace the + with the international access code of the country you're calling from (00 from Europe, 011 from the US or Canada).

Public Phones and Hotel-Room Phones

To make calls from public phones, you'll need a prepaid phone card. There are two kinds of phone cards: international and insertable. (Coin-op phones are virtually extinct.) Both types of phone card work only in France. If you have a live card at the end of your trip, give it to another traveler to use up.

International Phone Cards: Called "code cards" (*cartes à code,* cart ah code), these are the cheapest way to make international calls from Europe—with the best cards, it costs literally pennies a minute. They also work for local calls.

You can use international phone cards from any type of phone, even the one in your hotel room (but ask at the front desk if there are any fees for toll-free calls). The cards are sold all over; look for them at newsstand kiosks and tobacco shops *(tabacs).* Ask the clerk which of the various brands has the best rates for calls to America. Because cards are occasionally duds, avoid the more expensive denominations. Some shops also sell cardless codes, printed right on the receipt.

To use the card, scratch to get your code, then dial the free (usually 4-digit) access number. If the access code on the card doesn't work from your hotel-room phone, try the card's 10-digit, toll-free code that starts with 08. A voice in French (followed by English) tells you to enter your code. Before or after entering your code, you may need to press (or "*touche*," pronounced toosh) the pound key (#, *dièse*, dee-ehz) or the star key (*, *étoile*, eh-twahl). At the next message, dial the number you're calling (possibly followed by pound or star key; you don't have to listen through the entire sales pitch).

Remember that you don't need the actual card to use a card account, so it's sharable. You can write down the access number and code in your notebook and share it with friends.

Insertable Phone Cards: Called a *télécarte* (tay-lay-kart), this type of card can be used only at pay phones. It's handy and affordable for local and domestic calls, but more expensive for international calls. To use the card, physically insert it into a slot in the pay phone. They're sold in two denominations—*une petite* costs about €7.50; *une grande* about €15—at *tabacs*, newsstands, post offices, and train stations. While you can use a *télécarte* to call anywhere in the world, it's only a good deal for making quick local calls from a phone booth.

Hotel-Room Phones: Phoning from your room can be cheap for local calls (ask for the rates at the front desk first), but is often a rip-off for long-distance calls (unless you use an international phone card, explained earlier). Incoming calls are free, making this a cheap way for friends and family to stay in touch (provided they have a good long-distance plan for calls to Europe and a list of your hotels' phone numbers).

US Calling Cards: These cards, such as the ones offered by AT&T, Verizon, or Sprint, are the worst option. You'll nearly always save a lot of money by using a local phone card instead.

Mobile Phones

Many travelers enjoy the convenience of traveling with a mobile phone.

Using Your Mobile Phone: Your US mobile phone works in Europe if it's GSM-enabled, tri-band or quad-band, and on a calling plan that includes international calls. For example, with a T-Mobile phone, you'll pay $1 per minute to make or receive a call, and about $0.35 apiece for text messages.

You can save money if your phone is electronically "unlocked"—then you can simply buy a **SIM card** (a fingernail-sized chip that stores the phone's information) in Europe. SIM cards, which give you a European phone number, are sold at mobile-phone stores and some newsstand kiosks for about $5-10. When you buy the card, you'll also get some prepaid calling time

(€25 gives you about 30 minutes). Simply insert the SIM card in your phone (usually in a slot behind the battery), and it'll work like a European mobile phone. When buying a SIM card, always ask about fees for domestic and international calls, roaming charges, and how to check your credit balance and buy more time.

Many **smartphones,** such as the iPhone or BlackBerry, work in Europe—but beware of sky-high fees, especially for data downloading (checking email, browsing the Internet, watching videos, and so on). Ask your provider in advance how to avoid unwittingly "roaming" your way to a huge bill. Some applications allow for cheap or free smartphone calls over a Wi-Fi connection (see "Calling over the Internet," below).

Using a European Mobile Phone: Local mobile-phone shops all over Europe sell basic phones for around $50–100. You'll also need to buy a SIM card (explained earlier) and prepaid credit for making calls. If you remain in the phone's home country, domestic calls are reasonable, and incoming calls are free. You'll pay more if you're "roaming" in another country. If your phone is "unlocked," you can swap out its SIM card for a new one when you travel to other countries.

For more information on mobile phones, see www.ricksteves .com/phones.

Calling over the Internet

Some things that seem too good to be true...actually are true. If you're traveling with a laptop, you can make calls using VoIP (Voice over Internet Protocol). With VoIP, two computers act as the phones, and the Internet-based calls are free (or you can pay a few cents to call from your computer to a telephone). The major providers are Skype (www.skype.com) and Google Talk (www .google.com/talk).

Useful Phone Numbers

Understand the various prefixes. France's toll-free numbers start with 0800 (like US 800 numbers, though in France you dial a 0 first rather than a 1). In France, these 0800 numbers—called *numéro vert* (green number)—can be dialed free from any phone without using a phone card. But you can't call France's toll-free numbers from America, nor can you count on reaching US toll-free numbers from France.

Any 08 number that does not have a 00 directly following is a toll call, generally costing €0.10–0.50 per minute.

Embassies and Consulates

US Consulate in Nice: tel. 04 93 88 89 55, fax 04 93 87 07 38 (7 avenue Gustave V, does *not* provide visa services—Paris is the

nearest office for these services)
Canadian Consulate in Nice: tel. 04 93 92 93 22, fax 04 93 92 55 51 (2 place Franklin)
US Consulate in Marseille: tel. 04 91 54 92 00, fax 04 91 55 56 95 (place Varian Fry)
US Consulate and Embassy in Paris: tel. 01 43 12 22 22, passport services available Mon–Fri 10:00–11:00, online appointments possible, closed Sat–Sun (4 avenue Gabriel, to the left as you face Hôtel Crillon, Mo: Concorde, http://france.usembassy.gov)
Canadian Consulate and Embassy: tel. 01 44 43 29 00, reception open daily 9:00–12:00 & 14:00–17:00 (35 avenue Montaigne, Mo: Franklin D. Roosevelt, www.amb-canada.fr)
Australian Consulate: tel. 01 40 59 33 00, Mon–Fri 9:00–17:00, closed Sat–Sun (4 rue Jean Rey, Mo: Bir-Hakeim, www.france.embassy.gov.au)

Emergency Needs
Police: tel. 17
Emergency Medical Assistance: tel. 15
Riviera Medical Services: tel. 04 93 26 12 70. They have a list of English-speaking physicians and can help you make an appointment or call an ambulance (4 boulevard Maurice Maeterlinck).

Travel Advisories
US Department of State: tel. 202/647-5225, www.travel.state.gov
Canadian Department of Foreign Affairs: Canadian tel. 800-267-6788, www.dfait-maeci.gc.ca
US Centers for Disease Control and Prevention: tel. 800-CDC-INFO (800-232-4636), www.cdc.gov/travel

Directory Assistance
Directory Assistance for France (some English spoken): tel. 12
Collect Calls to the US: tel. 00 00 11

Airports
Nice: Aéroport de Nice—toll tel. 08 20 42 33 33 (€0.12/min), www.nice.aeroport.fr
Marseille: Aéroport Marseille–Provence—tel. 04 42 14 14 14, www.marseille.aeroport.fr
Paris: Aéroports Charles de Gaulle and Orly share the same numbers—toll tel. 3950 (€0.34/min), www.adp.fr; Beauvais—toll tel. 08 92 68 20 66, www.aeroportbeauvais.com
Lyon: Saint-Exupéry Airport—toll tel. 08 26 80 08 26 (€0.15/min), www.lyon.aeroport.fr

European Calling Chart

Just smile and dial, using this key:
AC = Area Code, LN = Local Number.

European Country	Calling long distance within ...	Calling from the US or Canada to ...	Calling from a European country to ...
Austria	AC + LN	011 + 43 + AC (without the initial zero) + LN	00 + 43 + AC (without the initial zero) + LN
Belgium	LN	011 + 32 + LN (without initial zero)	00 + 32 + LN (without initial zero)
Bosnia-Herzegovina	AC + LN	011 + 387 + AC (without initial zero) + LN	00 + 387 + AC (without initial zero) + LN
Britain	AC + LN	011 + 44 + AC (without initial zero) + LN	00 + 44 + AC (without initial zero) + LN
Croatia	AC + LN	011 + 385 + AC (without initial zero) + LN	00 + 385 + AC (without initial zero) + LN
Czech Republic	LN	011 + 420 + LN	00 + 420 + LN
Denmark	LN	011 + 45 + LN	00 + 45 + LN
Estonia	LN	011 + 372 + LN	00 + 372 + LN
Finland	AC + LN	011 + 358 + AC (without initial zero) + LN	999 + 358 + AC (without initial zero) + LN
France	LN	011 + 33 + LN (without initial zero)	00 + 33 + LN (without initial zero)
Germany	AC + LN	011 + 49 + AC (without initial zero) + LN	00 + 49 + AC (without initial zero) + LN
Gibraltar	LN	011 + 350 + LN	00 + 350 + LN
Greece	LN	011 + 30 + LN	00 + 30 + LN
Hungary	06 + AC + LN	011 + 36 + AC + LN	00 + 36 + AC + LN
Ireland	AC + LN	011 + 353 + AC (without initial zero) + LN	00 + 353 + AC (without initial zero) + LN
Italy	LN	011 + 39 + LN	00 + 39 + LN

European Country	Calling long distance within ...	Calling from the US or Canada to ...	Calling from a European country to ...
Montenegro	AC + LN	011 + 382 + AC (without initial zero) + LN	00 + 382 + AC (without initial zero) + LN
Morocco	LN	011 + 212 + LN (without initial zero)	00 + 212 + LN (without initial zero)
Netherlands	AC + LN	011 + 31 + AC (without initial zero) + LN	00 + 31 + AC (without initial zero) + LN
Norway	LN	011 + 47 + LN	00 + 47 + LN
Poland	LN	011 + 48 + LN (without initial zero)	00 + 48 + LN (without initial zero)
Portugal	LN	011 + 351 + LN	00 + 351 + LN
Slovakia	AC + LN	011 + 421 + AC (without initial zero) + LN	00 + 421 + AC (without initial zero) + LN
Slovenia	AC + LN	011 + 386 + AC (without initial zero) + LN	00 + 386 + AC (without initial zero) + LN
Spain	LN	011 + 34 + LN	00 + 34 + LN
Sweden	AC + LN	011 + 46 + AC (without initial zero) + LN	00 + 46 + AC (without initial zero) + LN
Switzerland	LN	011 + 41 + LN (without initial zero)	00 + 41 + LN (without initial zero)
Turkey	AC (if no initial zero is included, add one) + LN	011 + 90 + AC (without initial zero) + LN	00 + 90 + AC (without initial zero) + LN

- The instructions above apply whether you're calling a land line or mobile phone.
- The international access codes (the first numbers you dial when making an international call) are 011 if you're calling from the US or Canada, or 00 if you're calling from virtually anywhere in Europe (except Finland, where it's 999).
- To call the US or Canada from Europe, dial 00, then 1 (the country code for the US and Canada), then the area code and number. In short, 00 + 1 + AC + LN = Hi, Mom!

Airlines

The following 08 numbers are toll calls; the per-minute fee generally ranges from €0.10 to €0.50.

Aer Lingus: toll tel. 08 21 23 02 67
Air Canada: toll tel. 08 25 88 08 81
Air France: tel. 3654 or toll tel. 08 20 82 36 54
Alitalia: toll tel. 08 20 31 53 15
American Airlines: tel. 01 55 17 43 41
Austrian Airlines: toll tel. 08 02 81 68 16
BMI British Midlands: toll tel. 08 90 71 00 81
British Airways: toll tel. 08 25 82 54 00
Continental: tel. 01 71 23 03 35
Delta: toll tel. 08 11 64 00 05
EasyJet: toll tel. 08 26 10 33 20
Iberia: toll tel. 08 25 80 09 65
Icelandair: tel. 01 44 51 60 51
KLM: toll tel. 08 92 70 26 08
Lufthansa: toll tel. 08 92 23 16 90
Northwest: toll tel. 08 92 70 26 08
Olympic: tel. 01 44 94 58 58
Royal Air Maroc: toll tel. 08 20 82 18 21
SAS: toll tel. 08 25 32 53 35
Swiss International: toll tel. 08 92 23 25 01
United: toll tel. 08 10 72 72 72
US Airways: toll tel. 08 10 63 22 22

Car Leasing in France

Europe by Car: US tel. 800-223-1516, US fax 212/246-1458, www.europebycar.com
Auto France: US tel. 800-572-9655, US fax 201/393-7800, www.autofrance.net
Kemwel: US tel. 877-820-0668, www.kemwel.com

Hotel Chains

Huge Chain of Hotels: US tel. 800-221-4542, www.accorhotels.com (handles Ibis, Mercure, and Novotel hotels)
Ibis Hotels: tel. 08 92 68 66 86, US tel. 800-221-4542, www.ibishotel.com
Mercure Hotels: toll tel. 08 25 88 33 33, US tel. 800-221-4542, www.mercure.com
Kyriad Hotels: tel. 08 25 02 80 38, from US dial 011 33 1 64 62 59 70, www.kyriad.com
Best Western Hotels: tel. 08 00 90 44 90, US tel. 800-780-7234, www.bestwestern.com
Country Home Rental: www.gites-de-france.fr or www.gite.com; France Homestyle, US tel. 206/325-0132, www.francehomestyle

.com, info@francehomestyle.com; Ville et Village, US tel. 510/559-8080, www.villeetvillage.com, rentals@villeetvillage.com

Youth Hostels
Hostelling International, US Office: www.hiayh.org
Hostelling International, Canada Office: www.hostellingintl.ca

Cooking Schools
Maison d'Hôtes de Provence: In central Arles, you can take educational and convivial courses, either for several days or for a full week.

Cuisine de Provence: Charming Barbara Schuerenberg leads reasonably priced, easygoing cooking classes from her home in Vaison la Romaine (tel. 04 90 35 68 43, www.cuisinedeprovence.com, barbara@cuisinedeprovence.com, see page 158).

Jardin de Bacchus: Northwest of Avignon, in their Tavel bed-and-breakfast, Christine and Erik offer fun cooking classes (tel. 04 66 90 28 62, www.provence-escapade.fr, jardindebacchus@free.fr, see page 119).

Les Petits Farcis: In Old Nice, Rosa Jackson teaches a variety of cooking courses, some of which include visits to the city's markets (www.petitsfarcis.com, see page 276).

The Internet

The Internet can be an invaluable tool for planning your trip (researching and booking hotels, checking train schedules, and so on). It's also useful to get online periodically as you travel—to reconfirm your trip plans, check the weather, catch up on email, blog or post photos from your trip, or call folks back home (explained earlier, under "Calling over the Internet").

Many hotels offer a computer in the lobby with Internet access for guests. Smaller places may sometimes let you sit at their desk for a few minutes just to check your email, if you ask politely. For those traveling with a laptop, your hotel may have Wi-Fi (wireless Internet access, pronounced "wee-fee" by the French) or a port in your room for plugging in a cable to get online. Most hotels offer Wi-Fi for free; others charge by the minute.

If your hotel doesn't have access, ask your hotelier to direct you to the nearest place to get online. In the region's key cities—Nice and Avignon—you'll find plenty of coffee shops that offer Wi-Fi to travelers with laptop computers. Little hole-in-the-wall Internet-access shops, while common in the rest of Europe, are not prevalent in France. In smaller towns, post offices may offer Internet access *(cyberposte)*; buy a chip-card (about the same prices as phone cards) and you're in business.

Mail

French post offices are sometimes called PTT, for "Post, Telegraph, and Telephone"—look for signs for *La Poste*. Hours vary, though most are open weekdays 8:00–19:00 and Saturday morning 8:00–12:00. Stamps are also sold at *tabac* (tobacco) shops. It costs about €1 to mail a postcard to the US. Federal Express makes pricey two-day deliveries. One convenient, if expensive, way to send packages home is by using the PTT's Colissimo XL postage-paid mailing box. It costs about €33 for the international version, which allows you to send home all the goodies you can stuff into an 18" × 12" × 8" box (no weight limit).

While you can arrange for mail delivery to your hotel (allow 10 days for a letter to arrive), phoning and emailing are so easy that I've dispensed with mail stops altogether.

Transportation

By Car or Train?

Cars are best for groups of three or more (especially families with small kids), those packing heavy, and travelers scouring the countryside in search of the perfect hill town—a tempting plan for this region. Trains and buses are best for those going solo, blitz tourists, and city-to-city travelers.

If you plan to focus on Arles, Avignon, Aix-en-Provence, and seaside destinations along the Riviera, go by train. Stations are centrally located in each city, which makes hotel-hunting and sightseeing easy. Buses and taxis pick up where trains leave off. While bus service can be sparse, taxis are generally available and reasonable. If relying on public transportation, seriously evaluate the value of train or bus detours and focus on fewer destinations, or hire one of the excellent minivan tour guides I recommend (see "Tours of Provence," page 40).

I've included two sample itineraries—by car and by public transportation—to help you explore Provence and the French Riviera smoothly; you'll find these in the Introduction.

Trains

France's rail system (SNCF) sets the pace in Europe. Its super TGV (*train à grande vitesse;* tay zhay vay) system has inspired bullet trains throughout the world. The TGV runs at 170–220 mph. Its rails are fused into one long, continuous track for a faster and smoother ride. The TGV has changed commuting patterns in much of France and put most of the country within day-trip distance of Paris. TGV trains serve these cities in Provence and the Riviera: Avignon, Arles (very few trains), Nîmes, Marseille, Orange, Aix-en-Provence, Antibes, Cannes, and Nice. Avignon

French Railpasses

Prices listed are for 2009 and are subject to change. For the latest prices, details, and train schedules (and easy online ordering), see my comprehensive *Guide to Eurail Passes* at www.ricksteves.com/rail.

"Saver" prices are per person for two or more people traveling together. "Youth" means under age 26. The fare for children 4–11 is half the adult individual fare or Saver fare. Kids under age 4 travel free.

FRANCE PASS

	Adult 1st Class	Adult 2nd Class	Senior 1st Class	Youth 1st Class	Youth 2nd Class
3 days in 1 month	$293	$250	$268	$217	$186
Extra rail days (max 6)	45	37	40	33	28

Senior = 60 and up.

FRANCE SAVERPASS

	1st Class	2nd Class
3 days in 1 month	$249	$215
Extra rail days (max 6)	39	31

FRANCE RAIL & DRIVE PASS

Any 2 rail days and 2 car days in 1 month.

Car Category	1st Class	Extra Car Day
Economy	$264	$47
Compact	267	50
Intermediate	277	60
Full-size	306	89
Premium Automatic	322	105
Minivan	335	118

Prices are per person, two traveling together, except that extra-car-day prices are paid by only one person. Solo travelers pay about $100 extra. Third and fourth persons sharing the car can buy just a regular railpass. Extra rail days (3 max) cost $39 per day. To order a Rail & Drive pass, call your travel agent or Rail Europe at 800-438-7245.

This pass is not sold by Europe Through the Back Door.

Map key:
Approximate point-to-point one-way second-class rail fares in US dollars. First class costs 50 percent more. Add up fares for your itinerary to see if a railpass will save you money.

and Aix-en-Provence have separate TGV stations outside of town (with easy bus connections into the center)—note carefully which station your train serves (either "Centre-Ville" or "TGV"; if it's not specified, then it's the central station).

At any train station, you can get schedule information, make reservations, and buy tickets for any destination.

Schedules

Schedules change by season, weekday, and weekend. Verify train schedules shown in this book—on the Web, check Germany's excellent all-Europe schedule site, http://bahn.hafas.de/bin/query .exe/en.

Bigger stations have helpful information agents (wearing red or blue vests) roaming the station and at *Accueil* offices or booths. They can answer rail questions more quickly than the information or ticket windows. Make use of their help; don't stand in a ticket line if all you need is a train schedule.

Railpasses

Long-distance travelers can save money with a France Railpass, sold only outside France (through travel agents or Europe Through the Back Door; see "French Railpasses" sidebar). For roughly the cost of a Paris–Avignon–Paris ticket, the France Railpass offers three days of travel (within a month) anywhere in France. You can add up to six more days for the cost of a two-hour ride each day. You'll save money by getting the second-class instead of the first-class version, but first class gives you more options when reserving popular TGV routes (seats are limited for passholders, so reserving these fast trains several weeks in advance is recommended). The Saverpass version gives two or more people traveling together a 15 percent discount. Each day of use allows you to take as many trips as you want on one calendar day (you could go from Paris to Beaune in Burgundy, enjoy wine-tasting, then continue to Avignon, stay a few hours, and end in Nice—though I don't recommend it). Buy second-class tickets in France for shorter trips and spend your valuable railpass days wisely.

Buying Tickets

If traveling *sans* railpass, inquire about the many point-to-point discount fares possible (for advance purchase, youths, those over 60, married couples, families, travel during off-peak hours, and more). Remember that second-class tickets provide the same transportation for up to 33 percent less (and many regional trains to less-trafficked places often have only second-class cars).

TGV: While there's no deadline to buy any train ticket, the fast, reserved TGV trains can fill up. It's wise to book ahead for

French Train Terms and Abbreviations

SNCF *(Société Nationale Chemins de Fer):* This is the Amtrak of France, operating all national train lines that link cities and towns.

TGV *(Train à Grande Vitesse):* SNCF's network of high-speed trains (twice as fast as regular trains), connecting major cities in France. These trains always require a reservation.

CORAIL: These trains are the next best compared to the TGV in terms of speed and comfort.

TER *(Trains Express Régionale):* These trains serve smaller stops within a region. For example, you'll find trains called TER de Bourgogne (trains operating only in Burgundy) and TER Provence (Provence-only trains).

Rapide and ***Express*:** Trains designated as ***Rapide*** stop only in major cities. ***Express*** trains serve long-distance destinations, stopping at both large and midsize cities.

any TGV you cannot afford to miss, especially on the busy Paris–Avignon–Nice line. Tickets go on sale 90 days in advance, and the cheapest tickets sell out early.

You can buy tickets online at www.raileurope.com (a US company that delivers tickets to your home but doesn't always have the lowest rates), or better, at www.tgv-europe.com/en/home. If you choose a country other than the US and outside of western Europe, you'll be able to print tickets at home or pick them up in the station (if you choose, say, France, the site will be in French, and if you choose the US, you'll be redirected to www.raileurope.com).

On the Train: You can buy tickets on the train for a €4 surcharge, but you must find the conductor immediately upon boarding; otherwise it's a €35 minimum charge.

Automatic Train Ticket Machines

The ticket machines available at most stations are great time-savers for short trips when ticket window lines are long (but your American credit card won't work, so you'll need euro coins). Some have English instructions, but for those that don't, here is what you are prompted to do. (The default is usually what you want; turn the dial or move the cursor to your choice, and press *Validez* to agree to each step.)

1. *Quelle est votre destination?* (What's your destination?)
2. *Billet Plein Tarif* (Full-fare ticket—yes for most.)
3. *1ère ou 2ème* (First or second class; normally second is fine.)
4. *Aller simple ou aller-retour?* (One-way or round-trip?)
5. *Prix en Euro* (The price should be shown if you get this far.)

Key Travel Phrases

Bonjour, monsieur/madame, parlez-vous anglais?
Pron: bohn-zhoor, muhs-yur/mah-dahm, par-lay-voo
ahn-glay?
Meaning: Hello, sir/madam, do you speak English?

Je voudrais un départ pour (destination), ***pour le*** (date),
vers (general time of day), ***la plus direct possible.***
Pron: zhuh voo-dray uhn day-par poor (destination), poor luh
(date), vehr (time), lah ploo dee-rehk poh-see-bluh.
Meaning/Example: I would like a departure for Avignon, on
23 May, about 9:00, the most direct way possible.

Reservations

Reservations, while generally unnecessary for non-TGV trains,
are advisable during busy times (e.g., Fri and Sun afternoons, Sat
mornings, weekday rush hours, and particularly holiday weekends;
see "Major Holidays and Weekends," page 25). Reservations are
required for any TGV train (usually about €3, more during peak
periods), for selected other routes, and for *couchettes* (berths, €15)
on night trains. Railpass-holders need reservations for the TGV
trains, and only a limited number of reservations are available for
passholders. Once the €3 reservations sell out, travelers with a
France pass (but not a multi-country Eurail pass) also have access
to additional reserved seats (about €12 each). To avoid the more
expensive fares, try not to travel at peak times; ask at the station.
You are required to validate (*composter*, kohm-poh-stay) all train
tickets and reservations. Before boarding any SNCF train, look for
a yellow machine nearby to stamp your ticket or reservation. (Do
not *composter* your railpass, but do validate it at a ticket window
before the first time you use it.) Watch others and imitate.

Baggage Check

Baggage check (*consigne*, or *Espaces Bagages*) is available only at the
biggest train stations (about €4–10/bag depending on size), and is
noted where available in this book (depends on security concerns,
so be prepared to keep your bag). For security reasons, all luggage
must carry a tag with the traveler's first and last name and current
address. This applies to hand luggage, as well as bigger bags that
are stowed. Free tags are available at train stations.

Train Tips

- Arrive at the station with plenty of time before your departure
  to find the right platform, confirm connections, and so on.
  Small stations have minimal staff; if you can't find an agent at

Coping with Strikes

Going on strike (*en grève*) is a popular pastime in this revolution-happy country. President Sarkozy is pushing unions to their limits, and since bargaining between management and employees is not standard procedure, workers strike to get attention. Truckers and tractors block main roads and autoroutes (they call it Opération Escargot—"Operation Snail's Pace"), baggage handlers bring airports to their knees, and museum workers make artwork off-limits to tourists. Métro and train personnel seem to strike every year—perhaps during your trip. What does the traveler do? You could *jetter l'éponge* (throw in the sponge) and go somewhere less strike-prone (Switzerland's nice), or learn to accept certain events as out of your control. Strikes in France generally last no longer than a day or two, and if you're aware of them, you can usually plan around them. Your hotelier will know the latest (or can find out). Make a habit of asking your hotel receptionist about strikes.

the station, go directly to the tracks and look for the overhead sign that confirms your train stops at that track. *Remember that Avignon and Aix-en-Provence have separate TGV stations that are outside the town center.*

- Larger stations have platforms with monitors showing each car's layout (numbered forward or backward) so you can figure out where your *voiture* (car) will stop on the long platform and where to board it.
- Try to check schedules in advance. Upon arrival at a station, find out your departure possibilities. Large stations have a separate information window or office; at small stations, the regular ticket office gives information.
- If you have a rail flexipass, write the date on your pass each day you travel (before you board your first train).
- Validate tickets (not passes) and reservations in yellow machines before boarding. If you're traveling with a pass and have a reservation for a specific trip, you must validate the reservation.
- Reservations for all TGV trains are required, and often sell out. You can reserve any train at any station or through SNCF Boutiques (small offices in city centers). A limited number of reservations are allocated for railpass users during peak times—reserve as far ahead as you can for Friday and Sunday afternoons and Saturday mornings.
- Before getting on a train, confirm that it's going where you think it is. For example, if you want to go to Antibes, ask the

conductor or any local passenger, *"À Antibes?"* (ah ahn-teeb; meaning, "To Antibes?").

- Some trains split cars en route. Make sure your train car is continuing to your destination by asking, for example, *"Cette voiture va à Avignon?"* (seht vwah-tewr vah ah ah-veen-yohn; meaning, "This car goes to Avignon?").
- If a non-TGV train seat is reserved, it will usually be labeled *réservé*, with the cities to and from which it is reserved.
- Verify with the conductor all of the transfers you must make: *"Correspondance à?"*; meaning, "Transfer to where?".
- To guard against theft, it's best to keep your bags directly overhead. If you want to store them in the lower racks (available in most cars), make sure you can see them from your seat. Your bags are most vulnerable to theft before the train takes off and whenever it stops.
- Note your arrival time so you'll be ready to get off.
- Use the train's free WCs before you get off (but not while the train is stopped).
- For mixing train and bike travel, ask at stations for information booklets *(Train + Vélo)*.

Buses

You can get nearly anywhere in Provence and the Riviera by rail and bus...if you're well-organized, patient, and not in a hurry. Review my bus schedule information, always verify times at the local tourist office or bus station, and call ahead when possible. Regional buses work well for some destinations not served by trains. A few bus lines are run by SNCF (France's rail system) and are included with your railpass (show railpass at station to get free bus ticket), but most bus lines are independent of the rail system and are not covered by railpasses. Train stations often have bus information where train-to-bus connections are important—and vice versa for bus companies. On Sunday, regional bus service virtually disappears.

Bus Tips

- Read the train tips above and use those that apply.
- Use TIs often to help plan your trip; they have regional bus schedules and are happy to assist you.
- Remember that service is sparse to nonexistent on Sunday. Wednesday bus schedules are often different during the school year, since school is out this day (and regional buses generally serve schools).
- Be at bus stops at least five minutes early.
- On schedules, *en semaine* means Monday through Saturday.

Renting a Car

To rent a car in France, you must be at least 18 years old and have held your license for one year. An International Driving Permit is recommended, but not required, if your driver's license has been renewed within the last year ($15 through your local AAA, plus two passport photos, www.aaa.com); however, I've frequently rented cars in France and traveled problem-free with just my US license.

Drivers under the age of 25 may incur a young-driver surcharge, and some rental companies do not rent to anyone 75 and over. If you're considered too young or old, look into leasing, which has less-stringent age restrictions (see "Leasing," later in this chapter).

Research car rentals before you go. It's cheaper to arrange most car rentals from the US. Call several companies and look online to compare rates, or arrange a rental through your hometown travel agent. For the best deal, rent by the week with unlimited mileage. I normally rent the smallest, least expensive model with a stick-shift (cheaper than an automatic). For a two-week rental, allow $700 per person (based on two people sharing a car), including insurance, tolls, gas, and parking. For a longer rental time, consider leasing (explained later in the chapter); you'll save money on insurance and taxes. Compare pick-up costs (downtown can be cheaper than the airport) and explore drop-off options. Returning a car at a big-city train station can be tricky; get precise details on the car drop-off location and hours. Except in major cities, rental offices are usually closed on Sundays.

When you pick up the car, check it thoroughly and make sure any damage is noted on your rental agreement. Find out how your car's lights, turn signals, wipers, and gas cap function. When you return the car, make sure the agent verifies its condition with you.

If you want a car for only a day or two (e.g., for the Côtes du Rhône wine route or Luberon villages), you'll likely find it cheaper to rent it in France—US-arranged rentals tend to make financial sense only for three days or more. You can rent a car on the spot just about anywhere. In many cases, this is a worthwhile splurge. All you need is your American driver's license and a major credit card (figure €65–80/day, including 100 kilometers, or 60 miles, per day).

A **rail-and-drive pass** (such as a EurailDrive, Selectpass Drive, or France Rail and Drive) allows you to mix car and train travel economically (sold only outside France, available from your travel agent). Generally big-city connections are best done by train, and rural regions are best by car. With a rail-and-drive pass, you can take advantage of the speed and comfort of the TGV trains for longer trips, and rent a car for as little as one day at a time for day trips that can't be done without one.

APPENDIX

The basic France Rail and Drive Pass comes with two days of car rental and two days of rail in one month. You can pick up a car in one city and drop it off in another. Though you're only required to reserve the first car day, it's safer to reserve all days, as vehicles are not always available on short notice.

Car Insurance Options

Accidents can happen anywhere, but when you're on vacation, the last thing you need is stress over car insurance. When you rent a car, you are liable for a very high deductible, sometimes equal to the entire value of the car. Limit your financial risk in case of an accident by choosing one of these three options: Buy Collision Damage Waiver (CDW) coverage from the car-rental company (figure roughly 25 percent extra), get coverage through your credit card (free if your card automatically includes zero-deductible coverage), or buy coverage through Travel Guard.

CDW includes a very high deductible (typically $1,000–1,500). When you pick up the car, you'll be offered the chance to "buy down" the deductible to zero (for $15–30/day; this is sometimes called "super CDW").

If you opt for **credit-card coverage**, there's a catch. You'll technically have to decline all coverage offered by the rental companies, which means they can place a hold on your card (which can be up to the full value of the car). In case of damage, it can be time-consuming to resolve the charges with your credit-card company. Before you decide on this option, quiz your credit-card company about how it works.

Finally, you can buy car-rental insurance from **Travel Guard** ($9/day plus a one-time $3 service fee covers you for up to $35,000, $250 deductible, tel. 800-826-4919, www.travelguard.com). It's valid everywhere in Europe except the Republic of Ireland, and some Italian car-rental companies refuse to honor it. Residents of Washington state aren't eligible for this coverage.

For all the fine print about car-rental insurance, see www.ricksteves.com/cdw.

Leasing

For trips of three weeks or more, consider leasing (which automatically includes zero-deductible collision and theft insurance). By technically buying and then selling back the car, you save lots of money on tax and insurance. Leasing provides you a brand-new car with unlimited mileage and a 24-hour emergency assistance program. You can lease for as little as 17 days to as long as six months. Car leases must be arranged from the US.

Three reliable companies offer 17-day lease packages from about $1,000 for a small car and $1,400 for a midsize. They are

Auto France (Peugeot cars only, US tel. 800-572-9655, www.autofrance.net), Europe by Car (Peugeot and Renault cars, US tel. 800-223-1516, www.europebycar.com), and Kemwel (Peugeot cars only, US tel. 877-820-0668, www.kemwel.com). Anyone age 18 or over with a driver's license is eligible. You can pick up or return cars in major cities outside of France, but you'll have to pay an additional fee.

Driving in Provence and the French Riviera

It's a pleasure to explore this region by car, but you need to know the rules.

Seat belts are mandatory for all, and children under age 10 must be in the back seat. Almost all rentals are manual by default, so if you need an automatic, you must request one in advance. Gas *(essence)* is expensive—about $7 per gallon. Diesel *(gazole)* is less—about $6 per gallon—and diesel cars get better mileage, so rent one if you can. Gas is most expensive on autoroutes and cheapest at big supermarkets (closed at night and on Sun). Many gas stations close on Sunday. Most drivers will spend about $150 per week in gas to prowl the roads in Provence and the French Riviera. Your US credit and debit cards won't work at self-serve pumps; either pay cash or find gas stations with attendants.

Four hours on the autoroute costs about €25 in tolls (American credit cards not accepted), but the alternative to these super "freeways" usually means being marooned in countryside traffic—especially near the Riviera. Autoroutes save enough time, gas, and nausea to justify the splurge. Mix high-speed "autorouting" with scenic country-road rambling (be careful of sluggish tractors on country roads). You'll usually take a ticket when entering an autoroute and pay when you leave. Shorter autoroute sections (including along the Riviera) have periodic toll booths, where you can pay by dropping coins into a basket (keep a good supply of coins handy so you don't have to drive to a booth with an attendant to get

STOP AND LEARN THESE ROAD SIGNS

Speed Limit (km/hr) — Speed Limit No Longer Applies — No Passing — End of No Passing Zone

SENS UNIQUE One Way — Intersection — Main Road — Freeway

Danger — No Entry — No Entry for Cars — All Vehicles Prohibited

Parking — No Parking — DOUANE Customs — Yield

Driving in Provence and the

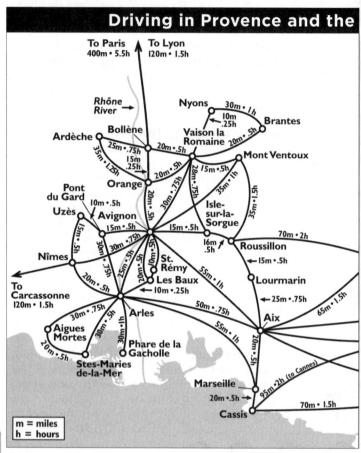

To Paris
400m • 5.5h

To Lyon
120m • 1.5h

Rhône River →

Nyons — 30m • 1h
10m
.25h — Brantes

Bollène
Ardèche — 25m •.75h
35m •1.25h
15m
.25h

Vaison la Romaine — 20m •.5h

Mont Ventoux

20m •.5h
28m •.75h — 15m •.5h
35m •1h
35m •1.5h

Orange — 30m •.75h

Isle-sur-la-Sorgue

Pont du Gard
Uzès — 10m •.5h
Avignon — 15m •.5h — 15m •.5h
16m
.5h — Roussillon — 70m • 2h

15m •.5h
30m •.75h
35m •.75h — 15m •.5h — Lourmarin

Nîmes — 30m •.75h
25m •.5h
10m
.5h
St. Rémy
55m • 1h

20m •.5h
20m •.5h — Les Baux — ← 10m •.25h — 25m •.75h

To Carcassonne
120m • 1.5h

50m •.75h — Aix — 65m • 1.5h

30m •.75h
30m •.5h — Arles
30m •.5h
55m • 1h
20m •.5h

Aigues Mortes
20m •.5h

Phare de la Gacholle

Stes-Maries de-la-Mer

Marseille
20m •.5h → — 95m •2h (to Cannes)

Cassis — 70m • 1.5h

m = miles
h = hours

change). Autoroute gas stations usually come with well-stocked mini-marts, clean restrooms, sandwiches, maps, local products, and cheap vending-machine coffee (€1.20—I dig the *cappuccino sucré*). Many have small cafés or more elaborate cafeterias with reasonable prices.

Roads are classified into departmental (D), national (N), and autoroutes (A). D routes (usually yellow lines on maps) are often slower but the most scenic. N routes and important D routes (red lines) are the fastest after autoroutes (orange lines). Green road signs are for national routes; blue are for autoroutes. Note that some key roads in France are undergoing letter designation and number changes (mostly N roads converting to D roads). If you are using an older map, the actual route name may differ from what's on your map. You may want to navigate by destination rather than road name...or buy a new map. There are plenty of good facilities,

French Riviera: Distance and Time

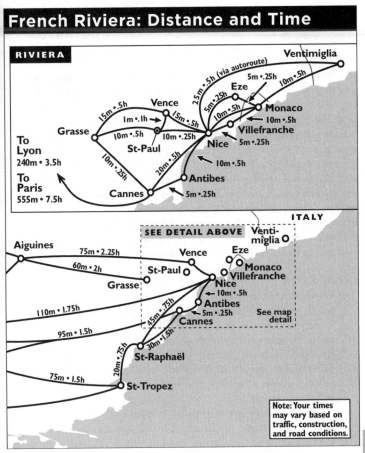

RIVIERA

Ventimiglia

25m • .5h (via autoroute)

5m • .25h

10m • .5h

Eze

5m • .25h

Vence

15m • .5h

15m • .5h

10m • .5h

Monaco

10m • .5h

Grasse

1m • .1h

Villefranche

10m • .5h

10m • .25h

10m • .25h

5m • .25h

St-Paul

Nice

To Lyon
240m • 3.5h

10m • .25h

20m • .5h

10m • .5h

To Paris
555m • 7.5h

Antibes

Cannes

5m • .25h

ITALY

SEE DETAIL ABOVE

Venti-miglia

Aiguines

75m • 2.25h

Vence

Eze

Monaco

60m • 2h

St-Paul

Villefranche

Grasse

Nice

10m • .5h

110m • 1.75h

45m • .75h

Antibes

See map detail

95m • 1.5h

5m • .25h

Cannes

30m • .5h

20m • .75h

St-Raphaël

75m • 1.5h

St-Tropez

Note: Your times may vary based on traffic, construction, and road conditions.

APPENDIX

gas stations (many closed Sun), and rest stops along most French roads.

Because speed limits are by road type, they typically aren't posted, so it's best to memorize them:

- Two-lane D and N routes outside cities and towns: 90 km/hour
- Divided highways outside cities and towns: 110 km/hour
- Autoroutes: 130 km/hour

If it's raining, subtract 10 km/hour on D and N routes and 20 km/hour on divided highways and autoroutes. Speed-limit signs are a red circle around a number; when you see that same number again in gray with a broken line diagonally across it, this means that limit no longer applies. Speed limits drop to 30–50 km/hour in villages (always posted) and must be respected.

France loves photo ticketing; movable cameras are carefully

placed to trap the unsuspecting driver. They seem most common in 30–50 km/hour zones, and you can get busted for going even a few kilometers over the limit (believe me).

Parking is a headache in the larger cities, and theft is a problem throughout southern France. Ask your hotelier for ideas, and pay to park at well-patrolled lots (blue *P* signs direct you to parking lots in French cities). Parking structures usually require that you take a ticket with you and pay at a machine (called a *caisse*) on your way back to the car. Overnight parking (usually 19:00–8:00) is generally very reasonable (except in Nice). Curbside metered parking also works (usually free 12:00–14:00 & 19:00–9:00, and all day and night in Aug). Look for a small machine selling time (called *horadateur*, usually one per block), plug in a few coins (€1.50 buys about an hour, though this varies by city), push the green button, get a receipt showing the amount of time you have, and display it inside your windshield. Keep a pile of coins in your ashtray for parking meters and short stints on autoroutes.

Driving Tips

- Be aware that in city and town centers, traffic merging from the right normally has the right-of-way *(priorité à droite),* even when you're driving on a major road. In contrast, cars entering the many suburban roundabouts must yield *(cédez le passage).*
- Be ready for many roundabouts—navigating them is an art. The key is to know your direction and be ready for your turn-off. If you miss it, take another lap.
- When navigating into cities, approach intersections cautiously, stow the map, and follow the signs to *Centre-Ville* (city center). From there, head to the TI *(Office de Tourisme).*
- When leaving or just passing through cities, follow the signs for *Toutes Directions* or *Autres Directions* (meaning "anywhere else") until you see a sign for your specific destination.
- Driving on any roads but autoroutes will take longer than you anticipate, so allow yourself plenty of time for slower traffic. (Tractors, trucks, traffic, and hard-to-follow signs all require patience.) First-timers should estimate how long they think a drive will take...then double it. I pretend that kilometers are miles (for distances) and base my time estimates accordingly. While locals are eating lunch (12:00–14:00), many sights (and gas stations) are closed, so you can make great time driving— but keep it slow when passing through villages.
- U-turns are illegal throughout France, and you cannot turn right on red lights.
- Be very careful when driving on smaller roads—many are narrow, flanked by little ditches that can lure inattentive drivers. I've met several readers who "ditched" their cars (and

Quick-and-Dirty Road Sign Translation

Instructional Signs that You Must Obey:

Cédez le Passage	Yield
Priorité à Droite	Right-of-way is for cars coming from the right
Vous n'avez pas la priorité	You don't have the right of way (when merging)
Rappel	Remember to obey the sign
Déviation	Detour
Allumez vos feux	Turn on your lights
Doublage Interdit	No passing
Parking Interdit/ Stationnement Interdit	No parking

Signs for Your Information:

Route Barrée	Road blocked
Centre Commercial	Grouping of large, suburban stores (not city center)
Centre-Ville	City center
Feux	Traffic signals
Horadateur	Remote parking meter, usually at the end of the block
Parc de Stationnement	Parking lot
Rue Piétonne	Pedestrian-only street
Sauf Riverains	Local access only
Sortie des Camions	Work truck exit

Signs Unique to Autoroutes:

Aire	Rest stop with WCs, telephones, and sometimes gas stations
Bouchon	Traffic jam ahead
Fluide	No slowing ahead ("fluid conditions")
Péage	Toll
Télépéage	Toll booths—automatic toll payment only
Toutes Directions	All directions (passing through a city)
Autres Directions	Other directions (passing through a city)
Par temps de Pluie	When raining (modifies speed-limit signs)

were successfully pulled out by local farmers).

- On autoroutes, keep to the right lanes to let fast drivers by, and be careful when merging into a left lane, as cars can be coming at very high speeds. Cars and trucks commonly keep their left blinker on while in a passing lane, indicating that they plan to get back over to the right.
- Motorcycles will scream between cars in traffic. Be ready—they expect you to make space to let them pass.
- Gas can be tricky to find in rural areas on Sunday, so fill up on Saturday. Autoroute filling stations are always open.
- Keep a stash of coins in your ashtray for parking and small autoroute tolls.

Biking

You'll find areas in Provence and the Riviera where public transportation is limited and bicycle touring might be a good idea. For many, biking is a romantic notion whose novelty wears off after the first hill or headwind—realistically evaluate your physical condition and be clear on the limitations bikes present. Start with an easy pedal to a nearby village or through the vineyards, then decide how ambitious you feel. Most find that two hours on a narrow, hard seat is enough. I've listed bike-rental shops where appropriate and suggested a few of my favorite rides. Local TIs always have addresses for bike-rental places. For a good touring bike, figure about €10 for a half-day and €16 for a full day. You'll pay more for better equipment; generally the best is available through bike shops, not at train stations or other outlets. French bikers often do not wear helmets, though most rental outfits have them (for a small fee).

Cheap Flights

If you're visiting one or more French cities on a longer European trip—or linking up far-flung French cities (such as Paris and Nice)—consider intra-European airlines. While trains are still the best way to connect places that are close together, a flight can save both time and money on long journeys. When comparing a flight to a train trip, consider the time it takes to get to the airport and how early you'll need to arrive to check in before the flight. Most flights make sense only as an alternate to a train ride of five or more hours in length.

One of the best websites for comparing inexpensive flights is www.skyscanner.net. Other comparison search engines include www.mobissimo.com and www.wegolo.com.

Airlines offering inexpensive flights to Provence and the Riviera include easyJet (www.easyjet.com), Ryanair (www.ryanair .com), and Vueling (www.vueling.com). Be aware of the potential drawbacks of flying on the cheap: nonrefundable and nonchangeable tickets, rigid baggage restrictions (and fees if you have more than what's officially allowed), trekking to airports far outside town, tight schedules that can mean more delays, little in the way of customer assistance if problems arise, and, of course, no frills. To avoid unpleasant surprises, read the small print—especially baggage policies—before you book.

Resources

Resources from Rick Steves

Rick Steves' Provence and the French Riviera 2010 is one of more than 30 titles in a series of **books** on European travel, which includes country guidebooks, city guidebooks (Paris, Venice, Florence, Rome, London, etc.), and my budget-travel skills handbook, *Rick*

Steves' Europe Through the Back Door. My phrase books—for French, Spanish, Italian, German, and Portuguese—are practical and budget-oriented. My other books are *Europe 101* (a crash course on art and history in full color), *Travel as a Political Act* (a travelogue sprinkled with advice for bringing home a global perspective), *European Christmas* (on traditional and modern-day celebrations), and *Postcards from Europe* (a fun memoir of my travels over 25 years). For a complete list of my books, see the inside of the last page of this book.

My **TV series**, *Rick Steves' Europe,* covers European destinations in 100 shows, with nine episodes on France. My weekly **public radio show,** *Travel with Rick Steves,* features interviews with travel experts from around the world, including several hours on France and French culture. All the TV scripts and radio shows (which are easy and free to download to an iPod or other MP3 player) are at www.ricksteves.com.

If you're traveling beyond Provence and the Riviera to Paris, England, or Italy, take advantage of my free self-guided **audio tours** of the major sights in Paris, Florence, Rome, Venice, and—coming in early 2010—London. Simply download them from www.ricksteves .com or iTunes (search for "Rick Steves' tours" in the iTunes Store), then transfer them to your iPod or other MP3 player. Interactive versions of my favorite Paris and Rome tours are for sale as **iPhone apps** on iTunes (for details, see www .ricksteves.com/iphonesupport).

Begin Your Trip at www.ricksteves.com

At our travel website, you'll find a wealth of free information on European destinations, including fresh monthly news and helpful tips from thousands of fellow travelers. You'll also find my latest guidebook updates (www.ricksteves.com/update) and my travel blog.

Our **online Travel Store** offers travel bags and accessories specially designed by me and my staff to help you travel smarter and lighter. These include my popular carry-on bags (roll-aboard and rucksack versions), money belts, totes, toiletries kits, adapters, other accessories, and a wide selection of guidebooks, planning maps, and DVDs.

Choosing the right **railpass** for your trip—amidst hundreds of options—can drive you nutty. We'll help you choose the best pass for your needs, plus give you a bunch of free extras.

Rick Steves' Europe Through the Back Door travel company offers **tours** with more than three dozen itineraries and about 300 departures reaching the best destinations in this book...and beyond. Our France tours include Paris and the South of France in 15 days, Paris and the Heart of France in 11 days (focusing on Paris, the Loire, and Normandy), Villages and Vineyards of Eastern France in 13 days, and the one-week Paris city tour. You'll enjoy great guides, a fun bunch of travel partners (with small groups of generally around 28), and plenty of room to spread out in a big, comfy bus. You'll find European adventures to fit every vacation length. For all the details, and to get our Tour Catalog and a free Rick Steves Tour Experience DVD (filmed on location during an actual tour), visit www.ricksteves.com or call us at 425/608-4217.

Maps

The black-and-white maps in this book, drawn by David Hoerlein, are concise and simple. Dave, who is well-traveled in France, designed the maps to help you locate recommended places and reach TIs, where you'll find more in-depth (and often free) maps of cities or regions. Better maps are sold at newsstands—take a look before you buy to be sure the map has the level of detail that you want.

Michelin maps are available throughout France at bookstores, newsstands, and gas stations (about €5 each, cheaper than in the US). The Michelin #528 map (1:1,000,000 scale) covers this book's destinations with good detail for drivers. The Michelin Local map #332 is good for the Luberon and the Côtes du Rhône, and #340 is best for the Bouches-du-Rhône (the southern area around Arles). Train travelers will do fine with the maps provided in this book. Drivers going beyond Provence and the Riviera should consider the soft-cover Michelin France atlas (the entire country at 1:200,000, well-organized in a €20 book with an index and maps of major cities). Spend a few minutes learning the Michelin key to get the most sightseeing value out of these maps.

Other Guidebooks

If you're like most travelers, this book is all you need. But if you're heading beyond my recommended destinations, $30 for extra maps and books can be money well spent.

Of the several guidebooks on Provence and the Riviera, many are high on facts and low on opinion, guts, or personality. For well-researched (though not annually updated) background information, try the Cadogan guide to Southern France. Serious learners prefer the Knopf guides to the Eyewitness guides' pretty pictures (which do not include hotel or restaurant recommendations). The popular, skinny green Michelin guides are dry but informative, especially for drivers. They're known for their city and sightseeing maps, and for their succinct, helpful information on all major sights. English editions, covering most of the regions you'll want to visit, are sold in France for about €14 (or $20 in the US).

Recommended Books and Movies

To get a feel for France in general, and specifically for Provence and the French Riviera, check out a few of these books or films:

Non-Fiction

For a good introduction to French culture and people, read *French or Foe* (Polly Platt) and *Sixty Million Frenchmen Can't Be Wrong* (Jean-Benoit Nadeau and Julie Barlow). The latter is a must-read for anyone serious about understanding French culture, contemporary politics, and what makes the French tick.

In *A Distant Mirror,* respected historian Barbara Tuchman takes readers back to medieval France. *The Course of French History* (Pierre Goubert) is a concise and readable summary. Ina Caro's *The Road from the Past* is filled with enjoyable essays on her travels through France, with an accent on history. And *The Yellow House* (Martin Gayford) vividly recounts Van Gogh and Gauguin's tumultuous stay in Arles.

Peter Mayle's bestselling memoirs, *A Year in Provence* and *Toujours Provence,* offer an evocative view of life in southern France. The travelogue *Portraits of France* (Robert Daley) includes chapters on Provence. In *At Home in France* (Ann Barry), an American author describes her visits to her country house. *Postcards from France* (Megan McNeill Libby) was written by an observant foreign exchange student. A mix of writers explores French culture in *Travelers' Tales: Provence* (edited by Tara Austen Weaver and James O'Reilly).

A Goose in Toulouse (Mort Rosenblum) provides keen insights on rural France through its focus on cuisine. Foodies may also enjoy *From Here, You Can't See Paris* (Michael S. Sanders), about a local restaurant where foie gras is always on the menu.

Da Vinci Code fans will enjoy reading that book's inspiration, *Holy Blood, Holy Grail* (Michael Baigent, Richard Leigh, and Henry Lincoln), which takes place mostly in southern France. *Labyrinth* (Kate Mosse) is an intriguing tale partly set in medieval southern France during the Cathar crusade.

If you'll be staying in France for a while, consider picking up *Living Abroad in France* (Terry Link) and/or *Culture Shock! France* (Sally Adamson Taylor).

Fiction

Written in the 1930s, *Joy of Man's Desiring* captures the charm of rural France. (The author, Jean Giono, also wrote the Johnny Appleseed eco-fable set in Provence, *The Man Who Planted Trees.*) *The Fly-Truffler* (Gustaf Sobin) features a character who studies the Provençal dialect. Peter Mayle, whose nonfiction books are recommended above, also writes fiction set in Provence, including *Hotel Pastis* and *A Good Year.* For a list of recommended books for children, see the chapter on Traveling with Children.

Films

To Catch a Thief (1955) features both the French Riviera and crackling performances by Grace Kelly and Cary Grant. In *La Grande Vadrouille* (1966), set during World War II, two French civilians aid the crew of a downed Allied bomber in crossing the demarcation line into southern France. *The Return of Martin Guerre* (1982) takes place during the Middle Ages.

Jean de Florette (1986), a marvelous tale of greed and intolerance, is about a city hunchback who inherits a valuable piece of property in rural France, only to have his efforts thwarted by his villainous neighbor. Its sequel, *Manon des Sources* (1986), continues the story, focusing on the hunchback's beautiful daughter.

Two films, based on the memoirs of writer/filmmaker Marcel Pagnol, show his early life in Provence: *My Father's Glory* (1991) and *My Mother's Castle* (1991).

Cyrano de Bergerac (1990), about a romantic poet with a large nose, has scenes filmed at the Abbaye de Fontenay. *French Kiss* (1995) includes scenes in the French countryside and Cannes, as well as Paris. *Chocolat* (2000), which was filmed in the Dordogne region, shows Juliette Binoche opening a chocolate shop and stirring up a tiny town. (*The Horseman on the Roof*, from 1995, is also set in southern France and features the beautiful Binoche.) *The Chorus* (2004), filled with angelic choir music, tells the story of a schoolteacher and the boys he brings together.

Holidays and Festivals

This list includes major festivals in the Provence and French Riviera region, plus national holidays observed throughout France. Many sights close down on national holidays, and weekends around those holidays are often wildly crowded with vacationers (book your hotel room for the entire holiday weekend well in advance). Note that this isn't a complete list; holidays often strike without warning.

Before planning a trip around a festival, make sure that you verify its dates via the festival's website or the France TI (US tel. 514/288-1904, www.franceguide.com, info.us@franceguide.com).

Jan 1	New Year's Day
Jan 6	Epiphany
Feb 12–28	Nice Carnival (Mardi Gras, parades, fireworks, www.nicecarnaval.com)
April 4	Easter Sunday
May 1	Labor Day
May 8	V-E Day
May 13	Ascension
May 23	Pentecost
May 12–23	Cannes Film Festival, in Cannes (www.festival-cannes.fr)
May 20–23	Monaco Grand Prix (auto race), in Monaco
June 21	Music festival (Fête de la Musique), concerts and dancing in the streets throughout France

2010

JANUARY

S	M	T	W	T	F	S
					1	2
3	4	5	6	7	8	9
10	11	12	13	14	15	16
17	18	19	20	21	22	23
24/31	25	26	27	28	29	30

FEBRUARY

S	M	T	W	T	F	S
	1	2	3	4	5	6
7	8	9	10	11	12	13
14	15	16	17	18	19	20
21	22	23	24	25	26	27
28						

MARCH

S	M	T	W	T	F	S
	1	2	3	4	5	6
7	8	9	10	11	12	13
14	15	16	17	18	19	20
21	22	23	24	25	26	27
28	29	30	31			

APRIL

S	M	T	W	T	F	S
				1	2	3
4	5	6	7	8	9	10
11	12	13	14	15	16	17
18	19	20	21	22	23	24
25	26	27	28	29	30	

MAY

S	M	T	W	T	F	S
						1
2	3	4	5	6	7	8
9	10	11	12	13	14	15
16	17	18	19	20	21	22
23/30	24/31	25	26	27	28	29

JUNE

S	M	T	W	T	F	S
		1	2	3	4	5
6	7	8	9	10	11	12
13	14	15	16	17	18	19
20	21	22	23	24	25	26
27	28	29	30			

JULY

S	M	T	W	T	F	S
				1	2	3
4	5	6	7	8	9	10
11	12	13	14	15	16	17
18	19	20	21	22	23	24
25	26	27	28	29	30	31

AUGUST

S	M	T	W	T	F	S
1	2	3	4	5	6	7
8	9	10	11	12	13	14
15	16	17	18	19	20	21
22	23	24	25	26	27	28
29	30	31				

SEPTEMBER

S	M	T	W	T	F	S
			1	2	3	4
5	6	7	8	9	10	11
12	13	14	15	16	17	18
19	20	21	22	23	24	25
26	27	28	29	30		

OCTOBER

S	M	T	W	T	F	S
					1	2
3	4	5	6	7	8	9
10	11	12	13	14	15	16
17	18	19	20	21	22	23
24/31	25	26	27	28	29	30

NOVEMBER

S	M	T	W	T	F	S
	1	2	3	4	5	6
7	8	9	10	11	12	13
14	15	16	17	18	19	20
21	22	23	24	25	26	27
28	29	30				

DECEMBER

S	M	T	W	T	F	S
			1	2	3	4
5	6	7	8	9	10	11
12	13	14	15	16	17	18
19	20	21	22	23	24	25
26	27	28	29	30	31	

July 3–25	Tour de France, the national bicycle race culminating on the Champs Elysées (www.letour.fr)
July 14	Bastille Day (fireworks, dancing, and revelry)
July	International Music and Opera Festival (www.festival-aix.com), Aix-en-Provence
July	Avignon Festival (theater, dance, music, www.festival-avignon.com), Avignon
Mid-July–early August	Chorégies d'Orange Music and Opera Festival (performed in a Roman theater, www.choregies.asso.fr), Orange
Mid-July	"Jazz at Juan" International Jazz Festival, Antibes/Juan-les-Pins
Late July	Jazz Festival (www.nicejazzfestival.fr), Nice

July and August	International Fireworks Festival (www .festival-pyrotechnique-cannes.com), Cannes
Aug 15	Assumption of Mary
Nov 1	All Saints' Day
Nov 11	Armistice Day
Dec 19–Jan 2	Winter holidays
Dec 25	Christmas Day

Conversions and Climate

Numbers and Stumblers

- Europeans write a few of their numbers differently than we do. 1 = 1, 4 = 4, 7 = 7.
- In Europe, dates appear as day/month/year, so Christmas is 25/12/10.
- Commas are decimal points and decimals commas. A dollar and a half is 1,50, and there are 5.280 feet in a mile.
- When pointing, use your whole hand, palm down.
- When counting with fingers, start with your thumb. If you hold up your first finger to request one item, you'll probably get two.
- What Americans call the second floor of a building is the first floor in Europe.
- On escalators and moving sidewalks, Europeans keep the left "lane" open for passing. Stay to the right.

Metric Conversions (approximate)

A kilogram is 2.2 pounds, and 1 liter is about a quart, or almost four to a gallon. A kilometer is six-tenths of a mile. I figure kilometers to miles by cutting them in half and adding back 10 percent of the original (120 km: 60 + 12 = 72 miles, 300 km: 150 + 30 = 180 miles).

1 foot = 0.3 meter	1 square yard = 0.8 square meter
1 yard = 0.9 meter	1 square mile = 2.6 square kilometers
1 mile = 1.6 kilometers	1 ounce = 28 grams
1 centimeter = 0.4 inch	1 quart = 0.95 liter
1 meter = 39.4 inches	1 kilogram = 2.2 pounds
1 kilometer = 0.62 mile	32°F = 0°C

Clothing Sizes

When shopping for clothing, use these US-to-European comparisons as general guidelines (but note that no conversion is perfect).

- Women's dresses and blouses: Add 30 (US size 10 = European size 40)
- Men's suits and jackets: Add 10 (US size 40 regular = European size 50)
- Men's shirts: Multiply by 2 and add about 8 (US size 15 collar = European size 38)
- Women's shoes: Add about 30 (US size 8 = European size 38½)
- Men's shoes: Add 32–34 (US size 9 = European size 41; US size 11 = European size 45)

Nice's Climate

First line, average daily high; second line, average daily low; third line, days of no rain. For more detailed weather statistics for destinations in this book (as well as the rest of the world), check www.worldclimate.com.

J	F	M	A	M	J	J	A	S	O	N	D
50°	53°	59°	64°	71°	79°	84°	83°	77°	68°	58°	52°
35°	36°	41°	46°	52°	58°	63°	63°	58°	51°	43°	37°
23	22	24	23	23	26	29	26	24	23	21	21

Temperature Conversion:
Fahrenheit and Celsius

Europe takes its temperature using the Celsius scale, while we opt
for Fahrenheit. For a rough conversion from Celsius to Fahrenheit,
double the number and add 30. For weather, remember that 28°C is
82°F—perfect. For health, 37°C is just right.

Hotel Reservation

To: _____   _____
               hotel   *email or fax*

From: _____   _____
               name   *email or fax*

Today's date: _____ / _____ / _____
                   day   *month*   *year*

Dear Hotel _____ ,
Please make this reservation for me:

Name: _____

Total # of people: _____   # of rooms: _____   # of nights: _____

Arriving: _____ / _____ / _____   My time of arrival (24-hr clock): _____
              day   month   year   (I will telephone if I will be late)

Departing: ____ / ____ / ____
               day   month   year

Room(s): Single ____   Double ____   Twin ____   Triple ____   Quad ____

With: Toilet ____   Shower ____   Bath ____   Sink only ____

Special needs: View ____ Quiet ____ Cheapest ____ Ground Floor ____

Please email or fax confirmation of my reservation, along with the type of room reserved and the price. Please also inform me of your cancellation policy. After I hear from you, I will quickly send my credit-card information as a deposit to hold the room. Thank you.

_____
Name

_____
Address

_____
City   *State*   *Zip Code*   *Country*

Before hoteliers can make your reservation, they want to know the information listed above. You can use this form as the basis for your email, or you can photocopy this page, fill in the information, and send it as a fax (also available online at www.ricksteves.com/reservation).

Essential Packing Checklist

Whether you're traveling for five days or five weeks, here's what you'll need to bring. Remember to pack light to enjoy the sweet freedom of true mobility. Happy travels!

- ❑ 5 shirts
- ❑ 1 sweater or lightweight fleece jacket
- ❑ 2 pairs pants
- ❑ 1 pair shorts
- ❑ 1 swimsuit (women only—men can use shorts)
- ❑ 5 pairs underwear and socks
- ❑ 1 pair shoes
- ❑ 1 rainproof jacket
- ❑ Tie or scarf
- ❑ Money belt
- ❑ Money—your mix of:
  - ❑ Debit card for ATM withdrawals
  - ❑ Credit card
  - ❑ Hard cash in US dollars ($20 bills)
- ❑ Documents (and back-up photocopies)
- ❑ Passport
- ❑ Printout of airline e-ticket
- ❑ Driver's license
- ❑ Student ID and hostel card
- ❑ Railpass/car rental voucher
- ❑ Insurance details
- ❑ Daypack
- ❑ Sealable plastic baggies
- ❑ Camera and related gear
- ❑ Empty water bottle
- ❑ Wristwatch and alarm clock
- ❑ Earplugs
- ❑ First-aid kit
- ❑ Medicine (labeled)
- ❑ Extra glasses/contacts and prescriptions
- ❑ Sunscreen and sunglasses
- ❑ Toiletries kit
- ❑ Soap
- ❑ Laundry soap
- ❑ Clothesline
- ❑ Small towel
- ❑ Sewing kit
- ❑ Travel information
- ❑ Necessary map(s)
- ❑ Address list (email and mailing addresses)
- ❑ Postcards and photos from home
- ❑ Notepad and pen
- ❑ Journal

If you plan to carry on your luggage, note that all liquids must be in three-ounce or smaller containers and fit within a single quart-size baggie. For details, see www.tsa.gov/travelers.

French Survival Phrases

When using the phonetics, try to nasalize the n sound.

Good day.	**Bonjour.**	bohn-zhoor
Mrs. / Mr.	**Madame / Monsieur**	mah-dahm / muhs-yur
Do you speak English?	**Parlez-vous anglais?**	par-lay-voo ahn-glay
Yes. / No.	**Oui. / Non.**	wee / nohn
I understand.	**Je comprends.**	zhuh kohn-prahn
I don't understand.	**Je ne comprends pas.**	zhuh nuh kohn-prahn pah
Please.	**S'il vous plaît.**	see voo play
Thank you.	**Merci.**	mehr-see
I'm sorry.	**Désolé.**	day-zoh-lay
Excuse me.	**Pardon.**	par-dohn
(No) problem.	**(Pas de) problème.**	(pah duh) proh-blehm
It's good.	**C'est bon.**	say bohn
Goodbye.	**Au revoir.**	oh vwahr
one / two	**un / deux**	uhn / duh
three / four	**trois / quatre**	twah / kah-truh
five / six	**cinq / six**	sank / sees
seven / eight	**sept / huit**	seht / weet
nine / ten	**neuf / dix**	nuhf / dees
How much is it?	**Combien?**	kohn-bee-an
Write it?	**Ecrivez?**	ay-kree-vay
Is it free?	**C'est gratuit?**	say grah-twee
Included?	**Inclus?**	an-klew
Where can I buy / find...?	**Où puis-je acheter / trouver...?**	oo pwee-zhuh ah-shuh-tay / troo-vay
I'd like / We'd like...	**Je voudrais / Nous voudrions...**	zhuh voo-dray / noo voo-dree-ohn
...a room.	**...une chambre.**	ewn shahn-bruh
...a ticket to ___.	**...un billet pour ___.**	uhn bee-yay poor
Is it possible?	**C'est possible?**	say poh-see-bluh
Where is...?	**Où est...?**	oo ay
...the train station	**...la gare**	lah gar
...the bus station	**...la gare routière**	lah gar root-yehr
...tourist information	**...l'office du tourisme**	loh-fees dew too-reez-muh
Where are the toilets?	**Où sont les toilettes?**	oo sohn lay twah-leht
men	**hommes**	ohm
women	**dames**	dahm
left / right	**à gauche / à droite**	ah gohsh / ah dwaht
straight	**tout droit**	too dwah
When does this open / close?	**Ça ouvre / ferme à quelle heure?**	sah oo-vruh / fehrm ah kehl ur
At what time?	**À quelle heure?**	ah kehl ur
Just a moment.	**Un moment.**	uhn moh-mahn
now / soon / later	**maintenant / bientôt / plus tard**	man-tuh-nahn / bee-an-toh / plew tar
today / tomorrow	**aujourd'hui / demain**	oh-zhoor-dwee / duh-man

In the Restaurant

I'd like / We'd like...	**Je voudrais / Nous voudrions...**	zhuh voo-dray / noo voo-dree-oh<u>n</u>
...to reserve...	**...réserver...**	ray-zehr-vay
...a table for one / two.	**...une table pour un / deux.**	ewn tah-bluh poor uh<u>n</u> / duh
Non-smoking.	**Non fumeur.**	noh<u>n</u> few-mur
Is this seat free?	**C'est libre?**	say lee-bruh
The menu (in English), please.	**La carte (en anglais), s'il vous plaît.**	lah kart (ah<u>n</u> ah<u>n</u>-glay) see voo play
service (not) included	**service (non) compris**	sehr-vees (noh<u>n</u>) koh<u>n</u>-pree
to go	**à emporter**	ah ah<u>n</u>-por-tay
with / without	**avec / sans**	ah-vehk / sah<u>n</u>
and / or	**et / ou**	ay / oo
special of the day	**plat du jour**	plah dew zhoor
specialty of the house	**spécialité de la maison**	spay-see-ah-lee-tay duh lah may-zoh<u>n</u>
appetizers	**hors-d'oeuvre**	or-duh-vruh
first course (soup, salad)	**entrée**	ah<u>n</u>-tray
main course (meat, fish)	**plat principal**	plah pra<u>n</u>-see-pahl
bread	**pain**	pa<u>n</u>
cheese	**fromage**	froh-mahzh
sandwich	**sandwich**	sah<u>n</u>d-weech
soup	**soupe**	soop
salad	**salade**	sah-lahd
meat	**viande**	vee-ah<u>n</u>d
chicken	**poulet**	poo-lay
fish	**poisson**	pwah-soh<u>n</u>
seafood	**fruits de mer**	frwee duh mehr
fruit	**fruit**	frwee
vegetables	**légumes**	lay-gewm
dessert	**dessert**	duh-sehr
mineral water	**eau minérale**	oh mee-nay-rahl
tap water	**l'eau du robinet**	loh dew roh-bee-nay
milk	**lait**	lay
(orange) juice	**jus (d'orange)**	zhew (doh-rah<u>n</u>zh)
coffee	**café**	kah-fay
tea	**thé**	tay
wine	**vin**	va<u>n</u>
red / white	**rouge / blanc**	roozh / blah<u>n</u>
glass / bottle	**verre / bouteille**	vehr / boo-teh-ee
beer	**bière**	bee-ehr
Cheers!	**Santé!**	sah<u>n</u>-tay
More. / Another.	**Plus. / Un autre.**	plew / uh<u>n</u> oh-truh
The same.	**La même chose.**	lah mehm shohz
The bill, please.	**L'addition, s'il vous plaît.**	lah-dee-see-oh<u>n</u> see voo play
tip	**pourboire**	poor-bwar
Delicious!	**Délicieux!**	day-lee-see-uh

For more user-friendly French phrases, check out *Rick Steves' French Phrase Book and Dictionary* or *Rick Steves' French, Italian & German Phrase Book*.

INDEX

INDEX

INDEX

INDEX

MAP INDEX

Rick Steves®
EUROPEAN TOURS

ADRIATIC • ATHENS & THE HEART OF GREECE • BARCELONA & MADRID • BELGIUM & HOLLAND • BERLIN, VIENNA & PRAGUE BEST OF EUROPE • BEST OF ITALY • BEST OF TURKEY • EASTERN EUROPE • ENGLAND FAMILY EUROPE • GERMANY, AUSTRIA & SWITZERLAND • HEART OF ITALY IRELAND • ISTANBUL • LONDON • PARIS PARIS & HEART OF FRANCE • PARIS & SOUTH OF FRANCE • PORTUGAL • PRAGUE ROME • SAN SEBASTIAN & BASQUE COUNTRY SCANDINAVIA • SCOTLAND • SICILY SOUTH ITALY • SPAIN & MOROCCO ST. PETERSBURG, TALINN & HELSINKI VENICE, FLORENCE & ROME • VILLAGE FRANCE • VILLAGE ITALY • VILLAGE TURKEY

VISIT **TOURS.RICKSTEVES.COM**

Great guides, small groups, no grumps

Start your trip a

Free information and great gear t

▶ Plan Your Trip

Browse thousands of articles and a wealth of money-saving tips for planning your dream trip. You'll find up-to-date information on Europe's best destinations, packing smart, getting around, finding rooms, staying healthy, avoiding scams and more.

▶ Eurail Passes

Find out, step-by-step, if a rail pass makes sense for your trip—and how to avoid buying more than you need. Get a bunch of free extras!

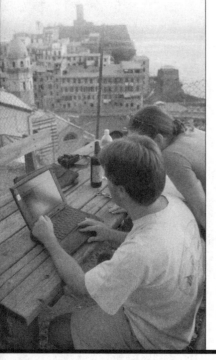

▶ Graffiti Wall & Travelers' Helpline

Learn, ask, share—our online community of savvy travelers is a great resource for first-time travelers to Europe, as well as seasoned pros.

Rick Steves' Europe Through the Back Door, Inc.

⌐rn your travel dreams into affordable reality

Free Audio Tours & Travel Newsletter

Get your nose out of this guide-book and focus on what you'll be seeing with Rick's free audio tours of the greatest sights in Paris, Rome, Florence and Venice.

Subscribe to our free *Travel News* e-newsletter, and get monthly articles from Rick on what's happening in Europe.

▶ Great Gear from Rick's Travel Store

Pack light and right—on a budget—with Rick's custom-designed carry-on bags, roll-aboards, day packs, travel accessories, guidebooks, journals, maps and DVDs of his TV shows.

---

130 Fourth Avenue North, PO Box 2009 • Edmonds, WA 98020 USA
Phone: (425) 771-8303 • Fax: (425) 771-0833 • www.ricksteves.com

Rick Steves
www.ricksteves.com

TRAVEL SKILLS
Europe Through the Back Door

EUROPE GUIDES
Best of Europe
Eastern Europe
Europe 101
European Christmas
Postcards from Europe

COUNTRY GUIDES
Croatia & Slovenia
England
France
Germany
Great Britain
Ireland
Italy
Portugal
Scandinavia
Spain
Switzerland

CITY & REGIONAL GUIDES
Amsterdam, Bruges & Brussels
Athens & The Peloponnese
Budapest
Florence & Tuscany
Istanbul
London
Paris
Prague & The Czech Republic
Provence & The French Riviera
Rome
Venice
Vienna, Salzburg & Tirol

PHRASE BOOKS & DICTIONARIES
French
French, Italian & German
German
Italian
Portuguese
Spanish

RICK STEVES' EUROPE DVDs
Austria & The Alps
Eastern Europe
England
Europe
France & Benelux
Germany & Scandinavia
Greece, Turkey, Israel & Egypt
Ireland & Scotland
Italy's Cities
Italy's Countryside
Rick Steves' European Christmas
Spain & Portugal
Travel Skills & "The Making Of"

PLANNING MAPS
Britain, Ireland & London
Europe
France & Paris
Germany, Austria & Switzerland
Ireland
Italy
Spain & Portugal

JOURNALS
Rick Steves' Pocket Travel Journal
Rick Steves' Travel Journal

NOW AVAILABLE

RICK STEVES APPS FOR THE iPHONE OR iPOD TOUCH

Map | Point Zero & Notre-Dame

Watch Video ▶

1. Point Zero & Notre-Dame 🔊

You're standing at the center of France, the point from which all distances are measured. It was also the center of Paris 2,300 years ago, when the Parisii tribe fished where the east–west riv...

Info

Info | Points of Interest | ☰

With these apps you can:

▶ Spin the compass icon to switch views between sights, hotels, and restaurant selections—and get details on cost, hours, address, and phone number.

▶ Tap any point on the screen to read Rick's detailed information, including history and suggested viewpoints.

▶ Get a deeper view into Rick's tours with audio and video segments.

Go to iTunes to download the following apps:

Rick Steves' Louvre Tour

Rick Steves' Historic Paris Walk

Rick Steves' Orsay Museum Tour

Rick Steves' Versailles

Rick Steves' Ancient Rome Tour

Rick Steves' St. Peter's Basilica Tour

Once downloaded, these apps are completely self-contained on your iPhone or iPod Touch, so you will not incur pricey roaming charges during use overseas.

Rick Steves books and DVDs are available at bookstores and through online booksellers.
Rick Steves guidebooks are published by Avalon Travel, a member of the Perseus Books Group.
Rick Steves apps are produced by Übermind, a boutique Seattle-based software consultancy firm.

Credits

Researcher

To help update this book, Rick and Steve relied on the assistance of...

Madeleine Vedel

Madeleine is a cook, a wine-lover, and a mom. She has lived in Provence for 15 years, leading tours, cultivating food artisans, and honing her southern accent.

Contributor

Gene Openshaw

Gene is the co-author of seven Rick Steves books. For this book, he wrote material on Europe's art, history, and contemporary culture. When not traveling, Gene enjoys composing music, recovering from his 1973 trip to Europe with Rick, and living everyday life with his daughter.

Rick Steves' Guidebook Series

Country Guides

Rick Steves' Best of Europe
Rick Steves' Croatia & Slovenia
Rick Steves' Eastern Europe
Rick Steves' England
Rick Steves' France
Rick Steves' Germany
Rick Steves' Great Britain
Rick Steves' Ireland
Rick Steves' Italy
Rick Steves' Portugal
Rick Steves' Scandinavia
Rick Steves' Spain
Rick Steves' Switzerland

City and Regional Guides

Rick Steves' Amsterdam, Bruges & Brussels
Rick Steves' Athens & the Peloponnese
Rick Steves' Budapest
Rick Steves' Florence & Tuscany
Rick Steves' Istanbul
Rick Steves' London
Rick Steves' Paris
Rick Steves' Prague & the Czech Republic
Rick Steves' Provence & the French Riviera
Rick Steves' Rome
Rick Steves' Venice
Rick Steves' Vienna, Salzburg & Tirol

Rick Steves' Phrase Books

French
French/Italian/German
German
Italian
Portuguese
Spanish

Other Books

Rick Steves' Europe 101: History and Art for the Traveler
Rick Steves' Europe Through the Back Door
Rick Steves' European Christmas
Rick Steves' Postcards from Europe
Rick Steves' Travel as a Political Act

Avalon Travel
a member of the Perseus Books Group
1700 Fourth Street
Berkeley, CA 94710

Text © 2009, 2008, 2007 by Rick Steves
Maps © 2009, 2008 by Europe Through the Back Door
Printed in the United States of America by Worzalla
First printing September 2009

Portions of this book were originally published in *Rick Steves' France, Belgium & the Netherlands* © 2002, 2001, 2000, 1999, 1998 by Rick Steves and Steve Smith; and in *Rick Steves' France* © 2010, 2009, 2008, 2007, 2006, 2005, 2004, 2003 by Rick Steves and Steve Smith.

ISBN (13) 978-1-59880-288-7
ISSN 1546-2749

For the latest on Rick's lectures, guidebooks, tours, public radio show, and public-television series, contact Europe Through the Back Door, Box 2009, Edmonds, WA 98020, tel. 425/771-8303, fax 425/771-0833, www.ricksteves.com, rick@ricksteves.com.

Europe Through the Back Door Reviewing Editors: Cameron Hewitt, Jennifer Madison Davis
ETBD Editors: Cathy Lu, Tom Griffin, Cathy McDonald, Sarah McCormic, Gretchen Strauch
ETBD Managing Editor: Risa Laib
Research Assistance: Madeleine Vedel
Avalon Travel Senior Editor and Series Manager: Madhu Prasher
Avalon Travel Project Editor: Kelly Lydick
Copy Editor: Judith Brown
Proofreader: Denise Silva
Indexer: Claire Splan
Production & Typesetting: McGuire Barber Design
Cover Design: Kimberly Glyder Design
Graphic Content Director: Laura VanDeventer
Maps & Graphics: David C. Hoerlein, Lauren Mills, Laura VanDeventer, Barb Geisler, Mike Morgenfeld
Front Cover Photo: Roussillon © David C. Hoerlein
Front Matter Color Photos: page i Lavender © Dominic Bonuccelli; page iv, Côtes du Rhône Wine Loop © Steve Smith
Photography: Steve Smith, Gene Openshaw, David C. Hoerlein, Rick Steves, Cameron Hewitt, Mike Potter, Robyn Cronin, Dominic Bonuccelli, Dorian Yates